Allaire Spectra e-Business

CONSTRUCTION KIT

Allaire Spectra e-Business

CONSTRUCTION KIT

Ben Forta
David Aden
Raymond Camden
Ashley King
Richard Ragan
John Stanard
Jeff Tapper

Allaire Spectra e-Business Construction Kit

International Standard Book Number: 0-7897-2365-4

Library of Congress Catalog Card Number: 99-068931

Printed in the United States of America

First Printing: May 2000

02 01 00 4 3 2 1

ASSOCIATE PUBLISHER
Michael Stephens

ACQUISITIONS EDITOR
Angela C. Kozlowski

DEVELOPMENT EDITOR
Susan Shaw Dunn

MANAGING EDITOR
Matt Purcell

PROJECT EDITOR
George E. Nedeff

COPY EDITOR
Gene Redding

INDEXER
Kevin Kent
Heather McNeil
Erika Millen

PROOFREADER
Candice Hightower

TECHNICAL EDITORS
Joshua Boughey
Amy Wong
Nicholas Calenda
Debbie Dickerson
Johnnie Mataska
Kurt Mossman
Robert "Skip" Klobucher

TEAM COORDINATOR
Pamalee Nelson

MEDIA DEVELOPER
Michael Hunter

INTERIOR DESIGNER
Ruth Harvey

COVER DESIGNER
Dan Armstrong

COPYWRITER
Eric Borgert

PRODUCTION
Stacey DeRome
Ayanna Lacey
Heather Hiatt Miller

Contents at a Glance

V Appendixes

Table of Contents

About the Authors

Ben Forta is Allaire Corporation's Product Evangelist for the ColdFusion product line. He has more than 15 years of experience in the computer industry in product development, support, training, and product marketing. Ben is the author of the best-selling *ColdFusion Web Application Construction Kit* (now in its third edition) and its sequel, *Advanced ColdFusion 4 Development* (both published by Que), as well as *Sams Teach Yourself HomeSite 4 in 24 Hours* and *Sams Teach Yourself SQL in 10 Minutes* (both published by Sams). Ben co-authored the official Allaire ColdFusion training courses, writes regular columns on ColdFusion and Internet development, and now spends a considerable amount of time lecturing and speaking on ColdFusion, Allaire Spectra, and Internet application development worldwide. Born in London, England, and educated in London, New York, and Los Angeles, Ben now lives in Oak Park, Michigan, with his wife, Marcy, and their five children. Ben welcomes your email at `ben@forta.com` and invites you to visit his Web site at `http://www.forta.com`.

As his mother is fond of recounting, **David Aden** started his computer experience (this lifetime anyway) with a small plastic and metal toy given to him for Christmas too many decades ago to admit. By placing thin plastic sheaths over strategically placed metal knobs and sliding an armature back and forth, the toy could be "programmed" to mimic basic binary calculations or the "logic" of an elevator. Many years later, after a long, fun, and rewarding stint in public affairs and community activism, David went on to work at H-P's now-defunct Distributed Computing Environment (DCE) lab in Massachusetts and an MCI Local development lab in Virginia. In 1997, he arrived at CareerBuilder, Inc., where he hooked up with current *webworld studios, inc.* partner, John Stanard, to work on his first ColdFusion project. Since then he's worked on various ColdFusion projects for Microsoft, CNET, Cable & Wireless USA, and others. John and he decided early in 1999 to make Spectra the focus of their business: to use it as a tool to help businesses achieve their tactical and strategic goals. They've been actively playing with Spectra ever since. Most of the time, they actually get paid for their antics.

Raymond Camden is a senior developer for Syntegra, Inc. He has worked with ColdFusion for three years and is a member of Team Allaire as well as a certified instructor. He has written numerous articles for both *CF Advisor* and the *ColdFusion Developer's Journal* and was a contributing author to Sybex's *Mastering ColdFusion 4*. Raymond has presented at multiple conferences, including the Allaire Developer's Conference in the fall of 1999. You can reach him at `morpheus@deathclock.com`.

Ashley King was a chief architect and senior engineer of the Allaire Spectra product and is the Spectra Evangelist for Allaire Corporation. He is a co-author of *The ColdFusion 4.0 Web Application Construction Kit* and *Advanced ColdFusion 4.0 Application Development* and is a contributor to *The ColdFusion Developers' Journal*. Ashley has served as director of technology at FamilyPoint.com (an iVillage company) and is former CEO of CreativeAspect, Inc., recently acquired by MedSite Publishing. He has built, advised, and managed numerous Web sites, including the first CD music store on the Web. He also enjoys windsurfing but regrets that most laptop computers aren't waterproof. His Web site is located at `http://ashleyking.com`.

Richard Ragan is a senior consultant with Syntegra, Inc. Richard began his career in computing as a high school junior. A chance to escape from American History class and learn FORTRAN programming at Florida State University was just too good to pass up. He's a veteran of the computer industry, with more than 30 years of experience, ranging from compiler construction, language design, user interface design, messaging, and directories to ColdFusion and now, of course, Spectra. Richard was involved in the Spectra beta test program and has been designing and implementing Spectra solutions ever since. Richard lives in Mountain View, California, in the heart of Silicon Valley. When not involved in the latest computer technology, he is a world traveler, student of natural languages, avid bicyclist, and practicing bibliophile.

John Stanard has more than nine years of consulting experience in the computer industry, the last five devoted exclusively to Internet consulting and application development. Most of the application development work was done with ColdFusion, starting at version 1.5 (although there was a short stint where John fell in with an ASP crowd, but he doesn't like to talk about that now). John's background includes management, public affairs, and design and print publishing, thus providing him a unique set of skills with which to approach Web application design and development. Since John formed *webworld studios, inc.,* with David Aden, clients have included CareerBuilder, Inc., NBC Interactive, and all the companies Dave cited in his biography.

Jeff Tapper is the Allaire Technologies Platform Head for the G Triad development corporation, where he has worked on projects for companies including Allaire, Toys 'R' Us, and Dow Jones. He has been working in ColdFusion since 1995 and has been a member of the G Triad team since 1998. Jeff is also known as a theatrical lighting designer and home brewer.

Dedication

Our contribution to this book is dedicated to L. Ron Hubbard, whose insights on the subject of study helped us get through what we needed to learn about Spectra and helped point out better ways to write about it.
—Dave Aden and John Stanard

To my wife, Jeanne Camden. Her strength and love kept me going throughout the process of getting this book to print. Also, to our future son or daughter.
—Raymond Camden

For Sally, Steven, and Nick.
—Richard Ragan

To my darling wife, Lisa. Without your love, support, encouragement, and patience, I wouldn't be here today.
—Jeff Tapper

Acknowledgments

From Ben Forta: First and foremost, I must thank the Allaire Spectra development team for creating a product that's destined to change the face of Web application development forever. Special thanks to Jeremy Allaire and Charles Teague for their invaluable input in planning this book as well as for providing the foreword and the cover quote.

Thanks to my co-authors, Ashley King, David Aden (with John Stanard), Jeff Tapper, Raymond Camden, and Richard Ragan for their outstanding contributions.

Thanks to Allaire Tech Support members and consultants Amy Wong, Debbie Dickerson, Johnnie Mataska, Joshua Boughey, Kurt Mossman, Nicholas Calenda, and Skip Klobucher for finding the time to check this book for technical accuracy.

Thanks again to everyone at Macmillan, especially Susan Dunn for yet another superb development job. A very special thank you to my acquisitions editor, Angela Kozlowski, who has the unenviable job of keeping me on track and on schedule—a task no mortal should have to endure.

And finally, thank you to my wife, Marcy, and our children for all the love, support, and encouragement a man could ask for. You are the reason, the motivation, and the inspiration.

From David Aden: I have a better understanding now of why authors always seem to want to thank their families and friends after working on a book—the thanks is well deserved. Special thanks goes to John Tilton and Andrew Hewitt, two very good ColdFusion (and now Spectra) developers: You guys are great to work with. I love your enthusiasm for taking on new challenges. To my sons, Jason and Jesse, who put up with their dad not being around most of the Christmas holiday—thank you very much. I'm not sure you guys know just how happy and proud I am to be your father. To my wife, who manages to both motivate me to keep my nose to the grindstone and help make the going fun—thank you.

From Ashley King: Thanks to Stephanie King, Mike Nimer, Libby Wilson, Sue Hove, Teri DeMarco, and all the amazing people at Allaire. And many thanks to Beck for keeping me company while I wrote.

From Richard Ragan: I would like to thank my parents, Jack and Janet Ragan, for everything they have done for me. They taught me perseverance, the joy of books, and the importance of learning. A special thanks to my wife, Sally, for all the support, love, and wonderful things she does. Thanks to Ben Forta for a chance to be an author.

From John Stanard: I want to thank my partner, David, for his dedication to getting this book done pretty much on schedule, even when I had to travel for most of December and thus was unable to help as much as we would have liked. He is either a very hard and dedicated worker or a glutton for punishment. I also want to thank the Allaire team for consistently working to improve their products and giving us something that's both functional and professional while being reasonably easy and fun to work with. That's a most unusual combination. Please keep up the good work!

From Jeff Tapper: Thanks is due to Gerry Libertelli, Adam Nowalsky, and David Unger, who have helped mold me into the programmer that I have become.

Tell Us What You Think!

As the reader of this book, *you* are our most important critic and commentator. We value your opinion and want to know what we're doing right, what we could do better, what areas you'd like to see us publish in, and any other words of wisdom you're willing to pass our way.

As an associate publisher, I welcome your comments. You can fax, email, or write me directly to let me know what you did or didn't like about this book—as well as what we can do to make our books stronger.

Please note that I cannot help you with technical problems related to the topic of this book, and that due to the high volume of mail I receive, I might not be able to reply to every message.

When you write, please be sure to include this book's title and author as well as your name and phone or fax number. I will carefully review your comments and share them with the author and editors who worked on the book.

Fax: 317-581-4770
Email: `michael_stephens@macmillanUSA.com`
Mail: Mike Stephens
Associate Publisher
201 West 103rd Street
Indianapolis, IN 46290 USA

INTRODUCTION

In this chapter

Who Should Use This Book

This book is written for anyone who wants to develop next-generation Web-based applications using Allaire's groundbreaking new development tool—Allaire Spectra.

Whether you are creating intranet-based content-management systems, high visibility e-commerce–based sites, or highly interactive user community portals, Spectra provides the building blocks to create, deploy, and manage every aspect of your application in ways never previously possible.

But all this power comes with a price. Unlike Allaire's other products (primarily ColdFusion and HomeSite), Spectra has a significant learning curve, and its use requires careful and methodical planning.

That's where this book comes in. Written by authors intimately familiar with Spectra (many were involved with Spectra's development), *Allaire Spectra e-Business Construction Kit* will walk you through every step of the Spectra application development process. From installation to application design to performance tuning to deployment, every facet of Spectra development is covered in detail, complete with real-world examples and tips.

If you want to develop applications in Spectra, if you are interested in learning how the latest application development technologies can simplify your own development, if you are ready to embrace the new and exciting world of e-business, then this book is for you.

What You Should Know

Allaire Spectra is built on top of Allaire's award-winning application server, ColdFusion. In addition to having basic Web skills (for example, HTML), you need a solid working knowledge of ColdFusion and the CFML language to develop Spectra applications. If you aren't a ColdFusion expert, I strongly suggest that you purchase the following two books:

- *The ColdFusion 4.0 Web Application Construction Kit* (ISBN 0-7897-1809-X)
- *Advanced ColdFusion 4 Development* (ISBN 0-7897-1810-3)

You should also have a good understanding of SQL basics; ColdFusion (and thus, Spectra) relies on SQL for all database interactions.

Links to these and other books that you'll find useful can be found on my Web site at `http://www.forta.com/books`.

How to Use This Book

This book is designed to be used in two different but complementary ways.

For starters, I recommend that you start with the first chapter and systematically work your way through all the book's contents. The best way to learn Spectra is by using Spectra, and by working through the chapters sequentially you'll get the chance to try out every major Spectra component.

Once you are comfortable with Spectra, this book will also serve as an invaluable reference tool. With a thorough index and extensive cross-referencing, you'll find tips, tricks, cautions, and useful bits of information scattered in every chapter.

The content of this book is divided into four primary parts.

Part I: Getting Started

Part I introduces Allaire Spectra and explains its relationship to ColdFusion. This part contains five chapters:

- Chapter 1, "Understanding Spectra," introduces Allaire Spectra and explains what it is and what it can do.
- Spectra is built on top of ColdFusion, and Chapter 2, "Understanding ColdFusion," discusses ColdFusion and the relationship between the two products.
- Chapter 3, "Spectra Concepts and Terminology," covers fundamental concepts and terms used with Spectra.
- Chapter 4, "Installing and Configuring Spectra," walks you through the Spectra installation process, pointing out tips and useful information along the way.
- Chapter 5, "Navigating the Spectra Design Tools," introduces the Webtop (Spectra's interactive design tool) and ColdFusion Studio extensions.

Part II: Building Spectra Applications

Part II covers basic Spectra application development from the ground up. This part contains five chapters:

- Chapter 6, "Introduction to Spectra Programming," explains how to use the COAPI, as well as how to work with basic objects and handlers—the building blocks of Spectra applications.
- Spectra sites require careful planning. Chapter 7, "Planning Spectra Sites," takes a step back and gives an overview of the planning process that must be used to build Spectra applications effectively.

- Chapter 8, "Building the Site Structure," shows you how to use the Layout and Site Object Models, as well as pages and containers.
- User experience is an important part of any application. Chapter 9, "Building Display Components," covers Spectra's user interface features in detail and teaches how to build displays that support the multiple browsers applying the unique capabilities of each.
- Chapter 10, "Creating and Managing Content," teaches content publishing in detail, including full coverage of categorizing content and scheduling publication.

Part III: Advanced Spectra

Part III builds on what has been learned thus far, teaching some of the more advanced and powerful features supported by Spectra. This part also has five chapters:

- Chapter 11, "Working with Meta Data," explains what meta data is and how to use it to build sites that can be searched and accessed with ease and flexibility.
- Chapter 12, "Using Process Logic Paths," covers Spectra's extensive support for multi-part processes and their creation and management.
- Workflow is an important part of all larger sites. Chapter 13, "Working with Workflow," explains Spectra's workflow features and how to use them within your own applications.
- Chapter 14, "Searching and Indexing," explains how to index content for flexible searching using the integrated Verity search engine.
- Chapter 15, "Using Message Queuing," covers the fundamentals of message queuing and how to build queuing systems in Spectra.

Part IV: Spectra Administration

Part IV covers Spectra administrative options, as well as features used in the creation of specific types of applications. This part contains nine chapters:

- Chapter 16, "Using Spectra Security Options," explains how to use Spectra's security services to secure your own applications.
- Chapter 17, "Site Reporting," covers the logging and reporting features that can be used to analyze site usage.
- Chapter 18, "Implementing Personalization," discusses implicit and explicit personalization and explains how to create personalized user experiences.
- Chapter 19, "Rules-Based Publishing," covers the use of rules to provide greater control of content publishing.
- *Syndication* is the mechanism used to share content (and even business logic) between different sites. Chapter 20, "Syndication," will teach you how to implement syndication technologies into your applications.

- Chapter 21, "Creating e-Commerce Sites," explains Spectra's e-commerce features, with real shopping cart–based examples.
- The Spectra user interface (the Webtop) is actually a Spectra application itself, and you can modify it as needed, or even write your own specialized user interfaces. Chapter 22, "Extending Spectra," explains how to do this and more.
- Chapter 23, "Administering Spectra," covers the management of a Spectra site, including the importing, exporting, and migration of data.
- Chapter 24, "Deploying Spectra Applications," covers the details of application deployment, including configuration options and performance optimization.

Part V: Appendixes

Three appendixes are included, primarily to be used as references:

- Appendix A, "Allaire Spectra Tags," is a complete and thorough list of every Spectra tag, sorted by service, and includes syntax and usage notes for each.
- Appendix B, "Spectra Structures," lists the data structures used by Spectra and their members.
- Appendix C, "COAPI Data Types," lists all the internal data types used by the Spectra COAPI.

The CD-ROM

The accompanying CD-ROM includes everything you need to get up and running with Spectra, including

- Evaluation versions of ColdFusion Enterprise
- Evaluation version of ColdFusion Studio
- Complete development version of Allaire Spectra
- All examples and source code used throughout this book
- Third-party add-on tags and components for use within your own applications

Conventions Used in This Book

The following typographic conventions are used in this book:

- Code lines, ColdFusion and Spectra tags, functions, variables, and any text you type or see onscreen appears in a `monospace` typeface. **`Bold monospace`** typeface is often used to represent user input.
- Placeholders in syntax descriptions appear in an *`italic monospace`* typeface. Replace the placeholder with the actual filename, parameter, or whatever element it represents.

- *Italics* highlight technical terms when they're being defined.
- The ➥ symbol is used before a line of code that's really a continuation of the preceding line. Sometimes a line of code is too long to fit as a single line on the page. If you see ➥ before a line of code, remember that it's part of the line immediately above it.

The book also contains notes, tips, and cautions to help you spot important or useful information more quickly. Some of these are helpful shortcuts to help you work more efficiently.

Enjoy the Book!

Having read this far, you are probably intrigued by the possibilities Spectra presents to you and are itching to start coding. So, turn the page and start reading; you'll be creating applications beyond your expectations before you know it.

PART I

Getting Started

CHAPTER

1

Understanding Spectra

In this chapter

Spectra Product Overview

As the Web evolves, more and more businesses seek to make it a center for doing business. Problems common to these businesses are solved daily by teams of developers and business people. To be successful in this highly competitive environment, developers need to build on the best practices rather than reinvent the wheel.

A system that encapsulates best practices and services is called a *framework*. More correctly, a framework is a series of modules that can be used as components in solving specific problems. Allaire Spectra is a packaged system that provides a framework, methodology, and services for the development of large-scale e-business applications for the Web. Spectra addresses key needs in the development, deployment, and management of these applications, including

- *Application modularity*. Maintaining applications becomes a problem in large-scale applications. In Spectra, code modules can be *packaged*, and functionality is modular, allowing for greater ease in developing and maintaining the code base. Application code can be packaged and installed on any Spectra server.
- *Code reuse*. In an enterprise, time-to-market pressures require the most efficient use of all resources, especially developers. Time spent re-tasking code for use elsewhere in an application is time taken away from an early deployment. When built, your Spectra application code is used from anywhere in the application, providing shorter development cycles and greater flexibility in deployment.
- *Enterprise-wide adoption*. As the Web becomes the center of business, those in management face technical dependency on an overtaxed IT department. Management of Spectra applications is provided through Web-based tools that allow developers and administrators to give control of the application to others in the enterprise, lessening dependence on those in IT.
- *Unified services*. Many Web applications in use today have high development and maintenance overhead, caused by the need to patch content management solutions with personalization and e-commerce systems. This dramatically increases deployment costs and complexity while reducing performance. In Spectra, content management, e-commerce, and personalization services are integrated into a single system.
- *Deployment flexibility*. Many systems cause Lock-IN, which is the forced dependence on one operating system or platform. This limits future choices and may cause nightmares in future deployments. A single Spectra code base runs on multiple OS platforms and relational database management systems (RDBMS) without modification. Tools for automated cross-platform database migration and application migration are provided for ease of deployment.

- *Team development.* IT shortages cause managers to be more flexible in the way teams work together. Individual developers also need to be able to be more productive by focusing on the tasks for which they are best suited. Spectra provides abstraction that lets teams work together on units (such as application code, content, and site design) that can be distributed to team members and then combined into a dynamic application.

At its simplest, Spectra is a package of more than 400 special ColdFusion tags and a ContentObject Database and runs atop the ColdFusion enterprise application server, inheriting the robust features and scalability of the leading application server. Chapter 2, "Understanding ColdFusion," details the features of the ColdFusion application server and its relationship to Spectra.

NOTE Spectra applications are coded with ColdFusion Markup Language (CFML) and make extensive use of CFML language features. To build Spectra applications, you should have a good understanding of CFML programming concepts. Some good resources for learning CFML include *The ColdFusion 4.0 Web Application Construction Kit* and *Advanced ColdFusion 4.0 Application Development*, both published by Que.

The Spectrum of Participants

Web application development has changed. Not long ago, these applications were developed by one programmer tucked away in a corner, high on caffeine, surrounded by tech books, and responsible for everything from content creation to Web site management to database administration.

But that (thankfully) has changed. Web-based applications are maturing and have gained acceptance as legitimate and necessary business tools. With this change has come the need for structure and discipline in the development process.

Web application development is now a team project consisting of graphic designers, content and copy editors, system administrators, database experts, business managers, corporate decision makers, business development personnel, marketing professionals, and more. All are now part of the design, rollout, and ongoing maintenance of the application at some level. Each has a distinct set of goals and objectives, and each has a different set of needs that must be met to accomplish these goals and objectives.

And this creates a whole new set of management problems. Most Web application development tools are designed for developers and assume a thorough and intimate knowledge of the low-level workings of what makes Web applications tick. Content creators, for example, can't simply write content unaware of formatting and presentation technologies (like HTML). Business decision makers can't run reports or perform analysis of trends and behavior without thoroughly understanding the workings of Web and application servers.

To truly facilitate group development, apply the talents and abilities of all the players in the team, and empower all team members to meet their objectives, new software is needed. Software like Allaire Spectra. In the Spectra view of the world, an application is created and maintained by a Spectrum of Participants, each with different needs and requirements, and each with the appropriate tools to accomplish those goals. Figure 1.1 shows the typical participant division.

FIGURE 1.1
The seven roles in the Spectrum of Participants.

The System Administrator

System administrators manage the Web and application servers, database servers (also known as relational database management systems, or RDBMSs), user directories, and other global resources for a Spectra application. System administrators also manage the ColdFusion application server and enterprise resources with which the Spectra application may interact.

In the example application you build in this book, the system administrator would be responsible for installation of software and the deployment environment. This participant would also create any application databases and security settings. If your role is that of a system administrator, pay close attention to Chapters 2, 3, 4, 16, 23, and 24.

The Interactive Developer

Interactive developers code application functionality and are responsible for implementing the application. This role requires a good knowledge of CFML and other development languages, standards, and environments that may be used to build application components such as ColdFusion eXtensions (CFXs) in C++ or Java, Servlets, COM, CORBA, and other components.

Interactive developers build workflows, multistep processes, and message queues and define the rules and logic used to select and personalize content on the site. Interactive developers also define syndication streams, which are rules that define how content and functionality from other sites are utilized in an application.

Interactive developers will code the Spectra application example in this book and will be writing CFML. Interactive developers will find the balance of the book to be quite relevant.

The Site Designer

Site designers create the site's user interface (UI) by creating graphic design elements as well as page templates with HTML. Site designers also manage the structure and navigation of the site and its sections and pages, defining areas where content can be published in pages.

In the a2zBooks example, the site designer will design the HTML layout and implement the site's organization. This means that this participant will determine all the sections and pages. Site designers should pay particular attention to Chapters 5, 8, and 9.

The Business User

Business users create and edit content in the Spectra application. They also participate in workflows and publish content to the site using Spectra's AnywhereAuthoring system or other Web-based tools. Business users may be writers, editors, subject matter experts, or any person who contributes and manages content in pages in the site. Business users also categorize content and choose what rules are used to publish content to pages.

The business users working with the a2z example enter the data for the books and authors and determine on what pages this content will be displayed. Chapter 10 is important for this role.

The Business Manager

Business managers define the site processes, including workflows and multistep processes. Business users participate in and manage all phases of design and development and define the business rules, data models, and categorization elements that are used by the interactive developer to create application functionality.

Business managers also initiate and manage workflows and obtain reports on site performance and manage site affiliate permissions. A2Z business managers determine the scope of the development and who participates in all the other roles. Business managers control the daily site operations by initiating workflows to create book content and monitoring the progress of everyone involved. A good understanding of the development process is essential for people in this role, along with familiarity with the site management tools. Review Chapters 3, 7, 10, 13, 16, 17, and 23 if this is your role.

The Site Member

Site members visit and interact with your site daily and interact with all the site functionality. Site members can choose personalization options and interact with tools according to their security permissions.

A site member in the a2zBooks application visits the Web site and interacts with the content. You will play this role frequently as you test and debug the site (and when you show it to your friends).

The Site Affiliate

Site affiliates use self-service tools to choose content from the site to be syndicated to their sites. Site affiliates may also provide content and site functionality to the site's syndication streams.

Functionality and processes developed for the site can also be syndicated to site affiliates, so that those components such as site processes can be available seamlessly on an affiliate Web site.

A2Z affiliates place books and information from the A2Z site in their own sites. Affiliates can log into the application and choose the content they want and how they want to receive it.

Spectra Architecture

The Spectra architecture organizes the features and framework of Spectra into three tiers, shown in Figure 1.2.

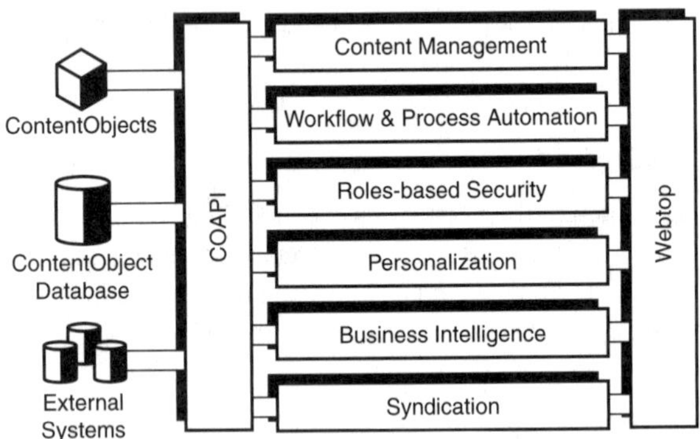

FIGURE 1.2
A conceptual diagram of Spectra's architecture.

The ContentObject API

The ContentObject API (COAPI) is the core of Spectra. It's the engine that runs your Spectra application and is also the point of integration with external systems in your enterprise. The COAPI also manages the invocation of the application functionality you create, as well as the retrieval and management of content and data in your application.

You can think of the COAPI as the operating system for your Spectra applications. If you write a Windows program, the operating system takes care of functions common to other applications, such as communications with external systems, security, and much more. You can also think of the COAPI as a set of foundation classes. Foundation classes in Windows programming provide common tools such as file browse windows, file management, and UI elements.

The COAPI manages security, content management tools, and connection to your external data. It also provides tools you use in your Spectra applications to do common tasks for you. If you are like most developers, you spend much of your time solving the same problems over and over. Spectra lets you move on to the real challenge: building a great application.

The ContentObject Database Part of the COAPI, the ContentObject Database (CODB), is where Spectra data structures, or ContentObjects, are stored. The ContentObject Database is an XML/relational hybrid database that uses Web Distributed Data eXchange (WDDX) to store complex structures of data in a static schema. This gives you the ability to develop and modify the data model for your application without making changes to the database. The CODB can be installed into Microsoft SQL Server 7, Oracle, Sybase, Informix, and DB2 databases and can be migrated between any of these supported platforms. As part of the COAPI, data access is managed for you, so you don't have to develop SQL queries for internally stored data.

▶ **See** Chapter 3, "Spectra Concepts and Terminology," for a discussion about ContentObjects and Chapter 6, "Introduction to Spectra Programming."

Multiple CODBs are managed within the COAPI and can be assigned to multiple Spectra applications. This means that you can store the content for each Spectra application separately, or you can share data between two applications if you need to (such as in an intranet/extranet). The whole process is transparent to your application, so you never have to change a database table or SQL queries.

What Is WDDX?

WDDX is an open standard, and SDKs for WDDX integration on multiple platforms and languages are available at `http://wddx.org`. WDDX is also covered extensively in Que's *Advanced ColdFusion 4.0 Application Development*. The ContentObject Database is discussed more in depth in Chapter 3 and in Chapter 6.

With WDDX, you can create variables in one environment (such as CFML) and share these variables with another environment (such as Java). The great part is that all you have to do is get the XML that WDDX creates to the other environment. The WDDX libraries take care of all conversions for you. As a result, it's very straightforward to use the data in the CODB from other languages and platforms. WDDX has many other cool uses. Visit the WDDX Web site for more examples.

For more information on XML, read Que's *Special Edition Using XML*, (ISBN 0-7897-1996-7) or *Sams Teach Yourself XML in 21 Days* (ISBN 1-575213966), both by Macmillan Computer Publishing.

External Resources and Databases Storing and accessing data from external sources also takes place within the COAPI. Your Spectra application can use any Microsoft SQL Server 7, Oracle, Sybase, or Informix database. If your database platform is different, you may want to check the Allaire Web site at `http://www.allaire.com` for an up-to-date list of supported systems. You can also use the internal CODB storage and multiple external databases at the same time within any Spectra application. Very rich and complex data models using multiple data storage methods can be created, providing great flexibility in application design.

Security Contexts Security in the COAPI is provided by the security services in ColdFusion, based on the Netegrity SiteMinder product. Very granular levels of security and the ability to use multiple user directories and assign roles-based permissions add to the robustness of Spectra COAPI security. User directories on ODBC, LDAP, and Windows NT resources can be used. Since the Spectra services are built atop the COAPI, your security model pervades all aspects of your application.

The Webtop

The Webtop allows those in the Spectrum of Participants to cooperatively develop, maintain, and manage the Spectra application in a Web-based environment. Tools based on roles in the Spectrum of Participants provide access to key Spectra services in a secure environment. The Webtop is a Spectra application and can be modified or adapted to specialized deployments for the highest degree of flexibility.

If you want to create your own Webtop, one tailored to the needs of your own organization, you can do so by using the one provided as a starting point.

To access the Webtop, from the Start menu choose Programs, Allaire, Spectra, and then Webtop. Log in with the username and password you created during installation. You'll now see the Webtop interface, shown in Figure 1.3, with the five sections of tools organized by role in the Spectrum of Participants.

NOTE If you haven't yet installed Spectra, just look at the figure for now. Installation is discussed in Chapter 4, "Installing and Configuring Spectra."

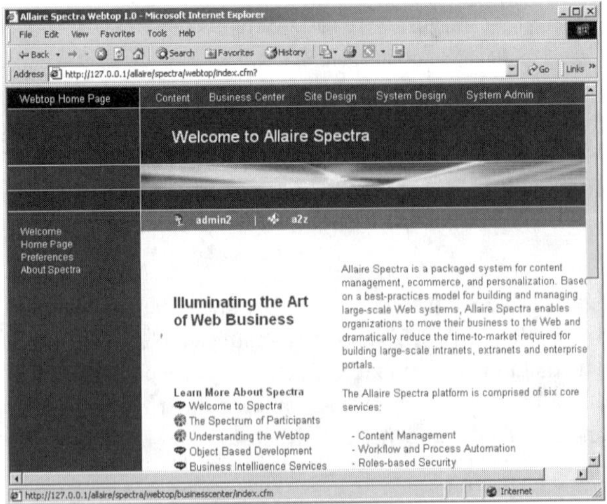

FIGURE 1.3
The welcome page of the Spectra Webtop.

Chapter 5, "Navigating the Spectra Design Tools," provides a tour of the Webtop and its five sections. Also, throughout the book these sections of the Webtop are detailed as the concepts and Spectra services are discussed.

Spectra Services (Not Processes)

Built atop the COAPI are six services that are part of all Spectra applications. These services are conceptual ways of understanding what the Spectra framework provides your applications, rather than actual "services" or "processes" running on your server. They are part of all Spectra application code that you build. Think of *services* in this context as "things already done for you," rather than as NT services. Figure 1.4 shows these Spectra services.

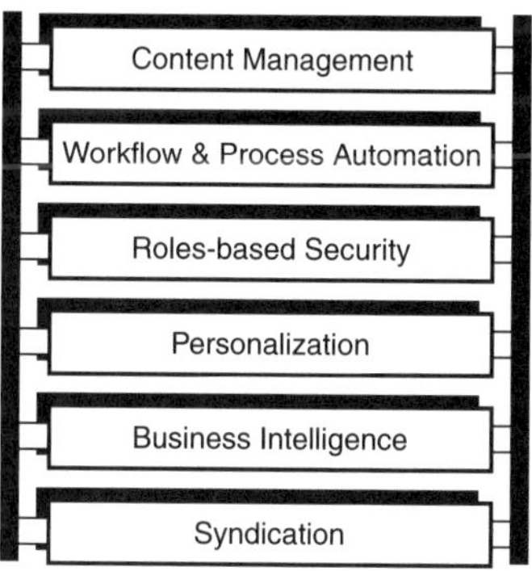

FIGURE 1.4
The six Spectra services.

These services are organized into three groups as shown in Table 1.1: the Site Object Model, the Site Layout Model, and the Site Process Model. These are described in more detail in Chapter 6.

Table 1.1 Organization of Spectra Services

Group	Services
Site Object Model	Underlying Spectra application functionality and the COAPI; roles-based security (see Chapters 3, 6, and 7)
Site Layout Model	Content management (see Chapters 8, 9, and 10)
Site Process Model	Workflow and process automation, personalization, syndication (see Chapters 11 through 21)

Content Management Spectra's content management service enables site designers to define the look-and-feel of the site as well as lay out the organization and navigation of the site. AnywhereAuthoring allows business users to create and edit content using a Web browser, whereas InContext Editing gives business users control over the content published in any area of the site.

Content management in Spectra applications is detailed in Chapter 8, "Building the Site Structure"; Chapter 9, "Building Display Components"; and Chapter 10, "Creating and Managing Content."

Workflow and Process Automation Business rules and business processes are encapsulated into Process Logic Paths (PLP) and workflows to allow the site to reflect business goals. These processes are defined by the business manager and implemented by the interactive developer for use throughout the application.

Process Logic Paths are detailed in Chapter 12, "Using Process Logic Paths." Workflow is discussed in Chapter 13, "Working with Workflow."

Roles-Based Security All areas of administration and management of a Spectra application are secured based on the role of the user, or at a more granular level. Each application function and process, as well as the site, sections, pages, and ContentObjects, can be secured from a central Webtop or tag-based control. Security permissions for those in the enterprise, affiliates, and site members can be managed using the same system.

Chapter 16, "Using Spectra Security Options," and Chapter 23, "Administering Spectra," provide detail about roles-based security in Spectra.

Personalization ContentObjects in a Spectra application can be categorized by using multiple hierarchies of meta data keywords, organized in nested categories for ease of management. These keywords then drive the selection of ContentObjects displayed on site pages by using publishing rules created by the interactive developer. These publishing rules provide great flexibility to create complex rules, including displaying content based on meta data associated with a user profile or displaying content based on external data.

The Personalization service is detailed in Chapter 18, "Implementing Personalization," and Chapter 19, "Rules-Based Publishing."

Integration with third-party collaborative filtering tools provides even greater personalization functionality. This is discussed in Chapter 22, "Extending Spectra."

Business Intelligence Spectra's Observation Architecture allows custom log objects to be generated to capture fine-grained information about user behavior and site performance. These custom log objects provide data for reports created by interactive developers, accessible anytime by business managers through a Web-based management interface.

Chapter 17, "Site Reporting," discusses implementation of the Business Intelligence service.

Syndication Based on the permissions assigned to site affiliates, sets of ContentObjects as defined by publishing rules are pushed to affiliate sites using multiple transport protocols. Site affiliates can enter the site in a self-serve mode and select sets of content to receive at any interval in WDDX or HTML format.

Syndication Streams define content from external sites and how the Spectra application will utilize this content. External content can be imported into the system or placed in message queues to be published at defined times. These Syndication Streams are defined by the interactive developer and allow content to be dynamically imported or retrieved at designated times.

Also, application logic such as order processing or catalog searches can be syndicated for use on external sites. By using WDDX and Spectra's Remote Invocation API (RIAPI), any platform that supports WDDX can utilize Spectra application functionality.

Syndication in Spectra is discussed in Chapter 20, "Syndication."

Goals and Objectives

You will find practical and relevant examples of building Web applications using Spectra's framework and services as you follow the creation of the a2z example application throughout this book. In Chapter 2, ColdFusion's features and how it is utilized in Spectra is discussed in detail. Chapter 3 introduces the terminology used throughout the book and is a good starting point for those already familiar with the ColdFusion application server.

To prepare for using the examples in this book, Chapter 4 will guide you through the process of installing the included Spectra evaluation version as well as provide instruction and tips for installing Spectra for deployment purposes. Chapter 5 will provide you with an understanding of the tools provided in the Webtop and in the ColdFusion Studio and HomeSite development environments.

The remaining chapters will guide you through the process of developing a Spectra application, including how to utilize the six services provided by the Spectra framework. In this book, the A2Z Online Bookstore application demonstrates the use of Spectra services and features. The code from this application is included in the CD that accompanies this book. Figure 1.5 shows the home page for this application.

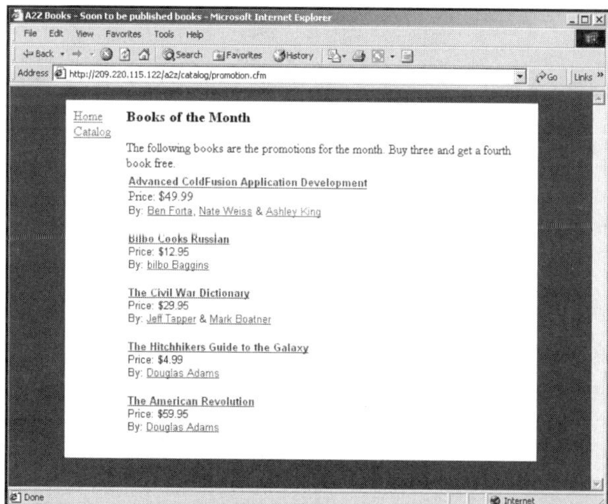

FIGURE 1.5
The A2Z Online Bookstore home page.

You can use the examples provided as a basis for developing your own Spectra application in conjunction with the discussions on Spectra development provided throughout this book.

Spectra is built to make your life easier by letting you focus on the work you do best. Others in your enterprise will find that they have the tools and the power to manage the parts of the application that they need to manipulate. Each feature of Spectra is an encapsulation of a solution to a problem. Your Spectra applications will be easy to manage and deploy, and you will find yourself remembering why you started developing in the first place.

Keep your enterprise in mind as you read this book. Think in terms of the real people who interact with your applications, their needs, and their skillsets. Have in mind the problems you've solved in the past and think about how you will solve these with the Spectra framework. If you are familiar with ColdFusion, you will find that Spectra development is simply a matter of understanding the tools you have to work with and how they all work. ●

CHAPTER 2

Understanding ColdFusion

In this chapter

ColdFusion and Its Relationship to Spectra

Allaire Spectra is a new product, but that doesn't mean it's unproven. Spectra is built on a reliable and proven foundation—ColdFusion.

At it's simplest, Spectra is actually nothing more than a ColdFusion application, probably the biggest and most complex ColdFusion application ever developed.

Understanding Spectra—and, indeed, writing Spectra applications—requires a solid understanding and working knowledge of ColdFusion. As such, this chapter gives a brief overview of ColdFusion and some of its technologies and explains how Spectra uses them.

NOTE This chapter briefly summarizes some key ColdFusion features and technologies that are important to Spectra developers. This book won't teach you ColdFusion, however, and a good working knowledge of ColdFusion is assumed. To learn ColdFusion, I strongly suggest that you buy two of my other books, *The ColdFusion 4.0 Web Application Construction Kit* (ISBN 0-7897-1809-X) and *Advanced ColdFusion 4.0 Application Development* (ISBN 0-7897-1810-3), both published by Que.

Understanding Application Servers

ColdFusion is an application server. To understand application servers, it's important to understand what Web servers are or, rather, what they aren't.

Web servers do just that—they serve. Web browsers make requests and Web servers fulfill those requests—they serve the requested information to the browser. These are usually HTML files and supported files (such as GIF and JPEG images).

And that's really all Web servers do. In the grand scheme of things, Web servers are actually pretty simple applications—they sit and wait for requests that they attempt to fulfill as soon as they arrive. Web servers don't let you interact with a database, personalize Web pages, or process the results of a user's form submission—they do none of that. All they do is serve pages.

So how do you extend your Web server to do the things I just listed and more? That's where Web application servers come into play. A *Web application server* is software that extends the Web server, allowing it to do things that it couldn't do by itself—kind of like teaching an old dog new tricks.

Here's how it works: When a Web server receives a request from a Web browser, it looks at that request to determine if it's a simple Web page or a page that needs processing by a Web application server. It does this by looking at the MIME type (or file extension). If the MIME type indicates that the file is a simple Web page (for example, it has an `HTM` extension), the Web server will fulfill the request and send the file to the requesting browser as is. But if the MIME type indicates that the requested file is a page that needs processing by a Web application server (for example, it has a `.cfm` extension), the Web server passes it to the appropriate Web application server and returns the result that it gets rather than the actual page itself. Figure 2.1 illustrates this concept.

FIGURE 2.1
Web servers pass requests to Web application servers, which in turn pass results back to the Web server for transmission to the requesting browser.

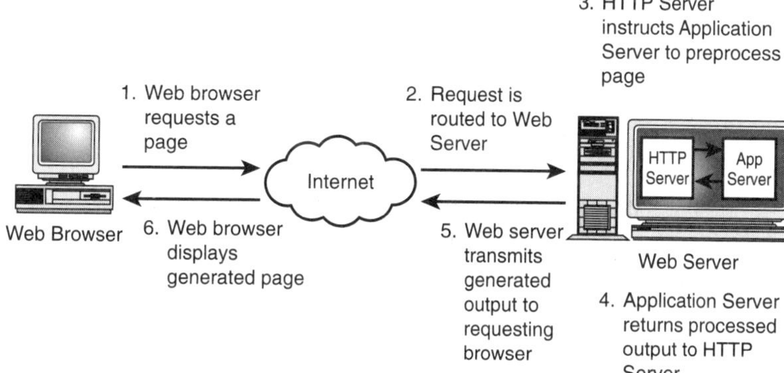

In other words, Web application servers are page preprocessors. They process the requested page before it's sent to the client (the browser), and in doing so they open the door to developers to do all sorts of interesting things on the server, such as

- Creating guest books
- Conducting surveys
- Changing your pages on-the-fly based on date, time, first visit, and whatever else you can think of
- Personalizing pages for your visitors and much more.

Why ColdFusion?

ColdFusion is the name of Allaire Corporation's award-winning family of Web application servers. It's worthwhile to note that ColdFusion helped define what Web application servers are—after all, ColdFusion was the very first Web application server commercially available (back in 1995). What this means is that the technology that you are about to learn is proven and reliable, one that hundreds of thousands of developers have already built their own applications on.

Why is ColdFusion so popular? This question has quite a few answers, but the most important answer is that it's incredibly easy to learn. ColdFusion uses the exact same language elements as HTML itself—tags and attributes. So if you are comfortable writing HTML, you already have all the skills you need to start writing CFML (ColdFusion Markup Language). That's not something that can be said about any other programming language out there.

Oh, and before I forget, don't let the simplicity and ease of use give you the wrong impression—CFML is a complete and powerful language, one that features all the language elements and components that you need to write world-class applications.

But there is more to it than simplicity.

Rapid Development I've already explained that ColdFusion's biggest claim to fame is its minimal learning curve. On top of that, ColdFusion Studio (the ColdFusion IDE) features a whole range of menus, toolbars, pop-up help options, and sophisticated interfaces to make rapid development even more rapid.

Scalable Deployment ColdFusion applications can scale, and scale well. By supporting clustering, fail-over and load-balancing, integration with hardware-based load-balancing products, and cluster-based session management, ColdFusion provides all the tools to build high-end scalable applications.

Of course, it's also possible to write ColdFusion applications that don't scale. ColdFusion is a tool, not a finished product. What you do with it is up to you.

Open Integration When building applications on the Web, the last thing you want is to be locked into a specific vendor's set of tools and technologies. ColdFusion is designed to integrate with any technologies you use. From extensive database support to support for distributed computing via COM, CORBA, and EJB to an extensive range of integration options (including a C/C++ API and Java integration), ColdFusion can be made to interact with whatever technologies you are currently using and with those you'll want to use in the future.

Complete System Security The more powerful and critical your applications are, the more important a solid and robust security system is. ColdFusion provides building blocks that you may use to build sophisticated and flexible security systems, using authentication and access control that work the way you need it.

NOTE Three different ColdFusion servers are actually available:

- *ColdFusion Express* is the freely available version of ColdFusion (the version you have). It supports a basic subset of ColdFusion's functionality and runs on computers with Windows or Linux.
- *ColdFusion Professional* is a commercial version that runs on computers with Windows or Linux. In addition to all the features offered by ColdFusion Express, ColdFusion Professional features integration with email and LDAP servers, support for all sorts of extensions, and the capability to write your own language extensions.
- *ColdFusion Enterprise* is a commercial version of ColdFusion that runs on computers with Windows, Linux, Solaris, or HP/UX. In addition to all the features offered by ColdFusion Professional, ColdFusion Enterprise also features high-end scalability and security options to ensure 100 percent uptime.

Spectra runs on ColdFusion Enterprise, not on Express or Professional. If you are currently running Express or Professional, you need to upgrade to the full Enterprise edition.

For all these reasons, ColdFusion has become the application server of choice for hundreds of thousands of developers the world over.

Custom Tags

CFML is a tag-based language that looks more like HTML and XML than it does a traditional script-based language.

CFML is made up of fewer than a hundred tags that do everything from database interaction to server-side HTTP calls to email sending and receiving to COM, CORBA, and Java integration and more.

But aside from the built-in tags, ColdFusion allows developers to write language extensions in the form of custom tags (often called CFXs). Hundreds of third-party custom tags are available, and many developers write their own tags for their own applications. Custom tags are the standard way to extend the ColdFusion server, and there is no limit to how many tags you can have and what they do.

NOTE This book won't teach you how to write and use ColdFusion custom tags. If you need help with this, refer to the ColdFusion documentation or my *Advanced ColdFusion 4.0 Application Development* book (ISBN 0-7897-1810-3).

Looking for third-party custom tags? Visit `http://www.allaire.com` and go to the Developer's Exchange in the Developer section. You'll find a searchable collection of hundreds of them that you can download.

Data Types, Variables, and Structures

Most computer languages support the use of variables, and CFML is no exception. But where CFML varies from most languages is that it has no real concept of data types. A ColdFusion variable is a variable, not a string variable or a numeric variable, it's just a variable that can hold any type of data. In other words, CFML is a *typeless* language.

There is good reason for this. Because HTML itself is typeless, the data you get back from forms and URLs is typeless—forcing you to use specific data types would be unnecessarily complex and add no real value.

ColdFusion is typeless, but SQL (the language used for ColdFusion database integration) isn't. When creating SQL statements in ColdFusion, correct data types must be used.

Although ColdFusion is typeless, it does support several advanced forms of variables.

Simple Variables Most variables are simple variables. These are named with unique names (not beginning with a numeric character) and may contain any data, including text, numbers, dates, and even entire files.

Simple variables are created using the ColdFusion `<CFSET>` or `<CFPARAM>` tag, like this:

```
<CFSET Name="Ben">
```

`<CFSET>` is used to both create and update variables.

Lists *Lists* are strings containing one or more elements. Lists are actually simple variables, too. What makes a list a list is that a delimiter may be used to simplify the manipulation of list elements. Lists are usually comma delimited, like this:

```
<CFSET Items="1,5,18,23">
```

But any character can be used as the list delimiter, so specifying a space as a delimiter, for example, will allow you to manipulate individual words in a sentence.

Lists are manipulated with a set of special functions (for example, `ListFirst()` and `ListGetAt()`), as well as via the `<CFLOOP>` tag that allows looping through list members.

TIP All list manipulation functions begin with the word `List`.

A list isn't an efficient form of storage (a list is essentially a long string), but it does provide a simple way of manipulating groups of data.

Arrays ColdFusion supports arrays of up to three dimensions, as well as arrays of arrays (and arrays of lists, and any other combination). Arrays are manipulated with array functions (for example `ArrayNew()` and `ArrayAppend()`) and can contain any type of data.

TIP All array manipulation functions begin with the word `Array`.

Arrays can be resized as needed and can grow automatically as elements are added to them. Functions also are provided to allow the conversion of a list to an array or an array to a list.

Structures A *structure* is a special form of variable, one that contains other variables. Also known as *associative arrays*, structures are the most flexible form of variable in ColdFusion because they allow complex sets of data to be grouped and manipulated as a group.

Unlike in an array, structure member variables are named or numbered. Structure elements can contain any form of data: simple variables, lists, arrays, and even other structures. Structure members can be assigned by using the `<CFSET>` tag or any of the special structure functions.

Structures are created by using the `StructNew()` function:

```
<CFSET user=StructNew()>
```

TIP All structure manipulation functions begin with the word `Struct`.

Scope *Scope* defines the lifetime and visibility of a variable. ColdFusion supports multiple scopes, all of which are used by supplying a scope prefix before the variable reference. The primary scopes are as follows:

- `APPLICATION` persists across all sessions application-wide (it doesn't span multiple applications).
- `SERVER` persists across all sessions and all applications on a server.
- `VARIABLES` persists for a single request and is visible only in the page in which it's created.
- `REQUEST` persists for a single request and is visible to all pages (and custom tags) processed in that request.
- `SESSION` persists for a single user session and is visible to all pages and requests processed for that session. It's highly flexible but limited to a single server.
- `CLIENT` persists for a single user session and is visible to all pages and requests processed for that session. It's not as flexible as `SESSION` but can span servers in a cluster.
- `FORM` persists for a single request and is visible only in the page to which its fields were submitted.
- `URL` persists for a single request and is visible only in the page to which `URL GET` parameters were submitted.

If no scope is specified when creating a variable, the default scope of `VARIABLES` is used. When variables are accessed, a specific order of evaluation is used to determine the variable being accessed if no scope prefix is provided.

Aside from the last three (which essentially can contain just strings), all ColdFusion scopes can contain any type of data, including all the variable types listed above.

WDDX

WDDX, or Web Distributed Data eXchange, is an XML format used to share structured data between applications and servers. Since it is XML, WDDX format data can be used by applications and languages other than ColdFusion.

XML is normally used to define specific types of data. WDDX is used to define data itself (including all the properties associated with raw data, including type, name, and other constraints). WDDX is designed to deliver the promise of XML without having to wait for standard XML vocabularies to evolve and gain acceptance.

The beauty of WDDX lies in the fact that it's XML but can be used without having to manipulate (or even know how to manipulate) XML structures directly.

To use WDDX within ColdFusion, a single tag is used, `<CFWDDX>`. This tag handles all the conversions of data into and out of WDDX format. Similar wrappers are available for other languages and platforms.

NOTE WDDX was created by Allaire Corporation but has been released for public use by any application. More information on WDDX is available at `http://www.wddx.org/`.

Working with Spectra and ColdFusion

As explained earlier, Spectra is written in ColdFusion. This means that the features and options available to ColdFusion, the strengths that have made ColdFusion a leading player in the application server space, and the experience and expertise that have been acquired in developing ColdFusion code apply to Spectra, too.

Although I didn't cover all of ColdFusion in this chapter (that would just not be possible), I did list some of the important technologies that ColdFusion offers, technologies that need to be understood by Spectra developers, technologies that Spectra applies extensively.

Custom Tags

As mentioned earlier, Spectra is implemented as ColdFusion custom tags, more than 200 of them (as listed in Appendix A, "Allaire Spectra Tags"). Every Spectra feature is invoked by using one or more tags. When you write Spectra code, you'll actually use three types of tags:

- Tags beginning with `CF` are standard CFML. These are documented in the ColdFusion documentation.
- Tags beginning with `CF_` are custom tags, either your own or from a third party.
- Tags beginning with `CFA_` are Spectra-specific tags. These are documented in the Spectra documentation, as well as in Appendix A of this book.

Some tags are simple tags, others are tag pairs (a beginning and an end tag), and yet others are tag families (tags used within the body of other tags). Regardless of the tags used, they all function the same way. They are called with a < before and a > after, and attributes are passed to them as standard XML format attributes (*`name=value`* pairs).

Knowing how to use tags is a prerequisite, although if you are comfortable writing HTML and CFML (as you should be), the only thing you'll need to learn is all the Spectra tags. That's what most of this book covers.

Want to see examples of world-class ColdFusion code? Almost all the Spectra tags are provided in source code form and are well commented. You can open and read any of them to see how Spectra does what it does, or just to learn ColdFusion tips and techniques used by some of the best ColdFusion developers out there—the team that wrote Spectra.

Structures

Spectra makes extensive use of structures, which are the most powerful and flexible type of variable. Many Spectra tags take structures as attributes. This makes parameter passing simpler; rather than pass dozens of attributes to a tag, you can create and populate a structure and then pass it to the tag.

Structures were introduced in ColdFusion 4, and even some experienced ColdFusion developers aren't familiar with using them. Spectra developers, however, must be comfortable using structures. It's close to impossible to use Spectra without knowing how to use structures.

When looking at Spectra tag syntax, attributes that accept structures usually are named with an `st` prefix. Attributes that take the name of a structure to be returned usually are named with an `r_st` prefix.

WDDX

Internally, Spectra uses WDDX extensively; much internal data is stored in this format. While you can write entire Spectra applications without even seeing this underlying format, a basic understanding of what WDDX is and what it looks like will be invaluable in debugging and troubleshooting. In addition, if you plan to work with syndication (described later in this book), understanding WDDX is required. ●

CHAPTER 3

Spectra Concepts and Terminology

In this chapter

Understanding Spectra's Terminology

Before you delve into building a Spectra application, learning about Spectra's terminology is very helpful. In this chapter, you will gain an understanding of what all the terms you will see throughout this book mean and how the concepts they represent relate to each other. Each term and concept is covered in much greater detail in subsequent chapters, as is additional terminology as needed.

You may be tempted to skip some of the items in this chapter. Even if you are a seasoned ColdFusion programmer, knowing the terminology will help you develop the example A2ZBooks application throughout this book and your own Spectra applications.

Tag Usage

Allaire Spectra consists of more than 400 custom tags. Spectra tags are designated by the prefix `cfa_`, unlike standard CFML custom tags, which are prefixed by `cf_`. This avoids naming conflicts with any custom tags that you may use in your applications. Just like standard CFML, Spectra tags have attributes and may or may not require end tags. Always refer to the tag help or Appendix A, "Allaire Spectra Tags," if you are unsure.

When you choose to install the client tools, help files and tag insight scripts are installed into ColdFusion Studio. The complete Allaire Spectra documentation set is then accessible from the Help tab.

Naming

To reduce confusion, Spectra tags are named by using the formula *object-action*. This means that if you need a tag to retrieve a ContentObject, the most likely name would be `cfa_ContentObjectGet`. Similarly, if you needed to copy a ContentObject to another ContentObject as an embedded object (which you'll learn about later in this chapter), you would use `cfa_ContentObjectCreateEmbeddedFromOriginal` (*object-action-object-action*).

Attributes

Spectra tags expect two kinds of attributes: input and output. Input attributes are further divided into data types for efficient processing. Characters that denote what data type the attribute will accept prefix each attribute name. Table 3.1 shows these attribute prefixes and what these tags will validate.

Table 3.1 Attribute Prefixes

Prefix	Example	Expected Result
a	aObjects	Array
st	stProperties	Structure or associative array
n	nValue	Number or float
i	iMaxItems	Integer
o	oProfile	Object. Since objects exist as structures in Spectra, this isn't used.
dt	dtLastModified	Date or date-time
(none)		String
w	wstProperties	In combination with any other prefix, this means a WDDX packet of the data type indicated by the secondary prefix is expected.
r_	r_result	Variable name. This is similar to the NAME attribute in CFML tags such as CFQUERY. The result of the tag execution will be placed in the specified variable.

CAUTION

The Spectra tag naming conventions are generally followed, but there are exceptions to the rule. Be sure to refer to documentation or use the appropriate Studio Tag Editors; don't make any assumptions about naming conventions.

Encapsulation

Just like other CFML tags, Spectra tags can be encapsulated inside your own custom tags. Typically, you would encapsulate Spectra tags to provide clearer meaning to what these tags are supposed to do in specific circumstances. For instance, the Spectra tag <cfa_container> allows you to create a container. If you want to refer to a specific container that contains news items, you would use the attribute containerID. The following shows how you could encapsulate the <cfa_container> tag in your own custom tag, <cf_news>:

```
<!--- Call the container by ID to preserve settings --->
<cfa_container
 containerID="F345D34-4763-DC8788B2A980"
>
```

A site designer could intuitively use this in a document without looking for the actual container ID.

Object-Based Development

Spectra applications consist of ContentObjects and ContentObject Types. Object-Based Development is the process of creating and maintaining these application components. Object-Based Development is not just a methodology for developing application code; it's also a methodology for creating your data model and data storage.

The core of Object-Based Development is the ContentObject Type. The ContentObject Type defines what will be stored in each ContentObject (properties), what can be done with each ContentObject (methods), and how each possible action that can be performed on a ContentObject relates to the code you write (handlers). The Object-Based Development model can be much more flexible and maintainable than standard ColdFusion development techniques, as shown in Table 3.2. Object-Based Development also allows you to take full advantage of all the services Spectra provides.

Table 3.2 Differences Between ColdFusion and Spectra Applications

Task	ColdFusion Approach	Spectra Approach
Rendering of the data model	A database schema is created in an RDBMS	Property definitions, ContentObject Types, and type properties are created.
Providing data access	SQL queries are generated and encapsulated in `CFQUERY` tags.	Data access is provided by the system.
Modifying the data model	Changes are made to the database schema and the SQL queries.	Type properties are modified as necessary. Complex changes can be made without database modifications.

Differences from Object-Oriented Development

Although *objects*, *properties*, and *methods* are common terms in object-oriented programming, Object-Based Development has key differences from this model. There are no class libraries or inheritance, and object instances vary in their behavior and life cycle. Object-Based Development isn't meant as a replacement—it's an encapsulation of the best practices in developing application logic and presentation layers for Web applications. Object-oriented development (using Java or C++) complements object-based Spectra applications very well, and Spectra and ColdFusion both fully support integration.

The ContentObject API (COAPI)

The core of Spectra and Object-Based Development is the ContentObject API (COAPI). This set of tags and services comprises the data access and application organization of Spectra.

The COAPI tags reside in the `/Program Files/Allaire/Spectra/Customtags/COAPI/` directory as well as the `/Program Files/Allaire/Spectra/Customtags/tier0/` directory. The `COPAI` directory contains system-level tags such as ContentObject storage and retrieval and Process Logic Path instantiation. The `tier0` directory contains the tags you are most likely to use, such as those used in the creation of ContentObject Types and ContentObjects, meta data services, security, and other services.

The COAPI is also the point of integration with external systems such as user databases, external databases, and legacy applications. All other Spectra systems and services are built atop the COPAI and use the tags and services it provides.

The Application *Applications* are sets of resources available to your Spectra applications. The resources you define in an application are the Security Context, the Spectra Database (ContentObject Database), and the Logging Object:

- The *Security Context* is the user databases, rules, and policies that form the basis of the security model for your application. This is covered in more detail in Chapter 16, "Using Spectra Security Options."
- The *ContentObject Database* is where all your application data will reside, including ContentObject Types, Process Logic Paths, and Site Layout Model data. Spectra manages the data access for this database. You will create one for each of your applications, as described in Chapter 6, "Introduction to Spectra Programming."
- The *Logging Object* defines what data from your application will be logged and where the log will reside. This is defined in the System Administration portion of the Webtop and is described in Chapter 17, "Site Reporting."

ContentObject Types *ContentObject Types* are the ContentObject definitions. ContentObject Types define what data is contained in ContentObjects of that type, as well as what actions can be performed on those ContentObjects. A ContentObject Type consists of a set of type properties, a set of methods, a handler root, and a label. The ContentObject Type becomes a template for all the ContentObjects of its type, otherwise known as its *instances*.

Properties *Properties* are the place where data is stored in a ContentObject. For instance, if you wanted to store and retrieve articles in your application, normally you would create a database table with columns for each component of an article. These components could be Tile, Body, and Author. In Spectra, the creation of a database table isn't necessary; your data is stored in the ContentObject. Three components make this possible: the Property Definition, the Type Property, and the Property itself.

NOTE You aren't limited to data storage in properties. You can also store data in external databases. This is covered in Chapter 6.

The *Property Definition* is a global definition of what the property will eventually be. Property Definitions contain a data type, a label, and validation information to be used by Spectra's default handlers. For the article example above, you would create Property Definitions for each component of the article. They would vary significantly from each other in their use in an application. A title, for example, is most likely a short string, whereas a body would probably be a very long set of text. In creating Property Definitions, you also consider how they will be used in all your ContentObject Types. You may have both articles and products as ContentObject Types, but both will have a body property. To enable your users to search both the body property of all the articles and the body property of all the products, you would create a Property Definition like the one shown in Table 3.3 and relate it with both ContentObject Types. This related Property Definition is called a *Type Property*.

Table 3.3 Example Property Definitions

Label	Data Type	Input Type	Validate
Title	`char`	`text`	required
Body	`longchar`	`textarea`	none
DueDate	`datetime`	`text`	date
OrderStatus	`char`	`select` (provide options)	

Each ContentObject Type contains a set of Type Properties. Each Type Property can be multilingual, can contain multiple values, and can be indexed by the Verity engine or stored in a normalized table. Type Properties can even contain other ContentObjects. Type Properties are limited only by the data type defined in the related Property Definition. The Type Property is a template for what can be stored in any ContentObject of that type. When a ContentObject of that type is created and the actual text of an article is stored with its title and author, a property is created.

Methods and Handlers All the actions that can be performed on a ContentObject are called *methods*. For the article example, you would create, edit, and display each ContentObject. You would create a method for each action. Each method has a label and an associated handler. *Handlers* are ColdFusion templates that you create. So, to allow users to edit your ContentObjects, you code a handler that contains a form for modifying the ContentObject and an action to persist the changes.

The system provides special handlers to enable you to build your application more quickly and also to take care of common tasks. The most commonly encountered are the `create`, `edit`, and `display` handlers. If you don't create named methods for these, Spectra will create default handlers. Once you create named methods for these tasks, your new handlers will override the default system handlers. One exception to this is the `create` handler; if you create a named method for this, Spectra will execute your code sequentially after the system `create` handler (the constructor). This allows you to perform complex initialization of a ContentObject if you need to. Table 3.4 lists the default handlers in Spectra.

Table 3.4 Spectra's Default Handlers

Handler	Function
`create`	Creates a new ContentObject. Can't be overridden.
`edit`	Renders a form for editing any ContentObject.
`delete`	Deletes a ContentObject.
`display`	Displays ContentObject properties and values.
`editattributes`	Allows for changing the `Active` and `Published` status for a ContentObject.
`editmetadata`	Allows categorization of a ContentObject.
`editsecurity`	Manages the permissions for all methods for a ContentObject.
`get`	Retrieves a ContentObject.
`preview`	Previews a ContentObject.

UML and Documentation After you create your ContentObject Type, you can use several strategies for documentation. UML provides a good set of tools for documenting your ContentObject Types because of their similarity to objects in object-oriented languages. However, if you are unfamiliar with UML, you can use techniques derived from UML, as shown in Table 3.5.

NOTE *UML* is the acronym for the *Unified Modeling Language*,an industry-standard language for documenting and visualizing software systems. A good primer on UML is *Sams Teach Yourself UML in 24 Hours* (ISBN 0-6723-1636-6).

Table 3.5 Example of a Documented Object

Object	Type Properties	Methods
Article		
	Title	`displayTeaser`
	Body	`displayFull`
	Author	
	Byline	

ContentObjects

ContentObjects are instances of ContentObject Types. In object-based development, ContentObjects are really sets of data that have been constrained by a ContentObject Type. These data sets can then be acted on or invoked by using the defined methods of the ContentObject Type. Put simply, ContentObjects are to ContentObject Types as rows are to tables in a database.

Invocation Passing the data from a ContentObject to a method is the process of invocation. Invocation occurs throughout the lifecycle of a ContentObject. Any time you want to do something with a ContentObject, you invoke it with a method, as shown in Figure 3.1. If you want to edit ContentObject x, you would invoke object x by using the `edit` method. The data contained in the ContentObject would be passed to the handler you associated with the `edit` method (or the default handler), and the result would be output to the page.

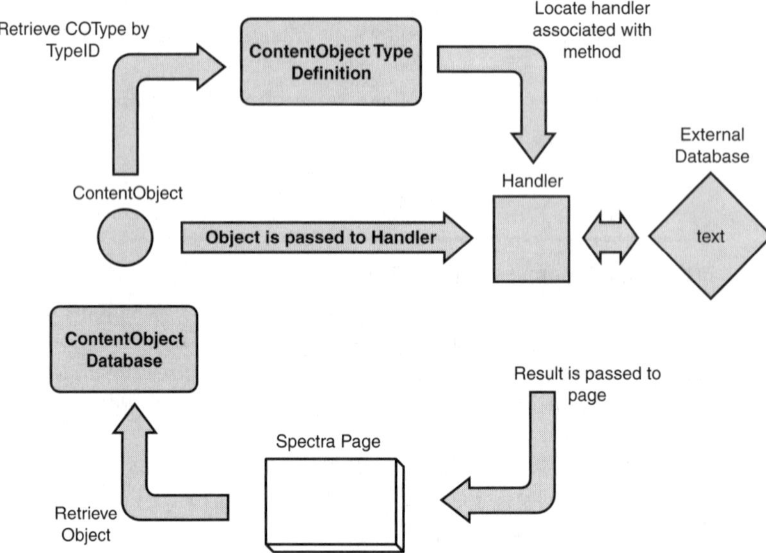

FIGURE 3.1
Object invocation consists of four steps.

Remote Invocation ContentObjects can also be invoked remotely, allowing interaction with other Spectra servers or applications. In fact, any application on virtually any platform can invoke a ContentObject remotely. This is the basis of Application Syndication, which allows Spectra application functionality to be shared securely with other Web applications.

Embedded Objects A Property Definition can have a data type that's actually a ContentObject Type. When this Property Definition is related to a ContentObject Type, any ContentObjects of this type will contain an Embedded Object. One property will fully contain another object. In our article example above, you could now place the author's name, email address, and biography in each article, all contained within a single property.

Embedded Objects can be shared or standalone. Shared Embedded Objects are objects that exist on their own and are embedded into multiple ContentObjects. When the master object is updated, all embedded versions are also updated. Standalone Embedded Objects exist only within a single ContentObject and must be accessed through the embedding object.

TIP For both shared and standalone Embedded Objects, the Embedded Objects have an `objectID` or unique identifier of `{`*`embedding objectid`*`}.{`*`property`*`}`.

Container-Oriented and Rules-Based Publishing

In a Spectra application, you organize areas of the page that are designated for content publishing into containers. Each of these containers is assigned one or more rules. These rules determine the logic used to select the objects in that container. You create these rules based on criteria you select, such as "surface all content that has meta data similar to that stored in the User Profile." Rules-based publishing is covered in detail in Chapter 19, "Rules-Based Publishing."

The Site Object Model

Your Property Definitions, ContentObject Types, and Content Objects are your Site Object Model. Your Site Object Model forms the basis for the application logic of your site and allows you to separate this from your presentation layer. The Site Object Model components have their own security that doesn't rely on presentation layer security, allowing fine control over functionality permissions.

All components of your Site Object Model are uniquely identified and are portable, allowing you to migrate easily from development to staging and on to production. The Site Object Model is constructed by the Interactive Developers and is used as underlying functionality by all other roles in the Spectrum of Participants.

The Site Layout Model

The Site Layout Model is the organization of the presentation layer and navigation of your site. Containers, pages, sections, and the site are all components of the Site Layout Model. Each of these components can be secured individually as a layer above Site Object Model security. Each element can also be cached individually, allowing you to cache sections within a page to improve performance without sacrificing interactivity.

The Site Object Model is constructed by site designers and can be managed by business users. The burden of site maintenance now becomes the power of site control by giving the tools to manage the site directly to those who need them.

The Site Process Model

Publishing Rules, Process Logic Paths (PLPs), and Workflows comprise the Site Process Model. Logging and Reporting are also components of this model. The Site Process Model unites the Site Object Model and the Site Layout Model and provides broad application functionality and management.

Interactive developers construct the Site Process Model based on the requirements and business rules defined by the business managers. Elements of both the Site Layout Model and the Site Object Model access this functionality to help the site reflect the business objectives of the enterprise.

Services

The six services Spectra provides are detailed throughout the book and are overviewed in Chapter 1, "Understanding Spectra." These services span the three models and are a part of all Spectra application code.

You will learn about each of Spectra's services and features in the following chapters.

CHAPTER 4

Installing and Configuring Spectra

In this chapter

Supported Platforms and System Requirements

Allaire Spectra is currently available for the Windows NT, Windows 2000, and Solaris operating systems, with support for Linux and HP-UX expected soon.

The system requirements for running Spectra on Windows NT are as follows:

- Window NT 4, Workstation, or Server, Service Pack 3 or greater
- ColdFusion Application Server Enterprise Edition 4.01 or higher with Advanced Security installed and enabled
- 100MB disk space
- 64MB RAM (256 recommended)
- Microsoft SQL Server, Sybase (SQL Anywhere, system 10, system 11), or Oracle (7.3 or 8.0) database

NOTE For Windows NT installations, ColdFusion Application Server 4.5 is required for use with an Oracle database.

- Version 4 or higher of Internet Explorer or Netscape Navigator
- CD-ROM drive
- Account with administrative privileges

The system requirements for running Spectra on Solaris are

- SPARC Solaris 7, 2.6, or 2.5.1 with all required patches
- ColdFusion Application Server Enterprise Edition 4.01 or higher with Advanced Security installed and enabled
- 150MB disk space
- 256MB RAM (512 recommended)
- Microsoft SQL Server, Sybase (SQL Anywhere, system 10, system 11), or Oracle (7.3 or 8.0) database

NOTE For Solaris installations, ColdFusion Application Server 4.5 is required for use with Oracle or Microsoft SQL Server databases.

- Version 4 or higher of Internet Explorer or Netscape Navigator
- CD-ROM drive
- X Windows platform software
- XCU4 utilities
- pkgadd, pkgrm, and pkginfo utilities
- Root level access

NOTE Although IE4 or Netscape 4 (or later) is required for use with the Webtop, sites can be built with Spectra for use with all browsers.

TIP While the Webtop is accessible to IE4+ and Netscape 4+, it has been optimized for use with IE5.

Before Spectra is installed, you must first install ColdFusion Application Server Enterprise Edition 4.01 or 4.5. See *The ColdFusion 4.0 Web Application Construction Kit*, published by Que Corporation, for details on installing the application server.

Also, be sure to verify that ColdFusion 4.01 or later is running properly before proceeding with the Spectra installation. You can check your version of the ColdFusion Application Server by going into the ColdFusion Administrator and clicking on the Version link.

Installing Spectra on Windows NT

Before installing Spectra on a Windows NT machine, log in to that machine with an administrative account. Also make sure that all program files are closed and that any database servers running on that machine are closed. Then, follow these steps:

1. If you are installing Spectra from a CD, place the Spectra 1.0 CD in the CD-ROM drive and run `Setup.exe` from that CD. Otherwise, run the executable that you downloaded from Allaire.

NOTE If your system has a previous installation of Spectra, running `Setup.exe` will replace Spectra program files but won't affect any existing data or applications. However, it's always safest to back up any existing databases before re-installing Spectra.

2. The Welcome screen should appear (see Figure 4.1). Click Next to begin.

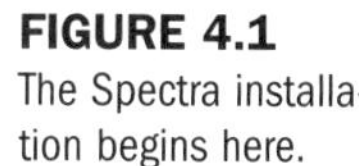

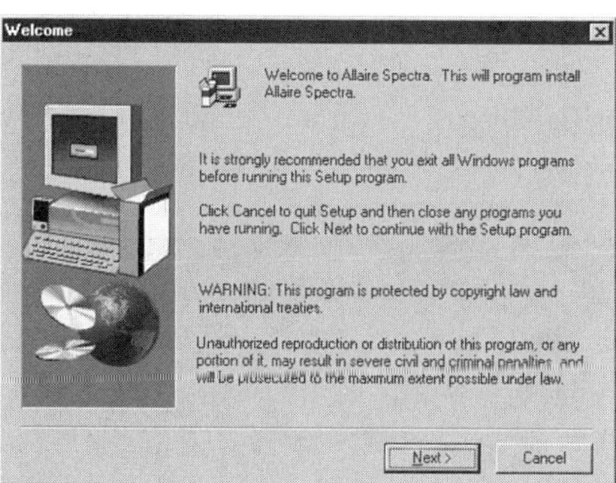

FIGURE 4.1
The Spectra installation begins here.

3. Read the software license agreement and choose Yes to accept it (see Figure 4.2).
4. The Spectra installer requires that you provide a valid serial number to install the product in production mode. To install an evaluation version, use the word `evaluation` as the serial number. Enter your name, company name, and Spectra serial number into the form, then click Next to continue.

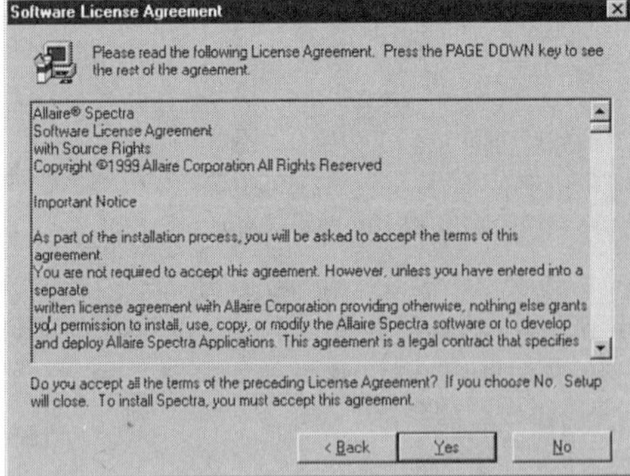

FIGURE 4.2
Read and agree to the Software License Agreement to continue.

5. Select the components you want to install. You can choose to install only the Spectra Server files, only the ColdFusion Studio for Spectra files, or both (see Figure 4.3).

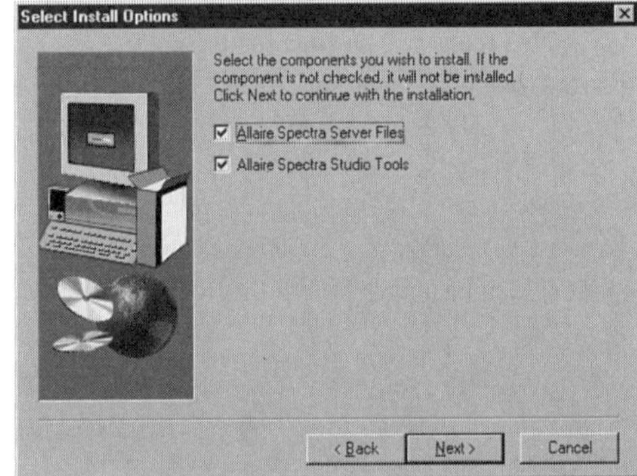

FIGURE 4.3
Choose which components you want to install. It is recommended that you not install the studio files onto a production server.

6. If you are installing the Spectra Server files, choose a directory into which those files will be installed, or accept the default directory (see Figure 4.4).

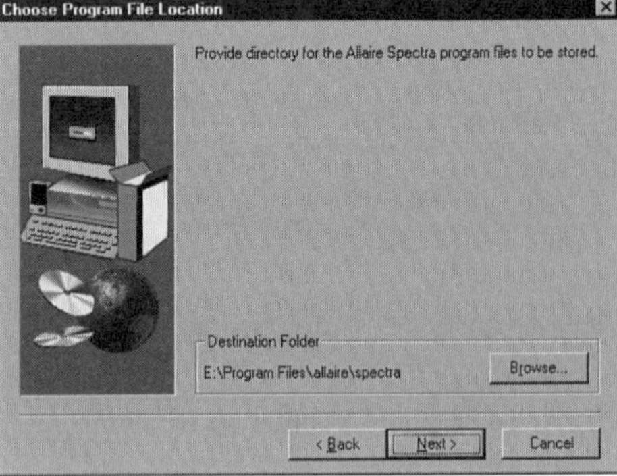

FIGURE 4.4
Provide a directory in which the Spectra program files should be stored.

7. If you are installing the Spectra Server files, the Setup Wizard will attempt to discover the Web root for the Web server installed. You will then be prompted to confirm this Web root (see Figure 4.5).

NOTE The Spectra Webtop and RestoreNet sample application will be installed in an `/Allaire/spectra/` subdirectory of the directory specified here. The i-Build sample application will be installed in an `/i-build/` subdirectory of this Web root.

FIGURE 4.5
Verify your Web root and click Next to continue.

8. You are prompted to enter the program folder of the Start menu, in which a shortcut to Spectra should be placed (see Figure 4.6). You can enter a new folder name or choose to install into one that already exists.

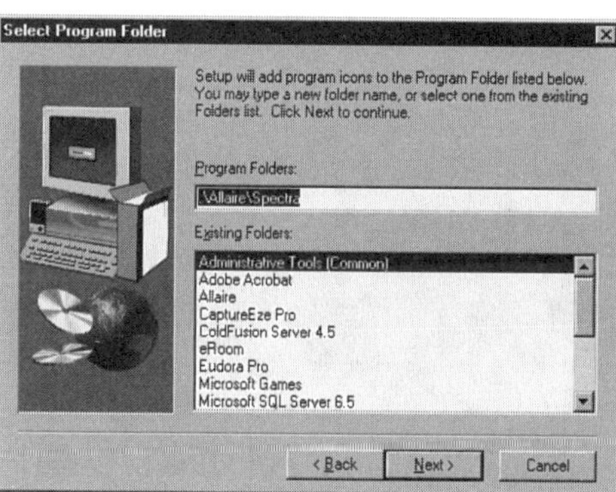

FIGURE 4.6
Choose the program folder that you want to use to access the Spectra menu from the Windows Start button.

9. You are asked to confirm the previous three selections (see Figure 4.7). If they all appear correctly, click Next; otherwise, click Back and correct the information.

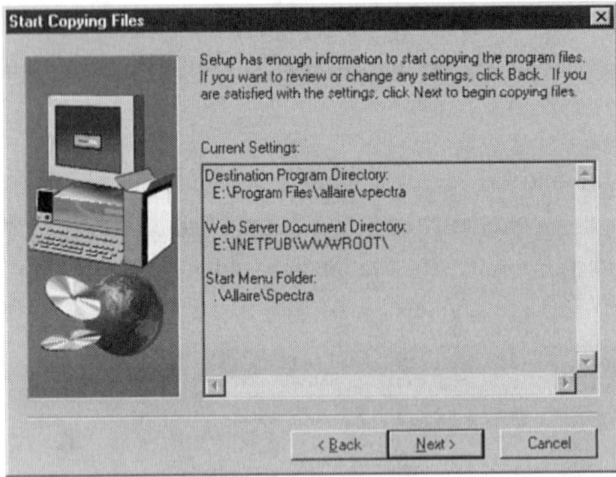

FIGURE 4.7
Confirm your entries and click Next to complete the installation.

CAUTION

If the ColdFusion installation on the server to which you are installing isn't a valid version or isn't installed properly, you may receive an error such as that shown in Figure 4.8 or 4.9. If you receive either message, be sure to remove the files from the directories specified in steps 6 and 7 above, ensure that ColdFusion Application Server Enterprise Edition 4.01 (or greater) is installed and its services are running, and attempt the installation again.

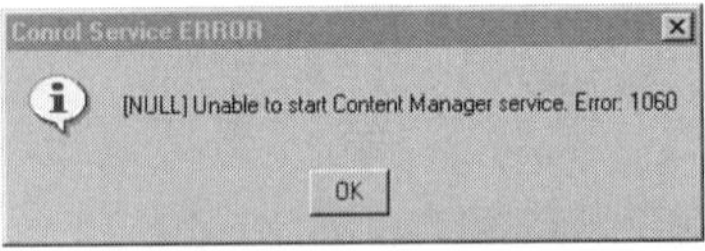

FIGURE 4.8
An error in installation sometimes results in the Content Manager not installing properly. This results in the error message seen here.

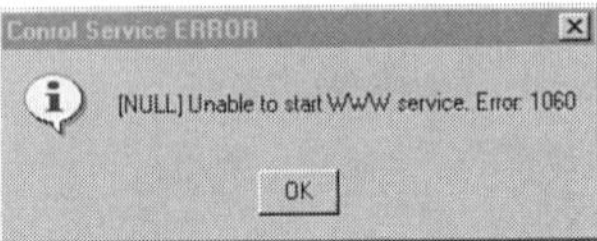

FIGURE 4.9
A failed Spectra installation can result in the Web server not properly restarting.

10. To complete the installation, your system needs to be restarted. You can let the installer restart the system for you or restart it manually (see Figure 4.10). Either way, you must click Finish to complete the installation.
11. After the machine is done rebooting, log back into Windows NT and choose the Allaire Spectra Webtop from the Start menu. You will next need to continue with the "Configuring the Webtop" section later in this chapter.

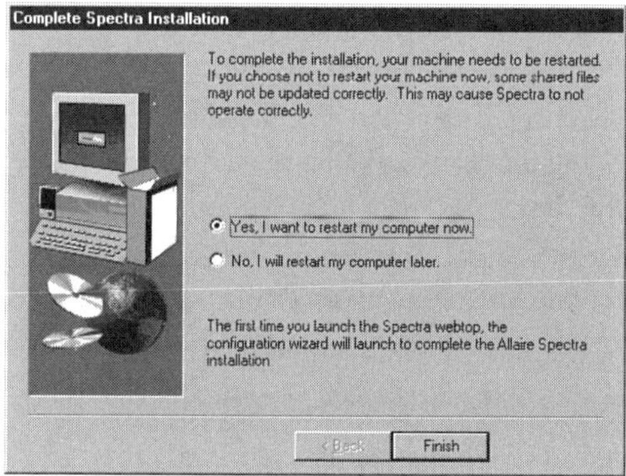

FIGURE 4.10
To complete the installation, you must reboot your server.

CAUTION

For security reasons, Allaire doesn't recommend installing sample applications or documentation on production servers or servers available across the public Internet. To remove these, delete the following directories:

- `webroot/I-build`
- `webroot/spectra`
- `webroot/spectra/docs`
- `webroot/spectra/restorenet`

Installing Spectra on Solaris

Before beginning to install Spectra on Solaris, you need to verify the following:

- That a Web server is installed and properly configured.
- That ColdFusion Application Server Enterprise Edition is installed and has enabled Advanced Security. You can verify the version of the ColdFusion Application Server by going into the ColdFusion Administrator and clicking the Version link.
- That you have an LDAP server installed and have the LDAP IP address, port, and admin user ID and password available.

Allaire Spectra for Solaris is distributed as a package file. As with other package files, you install and manage Allaire Spectra by using the pkgadd, pkgrm, and pkginfo utilities.

To install Allaire Spectra on Solaris, follow these steps:

1. Log in as `root`.

   If you are not installing from a CD, you can skip to step 5.
2. Load the Allaire Spectra CD-ROM into your CD drive.
3. Mount the CD-ROM on `/cdrom/cdrom0` if necessary. (If the Solaris Volume Manager is active, you won't need to mount the CD.)

4. Type **`pkgadd -d /cdrom/cdrom0`** to start the installation process. Solaris returns the names of the package files on the specified volume.
5. Select the Allaire Spectra package file. The installation begins by checking for appropriate OS patches and looking for a previous release (such as an evaluation copy) of Allaire Spectra on the machine.
6. Enter the Allaire Spectra Serial ID when prompted. You can use the word `evaluation` as a serial number if you are installing an evaluation version.
7. Accept the default directory for Allaire Spectra program files.
8. Select the Web server for Allaire Spectra.
9. Press Enter to have the program automatically configure the Web server.
10. Accept the default directory for the Web server.
11. Press Enter to begin the installation.

    When the installation is complete, observe the instructions regarding modifications that need to be made to ColdFusion's start/stop scripts with the appropriate database start/stop information.
12. Restart SiteMinder and the ColdFusion services.

If you're running Spectra on ColdFusion Application Server 4.5, you need to have the Variable Scope Lock settings in the ColdFusion Administrator set to No Automatic Checking or Locking. This may be changed in future releases of Spectra.

Configuring the Webtop

After installing Spectra on Windows NT or Solaris, launch the Webtop by opening a browser to `http://127.0.0.1/allaire/spectra/webtop/index.cfm`. You will come to the Webtop introduction page (see Figure 4.11). Clicking the Spectra box will bring you to the opening page of the Configuration Wizard. Click Continue to begin the configuration.

The Spectra configuration process continues where the installation left off and creates the necessary framework for Spectra to work on your server. Figure 4.12 shows an overview of the configuration process.

To configure Spectra, follow these steps:

1. Build the Spectra Verity collections (see Figure 4.13). This may take a few minutes, as Verity is used to index all aspects of the core Spectra installation.

NOTE If you attempt to install Spectra on a version of ColdFusion prior to 4.01, you may receive an error message at this point similar to the one shown in Figure 4.14.

FIGURE 4.11
The introductory splash page for the Spectra Configuration Wizard. Clicking the box in the center of the page launches the wizard.

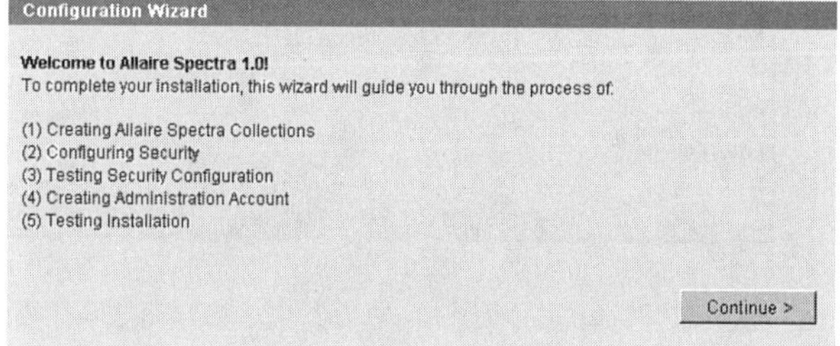

FIGURE 4.12
The Configuration Wizard gives a brief overview of the steps involved in configuring Spectra.

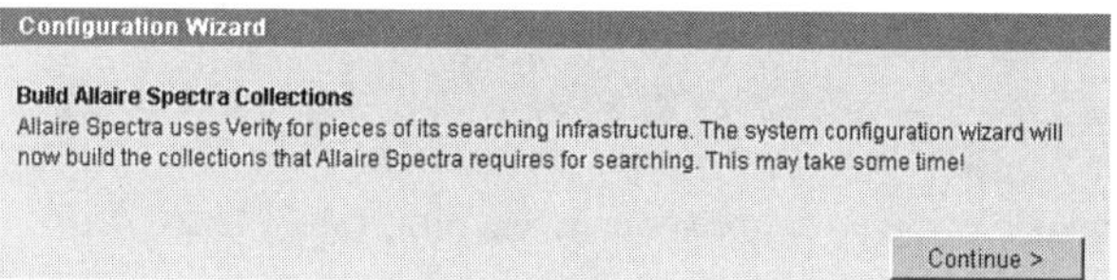

FIGURE 4.13
The Configuration Wizard builds Verity collections to enable searching of Spectra's core components.

2. If all went well with the collection building, you should see a screen telling you that the collections were successfully installed (see Figure 4.15). Click Continue to continue with the installation. If the collections weren't successfully built, go back and try to rebuild the collections.

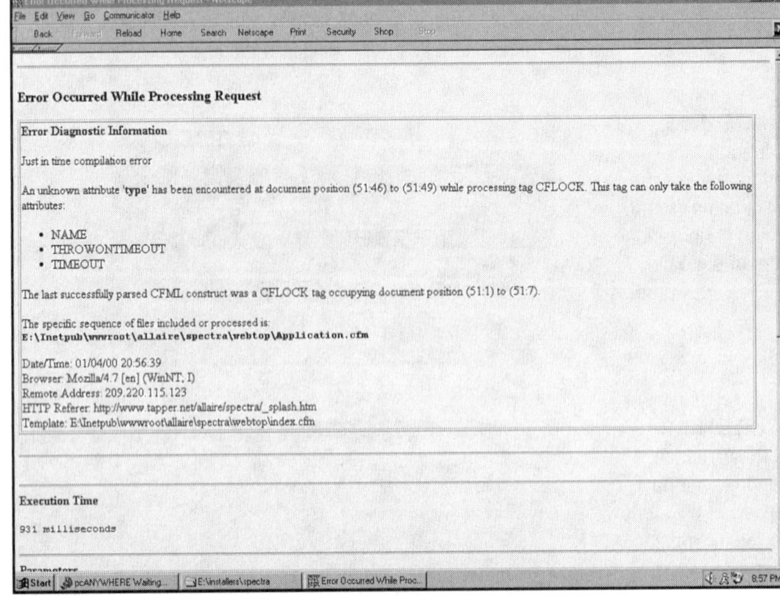

FIGURE 4.14
An error will be encountered if you attempt to install Spectra on a version of ColdFusion Application Server earlier than 4.01. The TYPE attribute of the CFLOCK referenced in the error message was added in CFAS 4.01.

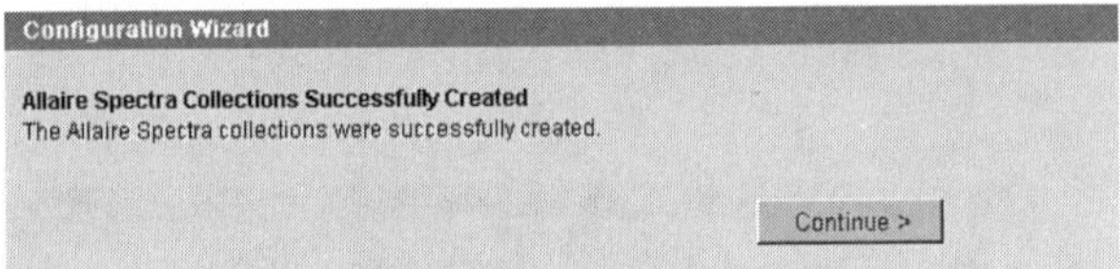

FIGURE 4.15
The Verity collections were successfully installed.

3. You are asked to configure security caching (see Figure 4.16). As Spectra uses ColdFusion Advanced Security to monitor all transactions with the system, interactions are performed more quickly if security information is cached. Allaire recommends using the Security Policy Store Cache, the Security Server Authorization Cache, and the ColdFusion Server Cache.

NOTE For even better performance, Allaire recommends loading the Security Server Policy Store Cache at startup. This way, all security information is readily available to Spectra without having to load the cache as the first user enters the system.

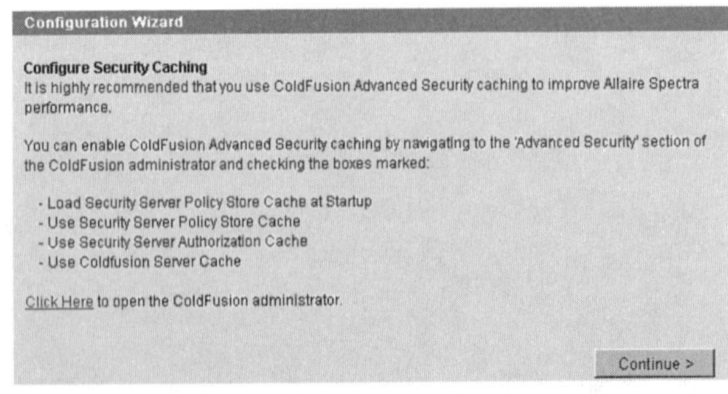

FIGURE 4.16
Allaire's cache recommendations are presented, along with a link to open the ColdFusion Administrator.

4. To enable these settings, launch the ColdFusion Administrator by clicking the Click Here link. Log in to the Administrator with the password you set up when first installing ColdFusion, and navigate to the Advanced Security page of the Server section (see Figure 4.17).

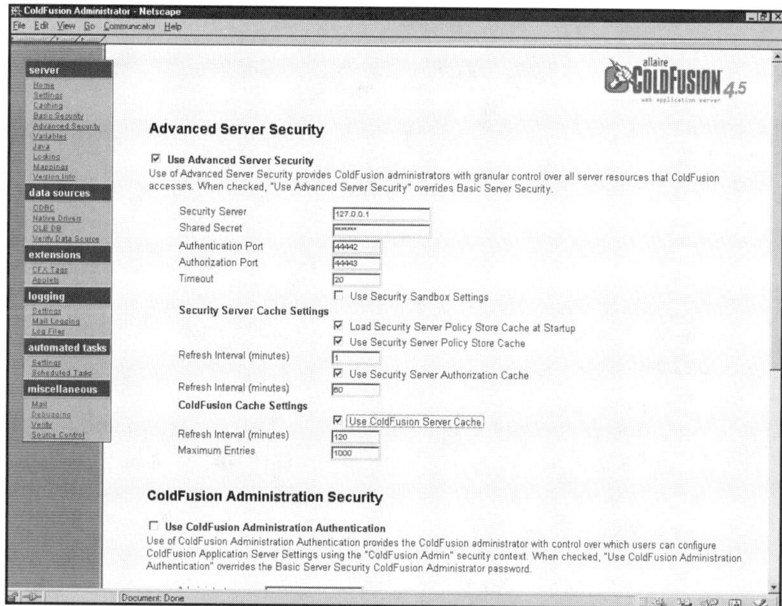

FIGURE 4.17
You can administer the Security Cache settings from the Advanced Server Security page.

Part I Ch 4

5. To enable these settings, check all three check boxes in the Security Server Cache Settings section and the check box labeled ColdFusion Cache Settings (refer to Figure 4.17).
6. Click the Apply button on the bottom of the page to return to the Configuration Wizard.
7. Spectra will want to verify that Advanced Security is enabled (see Figure 4.18). Click Test Security to begin the test.

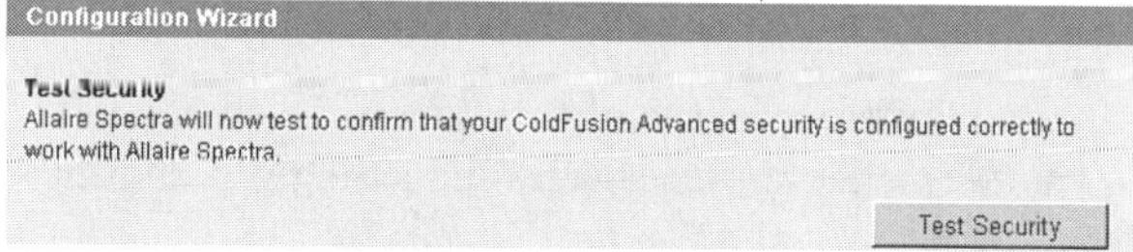

FIGURE 4.18
The Configuration Wizard is ready to test your security settings.

8. If Advanced Security is properly configured, you see a screen much like Figure 4.19. Click Continue to continue with the configuration. Otherwise, if Advanced Security isn't installed or is disabled, you see a screen such as that in Figure 4.20. You need to go back into the ColdFusion Administrator and verify that Advanced Security is enabled.

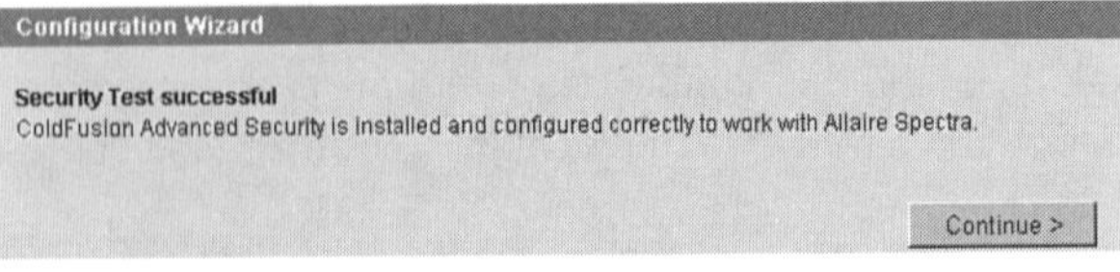

FIGURE 4.19
The Configuration Wizard has confirmed that Advanced Security is properly configured for Spectra.

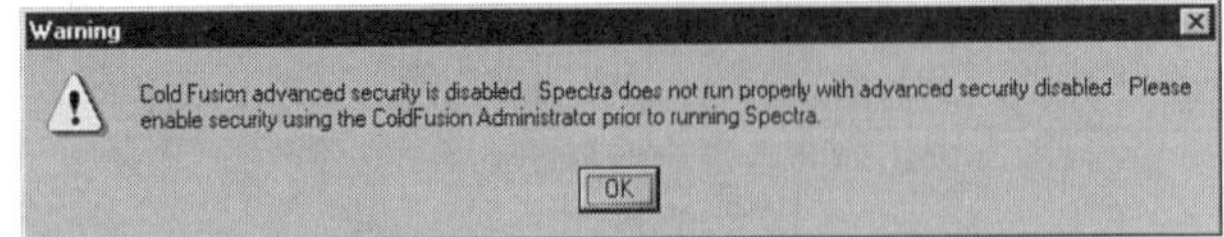

FIGURE 4.20
The security test has failed. Verify that you have Advanced Security installed and enabled.

NOTE Most Spectra Installation problems are related to problems in the Advanced Security setup. See Allaire Knowledgebase article #12498 (`http://www.allaire.com/Handlers/index.cfm?ID=12498&Method=Full`) for details on solving your particular problem.

9. You are prompted to choose an administrator username and password (see Figure 4.21). Whatever you choose, make sure that it's a username/password combination that you can remember, as it's the main administrative account for the Webtop. You need to enter your password twice: once in the Password text box, and once in the Confirm Password text box. Click the Create Account button to continue.

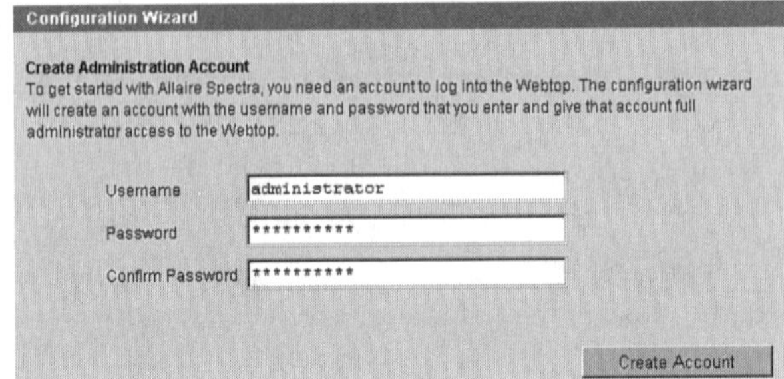

FIGURE 4.21
Don't forget your Administrator username and password. These are your keys to the system.

10. If you entered the same password both times, the screen in Figure 4.22 appears, confirming your Administrator username and letting you know it's the name to be used when you first log in to the Webtop.

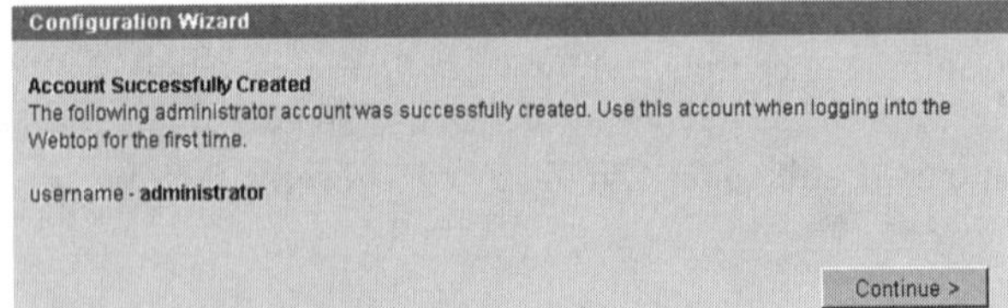

FIGURE 4.22
This shows the confirmation of your Administrators username.

11. Now you need to test that the ContentObject API (COAPI) has been installed successfully. The wizard will present a form asking you to click to test the COAPI (see Figure 4.23).

FIGURE 4.23
Test the COAPI.

12. If the COAPI tests successfully, you are presented with the screen shown in Figure 4.24. Otherwise, the wizard will walk you through reinstalling the COAPI. Click the Continue button on the COAPI Test Successful form to move to the final page of the Configuration Wizard.

FIGURE 4.24
COAPI test successful.

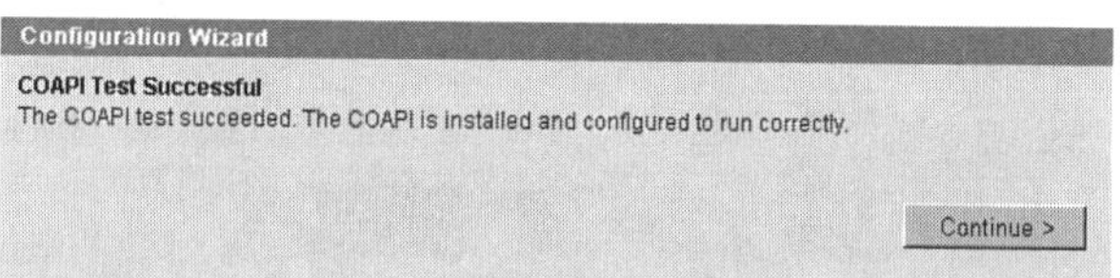

13. In the Allaire Spectra Successfully Configured form (see Figure 4.25), all that remains to be done is to launch the Webtop. Do so by clicking the Launch Allaire Spectra Webtop button.

FIGURE 4.25
Spectra configuration complete!

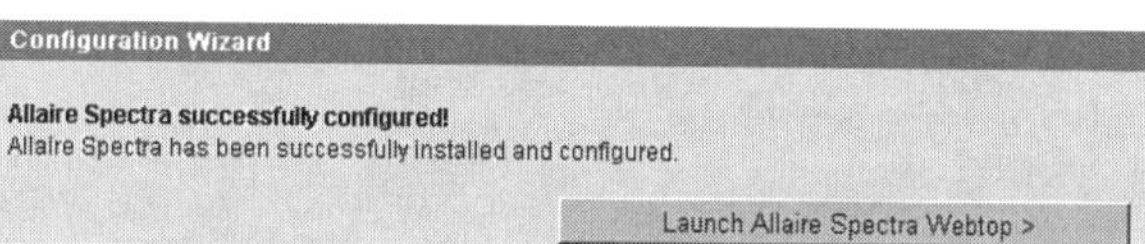

Uninstalling Spectra

To uninstall Spectra for Windows NT, launch the Uninstaller from the Add/Remove Control Panel.

To uninstall Spectra for Solaris, use the pkgrm utility.

Sample Application Walkthrough

The base Spectra installation comes with two sample applications: i-Build, a home improvement superstore, and RestoreNet, a sample e-commerce application for those who are doing home restoration. i-Build is installed into the `/webroot/ibuild directory`, and RestoreNet is installed in the `/webroot/allaire/spectra/restorenet/` directory.

Although these two sample applications aren't intended to showcase all of Spectra's features, they do give a nice overview of what's possible and provide a wealth of sample code on which you can base your applications.

i-Build

i-Build is a sample Spectra Web site aimed at the home improvement community. It simulates a content-driven Web site, with many how-to articles and a search engine to help find articles on topics of interest to you. It can be viewed by opening a browser and going to `http://127.0.0.1/i-build`.

On the home page (see Figure 4.26) are article summaries (referred to as *teasers* in Spectra) with links to the full articles. Included on the right side of the page are a search box and a pull-down menu that categorizes articles on the site.

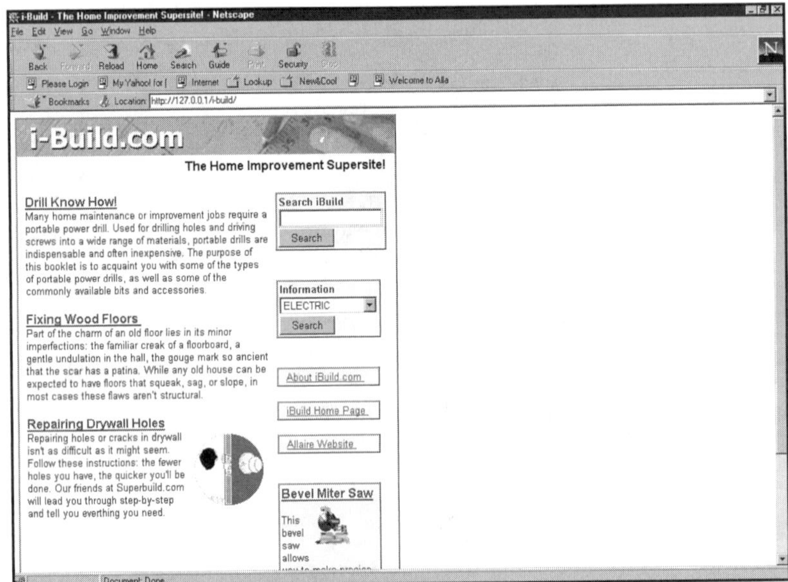

FIGURE 4.26
i-Build's home page.

By changing the URL to `http://127.0.0.1/i-build/index.cfm?designmode=1`, you can see Spectra's true power—the capability to edit a page without having to open files. Figure 4.27 shows the page in Design mode. From here you can add new articles, create new pages, edit existing articles, or add or change the navigation to the page. The icons above and to the left of each piece of content are used to add, edit, and maintain the content. This will be covered in greater detail throughout the book.

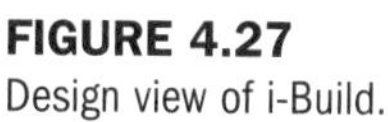

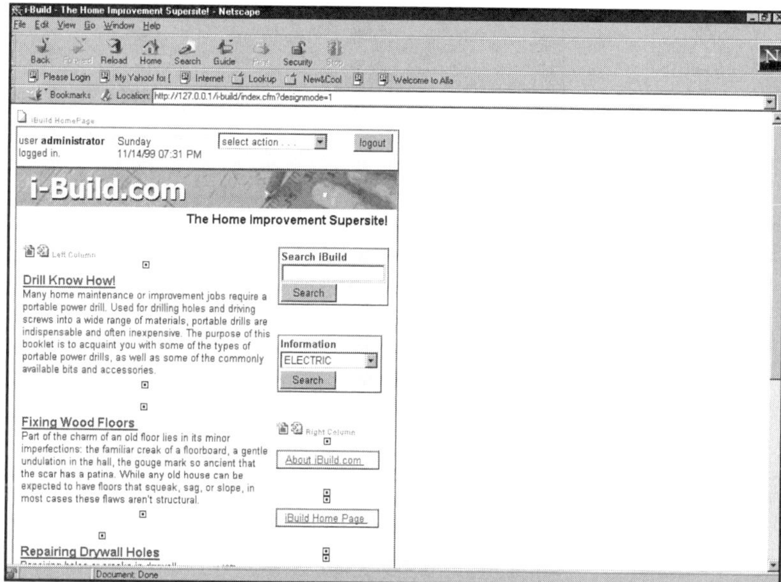

FIGURE 4.27
Design view of i-Build.

NOTE To enter Design mode, you will need to log in to the application with the administrative username and password you created when you configured Spectra.

RestoreNet

RestoreNet is another sample Spectra Web site aimed at the home improvement community. This site varies from i-Build in that it is a sample e-commerce application rather than a content-driven site. You can view RestoreNet by going to `http://127.0.0.1/allaire/spectra/restorenet` from a browser on your server.

The RestoreNet home page (see Figure 4.28) is comprised of three frames. The top frame has the site's logo and a banner ad. Below it, the center frame has introductory text about the site and displays a featured item. The bottom frame has links to the various sections of the site.

Clicking the More Info link below the featured item will bring you to the item's detail page (see Figure 4.29). Here you are presented with a link to add this item to your shopping cart.

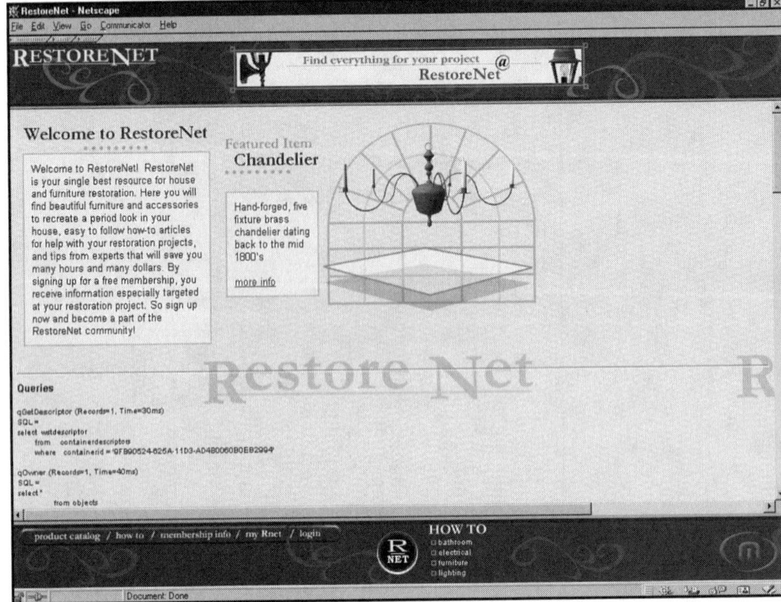

FIGURE 4.28
RestoreNet's home page.

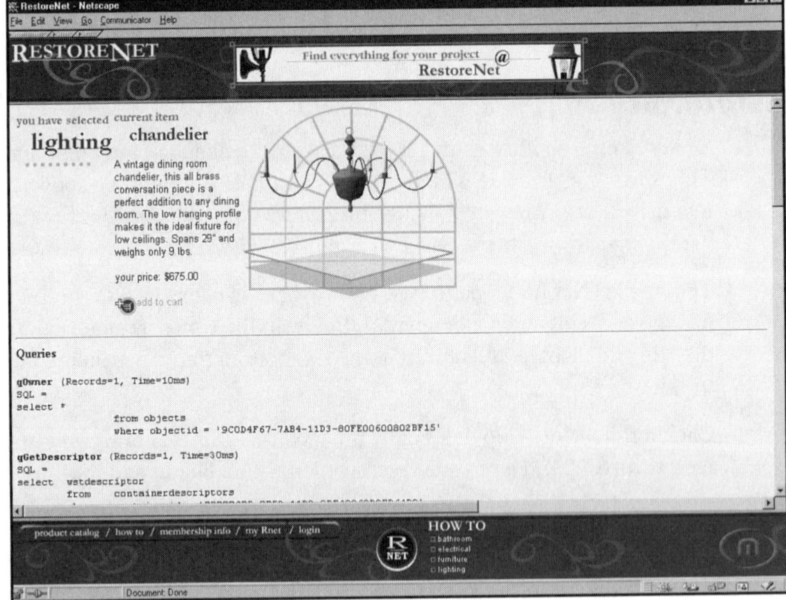

FIGURE 4.29
The chandelier detail page shows an image of the chandelier and has a descriptive paragraph and a link to add the item to your shopping cart.

CHAPTER 5

Navigating the Spectra Design Tools

In this chapter

Spectra Design Tools

Now that you have Spectra installed, you need to become familiar with the Spectra design tools that you'll use in creating your Spectra application. Since Spectra is based on ColdFusion, you probably won't be surprised to find that ColdFusion Studio remains a key development tool when it comes to writing the Spectra tags needed to implement your application. With Spectra comes a brand new tool that provides an out-of-the-box, Web-based environment suited to everyone in the Spectrum of Participants discussed in Chapter 1, "Understanding Spectra."

Spectra offers a rich set of services for dynamic content, personalization, e-business, and syndication, all supported by a ContentObject database. The Spectra services require a way for the participants to interact with the capabilities of Spectra. As Figure 5.1 shows, the Webtop is the connection to all the Spectra services for the interactive participant.

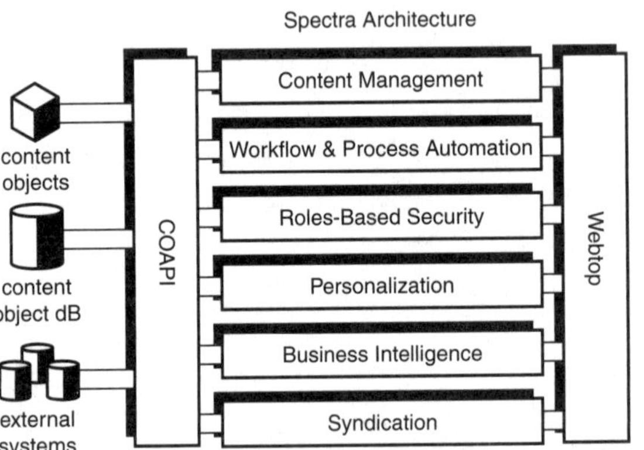

FIGURE 5.1
The Webtop provides the interface for the Spectrum of Participants to access Spectra services interactively.

Since the Webtop is Web based, all participants can use it from any Web browser anywhere, a concept dubbed *Anywhere Management*. The Webtop is built entirely using the Spectra COAPI tags and services. The Webtop code is open and available for you to look at and customize. This lets you give your environment a look-and-feel consistent with your organization's standards and lets you extend the Webtop's end user capabilities. Chapter 22, "Extending Spectra," shows you how to implement many of the capabilities you see in the Webtop, so this will be another key resource when you go to customize the Spectra environment.

Using the Webtop

Now start your browser so that you can follow along on this tour of the Webtop environment. From the Start menu, choose Programs, Allaire, Spectra, and then Webtop to launch your browser into the Webtop. If you want to add a link to the Webtop from other environments, the URL is `http://`*`yourserver.com`*`/allaire/spectra/webtop/index.cfm`, where *`yourserver.com`* identifies the system on which Spectra is installed. You should now see the Spectra Login window, shown in Figure 5.2.

FIGURE 5.2
Enter your username and password to access Spectra at the login prompt.

Login
You are attempting to access a protected system.
Please enter your username and password to continue.
username
password
Enter

NOTE If you are curious about the strings of ones and zeroes on the Spectra Login page and at the bottom of each Webtop section, here's a bit of Spectra trivia: The strings of ones and zeroes are there in homage to the movie *The Matrix*.

The Webtop Home Page

The Spectra Webtop is a secure system. You must provide a username and a password to gain access. Enter the Administrator username and password you established when you installed Spectra. Later in this chapter, you will learn how to create additional accounts that can use the Webtop.

After your successful login, you see a Spectra Webtop home page that looks like Figure 5.3.

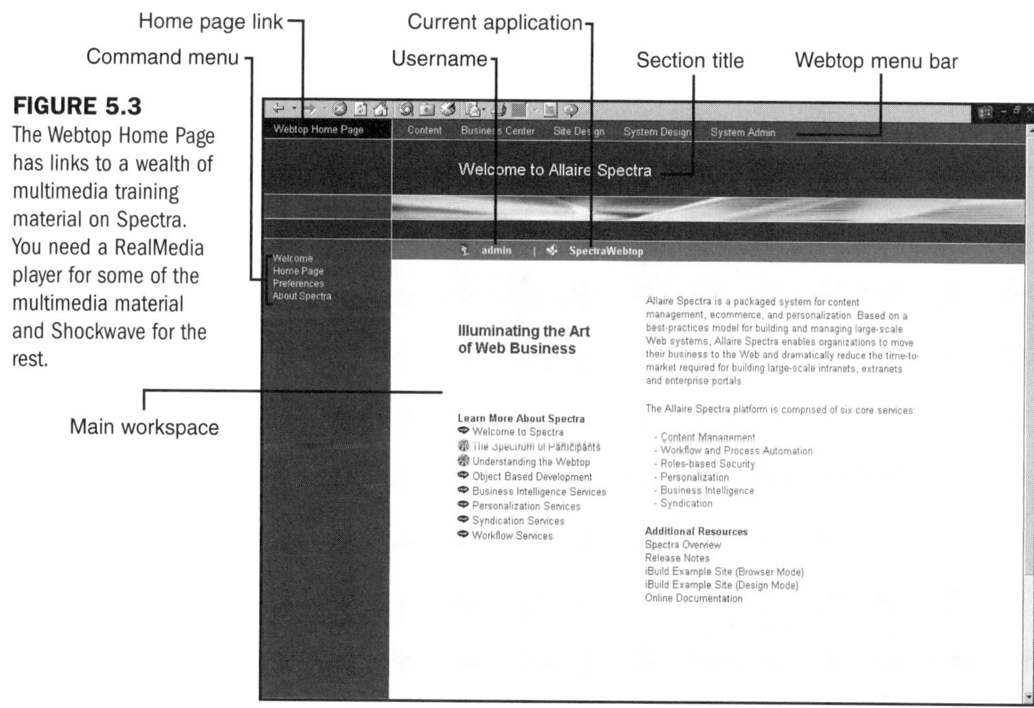

FIGURE 5.3
The Webtop Home Page has links to a wealth of multimedia training material on Spectra. You need a RealMedia player for some of the multimedia material and Shockwave for the rest.

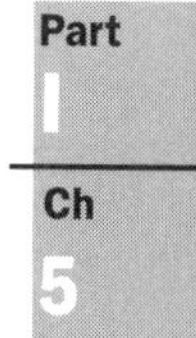

All Webtop sections have the same general layout, so let's start with the home page and learn about each of the parts of a Webtop page. Going across the top and then down the page, we first see the Webtop Home Page link. This appears on every Webtop page, and clicking it will bring you back to this page.

The Webtop menu bar is a key part of navigating the Webtop. If you are observant, you've probably already noticed that the menu bar has a passing resemblance to the Spectrum of Participants discussed in Chapter 1. Well, you're right, it does and for good reason. Each group of participants has a particular set of services and commands appropriate to that group's use of the Webtop. A system administration person is likely to find all he needs to do his job under the System Admin section of the Webtop, the rightmost menu item.

You are currently logged in as the administrator, so you can see all of the Webtop. It's very likely that, within the Spectrum of Participants, most will see and use only a portion of the Webtop. Thus, a user whose role is Business Manager might see only the Home Page and Business Center sections. You certainly wouldn't want him using the System Admin section.

▶ **See** Chapter 16, "Using Spectra Security Options," to learn how to set permissions to control access to sections of the Webtop.

The menu bar items relate to the Spectrum of Participants as follows:

Webtop Section	**Participant**
Content	Business User
Business Center	Business Manager
Site Design	Site Designer
System Design	Interactive Developer
System Admin	System Administrator

NOTE Site Members and Site Affiliates don't have a section of the Webtop devoted to them because they use the Web site/application produced by the other participants using the Webtop and other Spectra design tools. As such, they don't interact directly with the Webtop.

Below the menu bar is the section title. This clearly shows you where you are in the Webtop. The different sections are also color and motif coded. So if you see Van Gogh's *Wheatfield with Crows*, you'll know you are in the Site Design section. The motif in Figure 5.3 shows a spectrum that should remind you that you are on the Spectra home page.

Below the section title, you find the username and the current application. Together these make up the Preferences bar, providing links to the two sets of preferences. Another way to get to Preferences is via the link in the left frame.

The username shown is the one you are currently logged in as. If you click the username or the icon to the left of it, you get the User Profile form, where you can change your name and password and your email address.

To the right of the current username is the current application name. The initial application shown here is SpectraWebtop. When you have created your own application and are working with it, its name will appear here. Click the current application name or icon and you will see the Preferences form shown in Figure 5.4. You can also get to the Preferences form by clicking the Preferences tab on the User Profile form. The Preference form lets you change the current application and select Personal Page Content, something that will be covered shortly. You can also select Enable Personalized Home Page, which activates content on your personal home page in the Webtop, not the Webtop Home Page you are currently viewing. Choosing Enabling Webtop Help will add a vertical bar containing help information to the right side of every page.

Of all the reasons to use this form, you will find the most common to be to enable system entities. Spectra contains a number of system properties and object types that, by default, aren't displayed. Normally you see just the ones you've defined for your application. This is a good thing because the lists of types and properties can get very long and hard to navigate otherwise. Sometimes, though, you need to get information about a Spectra system entity, and that's when you want to remember how to turn this on. A little later in the tour of the Webtop, you will get a chance to turn it on and see the difference.

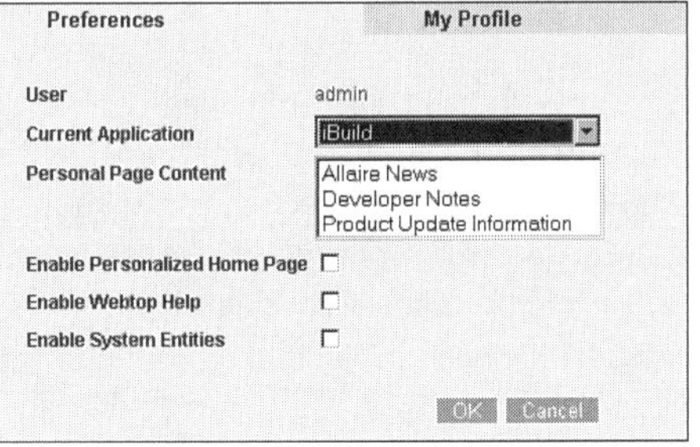

FIGURE 5.4
User Preferences dialog. Select your current application and set your Spectra preferences here.

Running down the left side of the page is the Command menu, also referred to as the *left-hand navigation area*. This is a tree control for easy navigation. On the Webtop Home Page, however, the tree is all leaves, so you have to wait until we get to the System Admin section discussion in this chapter to see how it provides quick access to all the command choices. Clicking an item in this menu causes it to be displayed in the main workspace, the large area to the right and filling most of the page. The workspace initially contains the result of the Welcome menu item at the top of the command list.

The Spectra Welcome command offers a set of multimedia links in the main workspace that you can use to learn more about the major services Spectra provides. Below the Welcome item in the command list is the Home Page command. Click this to see your own home page, as opposed to the Webtop Home Page. It should look like Figure 5.5.

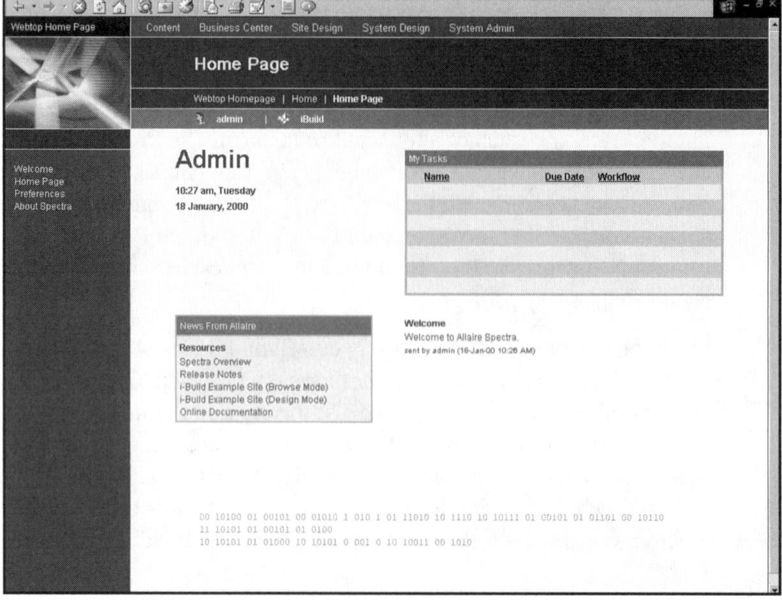

FIGURE 5.5
The user home page, your home base to see if you have tasks assigned and to get the latest news and messages.

Spectra provides a home page for each user. The home page provides an "at a glance" status of Spectra-related activities that the user might be interested in. In the My Tasks area he can see any workflow tasks assigned to him. If any Spectra system messages have been issued to all users, they are displayed in the lower-right corner of the main workspace. You probably don't have any right now, but we will put a message there later.

TIP Bookmark your Spectra home page and always use the bookmark to access Spectra. Provide others in your Spectrum of Participants with a link and encourage them to bookmark the page.

In the lower-left corner is News From Allaire. This contains a set of useful Spectra-related links. If you selected Personalization in the Preferences form earlier, the selected items appear at the end of this area. The personalized material is set up to be syndicated to your site from the Allaire site and can include Allaire News, Product Notes, and Product Update Information.

Click the Preferences command now. "I've seen that before," you say. Well, you are right. This is another way to get to the user profile and preferences, which you accessed earlier via the Preferences bar. Using the Preference bar is the better method because it's available from any section of the Webtop. Notice in Figure 5.5 one more feature of the Webtop that's not visible on the Webtop Home Page—the area directly above the Preferences bar. It shows the context of the current page in the overall structure of the Webtop.

The last command is the About Spectra command. Click this command to see information in the main workspace identifying the version level of Spectra, along with other useful environmental values and the product credits.

The System Admin Section

Let's now start looking at the Webtop sections where the real work takes place. First we are going to go to the System Admin section. Click System Admin on the Webtop menu bar. You will see a page that looks like Figure 5.6.

The first thing you will notice is that this section of the Webtop has all the components we discussed on the home page. What's different is the set of commands available to you. These commands support the system administration tasks you need to perform in support of a Spectra site or application.

You can now see the tree structure control in the command list. Try clicking the arrow to the left of Database Manager. Voilà, you see the subcommands provided for database management. Click the arrow again. Poof, they're hidden. Now click the Database Manager name to the right of the arrow. You get almost the same result as you did the first time—the subcommands are accessible. But you now see a brief summary of each subcommand in the main workspace. This is handy until you get used to the Webtop and don't want to wait for the extra page delivery that it takes to get this additional information. Ultimately, you are most likely to just use the disclosure arrows in the tree.

▶ **See** Chapter 23 for all the administration commands.

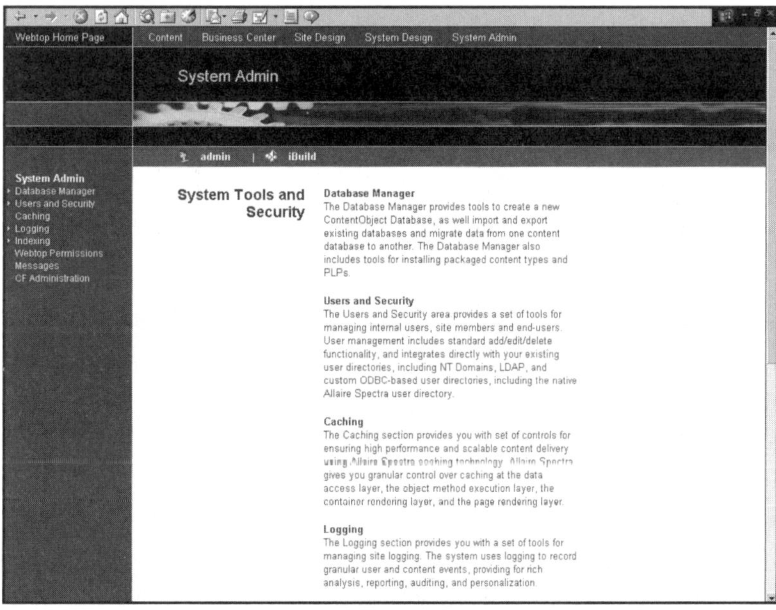

FIGURE 5.6
The System Admin page is where you manage your Spectra databases, Spectra user accounts and security, caching, logging, and indexing and where you set up Webtop access permissions.

Database Manager Database management tasks don't vanish with Spectra, but they are probably simpler than you are used to. Click the Database Manager command and you can see the facilities available to you.

The Install command lets you create a new empty ContentObject database. You would use this when you are creating a new Spectra application and need a database to keep all the content objects making up your application.

You definitely want to make a new ContentObject Database for a new application. Don't keep your application in the same database as the Webtop. This will ensure that your application's properties and types won't get overwritten by new additions in later releases of Spectra.

The Migrate command lets you make a copy of a ContentObject database. It will copy all the content objects from a source ContentObject database to a new target ContentObject database.

When you get ready to build a Spectra production application, use a production-quality database system to be sure your application performs well and is scalable. Besides, the Sybase Adaptive Server SQL Anywhere that comes with Spectra is licensed only for training and sample applications. Consult Chapter 23 and Chapter 24, "Deploying Spectra Applications," for more details.

CAUTION

The Install and Migrate commands will overwrite any existing tables with the same name in the target database.

The Export and Import commands are a pair. Use Export to write the entire contents of a ContentObject database to a file. You can then take that file to another Spectra machine and use Import to re-create the ContentObject database.

The remaining two commands, Import Types and Import PLP, allow you to incorporate prepackaged Spectra types with all their properties and methods into your Spectra system. If you are familiar with the Allaire ColdFusion Developer's Exchange, you know how valuable sharing packaged solutions can be. It's anticipated that before long there will be a number of prepackaged Spectra types in the Developer's Exchange that you can just pick up and use if they suit your needs.

NOTE PLPs (Process Logic Paths) are discussed in detail in Chapter 12, "Using Process Logic Paths." For now, all you need to know is that they provide a multi-step process for accomplishing a task. An example of a PLP would be a multi-step process to gather data and use it to make an object of a particular type. Like types, PLPs are expected to be shareable as packaged solutions, and the Import PLP command provides the mechanism to add them to your system.

Users and Security An important task for system administrators is to ensure security for a site. This can include registering users so they can access the site with a username and password, assigning them to groups to facilitate managing rights, and establishing security policies by area of the site and by the type of objects being manipulated. Click the Users and Security link to see the commands: Security Contexts, User Directories, Site Security, and Type Security, as shown in Figure 5.7.

Click the Security Contexts command in the left-hand navigation area. This command lets you create new security contexts and delete existing ones. A security context isn't new with Spectra. Rather, it's a feature of ColdFusion Advanced Security. For most of what you are likely to do now, just use the existing security context named `sc1` created with the Spectra install.

Click User Directories to see a list of all the currently defined directories. There should be only one, named `UserDirectory`. The default directory is ODBC based. You can create additional directories, and you might want to consider having one directory for Webtop users and a separate one, maybe an LDAP directory, for all the site members you register.

Go ahead and click the Single Person icon under the title Users. This will bring up a display of all the users registered in this directory. Your list of users will be different than the list in Figure 5.7; most likely it will contain only the single user you defined as Administrator. The pull-down list at the top lets you view the users filtered by group membership.

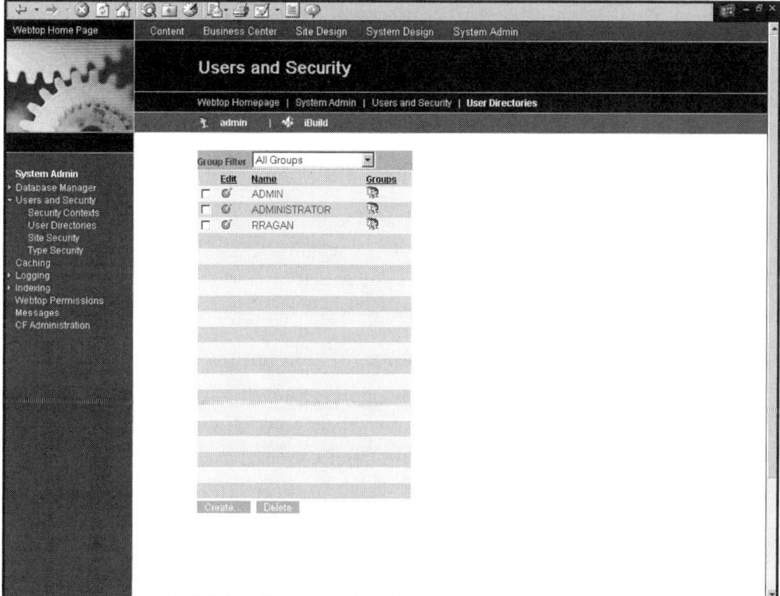

FIGURE 5.7
This lists all the users defined in the selected directory.

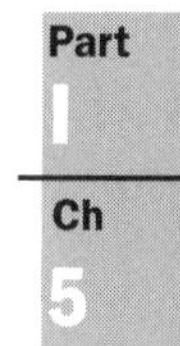

All this looking and not doing must be getting boring. Let's take a browsing break and make a new user. Click the Create button and you will get a simple form where you enter a username for the new user you want to create, provide a password, and verify the password. Finally, you can enter a description of the user if you want. Now click the Create button to make the new user.

CAUTION

Don't put a space in your username; otherwise, you won't be able to delete it. This is a bug in Spectra 1.0.

If you click the Multiple Heads icon under the Groups heading, you can place your new user into the groups you select.

You assign a user to a group by selecting the group from the list on the right, Ctrl+clicking for multiple groups, and then click the left arrow to move the group or groups from the Available Groups column to the Current Group Column. You can reverse the process to remove a user from a group.

Choose OK button the Groups dialog box to return to the list of users. If you want to delete a user, you just need to click the check box next to his name and choose the Delete button. There is no Undo, so be careful when you do this.

The two remaining security commands will be covered in more depth in Chapter 16. For now, here is a short summary of what they do:

- The Site Security command lets you assign security controls to sections and pages of your site.
- The Type Security command provides security controls on which methods can be used on an object type.

Another way to think about these two security commands is that Site Security controls who can go where on the site, and Type Security controls who can do what with objects of a particular type.

Caching The next major command is Caching. It gives you an overview of the settings of section- and page-level caching. Click the command to see how caching is set. The indicators to the right of each part of the site let you see at a glance the state of caching. The whole subject of caching will be covered in Chapter 24.

Logging The Logging area includes four commands: Site Logging Settings, Log Files, Reports, and Install Reports DB. Spectra includes a rich set of logging capabilities with granular control. Logging is crucial if you want to understand how your site is performing. From a business standpoint, logging can expose usage patterns that you can use to enhance personalization or to identify certain areas of the site that receive a lot of traffic.

- Click the Site Logging Settings command to see what logging you are doing. This command uses a tree format to show logging settings on your site. By selecting an item in the tree and choosing Edit, you can adjust the logging settings to collect more information or less, according to your needs.
- The Log Files command allows you to specify where your site logs are kept. In a clustered Spectra environment in which multiple servers might share a ContentObject database, the settings can be used to ensure that you get a single log file rather than one from each machine in the cluster.
- The Reports command provides a way to add new reporting to your site. The reports you produce are based on the Spectra log files specified in the previous command. You can schedule the creation of reports from logs or trigger a log processing run manually at any time.
- Install Reports DB is used to install a Reports database into an ODBC database you have set up. All you have to do is select the target datasource and choose Install Reporting Database—but don't do it right now. Later, when you get to Chapter 17, "Site Reporting," you will learn more about logging and reporting.

Indexing If searching is to run efficiently, a system administrator must establish regular care and feeding schedules for the Verity indexes. This can include reindexing the whole site, optimizing existing indexes, and even repairing them. Click Indexing to see the three commands it offers:

- The Type Collections command provides a place to define schedules for indexing, optimization of indexes, and repair on a type-by-type basis.
- The Meta Data Collections command provides a similar set of scheduling capabilities but applies to the Verity indexes generated when meta data is assigned to objects. These indexes provide the underlying mechanism for searching meta data.
- The Datasource Collections command also provides index management scheduling, like the other two commands. What's different here is that the actions are applied to all the collections in the datasource.

Webtop Permissions A lot of capabilities are available through the Webtop interface. It wouldn't do to let everyone have access to all the power of the Webtop. The next command, Webtop Permissions, provides a way to specify which groups and users are permitted access to which sections of the Webtop. Click Webtop Permissions to see the interface for setting the permissions. You should see a display similar to Figure 5.8. Details on how to use Webtop Permissions are covered in Chapter 16.

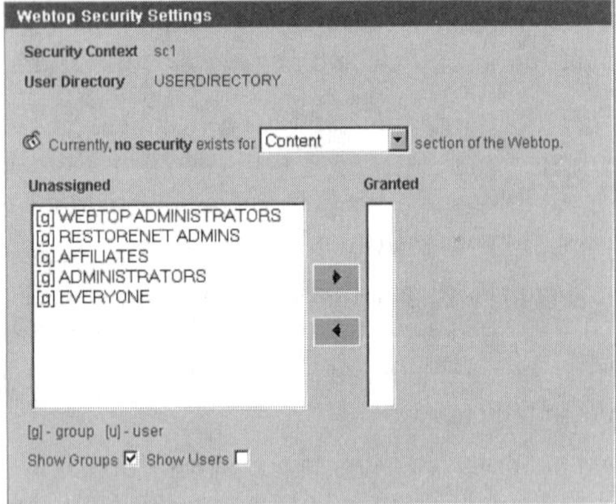

FIGURE 5.8
Webtop Security Settings lets you specify which users and groups can use which parts of the Webtop.

Messages The Messages command will let you place up to five messages at a time on the user's home page in the Webtop. If you specify more than five messages, the oldest won't be shown. This is a useful way to send messages to all Webtop users.

Go ahead and post a message. Title the message something like "Welcome" and put anything you want in the Message part, keeping in mind that what you put there will be seen by all your Webtop users. "Welcome to Allaire Spectra" might be appropriate. Then click OK.

When it says your message has been sent, click the Webtop Home Page link in the upper-left corner of the screen and on the Webtop Home Page, click the Home Page link in the command list. You will see something like Figure 5.5, with your message in the lower-right corner.

Once you post a message, there is no Webtop interface to delete the message. The following script will remove all the messages. The script retrieves all the message objects, based on type, and then deletes each of them, using the object IDs. Note that the System Message objects are stored in the Webtop's ContentObject database, `cfaobjects`, not in your application's database.

```
<CFSET messageTypeID = "EB1D6AAD-5E3B-11D3-AD4A0060B0EB2994">
<!--- Get all the System Message Objects --->
<cfa_contentObjectGetMultiple
   dataSource="cfaobjects"
   typeID="#MessageTypeID#"
   bActiveOnly="No"
   bNonArchivedOnly="No"
   r_qObjects="SysMessages">

<!--- Loop and delete each message object --->
<CFLOOP QUERY="SysMessages">
     <cfa_contentObjectDelete
        dataSource="cfaobjects"
        objectID="#SysMessages.ObjectID#">
</CFLOOP>
```

CF Administration Last but not least is the CF Administration command. This provides a convenient shortcut to start the ColdFusion Administrator, a useful feature since all the things you do in Spectra ultimately depend on ColdFusion.

The System Design Section

For many of you, this is the section where you will spend the most time in your development of a Spectra site. The System Design section gives you the tools to create all the basic object types your site will use. It's here that you create your application, implement your design decisions about the properties your types will have, what methods they will support, and how instances of the types will be created. You will also define the business workflows needed to support creation and use of your objects, what the meta data for your objects should be, and the rules that allow objects to be dynamically published.

That's a load of things to do in one section. Don't worry, though, we will take you through them one at a time and, before you know it, this section will feel like home to you. Go ahead and click the System Design link in the Webtop menu bar. You will see a screen like Figure 5.9.

Applications This is where it all begins. The first step in building a Spectra application is to create the application object. Click the Applications link and you will see the window shown in Figure 5.10.

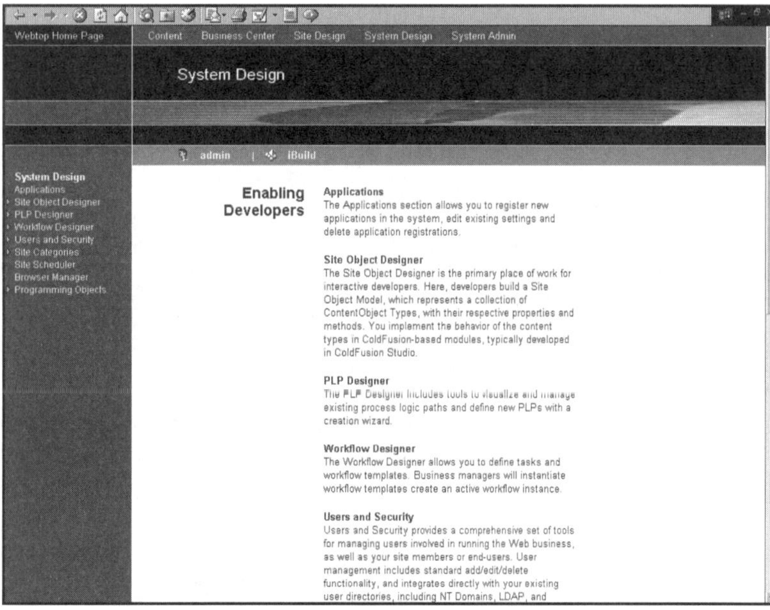

FIGURE 5.9
The System Design section is where interactive developers create all the properties, types, PLPs, workflows, and rules that establish a Spectra site's overall behavior.

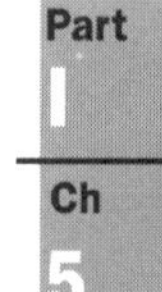

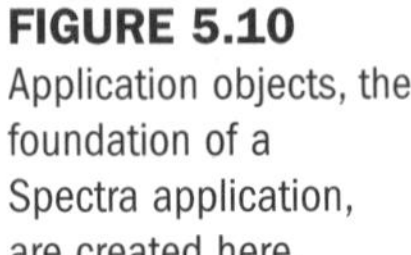

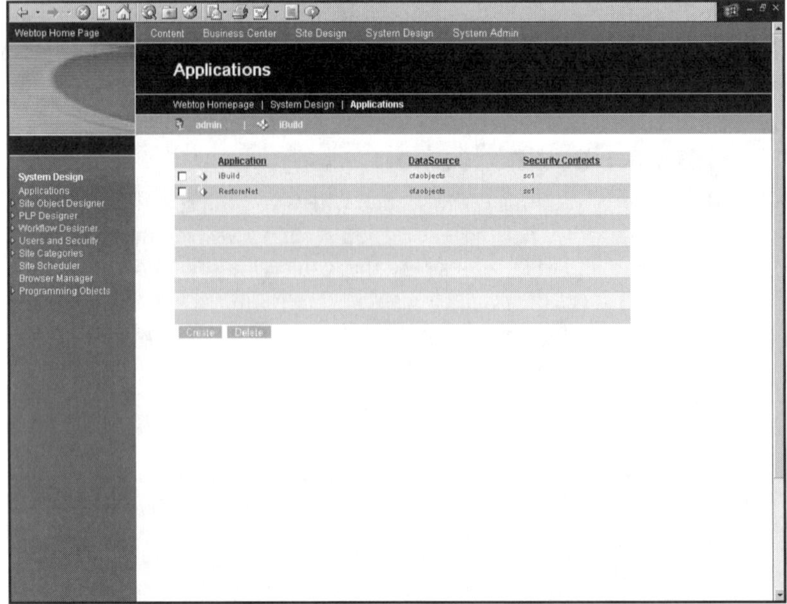

FIGURE 5.10
Application objects, the foundation of a Spectra application, are created here.

You should see the sample applications i-Build and RestoreNet. Here you can use the Create button to set up the foundation of a new Spectra application (which you will actually do in Chapter 6, "Introduction to Spectra Programming").

TIP If you can't figure out how to do something with Spectra, consider looking at code in i-Build or RestoreNet that does something like what you are trying to do. Chances are this will answer your question. If not, look at code in the Webtop. It does pretty much everything you might want to do in Spectra.

CAUTION

If you delete an application, make sure that you don't have any users with that application set as Current Application in their preferences. Otherwise, they won't be able to log in to Spectra after the deletion.

Site Object Designer Go ahead and click the Site Object Designer link. The Site Object Designer commands deal with three key parts of a content object: the properties, the type definition, and an instance of an object of a particular type. These three facets are mirrored in the Object Finder command, the Type Designer and Type Wizard commands, and the Property Definitions and Property Def Wizard command. We are going to start with properties because they are fundamental to building a type, and a type is needed to create an object of that type.

Property Definitions and the Property Def Wizard Click the Property Definitions command to see the existing set of defined properties. It should look something like Figure 5.11.

▶ **See** Chapter 6 for detailed use of the commands dealing with properties and types. Right now, we just want you to get a feel for what capabilities the various Webtop command links provide.

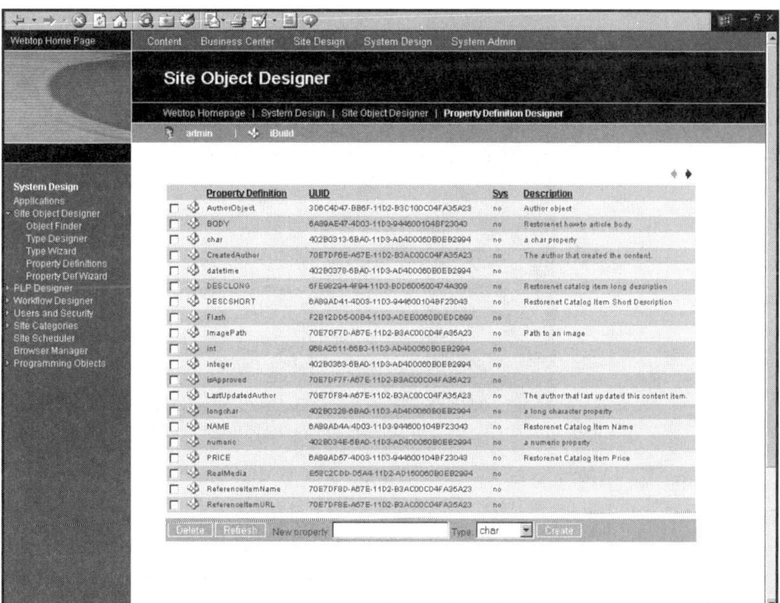

FIGURE 5.11
The Property Definitions command shows a list of all defined properties. You can create new properties here or delete existing ones.

We aren't going to do anything more with properties right now, but in the next chapter, "Introduction to Spectra Programming," you will get a chance to create some. The Property Def Wizard is just a wizard-style mechanism for creating a property definition, so we won't spend time going through it here because we don't want to create any new properties just yet.

Type Designer and Type Wizard Click the Type Designer command to see the existing set of defined object types. It should look something like Figure 5.12.

One type you should see is `iBuildContent`. This is the object type defined for the i-Build sample application that comes with Spectra. The `rn_` prefixed types are associated with RestoreNet, the other sample application. To the right of the Type column is a column labeled UUID (Universally Unique Identifier). Every object in a Spectra system has its own UUID that you can use to identify it. The UUID is unique across all systems, so you can safely package a type definition, move it to any other Spectra system, and be sure that it won't conflict with existing ones on the new system.

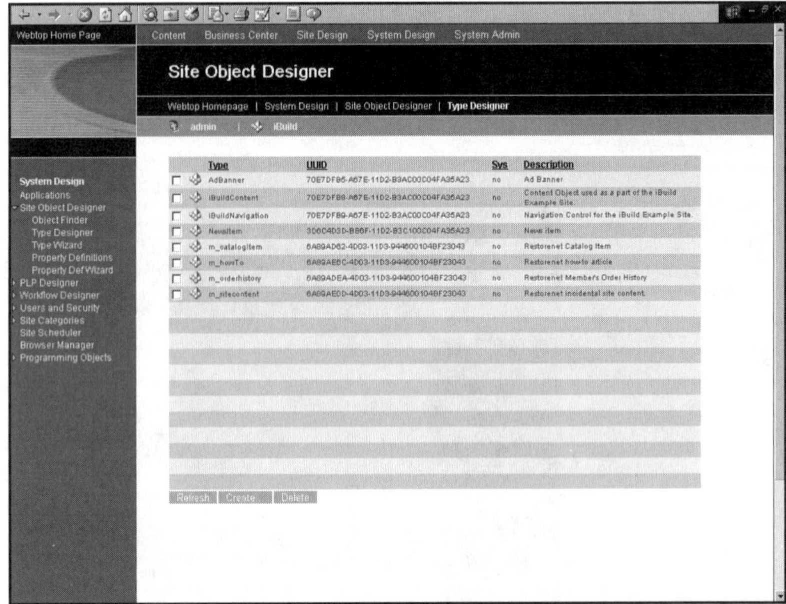

FIGURE 5.12
The Type Designer command shows a list of all defined object types. You can create new types here and edit or delete existing ones.

The UUID for a type like `iBuildContent` is used in Spectra tags where you need to perform an action based on type. For example, a search to find all objects of type `iBuildContent` would use the UUID 70E7DFB8-A67E-11D2-B3AC00C04FA35A23. Okay, got that committed to memory along with your driver's license number, postal code, passport number and other useful numeric trivia? What? You don't have any spare brain cells left to memorize 20 or so UUIDs? Then you had better do what all good Spectra programmers do: assign the UUID value to a name you can remember and use the name.

The next column to the right specifies whether a type is a Spectra system type. Unless you have turned on the Enable System Entities preference, you will see only user types. Go ahead and click the application name in the Spectra Preferences bar, click Enable System Entities in the form, and choose OK. Unfortunately, Spectra 1.0 takes you to the Webtop Home Page after any change to Preferences, so click the System Design link in the menu bar, the Site Object Designer link in the commands list, and the Type Designer command below that. You should now see many more types, something like Figure 5.13.

There are now more types than will comfortably fit in the display area, so the Webtop adds forward/backward arrows in the upper-right corner to let you see a page of types at a time. The other feature worth noting is that you can click a column heading to sort on that column. Clicking again will reverse the order of the sort. Try it. Click the UUID column. Now click the Type column. Click the Type column again to reverse the sort order. Sometimes it's easier to sort the end of a long list of type names to the first page than to use the arrows to move to the last page.

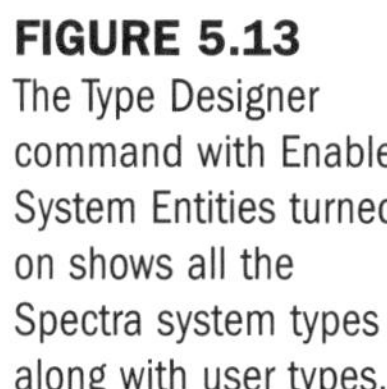

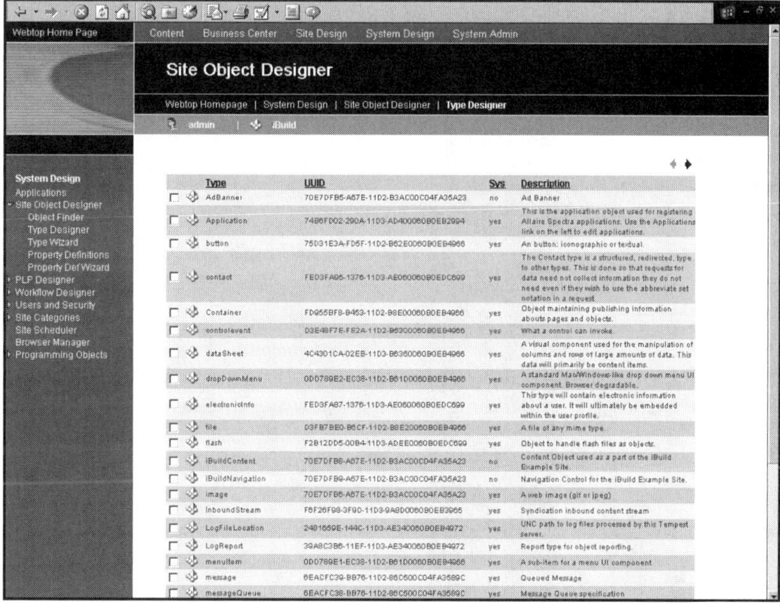

FIGURE 5.13
The Type Designer command with Enable System Entities turned on shows all the Spectra system types along with user types.

Now click the application name again, turn off Enable System Entities, and navigate your way back to System Design page as you did earlier. You should be looking at a display like that of Figure 5.12 now.

The Type Wizard, like the Property Def Wizard, is a step by step, handholding way to build types until you get comfortable with the process. Again, we will leave use of the wizard until the next chapter, when you build your own types.

Object Finder We've looked at properties that are used to form types. After you define an object type, you can create and work with objects of that type. The Object Finder, in Figure 5.14, lets you create, edit, and delete objects of a specified type. After you click Object Finder, be sure you use the pull-down menu labeled Filter by Type to select the `iBuildContent` object type. Now your screen should resemble Figure 5.14, because only objects of `iBuildContent` type are shown. Don't do this now but, by using the check boxes to the left of the objects, you can select some and delete them.

The text box labeled Filter by UUID is handy if you know the UUID of an object and want to find it. Just enter the UUID and press Enter to limit the display to the single UUID. The far-right pull-down menu lets you select from predefined views. If you define a view, you can select by type, date range, label filter, and owner. After you define the view, you can use it later.

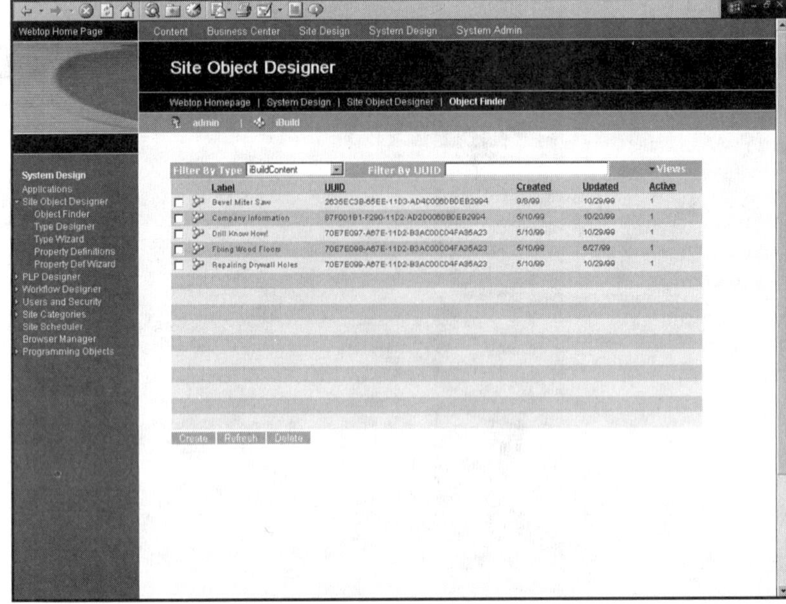

FIGURE 5.14
The Object Finder lets you view and edit objects of a selected type, create objects of that type, and delete objects.

PLP Designer *Process logic paths* (PLPs) are a very useful tool for building complex Spectra objects. A PLP is really nothing more than a predefined set of actions that pass a piece of data along from step to step. Some systems call it a *pipeline*, but PLPs are more flexible than the linear pipelines offered by other systems. Click PLP Designer to see the commands that relate to PLP operations.

NOTE You need to have done your design of the steps and the data they manipulate *before* you set out to create the PLP. If you don't, you will find it hard to get it right on-the-fly and end up doing extra work to make changes.

▶ **See** Chapter 12 for everythin you ever wanted to know about PLPs.

Like the Property and Type commands we just saw, the PLP Designer commands come in wizard and non-wizard flavors. Click the PLP Manager command, and you'll see a display that resembles Figure 5.15.

The PLP Manager shows you an icon, all the defined PLPs by name, their UUIDs, and a Packaging icon. If you click the icon to the left of the name, you get a flowchart depiction of the logic of your PLP. Go ahead, pick one and look at it.

After you have a chance to look at the flowchart, click the Back button in your browser. Clicking the name of the PLP will take you through a multi-step editing process, something best left until you know more about PLPs. The UUID to the right of the name is the unique identifier of the PLP. You will need to reference this identifier to initiate the PLP. Finally, the icon to the far right will package the PLP into a file that's downloaded to your machine. This file can then be imported into another Spectra system to add the functionality of the PLP to that system.

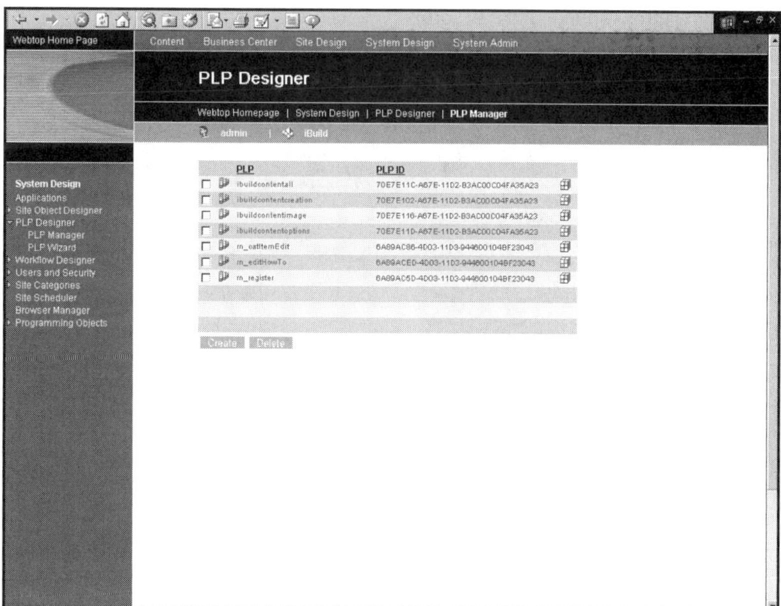

FIGURE 5.15
The PLP Manager lets you create a new PLP or edit properties of an existing PLPs. You can also delete a PLP.

Workflow Designer Whereas a PLP is a synchronous step-by-step process, a *workflow* is just the opposite. It is a number of loosely coupled tasks, some of which may be done in parallel and others of which can't proceed until all the tasks prior to them are complete. A PLP usually involves only a single person following a multi-step process that typically lasts for a brief period of time—minutes to hours. Workflows often involve multiple people doing a series of tasks that may take days or weeks before they are all completed. Click the Workflow Designer command.

The Workflow Designer area provides two commands: Workflow Templates and Tasks. You will usually want to use the Tasks command to define all the tasks that make up a workflow before defining the workflow itself.

Since workflows are composed of tasks, the first command you would normally use is Tasks. Click the Tasks command. For i-Build you see three tasks: Add Content, Add Image, and Edit/Approve Content and Image. At this level of definition, the tasks have no dependency relationships between them, although you might guess that adding content and image has to be done before the approval task can start. As with PLPs, you need to have a complete design for the tasks that make up the workflow and the dependencies between them done before you start creation of the workflow.

▶ **See** Chapter 13, "Working with Workflow," to define the tasks that you will then arrange into your workflow.

OK, let's look at how tasks are arranged to make a workflow. Click the Workflow Templates command under the Workflow Designer area. You will get a display that looks like Figure 5.16. Other than the name, the default owner of the workflow, and a Last Updated column, there's nothing of interest on this screen, although you can expect to see the UUID of the workflow appear here in future releases of Spectra.

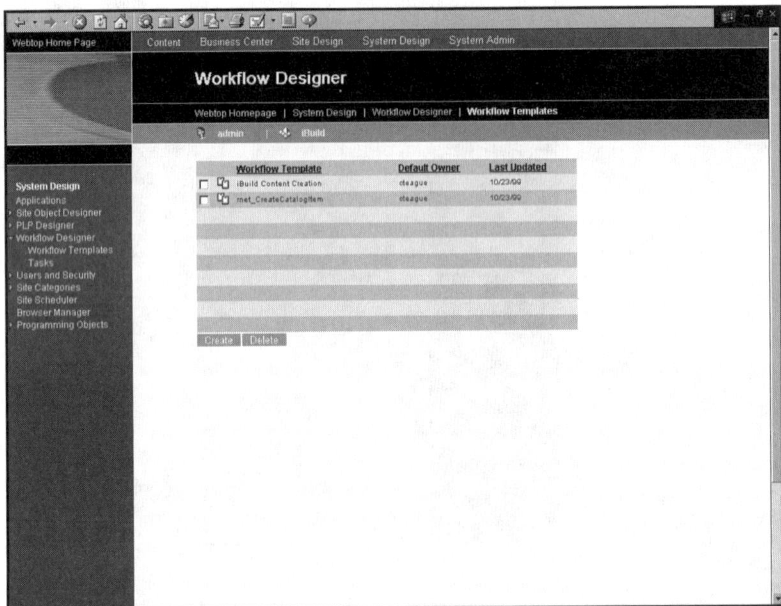

FIGURE 5.16
The Workflow Templates area lists all defined workflows.

Let's take a peek at the innards of a Workflow object, although you will handle this in depth in Chapter 13. Click the icon to the left of the workflow name to view a workflow. Here you see various properties of the workflow, including the tasks used to implement it.

We will stop here and not delve into how to establish dependencies between the tasks. After all, we have to leave something for Chapter 13.

Users and Security The next command in the list is Users and Security. Click it. Are you having that feeling of *déjà vu*? Well, you are seeing the same thing again. Several of the command areas are duplicated in different sections of the Webtop because more than one role in the Spectrum of Participants has good reason to need those commands. For example, you find the Users and Security functions in the System Admin, System Design, and Business Center sections of the Webtop. On the plus side, this means you already know this area and we can move right along.

Site Categories Meta data, as you learned in the definitions in Chapter 3, "Spectra Concepts and Terminology," is data about data. The Site Categories section is where you create the categories and keywords that are the basis for assigning meta data to objects. Click Site Categories to see the two available commands: Type Hierarchy Manager and Keyword Manager.

The Type Hierarchy Manager command lets you create a new meta data hierarchy. You can also associate one or more meta data hierarchies with an object type in the Type Hierarchy Manager. Bring up the screen by clicking Type Hierarchy Manager; what you see should be similar to Figure 5.17.

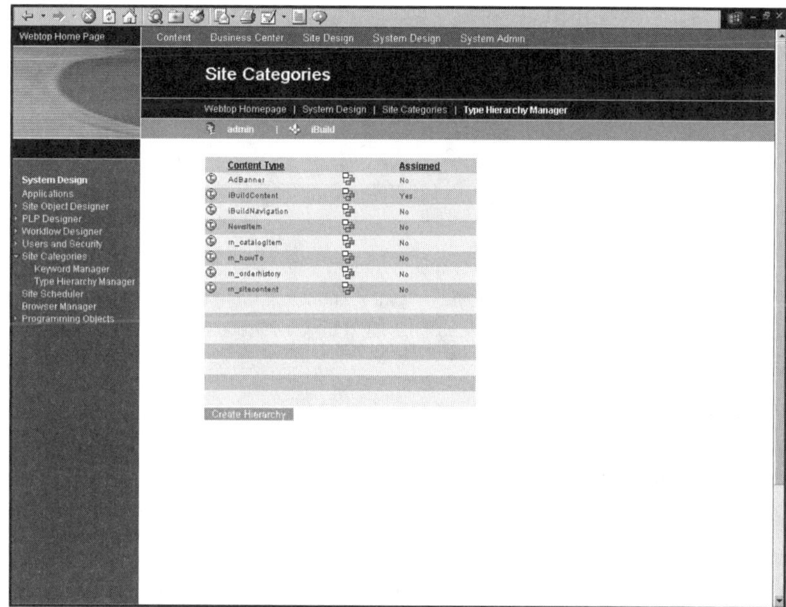

FIGURE 5.17
The Type Hierarchy Manager area is used to create new meta data hierarchies and to assign types to particular hierarchies.

If you want to create a new meta data hierarchy, you would use the Create Hierarchy button at the bottom of the screen (but not now). The icon to the left of the Content Type name will bring up a form that lets you select the meta data hierarchies that should be associated with the Content data type. Click the Keyword Manager command to see the form in Figure 5.18. What you see might not look exactly like Figure 5.18, so let's straighten that out before going on. If you see RestoreNet Meta Data on the pull-down (before pulling it down) and the i-Build hierarchy shown below, this is OK, since we are interested in looking at i-Build. If you see the RestoreNet Meta Data hierarchy, you will need to use the pull-down to switch to the i-Build meta data hierarchy. Just pull down, select i-Build, and release the mouse button. (There's a little confusion here in the way the pull-down works initially that should be corrected in a later release of Spectra.)

Now that your screen shows the i-Build meta data hierarchy, let's continue. i-Build has two categories: By Room and By Department. A *category* is just a structuring object, much like a directory in a file system. Just as a directory can contain other directories, a category can contain other categories. Just as a directory can contain files, a category can contain keywords. Click the arrow to the left of By Room. You now see four keywords: `BATHROOM`, `BEDROOM`, `GAMEROOM`, and `KITCHEN`. With categories and keywords you can build any hierarchy you need to support your site with meta data.

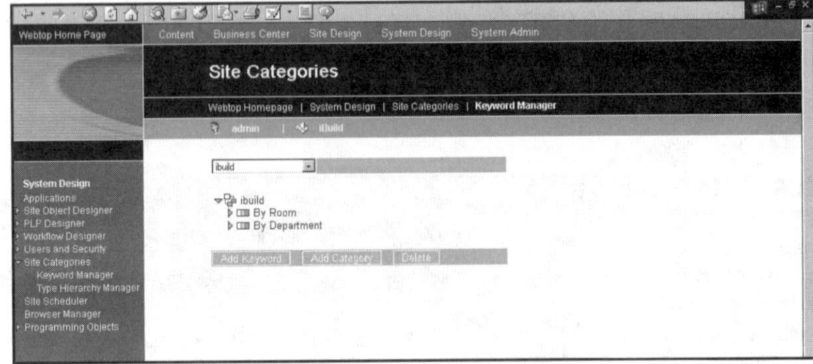

FIGURE 5.18
The Keyword Manager area is used to add new categories and keywords to a meta data hierarchy.

NOTE There's no button to delete a meta data hierarchy. If you need to delete one, you will need to turn on Enable System Entities in Preferences and use the Object Finder to select the `metaDataHierarchy` type. Find the one you want to delete, select it, and choose the Delete button.

▶ **See** Chapter 11, "Working with Meta Data," to learn how to create meta data hierarchies, add categories and keywords, and a number of good ways to use meta data to enhance your Spectra site.

Site Scheduler Click the Site Scheduler link to see an exceedingly dull display, since there are no scheduled events defined right now. To define an event, use the Create button. The form you then fill in lets you provide an object ID (UUID) and a method to invoke the object with. All the other values you can set that control the schedule are exactly those provided by the ColdFusion Scheduler, since that is what is being used. When a scheduled time is reached, the method you specified will be invoked with the object ID you provided. The Delete button is how you get rid of a scheduled action when you no longer need it.

Browser Manager One piece of drudge work every Web developer hates to face is the need to make Web solutions work on Netscape, Internet Explorer, and several other browsers, with different versions of each browser on different operating systems, all of which can be subtly different. If you see a Web programmer pounding his head against the wall, it might well be due his having to cope with this problem.

Spectra's Browser Manager attempts to make this nasty task a bit easier. Spectra has a tag called `<CFA_BROWSER>` that automatically sets a number of variables based on browser properties. Later, these variables can be used with different features of different browsers and different versions of the same browser. If `<CFA_BROWSER>` doesn't know the browser, an entry is added to the database. A graphical interface to the database is provided by the Browser Manager command. Click it to see the interface.

Versions of each major browser are shown. Sub-versions of browsers are supported and automatically inherit feature settings based on the parent entry. If you click the arrow to the left of a parent entry, you can see the defined sub-versions.

Let's say you discover from the logs that your site is being hit a lot by a new browser, the Browse-amatic 2000. You need to determine the capabilities of the Browse-amatic and specify those in its entry in the Browser Manager. Then the next time all those Browse-amatic 2000 users visit you, your Spectra application can exploit Browse-amatic 2000 features and avoid capabilities it lacks.

NOTE The Spectra User Interface tools are browser aware and use the Browser Manager information to customize their behavior to provide the best interface, given the capabilities of the browser—all without you worrying about it.

Programming Objects You are on the home stretch now in one of the more feature-rich sections of the Webtop. Click the Programming Objects command. It contains three fairly unrelated commands under one heading: Reports, Syndication Streams, and Rules. Since each of these three tasks requires writing code to implement the functionality, we must assume this to be the logical reason for grouping them. Logic aside, this is where they are.

The first of these three commands, Reports, is used to create `logReport` objects. A `logReport` object has properties that specify the handlers required to make the report and scheduling information about when to make the report. Under the heading Report Name would be the name you give the report. The Schedule column allows you to create a schedule for the report, and the OneClick column lets you run it immediately.

▶ **See** Chapter 17, to learn how to create custom reports for your site.

The second command, Syndication Streams, lets you set up inbound syndication of content from other sites to your Spectra site. In other words, you can have automated retrieval from other Web sites of information that you can then use on your site. It does this by invoking a handler that uses the `<CFHTTP>` tag to retrieve content from another Web site.

The third command, Rules, is one that you will use quite a bit. It lets you define the rules that govern dynamic content publishing on your site. Click the command to see the screen in Figure 5.19. In the figure, you see the rules currently defined. The Schedule Content rule and the Search Properties rule are general-purpose rules that you can use when you don't need anything fancy. They will be discussed later, in Chapter 19, "Rules-Based Publishing." The other rules you see are defined for the RestoreNet sample application.

The Site Design Section

The System Design section focused on creating and managing the object types, object instances, processes, workflows, and rules that provide the dynamic content that a Spectra site offers. This section is targeted at how the site looks and how the parts of the site relate to one another structurally. The site's physical and logical hierarchy is called the Site Layout Model. This model provides the hierarchical structure of the site, starting at the highest level with the Site object. The Site object contains one or more Section objects. Section objects contain Page objects and Page objects hold Container objects.

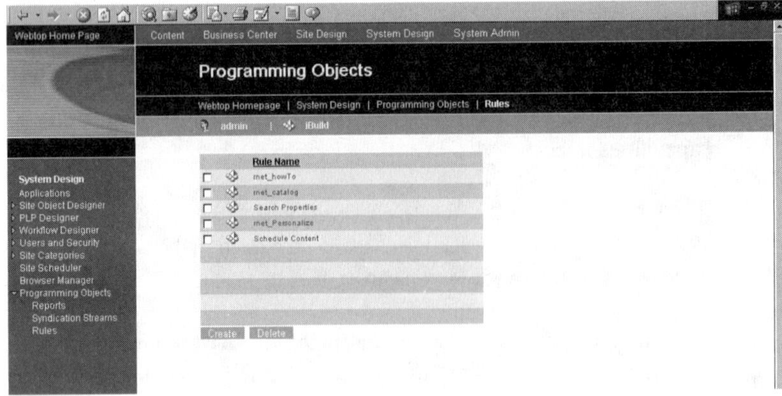

FIGURE 5.19
The Rules command lets you specify the properties of a rule. However, the bulk of the work of creating a functioning rule is writing the ColdFusion code that implements it.

The Site object corresponds to your intuitive notion of a site—a collection of all the Web information and capabilities making up one "logical" Internet site.

The Page object corresponds with your notion of a Web page—a single collection of information delivered by the server to the browser in a single request. People talk about writing Web pages, and in Spectra it's no different—you still write a Web page like you did in ColdFusion.

The Section object has no physical counterpart like pages do. Instead, sections can be thought of as a structuring or organizing mechanism to group a number of related pages together. Sections might well correspond to high-level links from the home page. For example, Products, Customer Support, and Investor Relations might be links to a collection of pages, all related, and thus fit the concept of a section.

The last item, the Container object, like sections has no direct correlation with anything tangible in the ColdFusion sense of putting data on a Web page. A container is the area of a Spectra page where dynamic content is published using rules.

Click the Site Design link in the Webtop menu bar. You will see a screen like Figure 5.20.

Site Layout Manager The Site Layout Manager area provides two commands for viewing and managing the Site, Section, Page, and Container objects and one command for defining standard page templates to be used when making new pages for the site.

Site Layout Model The Site Layout Model (see Figure 5.21) is a tree-structured map of the entire site. It lets you see the overall structure of the site all the way down to the container level and quickly see and edit all the logging, caching and security settings for each part of the site. What's more, most of this map is built automatically for you, as you will later learn.

Site Elements The Site Elements command lets you view and create the four site objects—Site, Section, Page, and Container. Click the command to see the site objects for the two sample applications. When you first create your site, you will make the Site object here as well as the Section objects. You rarely make Page and Container objects here because Spectra builds those for you automatically as you reference the pages that make up your site. Pull down the Element Type menu and select Section to see Section elements; you will see the display in Figure 5.22. The Label column names the Site element, and the Absolute Path column shows where relevant files for that element are to be found.

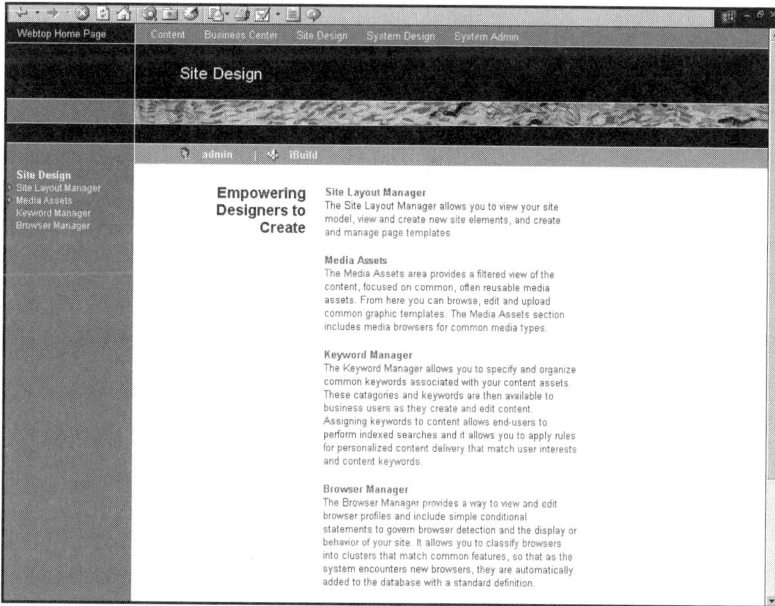

FIGURE 5.20
The Site Design section is where the Site Layout Model is created and managed. Page layout templates that can be created here provide consistency in site pages.

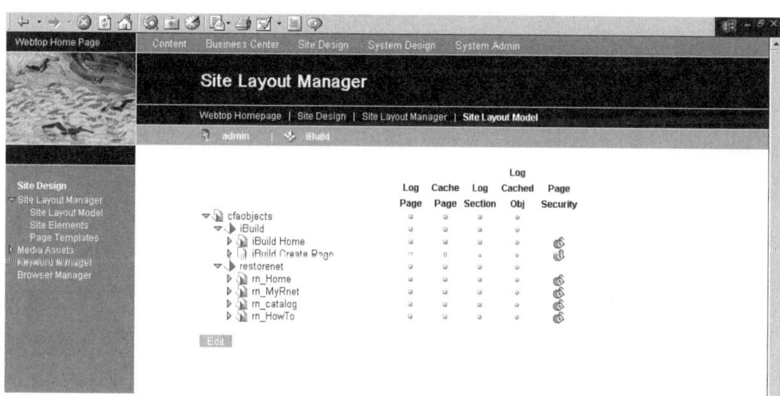

FIGURE 5.21
The Site Layout Model command encapsulates in one screen the complete layout of your site and all the key properties relating to caching, logging, and security.

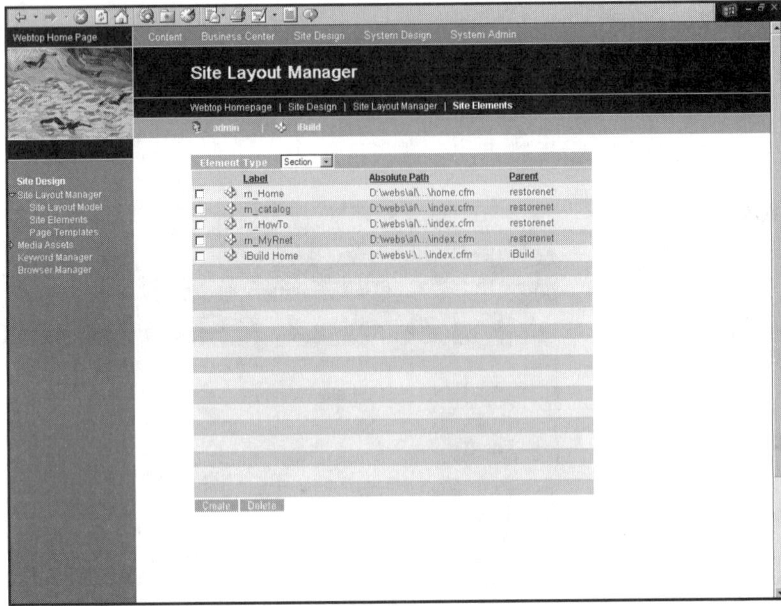

FIGURE 5.22
The Site Elements command, at the Section level, shows you all the sections. Similarly, you can view pages and containers when you select those element types.

Finally, the Parent column displays the parent element of this one. Here you can see that a Section in i-Build shows a Parent element of i-Build, and a page in the i-Build Home section would show a parent of that name.

Page Templates The Page Templates command provides a way to predefine canned page layouts and ensure consistency in site pages. If you click the command, you will see that the first two layouts are for i-Build and define a single-column page format and a three-column page format.

Media Assets The Media Assets area provides a place to upload and manage simple files as well as media in image, RealMedia, and Flash formats. You can have a library of loaded files and augment that by uploading new files. As soon as the files are on the Spectra server, they can be used in content objects. Details on how to do this will be in Chapter 10.

Files Click the Files command. Exciting, isn't it? Well, right now you don't have any files, or for that matter any other media types, on your freshly installed Spectra server. If you did, this is where you would see and manage them. The columns tell you the name of the file, when it was created, when it was last updated, who owns it, and whether it's active. An inactive file is one that's on the server but isn't available for use. We could go on here and take you through the Images, RealMedia, and Flash commands, but we don't want to bore you—they all look as empty as the Files list.

The Business Center Section

The Business Center section is aimed at a participant who worries more about how the business supported by the Spectra environment functions. Contrast this with the previous three sections, where the interests of the participants are focused on keeping the site running well, building the site, and designing the site. The Business Center user is far more interested in what the Spectra site can do to make the business more productive or perhaps more lucrative.

Let's look at the areas covered by the Business Center. Click the Business Center link on the Webtop menu bar to see the screen in Figure 5.23. Two areas will be familiar: Users and Security, and Site Categories. They are almost identical to what we've already covered, so we won't spend time going through them again. Users and Security is duplicated in this section because Business Center users may assign rights to those who need to perform assigned tasks. Site Categories, if you recall, is where you create site meta data hierarchies. Since meta data is crucial to the business-related aspects of the site like personalization, it seems appropriate to duplicate access to the command here. Remember that a Business Center user may not be able to see the System Design section of the Webtop at all, so some redundancy is needed.

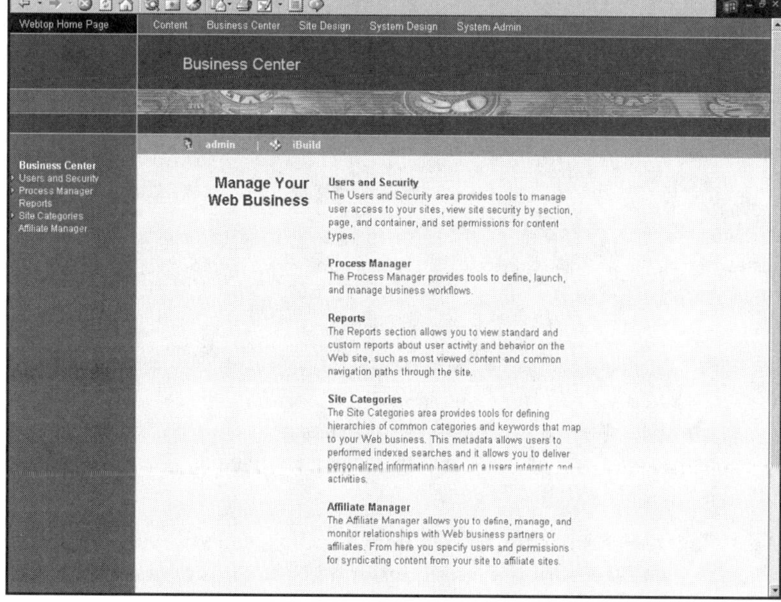

FIGURE 5.23
The Business Manager section is aimed at users who worry more about how the Spectra site can help the business than how the site might be constructed or kept running well.

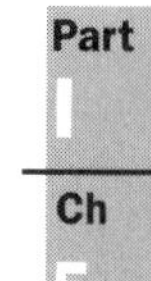

Process Manager The Process Manager area is devoted to starting and managing workflows. Click the Process Manager command to see workflow-related commands. Workflows provide an orderly, repeatable, traceable way to perform business processes. Any non-trivial site will soon find that the creation of content is likely to require an associated workflow. In most businesses, creating some kinds of content, such as product announcements, will require steps such as creating artwork, writing content, reviewing with marketing and legal, and getting final approval.

If these creation steps can be codified as a workflow, then when a new product launch is required, the marketing manager can start the workflow. The participants will receive notification of tasks and deadlines, usually by email. The marketing manager can then monitor the workflow and see if the tasks are being completed in a timely manner. If changes are made and parts of the workflow must be repeated, the manager can reset it so that the tasks are done again.

Start Workflow Let's take these out of order from how they are listed in the Webtop command list. After all, it makes sense to think about starting a workflow before you think about managing one that has already started. Click the Start Workflow command to get the screen in Figure 5.24. This command provides a list of available workflows and lets you select one to start, using the radio buttons in the left column. We aren't going to start one right now, but you will get a chance to do so in Chapter 13. The second step in this interface lets you assign a person to perform each task and set deadlines. The final step starts the workflow.

FIGURE 5.24
The Start Workflow command lets you select a workflow to be started, specify the task owners, and set deadlines for completion of each task.

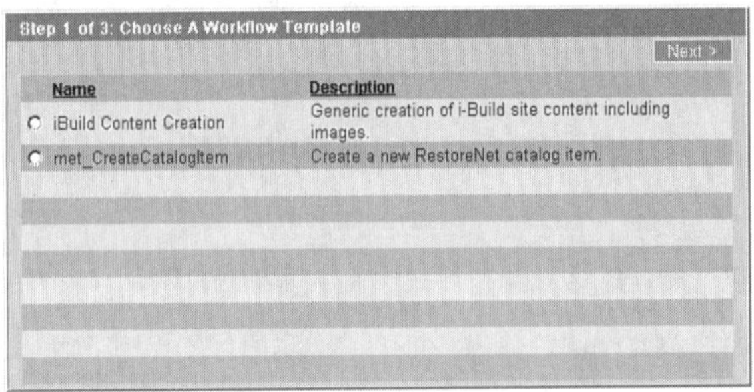

Workflow Manager The Workflow Manager command shows you workflows that are in progress as well as those that have been completed. There are no workflows listed, since this is a freshly installed system.

Reports Back in the System Admin section, you saw where logging and reports were defined. Well, now you have transformed into a business manager who wants to see those reports. Click the Reports command to see the built-in report types that come with Spectra. If you create new kinds of reports, they will appear in this list.

A Business Center user might be very interested in which content items get the most hits in a catalog shopping site, for example. Knowing the most popular pages or sections can also provide valuable insights that can lead to making the site even more popular.

Affiliate Manager If you want to syndicate content from this Spectra site, you have to be registered as a user with a password and be a member of the Affiliates group. The Affiliate Manager command is simply an alternate interface to put selected users into the Affiliates group. It can also be done in the Users and Security area using groups.

The Content Section

The Content section is the last of the Webtop's major sections. Click it on the Webtop menu bar to bring up the screen in Figure 5.25. This section is intended for the person responsible for creating, editing, and publishing the content of a Spectra site. Often, content creators will be the persons who perform the tasks that are part of the workflows we saw in the Business Center section. Let's get on with the commands of this section so we can finish this tour of the Webtop.

Content Finder Click the Content Finder command. The Content Finder is nearly identical to the Object Finder you saw in the System Design section. The only real difference is that the Object Finder will show all objects of the type you select. The Content Finder will show only objects marked as active. This behavior is convenient because it allows a Spectra system to have objects that are in progress but not ready for publication. Such objects are usually partially through the creation process, not yet approved, or in some sense shouldn't be considered as final content. By omitting inactive objects, the Content Finder helps prevent content that's not yet ready from being displayed.

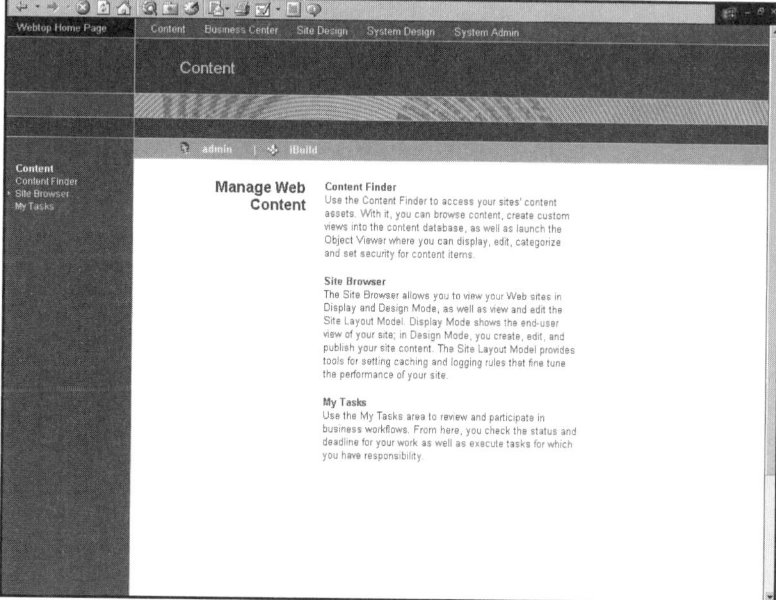

FIGURE 5.25
The Content section is where content creation, content editing, and publishing take place on a Spectra site.

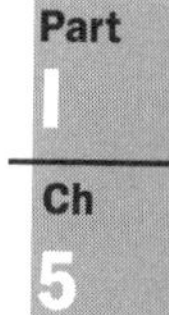

Site Browser Click the Site Browser command. The Site Browser provides the content provider with easy access to the two ways he might want to view the site, plus the Site Layout Model view that we saw back in the Site Design section.

Display Mode This command sends the browser to the URL associated with your Spectra site's top level URL, with a parameter of `designmode=false` passed on the URL. This will open a new window and let you see the site as an end user would see it. For example, doing this for i-Build gives you the end user view of the i-Build home page. Close this i-Build window when you are done with it.

Design Mode This command sends the browser to the URL associated with your Spectra site's top level URL, with a parameter of `designmode=true` passed on the URL. If you have coded your `Application.cfm` page to accept this parameter and set Spectra's mode to Design, clicking this command will take you to the same page as Display Mode, but you will have administrative editing capabilities while browsing the site. For example, doing this for i-Build gives us the screen in Figure 5.26. Notice the extra icons that have appeared around the content and the administrative bar that has appeared at the top of the page. Details on how to use the various Anywhere Editing controls will be covered in Chapter 10. Go ahead and close this i-Build window.

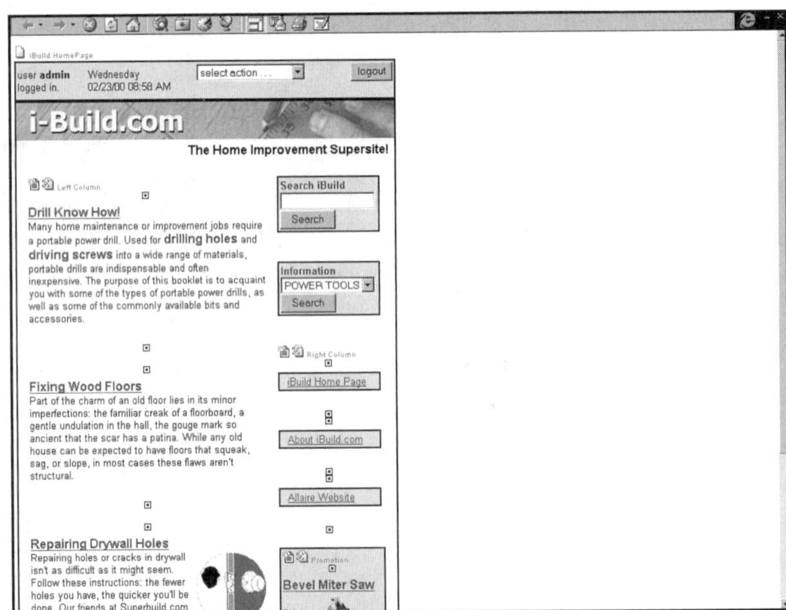

FIGURE 5.26
The Design Mode command takes you to your site in a mode that Allaire calls Anywhere Editing because you can navigate the site as you normally do but perform administrative publishing-related functions as you traverse the site.

Site Layout Model The Site Layout Model command is very similar to the version you saw in Site Design. The big difference here is that the site elements are read-only; you can't make new sections or change properties of sections. The one permitted change is the addition of new pages to the Site Layout. If you want to let your content creators add pages, you will need to have defined page templates in the Site Design section. Making everyone use the same templates ensures a consistent look-and-feel to the site.

My Tasks The very last command on your tour of the Webtop is My Tasks. It's this display and a similar one on the user's Webtop Home Page that list outstanding workflow. Right now there's nothing to show because no tasks are waiting to be performed. A task can be initiated by clicking the icon next to the task name.

▶ **See** Chapter 13 to learn how to create workflows, tasks, and notifications. You will get a chance to use this display to initiate tasks that you have organized into a workflow.

ColdFusion Studio Integration

When you look under the hood of a Spectra application, you find a lot of ColdFusion code. The application code is much shorter than traditional ColdFusion applications because you get to use the power of the Spectra custom tags to build your application. Nevertheless, you will still be writing ColdFusion to implement your handlers, PLPs, rules, custom tags, and templates, so ColdFusion Studio will still be your tool of choice.

ColdFusion Studio has been extended to provide integration with Spectra to improve your productivity, reduce errors, and generally minimize the number of side trips you have to make to the Webtop while coding in ColdFusion Studio.

If you have Studio on the server where you are installing Spectra, this will be detected automatically and ColdFusion Studio integration will be installed. If you need to install just the integration tools on a client system, there is a client install option for this purpose.

The Allaire Spectra Toolbar

After you install Spectra and bring up ColdFusion Studio, you will see a floating toolbar titled Allaire Spectra in the upper-right corner (see Figure 5.27). If you don't see the floating toolbar you need to install the

Allaire Spectra Studio Tools.

Installing Allaire Spectra Studio Tools on a ColdFusion Studio Client

To use the Allaire Spectra toolbar, you must have ColdFusion Studio installed on the machine. Then follow these steps:

1. Run a copy of the Allaire Spectra install file.
2. Click Next on the Install Welcome screen and on the License Agreement screen.
3. Deselect the Allaire Spectra Server Files check box in the list of components to install, and ensure that the Allaire Spectra Studio Tools check box is selected.
4. Click Next to advance to the Start Copying Files screen.
5. Click Next again to install and then Finish when done.

Now when you start ColdFusion Studio, you will see the Allaire Spectra toolbar.

Click the leftmost button on the toolbar, Register Allaire Spectra Application. This is where you register Spectra applications with ColdFusion Studio so that Studio can access the information from the Spectra environment. The Register dialog also lets you edit the application information and delete an application registration.

When you want to register an application, choose the Add App button. You will get the dialog box shown in Figure 5.28, except that you need to type in the data shown there, since we are going to register the RestoreNet application. If you didn't register i-Build in Figure 5.27, you should register i-Build here rather than RestoreNet. Just substitute the i-Build name for the RestoreNet name in the Register Application dialog box. After you enter the last field (the Password field), press Enter and ColdFusion Studio will validate your access to the Spectra environment. If this succeeds, you can then choose an application to add from the pull-down menu below the Password field. Select either i-Build or RestoreNet, depending on which one you are registering. Don't check the Display System Types box, but remember that this is where you can change it if you want to later. Finally, choose the Save button to save your application registration.

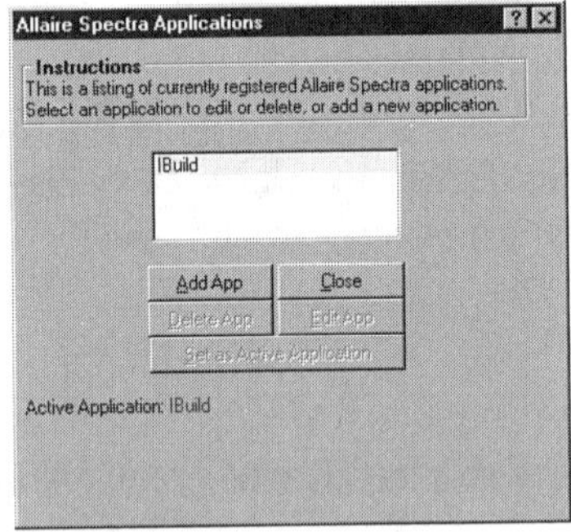

FIGURE 5.27
The Allaire Spectra Applications dialog is where you specify access information about your Spectra application to ColdFusion Studio.

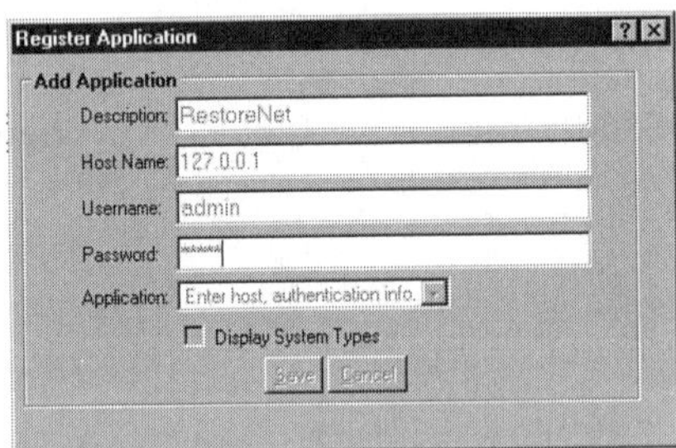

FIGURE 5.28
The Register Application dialog box needs to know how to contact the Spectra server (the Host Name field) and a valid username and password for the Spectra system.

After registering your application, you should see a dialog box like the one in Figure 5.29, showing the list of registered applications. If i-Build isn't the active application at the bottom of the dialog box, select it and choose the Set as Active Application button to make it active. Click Close to shut the dialog.

Let's move to the Type Browser. Click the second button from the left on the Spectra toolbar, the one with the T (for *type*) on the icon. Use the pull-down Type menu at the upper-left to select the `iBuildContent` object type and make your display look like that of Figure 5.30. This dialog box has three tabs: Details, Properties, and Methods. You see a description of the type, the path to where handlers for the type are stored, the UUID of the type, and some controls.

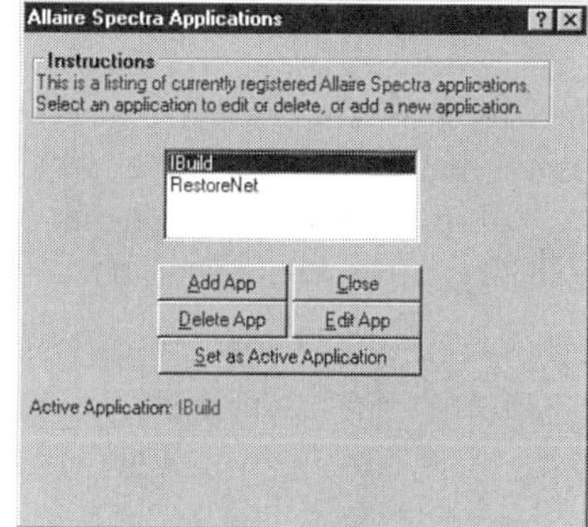

FIGURE 5.29
The Allaire Spectra Applications dialog lets you select which application is active.

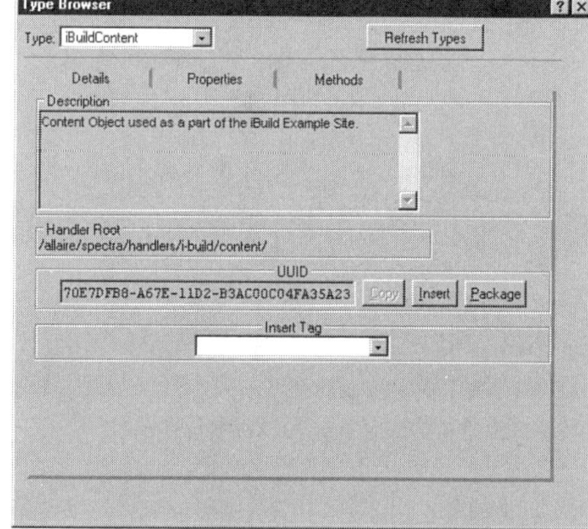

FIGURE 5.30
The Type Browser provides information as well as features such as inserting the UUID for you or even inserting complete tags.

If all you need is the UUID of the type inserted into your code, choose the Insert button and it will be entered for you. Depending on your browser's capabilities, the Copy button may or may not be active. This copies the UUID to the Clipboard. The Package button lets you package the object type for export to another Spectra system.

The Insert Tag pull-down at the bottom will insert the boilerplate parts of a selected Spectra tag for you, including the UUID of the type you are viewing. Go ahead and pull down to `cfa_contentObjectFind` and then release the mouse.

Wow, that was fast typing. You just had the following typed for you:

```
<CFA_CONTENTOBJECTFIND DATASOURCE=""
  TYPEID="70E7DFB8-A67E--11D2-B3AC00C04FA35A23" STPROPERTIES=""
  LPROPERTIESPRECEDENCE="">
```

If you click the Properties tab near the top of the dialog, you will see the screen in Figure 5.31. The Properties tab allows you to select a property by name from the list and see its settings. Go ahead and select one or two and see what information you get.

The last tab in the Type Browser is the Methods tab. Click it to see the screen in Figure 5.32. Here you have a list of all the methods defined for the type. After you select a method, choose the Edit Current Handler button at the bottom, and the code for that handler will be loaded into ColdFusion Studio for you. Close the Type Browser dialog box.

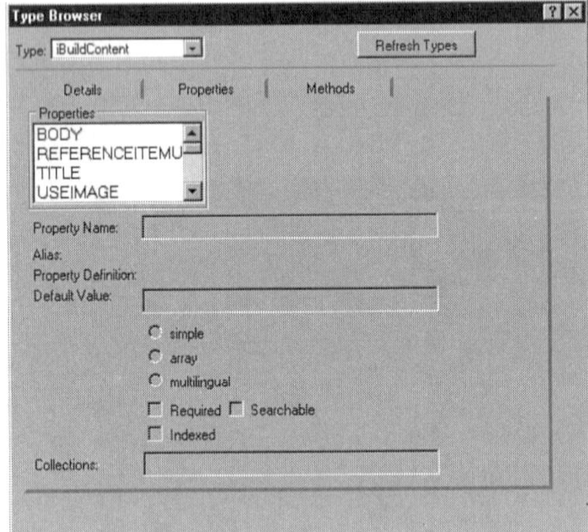

FIGURE 5.31
The Properties tab shows the attribute settings for the selected property.

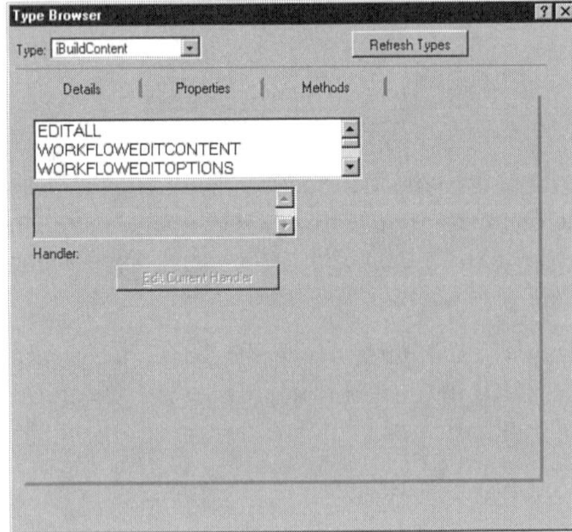

FIGURE 5.32
The Methods tab shows the defined methods for the type and allows you to edit the handler code for a method easily.

The third button on the Spectra toolbar has an icon like a molecule and is the Object Browser button. Click this button to see the Object Browser dialog (see Figure 5.33). You should use the pull-down to set the type to `iBuildContent`. This will display all the `iBuildContent` type objects as links. If you click one of the links, ColdFusion Studio will open the object in the Spectra Object Viewer.

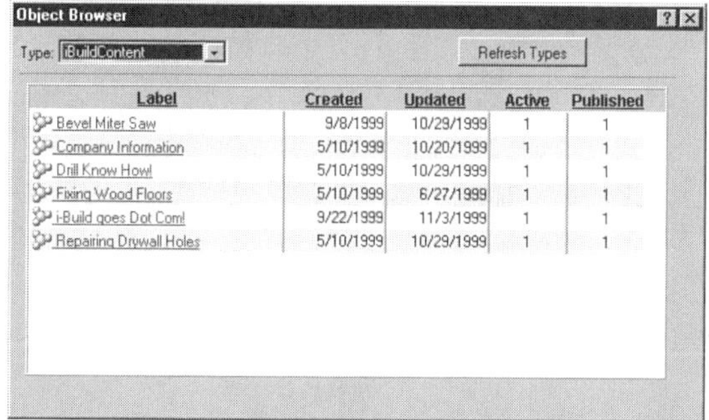

FIGURE 5.33
The Object Browser shows objects of the selected object type. You can launch the object into the Spectra Object Viewer by clicking the link in this dialog.

The fourth button is the Type Creation Wizard. Click it to open the wizard to the first step of a multi-step dialog. The process is similar to the one provided by the Webtop. The gain in having it here is that you don't need to start the Webtop if you suddenly find you need to define a type. We won't have you define one right now, but feel free to experiment later when you know more about creating types. For now, just close the window.

The last button in the Spectra toolbar is the Webtop Auto-Update tool. This automatically updates any new capabilities from Spectra into the toolbar. If everything is up to date, it tells you so.

ColdFusion Studio User Assistance Options

Several other forms of help are available for Spectra in the ColdFusion Studio environment. If you select the Help tab, you can access all the online documentation on Spectra. You can see the available documentation tree on the left and a detail page on the right once you select a page to view.

The Tag Insight feature of ColdFusion Studio has been extended to include the most common Spectra tags. An example of using this with the `<cfa_contentObjectFind>` tag is shown in Figure 5.34.

If you right-click the typed tag name and choose Edit Tag or press Ctrl+F4, you will get Tag Editor, with a property sheet and embedded help on the tag, as shown in Figure 5.35.

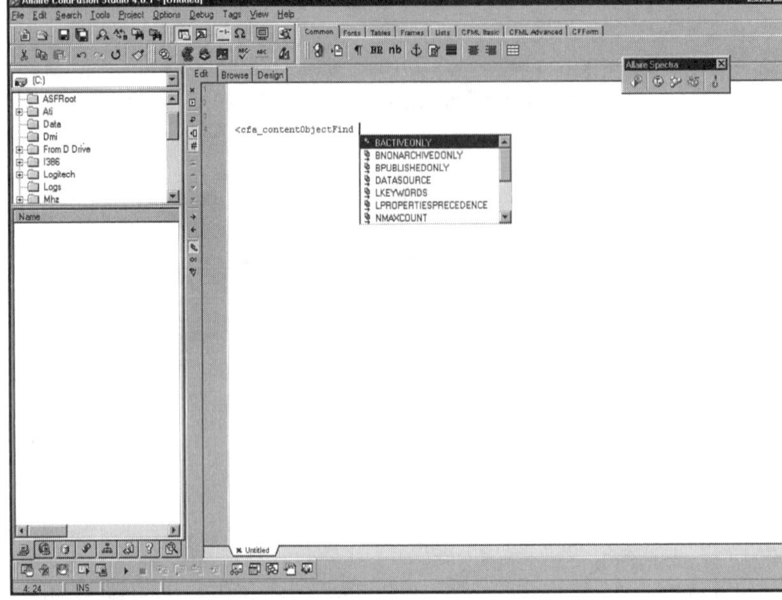

FIGURE 5.34
Tag Insight for Spectra tags shows available attributes you might want to add to the tag you are writing.

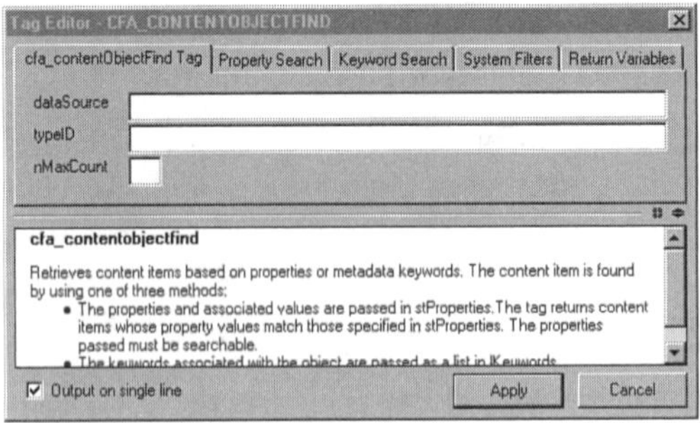

FIGURE 5.35
Tag Editor for Spectra provides a tabbed interface with embedded help to aid you in entering Spectra tags.

PART II

Building Spectra Applications

CHAPTER 6

Introduction to Spectra Programming

In this chapter

Creating and Initializing the Application

Getting started with a Spectra application involves some basic steps. Using the a2zBooks example application, you'll create Property Definitions, ContentObject Types, and handlers, all the basic building blocks of a Spectra application. The basic a2zBooks application has three ContentObject Types: Author, Publisher, and Book.

In a database-driven application, you would normally create a database schema with three or more tables with relationships between them to store the same data. You would then build a series of queries and create application logic around them for display and maintenance.

In your Spectra application, each data element is treated as an autonomous object with its own logic, and the data is stored as WDDX (XML) so you don't have to build a schema. Embedding Author and Publisher objects within each Book object creates the relationship between the three entities (Author, Publisher, and Book).

The application is the set of resources to be used in your Spectra application. It can be defined through the Webtop or programmatically. Programmatic creation of the application is advantageous for portability because it can become part of the application's logic. Webtop creation is advantageous for its simplicity.

Using the Webtop

Figure 6.1 shows the Applications screen in the Webtop. To get here, choose System Design and then Applications from the menu. Click Create on the lower portion of the page to open the Application Edit window. Clicking the Create button actually creates an empty Application object, then invokes the Application object's edit handler. Enter this information to create the a2z sample Application object:

Name	`a2z`
DataSource	`a2z`
Security Context	`sc1`
URL	`/a2z/index.cfm`

Click Create to update the Application object.

Using Spectra Tags

An alternative way to begin a new application by using code is to create a ContentObject with the same properties that you used above. All you need to remember is to use the ContentObject TypeID (which is also referred to simply as a TypeID) of Application objects. This TypeID is always the same. Listing 6.1 details an encapsulated version of this in a custom tag. Listing 6.2 uses this custom tag to create the a2z application.

FIGURE 6.1
The Webtop Application Manager screen.

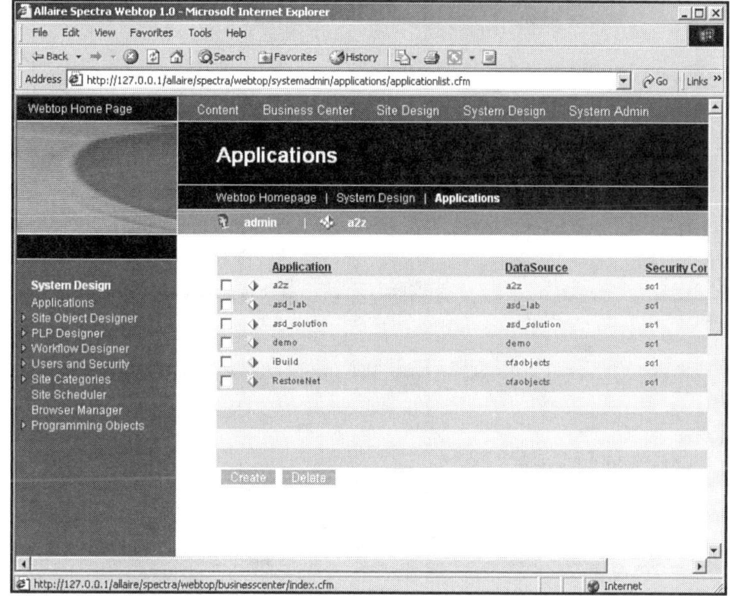

Listing 6.1 ***create_app.cfm*****—Custom Tag for Creating Spectra Application Objects**

```
<cfparam name="attributes.name">
<cfparam name="attributes.datasource">
<cfparam name="attributes.securityContext">
<cfparam name="attributes.applicationURL" default="">
<cfparam name="attributes.r_applicationID" default="">

<!--- Create a structure --->
<cfscript>

    stApplication = StructNew();

    stApplication.datasource = attributes.datasource;
    stApplication.lSecurityContexts = attributes.securityContext;
    stApplication.applicationPath = attributes.applicationURL;

</cfscript>

<!--- Create the object --->
<cfa_contentObjectCreate
 datasource="cfaobjects"
 typeid="74B6FD02-290A-11D3-AD400060B0EB2994"
 stproperties="#stApplication#"
 label="#attributes.name#"
```

continues

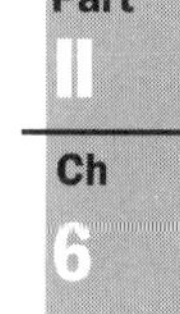

Listing 6.1 Continued

```
 r_id="applicationID"
>

<!--- Return the ID --->
<cfif attributes.r_applicationID neq "">

    <cfset "caller.#attributes.r_applicationID#" = applicationID>

</cfif>
```

Listing 6.2 *app.cfm*—Using *<cf_createApp>* to Create an Application

```
<cf_createApp
 name="A2Z"
 datasource="A2Z"
 applicationURL="/a2z/index.cfm"
 securityCOntext="sc1"
>
```

Initializing the Application

Now that the Application object has been created, the application must be initialized. Creating an `Application.cfm` file with a `<CFAPPLICATION>` tag within it initializes ColdFusion applications. Spectra application initialization is similar; you create an `Application.cfm` file and add a `<CFA_APPLICATIONINITIALIZE>` tag. The `<CFA_APPLICATIONINITIALIZE>` tag uses the application name (or ID) to determine which portions of the memory-resident Spectra system cache are to be passed to the request scope for page execution. Listing 6.3 shows the `Application.cfm` file with the `<CFA_APPLICATIONINITIALIZE>` tag. You'll be adding to this later to enable Design mode and also to enable security in your application.

You can add the Application object creation custom tag to the logic of your `Application.cfm` file to create a self-registering application. Use the server scope to set a flag after you check for the existence of the Application object.

The Request Scope As mentioned before, Spectra stores data in memory-resident caches for faster performance. Data such as type definitions, container descriptors, and cached objects is stored in the server scope. The relevant data from these caches, as well as runtime variables, needs to be accessible from all application elements, including custom tags. In ColdFusion 4.1 and above, the request scope does just that. The request scope is visible for the duration of page execution to all CFML that executes, including custom tags. Because the request scope doesn't persist after a page request, no special treatment is necessary in a clustered environment. The `<CFA_APPLICATIONINITIALIZE>` tag, as well as other areas of Spectra code, stores information for use in your application in the structure `request.cfa`.

Spectra Variables Looking at some example request scope variables and their values, shown in Table 6.1, you see that Spectra variables have prefixes to show the data type of the values stored in them. These prefixes are detailed in Chapter 3, "Spectra Concepts and Terminology."

To view all the data in any variable, use the <CFA_DUMP> tag. This handy utility takes any variable and dumps all values in a table. As soon as Spectra is installed on your system, you can use this utility just like any other custom tag in your ColdFusion applications.

Creating Property Definitions

Now that your application is created and initialized, you are ready to begin creating ContentObject Types. The first step in the creation of a ContentObject Type is to create Property Definitions. Property Definitions and their role in Spectra applications are detailed in Chapter 3.

Using the Webtop

Creating Property Definitions using the Webtop is an easy and straightforward process. As with all functions in the Webtop, it can also be done programmatically. You can choose your method according to your needs. Typically, you'll use the Property Definition Wizard the first few times you create Property Definitions. The Property Definition Manager is faster to use but less informative. Tags are a fast way of creating them, especially if you use ColdFusion Studio dialogs.

The Property Definition Wizard In the System Design section of the Webtop under the Site Object Designer menu, you'll find the Property Definition Wizard. After clicking it, you'll see the welcome screen in Figure 6.2. Click Next to continue.

You now see the Property Definition Settings screen (see Figure 6.3). Enter **`Email`** in the Label field. In the Description field, enter **`An Email Address`**. Under Data Type, choose `Char`. Click Next to move on.

The screen you see now (in Figure 6.4) allows you to choose the way a default edit handler will render this particular Property Definition in a form. Choose Text, then click Next to continue.

Now you will see validation options for your Property Definition (see Figure 6.5). These are used only with the default handlers, so anything you enter here will most likely be used only during development of your application. In the Server-Side Validation Expression field, enter **`(value contains '@')`** to check for the `@` as a sign of a valid email address. In the Validation Error Message field, enter **`Please enter a valid email address.`**.

You can now test the validation code. Enter **Blah** in the Test field and click Validate. A JavaScript alert will pop up. Click OK. You'll see the error message field in Figure 6.6. Now, enter a valid email address in the Test field. Click Validate, and the message will show that validation has passed. Click Next to continue.

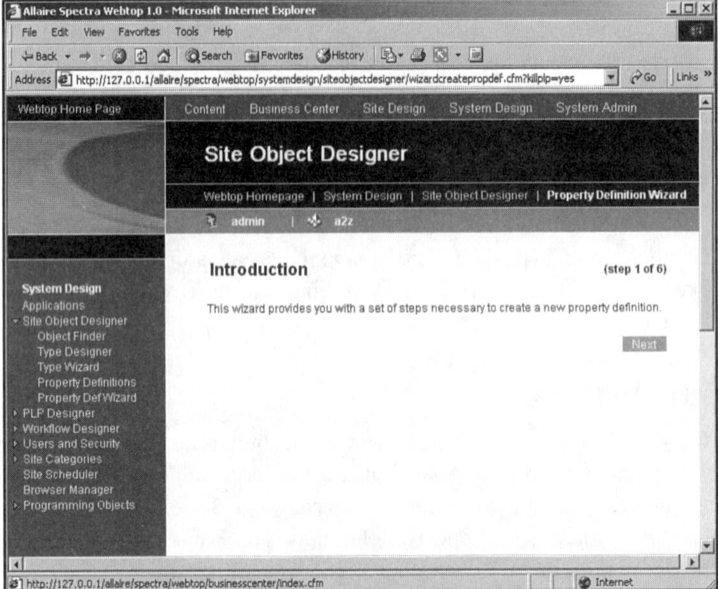

FIGURE 6.2
The Property Definition Wizard's main screen.

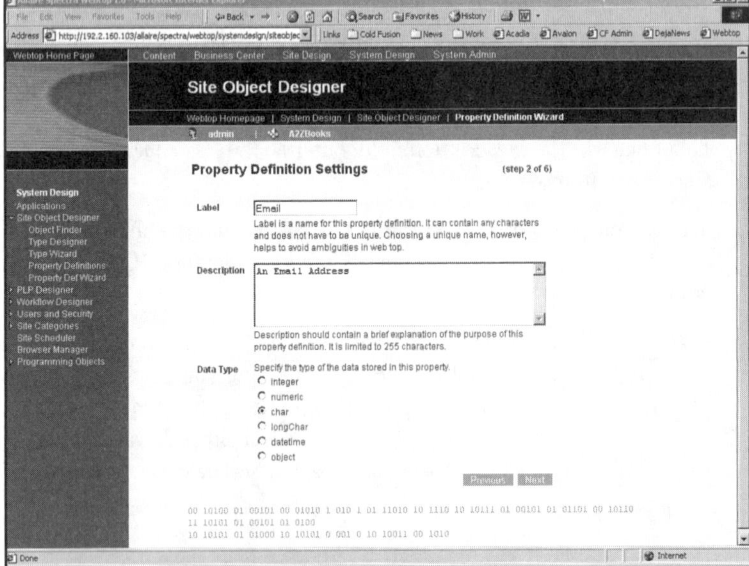

FIGURE 6.3
The Property Definition Settings screen from the Property Definition Wizard.

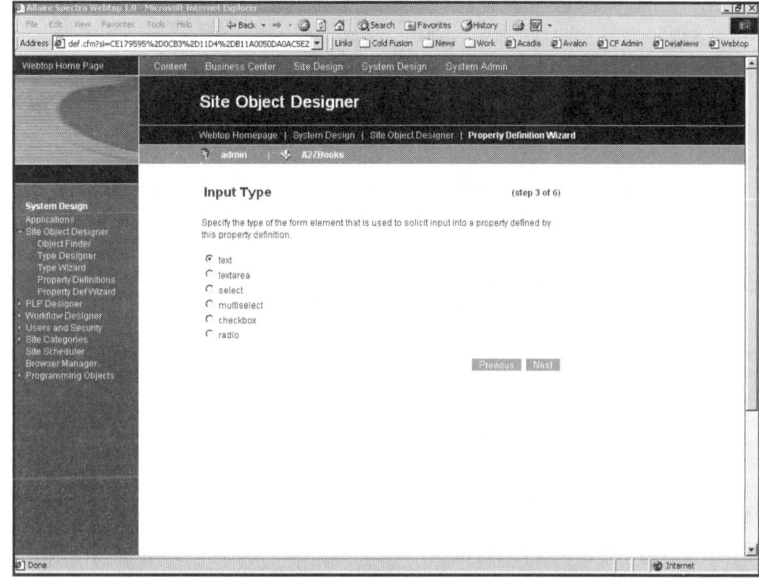

FIGURE 6.4
Default handler settings for the Property Definition Wizard.

FIGURE 6.5
Validation options for Property Definitions and default handlers.

Part II

Ch 6

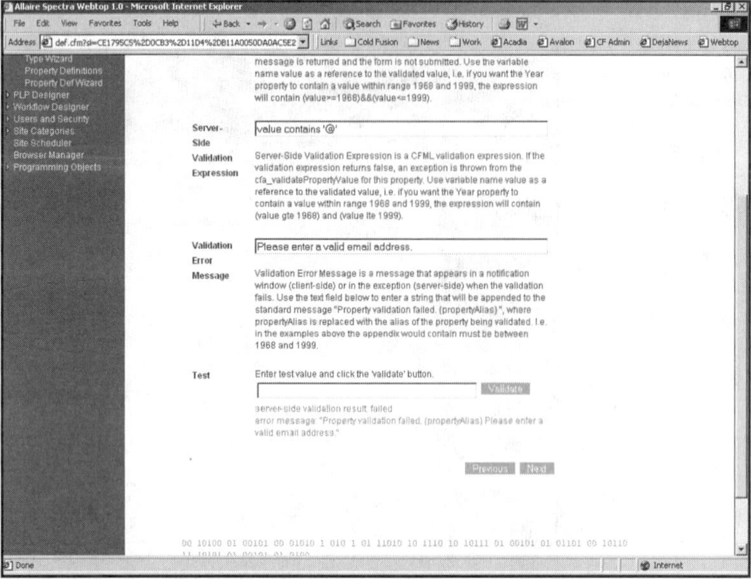

FIGURE 6.6
Testing the validation expressions in the Property Definition Wizard.

Figure 6.7 shows the Summary screen that details your Property Definition. Verify that all your information is correct, and then click Finish if everything is okay. If you need to change any values, you can still click Previous to go back and fix them. After you click Finish, the Property Definition ID will be shown. Property Definition IDs are generally used internally to relate the correct Property Definition with a Type Property, regardless of its label. Click OK to move on to the Property Definition Designer, shown in Figure 6.8.

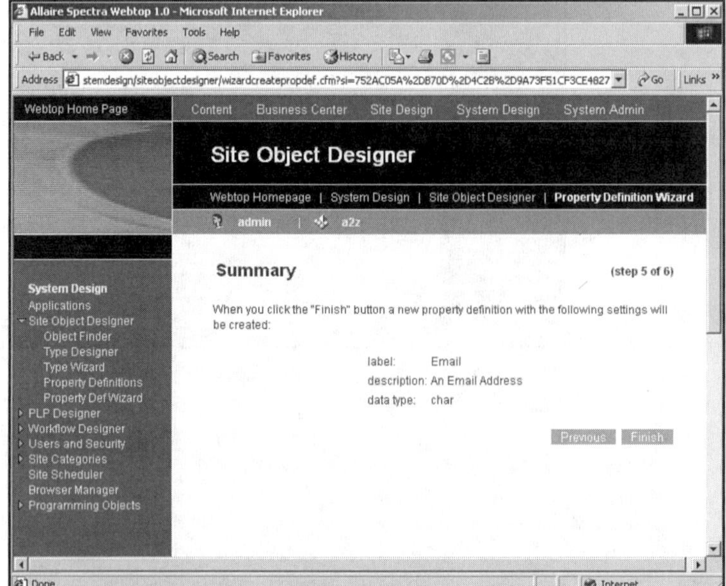

FIGURE 6.7
The Property Definition Wizard Summary screen shows all the information entered.

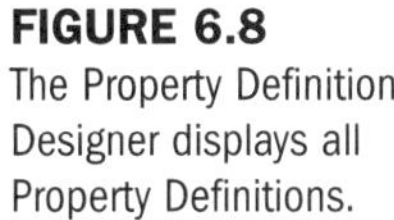

FIGURE 6.8
The Property Definition Designer displays all Property Definitions.

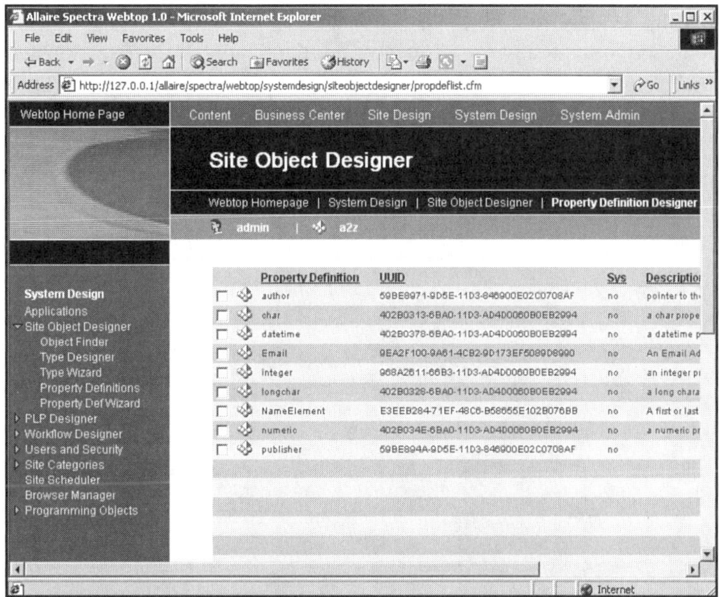

The Property Definition Manager A faster way to create Property Definitions uses the Property Definition Manager. At the bottom of the list, you'll find the New Property form. Enter **`NameElement`**, choose `char` from the data type list, and then click Create. This brings you to the New Property Definition form, shown in Figure 6.9.

Choose Text as the input type. Enter **`A first or last name`** in the Description field. For validation, enter **`(len(value) gt 0)`** in the CFML Expression field. Enter **`Please enter a name`** in the Error Message field. Click OK to complete the Property Definition and return to the Property Definition Manager.

FIGURE 6.9
The New Property Definition form is a fast way to create Property Definitions.

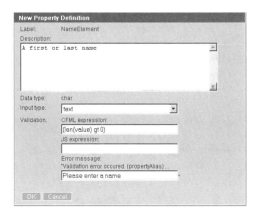

New Property Definition
Label: NameElement
Description:
A first or last name
Data type: char
Input type: text
Validation: CFML expression:
(len(value) gt 0)
JS expression:
Error message:
"Validation error occured. (propertyAlias)...
Please enter a name
OK Cancel

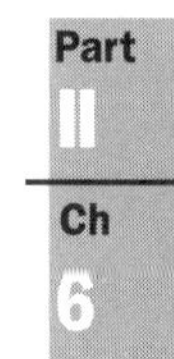

Editing and Viewing Property Definitions To view any Property Definition, click the pyramid icon to the left of the Property Definition label in the list shown in Figure 6.8. This will take you to the Property Definition Edit screen seen in Figure 6.10. Here you can modify all the elements and view all information in a Property Definition.

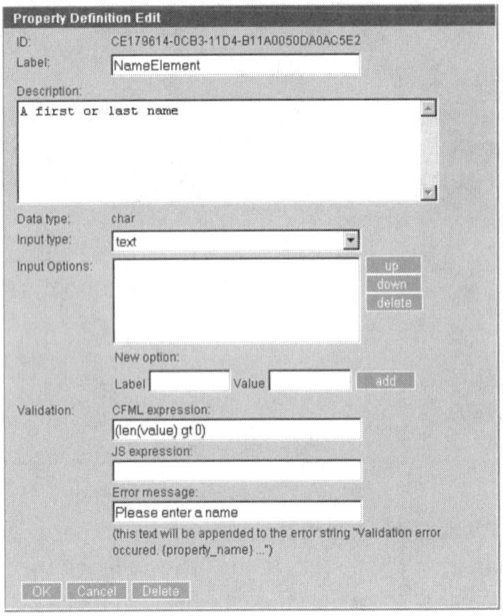

FIGURE 6.10
The Property Definition Edit screen provides an interface for editing Property Definitions.

Using Spectra Tags

Property Definitions are managed in Spectra with the `<CFA_PROPERTYDEFINITION>` tag. Using this tag to create a Property Definition is very fast, especially when you need to create many at a time. Listing 6.3 shows the creation of Property Definitions using this tag. You'll create two more Property Definitions later that will enable you to create embedded objects in your application.

Listing 6.3 ***create_definitions.cfm*****—Creating Property Definitions with Spectra Tags**

```
<!--- Create Property definitions for A2Z --->

<cfa_propertyDefinition
  action = "Create"
  dataSource = "#request.cfa.objectStore.dsn#"
  label = "City"
  description = "A City"
  dataType = "Char"
  inputType = "text"
  bRequired = "yes"
```

```
    bSearchable = "no"
    bIndexed = "no"
    defaultValue = ""
    r_id = "NewID"
  >

  <cfa_propertyDefinition
    action = "Create"
    dataSource = "#request.cfa.objectStore.dsn#"
    label = "Title"
    description = "A Title"
    dataType = "Char"
    inputType = "text"
    bRequired = "no"
    bSearchable = "no"
    bIndexed = "no"
    defaultValue = ""
    r_id = "NewID"
  >
```

Creating the ContentObject Type

With the basic Property Definitions created, you are ready to create the ContentObject Types for the a2z example application. ContentObject Types and their function are explained in both Chapter 1, "Understanding Spectra," and Chapter 3. ContentObject Types are created through the Webtop, programmatically with tags, or by using ColdFusion Studio.

Using the Webtop

You will most often create and manage your ContentObject Types by using the Webtop, because it's easy and offers the most management options. The Type Designer, shown in Figure 6.11, is the center of all Webtop functions for ContentObject Types and is found in the System Design section under the Site Object Designer.

The ContentObject Type Wizard The first time you create a ContentObject Type, it's helpful to be guided by the ContentObject Type Wizard. Later, you will most likely settle on one of the other methods of creating ContentObject Types. To access the ContentObject Type Wizard, choose Type Wizard from the Site Object Designer menu in the System Design section of the Webtop. You'll see the Introduction screen shown in Figure 6.12. Click Next to continue.

In the Type Settings screen in Figure 6.13, you'll enter the main information needed for creation of your new ContentObject Type. In the Label field, enter `Author`. Enter `Author` in the Alias field also. The alias is used in the Type Designer listings and can be different from the label. Consider making this field more descriptive if your Business Users may need it.

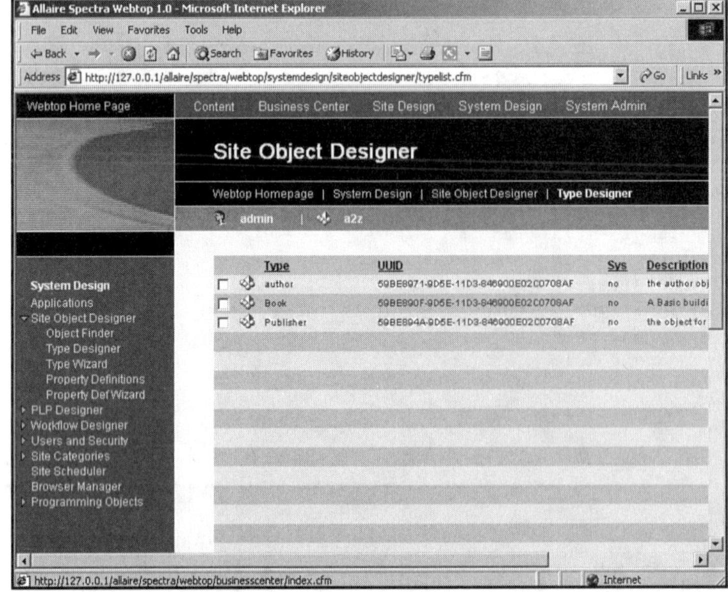

FIGURE 6.11
The Type Designer lists all ContentObject Types.

FIGURE 6.12
The Type Wizard Introduction screen provides some basic information.

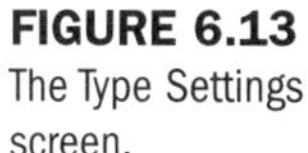

FIGURE 6.13
The Type Settings screen.

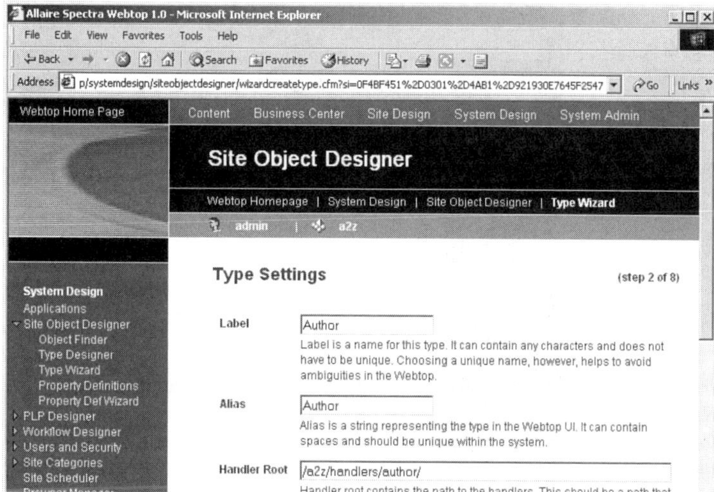

In the Handler Root field, enter **`/a2z/handlers/author/`**. This is the ColdFusion mapping where your handler files will reside. You'll create this directory and the mapping later in this chapter; Spectra doesn't create it for you.

Enter **`A book author.`** in the Description field. Click Next to move on.

The Type Properties screen shown in Figure 6.14 is where you create all the Type Properties needed for your ContentObject Type. You will create three Type Properties. Follow these steps:

1. Enter **`Email`** in the Name field and choose Email from the Definition field. This relates the Type Property to the Property Definition you created earlier.
2. Click Add.
3. Enter **`FirstName`** in the Name field and choose NameElement from the Definition field.
4. Click Add.
5. Enter **`LastName`** in the Name field and again choose NameElement from the Definition field.
6. Click Add, and then check your Type Properties in the list.
7. If you need to make changes, click Remove with the Type Property highlighted, and then re-create the Type Property.
8. When you are ready, click Next to save your changes.

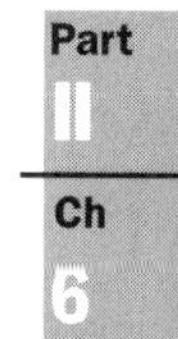

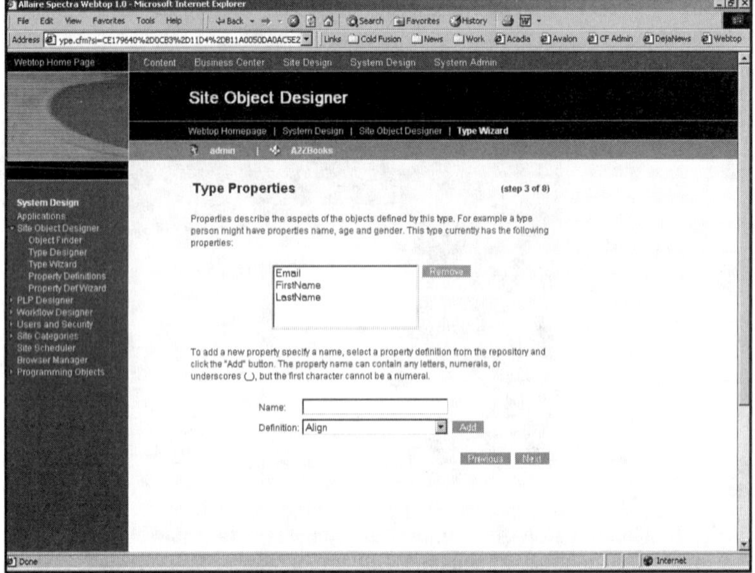

FIGURE 6.14
The Type Properties screen allows you to create Type Properties.

The next three screens are Property Detail screens where you set specific parameters for each Type Property. As you see in Figure 6.15, set the following options for each Type Property:

- Leave Default Value blank.
- For Multiplicity, choose One Value or Embedded Object.
- Check the check box next to Required to make the default edit handler validate that a value was entered.
- Check SQL Search Enabled to cause Spectra to store values in the Properties table in the ContentObject Database in addition to the Object packet in the Objects table.
- Check Verity Search Enabled to index this property in a Verity collection.

After completing the Property Detail configuration for all three properties, you will see the Type Methods screen, shown in Figure 6.16. You will create two methods for this ContentObject Type:

1. Enter **`Display`** in the Method field, and then click Add. This method will override the default Display method.
2. Enter **`EditSingle`** in the Method field and click Add.
3. Check your methods in the list, and then click Next.

▶ **See** Chapter 3 for more information on default methods and handlers.

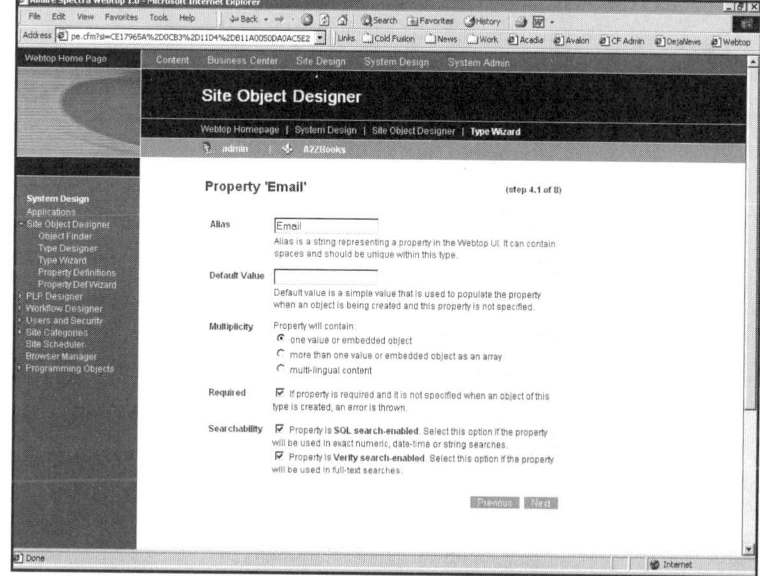

FIGURE 6.15
The Property Detail screens determine storage and searchability.

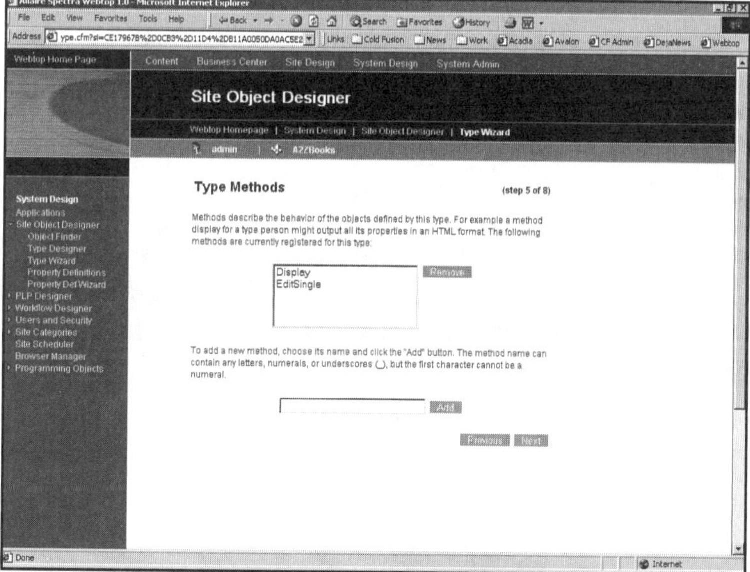

FIGURE 6.16
The Type Methods screen has fields for method creation.

Figure 6.17 shows the method detail screen. For each method, leave the defaults and click Next. You can enter a description if you want. These screens determine which file in the `/a2z/handlers/author/` directory will be called when the method is invoked.

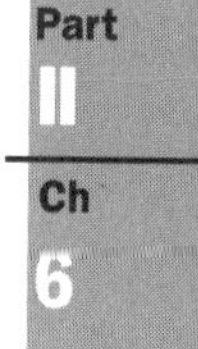

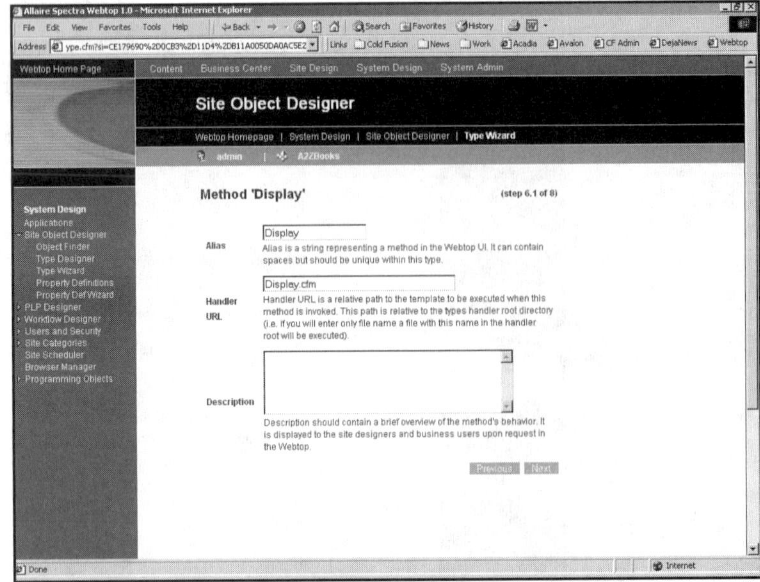

FIGURE 6.17
In this method detail screen, enter the handler filename.

The Summary screen in Figure 6.18 will appear after you complete the method detail screens. Check to see that all the information is correct, and then click Finish. The new ContentObject Type is created. Click OK to return to the Type Designer.

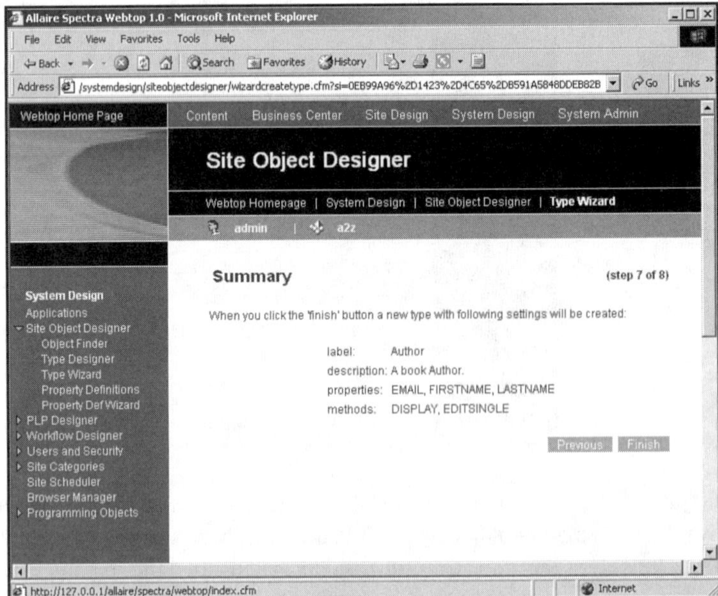

FIGURE 6.18
The Type Wizard Summary screen confirms your entries.

The Type Designer As with Property Definitions, there's a faster way to create ContentObject Types through the Webtop. Follow these steps:

1. From the Type Designer, scroll to the bottom of the screen shown earlier in Figure 6.11 and click Create. This brings you to the New Type form (see Figure 6.19).

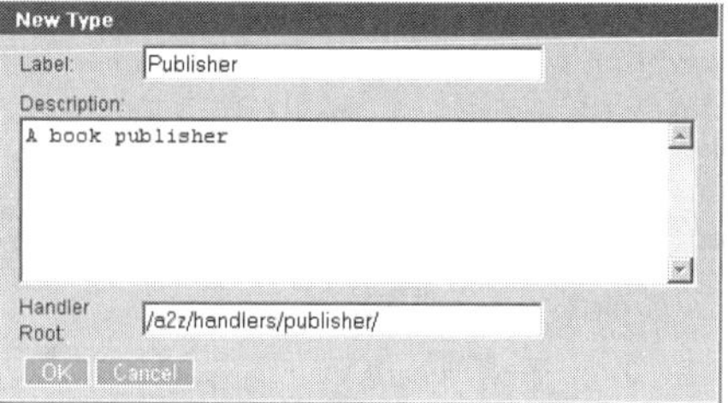

FIGURE 6.19
The New Type screen lets you create a ContentObject Type faster than the wizard.

2. Enter **`Publisher`** in the Label field and **`A book publisher`** for the description. In the Handler Root field, enter **`/a2z/handlers/publisher/`**. Click OK to continue.

   The Edit Type form in Figure 6.20 appears. Your new type has been created, so you'll now edit it as though you selected it from the Type Designer.

3. Click the Properties tab to see the form in Figure 6.21. Enter **`City`** in the New Property field, and choose City from the Property Definition list. Click Add.

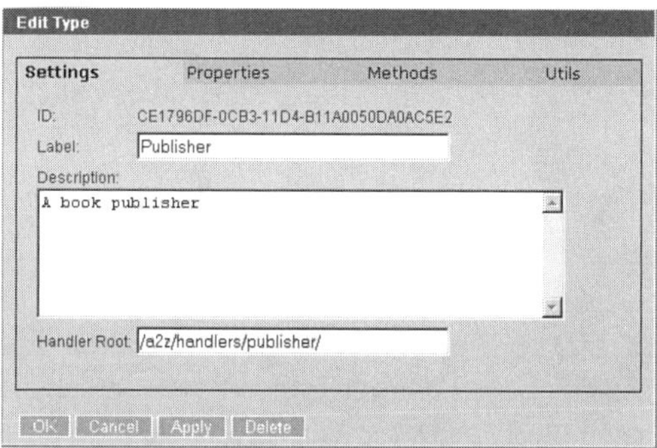

FIGURE 6.20
The Edit Type form lets you edit a new ContentObject Type.

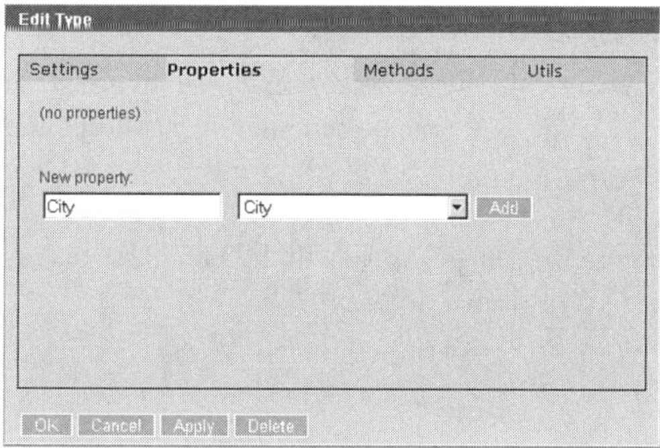

FIGURE 6.21
The Properties tab of the Edit Type form lets you enter new properties.

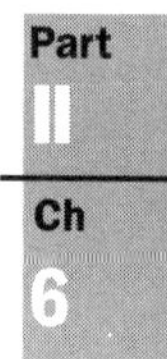

4. The New Type Property Definition form seen in Figure 6.22 appears. Check the check box next to Indexed, then click OK to return to the Edit Type form.
5. Click the Properties tab again to take you to the properties screen in Figure 6.21. Enter **Name** in the New Property field and choose NameElement from the Property Definition list. Click Add.
6. In the New Type Property Definition, check the check boxes next to both Searchable and Indexed. These selections will SQL search–enable and Verity search–enable the Type Property, respectively. Click OK to return to the Edit Type form.

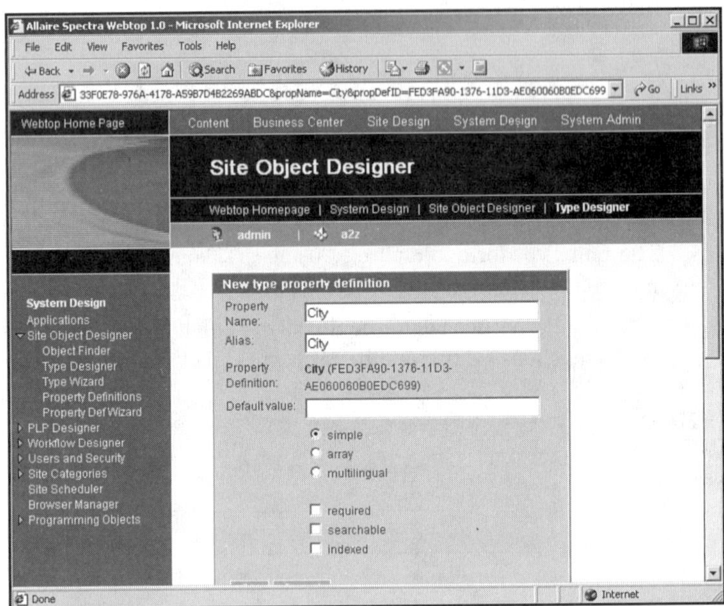

FIGURE 6.22
The New Type Property Definition screen is where you configure each Type Property.

7. To add methods to this ContentObject Type, choose the Methods tab and enter the methods there. For this ContentObject Type, we won't create any methods initially. Click OK to return to the Type Designer.

Using ColdFusion Studio Integration

Before creating the Book ContentObject Type, you'll need to create Property Definitions for each object you created. This is how you embed one object within another. Return to the Property Definition Designer in Figure 6.8 by choosing Property Definitions in the Site Object Designer menu. At the bottom of the list, you'll find the New Property form. Enter **Author**, choose Object from the Data Type list, and then click **Create**. This brings you to the New Property Definition form, shown in Figure 6.9.

Enter **`An author object`** in the Description field. Choose Author from the ContentObject Type list. Click OK to complete the Property Definition and return to the Property Definition Designer. At the bottom of the list, enter **`Publisher`** in the New Property field, choose Object from the Data Type list, and then click Create. This brings you again to the New Property Definition form, shown in Figure 6.9.

Enter **`A Publisher Object`** in the Description field, and then choose Publisher from the ContentObject Type list. Click OK.

Now you are ready to create the Book object. Open ColdFusion Studio and choose the Allaire Spectra toolbar. If you haven't already, register the current application (a2z) in the toolbar as discussed in Chapter 5, "Navigating the Spectra Design Tools." Click the Type Creation Wizard button to see the dialog box shown in Figure 6.23. Click Next to continue.

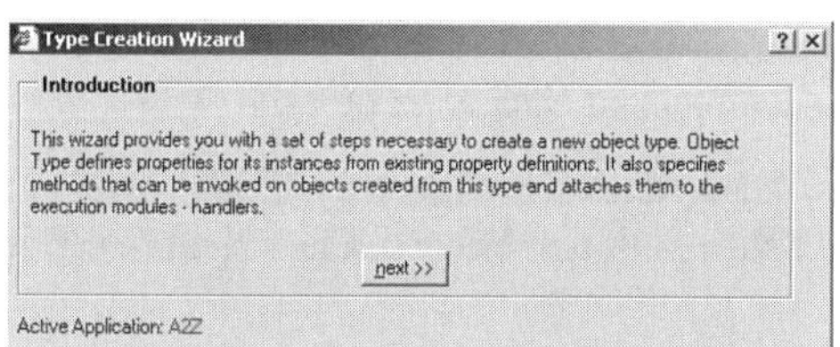

FIGURE 6.23
ColdFusion Studio's Type Creation Wizard is similar to the Webtop Type Wizard.

In the Type Settings dialog box, seen in Figure 6.24, enter **`Book`** in both the Label and Alias fields. In the Handler Root field, enter **`/a2z/handlers/book`**. In the Description field, enter **`The Book Object`**. Click Next to continue.

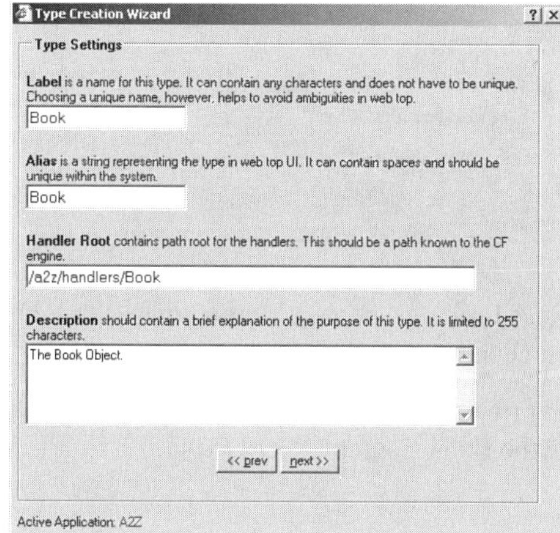

FIGURE 6.24
The Type Settings dialog box of the Type Creation Wizard.

In the Properties dialog box shown in Figure 6.25, create the following properties:

- `Author` with a definition of `Author`
- `Edition` with a definition of `Char`
- `ISBN` with a definition of `Char`
- `Pages` with a definition of `Integer`
- `Price` with a definition of `Numeric`
- `Published` with a definition of `Datetime`
- `Publisher` with a definition of `Publisher`
- `Title` with a definition of `Title`

Click Next to continue.

Each Type Property that you created now has its own dialog box, as shown in Figure 6.26. Leave each of them set to defaults and click Next on each.

You now see the Methods dialog, shown in Figure 6.27. Enter two methods—**`Display`** and **`Teaser`**—and click the Add New button after each. Click Next to continue.

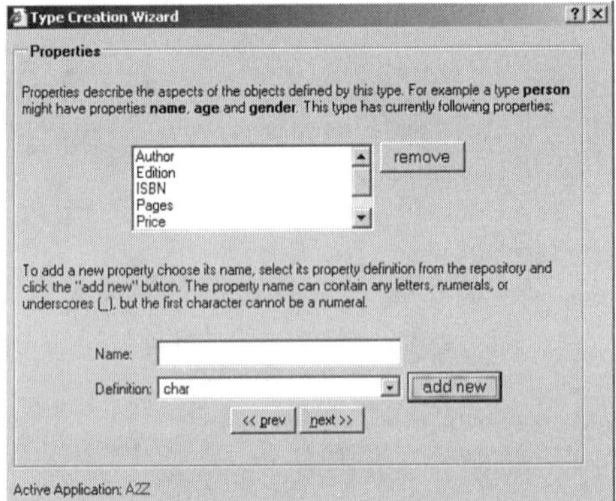

FIGURE 6.25
The Properties dialog is where you create Type Properties.

Each method that you entered will now show a Method dialog (see Figure 6.28). Accept the defaults in each dialog and click Next on each to continue.

The Summary dialog in Figure 6.29 shows the major information you've entered. If it's all correct, click Finish to create the Book ContentObject Type.

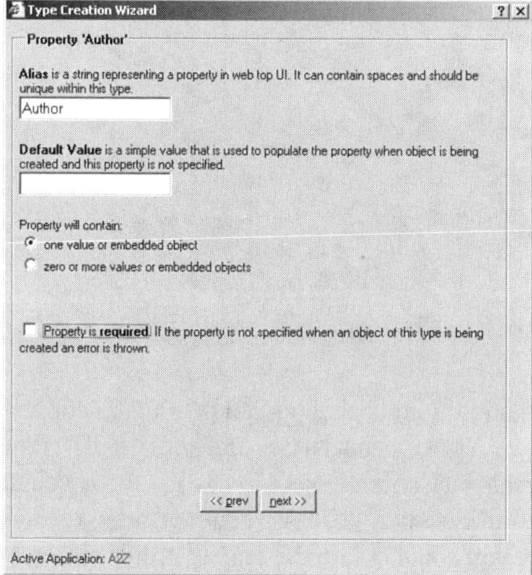

FIGURE 6.26
The Property detail dialog lets you configure each Type Property.

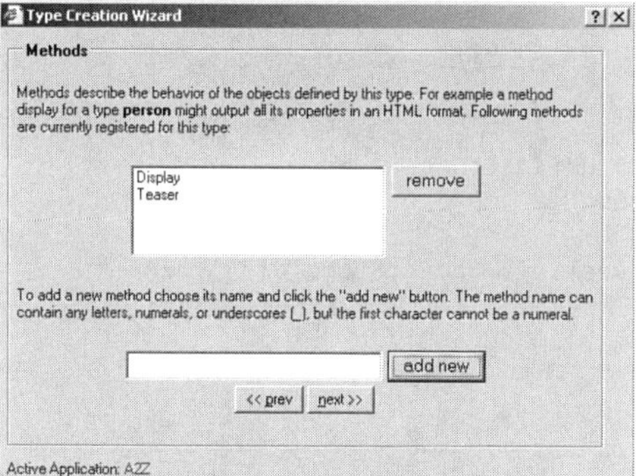

FIGURE 6.27
The Methods dialog controls new method creation.

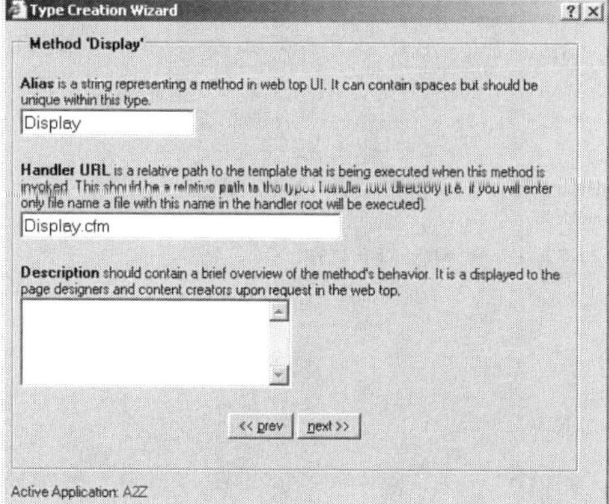

FIGURE 6.28
The Method detail dialog sets filenames for handlers.

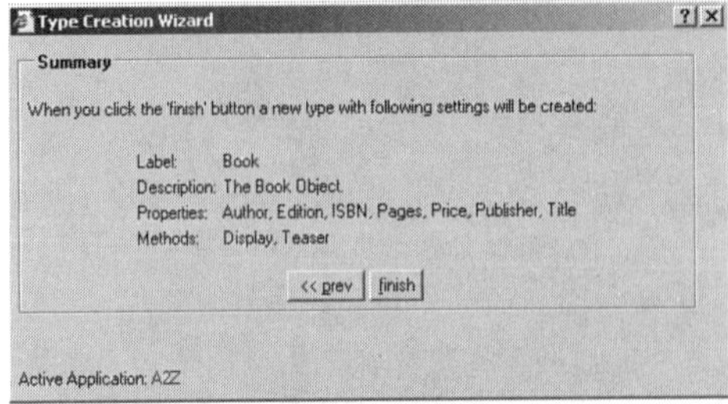

FIGURE 6.29
The Summary dialog shows all the information you've entered.

Using Tags

All the steps you've taken so far in this chapter can be done in one template using the <CFA_OBJECTTYPE>, <CFA_OBJECTTYPEPROPERTY>, and <CFA_OBJECTTYPEMETHOD> tags. The <CFA_OBJECTTYPE> tag creates a ContentObject Type. The <CFA_OBJECTTYPEPROPERTY> tag creates a Type Property, and the <CFA_OBJECTTYPEMETHOD> tag creates a method. Listing 6.4 shows an example of how you could create the entire Author object, Property Definitions and all.

Listing 6.4 *CREATE_TYPE.CFM*—Creating a ContentObject Type with Spectra Tags

```
<!--- Create Property definitions --->
<cfa_propertyDefinition
  action = "Create"
  dataSource = "#request.cfa.objectStore.dsn#"
  label = "Email"
  description = "An Email address"
  dataType = "Char"
  inputType = "text"
  bRequired = "yes"
  bSearchable = "no"
  bIndexed = "no"
  defaultValue = ""
  r_id = "emailDefID"
>

<cfa_propertyDefinition
  action = "Create"
  dataSource = "#request.cfa.objectStore.dsn#"
  label = "nameElement"
  description = "A First name or last name"
  dataType = "Char"
  inputType = "text"
  bRequired = "no"
  bSearchable = "no"
  bIndexed = "no"
  defaultValue = ""
  r_id = "nameElementDefID"
>
```

```
<!--- Create the ContentObject Type --->
<cfa_objectType
  dataSource="#request.cfa.objectstore.dsn#"
  action="CREATE"
  label="Author"
  description="An Author Object"
  handlerRoot="/A2Z/handlers/author"
  bSystemEnabled = "no"
  r_typeID = "AuthorTypeID"
>

<!--- Relate the Type Properties --->
<cfa_objectTypeProperty
  action = "CREATE"
  dataSource="#request.cfa.objectstore.dsn#"
  typeID = "#AuthorTypeID#"
  propertyDefinitionID = "emailDefID"
  propertyName = "Email"
  alias = "Email"
  defaultValue = ""
  bSearchable = "yes"
  bRequired = "yes"
  bIndexed = "yes"
  bArray = "no"
  bMultilingual = "no"
  bSystemEnabled = "no"
>

<cfa_objectTypeProperty
  action = "CREATE"
  dataSource="#request.cfa.objectstore.dsn#"
  typeID = "#AuthorTypeID#"
  propertyDefinitionID = "nameElementDefID"
  propertyName = "FirstName"
  alias = "FirstName"
  defaultValue = ""
  bSearchable = "yes"
  bRequired = "yes"
  bIndexed = "yes"
  bArray = "no"
  bMultilingual = "no"
  bSystemEnabled = "no"
>

<cfa_objectTypeProperty
  action = "CREATE"
  dataSource="#request.cfa.objectstore.dsn#"
  typeID = "#AuthorTypeID#"
  propertyDefinitionID = "nameElementDefID"
  propertyName = "LastName"
  alias = "LastName"
  defaultValue = ""
```

continues

Listing 6.4 Continued

```
    bSearchable = "yes"
    bRequired = "yes"
    bIndexed = "yes"
    bArray = "no"
    bMultilingual = "no"
    bSystemEnabled = "no"
>

<!--- Add a Method --->
<cfa_objectTypeMethod
    action = "CREATE"
    dataSource="#request.cfa.objectstore.dsn#"
    typeID = "#AuthorTypeID#"
    method = "showName"
    alias = "showName"
    description = "Show the name only"
    handlerURL = "/A2Z/handlers/showName.cfm"
    bSystemEnabled = "no"
>
```

Coding Handlers

The final step in creating Spectra ContentObject Types is the creation of handlers for each method. As discussed in Chapter 3, a handler consists of a `<CFA_HANDLER>` tag and application code. The `<CFA_HANDLER>` tag takes an object retrieved from the ContentObject Database and makes it a local structure variable with a name that is the same as what you've passed in the `OBJECT` attribute. You can then output the ContentObject properties, edit them, or even pass them to a PLP.

Storing Handlers

Before creating any handlers, you'll need to create the directory structure to store them in. Create a directory called `A2Z` in your root. It's best to keep your handlers out of your Web root for security reasons. Create a subdirectory called `Handlers`, and create subdirectories under `Handlers` named `Book`, `Publisher`, and `Author`. Now, open your ColdFusion Administrator and choose Mappings from the menu on the left. Create a mapping named A2Z for your new directory (see Figure 6.30). You can now create your handlers in their correct directories.

Handler Code

Handler code is very straightforward but can become complex, depending on your application. The basic handlers for the Book type are very simple. Listing 6.5 shows the code for the `Display` method for the Book type. Notice the `<CFA_HANDLER>` tag encloses the whole block of code. Remember that this is necessary in case multiple objects are being invoked, because

<CFA_HANDLER> loops over the code between it once for each object. You access the embedded object properties by using *object.property.property* notation.

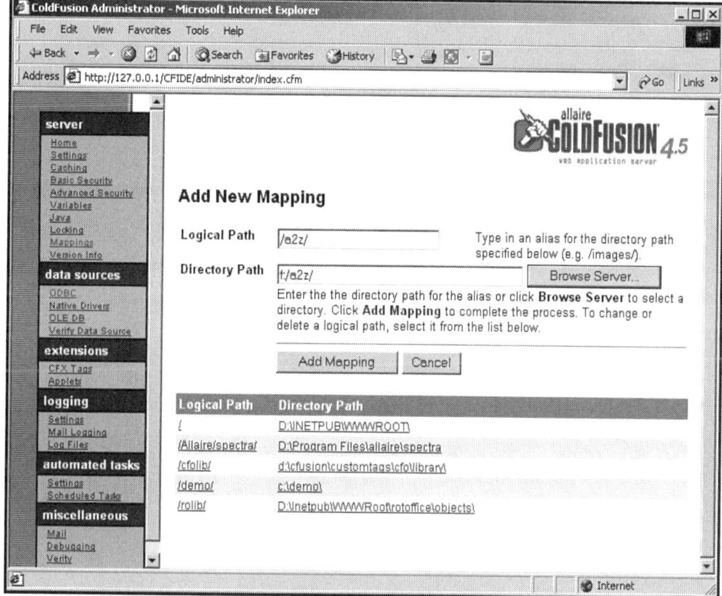

FIGURE 6.30
Adding a mapping in the ColdFusion Administrator.

Listing 6.5 *DISPLAY.CFM*—The Display Handler Outputs the Full Object

```
<cfa_handler
 object="Book"
>

<cfoutput>

<table>
<tr>
    <td><b>Title</b></td>
    <td>#Book.title#</td>
</tr>
<tr>
    <td><b>Author</b></td>
    <td><a href="mailto:#Book.Author.Email#">#Book.Author.FirstName#
                #Book.Author.LastName#</a></td>
</tr>
<tr>
    <td><b>Price</b></td>
    <td>#Book.Price#</td>
</tr>
```

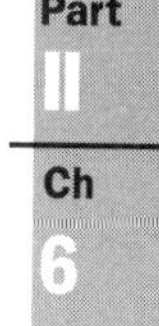

continues

Listing 6.5 Continued

```
<tr>
    <td><b>Publisher</b></td>
    <td>#Book.Publisher.Name#</td>
</tr>
</table>

</cfoutput>

</cfa_handler>
```

Listing 6.6 shows the code for the `Teaser` method for the A2Z Book ContentObject Type. Notice here that only a few properties are displayed and that the format is slightly different.

Listing 6.6 *teaser.cfm*—The *Teaser* Handler Displays Only Part of the Object

```
<cfa_handler
 object="Book"
>

<cfoutput>

<table>
<tr>
   <td><b>Title</b></td>
   <td>#Book.title# by #Book.Author.FirstName# #Book.Author.LastName#</td>
   <td><b>#Book.Price#</b></td>
</tr>
</table>

</cfoutput>

</cfa_handler>
```

Creating Objects

Creating ContentObjects or instances in Spectra is analogous to populating database tables. First, you create an empty object, then you pass the empty object to an edit handler (in this case, the default edit handler). You then complete the fields and update the existing object. This is done by using the Webtop or programmatically using `<CFA_CONTENTOBJECTCREATE>` and `<CFA_CONTENTOBJECTDATA>`.

Using the Webtop

You can use the Webtop to create test objects for the a2z application. In the System Design section of the Webtop, choose the Site Object Designer and then the Object Finder. You'll see the Object Finder screen in Figure 6.31. Choose Book from the Filter By Type list. The screen will refresh. Click Create at the bottom of the list to create a ContentObject.

FIGURE 6.31
The Object Finder lists available objects.

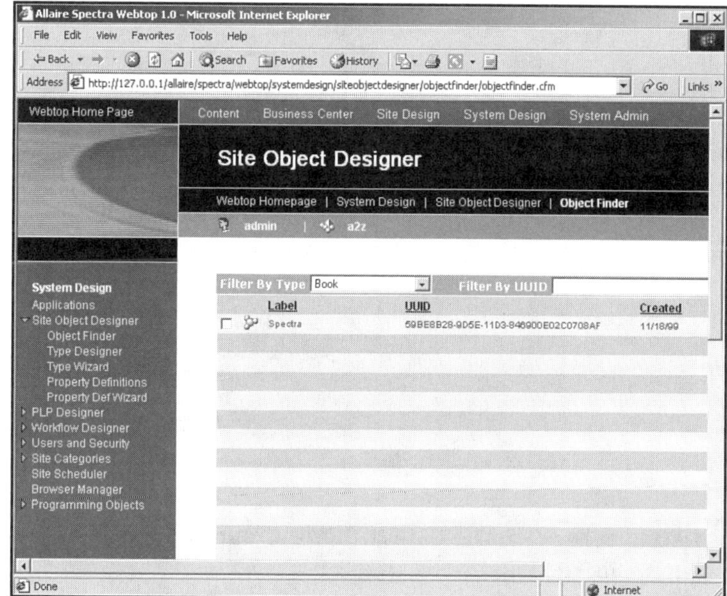

The Edit page of the Object Viewer will appear (see Figure 6.32). At this point, your empty object is already created. Fill out the form and click OK to update the object with your new data.

Using Spectra Tags

You can create objects in two ways with Spectra tags. The two-step method is generally used throughout your Spectra application when new objects are created that require user interaction for data. This is done in this manner because methods can be invoked only against an existing object. You can't override your create method, so you reuse your `Edit` method to update the object. First, an object is created with empty properties. You then invoke the empty object's `Edit` method. In the `Edit` method, you use `<CFA_CONTENTOBJECTDATA>` to update the properties. Listing 6.7 shows the object creation, and Listing 6.8 shows an example of the edit handler.

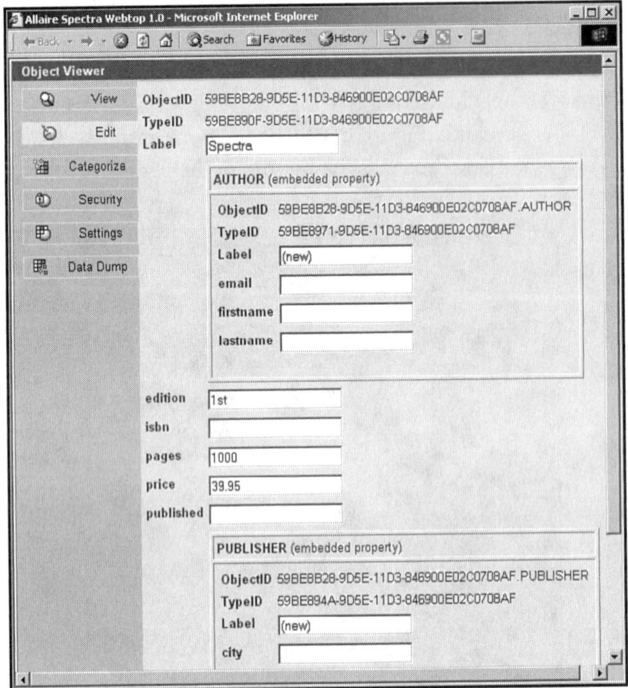

FIGURE 6.32
The Object Editor manages the properties of a ContentObject.

Listing 6.7 ***CREATE_EMPTY.CFM*—Create an Empty Object and Invoke the *editSingle* Handler**

```
<!--- Create the object (Repalce the TypeID with your Author typeID) --->
<cfa_contentObjectCreate
 datasource="#request.cfa.objectstore.dsn#"
 typeid="A4B6FC01-290A-11D3-AD400060B0EB2994"
 label="(New Object)"
 r_id="objID"
>

<!--- Invoke editSingle method on empty object --->
<cfa_contentObject
 datasource="#request.cfa.objectstore.dsn#"
 objectid="#objID#"
 method="editSingle"
>
```

Listing 6.8 *EDIT_SINGLE.CFM*—A Very Simple Edit Handler

```
<cfa_handler
 object="Author"
>

<cfif IsDefined('form.submit')>

    <cfa_contentObjectData
     datasource="#request.cfa.objectstore.dsn#"
     objectid="#Author.objectID#">

        <cfa_contentObjectProperty
         name="Email"
         value="#form.email#"
        >

    </cfa_contentObjectData>

    <cflocation = "./">

<cfelse>

    <!--- The form section --->
    <cfoutput>
    <form action="#cgi.script_name#" method="POST">

    <table>
    <tr>
        <td>Email Address:</td>
        <td>
        <input type="text" name="Email" value="#Author.email#">
        </td>
    </tr>
    <tr>
        <td colspan="2">
        <input type="submit" name="submit" value="Update">
        </td>
    </tr>
    </table>

    </form>
    </cfoutput>

</cfif>

</cfa_handler>
```

The one-shot method is used when you are creating objects and already have the data to populate them. This requires only the <CFA_CONTENTOBJECTCREATE> tag. You simply pass a structure that matches the Type Property structure of the object, and the creation occurs in one step. Listing 6.9 shows an example of one-shot ContentObject creation.

Listing 6.9 *one_shot.cfm*—Creating and Populating an Object in One Step

```
<!--- Create a structure --->
<cfscript>

    stProperties = StructNew();

    stProperties.FirstName = 'Larry';
    stProperties.LastName = 'Niven';
    stProperties.email = 'lniven@ringworld.com';

</cfscript>

<!--- Create the object (replace TypeID with Author TypeID) --->
<cfa_contentObjectCreate
 datasource="#request.cfa.objectstore.dsn#"
 typeid="A4B6FD05-290A-11D3-AD400060B0EB2994"
 stproperties="#stProperties#"
 label="#stProperties.FirstName# #stProperties.LastName#"
 r_id="objID"
>
```

Invoking Objects

You can now test your ContentObjects by invoking them directly. You'll need the ObjectID of an existing object to do this, and you'll find this in the Object Finder. Listing 6.10 shows an example of invoking an object directly by using `<CFA_CONTENTOBJECT>`. This isn't typically done within an application page. Generally, you would invoke directly from inside a handler, much like you would use a `cfinclude` or a `cfmodule` to reuse code in a ColdFusion application. You will be building containers to invoke these objects later, in Chapter 7, "Planning Spectra Sites."

Listing 6.10 *invoke_direct.cfm*—Invoke an Object Directly and Replace the ObjectID with One Found in Your Object Finder

```
<!DOCTYPE HTML PUBLIC "-//W3C//DTD HTML 4.0 Transitional//EN">

<html>
<head>
    <title>Untitled</title>
</head>

<body>
```

```
<!--- Invoke display method on object --->
<cfa_contentObject
 datasource="#request.cfa.objectstore.dsn#"
 objectid="59BE8B28-9D5E-11D3-846900E02C0708AF"
 method="Display"
>

</body>
</html>
```

CHAPTER 7

Planning Spectra Sites

In this chapter

Planning an Application

Application development is generally broken into five phases: planning, prototyping, implementing, testing, and revising. Each phase should end with a client review of the work produced by that phase. By having explicit approval of each phase, as well as the client's understanding of the development phases, the project can proceed in an orderly manner. This chapter will detail the specifics of the planning phase of applications development.

NOTE Throughout this chapter, the term *client* is used to describe the individual (or group) who has final approval of the work performed.

Defining the Problem

The first step in a successful development project is to clearly determine the purpose of the application you are going to build. The purpose of a well-defined application usually can be identified simply by specifying the problem the application is intended to solve. Only with a clear understanding of the problem can you truly judge the project's success.

Without a clear idea of the problem to be solved, time and resources are often spent solving the wrong problem. When you're armed with a definition of the problem, you can determine the application's purpose and be ready to begin the discovery phase to determine the application's requirements.

Discovering the Project's Needs

Armed with an understanding of the problem you intend to solve, you use the discovery phase to detail the system's requirements. The time needed for a discovery phase will vary, depending on the application's size. It's not uncommon for complicated applications to have discovery time frames measured in weeks and months rather than hours or days.

NOTE Generally, as applications increase in complexity, more time will be needed to fully define a project's requirements.

For Spectra applications, the business manager and the interactive developer for the project should lead the discovery phase. Through a series of interviews, meetings, focus groups, and brainstorming sessions with system end users, the business manager and interactive developer will begin to identify the application's feature set.

Determining the Feature Set One key component of the discovery phase is determining the feature set. The features of an application are the tools with which the application will solve its targeted problem. If you can't envision how a particular feature applies to solving the problem at hand, it probably shouldn't be included in the application.

Determining the Intended Audience and Tone Knowing your audience is crucial to meeting your users' needs. This is true in a site's content, navigation, and features. Some questions to ask as you are determining the site's tone are

- What is the general age group of the audience?
- What occupations will audience members have?
- What experiences are common to all members of your audience?
- Who are the role models to your audience?
- What other sources of information do members of your audience have in common? How do they present the information?
- Who are your audience members currently using for the services you plan to provide? Why should they use your services instead?
- What is your audience's technical ability?

You will find that some of these questions are more pertinent to your application than others. Intranet developers don't need to be concerned with competition, whereas sites aimed at students are probably less concerned with their audience's current occupations.

NOTE As you can imagine, feature sets vary greatly from one application to the next. The features you would find in an application aimed at helping students choose a college would be quite different from those of a community site for conspiracy theorists. Determine tone by knowing your intended audience.

Compiling the Information After the features and tone of the application are decided, the interactive developer and business manager will begin to determine the core object types, process logic paths (PLPs), workflows, users, groups, and security models required for those features. The interactive developer will take this information and begin to lay out the Site Object Model, identifying properties and methods of all the core objects. The business manager will begin to design the Site Layout Model, determining sections, pages, and containers, as well as meta data hierarchies and workflows.

Writing the Specification

When all of this is done, the interactive developer needs to write a functional specification, clearly laying out the Site Object Model, the methods needed for each object, and the individual steps of the process logic paths. Also, any external datasources to be used by the application need to be identified, and notes should be made of how they will be used in the application. This functional specification should include all the details necessary to build the project's infrastructure.

Determining the Budget

Based on the functional specification, the interactive developer and business manager need to determine the budget for the project. To do this, they need to take into account several factors:

- The number of man-hours needed to develop the application as specified
- Who will develop the application—internal employees or hired consultants
- The rates at which different participants in the application build are to be paid
- The application's hardware requirements
- The application's software requirements
- The application's due dates

One of the most important aspects of applications development is knowing the project's budget and how it applies to the development process. The budget not only determines what type of hardware can be purchased, but often it also determines how many people can be hired or assigned to the project, the amount of consultant time that can be used on the project, and so forth. Often, adequate time is not left for all the phases of software development, and the later phases are often cut short because of misjudgments in budgeting the earlier phases. Budgets are also severely affected by the project's timeframe. An old adage says that between doing a project well, doing it cheaply, and doing it quickly, project leaders are free to choose any two.

Writing the Scope

When the functional specifications and budget are determined, the business manager develops a scope of work. This scope of work is a proposal to the decision makers, identifying all the site's processes, procedures, and features, as well as the estimated production budget. Having all parties agree to the specifics of a project before development begins helps minimize changes to the project during development. Over the years, many studies have shown that the earlier in the development process a change is introduced, the cheaper it is to implement that change. A change introduced in the planning phase may cost as much as 100 times less to implement than a change introduced during the testing phase.

NOTE While having all parties agree to a scope before development begins helps to reduce the number of changes introduced during development, it should never be assumed that requirements are static. It should be remembered that software development is an iterative process, and refining expectations is part of the process. Having a scope in place helps make all parties realize the time and budget effects of such changes.

Setting Up an Application Checklist

Before development of a Spectra application begins, you should ensure that most (if not all) of the following are completed:

- Defining the problem the application intends to solve
- Defining the application's required features
- Defining the application's fundamental objects, their properties and required handlers, and what will be required of the handlers
- Defining the fundamental process logic paths to be used in the application
- Defining the sections, pages, and containers to be used in the application
- Identifying all outside datasources to be used in the application
- Identifying the application's target audience and the impact it will have on the layout, content, and design
- Determining the reports to be generated by the system
- Determining publishing rules that will be used in the application, including personalization
- Determining the application's syndication requirements
- Writing a functional specification that encompasses all these definitions
- Determining the development timeline
- Determining the applications budget
- Writing a scope
- Getting agreement on the scope by all parties involved

Planning Participants

Chapter 1, "Understanding Spectra," introduced you to Spectra's Spectrum of Participants. While the distinction between one participant and the next is completely arbitrary, at this point you should be listing what participants you'll need for your own application and assigning the resources required.

Business Managers Business managers work closely with interactive developers during the discovery phase in determining the core functionality of the system, including

- Identifying core object types
- Identifying process logic paths required by the application's features
- Identifying the reports that will be used to determine patterns of usage, success of changes, and so on
- Determining the publishing rules that will be used to decide what content gets shown to which users, and when

- Developing relationships with outside parties to syndicate content
- Identifying the Site Layout Model
- Identifying workflows and business logic as it applies to the site
- Determining the budget of the project

Interactive Developers Interactive developers bear much of the burden in planning and building a Spectra application. In the planning phase, they are responsible for

- Developing the Site Object Model
- Developing the Site Process Model
- Developing report specifications
- Developing publishing and personalization specifications
- Developing syndication specifications
- Identifying outside datasources and their interaction with the application

Site Designers Site designers will share with the business managers the burden of creating the Site Layout Model. As information architects, their input into the sites, sections, pages, and containers of the application will be invaluable:

- Helping to develop the Site Layout Model
- Developing the navigation flow
- Developing the interface

System Administrators System administrators bear the burden of creating the user/security framework and integrating the outside datasources:

- Working with the business manager to establish the application's users and groups
- Securing the Webtop
- Integrating outside datasources

Planning an Intranet for A2Z Books

In this section, you will be planning an intranet for the A2Z Books bookstore. This will help you understand the concepts behind building internal applications with Spectra.

Problem Definition

The employees in the Customer Service department don't have easy access to the information they need for their jobs.

Proposed Solution

A2Z Books needs a central place where employees can find information they need for their jobs. This information includes managing contacts, finding the status of current orders, and managing employee work schedules.

Identifying the Feature Set

To best meet the needs of the Customer Service department of A2Z Books, the application will require the following features:

- *Contact directory.* A central repository of names, phone numbers, addresses, email addresses, and so on for employees, customers, and vendors.
- *Order tracker.* A place to find the entire history of orders made by a user. This includes details of where any current orders are in the process of fulfillment.
- *Schedule manager.* A place for the Customer Service manager to plan the work schedule for upcoming weeks and track the hours worked by employees and the number of client issues each employee can handle during a given time.

Identifying the Site Layout Model

As shown in Figure 7.1, the A2Z Books intranet is divided into three sections, each of which is divided into pages. The top-level application flow is quickly discernable from the Site Layout Model. It's easy to see that this application is divided into Contact Directory, Order Tracking, and Schedule Manager sections. The various tasks in each section are also readily apparent.

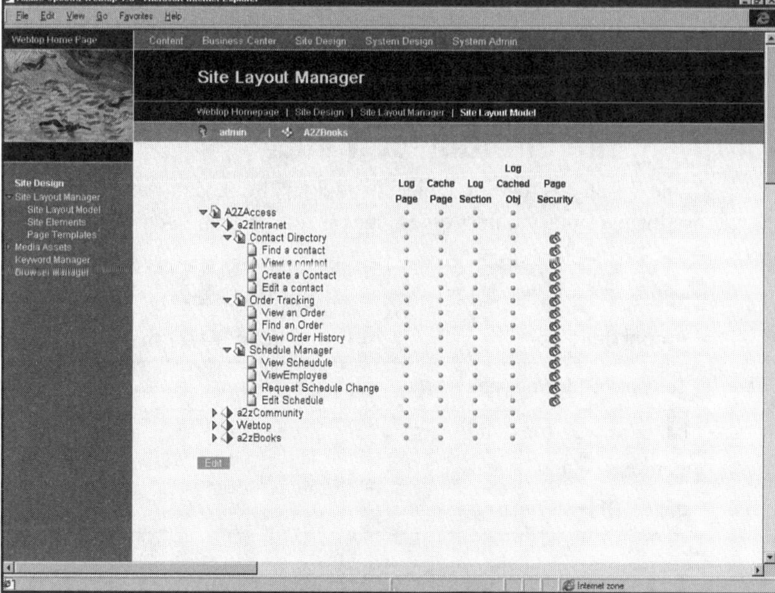

FIGURE 7.1
The A2Z Books intranet Site Layout Model.

Identifying Workflow

As you can see from the project requirements, the following workflows will be needed:

- Tracking a current order
- Refunding an order
- Requesting a schedule change

The order tracking workflow will interface with the order fulfillment workflow of the A2Z Books e-commerce application. This tracking workflow will determine the participants of the e-commerce workflow who currently have outstanding tasks for a client and will send that employee a message asking for an update on the order's status.

A Client Services member instantiates the order refund workflow. It needs to notify members of the fulfillment team to cancel an order and members of the accounting team to credit the customer's account.

The schedule change workflow is instantiated by an employee, sending a notification to the Client Services manager about a requested change. The Client Services manager will determine whether the change is reasonable and feasible and, if so, will launch the *edit schedule* process logic path. If the Client Services manager declines the change, a notification will be sent to the requesting employee.

Identifying Process Logic Paths

The following process logic paths will be used by this application:

- Creating a schedule
- Changing a schedule
- Adding a contact
- Finding a current order

Identifying the Site Object Model

Table 7.1 shows the Site Object Model for the A2Z intranet application. As you can see, there are three primary object types: `Contact`, `Order`, and `Schedule`.

Table 7.1 The A2Z Intranet Object Model

Properties	Public Methods	Secure Methods
`Contact` Object Type		
`ContactType` (nested object)	`Create`	`Edit`
Person (nested object)	`View`	`Delete`
`Order` Object Type		

Properties	Public Methods	Secure Methods
CustomerID	View	Cancel
ProductID	ViewHistory	Edit
OrderStage (nested object)		
OrderDate		
Schedule Object Type		
Shift (nested object)	Find	Create
Date	View	Edit
Employee (object array)		Delete
Manager (nested object)		

As you can see, most core object properties are objects themselves or are pointers to objects. To properly implement this Site Object Model, object types need to be created for the three core object types, the five nested objects, as well as the objects pointed to by other objects. The methods are also broken into two groups for each object: the public methods, which any user of the site can invoke, and the secure methods, which are available only to authorized users.

Identifying Users, Groups, and Security

With any application, it's necessary to determine who the users are and what permissions they will have to access the system. The application you are currently planning is an intranet, and by definition it's not accessible to the general public. In this case, employees are the main users who need access to the objects' "public" methods. Managers require access to the secure methods of the properties. Although there are objects for customers and outside contacts, these are pointers to user records, not active users of the system.

User records will be broken into the groups in Table 7.2.

Table 7.2 Users and Groups

Group	Members
Employees	Client Services, Order Fulfillment, Accounting, and Administrative personnel.
Managers	Decision makers who decide weekly schedules and are authorized to issue refunds.
Client Services	Each individual in the Client Services department, including managers.
Order Fulfillment	Individuals responsible for each step of the order fulfillment process, from billing to shipping, including managers.
Outside Contacts	Publishers, authors, shippers, and so on.
Customers	Registered users of the A2Z public Web site.

Table 7.3 shows how permissions are allocated to groups of users for the intranet.

Table 7.3 Groups and Security

Group	Security Procedures
Employees	Permission to use public methods of all objects.
Managers	Permission to access secure methods of objects.
Client Services	Permission to view workflow for the Client Services department, as well as a customer's current order or order history.
Order Fulfillment	Access to the order fulfillment workflow; can mark tasks as completed.
Outside Contacts	No access to this system.
Customers	No access to this system.

Planning an e-Commerce Site for A2Z Books

Much of the rest of this book will show you how to build an application for the A2Z Bookstore. Here you will see how the requirements for this application have been determined.

Problem Definition

It's too difficult to maintain the current A2Z Books Web site. There's no orderly procedure for adding new books to the Catalog or for adding content to the News section. There's also no way to deliver customized content to a user based on knowledge previously acquired.

Proposed Solution

By building the A2Z Books e-commerce site with Allaire Spectra, the Marketing department will be able to enter content about the products without having to become involved in the code. The user experience can be customized based on user preferences, and clear workflows can be established for adding new products to the Web site, adding new marketing materials to the products, and shipping orders.

Identifying the Feature Set

To help make the A2Z site a successful one, the following features will be needed:

- *Product news.* By providing timely news about the book industry, including new releases, best sellers, and book reviews, it's hoped that we can keep customers returning and using A2Z Books for all of their book buying.

- *Customizable Catalog.* An easily customizable Catalog will allow business managers to highlight particular products, identify products as being of interest to a particular group of people, and keep the Catalog current. This should also include a shopping cart system to facilitate users purchasing items.
- *Personalization.* The intention is to present users with news and products specifically tailored to their needs. By minimizing the number of products presented to the user in which they aren't interested, we hope to be able to increase the percentage of users who purchase products, as well as the number of repeat customers.

Identifying the Site Layout Model

As shown in Figure 7.2, the A2Z Books site is divided into three sections: News, Catalog, and Admin. Each section is divided into two or more pages.

FIGURE 7.2
The A2Z Books Site Layout Model.

See Chapter 8, "Building the Site Structure," for complete details on creating the Site Layout Model for the A2Z Books e-commerce application.

Identifying Workflow

As identified in the requirements for this application, a workflow will be needed for each of the following:

- Publishing news articles
- Adding new products to the Catalog
- Filling orders

The publishing news articles workflow begins with the site editor determining that a particular article is needed. He starts the workflow, which notifies the article author of the story needed and the deadline. At the same time, notification is sent to the graphic artist, indicating the image that will be run with the article. When each task is completed, the editor is notified, and either approves the materials or sends them back to their creator for changes. When the material is approved, the business manager is notified that a new article is ready for publishing. The BM determines the scheduling and rules of publishing the article and sends this information to the interactive developer. The interactive developer deploys the content to the development server and, once the approval of the business manager is received, pushes it to the live server.

The workflow for adding a product to the Catalog works in much the same way as adding a news article.

The order fulfillment workflow, however, is somewhat different. Unlike the others, it's instantiated by the system as a result of a customer having successfully purchased a product. This sends notification to the Billing department to process the payment. When the payment is processed, warehouse personnel are notified of the product and shipping address of the customer. After they fill the order, the Shipping department takes the package, ships it, and enters the shipping tracking number into the system.

▶ **See** Chapter 13, "Working with Workflow," for complete details on creating these workflows.

Identifying Process Logic Paths

To meet the functional requirements of the A2Z Bookstore, the following process logic paths will be necessary:

- Customer registration
- Customer checkout

Each task will take several steps to accomplish, which are best handled with process logic paths.

▶ **See** Chapter 12, "Using Process Logic Paths," for complete details on creating these PLPs.

Identifying Site Object Model

The A2Z Bookstore, as determined above, has four primary objects: a `Book`, a `Customer`, a `News Item`, and an `Order`. Their definitions are shown in Table 7.4.

NOTE Although we've identified only four primary object types, the application, when completed, will have many more objects, some of which will be used to construct these four main objects.

Table 7.4 The A2Z e-Commerce Application Object Model

Properties	Public Methods	Secure Methods
`Book` Object Type		
`Author` (object array)		`Edit`
`Publisher` (nested object)	`View` `Purchase`	`Delete` `Create`
`Publication Date`		`Add`
`Number of Pages`		
`Price`		
`Title`		
`ISBN`		
`Customer` Object Type		
`First Name`	`View Own Record`	`View`
`Last Name`	`Edit Own Record`	`Edit`
`Email Address`		`Delete`
`Street Address`		`Add`
`City`		`Search`
`State`		
`Zip Code`		
`Home Phone`		
`Office Phone`		
`News Item` Object Type		
`Author` (nested object)	`View`	`Add`
`Title`	`View Teaser`	`Delete`
`Teaser`	`View History`	`Edit`
`Body`		
`Image`		

continues

Table 7.4 Continued

Properties	Public Methods	Secure Methods
`Order` **Object Type**		
`Customer ID`	`View Order Status`	`Edit`
`Product ID` (array)		`Delete`
`Purchase Date`		
`Purchase Price`		

▶ **See** Chapter 8 for complete details on creating the Site Object Model for the A2Z Books e-commerce application.

Identifying Users, Groups, and Security

As you can see in Tables 7.5 and 7.6, the site's access is broken into users and groups. Access rights are then assigned to groups to ensure that only those who need access to a secure method are granted it.

Table 7.5 Groups and Users

Group	Users
Employees	Shipping, writers, designers, Marketing department, managers, Billing department, and interactive developers
Business Managers	Marketing department, managers, and editors
Content	Writers, designers, and editors
Order Fulfillment	Billing and Shipping departments
Administrators	Business managers and interactive developers
Customers	Any registered user of the site

Table 7.6 Groups and Security

Group	Security Procedures
Employees	Access to all public methods and can view order secure methods.
Business Managers	Access to all public and secure methods, as well as to site customization rule creation.
Content	Access to all secure methods of `Book` and `News Item` objects.
Order Fulfillment	Access to all secure methods of `Order` object.
Administrators	Access to all public and secure methods.
Customers	Access to all public methods.

▶ **See** Chapter 16, "Using Spectra Security Options," for complete details on creating the users and groups for the A2Z Books e-commerce application.

Planning a Community Site for A2Z Books

Along with intranets and e-commerce applications, there is a great demand for community sites. This section will walk you through the process of planning such a site.

Problem Definition

There are fewer repeat customers than is desired. Those that do return complain that while they are dedicated customers, there's no sense of community among them.

Proposed Solution

By using the information already known about each customer, including preferences and demographics, we can help build a community among users with similar interests.

Identifying the Feature Set

Here are some of the features that might be required by a community site:

- *Syndicated content.* By bringing in content from outside sources, we can develop sections of the site for a community of users interested in a particular genre of book, without needing staff members with expertise in every genre.
- *Discussion forums.* By providing a forum for users to compare their own opinions of books, authors, publishers and genres, the needs of our clients can be better determined, while at the same time offering a wealth of user-driven content for all.
- *Personalized news.* By letting users customize a portal page for themselves, an even greater degree of insight into the users' preferences can be gained, while at the same time offering a valuable service to clients and encouraging repeat business.
- *Scheduled Chat.* One very popular feature on the Web today is chat rooms. These allow users with similar interests to interact with each other in real-time. In the A2Z Bookstore, chats can be scheduled with popular authors to give readers a chance to interact with the author.

Identifying the Site Layout Model

Rather than develop a different section for each genre of book, you can see in Figure 7.3 that there's one general section that will display any genre passed to it. Since the components of a science fiction section are no different than those of a romance section, the section is a genre section, with the specific content for that genre determined by the genre ID. There is also a User Home Pages section, which will be portals to the site for individual users. Within that section is a section for user-specific news and threads for forums in which the user has expressed an interest.

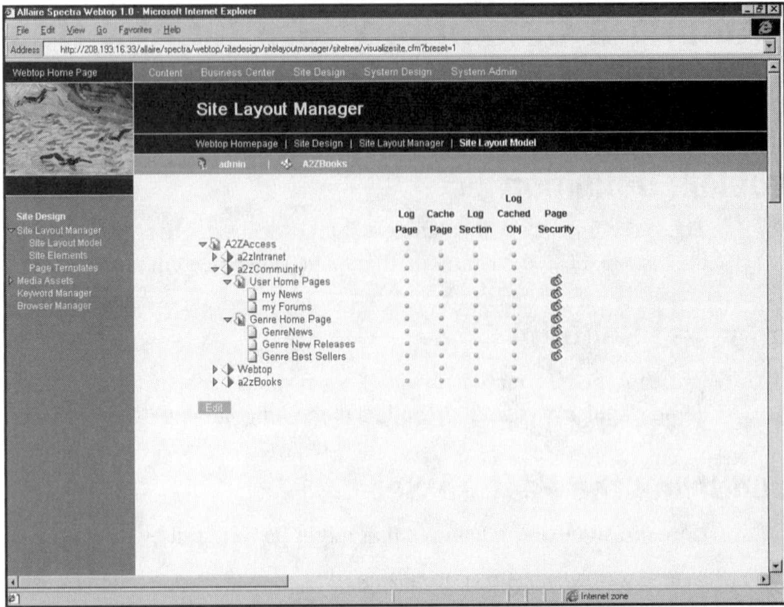

FIGURE 7.3
The A2Z community Site Layout Model.

Identifying the Workflow

The A2Z Books community site will require a workflow to secure new syndicated content. This workflow starts with a business associate first contacting an outside provider of content and coming to an understanding of the terms of the syndication. When this is marked as complete, a member of the Legal department draws up a contract based on the terms of the agreement. There is an iterative process during which the details of the contract are hammered out. Once the Legal department receives the signed contract, the interactive developer is notified that a new syndication agreement has been reached. The interactive developer needs to contact the content provider to determine the specifics of how the content is to be delivered. Once this is determined, the business manager determines a hierarchy, which will be applied to content from this vendor. Finally, the new content is programmatically scheduled into the site.

Identifying the Process Logic Paths

In the A2Z community site, a process logic path will be used to walk consumers through the process of creating their own custom home pages. Several steps are involved in this process, starting with choosing layout and colors, continuing on to choosing genres about which they want news stories, and concluding with their choices about which forums they want to track.

Identifying the Site Object Model

The Site Object Model for the A2Z community site is an extension of the model of the A2Z Bookstore. A few new object types in Table 7.7 are specific to the ideas of incoming syndicated content and forums. The idea is that a forum is comprised of several threads (user-published articles).

Table 7.7 The A2Z Community Application Object Model

Properties	Public Method	Secure Method
`Syndicated Story` Object Type		
`Title`	`Create`	`Edit`
`Teaser`	`View`	`Delete`
`Body`	`View Teaser`	`Add`
`Image`		
`Genre` (array)		
`Source`		
`Forum` Object Type		
`Title`	`View`	`Edit`
`Section`	`Add`	`Delete`
`Threads` (object array)		
`Genre`		
`Thread` Object Type		
`Author` (nested object)	`View`	`Edit`
`Subject`	`Add`	`Delete`
`Body`		
`InResponseToThread`		

NOTE The `Syndicated Story` object type has the `Genre` field set to an array of values so that one story can be assigned to several genres.

Identifying Users, Groups, and Security

In the community site is a separate group for each genre that has a section in the site. Customers are allowed to be part of several of these groups, should they choose to be. There is a third security category of methods for this site, which is Group Member Methods.

This represents a method accessible to authenticated members of a group but not to the public at large. In these forums, anyone can read the content, but only members of the group can post messages.

NOTE For brevity, only two genres are shown as groups in Tables 7.8 and 7.9 (Science Fiction and Politics); in actuality, there may be dozens of such groups.

Table 7.8 Groups and Users

Group	Users
Science Fiction	Customers who have registered as fans of this genre.
Politics	Customers who have registered as fans of this genre.
Business Managers	Employees responsible for classifying syndicated content.
Forum Administrators	Employees responsible for administering the forums, removing inappropriate posts, and so on.

Table 7.9 Groups and Security

Group	Security Procedures
Science Fiction	Access to all public methods and group member methods for the Science Fiction forum and `Thread` objects.
Politics	Access to all public methods and group member methods for the Politics forum and `Thread` objects.
Business Managers	Access to all public and secure methods, as well as to content classification methods.
Forum Administrators	Access to all methods of forums and threads.
Interactive Developer	Access to the secure methods for the `Syndicated Story` objects.

CHAPTER 8

Building the Site Structure

In this chapter

Creating a Site Object Model

As discussed in Chapter 7, "Planning Spectra Sites," once the project is fully specified and scoped, the next step is to build the site infrastructure. In Spectra, this starts with assembling the Site Object model and Site Layout model.

In this chapter, you will build the object types for the Book, Author, and Publisher objects of the a2zBooks application that you planned in Chapter 7. You will also build the Site Layout model discussed there.

The Site Object model offers a way to design and organize the data and activities that comprise your Web applicaton. It serves as the framework for integrating services and content, such as workflows, and reporting. The Site Object model is a blueprint of the site-specific ContentObject Types developed for your site.

The interactive developer begins a new project in the Site Object Designer. It is here that you will create and manage the objects, object types, and property definitions used for your application.

Creating Object Types

There are two ways to create an object type: either with the Object Creation Wizard, or through the Object Type Designer.

Creating the Author Object with the Object Creation Wizard To create an object with the Object Creation Wizard, navigate to the Site Object Designer link of the System Designer section of the Webtop and click the Type Designer link. This will bring you to the screen shown in Figure 8.1.

Click Next to add the type settings for your new type (see Figure 8.2). The Label field can consist only of letters; no numbers, punctuation, or spaces are allowed. The Alias is a friendly name of the object type, which will be used in the Webtop to refer to the object. The handler root is the path on the system that ColdFusion will use to find the handlers for this object. In this example, `/allaire/spectra/handlers/a2z/author` is used, so there must be an existing mapping in the ColdFusion Administrator for `/Allaire/`.

Next, enter the properties of this object. Figure 8.3 shows the property entry screen for the Author object. Properties are entered by assigning them a name and choosing the definition type from the pull-down menu. In Figure 8.3 you can see the `Bio` property being created as a `longChar`. The `email` field has already been created with the definition `Email`, while `firstname` and `lastname` have been created with the `Text` definition.

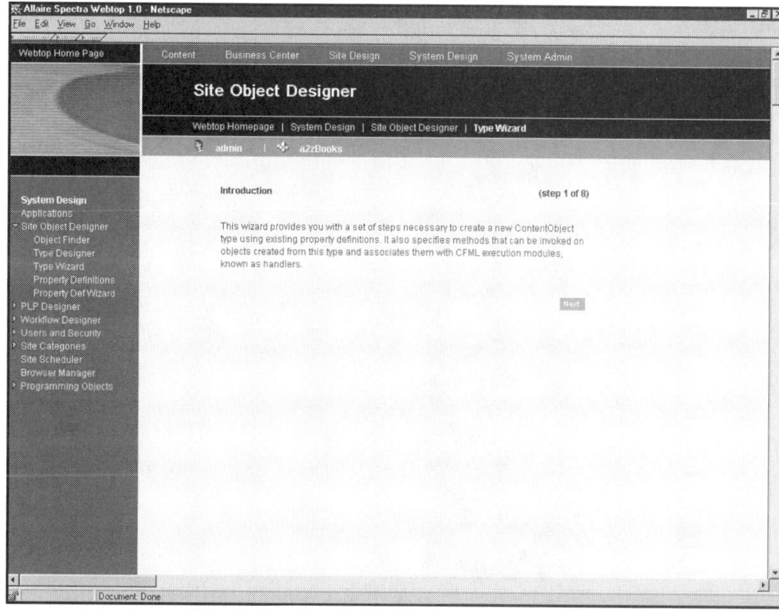

FIGURE 8.1
The Type Wizard will help automate the process of creating object types.

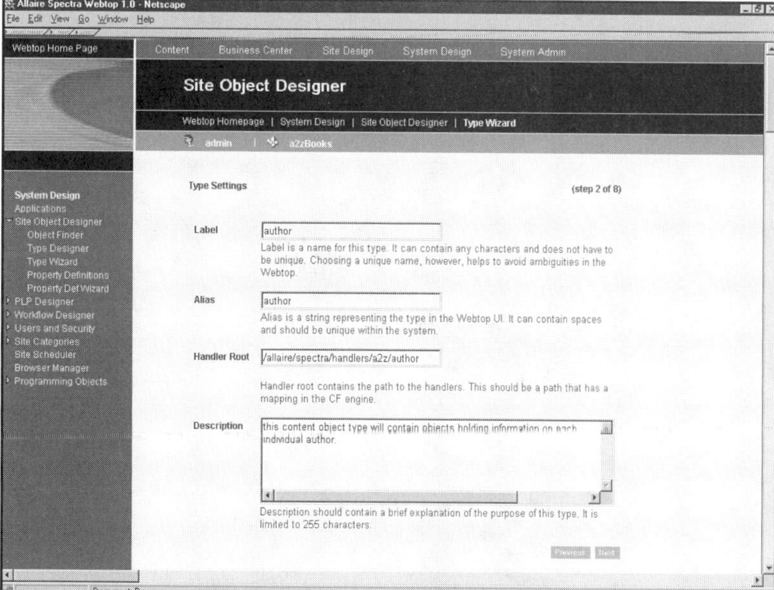

FIGURE 8.2
The first step in creating an object type with the Type Wizard is choosing the type settings for the object.

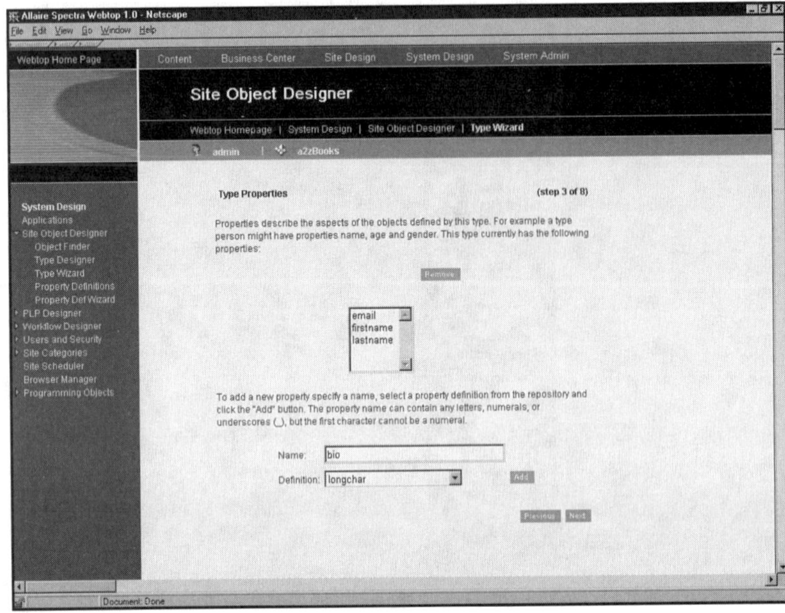

FIGURE 8.3
The `Bio` property is being defined here for the Author object. You can see that the `firstname`, `lastname`, and `email` properties have already been created.

After all the properties are named for the object, the wizard will walk you through the specifics of each property. In addition to the name and definition, which you have already assigned to each property, you can now define an alias and a default value, as well as Multiplicity, Required, and Searchability settings (see Figure 8.4).

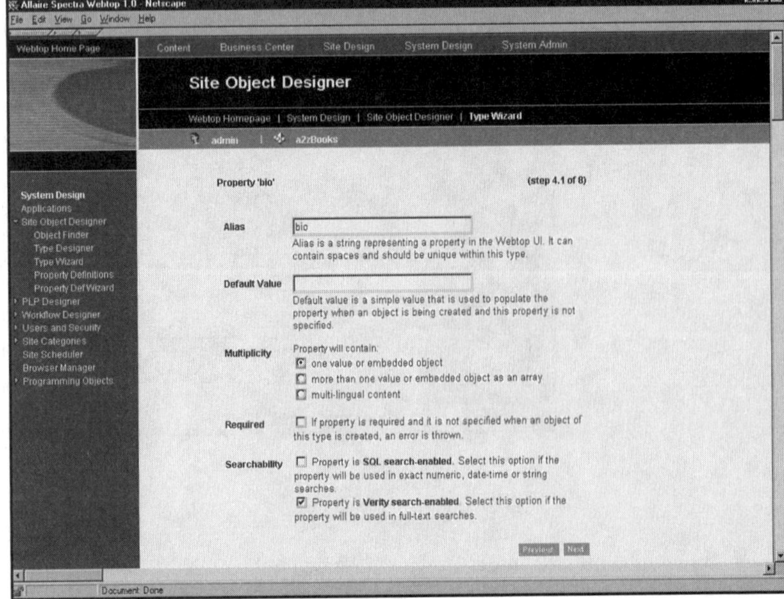

FIGURE 8.4
The `Bio` property definition page. This object is defined as a single entity, which is verity search-enabled but not indexed for a SQL search.

The optional alias allows you to assign the property a friendlier name, which will be used to identify the property in the Webtop. Unlike the `Label` attribute, properties can contain any kind of character, including numbers, spaces, and punctuation.

The `default` value is also optional. If a `default` value is provided, new objects of this type will use this value if they aren't specifically provided with a value for this property.

In addition to simple values and objects, Spectra will allow you to store either arrays of values or data in other languages. The Multiplicity setting indicates what is to be stored in this property. For multilingual values, Spectra uses the ISO 639 two-character language codes to specify the character set. Information of these codes can be found at `http://www.ics.uci.edu/pub/ietf/http/related/iso639.txt`.

In Figure 8.4, `Bio` is set so that it can contain a single value, it is not required, and it is searchable with verity, but not through SQL searches.

Spectra can also allow for an array of values to be stored as a property. In Figure 8.5, you can see that the property `email` has been set to accept an array of values, to accommodate the possibility that an author may have more than one email address.

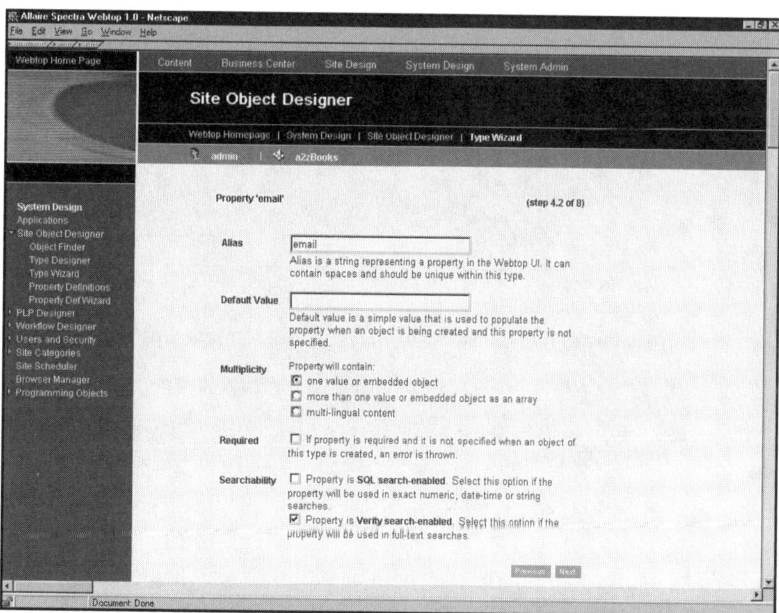

FIGURE 8.5
The `email` property definition page. Note that this is defined as an array of values, to allow for the possibility that an author may have more than one email address.

The `email` property details are defined here. Since a person can have more than one email address, this property is defined to allow an array of values as an email address.

As part of the property definition, you can decide if the field is required. If a field is marked as required and you attempt to create an object without this field present, Spectra will throw an exception.

Next, you will be asked to define the settings for the `firstname` property. This is a good example of a property that is required, as well as Verity- and SQL search–enabled, to allow users to easily find authors of their choice.

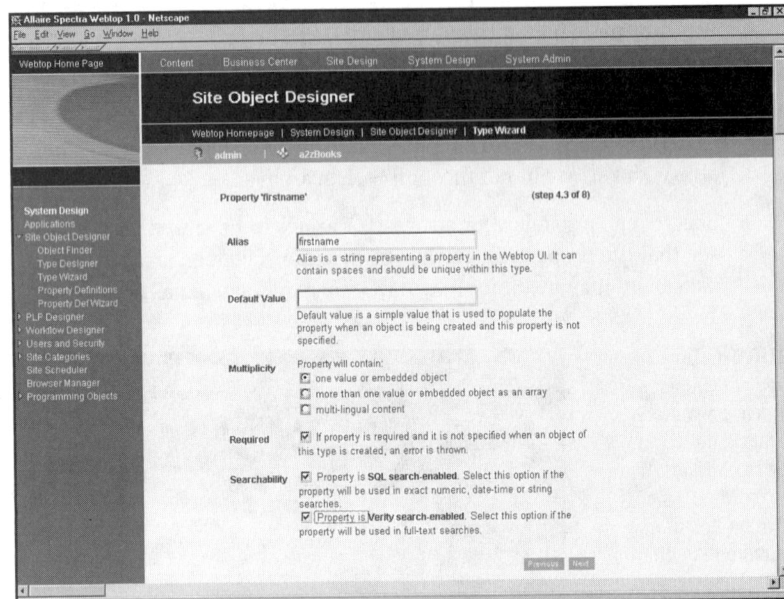

FIGURE 8.6
The `firstname` property is defined as a simple value, which is required, indexed, and searchable.

Lastly, you can decide if the property is to be indexed or searchable:

- An *indexed property* is included in a Verity collection for searching.
- A *searchable property* can be searched with a SQL query against the Properties table in the object store.

See Chapter 14, "Searching and Indexing," for more information on indexed and searchable properties.

The `lastname` property is also set as indexed, searchable, and required for the same reasons as the `firstname` property. Its definition can be seen in Figure 8.7.

After you set the details of all the object's properties, the wizard will ask you to define type methods. Later in this chapter, you will learn about creating a `display` method and handler; in Chapter 10, "Creating and Managing Content," you will learn about creating edit methods and handlers. Anticipating the creation of the `display` method, you can enter **`display`** as a new method here.

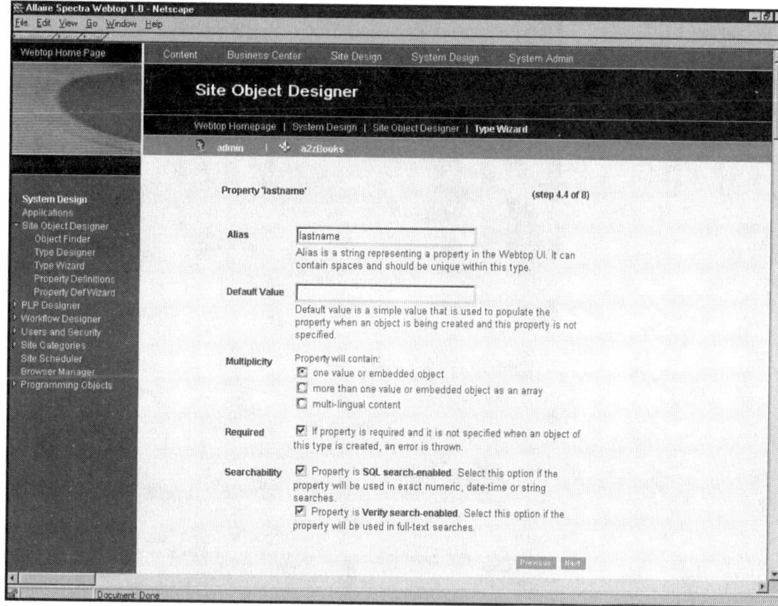

FIGURE 8.7
The `lastname` property is defined as a required, indexed, and searchable field.

NOTE If you don't provide any methods for an object, Spectra will allow you to use its default methods. These methods are serviceable for a development phase, but you probably wouldn't want to launch a site by using only default methods.

To add a new method for the object Type, type the method name and click the Add button (see Figure 8.8). When you are done naming your methods, clicking the Next button will allow you to define them.

The wizard will then ask for details on this method, as shown in Figure 8.9. These details include an alias, a handler and a description. The handler is the name of the file that contains the CFML code that details how the method is handled. This file should reside in the directory you specified as the handler root of this object. The description acts as a comment on the method, giving a brief overview of what the method does.

Now that all properties and methods are defined for this object, the wizard will ask you to confirm the data that you have entered (see Figure 8.10).

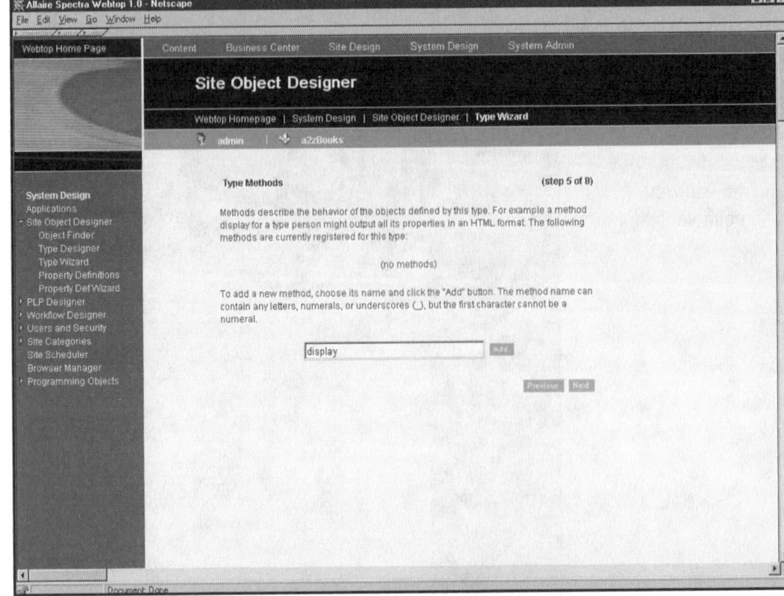

FIGURE 8.8
This is the Type Methods page of the Type Creation Wizard. The `display` method is being defined.

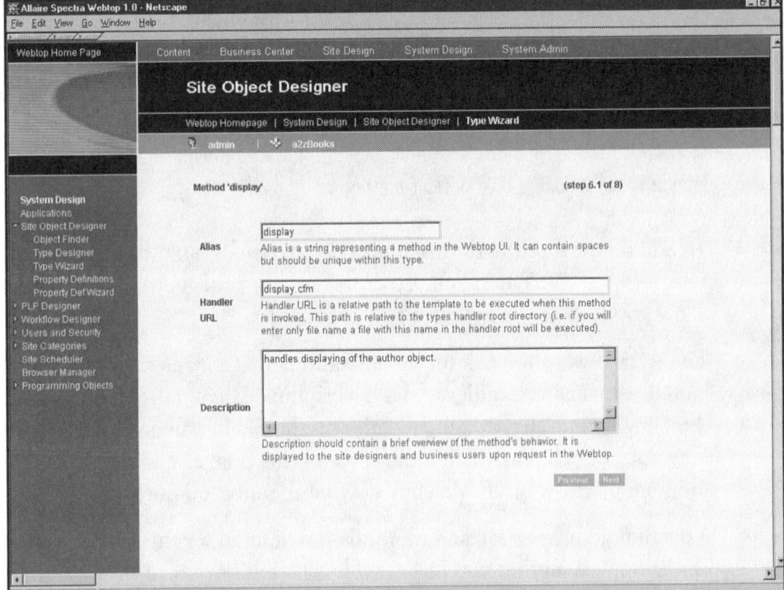

FIGURE 8.9
The details of the `display` method include the name of the handler file, as well as a description of the task performed by this file.

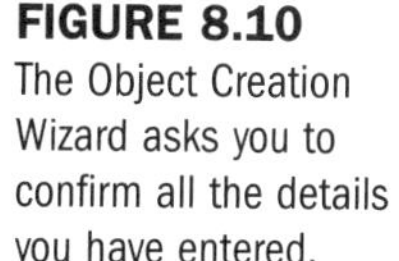

FIGURE 8.10
The Object Creation Wizard asks you to confirm all the details you have entered.

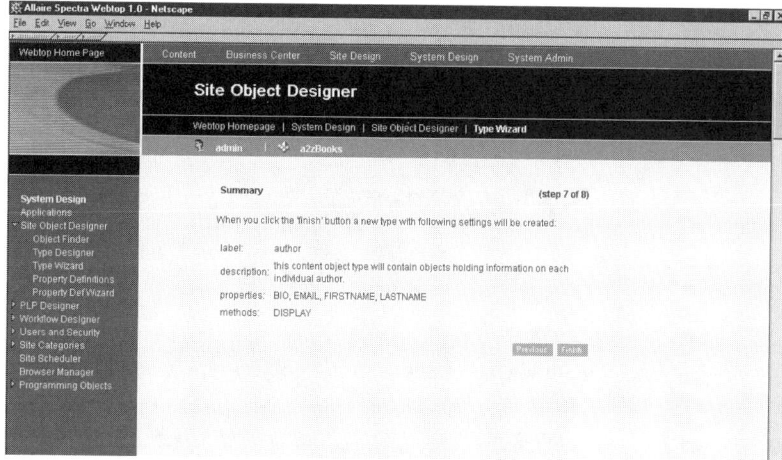

If the details all look correct, click Finish and the wizard will create the object type. Figure 8.11 shows the results of the object creation.

FIGURE 8.11
The object has been created successfully.

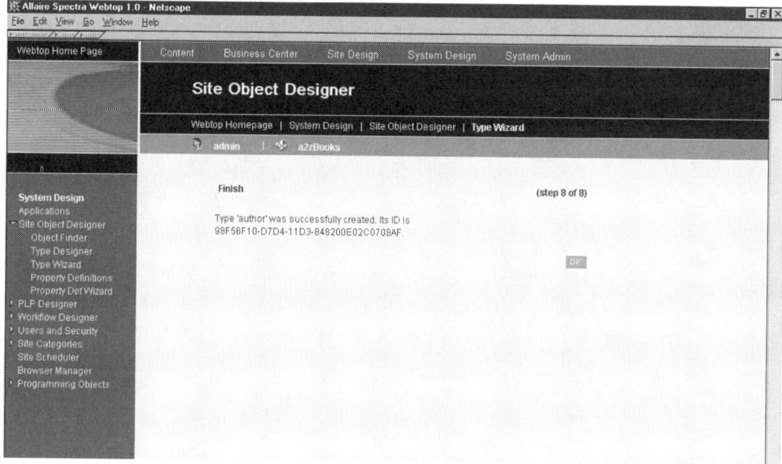

NOTE The object ID shown in Figure 8.11 is unique to the system it is created on. Don't be alarmed that your object ID is different from the object ID shown.

Creating the Book Object with the Object Finder You can also create new object types directly through the Type Designer of the Site Object Designer. To begin, click the Create button on the bottom of the Type Designer page. This will bring you to the form shown in Figure 8.12.

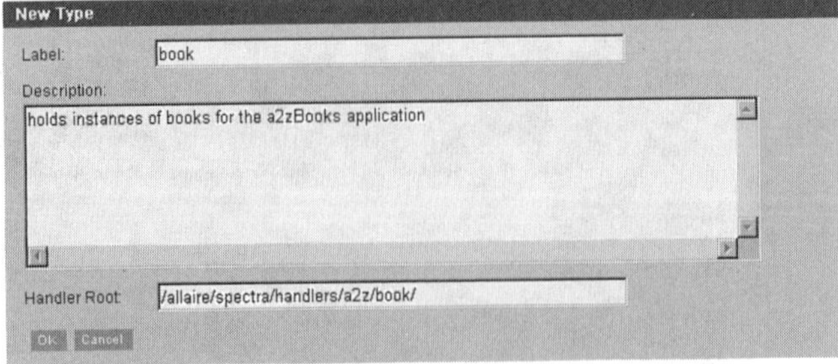

FIGURE 8.12
To begin creating a new object type in the Object Designer, give the object a label, description, and handler root.

After you click OK, you return to a very similar form, with the addition of navigation to the properties, methods, and utilities for this object type (see Figure 8.13).

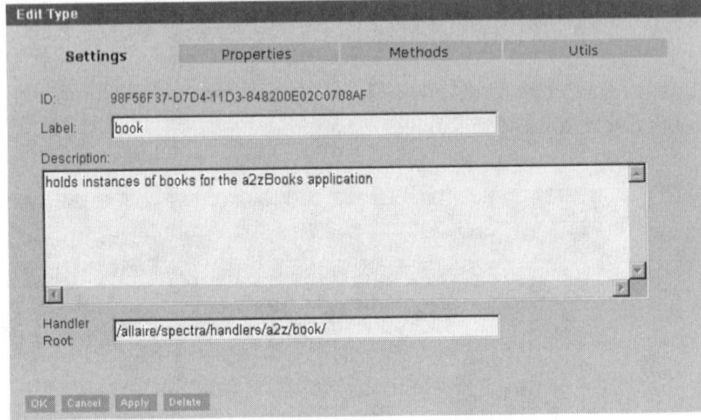

FIGURE 8.13
Once the new object has its basic settings of Label, Description and Handler Root, you are presented with the new tab options of Properties, Methods, and Utils.

Clicking the Properties tab will allow you to begin assigning the properties of this object type. As defined in Chapter 7, you will want to create the following properties for the Book object: `author`, `edition`, `ISBN`, `pages` (which defines the number of pages in the book), `price`, `published` (which defines the date the book was published), `publisher`, and `title`. In Figure 8.14, these properties have all been created.

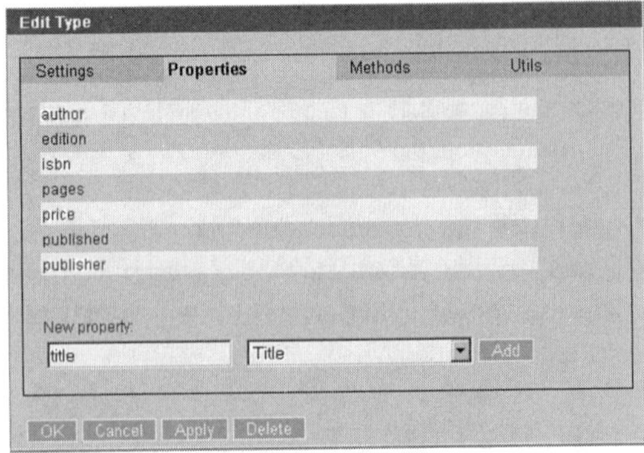

FIGURE 8.14
A new property named `title` of the type `Title` is assigned to the object. It's not necessary for the property name to match the property type name, although often that is the case.

Clicking the Add button will bring you to the Property Definition form (see Figure 8.15). Here, you can set Alias, Default Value, Multiplicity, Required, and Searchability settings for this property. These settings mirror the settings you used in the Object Type Wizard earlier in this chapter.

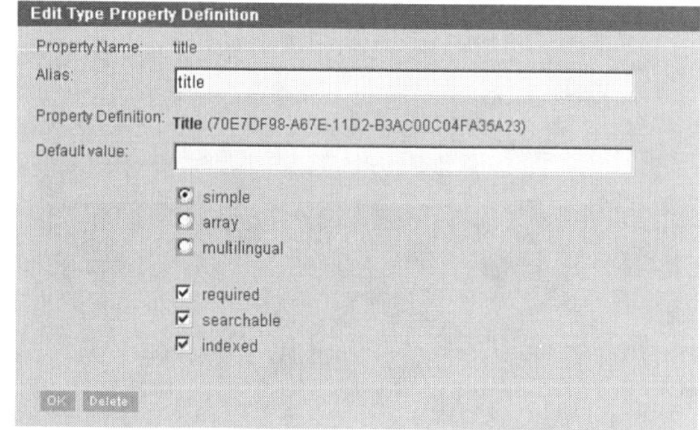

FIGURE 8.15
The `title` property is defined as a simple value that is required, searchable, indexed, and has no default value.

After you make these entries for the `title` property, click OK to return to the Edit Type form, as shown in Figure 8.13. Click the Properties tab again to continue adding properties to this object. You will need to add the `edition`, `ISBN`, `pages`, `price`, and `published` properties, as you just did above. For the moment, leave out the `author` and `publisher` properties. These special properties will be used to embed an Author object and a Publisher object, as discussed in more detail later, in the section "Creating Custom Properties."

The `edition` and `ISBN` properties should be set to the `char` property type, `pages` should be an `Integer` property type, `price` should be numeric, and `published` should be a `datetime` and be marked as searchable.

When the properties are set, you can start entering the methods for this object. You will learn more about creating display handlers later in this chapter but, for now, enter method information for two different `display` methods. One will display the full information of the book (let's call this one `Display`), and one will display only the title and author, which we'll call `Teaser`. Figure 8.16 shows the details of the `Teaser` method, Figure 8.17 shows the `Display` method details, and Figure 8.18 shows the summary of all existing `Teasers` for this object.

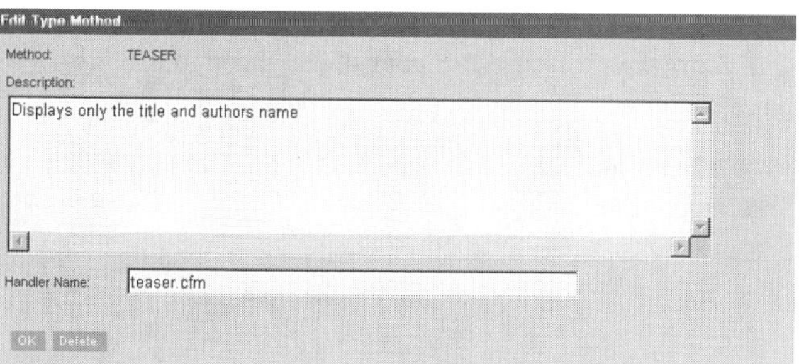

FIGURE 8.16
The `Teaser` method of the Book object type will display the title and author of the book. This will be used when several books are displayed at once.

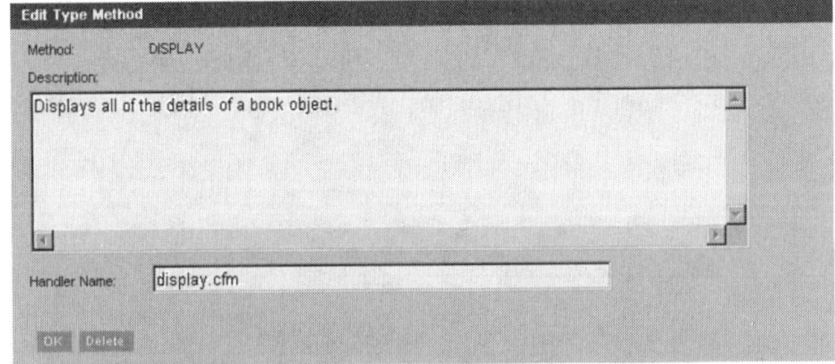

FIGURE 8.17
The `Display` method of the Book object will display all the details about a book.

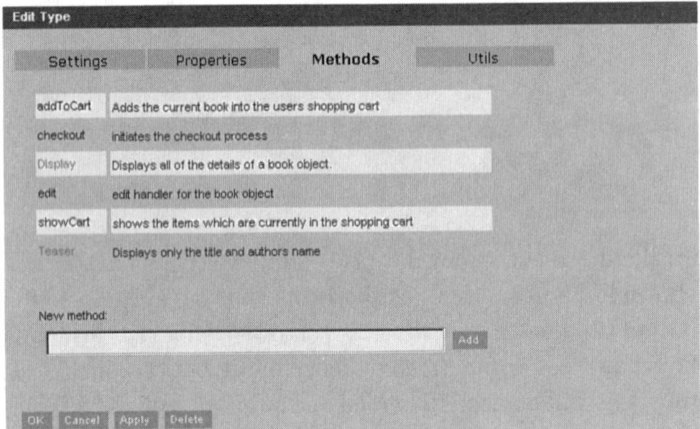

FIGURE 8.18
The Methods page for the Book object now shows both the `Teaser` and `Display` methods.

▶ **See** Chapter 21, "Creating e-Commerce Sites," for details on creating the `Addtocart`, `Checkout`, and `Showcart` methods.

By following the same steps above, you should also create an object type to hold information about a book's publisher, named Publisher. The handler root should be `/allaire/spectra/handlers/a2z/publisher`, to keep consistency within your application. Two properties will be required: `city`, a `char` representing the city in which the publisher is located, and `name`, to indicate the name of the publishing company.

Creating Properties

As you've already seen, ContentObject Types are constructed of properties and methods. You can define your own properties for your object through the Property Definition pages of the Site Object Designer.

Basic Property Definitions All properties in Spectra can be broken down to one of six basic definitions, as seen in Table 8.1.

Table 8.1 Spectra Property Definitions

Data Type	Definition
`Char`	Variable length string up to 255 characters
`DateTime`	A date in the *mm/dd/yyyy* format
`Integer`	A whole number
`LongChar`	A variable-length string, which can be longer than 255 characters
`Numeric`	A number with floating decimal point
`Object`	An embedded instance of a Content object type

NOTE `LongChar` length is limited by the upper limit of the database and the driver for that database. For example, while a SQL Server 6.5 `Text` field will hold 2 gigabytes, the ODBC driver has trouble handling more than 16KB.

`Numeric` and `Integer` data types are based on the integer and float specifications of the database.

Creating Custom Properties Like many programming environments, Spectra allows you to create custom properties based on the six core property types. With these custom properties, you can determine how they are input through an HTML form, handle data validation with JavaScript or with CFML, and choose the error message to be thrown, should the entered data not meet the data validation criteria.

Creating Properties with the Property Wizard To create a new property with the Property Definition Wizard, navigate to the Site Object Designer page of the System Designer section and click the Property DefWizard link. The wizard will launch, as seen in Figure 8.19.

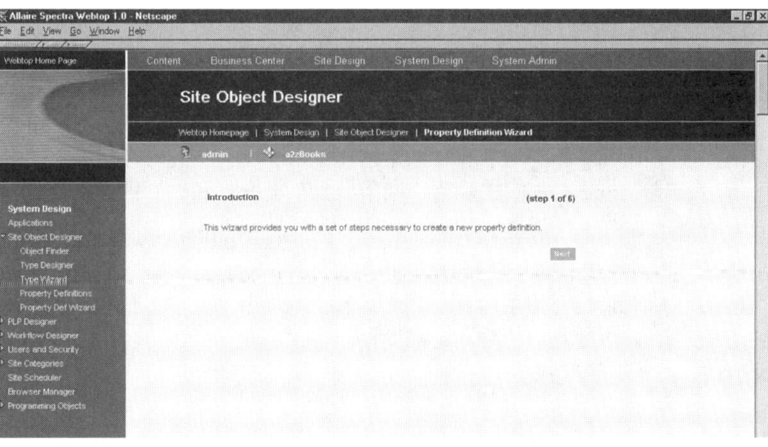

FIGURE 8.19
The Property Definition Wizard simplifies creating custom properties by breaking it down into several easy-to-understand tasks.

To create a property with the Property Definition Wizard, follow these steps:

1. Open the Site Object Designer menu on the System Design page.
2. To create a new property type, `email address`, open the Property Definition Wizard and enter the Label, Description, and Data Type, as shown in Figure 8.20.

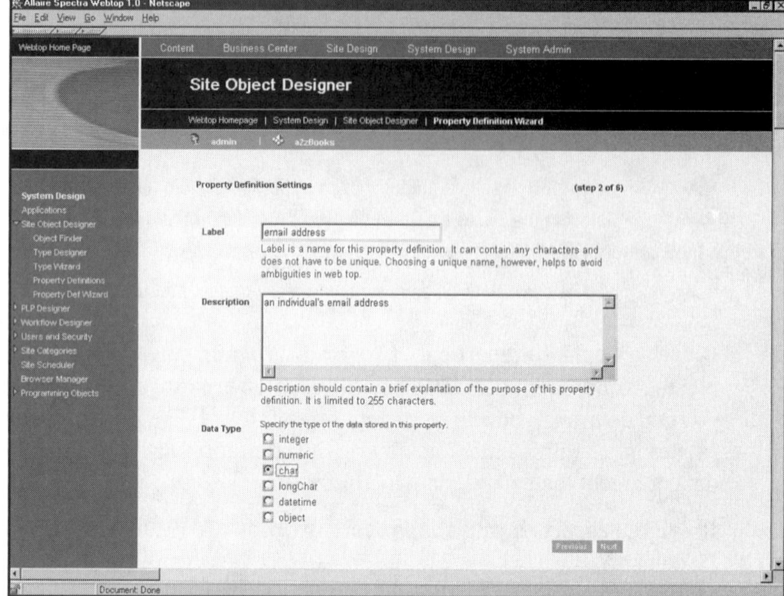

FIGURE 8.20
The first step in creating a new property type with the wizard is to choose a Label, Description, and Data Type.

3. Choose the input type to be used with this property. These input types refer to HTML form elements. Because a text field makes the most sense for an `email` property, that's what will be used. This can be seen in Figure 8.21. Click Next.
4. Each custom property type allows you to choose a JavaScript or CFML expression to be used to validate the data. In Figure 8.22, the CFML expression is

   `(len(value) gte 6) and (value contains '@') and (value contains '.').`

   These validation rules are used to ensure that any entry made could potentially be a valid email address. To be valid, an email address must be at least six characters long (the shortest potentially valid address is *`x@y.ch`*) and must contain an at sign (the `@` character) as well as a period.

NOTE The word `value` is used in the validation expressions to represent the value entered by a user.

5. To test the validation, enter the phrase **`this should fail`** into the text box and click the Validate button (see Figure 8.23). An error message is returned, with the message entered in the Validation Error Message text box. Be sure to test both valid and invalid entries to ensure that your validation works as you believe it should.

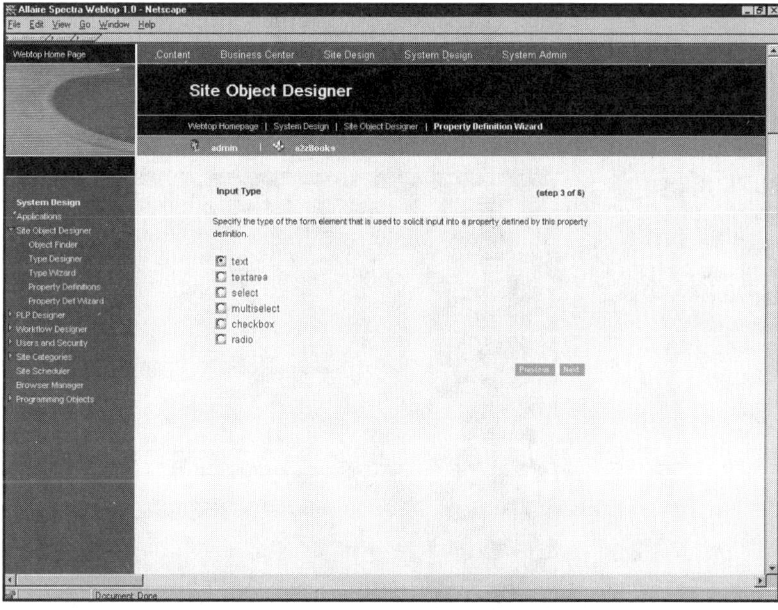

FIGURE 8.21
The `Text` input type is chosen for the new `email` property.

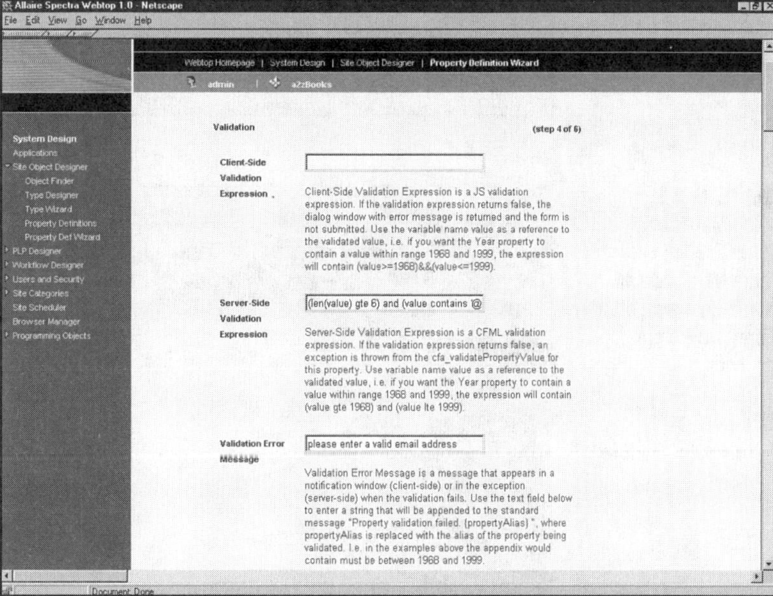

FIGURE 8.22
Entering validation.

6. The wizard will summarize your entries, giving you a final chance to go back and make changes before the new property type is entered into the system (see Figure 8.24). Click Previous if you need to go back and make any changes; click Finish if the property type is correct.

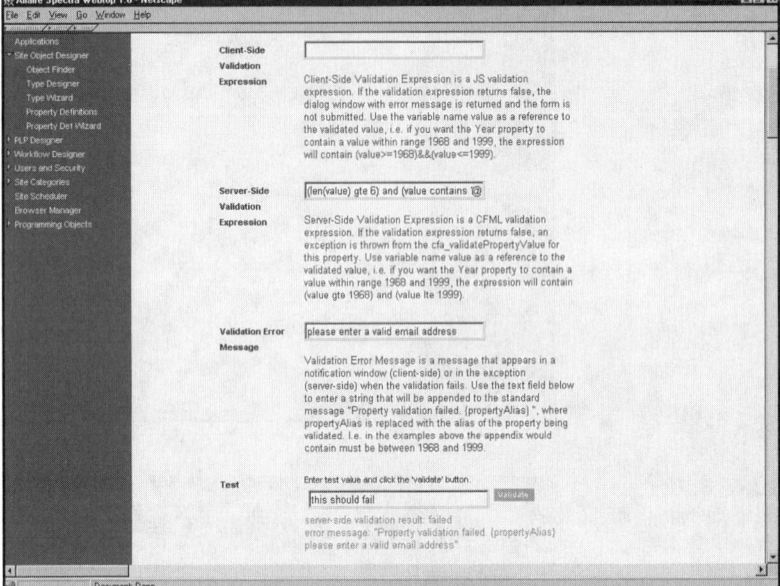

FIGURE 8.23
The phrase `this should fail` is entered into the test validation box and, as expected, fails.

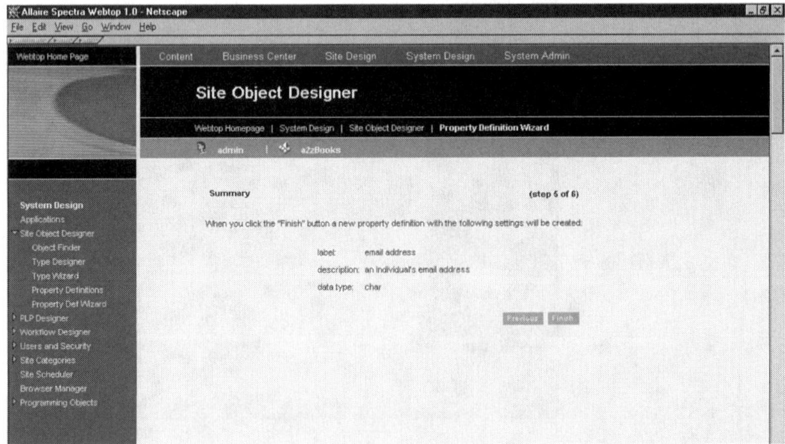

FIGURE 8.24
The summary gives you a chance to confirm the label, description and data type of the property before committing it.

After you confirm your entries from the Summary page, the property is created, and the new property type ID is displayed (see Figure 8.25).

Creating Properties with the Property Definition Designer You can also create properties without the wizard by entering a new property name and data type in the form at the bottom of the Property Definitions page (see Figure 8.26).

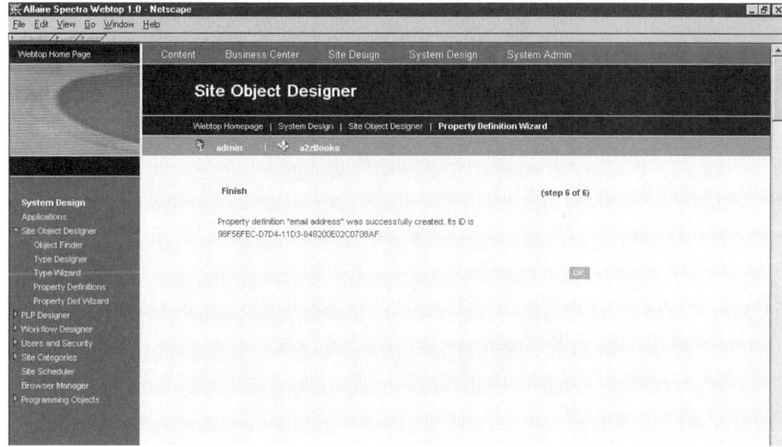

FIGURE 8.25
Once the property definition is created, the wizard will let you know the new property definition ID.

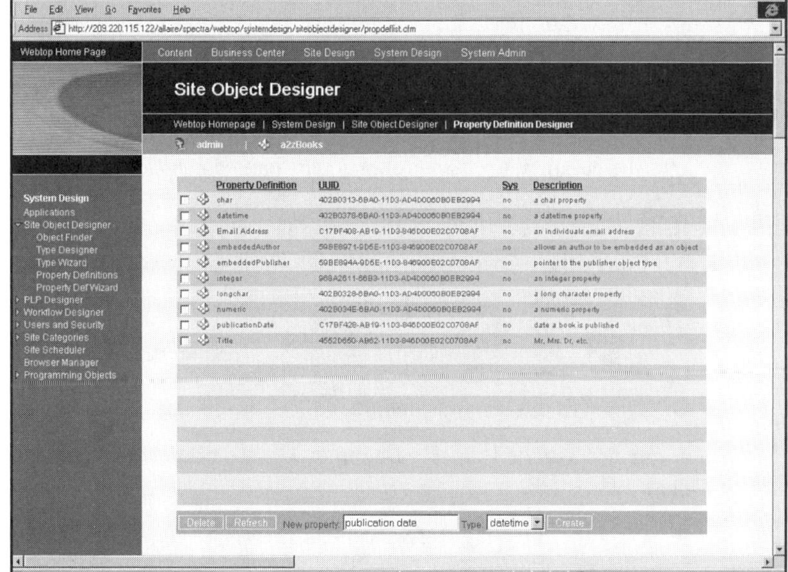

FIGURE 8.26
Creating a new `publicationDate` property.

Next you will be prompted for the details of this property, as shown in Figure 8.27. You can add an optional description, to make it easier for other users to understand what this property does. You also need to specify the input type to be used for entering data for this property. You can also enter data validation expressions and error messages to be displayed should the validation fail.

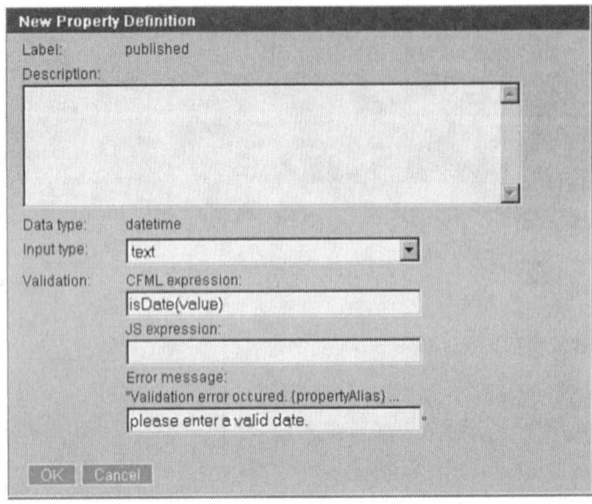

FIGURE 8.27 The `publicationDate` property needs to be a valid date, so the CFML expression `isDate(value)` is used.

Creating Objects as Properties Sometimes an object is used as a property of another object. In the a2zBooks application, the Book object needs to contain an `author` property. As there is more information about authors than merely their names, it will become necessary to embed an Author object into the Book object. This way, an author's `name`, `email`, and `Bio` properties are all available to the Book object.

To create a property for an embedded object, you begin in the same way you would any other property, with the exception that the type of the new property is set to `object`. Figure 8.28 shows the creation of a new property type named `embeddedAuthor`.

Then follow these steps:

1. Click Create next to the Type drop-down list.
2. You are asked for a description of the property and which object it will contain. In Figure 8.29, the new property `embeddedAuthor` is set as a property containing the Author object type.
3. Click OK to save your definition.

You can also use the Property Definition Wizard to create an embedded object property type. Follow these steps:

1. Click the Property DefWizard link in the Site Object Designer section of the navigation area.

Part II
Ch 8

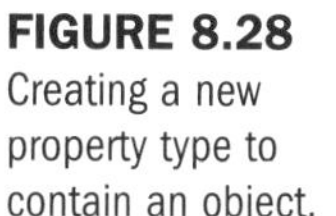

FIGURE 8.28
Creating a new property type to contain an object.

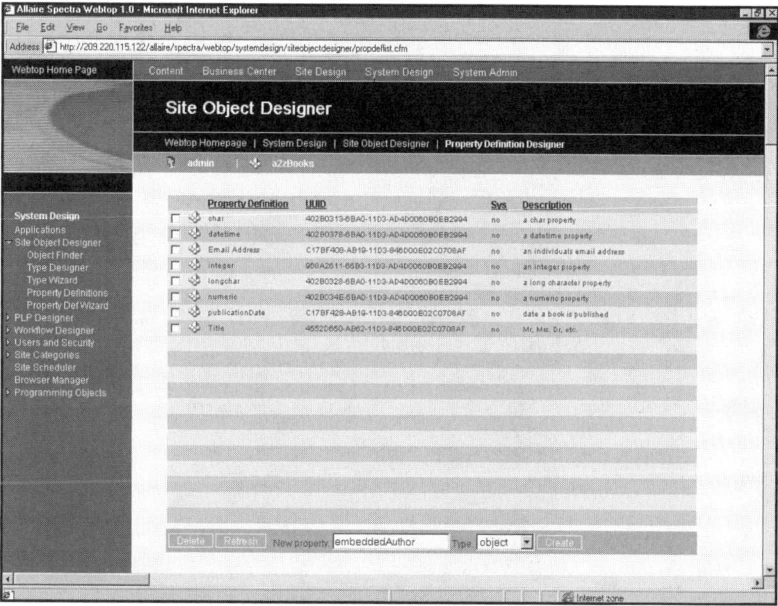

FIGURE 8.29
The description and object type to be embedded are specified.

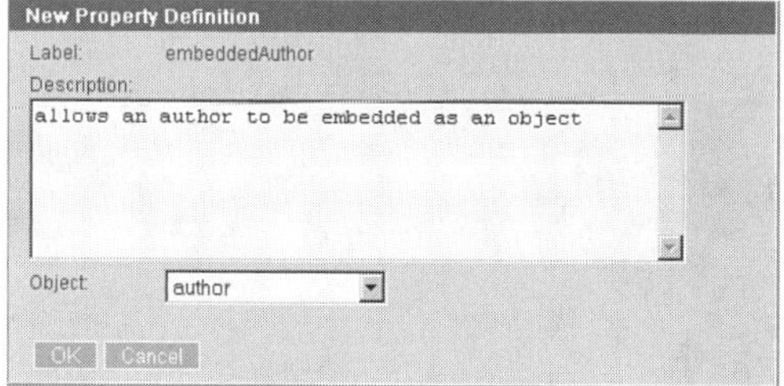

2. The introduction to the Property Definition Wizard will appear, as you saw earlier in Figure 8.19. Clicking the Next button will bring you to the Property Definition Settings page (see Figure 8.30).
3. You are prompted for a label, description, and data type for the new property. To use the wizard to create an embedded object type, choose the `object` data type.
4. You are presented with a list of objects that you can embed (see Figure 8.31). Choose the Publisher object.

NOTE An object can be embedded only into a single property. If you want to create a new property type of an object that's already defined in another property, you must first delete the existing property before you are allowed to create a new one.

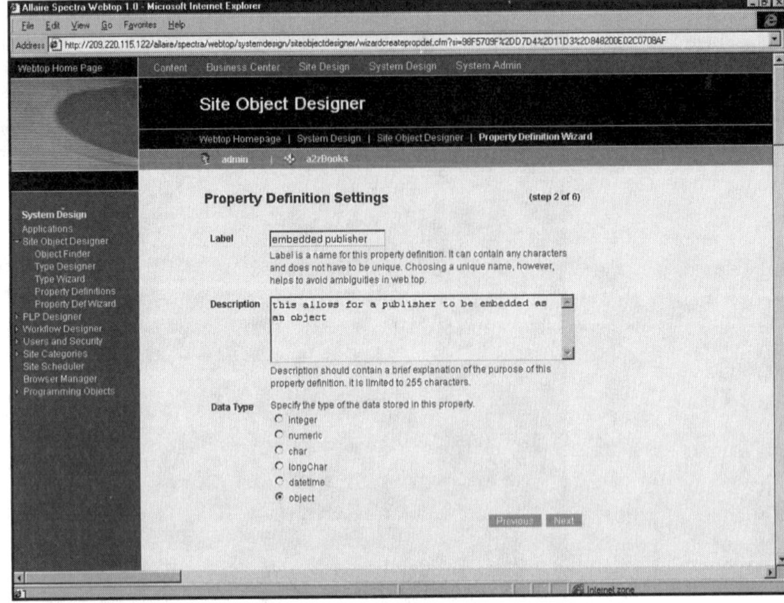

FIGURE 8.30 The new type `embedded publisher` is created, with a Data Type `object`.

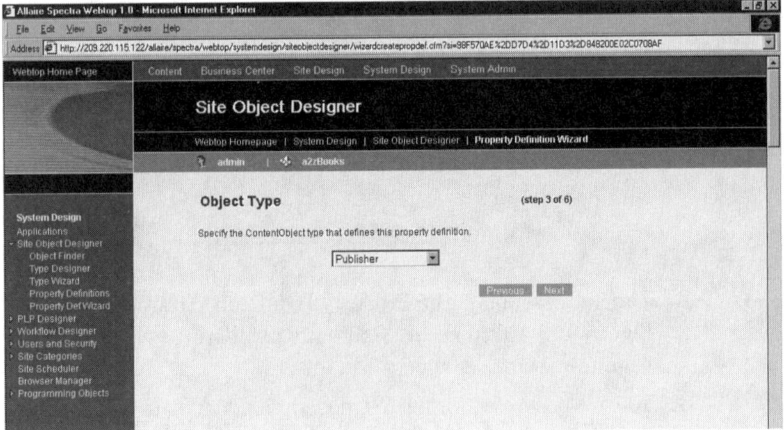

FIGURE 8.31 The object to be embedded—in this case, Publisher—is specified.

5. You are asked to confirm your entries before they are committed to the system (see Figure 8.32).

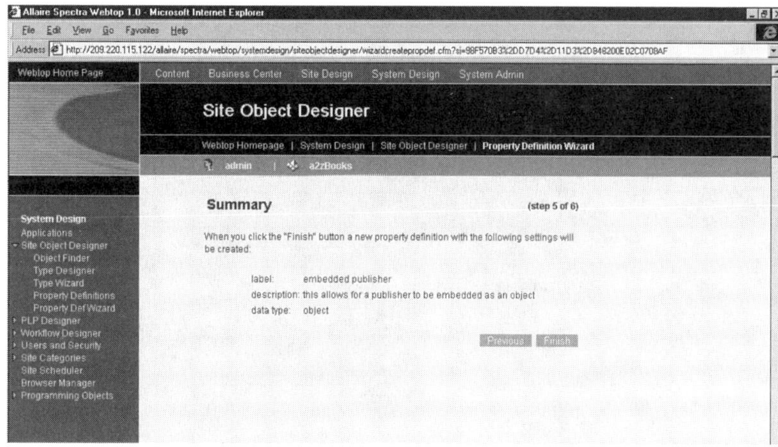

FIGURE 8.32
The summary of the newly created `embedded publisher` property is displayed.

After you create the property types for the Author and Publisher object types, you can go back to the Object Type Designer and add these properties to the Book object. Follow these steps:

1. Click the Type Designer link in the Site Object Designer menu.
2. Click the widget next to the Book object type.
3. From the Edit Type page, click the Properties link.
4. In the New Property text box, enter the property name **`publisher`**, choose the `embeddedPublisher` property type from the pull-down menu, and click Add.
5. On the New Type Property Definition page, choose an alias for the property, set it as a simple value, and click OK.

Repeat these same steps to create the `author` property of the book as an `embeddedAuthor` property type. However, you will want to set the `author` property as an array so that a book can have more than one author.

Using the Site Layout Model

The Site Designer will begin the development process in the Site Layout model. From here, you can create sites, sections, and pages, manage logging, caching, and security settings for these, and manage page templates.

The first step in beginning a new application in the Site Layout model is to create a new site. To do this, follow these steps:

1. Go to the Site Design section of the Webtop, expand the Site Layout Manager menu, and click the Site Elements link.

2. Choose Site from the pull-down menu and click Create. This will bring you to the Site Component Editor for creating a site (see Figure 8.33).

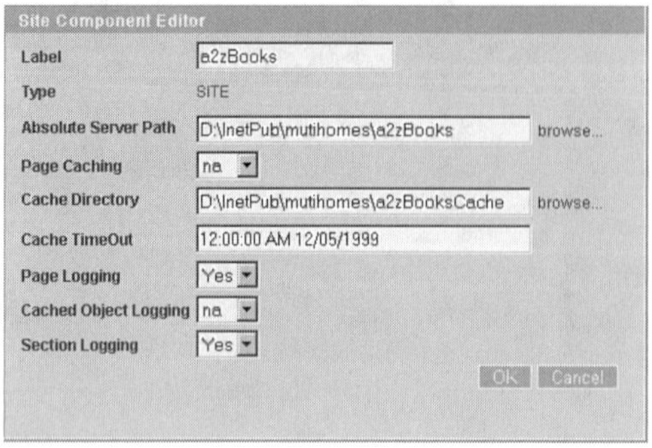

FIGURE 8.33
Using the Site Component Editor to create a new site.

Site Component Editor

Label	a2zBooks
Type	SITE
Absolute Server Path	D:\InetPub\mutihomes\a2zBooks browse...
Page Caching	na
Cache Directory	D:\InetPub\mutihomes\a2zBooksCache browse...
Cache TimeOut	12:00:00 AM 12/05/1999
Page Logging	Yes
Cached Object Logging	na
Section Logging	Yes

OK Cancel

NOTE If you want to edit an existing site, click the widget icon next to the site name to edit it.

Sites

In Figure 8.33, a new site named `a2zBooks` is created. The Absolute Server Path is a required field that specifies where on the server the code base for this application will reside. This needs to be set as an absolute path to the root directory for the application. In this example, the application will sit in the `d:\inetpub\multihomes\a2zBooks` directory. You can also specify caching and logging details for the application.

▶ **See** Chapter 24, "Deploying Spectra Applications," for more information on caching and logging.

Sections

To create a new section in the Site Component Editor, choose Section from the Element Type pull-down menu and click the Create button. This will bring you to the form shown in Figure 8.34

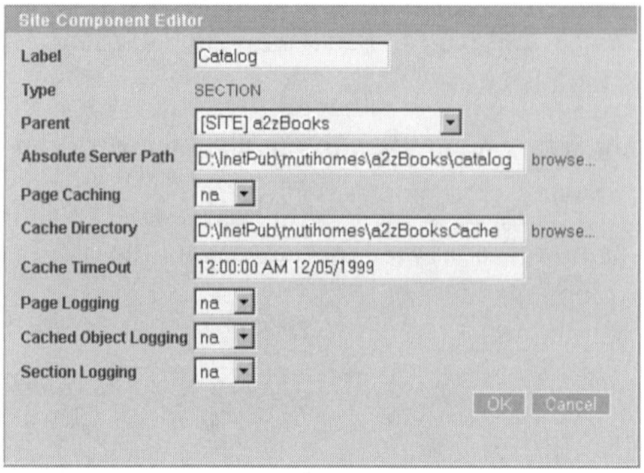

FIGURE 8.34
Using the Site Component Editor to create a new section.

Site Component Editor

Label	Catalog
Type	SECTION
Parent	[SITE] a2zBooks
Absolute Server Path	D:\InetPub\mutihomes\a2zBooks\catalog browse...
Page Caching	na
Cache Directory	D:\InetPub\mutihomes\a2zBooksCache browse...
Cache TimeOut	12:00:00 AM 12/05/1999
Page Logging	na
Cached Object Logging	na
Section Logging	na

OK Cancel

You will be prompted for all the same fields as you were for creating a site, with the addition of the Parent field. A section can have either a site or another section as a parent.

Pages and Page Templates

Creating a page in the Site Component Editor is similar to creating a section in that pages can have either a section or a site as a parent. To work with pages, choose Page in the pull-down menu. Figure 8.35 shows the page creation form for the home page.

Site Component Editor

Label	Homepage
Type	PAGE
Parent	[SITE] a2zBooks
Absolute Server Path	d:\inetpub\multihomes\a2zBooks\index.cfm browse...
Page Caching	Yes
Cache Directory	d:\inetpub\multihomes\a2zBooksCache browse...
Cache TimeOut	7:29:00 AM 11/26/1999
Page Logging	No
Cached Object Logging	No
Section Logging	No

OK Cancel

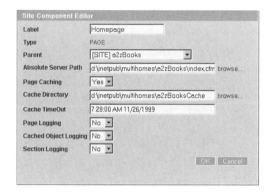

FIGURE 8.35
Using the Site Component Editor to create a new page.

Page templates can be created in the Webtop to help designers, business managers, and content personnel deploy new pages quickly. To create a page template, click the Page Templates link in the Site Layout Manager section of the Site Design portion of the Webtop. Click Create to create a new page template, or click the page icon next to an existing page template to edit it. Figure 8.36 shows the page template form. As with all elements of the Webtop, you start by giving your page template a label. Next, choose the site or section to act as the owner of this page. A description can be entered to help other users understand this template. Finally, you must specify at least one of the three template files to be used. These are files that will be `CFIncluded` into the page. Click OK to complete page template creation.

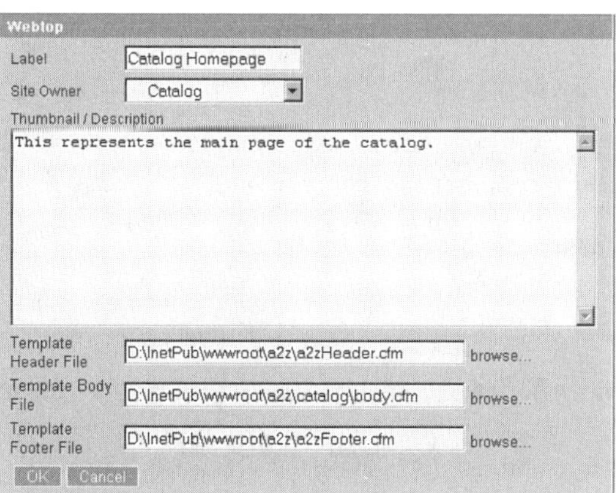

Webtop

Label	Catalog Homepage
Site Owner	Catalog
Thumbnail / Description	This represents the main page of the catalog.
Template Header File	D:\InetPub\wwwroot\a2z\a2zHeader.cfm browse...
Template Body File	D:\InetPub\wwwroot\a2z\catalog\body.cfm browse...
Template Footer File	D:\InetPub\wwwroot\a2z\a2zFooter.cfm browse...

OK Cancel

FIGURE 8.36
Creating a page template.

Spectra offers two ways for pages to be created: either through the Page Templates section of the Site Layout Manager or with the `<cfa_page>` tag. To create a page from the Webtop, go to the Page Templates page of the Site Layout Manager, choose a radio button next to one of the page templates you've created, and click the Create Page button at the bottom of the page. This will bring you to a form, as shown in Figure 8.37.

The page name you specify will appear in the Site Layout Model. You can also specify a section and site, which are the parents to this page. You also need to specify the datasource into which this page will be stored and the file path and URL at which this page will be accessible. Clicking Create Page will create a ColdFusion template on your system in the path specified.

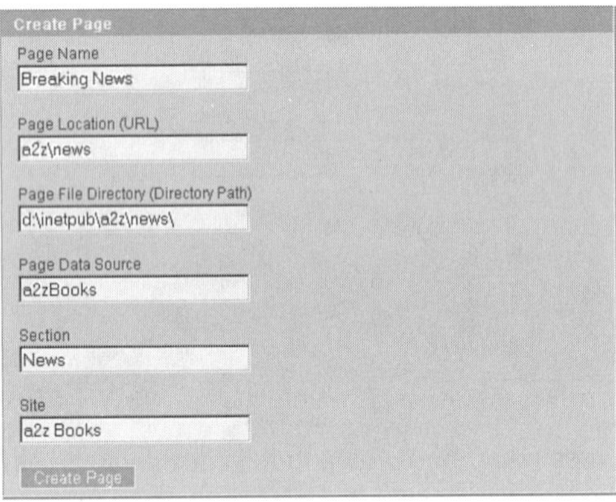

FIGURE 8.37
Creating a page from a page template.

Listing 8.1 shows the page created by Spectra when the form in Figure 8.37 was submitted.

Listing 8.1 The Result of the Form in Figure 8.37

```
<!--- This page was generated by Allaire Spectra --->
<!--- page template: 7DCD84AD-AA6D-11D3-846D00E02C0708AF --->
<!--- created: {ts '1999-12-11 17:41:26'} --->
<!--- created by: admin --->
<!--- Application: a2zBooks --->
<cfa_page
     pagename = 'Breaking News'
     SectionName = 'News'
     siteName = 'A2Z Books'
     datasource = 'a2zAccess'>
<cfinclude template='/a2z/a2zHeader.cfm'>
     <cfinclude template='/a2z/catalog/body.cfm'>
     <cfinclude template='/a2z/a2zFooter.cfm'>

</cfa_page>
```

This code begins with a series of comment tags, indicating that the page was generated automatically by Spectra and giving the ID of the page template used, as well as the date created, the user who created it, and the application for which it is intended.

Next, a `<cfa_page>` tag indicates that this page is part of the a2zBooks application, in the News section, and has a page name of Breaking News. The datasource for this application is also provided.

Between the `<cfa_page>` and `</cfa_page>` tags are three `<cfinclude>` tags, indicating the `header`, `body`, and `footer` files to be used for this page.

You can also create pages in Spectra through code by including a `<cfa_page>` tag in a ColdFusion template. In Listing 8.1, the home page for the a2zBooks catalog is created. Notice the `<cfa_page>` tag on top of the template, which informs Spectra that this is the a2zBooks catalog home page of the Catalog section of the a2zBooks application. The settings also indicate that this page should not be cached, that page objects should not be preloaded, that the page should not be logged, and that cached objects should not be logged. (You can find more information on caching and logging in Chapters 17 and 24.) As with all tags in Spectra, you need to include the datasource in which this application's objects are stored. In the `application.cfm` file, you will find the lines

```
<cfa_applicationInitialize
    name="a2zBooks"
    mode="#variables.mode#">
```

which indicate that the application name is a2zBooks. Among other things, the `cfa_applicationInitialize` tag will read the name of the datasource assigned to this application and set it into a request variable named `request.cfa.`*`<applicationname>`*`.datasource`. By setting the variable to the request scope, it is available to every template that is encountered in the course of an HTTP request. Listing 8.2 shows the `index.cfm` page of the catalog.

Listing 8.2 Using *<cfa_page>*

```
<!---
File:          /catalog/index.cfm
Author:        jeff tapper (jeff@tapper.net)
Date:          12/5/1999
Description: homepage of the a2z Books Catalog
Notes:
--->

<CF_a2zFormatting SubTitle="howdy-hoe">
    <cfa_page
        dataSource="#REQUEST.CFA.a2zBooks.DATASOURCE#"
        pageName="a2z catalog homepage"
        sectionName="catalog"
        siteName="a2zBooks"
        cachePage="No"
        bPreLoadPageObjects="No"
        logPage="No"
        logCachedObjects="No" >

    <table width="500">
        <tr>
```

continues

Listing 8.2 Continued

```
            <td>
            <cfa_container
                datasource="#request.cfa.a2zbooks.datasource#"
                name="catalogt"
                busecache="no"
                cachetype="server"
                cachedir="d:\inetpub\multihomes\a2zbookscache"
                dtcachetimeout="#createTimeSpan(1,0,0,0)#" >
            </td>
        </tr>
    </table>
    </cfa_page>
</CF_a2zFormatting>
```

This code begins with a `<cfa_page>` tag, as described above, indicating the `pageName`, `siteName`, `sectionName`, and `dataSource`. The optional attributes `cachePage`, `bPreLoadPageObjects`, `logPage`, and `logCachedObjects` are all set to `NO`.

Inside the `<cfa_page>` tags is a simple HTML table, containing a single cell with a `CFA_Container` tag into which content can be published.

After this code is run, the Site Object model now reflects an a2z catalog home page in the Catalog section of the a2zBooks application.

Containers

In Listing 8.2 is the `<cfa_container>` tag. This tag tells Spectra that this position on the page can contain content objects. This will manage the retrieval of content items, as well as the interface to the publishing system. When browsing the site in Design mode, a scheduling widget will be placed in the upper-left corner of any containers you encounter. Clicking this widget will allow you to publish content objects to this container. If there is any content published to that container, you will find boxes above and below the center of each content item. Clicking one of those boxes will allow you to view, edit, or categorize the data inside the selected object.

The `<cfa_container>` tag takes the attributes listed in Table 8.2.

Table 8.2 *<cfa_container>* Attributes

Attribute	Required?	Description
`Datasource`	No	The Content Object Database from which objects will be chosen. If none is specified, `request.cfa.contentobject.dsn` is used.
`Name`	Yes	The name given to the container that will appear in the Site Object model. This must be unique within the `cfa_page` tag.

Attribute	Required?	Description
bUseCache	No	Indicates whether to use caching for content items in this container. If no cached version exists, this will create one. The default is no.
cacheType	No	Specifies the scope into which the content is cached. Available options are `Session` (default), `Request`, `Scope`, and `File`.
cacheDir	Yes if `cacheType` is `File`	Specifies the directory into which the container's cache file will be written.
dtCacheTimeout	No	The date/time when the cache was last reset.

Figure 8.38 shows the catalog home page in Design mode. Notice that the container is currently empty, as no content has yet been scheduled to it. By clicking the icon next to the text `catalog`, you will enter the container editor (see in Figure 8.39).

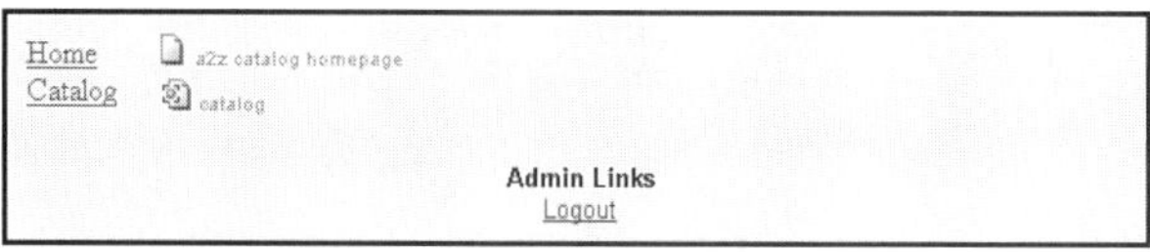

FIGURE 8.38
The Design Mode view of the catalog page before any content is added to the container.

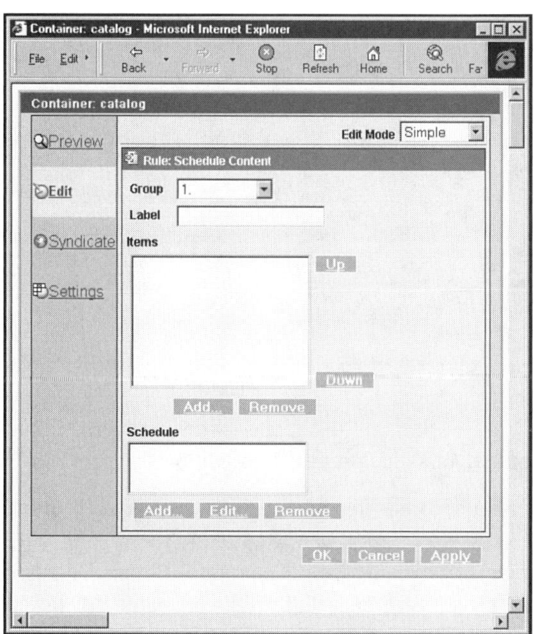

FIGURE 8.39
From the simple container editor, you can add, schedule, and group content objects.

To add content to this container, follow these steps:

1. Click the Add button below the Items text box. This will bring you to an object finder.
2. Select the object type whose content you want to schedule. As this is a book catalog, you should choose the Book object type from the pull-down menu.
3. Check the boxes next to the books you want to display on the catalog home page. If you haven't yet created any book objects, there will not be any books available to add.
4. Choose the method that should be used with these books. In this case, you should choose `Teaser`, which displays the title and author(s) of the book. (The `Teaser` method is a specific type of `display` method and will be discussed in greater detail later in the section "Basic Display Handler.") You can see the complete form in Figure 8.40.
5. Once you click Add in the object finder, you will return to the simple container editor. Now, you can see the books that have been chosen and the methods that will be executed.

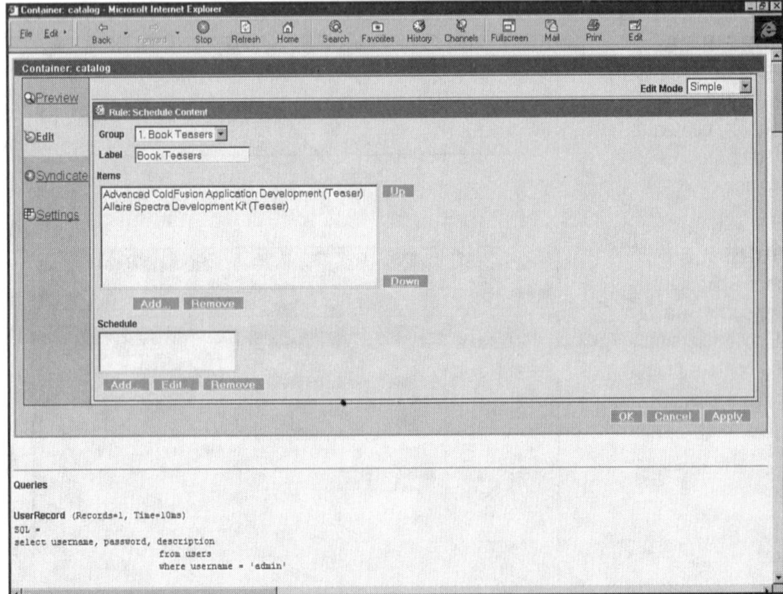

FIGURE 8.40
Two books have been scheduled with the `Teaser` method.

6. Clicking the Preview link on the left side of the container editor will show you what the scheduled content looks like in your new container, as seen in Figure 8.41.

The container editor can also be used to schedule a content object to appear at a specific time. Suppose that a new book was recently added to the system, and the editors want it to appear in the catalog every evening from 6 p.m. until 10 p.m. To facilitate this, click the Edit button. Create a new group of content that will be scheduled so that the initial group will

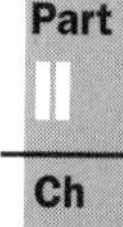

always appear and the new group will be added for its scheduled hours. To do this, choose Add Group from the Group pull-down menu, and name the new group. Next, click the Add button to choose a new content object to display as this group. As above, you can only add Content Items that have previously been created.

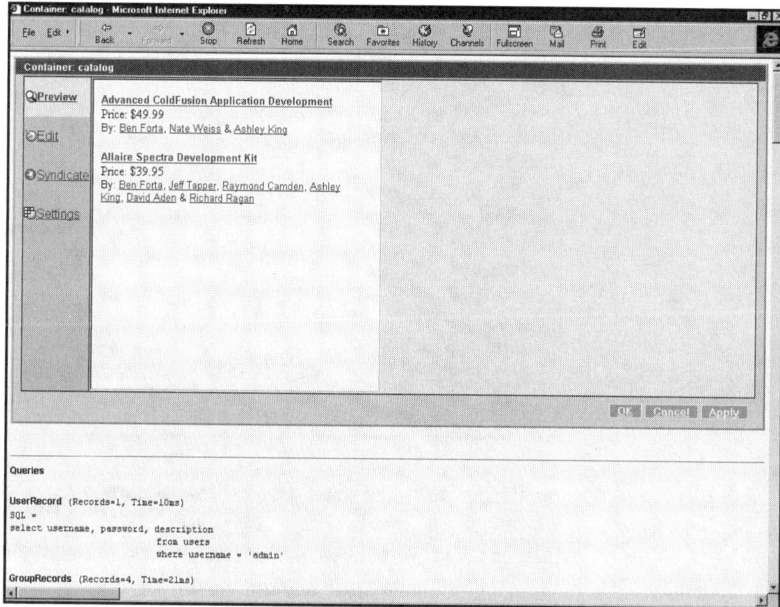

FIGURE 8.41
A preview of the container.

After you choose the object and method, click Add. Back in the container editor, while the new group is still chosen in the group pull-down menu, click the Add button below the Schedule box to add a schedule for displaying this content. Figure 8.42 shows the content scheduling form.

Times of day need to be referenced using a 24-hour clock. A start time of 18:00 and end time of 22:00 indicate that the content will appear from 6 to 10 p.m.

To schedule this book to appear from 6 to 10 p.m daily, first choose the Daily radio button at the top of the form. Next, enter the start time, in 24-hour time format. For 6 p.m., the start time should be entered as 18:00. The end time is entered in the same format. The start date is also required. This is the day when the content should first be displayed. The end date is optional.

Looking at the page at the scheduled time shows that the new book has been added to the catalog, as shown in Figure 8.43. During the specified hours, the catalog will appear as shown in Figure 8.44.

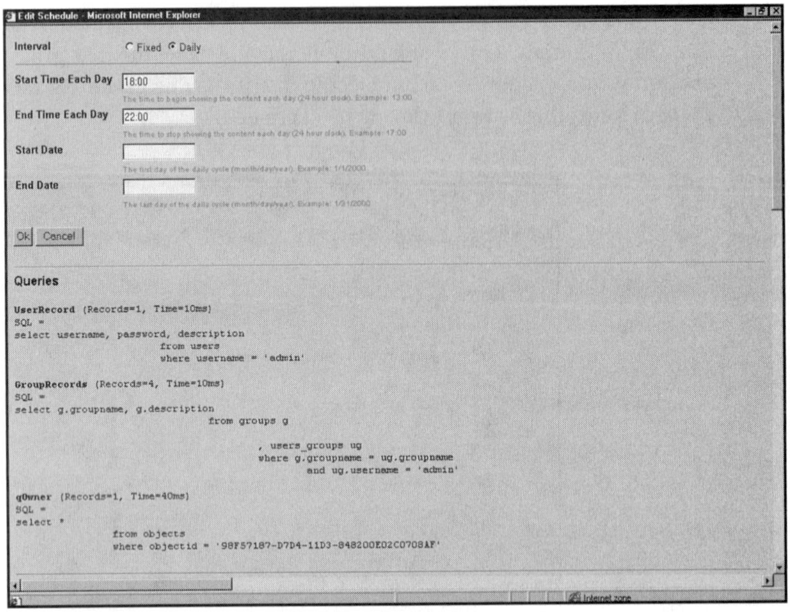

FIGURE 8.42
The scheduling screen.

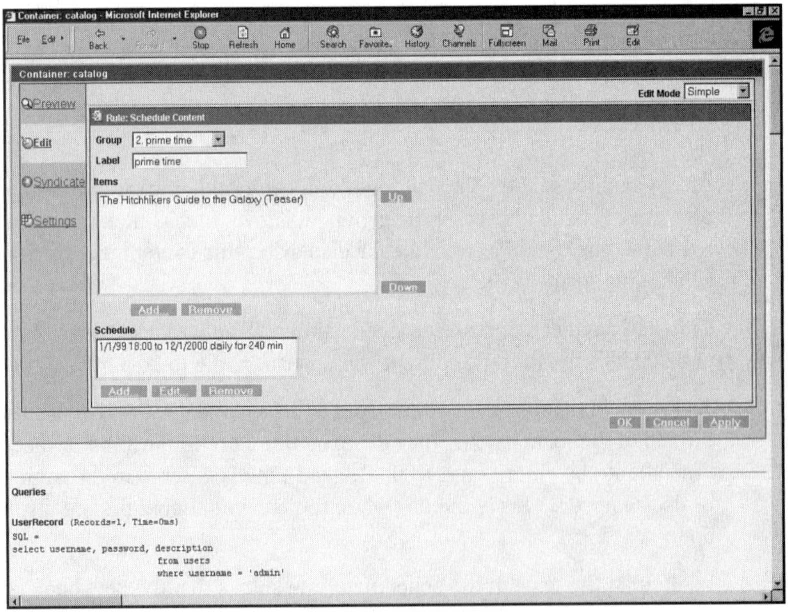

FIGURE 8.43
When the schedule is entered, the Edit screen displays the schedule for this group.

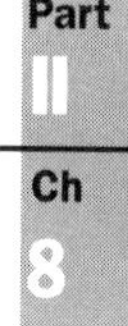

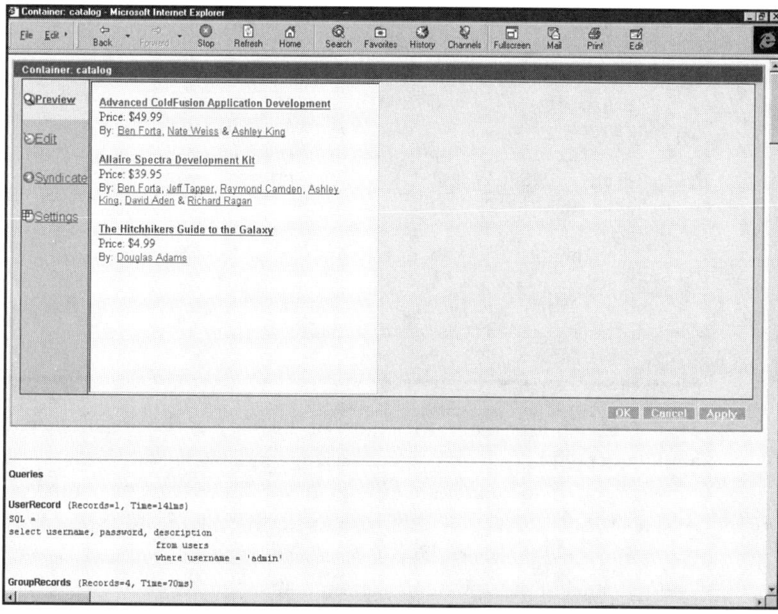

FIGURE 8.44
It's after 6 p.m. but before 10 p.m., and the newly added book appears in the catalog with the books that always appear.

NOTE Scheduling is one type rule available in Spectra. There are also other built-in rules and the capability to create custom rules to truly personalize your application. Chapter 19, "Rules-Based Publishing," covers how to create rules in detail.

Basic Display Handlers

Figure 8.48 shows Spectra's default display handler. Listing 8.3 shows the source code for this handler, which can be found in the `/allaire/spectra/handlers/system/default/` directory.

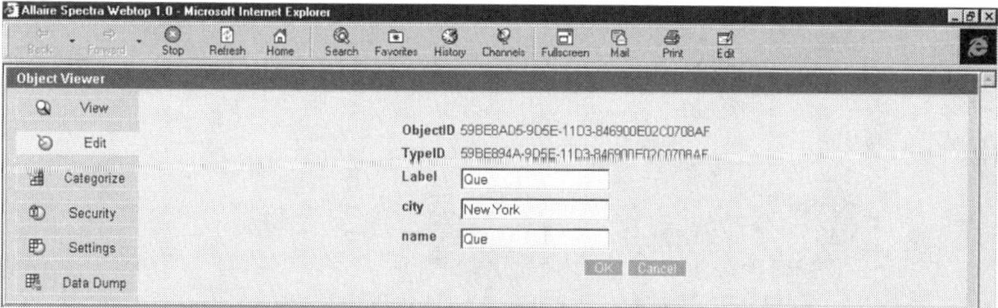

FIGURE 8.45
A Publisher content object displayed using the default display handler.

Listing 8.3 The Default Display Handler

```
<!---
    Template:            display.cfm
    Author:                Peter Muzila
    Description:
    Default DISPLAY handler. Invoked for objects of types that do not
    have their own DISPLAY handler
--->
<cfa_handler object="object" separator="<p>">
<cfa_displayFullObject
    objectID = "#object.objectID#"
    datasource="#attributes.dataSource#">
</cfa_handler>
```

`<cfa_displayFullObject>` does most of the work of the default display handler, but what should be noted here is the `<cfa_handler>` tag, which assigns a scope to the current object. In the case of the default handler in Listing 8.3, the scope is named `object`. With this, you can refer to any property of this object with the syntax `object.`*`propertyname`*. As an added benefit, if passed multiple objects, `<cfa_handler>` will loop over those objects and insert the value specified in the optional `separator` attribute between each object.

Listing 8.4 shows a custom display handler for the Author object, with its output visible in Figure 8.46.

Listing 8.4 The Display Handler for Author Objects

```
<!---
File:       display.cfm
Author:       jeff tapper (jeff@tapper.net)
Date:       12/5/1999
Description:  Display Handler for a2zBooks author object type
Notes:
--->
  <!--- use the handler tag to set the scope up --->
<CFA_HANDLER
  OBJECT="Author"
  SEPARATOR="<p>"     >

<CF_A2ZFORMATTING>
  <CFOUTPUT>
  <TABLE>
  <!--- Display the authors name --->
  <TR><TD ALIGN="center" COLSPAN="2">
    <B>#author.firstName# #author.lastname#</B>
  </TH></TR>

  <!--- Check to see if there is any entries in the email array--->
  <CFIF ISARRAY(AUTHOR.EMAIL)>
    <TR><TD COLSPAN="2">
```

```
    <!--- Loop over the email array --->
    <CFLOOP FROM="1" TO="#arrayLen(author.email)#" INDEX="counter">

      <!--- Display this email address, with a mailto link --->
      <A HREF="mailto:#author.email[counter]#">#author.email[counter]#</A><BR>

    </CFLOOP>

    </TD></TR>

  </CFIF>

  <!--- display the authors bio --->
  <TR><TD COLSPAN="2">#author.bio#</TD></TR>

  </TABLE>

  </CFOUTPUT>
</CF_A2ZFORMATTING>
</CFA_HANDLER>
```

The handler begins with the `<cfa_handler>` tag, establishing the scope `author`. Next, a basic HTML table is laid out. In the first row of the table, the author's name is displayed by referencing the variables `author.firstName` and `author.lastname`. Then, a check is made to see whether the `email` field is an array; if it is, the handler loops from 1 to the number of elements in the array and displays each email address in the array, with a `<BR>` tag between each one. The syntax `author.email[1]` will display the first entry in the `email` array of the Author object. Finally, the author's bio is displayed by referencing `author.bio`.

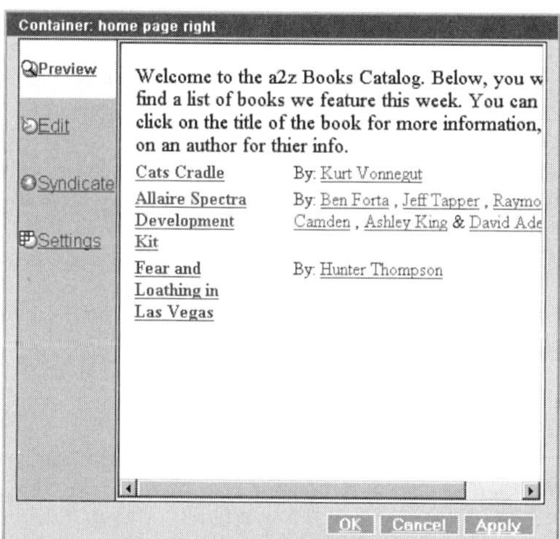

FIGURE 8.46
An Author object, displayed with the display handler shown in Listing 8.4.

The Book object display handler is more complicated, as it contains an array of embedded Author objects. The Book display handler's code is shown in Listing 8.5; Figure 8.47 shows the resulting output.

Listing 8.5 The Display Handler for Book Objects

```
<!---
File:        display.cfm
Author:      jeff tapper (jeff@tapper.net)
Date:        12/5/1999
Description: Display Handler for a2zBooks Book object Type
Notes:
--->
<!--- restrict white space --->
<CFSETTING enableCFoutputonly="yes">

    <!--- use the handler tag to establish the "book" scope--->
    <CFA_HANDLER
        OBJECT="Book"
        SEPARATOR="<p>">
<cf_A2zFormatting>
    <CFOUTPUT>
    <TABLE>
        <!--- display the books title --->
        <TR><TD ALIGN="center" COLSPAN="2"><B>#book.title#</B></TH></TR>
        </CFOUTPUT>

        <!--- If any authors are defined, display them --->
        <CFIF ARRAYLEN(BOOK.AUTHOR)>
            <CFOUTPUT>
            <TR><TD COLSPAN="2"><B>By:</B>
            </CFOUTPUT>

            <!--- loop through array of authors --->
            <CFLOOP FROM="1" TO="#arraylen(book.Author)#" INDEX="count">
                <!--- get this author --->
                <CFA_CONTENTOBJECTGET
                 DATASOURCE="#request.cfa.a2zbooks.datasource#"
                 OBJECTID="#book.author[count]#"
                 R_STOBJECT="author">

                <!--- display authors first name and lastname --->
                <CFOUTPUT>
                    #author.firstname# #author.lastname#
                </CFOUTPUT>

                <!--- if we've displayed the penultimate author,
                add an ampersand before the final person --->
                <CFIF COUNT + 1 EQ ARRAYLEN(BOOK.AUTHOR)>
                        <CFOUTPUT> & </CFOUTPUT>

                <!--- if there are more authors to display,
                separate them with a comma --->
```

```
                <CFELSEIF COUNT LT ARRAYLEN(BOOK.AUTHOR)>
                          <CFOUTPUT>, </CFOUTPUT>
                </CFIF>

            </CFLOOP>

            <CFOUTPUT>
                </TD></TR>
            </CFOUTPUT>

        </CFIF>

        <CFOUTPUT>
        <!--- Display the ISBN --->
        <TR><TD><B>ISBN</B>:</TD><TD>#book.isbn#</TD></TR>
        <!--- Display the Publication Date--->
        <TR><TD><B>Publication Date:</B></TD>
        <TD>#dateFormat(book.published,"mm/dd/yyyy")#</TD></TR>
        <!--- Display the Number of pages and price--->
        <TR><TD>#book.pages# pages.</TD>
        <TD>#dollarFormat(book.price)#</TD></TR>
    </TABLE>
    </CFOUTPUT>
</cf_A2zFormatting>
</CFA_HANDLER>
```

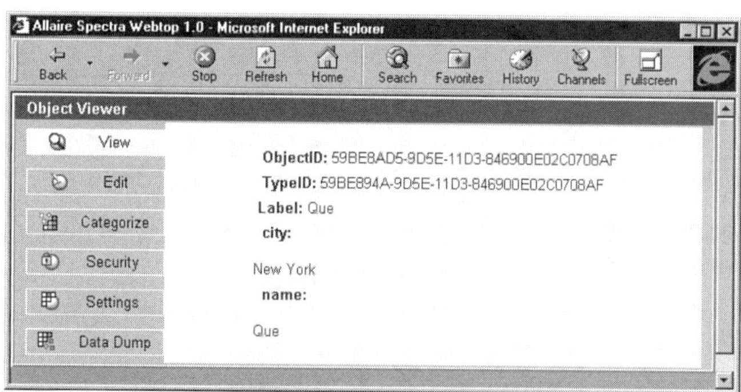

FIGURE 8.47
A Book object displayed with the display handler shown in Listing 8.5.

This handler begins in much the same way as the Author display handler, with a `<cfa_handler>` tag, this time defining the scope `book`. Then, the title of the book, accessible via the variable `book.title`, is output. Next is a check to see if the Author object array has any elements.

If there are authors for this Book object, the handler loops through the Author array. For each author in the array, you need to use the `<CFA_CONTENTOBJECTGET>` tag to retrieve the embedded Author object. The syntax `#book.author[1].objectID#` refers to the first author in the array. The `R_STOBJECT` attribute of the `<CFA_CONTENTOBJECTGET>` tag establishes the variable into which the retrieved object's information will be stored.

In this instance, the name `author` is used to store the information. With this returned information, you can access the author's name with the variables `author.firstName` and `author.lastname`.

This is followed by a few lines of code that determine if a comma or ampersand needs to be placed between the authors. Finally, the ISBN, publication date, number of pages, and price of the book are output by accessing those variables with the `book.variable_name` syntax.

If you are unsure of what variables are available to you for a particular object, the `<cfa_dump>` tag is of immense value, as it will show you every piece of data stored within the object you pass to it.

`teaser.cfm` is another display handler for the Book object, although its purpose is to display just the title and authors of each book. This will be useful for creating the online catalog, enticing users to click a book's title for the detailed information about the book. Listing 8.6 shows the source of `teaser.cfm`.

Listing 8.6 The *Teaser* Handler for Books

```
<!---
File:         teaser.cfm
Author:       jeff tapper (jeff@tapper.net)
Date:         12/5/1999
Description: Teaser Handler for a2zBooks Book object Type
Notes:        displays book title and books authors,
               with links to details on the book or the authors.
--->

<cfsetting enablecfoutputonly="yes">

<!--- use the handler tag to set the scope up for me --->
<CFA_HANDLER
     OBJECT="Book"
     SEPARATOR="<p>"
>

<CFOUTPUT>
     <FONT FACE="Arial" SIZE=2><B>
     <A href="/a2z/invoke.cfm?method=display&objectID=#book.objectID#">
     #book.title#</a></B></FONT>
     <BR>
     Price: #DollarFormat(book.price)#
</cfoutput>

     <!--- If any authors are defined, display them --->
     <CFIF ARRAYLEN(BOOK.AUTHOR)>
          <CFOUTPUT>
               <BR><FONT FACE="Arial" SIZE=2>By:
          </cfoutput>

          <!--- loop through array of authors --->
          <CFLOOP FROM="1" TO="#arraylen(book.Author)#" INDEX="count">

               <!--- get this author --->
```

```
            <CFA_CONTENTOBJECTGET
             DATASOURCE="#request.cfa.a2zbooks.datasource#"
             OBJECTID="#book.author[count]#"
             R_STOBJECT="author">

            <!--- display authors first name and lastname --->
            <cfoutput>
    <a href="/a2z/invoke.cfm?method=display&objectID=#author.objectID#">
    #author.firstname# #author.lastname#</a></cfoutput>

            <CFIF COUNT + 1 EQ ARRAYLEN(BOOK.AUTHOR)>
            <!--- if we've displayed the penultimate author,
            add an ampersand before the final person --->
                 <cfoutput> & </cfoutput>
            <CFELSEIF COUNT LT ARRAYLEN(BOOK.AUTHOR)>
            <!--- if there are more authors to display,
            seperate them with a comma --->
                <cfoutput>, </cfoutput>
            </CFIF>

        </CFLOOP>
        <cfoutput></FONT><P></cfoutput>

    </CFIF>

</CFA_HANDLER>
<cfsetting enablecfoutputonly="no">
```

As you can see, this is very similar to the display handler, although it only displays the title, author(s), and price of the book. Also notice that `invoke.cfm` is used to create links to invoke the `display` methods of both the books and the authors.

▶ **See** Chapter 10 for more information on invoking methods.

Creating display handlers may seem a daunting task when you first begin, but for a seasoned ColdFusion developer familiar with structures and arrays, it will take little time to get up to speed to create robust display handlers. Don't forget that it's through your display handlers that your end users will view your objects. ●

CHAPTER 9

Building Display Components

In this chapter

The User Interface Toolkit

Spectra includes tags to help designers and developers construct a rich interface for users. These tags provide the means to design and place the Spectra Display Components. These components use advanced client-side DHTML for current browsers and a simpler version of HTML for earlier browser versions. Spectra provides the framework for the following UI components:

- Menus
- Buttons
- Trees
- HTML Editors
- Tabs

While it's true that the site designer is responsible for much of a Spectra application's look-and-feel, the interactive developer can help the designer by wrapping Spectra user interface tags in custom tags so that the site designer can more easily place user interface elements. You can also code UI tools, such as the HTML control, directly into a handler to help those responsible for the content mark up their text into HMTL.

Spectra user interface tags are built by using ContentObject Types. In addition to providing flexible options for invoking these controls, this also allows you to implement Spectra's role-based security.

Invoking UI Controls

Two different methods are available for invoking UI components. To invoke them dynamically, define the user interface elements as instances of the appropriate ContentObject Type and then display them by calling the `<CFA_CONTENTOBJECT>` tag. For example, you might define an instance of the button ContentObject Type and display it via `<CFA_CONTENTOBJECT>`. You can also invoke UI items statically by coding tags directly. Listing 9.1 later in this chapter shows an example of the Menu control invoked statically.

Cascading Style Sheets and UI Controls

With the introduction of cascading style sheets (CSS) to HTML, designers can create highly customized interfaces for their applications. However, CSS creation is complicated and often poorly coded. To help create and maintain CSS, Spectra implements this through the *Style objects*, a ContentObject Type whose properties represent attributes of a cascading style sheet. The Style object automatically handles HTML degradation for browsers that don't support cascading style sheets.

You can use these style tags in the UI controls provided by Spectra. To create a new style, follow these steps:

1. Navigate to the Site Object Designer menu of the System Design section of the Webtop.
2. From the Object Finder, choose the Style object type from the pull-down menu.

NOTE You must enable system objects in the preferences of the Webtop to see the Style ObjectType in the pull-down menu.

3. Click Create.
4. Define the style as shown in Figure 9.1. All the fields in Figure 9.1 correspond to similarly named cascading style sheet properties. For more information on cascading style sheets, see `http://www.w3.org/Style/CSS/`.
5. Click Apply to see a preview of your new style.

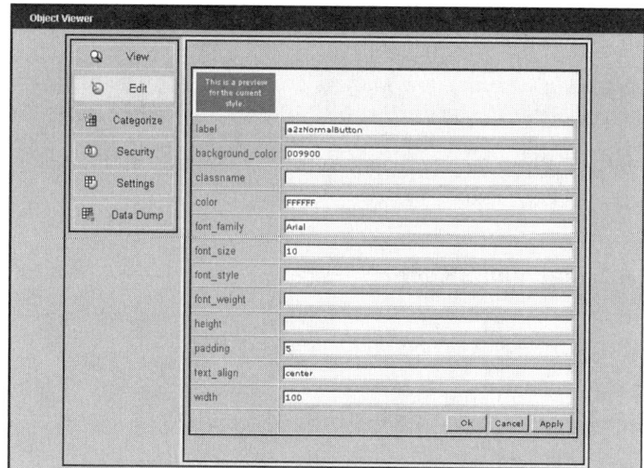

FIGURE 9.1
Here is a style definition page. Shown is the definition for the `a2zNormalButton` style.

Using the UI Controls

Although Spectra provides a variety of UI controls, you will find similarities in how they are coded into your applications.

Menus

Spectra provides an interface for building menus and menu items. The menus can appear as HTML select menus (see Figure 9.2) in older browsers, or as DHTML select menus (see Figure 9.3) in newer browsers. Menu items can link to a URL, trigger a JavaScript function, or trigger a control event handler.

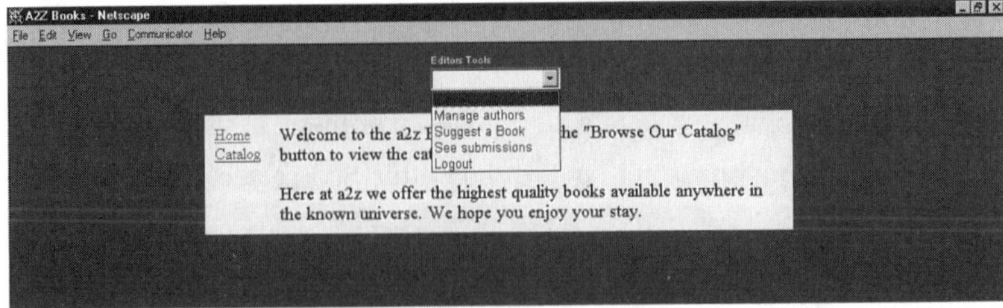

FIGURE 9.2
The Editors Tools menu displayed as an HTML Select box in an older browser.

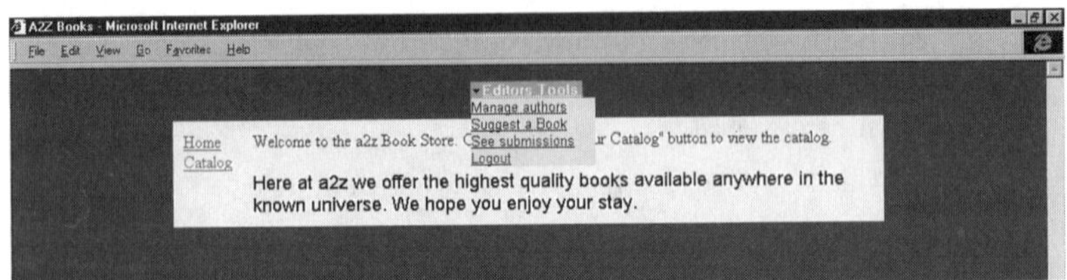

FIGURE 9.3
The same menu is displayed using DHTML in the latest version of Internet Explorer.

▶ **See** Chapter 10, "Creating and Managing Content," for full details on the <CFA_CONTROLHANDLER> and <CFA_CONTROLHANDLEREVENT> tags.

In Listing 9.1, a custom tag is created to display a menu linking to various administrator tools for the a2zBooks application.

Listing 9.1 *adminNav.cfm*

```
<!---
File:           \customtags\a2z\adminnav.cfm
Author:         Jeff Tapper
Date:           1/15/00
Description:    Displays Administrator Menu
Notes:
--->

<CFA_CONTROLHANDLER NAME="AdminMenu">
    <TABLE CELLPADDING="0" CELLSPACING="0">
        <TR>
        <TD>

        <CFA_DROPDOWNMENU
                DATASOURCE="#REQUEST.CFA.A2ZBOOKS.DATASOURCE#"
                ID="5E6F2170-F1CF-11D2-B6280060B0EB4966"
                LABEL="Editors Tools">

                <CFA_MENUITEM
                    LABEL = "Manage authors"
                    DESCRIPTION = "Manage authors"
```

```
                    URL = "/a2z/catalog/manageAuthors.cfm"
                    SELECTED="false">

                <CFA_MENUITEM
                    LABEL = "Suggest a Book"
                    DESCRIPTION = "Creating a submission
                    for a suggested book"
URL = "/a2z/submission/makeSubmission.cfm"
                    SELECTED="false">

                <CFA_MENUITEM
                    LABEL = "See submissions"
                    DESCRIPTION = "review submitted suggestions"
                    URL = "/a2z/submission/AssignSubmission.cfm"
                    SELECTED="false">

        </CFA_DROPDOWNMENU>
        </TD>
        </TR>
    </TABLE>
</CFA_CONTROLHANDLER>
```

Part II Ch 9

Listing 9.1 begins by opening a Control Handler tag to contain the menu. Inside a basic HTML table, a <CFA_DROPDOWNMENU> tag is opened with a datasource, ID, and label. The variable REQUEST.CFA.A2ZBOOKS.DATASOURCE represents the datasource for the a2zBooks application. The ID needs to be a UUID, which is unique to this page. It doesn't need to reflect a UUID of an object registered in the system. A label is also provided that is used in the menu display, as you saw in Figures 9.2 and 9.3. Optional attributes of the <CFA_DROPDOWNMENU> tag aren't in use here; these attributes define styles of the menu's background area, the normal style, and the style when an item is moused over.

▶ **See** Appendix A, "Allaire Spectra Tags," for full details on the <CFA_DROPDOWNMENU> tag.

Next, the three menu items are specified, along with the attribute's label, URL description, and the selected attribute.

▶ **See** Appendix A for full details on the <CFA_MENUITEM> tag.

▶ **See** Chapter 10 for details on using control handlers.

Finally, the <CFA_DROPDOWNMENU>, <TABLE>, and <CFA_CONTROLHANDLER> tags are closed.

Buttons

In Spectra, you can use *link buttons* and *image buttons* to invoke a URL, JavaScript, or control event handler. A link button is displayed as a button in current browsers and as a simple link in earlier browsers. Image buttons display the specified image as a button in current browsers and as a text link in earlier browsers. Both of these are created with the <CFA_BUTTON> tag.

▶ **See** Appendix A for details on the attributes of the <CFA_BUTTON> tag.

The *ACTION* and *ACTIONDATA* Attributes Link and image buttons include `ACTION` and `ACTIONDATA` attributes. You use these attributes to control the processing performed when the user clicks the link, as indicated in Tables 9.1 and 9.2.

Table 9.1 *CFA_Button* Tag Actions

Action	Description
`URL`	Link to the URL specified in the `ACTIONDATA` attribute.
`JavaScript`	Perform the JavaScript listed in the `ACTIONDATA` attribute.
`ControlHandlerEvent`	Invoke the server event listed in the `ACTIONDATA` attribute.

Table 9.2 The *ACTIONDATA* Attribute of the *CFA_Button* Tag

Action	Description
`URL`	The URL to invoke when the button is pressed.
`JavaScript`	The JavaScript to invoke when the button is pressed.
`ControlHandlerEvent`	The server event to invoke when the button is pressed.

Button States Buttons can have any of the following states, which you control with attributes (static invocation) or properties (dynamic invocation):

`Normal`	Default button display.
`Over`	When the mouse cursor is over the button.
`Down`	While the button is clicked.
`Pressed`	When the button is used as a toggle and is in the enabled state.
`Unavailable`	When the button isn't available for use.
`PressedUnavailable`	When the button is used as a toggle, is in the enabled state, but not available for use.

Using the Link Button You can use the link button to provide visually highlighted links to other URLs. The link button adjusts its display characteristics based on the browser type.

You can make any link into a link button by replacing the `<A HREF=...></A>` tags with a `<CFA_BUTTON>` tag. Listing 9.2 shows a static invocation of a link button to link into the a2zBooks Catalog. Figure 9.4 shows this button in use.

Listing 9.2 *index.cfm*—Invoking a Link Button

```
<cfa_button
    dataSource = "REQUEST.CFA.a2zBooks.DATASOURCE"
    id = "D3E48F89-FE2A-11e2-B6300060B0fB4967"
```

```
label = "Browse our Catalog"
action="url"
actionData="/a2z/catalog/index.cfm"
description="Browse the a2zBooks catalog"
state="normal">
```

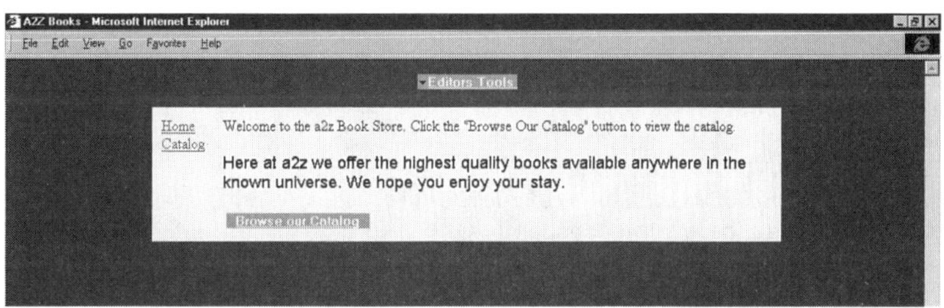

FIGURE 9.4
The link button is now used to link to the Catalog.

You can also display a button dynamically by defining the button in the ContentObject Database.

▶ **See** Appendix A for details on the properties of the button object.

The button ContentObject Type is used for both link buttons and image buttons. The `buttonText` property determines whether the button appears as a link button or an image button. If you specify a value for the `buttonText` property, Spectra displays a link button; otherwise, it will display an image button. The following code snippet invokes a link button dynamically:

```
<cfa_contentObject
    dataSource="REQUEST.CFA.A2ZBOOKS.DATASOURCE"
    lobjectids="D3E48F82-FE2A-11D2-B6300060B0EB4966"
    method="display"
    busecache="#cache#"
    >
```

Here, you are invoking the `display` method of a specific image object in the a2zBooks datasource. The `bUseCache` tag is set as a global variable, so that you can turn off object caching in one convenient location.

You can use images instead of text on buttons as well. While the Link button uses six styles for its text, the image button uses six images to represent each of the button's potential states.

The code in Listing 9.3 displays an image button statically:

Listing 9.3 *imageButton.cfm*—Displaying a Button Image Statically

```
<!---
File:           \customtags\a2z\imageButton.cfm
Author:         Jeff Tapper
Date:           1/15/00
Description:    Creates structures for each of the six images,
                 and displays them as an image button.

Notes:
--->

<CFSCRIPT>
     stNormalimage = structNew();
     stNormalimage.border = "0";
     stNormalimage.height = "100";
     stNormalimage.width = "200";
     stNormalimage.file.fileurl = "/images/blue.GIF";

     stoverimage = structNew();
     stoverimage.border = "0";
     stoverimage.height = "100";
     stoverimage.width = "200";
     stoverimage.file.fileurl = "/images/green.GIF";

     stpressedimage = structNew();
     stpressedimage.border = "0";
     stpressedimage.height = "100";
     stpressedimage.width = "200";
     stpressedimage.file.fileurl = "/images/orange.GIF";

     stUnavailableimage = structNew();
     stUnavailableimage.border = "0";
     stUnavailableimage.height = "100";
     stUnavailableimage.width = "200";
     stUnavailableimage.file.fileurl = "/images/purple.GIF";

     stUnavailablePressedimage = structNew();
     stUnavailablePressedimage.border = "0";
     stUnavailablePressedimage.height = "100";
     stUnavailablePressedimage.width = "200";
     stUnavailablePressedimage.file.fileurl = "/images/yellow.GIF";

     stDownImage = structNew();
     stDownImage.border = "0";
     stDownImage.height = "100";
     stDownImage.width = "200";
     stDownImage.file.fileurl = "/images/red.GIF";

     urlPath = "somePage.cfm";
     description = "The magical mystery button.";
</CFSCRIPT>
```

```
<!--- get #thispath# --->
<CFPARAM NAME="attributes.buttonstate" DEFAULT="normal">

<CFA_BUTTON
    DATASOURCE = "#REQUEST.CFA.a2zBooks.DATASOURCE#"
    ID = "D3E48F89-FE2A-11D2-B6300060B0EB4967"
    ACTION="url"
    ACTIONDATA="#variables.urlpath#"
    DESCRIPTION="#variables.description#"
    STNORMALIMAGE="#variables.stNormalImage#"
    STOVERIMAGE="#variables.stOverImage#"
    STDOWNIMAGE="#variables.stDownImage#"
    STPRESSEDIMAGE="#variables.stPressedImage#"
    STUNAVAILABLEIMAGE="#variables.stUnavailableImage#"
    STUNAVAILABLEPRESSEDIMAGE="#variables.stUnavailablePressedImage#"
    STATE="#attributes.buttonstate#"
    >
```


The first step in creating an image button is to build a structure for each image. Each structure should have a height, width, border, and `file.fileURL` entry. `file.fileURL` points to the URL of the graphic file on the server. There are also settings at the end of the `<CFSCRIPT>` block that set the click-through URL for the button, as well as the description that will be used in the `<ALT>` tags of the images

Next, with the `<CFPARAM>` tag, we set a default value for the state of the button. If no attribute is passed to this tag, the button will be displayed as normal.

Finally, the variables are all fed into the `<CFA_BUTTON>` tag, and the image button is created. Figure 9.5 shows the image button in the normal state.

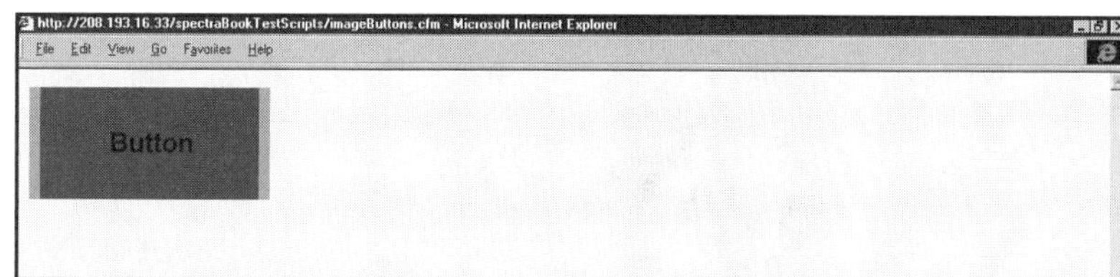

FIGURE 9.5
The image button here displays the normal state.

Trees

Spectra provides a tree control to enable you to display hierarchical data.

The tree control is displayed with the `<CFA_TREE>` tag. This tag has attributes that allow you to choose the display and selection.

Skins Three display styles for trees ship with Spectra, and you can easily create your own customized style. In Spectra, these styles are referred to as the skins attribute. The built-in skins emulate the tree structures of Windows Explorer (`WIX`), Macintosh (`MAC`), and Visual Source Safe (`VSS`). Figures 9.6, 9.7, and 9.8 show the three skins in use.

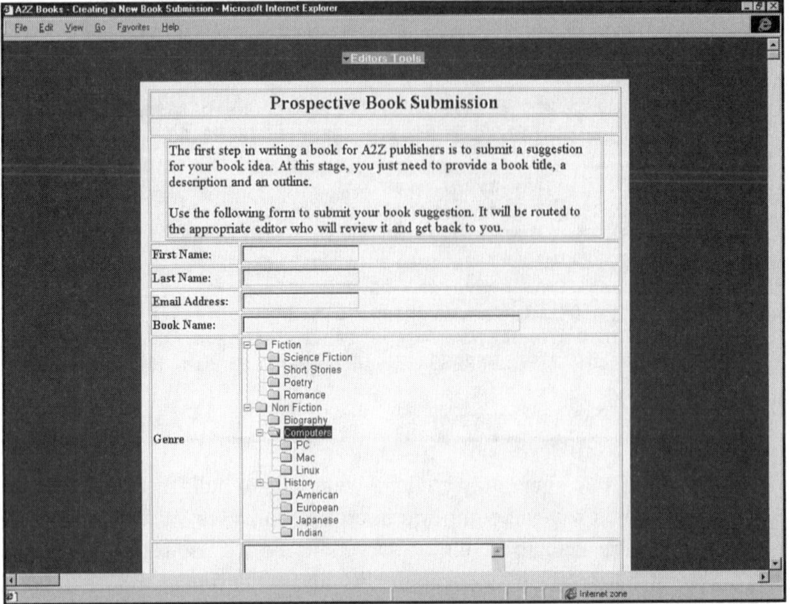

FIGURE 9.6
The `WIN` skin applied to a genre hierarchy.

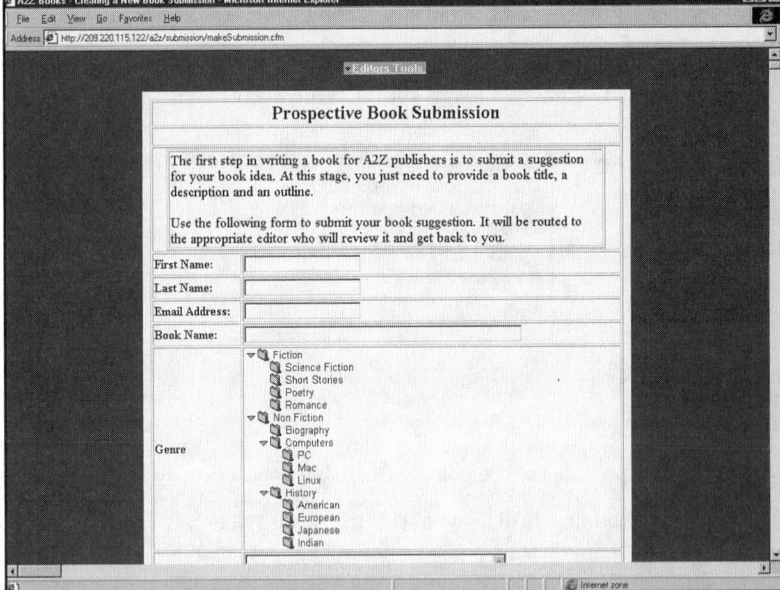

FIGURE 9.7
The `MAC` skin applied to a genre hierarchy.

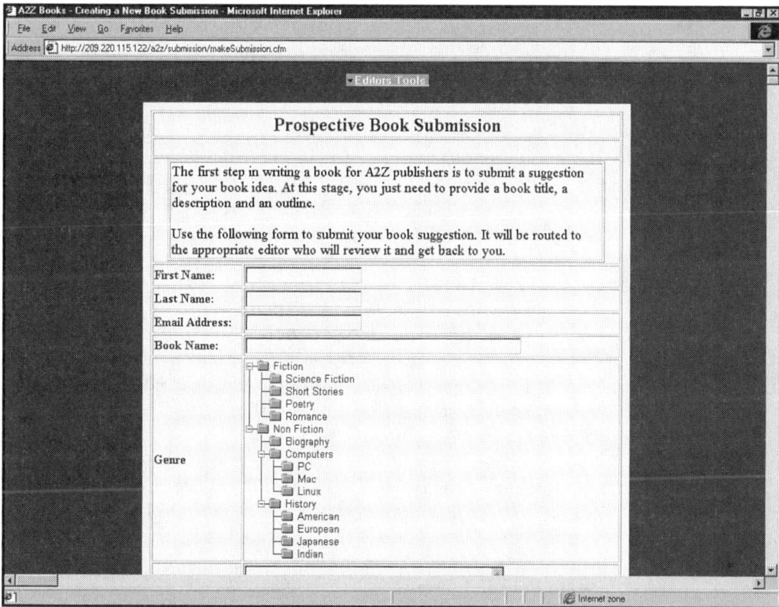

FIGURE 9.8
The VSS skin applied to a genre hierarchy.

The *MODE* Attribute A tree is normally used to display hierarchical data so that a user can select within it. The selection process can work in three ways:

NAV	It can be used as a basic navigation element, in which any item clicked from the tree will redirect you to the URL associated with the selection.
SELECT	A tree can be used as a form element, submitted a single choice to the next page only when the user submits the form.
MULTISELECT	A tree can allow the user to choose multiple selections on a form, submitted as a single choice to the next page only when the user submits the form.

Listing 9.4 shows a sample tree control, which uses `<CFA_TREEITEM>` tags to statically populate a tree.

Listing 9.4 *genreTree.cfm*—A Sample Tree Control

```
<!---
File:          /customtags/a2z/genreTree.cfm
Author:        jeff tapper
Date:          01/15/2000
Description:   CFA_Tree to display Genres of a book store, and indicate
                whether the publishers are currently accepting submissions
                of that genre.
```

continues

Listing 9.4 Continued

```
Notes:
--->

<cfa_tree name="genreTree" skin="vss" mode="multiselect" bReset=1>
    <cfa_treeColumnHeader name="A"
            label="<font face=arial size=1>Accepting Submissions?</font>"
            width="40">

    <cfa_treeItem label="Fiction" value="Fiction" expand=TRUE>
        <cfa_treeColumn name="A" icon="na"/>
        <cfa_treeItem label="Science Fiction" value="SciFi"/>
        <cfa_treeItem label="Short Stories" value="ShortStories"/>
        <cfa_treeItem label="Poetry" value="Poetry"/>
        <cfa_treeItem label="Romance" value="Romance"/>
    </cfa_treeItem>

    <cfa_treeItem label="Non Fiction" value="Non-Fiction" expand=TRUE>
        <cfa_treeColumn name="A" icon="na"/>
        <cfa_treeItem label="Biography" value="Biography">
            <cfa_treeColumn name="A" icon="off"/>
        </cfa_treeItem>

        <cfa_treeItem label="Computers" value="Computers" expand=TRUE>
            <cfa_treeColumn name="A" icon="on"/>
            <cfa_treeItem label="PC" value="PC"/>
            <cfa_treeItem label="Mac" value="Mac"/>
            <cfa_treeItem label="Linux" value="Linux"/>
        </cfa_treeItem>

        <cfa_treeItem label="History" value="History" expand=TRUE>
            <cfa_treeItem label="American" value="American">
                <cfa_treeColumn name="A" icon="off"/>
            </cfa_treeItem>

            <cfa_treeItem label="European" value="European">
                          <cfa_treeColumn name="A" icon="off"/>
            </cfa_treeItem>

            <cfa_treeItem label="Japanese" value="Japanese">
                <cfa_treeColumn name="A" icon="on"/>
            </cfa_treeItem>

            <cfa_treeItem label="Indian" value="Indian">
                <cfa_treeColumn name="A" icon="on"/>
            </cfa_treeItem>
        </cfa_treeItem>

    </cfa_treeItem>

</cfa_tree>
```

The tree definition begins with the <CFA_TREE> tag, which is called with a name genreTree, the VSS skin, and in MULTISELECT mode. Also provided is the bReset=1 attribute, indicating that this tree should be reset when it is loaded. Without the bReset value, the tree will be stored as a session variable and loaded from memory for subsequent requests. Earlier, Figure 9.8 showed the tree created with the code in Listing 9.5.

While you are still in development, it's a good idea to leave bReset set to 1; however, before launching the site, setting this flag to 0 (off) will help performance.

Just below the tree tag is a <CFA_TREECOLUMNHEADER> tag, indicating that there is one column, which should be labeled Accepting Submissions. If you need to have multiple columns next to the tree, you will need a <CFA_TREECOLUMNHEADER> tag for each column. There is no limit to the number of columns you may use. This will give you the option of putting a Yes (green dot), No (red dot), or Not Applicable (gray dot) next to any item.

Inside the tree are several <CFA_TREEITEM> tags, each with a label that appears to the user and a value that's passed with the form. The first of these tree items, labeled Fiction, also has the expand="true" attribute, indicating that any items in folders below this item should be displayed as well. If an item is to have other items under it—such as Fiction has Science Fiction, Poetry, Short Stories, and Romance under it—the sub-items must be placed between the <CFA_TREEITEM> and </CFA_TREEITEM> tags. Items without sub-items can be coded either as <CFA_TREEITEM label="American" value="American"></CFA_TREEITEM> or, more succinctly, <CFA_TREEITEM label="American" value="American"/>. As such, we create the hierarchy.

To put a Yes, No, or NA dot in a column next to a TreeItem, you must use a <CFA_TREECOLUMN> tag between that item's opening and closing <CFA_TREEITEM> tags. For trees with multiple columns, you must use a <CFA_TREECOLUMN> tag for each column. This is done throughout to indicate in which genres publishers are currently accepting submissions. As you can see, they are accepting no submissions in fiction, but they are accepting some computer and non-Western history submissions.

Style Attributes <CFA_TREE> has four optional style-related attributes, as shown in Table 9.3.

▶ Appendix A details all attributes for <CFA_TREE>.

Table 9.3 <CFA_TREE> Style Attributes

Attribute	Description
bShowItemIcon	Specifies whether to display the icon (the folder graphics in the included skins). Earlier in this chapter, Figure 9.8 showed the VSS skin with bShowItemIcon set to no.
stNormalStyle	Specifies the name of a structure holding style object property information for the normal item state.

continues

Table 9.3 Continued

Attribute	Description
`StHighlightStyle`	Specifies the name of a structure holding style object property information for the highlighted item state.
`StLinkStyle`	Specifies the name of a structure holding style object property information for the link item state if the `NAV` mode is selected.

Using the Tree Control Outside a Form When using a tree control in `MODE="nav"`, users can navigate to a tree item, click it, and go directly to another page. The URL of the page is set as the value of the TreeItem.

Using a Custom Display Style By default, the tree control uses images from `system/images/icons`. If you prefer to store your images in another directory, you can specify the directory in the `treeImagesDir` attribute.

To create your own display style, follow these steps:

1. Create the following icons, storing them all in the same directory:
   - `Folder.gif`
   - `Folder_open.gif`
   - `node.gif`
   - `connector.gif`
   - `branch.gif`
2. Call the `<CFA_TREE>` tag with the `TREEIMAGESDIR` attribute, indicating the directory where your custom graphics are located.

NOTE Tree icons must be 16×16 GIF images.

HTML Editor Control

When using handlers to edit information, you usually use basic form controls. Spectra offers the `<CFA_HTMLEDITOR>` tag as an alternative to the `TextEdit` control. This control embeds a WYSIWYG HTML editor into a text area, allowing users who don't know HTML to mark up text. At the click of a toolbar button, they can produce HTML formatting in the selected text. The control hides the HTML codes.

These controls can be coded into item handlers, PLP handlers, rule processor handlers, and in any other form that requires HTML text manipulation. The only requirement is that they be contained within a form.

TIP For more information on each button, position your mouse over the button until the ToolTip appears.

In Listing 9.5, you can see the HTML Editor Control used in the `Author` edit handler to allow an author to add HTML to his biography. Figure 9.9 shows the result of this code.

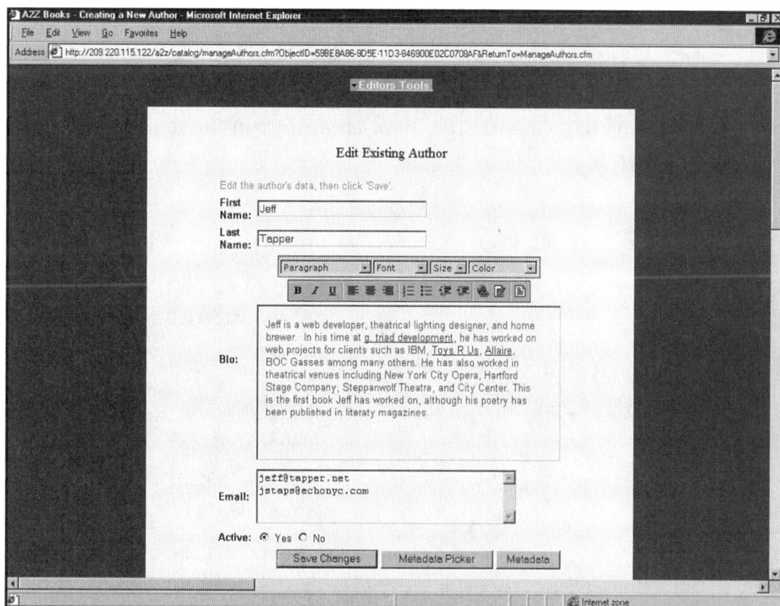

FIGURE 9.9
The HTML Editor Control used in the Author ObjectType edit handler.

Listing 9.5 ***editAuthor.cfm*—Allowing Authors to Personalize Their Bios with HTML**

```
<TR>
<TD><FONT FACE="arial" SIZE="-1"><b>Bio:</b></FONT></TD>
<TD>
<cfa_htmlEditor
        name = "Bio"
        height = "200"
        width = "400"
        value = "#Trim( Author.Bio )#"
        form = "AuthorForm">
</TD>
</TR>
```

▶ **See** Chapter 10 for the full listing of the edit handler for the Author object.

Customizing the Menu Bar Contents By default, `<CFA_HTMLEDITOR>` displays drop-down menus that contain the following items:

- *Paragraph.* Normal paragraph (`<P>`), Header 1 (`<H1>`) through Header 6 (`<H6>`), and Pre (`<PRE>`)
- *Font.* Arial, Verdana, Times, and Courier
- *Size.* 1 through 7
- *Color.* Black, Gray, Dark Red, Navy, and Dark Green

`<CFA_HTMLEditor>` also has an optional attribute, `STFORMATTING`, that will allow interactive developers to customize the items appearing on the toolbar. The `STFORMATTING` attribute contains four 2-dimensional arrays:

- `aParagraph` controls items displayed in the Paragraph drop-down listbox:

`[arrayindex][1]`	HTML value to be applied (for example, `<H1>`).
`[arrayindex][2]`	Text to be displayed in the Paragraph styles drop-down listbox (for example, `Header 1`).

- `aFont` controls items displayed in the Font drop-down listbox:

`[arrayindex][1]`	`FontName` value (for example, `arial,geneva, sans-serif`).
`[arrayindex][2]`	Text to display in the Font drop-down listbox (for example, Arial).

- `aSize` controls items displayed in the Size drop-down listbox:

`[arrayindex][1]`	`FontSize` value (for example, 3).
`[arrayindex][2]`	Text to display in the Size drop-down listbox (for example, 3).

- `aColor` controls items displayed in the Color drop-down listbox:

`[arrayindex][1]`	`FontColor` inline style setting (for example, `color: red`).
`[arrayindex][2]`	Text to display in the Color drop-down listbox (for example, Red).

CAUTION

If you provide a `stFormatting` structure, it must contain all options for all drop-down menus that you want to appear in the control. None of the default items will appear unless they are in your `stFormatting` structure.

Listing 9.6 shows a custom use of `<CFA_HTMLEDITOR>` with the `STFORMATTING` attribute.

Listing 9.6 *htmlEditor.cfm*—A Custom Use of *<CFA_HTMLEDITOR>*

```
<!---
File:           \customtags\a2z\htmlEditor.cfm
Author:         Jeff TapperDate:          1/15/2000
Description:    Displays an HTML Editor with a custom tool bar.
Notes:
--->
<CFSCRIPT>
// Initialize the structures
    stToolbar = StructNew();
    stToolbar.aParagraph = ArrayNew(2);
    stToolbar.aFont = ArrayNew(2);
    stToolbar.aSize = ArrayNew(2);
    stToolbar.aColor = ArrayNew(2);
// set the paragraph menu options
    stToolbar.aParagraph[1][1] = "<P>";
    stToolbar.aParagraph[1][2] = "Normal Paragraph";
    stToolbar.aParagraph[2][1] = "<TT>";
    stToolbar.aParagraph[2][2] = "Teletype";
    stToolbar.aParagraph[3][1] = "<PRE>";
    stToolbar.aParagraph[3][2] = "Pre-Formatted";
// set the font menu options
    stToolbar.aFont[1][1] = "serif";
    stToolbar.aFont[1][2] = "Serif";
    stToolbar.aFont[2][1] = "sans-serif";
    stToolbar.aFont[2][2] = "Sans Serif";
    stToolbar.aFont[3][1] = "cursive";
    stToolbar.aFont[3][2] = "Cursive";
// set the font size menu options
    stToolbar.aSize[1][1] = "7";
    stToolbar.aSize[1][2] = "Biggest";
    stToolbar.aSize[2][1] = "6";
    stToolbar.aSize[2][2] = "Bigger";
    stToolbar.aSize[3][1] = "5";
    stToolbar.aSize[3][2] = "Big";
    stToolbar.aSize[4][1] = "4";
    stToolbar.aSize[4][2] = "Normal";
    stToolbar.aSize[5][1] = "3";
    stToolbar.aSize[5][2] = "Small";
    stToolbar.aSize[6][1] = "2";
    stToolbar.aSize[6][2] = "Smaller";
    stToolbar.aSize[7][1] = "1";
    stToolbar.aSize[7][2] = "Smallest";
// set the color menu options
    stToolbar.aColor[1][1] = "FF0000";
    stToolbar.aColor[1][2] = "Red";
    stToolbar.aColor[2][1] = "00FF00";
    stToolbar.aColor[2][2] = "Green";
    stToolbar.aColor[3][1] = "0000FF";
    stToolbar.aColor[3][2] = "Blue";
    stToolbar.aColor[4][1] = "FFFFFF";
    stToolbar.aColor[4][2] = "White";
```

continues

Listing 9.6 Continued

```
    stToolbar.aColor[5][1] = "000000";
    stToolbar.aColor[5][2] = "Black";
</cfSCRIPT>

<!--- invoke the editor --->
<cfa_controlHandler name="htmlEditForm">
        <cfa_htmlEditor
            name = "teaser"
            height = "200"
            width = "400"
            value = ""
            form="htmlEditForm"
            stFormatting = "#stToolbar#"
        >
        <input type="submit">
</cfa_controlHandler>
```

Listing 9.6 begins by initializing a `stToolbar` structure and 4 two-dimensional arrays, one each for Paragraph, Font, Size, and Color. Next, the paragraph array is populated with three entries. The first sets a normal paragraph as being contained within `<P>` tags. The second sets a Teletype paragraph as being contained within `<TT>` tags. Finally, a Preformatted paragraph is defined as being contained within `<PRE>` tags.

Next, the Font menu is populated. In this instance, a user would have three font options: Serif, Sans-Serif, and Cursive.

The Font Size menu is then populated. While the array sets numerical values to represent each of the 7 available font sizes, the user is given options ranging from biggest to smallest.

Then, the Color menu is populated. The values used by the system are hexadecimal codes relating to the amount of red, green, and blue used to construct that color.

Finally, the HTML Editor is invoked and passed the `stToolbar` structure that you have created.

NOTE The HTML Editor works only in Internet Explorer 4 and 5. In other browsers it will appear as a text area.

Tab Dialogs

Spectra provides a Tab control that you can use to partition the display of complex data. The Tab control is defined through the use of `<CFA_TABAREA>` and `<CFA_TABPAGE>` tags. You've already seen tabbed dialogs used throughout the Webtop, in places such as the Object Type Designer (see Figure 9.10).

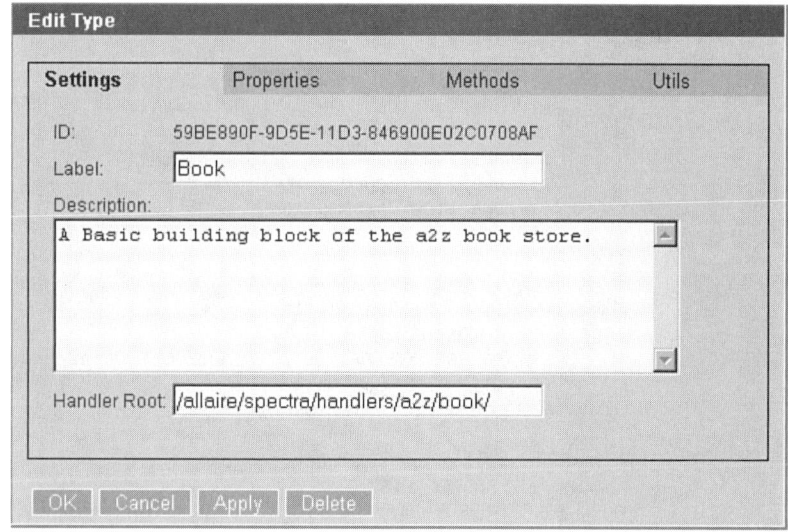

FIGURE 9.10
The Settings, Properties, Methods, and Utils links of the Object Type Designer are really a tabbed dialog.

Listing 9.7 shows a tab area control being integrated into the form of the edit handler for the `BookSubmission` object.

Listing 9.7 *AuthorEdit.cfm*—Integrating a Tab Area Control into a Form

```
<!---
File:            /catalog/AuthorEdit.cfm
Author:          david adenDate:          12/31/1999
Description:     Handler for the BookSubmission Object Type -- the
                  handler that is called when the anonymous user creates
                  a new Book Submission.
Notes:
Change History: 1/15/2000 (JT) - Added Tab Control to form
--->

<CFA_HANDLER
        OBJECT="NewSub" >

     <!--- Second time through (after we submitted) --->
     <CFIF ISDEFINED("FORM.SubmitSubmission")>

          <!--- Create a structure to use to update the
                submission object. --->
<CFSCRIPT>
               // create the struct
               stProperties = StructNew();

               // Populate the Struct from the form
               stProperties.Label = FORM.BookName;
```

continues

Listing 9.7 Continued

```
        stProperties.FirstName = FORM.FirstName;
        stProperties.LastName = FORM.LastName;
        stProperties.Email = FORM.Email;
        stProperties.BookName = FORM.BookName;
        stProperties.Genre = FORM.Genre;
        stProperties.Description = FORM.Description;
        stProperties.Outline = FORM.Outline;
    </CFSCRIPT>

    <!--- Update the Content Item --->
    <CFA_CONTENTOBJECTDATA
        DATASOURCE = "#REQUEST.CFA.A2ZBOOKS.Datasource#"
        OBJECTID="#NewSub.ObjectID#"
        STPROPERTIES="#stProperties#"/>

    <!--- Get the current workflow data --->
    <CFA_WORKFLOWGETLIST
        DATASOURCE="#REQUEST.CFA.A2ZBOOKS.Datasource#"
        WORKFLOWID="#SESSION.WorkFlowID#"
        R_STWORKFLOWAGENDA="stWorkFlowAgenda">

    <!--- We need to get ID for the Task this was called from
           by checking
for active tasks (there should only be 1). --->
    <CFIF LISTLEN(STWORKFLOWAGENDA.LACTIVETASKS) NEQ 1>
        <CFOUTPUT>
            Error! Instead of one active task, there's
                #ListLen(SESSION.stworkFlowAgenda.lActiveTasks)#!<BR>
        </CFOUTPUT>
        <CFABORT>
    <CFELSE>
        <CFSET ACTIVETASK = LISTFIRST(STWORKFLOWAGENDA.LACTIVETASKS)>
    </CFIF>

    <!--- Since this is being done as part of a Workflow, and so is
           called from a step, we need to mark the step as done. --->
    <CFA_TASKEND
        DATASOURCE="#REQUEST.CFA.A2ZBOOKS.Datasource#"
        TASKID="#ActiveTask#"
        WORKFLOWID="#SESSION.WorkFlowID#">

    <!--- Now update the Workflow (to kick off notification to
           the next step). --->
    <CFA_WORKFLOWEXECUTE
        DATASOURCE="#REQUEST.CFA.A2ZBOOKS.Datasource#"
        WORKFLOWID="#SESSION.WorkFlowID#">

    <CFOUTPUT>
        <!--- Show a success message --->
        Submission successfully updated!<BR>
        <BR>
```

```
            Someone will get back to you concerning your submission.<BR>
            <BR>
        </CFOUTPUT>

    <!--- First time through we're going to display the object. --->
    <CFELSE>

        <CFOUTPUT>
        <!--- Get the query string --->
<CFSET IIF( LEN(CGI.QUERY_STRING),
        "thisQueryString='?#cgi.query_string#'",
        "thisQueryString=''" )>

        <CFA_TABAREA WIDTH=400 HEIGHT=200 TABWIDTH=70>

        <CFA_TABPAGE NAME="OverView" SELECTED="Yes">
        <FORM NAME="BookSubForm"
        ACTION="#cgi.script_name##thisQueryString#" METHOD="post">

        <INPUT TYPE="Hidden"
        NAME="NewSubmissionID" VALUE="#NewSub.ObjectID#">

        <TABLE BORDER="1" WIDTH="620">
            <TR>
                <TD COLSPAN="2" ALIGN="CENTER">
                <FONT SIZE="+2">
                    <B>Prospective Book Submission</B>
                </FONT>
                </TD>
            </TR>
            <TR>
                <TD COLSPAN="2"> </TD>
            </TR>
            <TR>
                <TD COLSPAN="2" ALIGN="CENTER">
                <TABLE BORDER="1" WIDTH="575">
                    <TR>
                        <TD>
                <FONT SIZE="+1">
                    The first step in writing a book for A2Z publishers is
                    to submit a suggestion for your book idea. At this
                    stage, you just need to provide a book title, a
                    description and an outline.<BR>
                    <BR>
                    Use the following form to submit your book suggestion.
                    It will be routed to the appropriate editor who will
                    review it and get back to you.
                </FONT>
                        </TD>
                    </TR>
                </TABLE>
                </TD>
            </TR>
```

continues

Listing 9.7 Continued

```
        </TABLE>
    </CFA_TABPAGE>
    <CFA_TABPAGE NAME="About You" SELECTED="No">
        <TABLE>
        <TR>
            <TD><B>First Name:</B></TD>
            <TD><INPUT TYPE="Text" NAME="FirstName"
            SIZE="20" VALUE=""></TD>
        </TR>
        <TR>
            <TD><B>Last Name:</B></TD>
            <TD><INPUT TYPE="Text" NAME="LastName"
            SIZE="20" VALUE=""></TD>
        </TR>
        <TR>
            <TD><B>Email Address:</B></TD>
            <TD><INPUT TYPE="Text" NAME="Email"
            SIZE="20" VALUE=""></TD>
        </TR>
        </TABLE>
    </CFA_TABPAGE>
    <CFA_TABPAGE NAME="About the Book" SELECTED="No">
        <TABLE>
        <TR>
            <TD><B>Book Name:</B></TD>
            <TD><INPUT TYPE="Text" NAME="BookName"
            SIZE="50" VALUE=""></TD>
        </TR>
        <TR>
            <TD><B>Description</B></TD>
            <TD><TEXTAREA COLS=40 ROWS=5 NAME="Description">
            </TEXTAREA></TD>
        </TR>
        <TR>
            <TD><B>Outline</B></TD>
            <TD><TEXTAREA COLS=40 ROWS=5 NAME="Outline">
            </TEXTAREA></TD>
        </TR>
        <!--- NEED TO MAKE THIS A SELECTION BOX. --->
        <TR>
            <TD><B>Genre</B></TD>
            <TD>
                <CF_GENRETREE>
            </TD>
        </TR>
        </TABLE>
    </CFA_TABPAGE>
    <CFA_TABPAGE NAME="Submit">
        <TABLE>
        <TR>
            <TD COLSPAN="2" ALIGN="CENTER">
```

```
                    <INPUT NAME="SubmitSubmission"
                    TYPE="Submit" VALUE="Submit">
                    <INPUT NAME="Cancel" TYPE="Submit" VALUE="Cancel">
                </TD>
            </TR>
            </TABLE>
        </FORM>
        </CFA_TABPAGE>
    </CFA_TABAREA>
    </CFOUTPUT>

    </CFIF>

</CFA_HANDLER>
```


▶ **See** Chapter 13, "Working with Workflow," for the first half of this edit handler.

The tab area begins about halfway through, after it has been determined that `form.SubmitSubmission` isn't defined; therefore, the form should be displayed. The tab area is passed attributes for height, width, and tab width, defining the size in pixels that should be devoted to the tab area and the maximum width to allow each individual tab. Next, a tab page is defined, with a name that appears on the tab and a flag indicating that this is the selected tab. Then, the form is opened, and some introductory text is displayed before this tab page is closed. The next tab page is defined with the name About You, and the selected flag is set to No. Then, form fields are provided for users to enter their information, and the tab page is closed. A third tab page, named About the Book, solicits a name, description, outline, and genre from the user. For genre, the `<cf_genreTree>` tag you created back in Listing 9.4 is called. Finally, the fourth tab page is defined with the name Submit and contains the Submit button for the form.

When you run the code in Listing 9.7, by default, the introduction tab will be selected, and you will view the page as seen in Figure 9.11. Clicking the About You tab allows you to enter your personal information, as shown in Figure 9.12. Clicking the About the Book tab allows you to enter the details on the book you are submitting (see Figure 9.13). Finally, the Submit tab allows you to send in all the information.

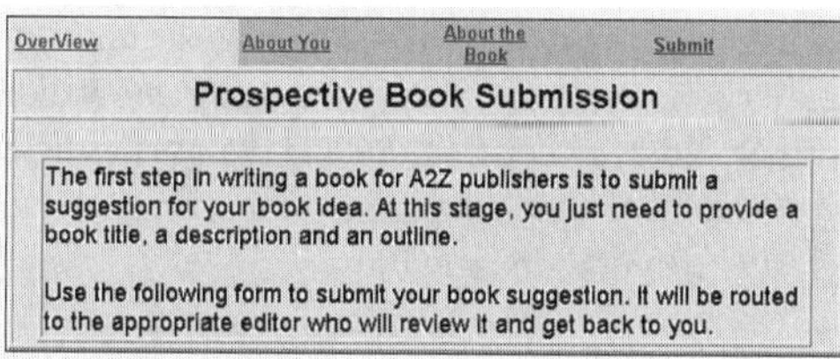

FIGURE 9.11
The Prospective Book Submission form begins with an introduction to the book submission process. Note that the OverView tab is selected.

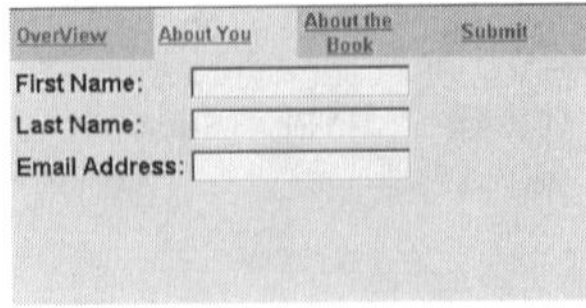

FIGURE 9.12
The About You tab asks a prospective author for his first name, last name, and email address.

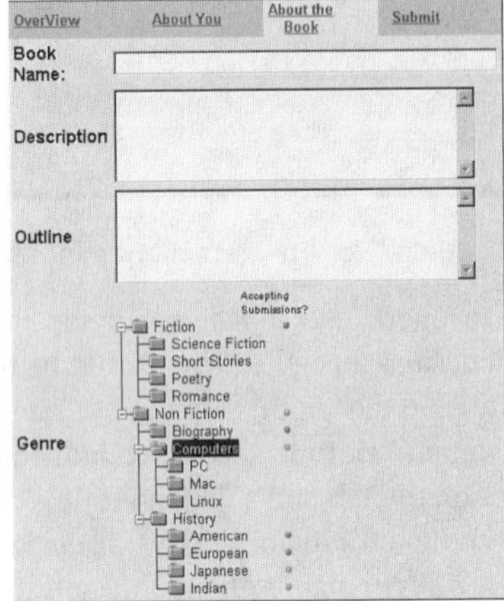

FIGURE 9.13
The About the Book tab provides form fields for the title, description, and outline and the tree to choose a genre.

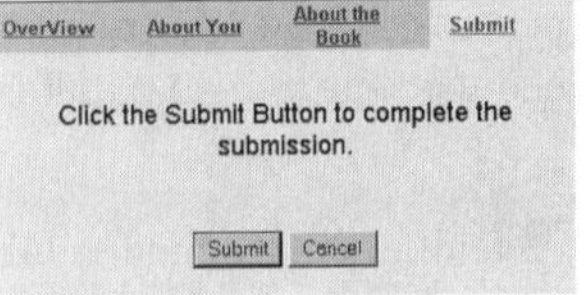

FIGURE 9.14
The Submit tab prompts a user to click the Submit button to complete his entry.

Using Browser Tools

A requirement for most modern Web applications is that their display is customized to make the best use of the capabilities of the user's browser. A user running the latest version of Internet Explorer can experience your site with formatting and validation through JavaScript and DHTML. A user with an old browser that doesn't support JavaScript should still be able to use your application. When he visits, any functions that were occurring on the client-side will need to be replaced with server-side functions.

The biggest difference among the browsers is in their differing levels of support for

- Cascading style sheets
- JavaScript and DHTML

- Tables
- Frames

To help designers and developers overcome these differences, Spectra provides the `<CFA_BROWSER>` tag, which detects the type of browser a user has and populates the `request.cfa.browser` structure with information about the capabilities of this user's browser.

Table 9.4 lists the keys in the `request.cfa.browser` structure:

Table 9.4 The Keys of the *request.cfa.browser* Structure

Key	Description
`Browser`	High-level browser identifier. Values include `MSIE`, `Mozilla`, `Opera`, and `Other`.
`Name`	Browser name.
`MinorVersion`	Browser minor version.
`MajorVersion`	Browser major version.
`ParentAgent`	The name of the browser from which this browser inherits its definition.
`UserAgent`	HTTP `UserAgent` string, as passed by the browser.
`Frames`	Boolean indicating whether the browser supports frames.
`Tables`	Boolean indicating whether the browser supports tables.
`Cookies`	Boolean indicating whether the browser supports cookies. This indicates only whether this browser version can support cookies. Users can disable this feature.
`JavaApplets`	Boolean indicating whether the browser supports Java applets. This indicates only whether this browser version can support Java applets. Users can disable this feature.
`JavaScript`	Boolean indicating whether the browser supports JavaScript. This indicates only whether this browser version can support JavaScript. Users can disable this feature.
`JavaScriptVer`	Version of JavaScript enabled on the browser.
`DHTML`	Boolean indicating whether the browser supports DHTML. This indicates only whether this browser version can support DHTML. Users can disable this feature.
`VBScript`	Boolean indicating whether the browser supports VBScript. This indicates only whether this browser version can support VBScript. Users can disable this feature.
`BackgroundSounds`	Boolean indicating whether the browser supports background sounds.
`StyleSheets`	Boolean indicating whether the browser supports cascading style sheets.
`ActiveXControls`	Boolean indicating whether this browser version can support ActiveX controls. Users can disable this feature.

Managing Browser Definitions

The <CFA_BROWSER> tag updates the browser definition database automatically each time it detects a new browser type. You can view the browser definitions in either the System Design or Site Design sections of the Webtop by clicking the Browser Manager link. From here, you can add, modify, or delete browser definitions. Figure 9.15 shows the browser tree.

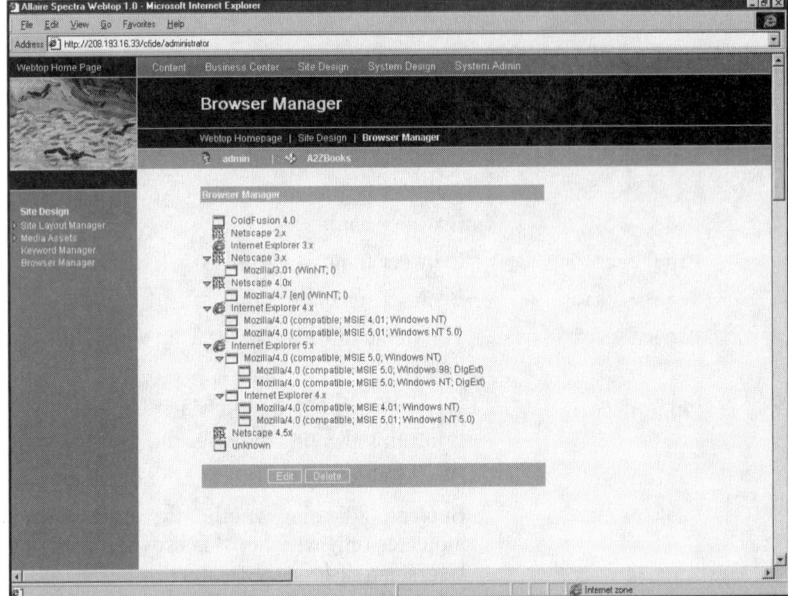

FIGURE 9.15
The browser tree shows the hierarchy of browsers.

The browser definition is based on a system of browser inheritance. As you saw in Figure 9.15, both the Windows NT and Windows 98 versions of Internet Explorer 5 inherit from the Internet Explorer 5.x entry.

To change the settings for a browser, select the browser to edit from the tree and click the Submit button. Figure 9.16 shows the Edit Browser page.

Spectra maintains its browser definitions in the `browser.wddx` file, found in the `spectrainstalldirectory/database` directory. Changes made in the Edit Browser screen will be written to this file.

CAUTION

Don't modify the `browser.wddx` file manually.

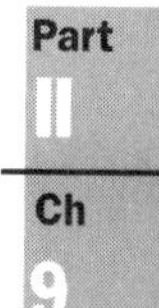

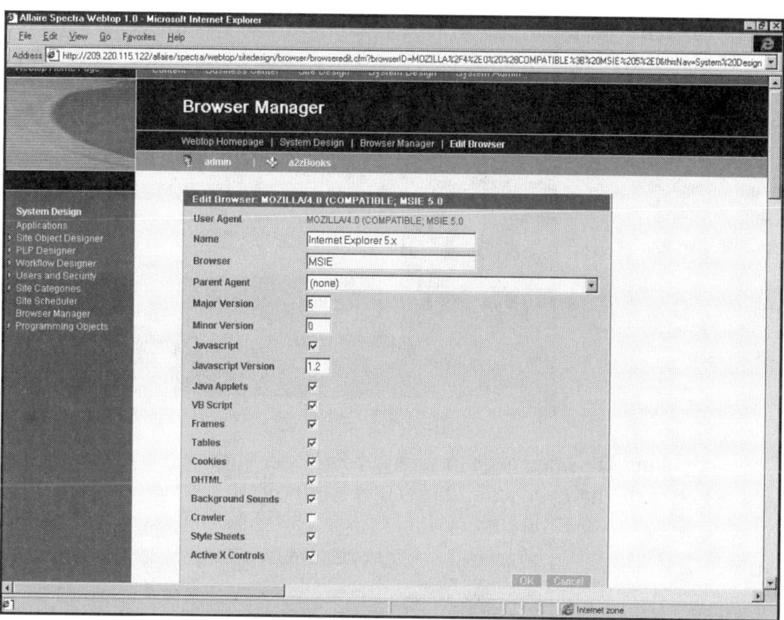

FIGURE 9.16
Here you see the settings for Internet Explorer 5.x.

Graceful Browser Degradation Handling

Once `request.cfa.browser` is populated, you can determine the browser capabilities of individual users and process the pages appropriately.

To facilitate this, add the following lines after the `<CFA_APPLICATIONINITIALIZE>` tag in your `application.cfm` file:

```
<CFIF NOT ISDEFINED("request.cfa.broswer")>
     <CFA_BROWSER>
</CFIF>
```

Then, we will drop in a `MARQUEE` tag (which is available only to browsers that support VBScript) on the home page:

```
<cfif isDefined("request.cfa.browser") AND
      request.cfa.browser.vbScript is TRUE>
     <MARQUEE BEHAVIOR='scroll' ALIGN='top'
          DIRECTION='left' WIDTH='400' HEIGHT='0'>
          Welcome to the a2z Book Store.  Click the "Browse Our Catalog"
          button to view the catalog.
     </MARQUEE>
</cfif>
```

First, this determines if the `request.cfa.browser` structure exists; if it does, it tests to see if the current browser supports VBScript.

Open the page created earlier in Netscape, and you will see a screen like the one in Figure 9.17. Since Netscape doesn't support VBScript, the welcome text appears as static text.

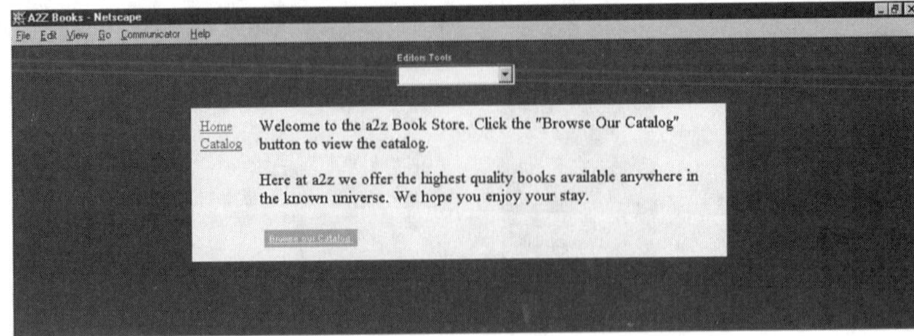

FIGURE 9.17
In Netscape, the text appears as text, since Netscape doesn't support VBScript.

Opening the same page in Internet Explorer shows the welcome text scrolling across the screen in marquee style, as seen in Figure 9.18.

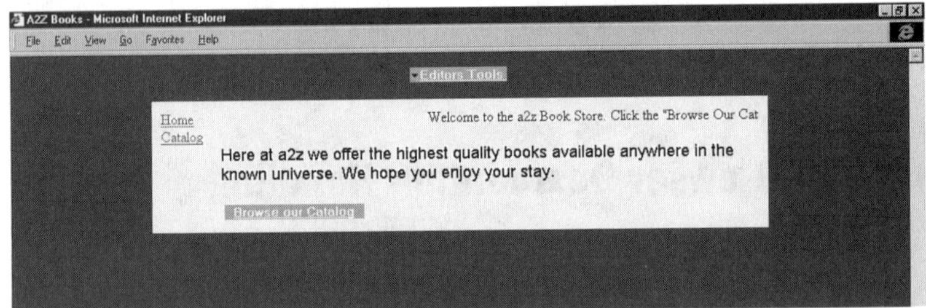

FIGURE 9.18
In Internet Explorer, the text scrolls marquee-style across the page.

Securing UI Controls

When Spectra user interface controls are implemented through ContentObject Types, you can use Spectra security to control access and display based on user ID. For a2zBooks, you can decide to display the HTML control only to users who are authorized to edit content.

To use Spectra security to restrict access to a user interface control, follow these steps:

1. Access the Object Finder and display a list containing the desired user interface ContentObject Type (for example, button).
2. Click the icon for the instance to be secured.
3. Click the Security link.
4. Choose the method to be secured (see Figure 9.19).
5. Choose the users or groups that are authorized to use the method, and click the arrow pointing to Granted.

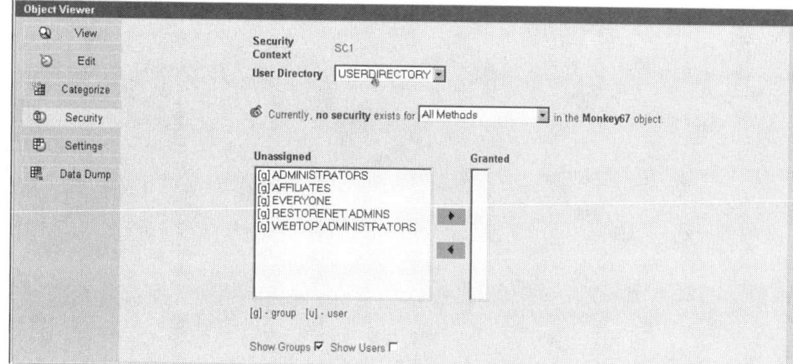

FIGURE 9.19
Choose the method to be secured and the users/groups who have permission to use that method.

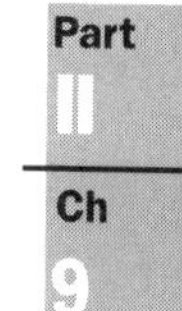

CHAPTER 10

Creating and Managing Content

In this chapter

Understanding Spectra Content Management

Content management is the heart of the Spectra system. In Spectra, virtually every element is implemented as a ContentObject (CO) Type, or simply an Object Type, with associated properties and methods that are used as the pattern from which individual Content Items (objects) are created. Using CO Types as the basis for storing and manipulating data gives you a tremendous amount of flexibility, because Object Types can be highly customized to fit your particular development needs. They also allow you to encapsulate functionality—such as handlers to edit or display an individual piece of content—into easily maintained CFML templates.

This chapter describes basic methods for creating, editing, and deleting Content Items. For an in-depth description of ContentObject Types, including how to define them, see Chapter 6, "Introduction to Spectra Programming."

The key terms to understand for Content Management (covered in Chapter 6 and in Chapter 11, "Working with Meta Data") include

- *ContentObject Type.* Defines a specific type of object. For example, "News Article" is a type of object, as is "User Profile," "Button," or "Workflow Task." In some cases this may be referred to as an "Object Type" or, if the context is obvious, a "Type."
- *Content Item, ContentObject, or Object.* An instance of a ContentObject Type. The ContentObject Type provides the pattern from which each individual instance of an object is created. For example, a News Article ContentObject Type would be used as the pattern from which an actual News Article Content Item (individual object) would be created. Most of the Allaire documentation uses the term Content Item, but the terms *Object* and *instance* are also used. In this chapter, Content Item and Object are used interchangeably.
- *Property.* A single element of data associated with a ContentObject Type; an attribute of a ContentObject Type. When you use Spectra tags to create a Content Item (a new object that is an instance of a ContentObject Type), it is created with all the properties of its parent ContentObject Type. For example, a News Article ContentObject Type would include properties such as `Title`, `Author`, `Teaser`, and `Copy Body`. Each individual News Article Content Item possesses these same properties.
- *Method.* An action that can be performed on the data held by a Content Item. Methods are associated with ContentObject Types and can be invoked on each Content Item. For example, the News Article ContentObject Type would have a `Display` method. You can then invoke this method on an instance of the News Article ContentObject Type to display an individual article (Content Item). Methods are implemented in CFML, and the templates you write to implement them are referred to as *handlers*. Spectra provides a set of default handlers that are automatically used if you don't define specific handlers for your ContentObject Types. For more information on default handlers, see Chapter 6.

- *Meta data*. Information or data that describes other information. For example, a News Article Content Item might hold a story about a new product release from our A2Z Company. When we enter the article into Spectra, we might want to categorize the article as "favorable press" or as a "review." Such categorization data is called *meta data* because it is information about other information, in this case the news article.

ContentObject Types

This chapter will cover how to use ContentObject Type methods to create, edit, and delete Content Items and associate meta data with Content Items. Spectra distinguishes between several flavors of ContentObject Types:

- *User-defined*. These are the ContentObject Types defined by the Interactive Developer and used in specific applications.
- *System-defined*. These are ContentObject Types defined by Allaire and shipped with Spectra. They include items such as the User Profile, which contains personalization information (see Chapter 18, "Implementing Personalization," for more information). Generally, interactions with system-defined ContentObject Types are accomplished through the Webtop or programmatically by using Spectra custom tags.
- *Core ContentObject Types*. Allaire distinguishes between most system-defined ContentObject Types and what it refers to as *Core* Object Types. Core Object Types are fully developed object types that are most often used as embedded objects. This category includes the *File* ContentObject Type (which can hold any MIME type file) and the *Flash* ContentObject Type for managing Flash files. Appendix C, "COAPI Data Types," defines these types and their associated properties and methods.

This chapter focuses primarily on user-defined CO Types, but the principles are largely the same for System and Core ContentObject Types.

Managing Webtop Content

Although the Webtop can be used to create, edit, or delete Content Items (Objects), it is most often used to handle a temporary administrative need. For most Spectra applications, you will code your own templates to allow users to create, edit, and delete content related to your application.

Creating Content Items

The following text refers to and uses the a2zBooks demonstration application included on the accompanying CD-ROM. This includes basic Author and Book ContentObject Types that are used throughout this chapter's examples.

To create a new Book Content Item, do the following:

1. Open the Webtop (logging in as required).
2. Click System Design.
3. Click Site Object Designer in the left column.
4. From the sublist, click Object Finder. A grid of Content Items appears.
5. In the Filter By Type drop-down, select Book. The screen refreshes and displays a list of existing Content Items that were previously created from the Book ContentObject Type (see Figure 10.1).

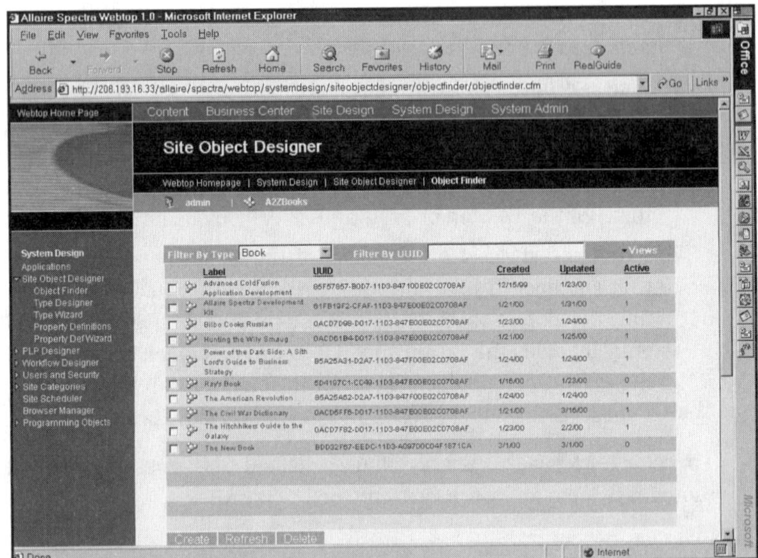

FIGURE 10.1
The Object Finder provides an interface for finding and displaying basic information on existing Content Items.

6. Click Create at the bottom of the grid display. The Object Viewer opens and provides a form that displays all the properties of the Book Content Item.
7. Enter **`My New Book`** in the Title and Label fields (see Figure 10.2). `Title` is a user-defined property of the Book ContentObject Type; `Label` is a Spectra-generated property created for all ContentObject Types. The Webtop displays the `Label` property in lists of Content Items.
8. Enter information into the Edition, ISBN, Pages, and Price fields. Select a publication date from the drop-down list and choose whether to display the book in the Catalog.
9. Click Save Changes to save the new Book data.
10. Close the Object Viewer.

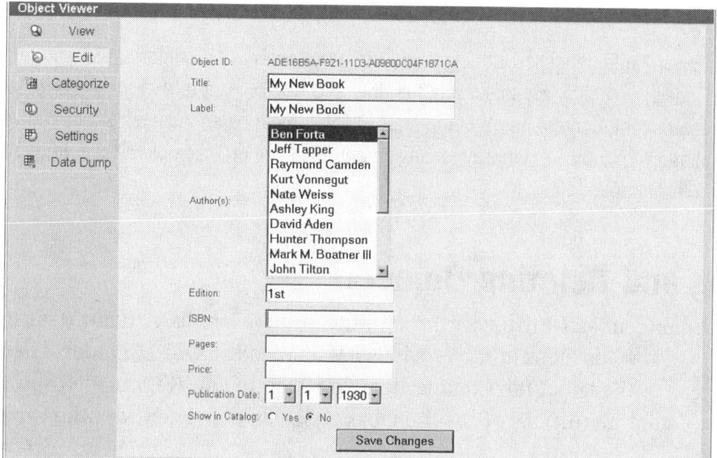

FIGURE 10.2
The Object Viewer allows you to enter and save data for a new Content Item.

11. In the Object Finder, click Refresh at the bottom of the page. The page updates and displays My New Book in the list of existing Book Content Items (see Figure 10.3).

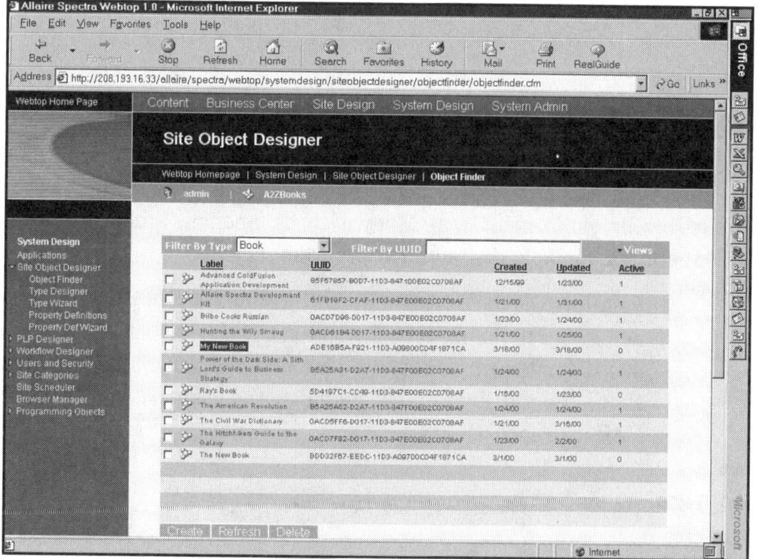

FIGURE 10.3
When the Object Finder is refreshed, it will show the new Book Content Item you created.

NOTE Behind the scenes, Spectra creates a new Book Content Item when the Object Viewer is open and then invokes its edit handler to add information to the new object. When the Content Item is created—but before you add the data specific to the new ContentObject Type—the

continues

continued

Object Finder refreshes. Until you add the new Content Item's information and refresh the Object Finder, it will show an object with no label and `Active` set to `0`. If for some reason you don't finish entering the Content Item's information, it will remain as an incomplete entry in your database. A strategy for programmatically managing and cleaning up incomplete Content Items is presented later in this chapter.

Editing and Deleting Objects

Editing an existing object through the Webtop entails virtually the same steps as creating one. Use the steps in the previous list to open the Object Finder. Then click the label or the icon to the left of the Content Item you want to edit (Figure 10.3 shows the icons next to each Content Item). This opens the Object Viewer, populated with the Content Item you clicked.

Delete Content Items by clicking the check box to the left of the Content Item you want to delete and then clicking Delete at the bottom of the Object Finder screen.

CAUTION

Use Delete with care. Deletions are final and can't be undone.

Categorizing, Setting Options, and Dumping a Content Item

The Object Viewer includes several other buttons that you use to perform additional actions on new or existing Content Items. Each button invokes a different handler or function related to the current Content Item. Many of these functions are described in greater detail elsewhere, but the following summarizes what they do:

- *View* invokes the `Display` method for the current Content Item and displays the results in the area to the right of the buttons. If you haven't created and defined your own handler to implement the `Display` method, the default `Display` handler is used. Figure 10.4 shows the way the Content Item displays using a `Display` handler created for the a2zBooks application.

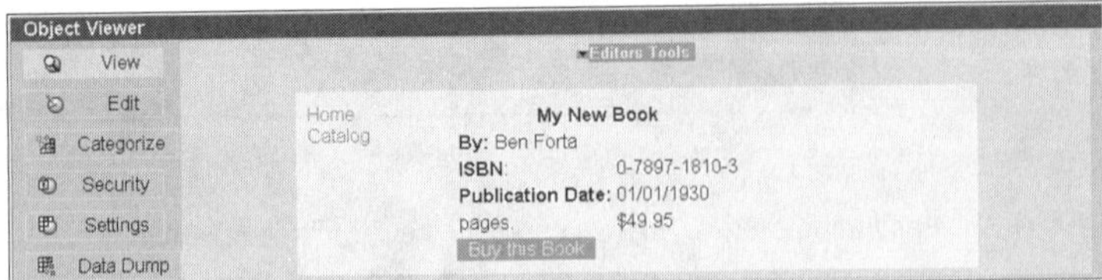

FIGURE 10.4 Clicking View in the Object Viewer invokes the `Display` method for the Content Item.

- *Edit* invokes the `Edit` method for the current Content Item.
- *Categorize* invokes the `EditMetaData` method for the current object. Meta data is information that helps describe, categorize, or summarize other information.

  In this case, the meta data we are using is a set of categories and keywords that can be associated with a book to use when doing searches. Click Categorize to see the available hierarchy of categories and keywords. Click the triangular icon to the left of *genre* to open it and then open Fiction. Click the keyword `Science Fiction` to select it; then click Assign/Unassign to assign the keyword `Science Fiction` to the Book Content Item.

  Figure 10.5 shows the window used to find and assign categories and keywords to Content Items. For complete information on meta data, see Chapter 11.

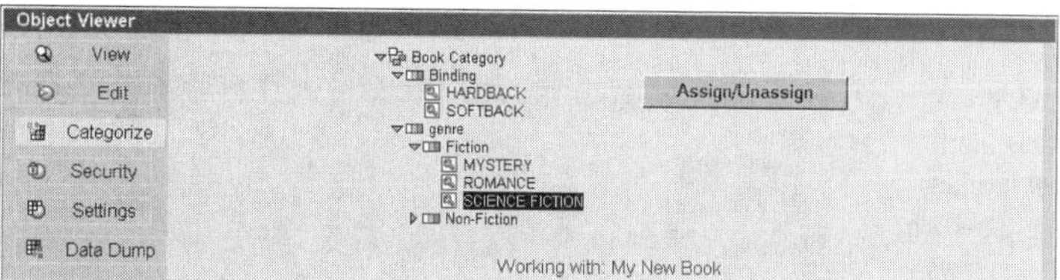

FIGURE 10.5 Clicking Categorize in the Object Viewer allows you to associate categories or keywords with your Content Item.

- *Security* invokes the `EditSecurity` method, which allows you to specify security data concerning the current Content Item. Figure 10.6 shows the form displayed by the default `EditSecurity` method with no security restrictions defined. This form allows you to restrict access to any Content Item's methods by specifying the users or groups that may invoke the method.

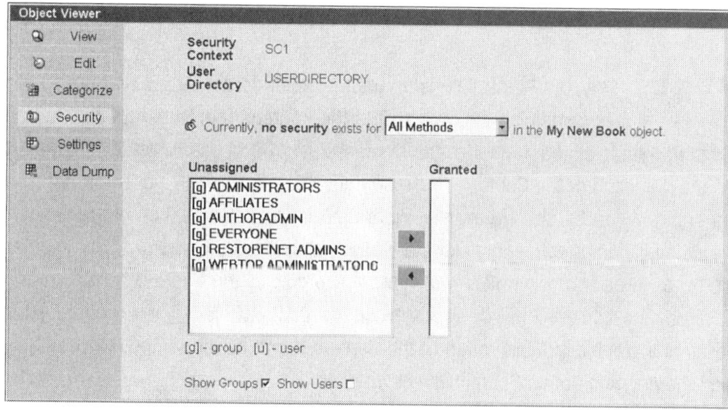

FIGURE 10.6 Clicking Security in the Object Viewer invokes the `EditSecurity` method, which allows you to adjust the security settings for your Content Item.

NOTE By default, a Content Item's methods can be invoked by anyone. However, as soon as you specifically grant access to any one user or group, security may be enforced and only those users or groups specifically granted access can invoke the method. For complete information on Spectra security, see Chapter 16, "Using Spectra Security Options."

- *Settings* invokes the `EditAttributes` handler. The default handler for this method allows you to set two system-generated properties associated with all ContentObject Types: `Active` and `Archive`. Both are used to control the display of Content Items in default handlers and may also be accessed by user-defined handlers to control which Content Items are displayed. For example, the `<CFA_CONTENTOBJECTFIND>` tag (which searches for Content Items matching criteria you supply) by default retrieves only Content Items that are active (`active = true`) and aren't archived (`archive = false`). Figure 10.7 shows the `EditAttributes` display.

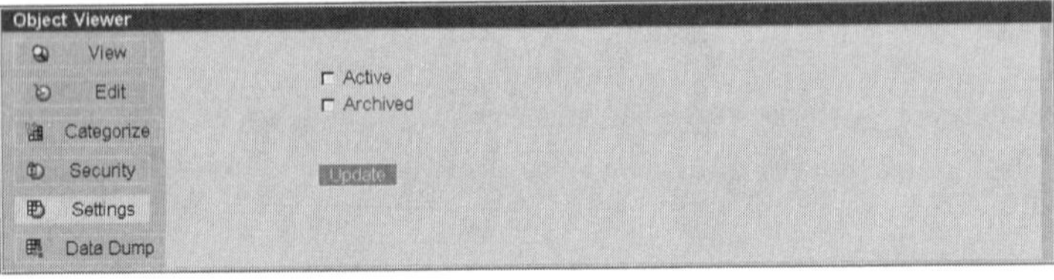

FIGURE 10.7 Clicking Settings in the Object Viewer invokes the `EditAttributes` method, which allows you to specify whether the Content Item is active and whether it should be archived.

- *Data Dump* calls the `<CFA_DUMPOBJECT>` tag, passing it the current object ID, to display a visual representation of the data it contains, as well as the ContentObject Type's properties and methods. Figure 10.8 shows part of the Data Dump for the My New Book Content Item.

NOTE `<CFA_DUMPOBJECT>` is an undocumented Spectra tag that expects to be passed attributes containing the object ID of the Content Item to dump and the datasource where that Content Item is stored. It queries the ContentObject Database to get the Content Item's data, as well as the definition of the Content Item's ContentObject Type. `<CFA_DUMPOBJECT>` uses `<CFA_DUMP>`, an extremely useful Spectra tag that creates a visual representation of any variable passed to it, including variables with complex data types such as structures, arrays, and queries. `<CFA_DUMPOBJECT>` invokes `<CFA_DUMP>` to display the Content Item's structure and data, followed by a second call to `<CFA_DUMP>` on the ContentObject Type's properties and methods. The result is a graphic representation of the Content Item's structure, the data contained in its properties, and the definition of its ContentObject Type.

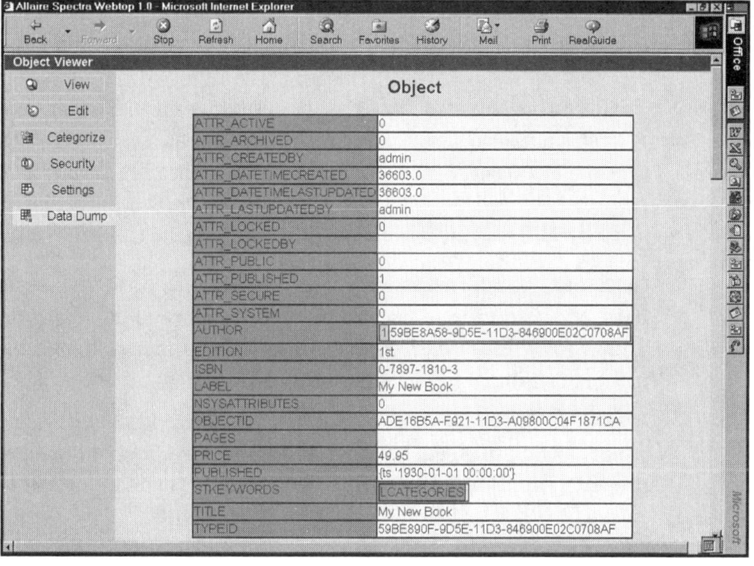

FIGURE 10.8
Clicking Data Dump in the Object Viewer invokes the <CFA_DUMPOBJECT> tag, which shows you a graphical representation of the structure and content of the Content Item.

Webtop Limitations

Although the Webtop is useful for initially creating, editing, and viewing ContentObject Types and individual instances of Content Items (objects), it might not serve well for large installations or complex day-to-day work. The most obvious difficulties with it are the following:

- The Object Finder displays a limited number of items. When you're working with Object Types with tens of thousands of Content Items, you will need to filter the display by the UUID (unique ID) or by a View.
- Finding Content Items tends to be slow, especially as the number of Content Items increases.

NOTE Although the Webtop in Spectra 1.0 may have limitations for use with large data sets or complex applications, Allaire has announced initiatives that could greatly improve Webtop performance for the Spectra 2.0 release. In the future, the Webtop may become a vital ingredient of packaged existing functionality that can be easily adapted to many different applications.

Managing Content Programmatically

Most Spectra applications require you to write your own code to manage Content Items. This section covers how to code templates to create, edit, and delete Content Items. It also covers some advanced topics, such as managing core Object Types, including Files, Images, and Flash animations, and how to manage Content Items that contain embedded objects.

NOTE The code examples in this section are taken from the a2zBooks demonstration application included on the CD-ROM. To use these templates, you will need to install that application. For more information about creating ContentObject Types, see Chapter 6.

Creating Content Items involves two general approaches:

- Gather all the information from the user that needs to be inserted into the new Content Item, and then call the Spectra tag that creates and populates the new Content Item. This is sometimes referred to as the *single-file* approach, because it's usually implemented as a single self-posting form that collects the information and creates the new Content Item.
- Create an empty object and then invoke its `Edit` method to allow the user to fill in the property data. This is often referred to as the "two-file" or *edit handler* approach.

Both methods are detailed in the following sections, including suggestions for working around their disadvantages, where possible.

Creating Content Items with a Single File

The single-file approach is conceptually and programmatically straightforward:

1. Code a CF template that presents the user with a form to gather the information needed to create the new Content Item. This template lives under the Web root and usually posts to itself.
2. Write code that receives the post from the form described in step 1 and uses that data to create and populate a new Content Item.

Listing 10.1 is an example of the single-file approach.

Listing 10.1 The Single-File Approach to Creating a New Content Item

```
<!---
File:         /catalog/authorcreateSingleFile.cfm
Author:       david aden (david@wwstudios.com)
Date:         12/15/1999
Description:  Creating an author object with a single file.
Notes:
--->

<!--- Display the basic a2z formatting. --->
<CF_A2ZFORMATTING subtitle="Creating a New Author">

<!--- Log the page. --->
```

```
<CFA_PAGE
    DATASOURCE="#REQUEST.CFA.a2zBooks.DATASOURCE#"
    PAGENAME="a2z Author Creation"
    SECTIONNAME="catalog"
    SITENAME="a2zBooks"
    CACHEPAGE="No"
    BPRELOADPAGEOBJECTS="No"
    LOGPAGE="No"
    LOGCACHEDOBJECTS="No">

    <!--- If we've submitted, then we need to run the handler to
          add a book. --->
    <CFIF IsDefined("FORM.CreateNewAuthor")>

        <!--- Create and populate the structure that holds the data to
              be inserted into the object. --->
        <CFSET stThisObject = StructNew()>

        <!--- Set the values from the FORM, except for Email --->
        <CFSET stThisObject.FirstName = FORM.FirstName>
        <CFSET stThisObject.LastName = FORM.LastName>
        <CFSET stThisObject.Bio = FORM.Bio>
        <CFSET stThisObject.Title = FORM.Title>
        <CFSET stThisObject.attr_active = FORM.attr_active>

        <!--- Create the array to contain the email addresses --->
        <CFSET stThisObject.Email = ArrayNew(1)>

        <!--- Loop through the email addresses and add them to the
              array --->
        <CFSET LoopCounter = 1>
        <CFLOOP LIST="#FORM.email#" index="CurrEmail">
            <CFSET stThisObject.email[LoopCounter] = CurrEmail>
            <CFSET LoopCounter = LoopCounter + 1>
        </CFLOOP>

        <!--- Create the object -- set the label to the first and
              last names --->
        <CFA_CONTENTOBJECTCREATE
            DATASOURCE="#REQUEST.CFA.a2zBooks.DATASOURCE#"
            TYPEID="#application.authorTypeID#"
            LABEL="#FORM.FirstName# #FORM.LastName#"
            STPROPERTIES="#stThisObject#"
            R_ID="NewBookID">

            <CFOUTPUT>
            <TABLE width="500">
                <tr>
                    <TD ALIGN="left">
                        New author #FORM.FirstName# #FORM.LastName#
                            successfully created!
                    </TD>
```

Part II Ch 10

continues

Listing 10.1 Continued

```
            <TR>
        </TABLE>
        </CFOUTPUT>

<!--- ELSE this is the first time through. --->
<CFELSE>

    <!--- Get the query string (so a stray question mark doesn't appear
          if there is no query string). --->
    <CFSET IIf( Len(cgi.Query_string) GT 0,
        "thisQueryString='?#cgi.query_string#'",
        "thisQueryString=''" )>

    <CFOUTPUT>
    <CFFORM NAME="CreateAuthor"
        ACTION="#cgi.script_name##thisQueryString#"
        METHOD="post">
        <TABLE width="500">
            <TR>
                <TD COLSPAN="2" ALIGN="center">
                    <B>Enter a New Author</B>
                </TD>
            <TR>
                <TD>First Name:</TD>
                <TD>
                    <CFINPUT TYPE="Text" NAME="FirstName"
                        MESSAGE="\'First Name\' is a required field."
                        REQUIRED="Yes"
                        SIZE="40">
                </TD>
            </TR>

            <TR>
                <TD>Last Name:</TD>
                <TD>
                    <CFINPUT TYPE="Text" NAME="LastName"
                        MESSAGE="\'Last Name\' is a required field."
                        REQUIRED="Yes"
                        SIZE="40">
                </TD>
            </TR>

            <TR>
                <TD>Title:</TD>
                <TD>
                    <CFSELECT NAME="Title" SIZE="1">
                        <option value="">
                        <option value="Mr.">Mr.
                        <option value="Mrs.">Mrs.
                        <option value="Ms.">Ms.
                        <option value="Dr.">Dr.
```

```
                        <option value="Atty.">Atty.
                    </CFSELECT>
                </TD>
            </TR>

            <TR>
                <TD>Bio:</TD>
                <TD>
                    <TEXTAREA COLS="40" ROWS="4" NAME="Bio"></TEXTAREA>
                </TD>
            </TR>

            <TR>
                <TD>Email1:</TD>
                <TD><INPUT TYPE="text" SIZE="40" NAME="email"></TD>
            </TR>
            <TR>
                <TD>Email2:</TD>
                <TD><INPUT TYPE="text" SIZE="40" NAME="email"></TD>
            </TR>
            <TR>
                <TD>Email3:</TD>
                <TD><INPUT TYPE="text" SIZE="40" NAME="email"></TD>
            </TR>

            <TR>
                <TD>Active:</TD>
                <TD>
                    <INPUT TYPE="Radio" NAME="attr_active"  VALUE="1"
                        CHECKED>Yes  
                    <INPUT TYPE="Radio" NAME="attr_active" VALUE="0">No
                </TD>
            </TR>

            <TR>
                <TD colspan="2" align="center">
                    <INPUT TYPE="Submit" NAME="CreateNewAuthor"
                        VALUE=" Create ">
                </TD>
            </TR>
        </TABLE>
    </CFFORM>
    </CFOUTPUT>
</CFIF>

</CFA_PAGE>

</CF_A2ZFORMATTING><!--- Close the page formatting --->

<SCRIPT LANGUAGE="JavaScript" TYPE="text/javascript">
<!--
```

continues

Listing 10.1 Continued

```
    // Focus on the first element
    if ( typeof(document.CreateAuthor) != 'undefined' ) {
        document.CreateAuthor.FirstName.focus();
    }

//-->
</SCRIPT>

</SCRIPT>
```

Figure 10.9 shows the form this template displays.

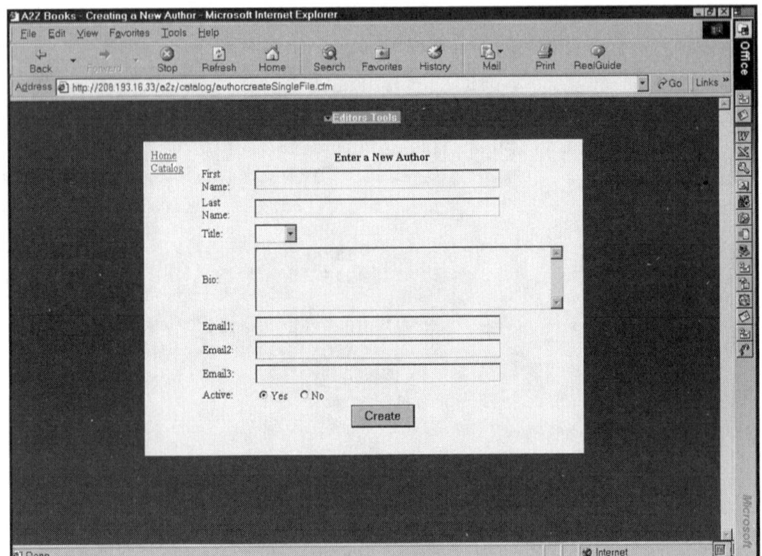

FIGURE 10.9
The `AuthorCreateSingleFile.cfm` template produces a simple interface for entering information about a new author.

Listing 10.1 begins with the custom `<CF_A2ZFORMATTING>` tag, which does basic formatting for the A2Z site. It calls the `CFA_Page` Spectra tag to include the page in Spectra's Site Model (see Chapter 8, "Building the Site Structure"). The rest of the template consists of a self-posting form and the code that handles form submissions. `<CFIF>` checks whether the form has been submitted; if not, the `<CFELSE>` section displays the form itself.

First look at the bottom half of the template—the `<CFELSE>` section. This begins by using the ColdFusion `Iif()` function to create a local variable, `thisQueryString`, that either holds the complete query string passed to this template (if one exists) or is set to an empty string (if no query string exists).

We then use thisQueryString as part of the ACTION attribute of the <CFFORM> tag. The body of <CFFORM> includes form elements for each property of the Author ContentObject Type. When the user submits the form, it self-posts and the <CFIF> near the top of the template catches the submission.

The top half of the template runs and does the following:

1. It creates a structure (stThisObject) to hold the properties that will be used to create the object.
2. It assigns the simple (non-array) properties to that structure. This includes attr_active, one of the system-generated properties common to all Content Items. The Webtop and some tags check this property to determine whether a particular object should be returned.
3. The template initializes an array to hold the email addresses. Because the email property of the Author ContentObject Type is defined as an array, we need to create and populate an array to pass to the Spectra tag we use to create the new Content Item.
4. The template loops through the list of email addresses passed from the form to populate the array.
5. When all the properties are assigned to the structure, the template calls the <CFA_CONTENTOBJECTCREATE> tag to create and populate the object. Its attributes are as follows:

TypeID	A required field that identifies the type of Content Item we're creating.
Label	The name to assign to the Content Item. Label is a system-generated property of all Content Items. It is used in the Webtop when Content Items are listed and is also used for searching and filtering.
StProperties	The structure containing the property data. Spectra populates the new Content Item's properties with the data contained in this structure.
r_id	The name of the variable in which the tag returns the new Content Item's UUID.

Creating and Populating Content Items with an Edit Handler

The second approach to creating and populating Content Items involves a more detailed understanding of how Spectra works with ContentObject Type methods, but the basic steps are simple:

1. Code a CF template, located in the Web root, that calls the <CFA_CONTENTOBJECTCREATE> tag to create a new Content Item. The <CFA_CONTENTOBJECTCREATE> tag optionally allows you to invoke a method on the Content Item it creates. We're going to invoke EditAuthor, a method defined for the Author ContentObject Type.

2. Code a handler to implement the `EditAuthor` method. The handler presents a form for entering the data to add to the newly created Content Item. It also includes code to update the database when the user submits the form.

Listing 10.2 demonstrates the first part: a template that calls `<CFA_CONTENTOBJECTCREATE>` to create a new, empty Content Item and then invokes the `EditAuthor` method on the newly created Content Item. The template, `ManageAuthorsMini.cfm`, isn't accessible from any menu within the a2zBooks application, although it's part of the installation. You can access it by pointing your browser to `<A2Z Install URL>/catalog/ManageAuthorsMini.cfm`. Later in the chapter, we'll modify this template and add functionality to it to create the `ManageAuthors.cfm` template.

Listing 10.2 The Two-File Approach for Creating Content Items

```
<!---
File:         /catalog/ManageAuthorsMini.cfm
Author:       david aden (david@wwstudios.com)
Date:         12/15/1999
Description:  Interface for creating, editing and deleting author
              objects.
Notes:
--->

<!--- Display the basic a2z formatting. --->
<CF_A2ZFORMATTING subtitle="Creating a New Author">

<!--- Log the page. --->
<CFA_PAGE
    DATASOURCE="#REQUEST.CFA.a2zBooks.DATASOURCE#"
    PAGENAME="a2z Author Management Mini"
    SECTIONNAME="catalog"
    SITENAME="a2zBooks">

    <!------------------------------------------------------------
    CREATE a new object and call the edit handler.
    ------------------------------------------------------------->
    <CFIF IsDefined("FORM.CreateObject")>

        <!--- Set the variables we're going to pass in. --->
        <CFSET stParams = StructNew()>
        <CFSET stParams.Title = "Create New Author">
        <CFSET stParams.Message = "Enter the data for the new author.">

        <!--- Let's create an empty object and call the edit handler. --->
        <CFA_CONTENTOBJECTCREATE
            DATASOURCE="#REQUEST.CFA.a2zBooks.DATASOURCE#"
            TYPEID="#application.authorTypeID#"
            LABEL="__NEWITEM__"
            METHOD="EditAuthor"
            STPARAMS="#stParams#"
            BACTIVATE="No"
            R_ID="thisobjectid"
```

```
        >

    <!------------------------------------------------------------------
    UPDATE - This runs when the edit handler submits to itself.
        (This could be after a new Content Item has been created and the
        edit handler was called to populate it or could be after editing
        an existing item.)
    ------------------------------------------------------------------->
    <CFELSEIF IsDefined("FORM.CommitChanges")>

        <!--- Set a ReturnTo variable which will be used to tell the code
              where to go after completing. --->
        <CFSET stParams = StructNew()>
        <CFSET stParams.ReturnTo = "ManageAuthors.cfm">

        <CFA_CONTENTOBJECT
          DATASOURCE="#REQUEST.CFA.a2zBooks.DATASOURCE#"
          OBJECTID="#FORM.ObjectID#"
          METHOD="EditAuthor"
          STPARAMS="#stParams#"
          BSECURE="No"
          BLOGGING="No"
          BUSECACHE="No">

    <!--- ELSE we're coming to the page for the first time. Display a
            list of the authors and buttons to create or delete them. --->
    <CFELSE>

        <CFOUTPUT>

        <!--- Get the query string --->
        <CFSET IIf( Len(cgi.Query_string),
                    "thisQueryString='?#cgi.query_string#'",
                    "thisQueryString=''" )>

        <CFFORM ACTION="#cgi.script_name##thisQueryString#" METHOD="post">
        <TABLE WIDTH="620" BORDER="0" CELLPADDING="0" CELLSPACING="0">
            <TR>
                <TD COLSPAN="3" ALIGN="center">
                    <INPUT TYPE="submit"
                        NAME="CreateObject"
                        VALUE="Create Author">
                </TD>
            </TR>

        </TABLE>
        </CFFORM>
        </CFOUTPUT>

    </CFIF>

</CFA_PAGE>

</CF_A2ZFORMATTING><!--- Close the page formatting --->
```

This template is a self-posting form with three sections. We're going to start with the <CFELSE> section, which runs the first time the template is requested.

Within <CFELSE> is a very simple form that contains only one element: a submit button named CreateObject. When the user clicks this, the form self-submits, and the first <CFIF> catches the submission. Next we create a structure, stParams, that's used to pass information into the handler that we'll use to add information to the new Content Item. The structure is assigned two keys, Title and Message, which we'll display to the user.

Next, we call <CFA_CONTENTOBJECTCREATE> and pass it the following attributes:

- TYPEID contains the UUID of the ContentObject Type for which we want to create a new Content Item.
- LABEL is the name displayed in the Webtop list of Content Items. We've set it to the string "__NEWITEM__" as a way of marking new Content Items in case the user doesn't complete the data. Later, we can search for Content Items with this string in their labels and delete them. For more information on deleting incomplete Content Items, see the section "Comparing Create Methods," later in this chapter.
- METHOD is the name of the method to invoke on the new Content Item after it is created.
- STPARAMS contains a structure that holds any parameters that need to be passed to the method specified in the METHOD attribute. Inside the method handler, stParams is accessible as Attributes.stParams.
- BACTIVATE specifies whether the Content Item's attr_active property will be set to active when it is created. We aren't activating this object yet, because we don't want it to show up in searches or other actions until after the user adds data to it.
- R_ID is the name of the variable in which we want Spectra to return the UUID of the new Content Item.

The <CFA_CONTENTOBJECTCREATE> tag creates a new Content Item, and then invokes the EditAuthor method, which is shown in Listing 10.3. EditAuthor is a self-posting form.

Listing 10.3 The *EditAuthor* Method of the Author ContentObject Type

```
<!---
File:         EditAuthor.cfm
Author:       david aden (david@wwstudios.com)
Date:         12/18/1999
Description:  Edit Handler for a2zBooks author object type
Notes:
--->
<!--- use the handler tag to set the scope up --->
<CFA_HANDLER
    OBJECT="Author"
    SEPARATOR="<p>">
```

```
<!--- Check if the user is submitting the form or displaying --->
<CFIF ISDEFINED("FORM.CommitChanges")>

    <!--- Initialze an array to hold the email addresses. --->
    <CFSET aEmail = ArrayNew(1)>

    <!--- There may be multiple email addresses, so we need to stick
          them into the Array since that's what the object expects.
          We allow the user to separate email addresses with new
          lines, commas or semicolons. --->
    <CFIF Len(FORM.Email)>
        <CFSET aEmail = ListToArray(FORM.email,"#chr(10)#,;")>
    </CFIF>

    <!--- update the object --->
    <CFA_CONTENTOBJECTDATA
        DATASOURCE = "#request.cfa.a2zbooks.datasource#"
        OBJECTID = "#objectid#">

        <!--- update the following properties --->
        <CFA_CONTENTOBJECTPROPERTY NAME="Label"
            VALUE="#Form.FirstName# #Form.LastName#">
        <CFA_CONTENTOBJECTPROPERTY NAME="FirstName"
            VALUE="#Form.FirstName#">
        <CFA_CONTENTOBJECTPROPERTY NAME="LastName"
            VALUE="#Form.LastName#">
        <CFA_CONTENTOBJECTPROPERTY NAME="Bio" VALUE="#Form.Bio#">
        <CFA_CONTENTOBJECTPROPERTY NAME="Email" VALUE="#aEmail#">
        <CFA_CONTENTOBJECTPROPERTY NAME="ATTR_ACTIVE"
            VALUE="#form.Active#">
    </CFA_CONTENTOBJECTDATA>

    <!--- return to the main page --->
    <CFIF StructKeyExists(Attributes.stParams, "ReturnTo")>
        <CFLOCATION URL="#Attributes.stParams.ReturnTo#">
    </CFIF>

<!--- Not submitting the form, so display instead --->
<CFELSE>

    <CFOUTPUT>

    <SCRIPT LANGUAGE="JavaScript" TYPE="text/javascript">
    <!--

        function AssignMD2(ObjID) {
            // new window feature
            myfeatures = 'width=450,height=450,toolbar=no,location=no,
                        ➥directories=no,status=no,menubar=no,
                        ➥scrollbars=yes,resizable=yes';

            // open a new window to pick the meta data.
```

continues

Part II Ch 10

Listing 10.3 Continued

```
        MDWin = window.open("ManageAuthorsMD2.cfm?ObjectID="
                ➥+ObjID,"MDWin",myfeatures);
    }

    function AssignMD(ObjID) {
        // new window feature
        myfeatures = 'width=450,height=350,toolbar=no,location=no,
                     ➥directories=no,status=no,menubar=no,
                     ➥scrollbars=yes,resizable=yes';

        // open a new window to pick the meta data.
        MDWin = window.open("ManageAuthorsMD.cfm?ObjectID="
                ➥+ ObjID,"MDWin",myfeatures);
    }
//-->
</SCRIPT>

<!--- Display the formatting information --->
    <BR><BR>
    <!--- Set the query string (So a stray question mark doesn't
            appear if there is nothing in the query string). --->
    <CFSET IIf( Len(cgi.QUERY_STRING),
        "thisQueryString='?#cgi.query_string#'",
        "thisQueryString=''" )>

    <CFFORM NAME="AuthorForm"
        ACTION="#CGI.SCRIPT_NAME##thisQueryString#" METHOD="POST">

        <!--- Pass along the ID for the object we're dealing
                with. --->
        <INPUT TYPE="hidden"
            NAME="ObjectID"
            VALUE="#Author.ObjectID#">

         <!--- Outside table --->
        <TABLE WIDTH="620"
            BORDER="0"
            CELLPADDING="0"
            CELLSPACING="0">
            <TR>
                <TD ALIGN="center">
                <FONT size="+1">
                    <CFIF StructKeyExists(Attributes.stParams,
                        "Title")>
                        #Attributes.stParams.Title#
                    <CFELSE>
                        Author Edit Form
                    </CFIF>
                    <BR><BR>
                </FONT>
                </TD>
```

```
</TR>
<TR>
    <TD VALIGN="top" ALIGN="Center">

        <CENTER>
        <!--- FORM table --->
        <TABLE BORDER="0"
            CELLPADDING=2
            CELLSPACING=2 WIDTH="455" >
            <CFIF StructKeyExists(Attributes.stParams,
                "Message")>
                <TR>
                    <TD COLSPAN=2>
                    <FONT FACE="arial"
                        SIZE="-1" COLOR="red">
                        #Attributes.stParams.Message#
                    </FONT></TD>
                </TR>
            </CFIF>
            <TR>
                <TD><FONT FACE="arial" SIZE="-1">
                    <b>First Name:</b>
                </FONT></TD>
                <TD><FONT FACE="arial" SIZE="-1">
                    <INPUT TYPE="text"
                      NAME="FirstName"
                      SIZE="30"
                      VALUE="#Trim(Author.FirstName)#">
                </FONT></TD>
            </TR>
            <TR>
                <TD><FONT FACE="arial" SIZE="-1">
                    <b>Last Name:</b></FONT>
                </TD>
                <TD><FONT FACE="arial" SIZE="-1">
                    <INPUT TYPE="text"
                      NAME="LastName"
                      SIZE="30"
                      VALUE="#Trim(Author.LastName)#">
                </FONT></TD>
            </TR>
            <TR>
                <TD><FONT FACE="arial" SIZE="-1">
                    <b>Bio:</b>
                </FONT></TD>
                <TD>

                <CFA_HTMLEDITOR
                    NAME="Bio"
                    HEIGHT="200"
                    WIDTH="400"
```

continues

Listing 10.3 Continued

```
                    VALUE="#Trim( Author.Bio )#"
                    FORM="AuthorForm">
                </TD>
            </TR>

            <TR>
                <!--- Initialze a var --->
                <CFSET lEmail = "">

                <!--- If the email address array has
                      stuff in it, then construct the
                      display version of it by
                      turning the array into a list
                      delimited with a New Line. --->
                <CFIF ArrayLen(Author.email)>
                <CFSET lEmail =
                ArrayToList(Author.email,"#chr(10)#")>
                </CFIF>
                <TD><FONT FACE="arial" SIZE="-1">
                    <b>Email:</b>
                </FONT></TD>
                <TD><FONT FACE="arial" SIZE="-1">
                    <TEXTAREA COLS=40
                      ROWS=4
                      NAME="email">#lEmail#</textarea>
                </FONT></TD>
            </TR>

            <TR>
                <TD ><FONT FACE="arial" SIZE="-1">
                    <b>Active:</b>
                </FONT></TD>
                <TD><FONT FACE="arial" SIZE="-1">
                    <INPUT TYPE="radio"
                        NAME="Active"
                        VALUE="1"
                        <CFIF Author.ATTR_ACTIVE >
                        CHECKED</CFIF>> Yes
                    <INPUT TYPE="radio"
                        NAME="Active"
                        VALUE="0"
                        <CFIF NOT Author.ATTR_ACTIVE>
                        CHECKED</CFIF>> No
                </FONT></TD>
            </TR>
            <TR>
                <TD COLSPAN=2 ALIGN="right">
                <FONT FACE="arial" SIZE="-1">
```

```
                                                <INPUT Name="CommitChanges"
                                                    TYPE="submit"
                                                    VALUE="Save Changes">
                                                <INPUT Name="AssignMetaData"
                                                    TYPE="Button"
                                                    VALUE="Metadata Picker"
                                                    onClick=
                                                      "AssignMD('#Author.ObjectID#')">
                                                <INPUT Name="AssignMetaData"
                                                    TYPE="Button"
                                                    VALUE="Metadata"
                                                    onClick=
                                                      "AssignMD2('#Author.ObjectID#')">
                                                </FONT></TD>
                                            </TR>
                                        </TABLE>    <!--- End FORM table. --->
                                        </CENTER>
                                    </TD>
                                </TR>
                            </TABLE> <!--- Outside table --->
                        </CFFORM>
                    </CFOUTPUT>
                </CFIF>
            </CFA_HANDLER>
```

Figure 10.10 shows the form that appears when you run `ManageAuthorsMini.cfm`. Figure 10.11 shows the form that appears when the `EditAuthor` method runs.

Part II Ch 10

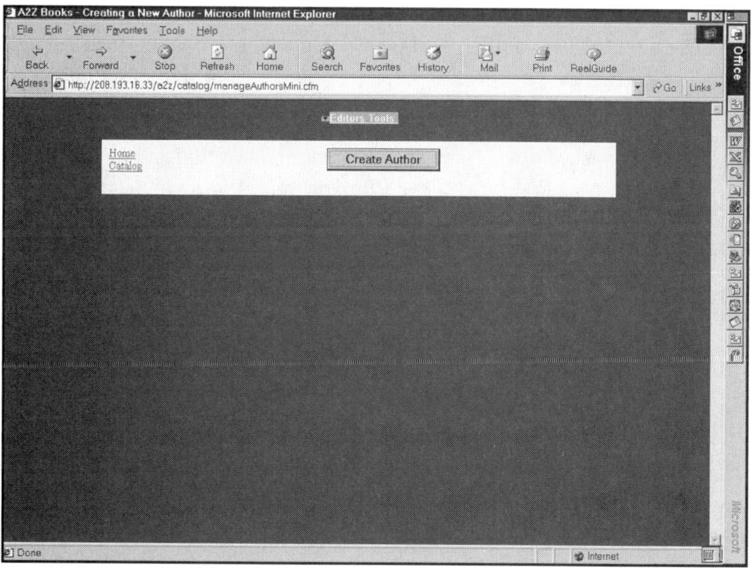

FIGURE 10.10
The `ManageAuthorsMini.cfm` template generates a simple form with a button for creating a new Author Content Item.

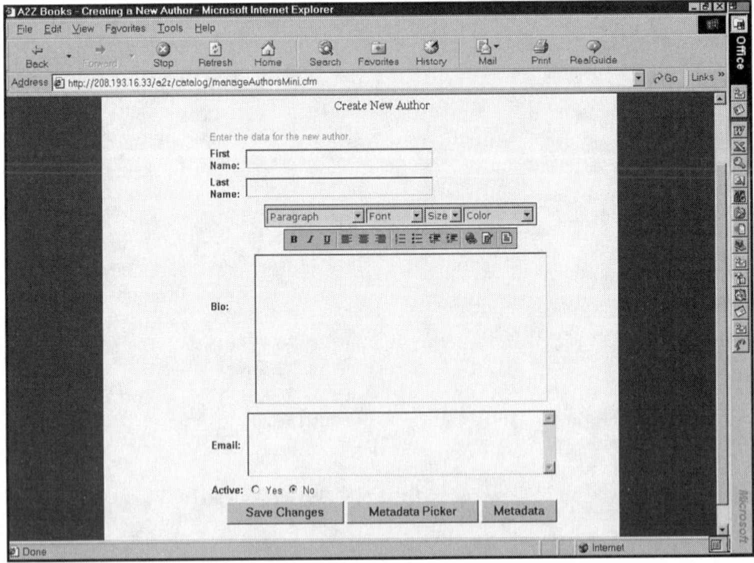

FIGURE 10.11
The `EditAuthor` method generates a form you can use to add data for a new Author Content Item.

When Spectra invokes the `EditAuthor` method after creating the Content Item, it passes the new Content Item's object ID to the handler. The `<CFA_HANDLER>` tag at the top of `EditAuthor` assigns a local name, `Author`, to the Content Item. This local name is a scope available only within the handler itself—a kind of shorthand notation for the Content Item passed to the handler.

The `EditAuthor` handler is implemented as a self-posting form, so the first thing it does is check whether it's receiving a form submission or if it should display a form for data entry. Because this is the first time into the handler, the bottom half executes, displaying a form.

The first part of the display section includes JavaScript that opens windows to allow the user to associate meta data with the Content Item. For a full description of meta data, see Chapter 11.

Although it's possible to code handlers without using `<CFA_HANDLER>`, it's almost always better to use it because it performs several important functions. It loops through any Content Items passed to it (it's possible to pass multiple Content Items to one handler) and allows you to specify a local name (also referred to as a *scope*) through which the passed Content Items can be accessed.

The rest of the display section is a `<CFFORM>` that allows the user to enter data for each of the properties of the Author ContentObject Type. It begins by setting a hidden field to hold the object ID for the current Content Item. This is needed by the handling code when the form is submitted.

The form accesses the Attributes.stParams structure that was passed to the <CFA_CONTENTOBJECTCREATE> tag to see if it contains a Title field. If so, the handler displays its value; otherwise, a generic title is displayed. Likewise, stParams is checked to see if it contains a message key; if so, it is displayed also. The first two display fields of the form—FirstName and LastName —are simple HTML elements. Their values are taken from the Author scope that was defined in the <CFA_HANDLER> tag.

Next we use the <CFA_HTMLEDITOR> tag, which encapsulates a browser-based WYSIWYG editor that runs in Internet Explorer 4.0 and greater. In Netscape browsers, <CFA_HTMLEDITOR> gracefully degrades to a <TEXTAREA>.

The eMail property of the Author Content Item is an array and is converted to a list (delimited by the newline character) and is displayed in a TEXTAREA.

When the user clicks Save Changes, the form self-submits. It's important to understand the sequence of events that occurs at this point:

1. The user clicks the Save Changes button, which is named CommitChanges.
2. The form is submitted to the template contained in the CGI variable SCRIPT_NAME, which contains the name of the script from which the edit handler was originally called—in this case ManageAuthorsMini.cfm. CGI.SCRIPT_NAME contains ManageAuthorsMini.cfm instead of EditAuthor.cfm because CGI variables are set at the beginning of a request and don't change across the entire request. ManageAuthorsMini.cfm is the Web root template that was originally requested by the browser, so its name is available in CGI.SCRIPT_NAME no matter how many custom tags or handlers are invoked as a result of that single request. The EditAuthor form submits to ManageAuthorsMini.cfm.
3. This brings us back to the ManageAuthorsMini.cfm template. Here, the POST is caught by

```
<cfelseif IsDefined("FORM.CommitChanges")>
```

4. In ManageAuthorsMini.cfm, we create a stParams structure and set its ReturnTo key to ManageAuthorsMini.cfm. The <CFA_CONTENTOBJECT> tag then reinvokes the EditAuthor method on the original Content Item by setting its ObjectID attribute to FORM.ObjectID.
5. This brings us back to the EditAuthor handler. Here, we catch the form submission with

```
<CFIF ISDEFINED("FORM.CommitChanges")>
```

   This works because form variables are also available across an entire request.
6. We then create an array to hold any email addresses passed in from the form, and a <CFIF> tests whether FORM.email contains anything (if its length is anything other than zero). If so, we convert the value of FORM.email to an array, creating a new array element for every newline, comma, or semicolon it contains.

7. The actual work of updating the Content Item is done with the <CFA_CONTENTOBJECTDATA> tag and its associated <CFA_CONTENTOBJECTPROPERTY> tags. This template uses one form of <CFA_CONTENTOBJECTDATA>; there is a second one available.
8. The code then checks for a ReturnTo key in Attributes.stParams and, if it exists, does a <CFLOCATION> to return the user to it.

Using <CFA_CONTENTOBJECTDATA>

<CFA_CONTENTOBJECTDATA> has two forms. In Listing 10.3, it's used with multiple <CFA_CONTENTOBJECTPROPERTY> tags, each of which sets the value for a property of the Content Item being updated. A second form of <CFA_CONTENTOBJECTDATA> doesn't use the <CFA_CONTENTOBJECTPROPERTY> tag, instead passing in a structure that holds the property values to update. With this second method, the same code would be written as

```
<CFSET stProperties = StructNew()>
<CFSET stProperties["Label"] = "#Form.FirstName# #Form.LastName#">
<CFSET stProperties["FirstName"] = Form.FirstName>
<CFSET stProperties["LastName"] = Form.LastName>
<CFSET stProperties["Bio"] = Form.Bio>
<CFSET stProperties["Email"] = aEmail>
<CFSET stProperties["ATTR_ACTIVE"] = form.Active>

<CFA_CONTENTOBJECTDATA
     DATASOURCE = "#request.cfa.a2zbooks.datasource#"
     OBJECTID = "#objectid#"
     stProperties="#stProperties#"/>
```

<CFA_CONTENTOBJECTDATA> requires an end tag, but this can be accommodated by using the shorthand notation for an end tag as in the preceding (note the use of the / at the end of the <CFA_CONTENTOBJECTDATA> tag). This shorthand is equivalent to including </CFA_CONTENTOBJECTDATA> after the opening tag.

Comparing Create Methods

Both the single-file and edit handler methods for creating objects have advantages and disadvantages, although the edit handler method is preferable.

The primary disadvantage of the single-file method is that it usually results in you having to maintain two files that contain essentially the same HTML form:

- The template that holds the form used to create a new Content Item
- The ContentObject Type's edit handler used to edit an existing Content Item

The primary advantage of the single-file method is that it reduces the chance of creating a Content Item that never gets populated, because it doesn't create a Content Item until the user has supplied the data to populate it. This helps prevent empty or incomplete Content Items from getting into and potentially cluttering up the Object Store database.

The primary disadvantage of the edit handler approach is that it may result in stray, incomplete Content Items in the database. This can happen for any number of reasons, including hardware, operating system, or network failure or simply because the user clicked Create Object but never got around to entering the data through the edit handler.

Despite this, the edit-handler approach has several important advantages:

- It doesn't require you to maintain two nearly identical templates (one for creating, the other for editing).
- The edit handlers are subject to built-in Spectra security and logging, whereas the Web root file used by the single-file method isn't.
- You may want to perform some actions with a Content Item in conjunction with data entry, such as categorizing it, for which you need to have an existing Content Item ID. Using the single-file approach, no Content Item ID is available until you submit the form.

Fortunately, the primary problem with the edit handler method—the chance of leaving stray, incomplete objects in the ContentObject Database—is easily resolved by periodically running a clean-up script to find and delete incomplete objects from the ContentObject Database. This is covered in the next section.

Cleaning Up Incomplete Content Items

By using a consistent convention when creating Content Items, you can easily create a script that will find and delete incomplete entries in the ContentObject Database.

The first step is to create all Content Items using a distinctive label. In the example in Listing 10.2, we set the label for new Content Items to `__NEWITEM__`, but this could be set to any string of characters that's unlikely ever to be used as the actual label for a Content Item.

The next step is to create a template that can be run periodically to look for items that fit two requirements:

- Their labels are set to `__NEWITEM__`.
- They are old enough that you can be reasonably certain they have been abandoned.

Listing 10.4 contains the code for a custom tag that finds Content Items that fit these requirements and then uses `<CFA_CONTENTOBJECTDELETE>` to delete them.

Listing 10.4 Finding and Deleting Abandoned, Incomplete Content Items

```
<!---
File:         CleanUpStrayObjects.cfm
Author:       david aden (david@wwstudios.com)
Date:         12/18/1999
```

continues

Listing 10.4 Continued

```
Description:  Custom tag that can be used in a scheduled template to
              clean up incomplete objects from the Object Database.
Notes:        This version cleans all stray objects -- this could be
              expanded to allow for deleting strays of selected
              Content Object Types.
--->

<!--- Set a default object expires time in minutes if none passed in. --->
<cfif IsDefined("Attributes.ObjectExpirationTime") >
    <CFSET ObjectExpirationTime =
        EVALUATE( "#Attributes.ObjectExpirationTime#/(24*60)" )>
<CFELSE>
    <CFSET ObjectExpirationTime = evaluate("30/(24*60)")>
</cfif>

<!--- If no data source, then abort. --->
<CFIF NOT IsDefined("Attributes.DataSource")>
    <CFTHROW MESSAGE="'Datasource' is a required attribute. Aborting...">
    <CFABORT>
</CFIF>

<!--- If no new object label passed in, abort. --->
<CFIF NOT IsDefined("Attributes.NewObjectLabel")>
    <CFTHROW MESSAGE="'NewObjectLabel' is a required attribute.
        Aborting...">
    <CFABORT>
</CFIF>

<!--- Forces converstion of the date to a number which is how the
      datetimecreated field is stored in the table Objects. --->
<CFSET CurrDate = 0 + Now()>

<!--- Get a list of the Objects where the label is the magic string
      for a new object and the date of creation is older than a
      configurable amount. --->
<CFQUERY Name="GetGarbageObjects" datasource="#Attributes.Datasource#">
    SELECT
        ObjectID,
        label,
        datetimecreated
    FROM objects
    WHERE label = '#Attributes.NewObjectLabel#'
    AND (#CurrDate# - datetimecreated) > #ObjectExpirationTime#
</CFQUERY>

<!--- Loop through the found items and delete them.  --->
<CFLOOP query="GetGarbageObjects">
    <CFA_CONTENTOBJECTDELETE
      DATASOURCE="#Attributes.Datasource#"
      OBJECTID="#GetGarbageObjects.ObjectID#">
</cfLOOP>
```

```
<CFIF IsDefined("Attributes.r_NumberDeleted")>
    <CFSET SetVariable("Caller.#Attributes.r_NumberDeleted#",
        GetGarbageObjects.RecordCount)>
</CFIF>
```

This custom tag starts by setting a default Content Item expiration period in minutes, unless a value is passed to it in the `ObjectExpirationTime` attribute. It then checks for the required `Datasource` and `NewObjectLabel` attributes. `NewObjectLabel` contains the unique label assigned to Content Items when they are created.

Next, it converts the current date and time to an integer, because that's the data type used to store a Content Item's time-of-creation in the ContentObject Database.

Using the value in `Attributes.NewObjectLabel` and the converted current date and time, we do a direct SQL query on the `Objects` table in the ContentObject Database to find orphaned Content Items. Once we have the list, we loop through the recordset and delete each Content Item using `<CFA_CONTENTOBJECTDELETE>`.

If a return variable was specified, the custom tag returns the total number of Content Items deleted. For the a2zBooks application, `<CF_CleanUpStrayObjects>` would be called, as follows:

```
<CF_CleanUpStrayObjects
  datasource="#REQUEST.CFA.a2zBooks.DATASOURCE#"
  NewObjectLabel="__NEWITEM__"
  ObjectExpirationTime="10"
  r_NumberDeleted="NumDel">
```

This clean-up custom tag could be periodically invoked by the ColdFusion scheduler or could be run at application startup.

Editing and Deleting Content Items

You edit or delete Content Items with procedures nearly identical to the edit-handler approach to creating Content Items described earlier. In fact, one great advantage of Spectra is the way it generalizes actions as ContentObject Type methods. Once you learn how to implement methods, you can adapt that skill to a wide variety of application requirements.

For example, to edit an existing Content Item, all we need to add to the existing code is a way to catch the user's request to edit and then call the same `EditAuthor` method that was used for populating a newly created Content Item.

We can apply the same approach to deleting a Content Item—you can write a `Delete` method for each ContentObject Type. However, the actual Content Item deletion is handled by a tag supplied with Spectra—`<CFA_CONTENTOBJECTDELETE>`. Our code just needs to give the user a way to identify the Content Item(s) he wants to delete and use `<CFA_CONTENTOBJECTDELETE>` to remove the objects from the ContentObject Database.

Deleting Content Items

Although the <CFA_CONTENTOBJECTDELETE> tag deletes Content Items from the ContentObject Database, it doesn't remove the Content Item from any Verity collections the item has been put into for searching purposes.

Search-related information about a Content Item can end up in two different collections: one used to associate meta data categories or keywords with the Content Item, the other to store Content Item properties defined as *indexed*. Both indexes need to be updated programmatically when a Content Item is deleted.

To remove any record of a Content Item from the meta data collection, use the <CFA_METADATAINDEXDELETE> tag. To remove any record of a Content Item from the index holding data on indexed properties, use <CFA_TYPEINDEXKEYDELETE>. The simplest way to accomplish this is to create a delete handler for your ContentObject Type that combines all three actions: removing the meta data index data by using <CFA_METADATAINDEXDELETE>, removing the object type index data by using <CFA_TYPEINDEXKEYDELETE>, and deleting the object with <CFA_CONTENTOBJECTDELETE>. The default delete handler in Spectra 1.0 isn't functional; however, the default delete handler for a later release will reportedly include code to update the Verity collections.

See Chapter 11 for more information on meta data. For more information on searching with Spectra, see Chapter 14, "Searching and Indexing."

Listing 10.5 contains a more complete version of the code in Listing 10.2. Conditional logic has been added to the top of the template to catch edit and delete requests, and a form has been added to the bottom to display a list of existing Content Items. This form includes check boxes to allow the user to select Content Items to delete.

Listing 10.5 The *ManageAuthors.cfm* Template

```
<!---
File:          /catalog/ManageAuthors.cfm
Author:        david aden (david@wwstudios.com)
Date:          12/15/1999
Description:   Interface for creating, editing and deleting author objects.
Notes:
--->

<!--- Display the basic a2z formatting. --->
<CF_A2ZFORMATTING subtitle="Creating a New Author">

<!--- Log the page. --->
<CFA_PAGE
    DATASOURCE="#REQUEST.CFA.a2zBooks.DATASOURCE#"
    PAGENAME="a2z Author Management"
    SECTIONNAME="catalog"
    SITENAME="a2zBooks">
```

```
<!-------------------------------------------------------------
CREATE a new object and call the edit handler.
------------------------------------------------------------->
<CFIF IsDefined("FORM.CreateObject")>

    <!--- Set the variables we're going to pass in. --->
    <CFSET stParams = StructNew()>
    <CFSET stParams.Title = "Create New Author">
    <CFSET stParams.Message = "Enter the data for the new author.">

    <!--- Let's create an empty object and call the edit handler. --->
    <CFA_CONTENTOBJECTCREATE
         DATASOURCE="#REQUEST.CFA.a2zBooks.DATASOURCE#"
         TYPEID="#application.authorTypeID#"
         LABEL="__NEWITEM__"
         METHOD="EditAuthor"
         STPARAMS="#stParams#"
         BACTIVATE="No"
         R_ID="thisobjectid"
        >

<!-------------------------------------------------------------
UPDATE - This runs when the edit handler submits to itself.
    (This could be after a new Content Item has been created and the
    edit handler was called to populate it or could be after editing
    an existing item.)
------------------------------------------------------------->
<CFELSEIF IsDefined("FORM.CommitChanges")>

    <!--- Set a ReturnTo variable which will be used to tell the code
          where to go after completing. --->
    <CFSET stParams = StructNew()>
    <CFSET stParams.ReturnTo = "ManageAuthors.cfm">

    <CFA_CONTENTOBJECT
      DATASOURCE="#REQUEST.CFA.a2zBooks.DATASOURCE#"
      OBJECTID="#FORM.ObjectID#"
      METHOD="EditAuthor"
      STPARAMS="#stParams#"
      BSECURE="No"
      BLOGGING="No"
      BUSECACHE="No">

<!-------------------------------------------------------------
DELETE an object (confirming the user wants to do that is done
client-side)
------------------------------------------------------------->
<CFELSEIF IsDefined("Form.DeleteObject")>

    <!--- Delete it. --->
    <CFLOOP LIST="#FORM.DeleteList#" index="CurrAuthor">
```

continues

Listing 10.5 Continued

```
        <CFA_CONTENTOBJECTDELETE
              DATASOURCE="#REQUEST.CFA.a2zBooks.DATASOURCE#"
              OBJECTID="#CurrAuthor#">
    </CFLOOP>

    <!--- Reload the original page. --->
    <CFLOCATION URL="#cgi.script_name#">

<!-------------------------------------------------------------
EDIT an object -- this displays the edit form when an OBJECT ID is
    passed in as either a URL or FORM variable.
-------------------------------------------------------------->
<CFELSEIF IsDefined("URL.ObjectID") OR IsDefined("FORM.ObjectID")>

    <!--- Set a message that's displayed in the Edit handler. --->
    <CFSET stParams = StructNew()>
    <CFSET stParams.Message =
        "Edit the author's data, then click 'Save'.">
    <CFSET stParams.Title = "Edit Existing Author">
     <CFIF IsDefined("URL.ReturnTo")>
        <CFSET stParams.ReturnTo = URL.ReturnTo>
    </CFIF>

    <CFA_CONTENTOBJECT
          DATASOURCE="#REQUEST.CFA.a2zBooks.DATASOURCE#"
          OBJECTID="#iif(IsDefined('URL.ObjectID'),
               'URL.ObjectID','FORM.ObjectID')#"
          METHOD="EditAuthor"
          STPARAMS="#stParams#"
          BSECURE="Yes"
          BABORTONUNAUTHORIZEDACCESS="No"
          BLOGGING="No"
          BUSECACHE="No"
          R_STPARAMS="stParams" >

<!--- ELSE we're coming to the page for the first time. Display a list
        of the authors and buttons to create or delete them. --->
<CFELSE>

    <!--- A convenient place to run the custom tag to clean up
          stray objects. Normally, this would be run as a scheduled
          process or at application start-up. --->
    <CF_CLEANUPSTRAYOBJECTS
      DATASOURCE="#REQUEST.CFA.a2zBooks.DATASOURCE#"
      NEWOBJECTLABEL="__NEWITEM__"
      OBJECTEXPIRATIONTIME="10"
      R_NUMBERDELETED="NumDel">

    <SCRIPT LANGUAGE="JavaScript" TYPE="text/javascript">
    <!--
```

```
    // Warn the user about a request to delete.
    var Warned = false;

    function DeleteWarn(currAuthor) {

        if( ! Warned ) {
            if ( confirm('Are you sure you want to delete
            this author(s)?') ) {
                Warned = true;
                return true;
            }
            else {
                currAuthor.checked = false;
                return false;
            }
        }
    }
//-->
</SCRIPT>

<!--- Get all the active authors --->
<CFA_CONTENTOBJECTGETMULTIPLE
      DATASOURCE="#REQUEST.CFA.a2zBooks.DATASOURCE#"
      TYPEID="#application.AuthorTypeID#"
      BACTIVEONLY="False"
      R_STOBJECTS="stAuthor">

<!--- Order the authors by last name --->
<CFA_STRUCTSORTCOMMONSUBKEYS
    STRUCT="#stAuthor#"
    COMMONSUBKEY="LastName"
    SORTTYPE="textNoCase"
    R_ASORTEDKEYS="aAuthor">

<CFOUTPUT>

<!--- Get the query string --->
<CFSET IIf( Len(cgi.Query_string),
    "thisQueryString='?#cgi.query_string#'",
    "thisQueryString=''" )>

<CFFORM ACTION="#cgi.script_name##thisQueryString#" METHOD="post">
<!--- Outside table --->
<TABLE WIDTH="620" BORDER="0" CELLPADDING="0" CELLSPACING="0">
    <TR>
        <TD ALIGN="center" colspan="4">
        <FONT SIZE="+1">
            <B>Managing Authors</B>
            <BR><BR>
        </FONT>
        </TD>
```

Part II

Ch 10

continues

Listing 10.5 Continued

```
<TR>

<!--- Column headings --->
<TR>
    <TH align="left">Delete</TH>
    <TH align="left">Name</TH>
    <TH align="left">Email</TH>
    <TH align="left">Active</TH>
</TR>

<!--- Loop through the array that holds an ordered set of
      keys to the stAuthor structure. --->
<CFLOOP FROM="1" TO="#ArrayLen(aAuthor)#" INDEX="Counter">

    <!--- Set a local variable to hold the UUID of the current
          author --->
    <CFSET CurrAuthor = aAuthor[Counter]>
    <TR>

        <TD>
            <CFINPUT type="checkbox" NAME="DeleteList"
                VALUE="#CurrAuthor#"
                onclick="DeleteWarn(this);">
        </TD>
        <TD>
            <!--- Call this form to edit a particular
                  author. --->
            <A HREF="#CGI.Script_name#?ObjectID=#CurrAuthor#&
            ReturnTo=ManageAuthors.cfm">
                #stAuthor[CurrAuthor].LastName#,
                #stAuthor[CurrAuthor].FirstName#</A>
        </TD>
        <TD>
            <!--- If we have an entry in the Email array, then
                  display the first element of the array. --->
            <CFIF ArrayLen( stAuthor[CurrAuthor].Email )
                GREATER THAN 0>
                #stAuthor[CurrAuthor].Email[1]#
            <CFELSE>
                None
            </CFIF>
        </TD>
        <TD>
            <!--- If the attr_Active property is set to Yes,
                  then show the author is active. --->
            <CFIF stAuthor[CurrAuthor].attr_Active IS 'Yes'>
                Yes
            <CFELSE>
                No
            </CFIF>
```

```
                    </TD>
                </TR>
            </CFLOOP>

            <TR>
                <TD COLSPAN="3"> </TD>
            </TR>

            <TR>
                <TD COLSPAN="3" ALIGN="center">
                    <INPUT TYPE="submit"
                        NAME="CreateObject" VALUE="Create Author">
                    <INPUT TYPE="submit"
                        NAME="DeleteObject" VALUE="Delete">
                </TD>
            </TR>

        </TABLE>
        </CFFORM>
        </CFOUTPUT>

    </CFIF>

</CFA_PAGE>

</CF_A2ZFORMATTING><!--- Close the page formatting --->

<SCRIPT LANGUAGE="JavaScript" TYPE="text/javascript">
<!--
    // Focus on the first element
    if ( typeof(document.CreateAuthor) != 'undefined' ) {
        document.CreateAuthor.FirstName.focus();
    }

//-->
</SCRIPT>
```


Figure 10.12 shows the output of `ManageAuthors.cfm` when the user first requests the page.

Listing 10.5 is based on Listing 10.2 with expanded functionality. The following description will focus on what has been added to the template, rather than repeat things covered in the explanation of Listing 10.2.

Like the earlier template, this one is a self-posting form, and the bottom half of the template runs when the user first requests the page. The display section begins by running the `<CF_CLEANUPSTRAYOBJECTS>` described earlier in the "Cleaning Up Incomplete Content Items" section. Normally this tag would be run as a scheduled item or at application startup, but it is here to demonstrate how it's called.

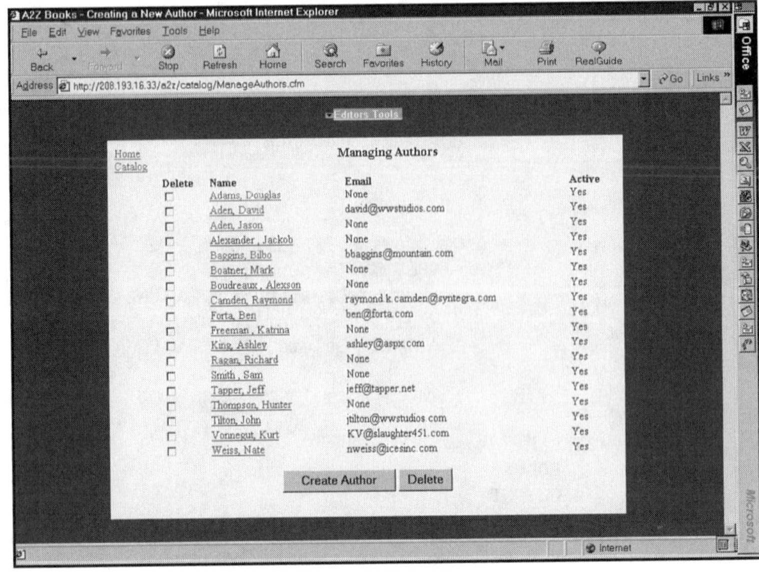

FIGURE 10.12
The `ManageAuthors.cfm` template displays a list of available authors, with access to add, edit, and delete functions.

The template uses JavaScript to caution the user that he is about to delete an author when he selects one for deletion.

NOTE The JavaScript warning box appears only when the user picks the first Content Item to delete. No further warnings are issued.

The template then calls the `<CFA_CONTENTOBJECTGETMULTIPLE>` tag to get all Author Content Items. The `bActiveOnly` attribute is set to `false`, so both active and inactive items are returned. The actual Content Items are returned in the variable specified in the `r_stObjects` variable—`stAuthor`.

Because the elements of ColdFusion structures aren't returned in any specific order, we use the `<CFA_STRUCTSORTCOMMONSUBKEYS>` tag to get an ordered list of structure keys. `stAuthor` is a structure made up of structures, as follows:

```
stAuthor[OBJECT UUID].OBJECTPROPERTIES
```

The top-level key (`OBJECT UUID`) is the UUID of each author found by `<CFA_CONTENTOBJECT-GETMULTIPLE>`. The subkeys are the properties for each Author Content Item, so part of a single Author element might look like this (this UUID is fictitious):

```
stAuthor[59BE8A58-9D5E-11D3-846900E02C0708AF].FirstName = 'Ben'
stAuthor[59BE8A58-9D5E-11D3-846900E02C0708AF].LastName = 'Forta'
stAuthor[59BE8A58-9D5E-11D3-846900E02C0708AF].Bio = 'Ben is the ....'
...
```

<CFA_STRUCTSORTCOMMONSUBKEYS> expects to be passed a subkey (such as LastName in the preceding) in its commonSubKey attribute and returns a regular array whose element values are the top-level keys (Author UUIDs in the preceding) ordered by the values in the subkey. When you loop through the array returned by <CFA_STRUCTSORTCOMMONSUBKEYS>, you get the top-level keys of the structure ordered by the subkey. In Listing 10.5, the returned array is named aAuthor. Looping through this array will give us a set of Author UUIDs in LastName order. This loop is done with the following:

```
<CFLOOP FROM="1" TO="#ArrayLen(aAuthor)#" INDEX="Counter">
    <CFSET CurrAuthor = aAuthor[Counter]>
```

The heart of the display section generates a table that contains all the authors found with <CFA_CONTENTOBJECTGETMULTIPLE> in order by last name. Each row contains a check box the user clicks to indicate that he wants to delete the author. Multiple authors can be selected for deletion.

After the user selects the authors to delete, he clicks a Delete button at the bottom of the page. This self-submits the form, which is caught by

```
<CFELSEIF IsDefined("Form.DeleteObject")>
```

The template then loops through the list of object IDs selected for deletion and calls <CFA_CONTENTOBJECTDELETE> on each one.

Back in the display section, each author's name is an anchor tag that links to the current template. When the user clicks a name, ManageAuthors.cfm is requested with the selected author's object ID passed as a URL variable. This is caught by the following statement:

```
<CFELSEIF IsDefined("URL.ObjectID") OR IsDefined("FORM.ObjectID")>
```

When this succeeds, we call <CFA_CONTENTOBJECT> to invoke the EditAuthor method on the Author Content Item as contained in the URL variable ObjectID. The EditAuthor handler works the same way here as it does in Listing 10.2. So, by adding additional handler sections and expanding the display section of ManageAuthorsMini.cfm, we've expanded the template's function to show a list of existing authors and provide users a way to edit or delete them.

Advanced Content Management: Multilingual Properties and Embedded Objects

Spectra provides some advanced capabilities for Content Management:

- Spectra supports multilingual properties of types char and longchar, which opens the door to providing versions of your site in more than one language, depending on the preferences set by the user. Date and number formatting for multiple languages isn't a Spectra-specific function, but it may be done by using the ColdFusion international functions such as LSDateFormat(). (For more information on ColdFusion international functions, see *The ColdFusion 4.0 Web Application Construction Kit* by Ben Forta.)

- Spectra allows you to embed Content Items within other Content Items. In some cases, this can simplify coding—especially if one Content Item needs to be shared by many different Content Items. In that case, you can create one original version of the Content Item and embed it as a shared object within other Content Items. Changes to the original are propagated to all the others.

This section introduces you to using multilingual properties and embedded objects by creating an object that contains both, the PressRelease ContentObject Type.

Creating Multilingual and Embedded Object Properties

This section assumes that you understand how to create ContentObject Types. Thus, it concentrates only on how to create properties that will hold multilingual and embedded properties.

▶ **See** Chapter 6 for more information on creating ContentObject Types.

Follow these steps:

1. In the Webtop, click System Design.
2. Open the Site Object Designer in the left column.
3. Click Type Designer. At the bottom of the form, click `Create`.
4. Enter **`PressRelease`** in the Label text box. Enter a description and then the handler path: **`/allaire/spectra/handlers/A2Z/PressRelease/`**

   Figure 10.13 shows the New Type definition for the PressRelease object.

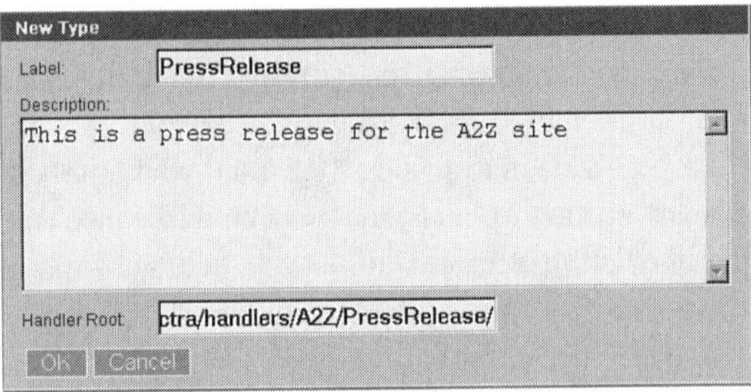

FIGURE 10.13
Use the New Type form to create a new ContentObject Type.

5. Click OK.
6. Click the Properties tab. Add a `Title` property of type `char`. Click Add.
7. In the New Type Property Definition form, select Multilingual (see Figure 10.14) and then click `OK`.
8. Create a `BodyText` property of type `longchar` and make it multilingual as well.
9. Create a `RelatedAuthor` property that will hold information on the author about whom the press release is written. Make this property of type `embeddedAuthor`. `embeddedAuthor` is a property definition that can be used to embed Author Content Items into other Content Items. It is created in Chapter 8, Building the Site Structure."

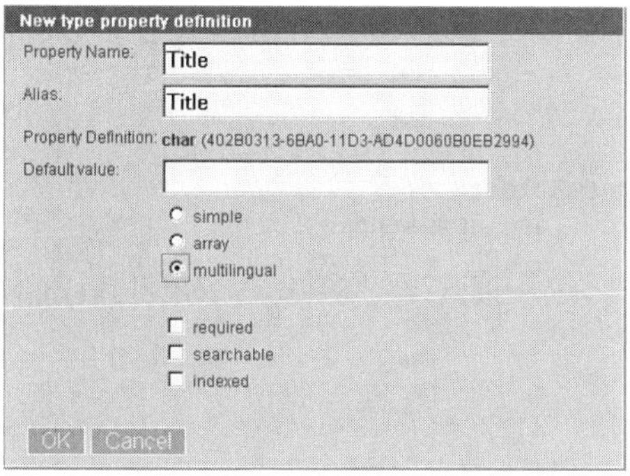

FIGURE 10.14
Setting a property as multilingual allows you to store more than one language version of the property.

10. For simplicity, allow users to specify only one embedded author by selecting `Simple`, although the New Type Property Definition form allows you to define a property as an array of embedded objects by selecting `Array`. Figure 10.15 shows the new `RelatedAuthor` property and the option for creating it as an array property. When you finish defining the property, click `OK`.

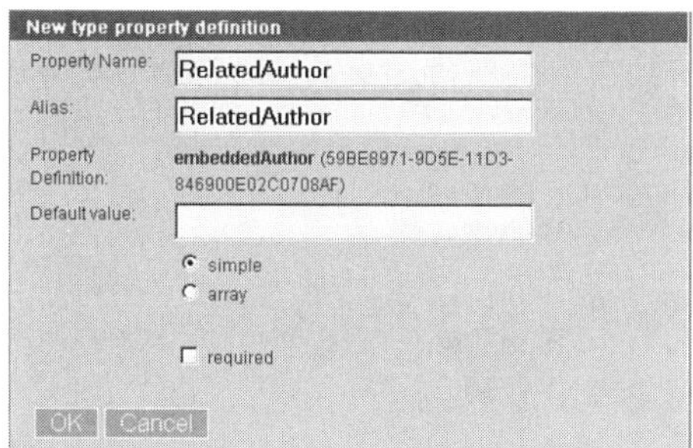

FIGURE 10.15
Embedded object properties can be single objects or arrays of embedded objects.

11. Use the Methods tab to define one method for this ContentObject Type: `PREdit`. The handler template name is `PREdit.cfm`.

NOTE Spectra uses the ISO 639 two-character language codes to manage its multilingual functions. You can get a complete list of these codes at `http://www.ics.uci.edu/pub/ietf/http/related/iso639.txt`.

Managing Objects with Multilingual and Embedded Object Properties

Our PressRelease ContentObject Type now contains two multilingual properties and an embedded object, so we need to build pages and handlers that will accommodate these. Listing 10.6 contains a Web root template for managing PressRelease Content Items. It's based on the template examined in Listing 10.5 for managing Author Content Items but has been adapted to the PressRelease ContentObject Type.

Listing 10.6 Managing the Interaction with the PressRelease ContentObject Type

```
<!---
File:         /news/PressRelease.cfm
Author:       david aden (david@wwstudios.com)
Date:         3/19/00
Description:  Interface for creating, editing and deleting press
              releases.
Notes:
--->

<!--- Display the basic a2z formatting. --->
<CF_A2ZFORMATTING subtitle="Managing Press Releases">

<!--- Log the page. --->
<CFA_PAGE
    DATASOURCE="#REQUEST.CFA.a2zBooks.DATASOURCE#"
    PAGENAME="Press Releases"
    SECTIONNAME="News"
    SITENAME="A2ZBooks">

    <!--- Set the Press Release Content Object Type --->
    <CFSET PressReleaseID = '10B781B5-FDFA-11D3-A09800C04F1871CA'>

    <!--- Populate a structure to translate between the language codes
            and full language names --->
    <CFSET stLanguages = StructNew()>
    <CFSCRIPT>
        stLanguages['en'] = 'English';
        stLanguages['es'] = 'Spanish';
        stLanguages['de'] = 'German';
    </CFSCRIPT>

    <!--- Set the default language to English --->
    <CFPARAM name="Session.Language" default="en">

    <!--- If we're passing a Language variable, then set it into a
            Session variable --->
    <CFIF IsDefined("FORM.Language")>
        <CFSET Session.Language = FORM.Language>
    <CFELSEIF IsDefined("URL.Language")>
        <CFSET Session.Language = URL.Language>
    </CFIF>

    <!---------------------------------------------------------------
    HANDLER SECTION: This is the section that catches all posts or
    links to this template.
    --------------------------------------------------------------->
    <!---------------------------------------------------------------
```

```
CREATE a new object and call the edit handler.
---------------------------------------------------------------->
<CFIF IsDefined("FORM.CreateObject")>

    <!--- Set the variables we're going to pass in. --->
    <CFSET stParams = StructNew()>
    <CFSET stParams.Title = "Create New Press Release">
    <CFSET stParams.Message = "You must create an English version of
        all press releases before creating other versions.">

    <!--- Let's create an empty object and call the edit handler. --->
    <CFA_CONTENTOBJECTCREATE
         DATASOURCE="#REQUEST.CFA.a2zBooks.DATASOURCE#"
         TYPEID="#PressReleaseID#"
         LABEL="__NEWITEM__"
         METHOD="PREdit"
         STPARAMS="#stParams#"
         BACTIVATE="No"
         R_ID="thisobjectid"
        >

<!----------------------------------------------------------------
CREATE a new language version of the object.
---------------------------------------------------------------->
 <CFELSEIF IsDefined("FORM.NewLanguage")>

    <CFIF NOT IsDefined("FORM.AddLanguage")>
        You need to select a press release to add a language to!<BR>
        <BR>
        Please go back.
        <CFABORT>
    </CFIF>

    <!--- Set the current object --->
    <CFSET ObjectID = FORM.AddLanguage>

    <!--- Set the variables we're going to pass in. --->
    <CFSET stParams = StructNew()>
    <CFSET stParams.Title = "Add a Language Version">
    <CFSET stParams.Message = "Add a #stLanguages[Session.Language]#
        press release.">

    <CFA_CONTENTOBJECT
         DATASOURCE="#REQUEST.CFA.a2zBooks.DATASOURCE#"
         OBJECTID="#ObjectID#"
         METHOD="PREdit"
         STPARAMS="#stParams#"
         BSECURE="Yes"
         BABORTONUNAUTHORIZEDACCESS="No"
         BLOGGING="No"
```

continues

Listing 10.6 Continued

```
           BUSECACHE="No"
           R_STPARAMS="stParams" >

<!-----------------------------------------------------------------
UPDATE - This runs when the edit handler submits to itself.
    (This could be after a new Content Item has been created and the
    edit handler was called to populate it or could be after editing
    an existing item.)
------------------------------------------------------------------>
<CFELSEIF IsDefined("FORM.CommitChanges")>

    <!--- Set a ReturnTo variable which will be used to tell the code
          where to go after completing. --->
    <CFSET stParams = StructNew()>
    <CFSET stParams.ReturnTo = "PressRelease.cfm">

    <CFA_CONTENTOBJECT
      DATASOURCE="#REQUEST.CFA.a2zBooks.DATASOURCE#"
      OBJECTID="#FORM.ObjectID#"
      METHOD="PREdit"
      STPARAMS="#stParams#"
      BSECURE="No"
      BLOGGING="No"
      BUSECACHE="No">

<!-----------------------------------------------------------------
DELETE an object (confirming the user wants to do that is done
client-side)
------------------------------------------------------------------>
<CFELSEIF IsDefined("Form.DeleteObject")>

    <!--- Delete it. --->
    <CFLOOP LIST="#FORM.DeleteList#" index="CurrPressRelease">
        <CFA_CONTENTOBJECTDELETE
              DATASOURCE="#REQUEST.CFA.a2zBooks.DATASOURCE#"
              OBJECTID="#CurrPressRelease#">
    </CFLOOP>

    <!--- Reload the original page. --->
    <CFLOCATION URL="#cgi.script_name#">

<!-----------------------------------------------------------------
If we're passing an AuthorID, let's display the data about the
    author.
------------------------------------------------------------------>
<CFELSEIF IsDefined("URL.ShowAuthor")>

    <CFA_CONTENTOBJECT
        DATASOURCE="#REQUEST.CFA.a2zBooks.DATASOURCE#"
        OBJECTID="#URL.ObjectID#.RelatedAuthor"
        METHOD="DisplayPlain">
```

```
<!------------------------------------------------------------------
EDIT an object -- this displays the edit form when an OBJECT ID is
    passed in as either a URL or FORM variable.
------------------------------------------------------------------->
<CFELSEIF IsDefined("URL.ObjectID") OR IsDefined("FORM.ObjectID")
    OR IsDefined("FORM.NewLanguage")>

    <!--- Set a message that's displayed in the Edit handler. --->
    <CFSET stParams = StructNew()>
    <CFSET stParams.Message =
        "Edit the press release data, then click 'Save'.">
    <CFSET stParams.Title = "Edit Existing Press Release">
     <CFIF IsDefined("URL.ReturnTo")>
        <CFSET stParams.ReturnTo = URL.ReturnTo>
    </CFIF>

    <CFA_CONTENTOBJECT
          DATASOURCE="#REQUEST.CFA.a2zBooks.DATASOURCE#"
          OBJECTID="#iif(IsDefined('URL.ObjectID'),
              'URL.ObjectID','FORM.ObjectID')#"
          METHOD="PREdit"
          STPARAMS="#stParams#"
          BSECURE="Yes"
          BABORTONUNAUTHORIZEDACCESS="No"
          BLOGGING="No"
          BUSECACHE="No"
          R_STPARAMS="stParams" >

<!------------------------------------------------------------------
DISPLAY SECTION: We're coming to the page for the first time.
    Display a list of the press release and buttons to create or
    delete them.
------------------------------------------------------------------->
<CFELSE>

    <SCRIPT LANGUAGE="JavaScript" TYPE="text/javascript">
    <!--
        // Warn the user about a request to delete.
        var Warned = false;

        function DeleteWarn(currPressRelease) {

            if( ! Warned ) {
                if ( confirm('Are you sure you want to
                     delete this Press Release(s)?') ) {
                    Warned = true;
                    return true;
                }
                else {
                    currPressRelease.checked = false;
                    return false;
```

continues

Listing 10.6 Continued

```
            }
        }
    }
//-->
</SCRIPT>

<!--- Get all the active press releases --->
<CFA_CONTENTOBJECTGETMULTIPLE
      DATASOURCE="#REQUEST.CFA.a2zBooks.DATASOURCE#"
      TYPEID="#PressReleaseID#"
      BACTIVEONLY="False"
      R_STOBJECTS="stPressRelease">

<CFOUTPUT>

<!--- Get the query string --->
<CFSET IIf( Len(cgi.Query_string),
    "thisQueryString='?#cgi.query_string#'",
    "thisQueryString=''" )>

<CFFORM ACTION="#cgi.script_name##thisQueryString#"
    METHOD="post"
    NAME="CreatePressRelease">
<!--- Outside table --->
<TABLE WIDTH="620" BORDER="1" CELLPADDING="0" CELLSPACING="0">
    <TR>
        <TD ALIGN="center" colspan="10">
        <FONT SIZE="+1">
            <B>Managing Press Releases</B>
            <BR><BR>
        </FONT>
        </TD>
    <TR>

    <!--- Column headings --->
    <TR>
        <TH ALIGN="Center" WIDTH="25">Delete</TH>
        <TH ALIGN="Center" WIDTH="25">New Lang</TH>
        <TH ALIGN="Left" WIDTH="25">Language</TH>
        <TH ALIGN="Left" WIDTH="300">Title</TH>
        <TH ALIGN="Left" WIDTH="50">Related Author</TH>
        <TH ALIGN="Left" WIDTH="25">Active</TH>
    </TR>

    <!--- Loop through the array that holds an ordered set of
          keys to the stPressRelease structure. --->
    <CFLOOP COLLECTION="#stPressRelease#" ITEM="CurrPressRelease">

        <!--- Loop through all the languages present for the
              current press release --->
```

```
            <CFLOOP
                COLLECTION="#stPressRelease[CurrPressRelease].Title#"
                ITEM="CurrLang">
            <TR>
                <TD ALIGN="Center">
                    <CFINPUT type="checkbox" NAME="DeleteList"
                        VALUE="#CurrPressRelease#"
                        onclick="DeleteWarn(this);">
                </TD ALIGN="Center">
                <TD>
                    <CFINPUT type="radio" NAME="AddLanguage"
                        VALUE="#CurrPressRelease#">
                </TD>
                <TD>
                  <A HREF="#CGI.SCRIPT_NAME#?ObjectID=#CurrPressRelease#
                   &Language=#CurrLang#">
                      #stLanguages[CurrLang]#</a>
                </TD>
                <TD>
                    <!--- Display the title for the current
                            language --->
                    #stPressRelease[CurrPressRelease].Title[CurrLang]#

                </TD>

                <!--- Display the related author name --->
                <TD>
<A HREF="PressRelease.cfm?ShowAuthor=1&ObjectID=#CurrPressRelease#">
  #stPressRelease[CurrPressRelease].RelatedAuthor.Label#</A>
                </TD>
                <TD>
                    <!--- If the attr_Active property is set to Yes,
                            then show the press release is active. --->
                    <CFIF stPressRelease[CurrPressRelease].attr_Active
                    IS 'Yes'>
                        Yes
                    <CFELSE>
                        No
                    </CFIF>
                </TD>
            </TR>
            </CFLOOP>
        </CFLOOP>

        <TR>
            <TD COLSPAN="10"> </TD>
        </TR>

        <TR>
            <TD COLSPAN="10" ALIGN="center">
                <INPUT TYPE="submit"
```

continues

Listing 10.6 Continued

```
                        NAME="CreateObject" VALUE="Create Press Release">
                    <INPUT TYPE="submit"
                        NAME="DeleteObject" VALUE="Delete">
                </TD>
            </TR>

            <TR>
                <TD COLSPAN="10" ALIGN="center">
                    <SELECT NAME="Language">
                        <OPTION VALUE="en" SELECTED>English
                        <OPTION VALUE="es">Spanish
                        <OPTION VALUE="de">German
                    </SELECT>

                    <INPUT TYPE="Submit" NAME="NewLanguage"
                        VALUE="Create New Language">
                </TD>
            </TR>

        </TABLE>
        </CFFORM>
        </CFOUTPUT>

    </CFIF>

</CFA_PAGE>

</CF_A2ZFORMATTING><!--- Close the page formatting --->
```

You can run `PressRelease.cfm` by requesting it in your browser:

`http://your_A2Z_install_machine/a2z/news/PressRelease.cfm`

Figure 10.16 shows the form as it appears when no press releases have been created.

At the top of the template we set the `PressRelease` ContentObject Type ID to a local variable for convenience. We then create a structure, `stLanguages`, that translates between the two-character codes Spectra uses to identify languages and the full name of the language. We've entered only three languages here, but in a production application this list would likely be much longer, and the structure would be populated at application startup in the `application.cfm` file.

NOTE A list of all the language abbreviations used by Spectra is available at `http://www.ics.uci.edu/pub/ietf/http/related/iso639.txt`.

Next, we set a default language into `Session.Language` and then check whether `Language` has been passed as either a `URL` or `FORM` variable. Then we have a series of `<CFIF>` and `<CFELSEIF>` statements that catch various actions the user may take. The first time the user requests the template, he falls through to the display section contained in the `<CFELSE>`.

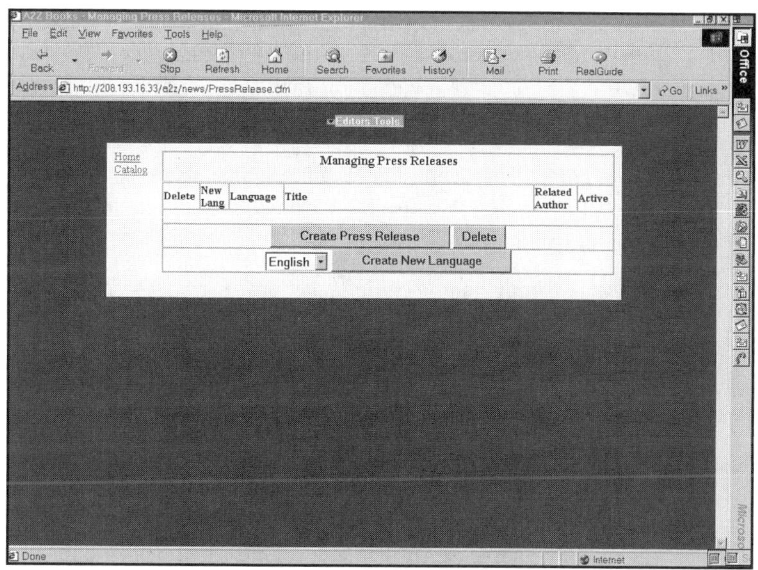

FIGURE 10.16 The `PressRelease.cfm` template provides an interface for adding, editing, or deleting press releases.

The display section begins with some JavaScript that pops up a warning box when the user selects a PressRelease for deletion.

After that we use a `<CFA_CONTENTOBJECTGETMULTIPLE>` to retrieve all the `PressRelease` Content Items into `stPressRelease`. The rest of the display section is a self-posting form. The first part of the form is standard HTML; the interesting part starts with the `<CFLOOP>` through the `stPressRelease` structure. Normally, one loop would be sufficient to cycle through the returned press releases but, because we have multilingual fields within the PressRelease Content Items, we need an inner loop that cycles through the keys for the multilingual `Title` property. `Title` has a key for each version of `Title`—the structure keys consist of the two-character identifier used to uniquely identify a language as described in the Note above.

Multilingual properties are implemented as structures. A key exists for each language for which a version of the property has been created. This flexible architecture allows you to add as many versions of a Content Item as needed for your application without having to change the code used to handle the Content Items.

The template displays each version of each PressRelease on its own row. The row includes a check box to mark the PressRelease for deletion. For the purpose of this demonstration, we will delete the Content Item as a whole, not individual versions of it.

Each row has a radio button the user clicks when he wants to create a new version of a press release. The use of this is covered later.

Next is an anchor tag that links back to the current template and passes URL variables containing the current object ID as well as the current language. Following this is a line that displays the title for the current version of each press release:

```
#stPressRelease[CurrPressRelease].Title[CurrLang]#
```

The last item of interest is another anchor tag that also links to the current template and passes the URL variable `ShowAuthor`. We'll use this link to demonstrate how you can invoke a method on an embedded object.

Now, let's walk through some common actions. First, let's create a new press release.

When the user clicks the `Create Press Release` button, the display section form self-submits and passes the form variable `CreateObject`. This is caught in the handling section of the template by

```
<CFIF IsDefined("FORM.CreateObject")>
```

Just as we did in Listing 10.5, we use `<CFA_CONTENTOBJECTCREATE>` to create a new Content Item and then invoke a method on it. In this case, we invoke the `PREdit` handler. Spectra creates an empty PressRelease with default (empty) English versions of both the `Title` and `BodyText` multilingual properties. Figure 10.17 shows the form generated by the `PREdit` handler.

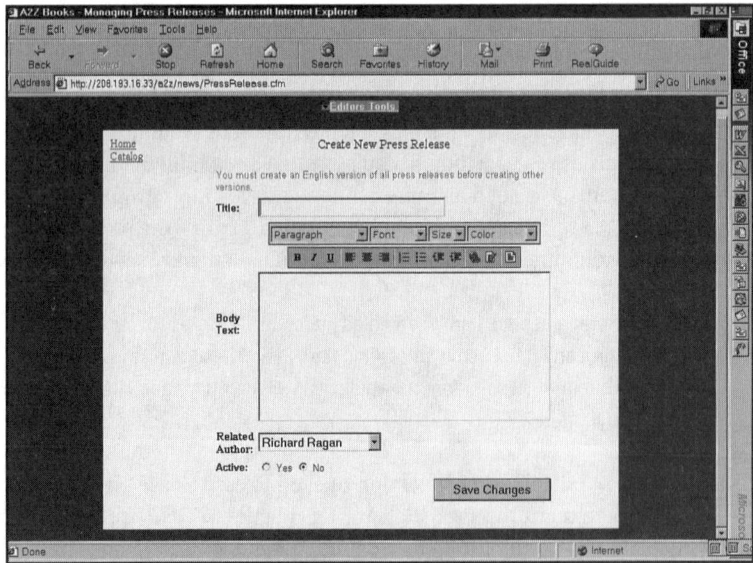

FIGURE 10.17
The `PREdit` handler displays a form for entering or editing information about a PressRelease Content Item.

When the user submits the form generated by the PREdit handler, it self-submits back to the PressRelease.cfm template. This is caught by

```
<CFELSEIF IsDefined("FORM.CommitChanges")>
```

which re-invokes the PREdit handler. Inside PREdit, the PressRelease information is updated.

We'll need to look at PREdit.cfm to understand how this works, but first look at the additions to the handler section that exist to accommodate the multilingual properties and the embedded Author object. When the user clicks the Create New Language button, the following catches the submission:

```
<CFELSEIF IsDefined("FORM.NewLanguage")>
```

This checks to see if the user selected a row using the radio button in the New Lang column and generates an error message if not. If a row was selected, it sets a local ObjectID variable to the value passed in the radio button, since this is the PressRelease for which we're going to create a new version. The selected language is passed from the Form drop-down box and is assigned to Session.Language near the top of PressRelease.cfm. The code then invokes the PREdit method and data entry proceeds as usual.

The only other new addition to the handler section displays the data contained in an embedded Author object. In this application, all press releases are required to relate to an author, and the related Author object is embedded directly into the PressRelease Content Item. The request to display the author information is caught with

```
<CFELSEIF IsDefined("URL.ShowAuthor")>
```

Displaying the embedded data consists of one step—invoking a method on the embedded Author object with

```
<CFA_CONTENTOBJECT
    DATASOURCE="#REQUEST.CFA.a2zBooks.DATASOURCE#"
    OBJECTID="#URL.ObjectID#.RelatedAuthor"
    METHOD="DisplayPlain">
```

This uses the familiar <CFA_CONTENTOBJECT> tag to invoke the method but, rather than pass it a simple object ID, we've passed it the object ID for our current PressRelease, concatenated with the property that holds the embedded object, RelatedAuthor. Spectra looks up the parent object (the PressRelease), and then finds the embedded object (the Author) and invokes the DisplayPlain method on that Author object. DisplayPlain is a method of the Author object and is defined the same way any other method is defined.

Coding Edit Handlers for Objects with Multilingual and Embedded Object Properties

Now let's look at the PREdit.cfm handler template in Listing 10.7 to see how the multilingual properties are updated and how we create an embedded Author object.

Listing 10.7 Providing a Form for Entering or Updating Information in the PressRelease Content Items

```
<!---
File:          PREdit.cfm
Author:        david aden (david@wwstudios.com)
Date:          3/19/00
Description:   Edit Handler for a2zBooks press release object type
Notes:
--->
<!--- use the handler tag to set the scope up --->
<CFA_HANDLER
    OBJECT="PressRelease"
    SEPARATOR="<p>">

<!-----------------------------------------------------------------
HANDLER SECTION: Check if the user is submitting the form or displaying
----------------------------------------------------------------->
<CFIF ISDEFINED("FORM.CommitChanges")>

    <!--- update the object --->
    <CFA_CONTENTOBJECTDATA
        DATASOURCE = "#request.cfa.a2zbooks.datasource#"
        OBJECTID = "#objectid#"
        ISOLANGUAGE="#SESSION.Language#">

        <CFA_CONTENTOBJECTPROPERTY NAME="Label"
            VALUE="#Form.Title#">

        <!--- update the following properties --->
        <CFA_CONTENTOBJECTPROPERTY NAME="Title"
            VALUE="#Form.Title#">
        <CFA_CONTENTOBJECTPROPERTY NAME="BodyText"
            VALUE="#Form.BodyText#">
        <CFA_CONTENTOBJECTPROPERTY NAME="ATTR_ACTIVE"
            VALUE="#form.Active#">

    </CFA_CONTENTOBJECTDATA>

    <!--- Check if there is anything in the RelatedAuthor property.
            If not, then we need to create the embedded object. --->
    <CFIF NOT IsStruct(PressRelease.RelatedAuthor)>

        <CFA_CONTENTOBJECTCREATEEMBEDDEDFROMORIGINAL
            DATASOURCE = "#request.cfa.a2zbooks.datasource#"
            OBJECTID="#ObjectID#.RelatedAuthor"
            ORIGINALOBJECTID="#FORM.RelatedAuthor#">

    </CFIF>

    <!--- return to the main page --->
    <CFIF StructKeyExists(Attributes.stParams, "ReturnTo")>
```

```
        <CFLOCATION URL="#Attributes.stParams.ReturnTo#">
    </CFIF>

<!-------------------------------------------------------------------
DISPLAY SECTION
------------------------------------------------------------------->
<CFELSE>

    <!--- Get a list of all the authors --->
    <CFA_CONTENTOBJECTGETMULTIPLE
        DATASOURCE="#request.cfa.a2zbooks.datasource#"
        TYPEID="#application.AuthorTypeID#"
        r_stObjects="stAuthors">

    <CFOUTPUT>

    <!--- Set the query string (So a stray question mark doesn't
            appear if there is nothing in the query string). --->
    <CFSET IIf( Len(cgi.QUERY_STRING),
        "thisQueryString='?#cgi.query_string#'",
        "thisQueryString=''" )>

    <CFFORM NAME="PressReleaseForm"
        ACTION="#CGI.SCRIPT_NAME##thisQueryString#" METHOD="POST">

    <!--- Pass along the ID for the object we're dealing
            with. --->
    <INPUT TYPE="hidden"
        NAME="ObjectID"
        VALUE="#PressRelease.ObjectID#">

     <!--- Outside table --->
    <TABLE WIDTH="620"
        BORDER="0"
        CELLPADDING="0"
        CELLSPACING="0">
        <TR>
            <TD ALIGN="center">
            <FONT size="+1">
                <CFIF StructKeyExists(Attributes.stParams,
                    "Title")>
                    #Attributes.stParams.Title#
                <CFELSE>
                    Press Release Edit Form
                </CFIF>
                <BR><BR>
            </FONT>
            </TD>
        </TR>
        <TR>
            <TD VALIGN="top" ALIGN="Center">
```


continues

Listing 10.7 Continued

```
<CENTER>
<!--- FORM table --->
<TABLE BORDER="0"
    CELLPADDING=2
    CELLSPACING=2 WIDTH="455" >
    <CFIF StructKeyExists(Attributes.stParams,
        "Message")>
        <TR>
            <TD COLSPAN=2>
            <FONT FACE="arial"
                SIZE="-1" COLOR="red">
                #Attributes.stParams.Message#
            </FONT></TD>
        </TR>
    </CFIF>
    <TR>
        <TD><FONT FACE="arial" SIZE="-1">
            <b>Title:</b>
        </FONT></TD>

        <!--- If the language already exists
            in the title property, then we
            should use it else set a
            default --->
        <CFIF StructKeyExists(PressRelease.Title,
          SESSION.Language)>
            <CFSET MyTitle =
              Trim(PressRelease.Title[SESSION.Language])>
        <CFELSE>
            <CFSET MyTitle = "">
        </CFIF>
        <TD><FONT FACE="arial" SIZE="-1">
            <INPUT TYPE="text"
              NAME="Title"
              SIZE="30"
              VALUE="#MyTitle#">
        </FONT></TD>
    </TR>
    <TR>
        <TD><FONT FACE="arial" SIZE="-1">
            <b>Body Text:</b>
        </FONT></TD>
        <TD>

        <CFIF StructKeyExists(PressRelease.BodyText,
          SESSION.Language)>
            <CFSET MyBodyText =
             Trim(PressRelease.BodyText[SESSION.Language])>
        <CFELSE>
            <CFSET MyBodyText = "">
        </CFIF>
```

```
        <CFA_HTMLEDITOR
            NAME="BodyText"
            HEIGHT="200"
            WIDTH="400"
            VALUE="#MyBodyText#"
            FORM="PressReleaseForm">
        </TD>
    </TR>

    <TR>
        <TD><B>Related Author:</B></TD>
        <TD>
            <CFIF NOT IsStruct(PressRelease.RelatedAuthor)>
                <SELECT NAME="RelatedAuthor">
                <CFLOOP COLLECTION="#stAuthors#"
                 ITEM="CurrAuthor">
                 <OPTION
                  VALUE="#stAuthors[CurrAuthor].ObjectID#">
                     #stAuthors[CurrAuthor].Label#
                </CFLOOP>
                </SELECT>
            <CFELSE>
                <B>#PressRelease.RelatedAuthor.Label#</B>
            </CFIF>
        </TD>
    </TR>

    <TR>
        <TD ><FONT FACE="arial" SIZE="-1">
            <b>Active:</b>
        </FONT></TD>
        <TD><FONT FACE="arial" SIZE="-1">
            <INPUT TYPE="radio"
                NAME="Active"
                VALUE="1"
                <CFIF PressRelease.ATTR_ACTIVE>
                CHECKED</CFIF>> Yes
            <INPUT TYPE="radio"
                NAME="Active"
                VALUE="0"
                <CFIF NOT PressRelease.ATTR_ACTIVE>
                CHECKED</CFIF>> No
        </FONT></TD>
    </TR>
    <TR>
        <TD COLSPAN=2 ALIGN="right">
        <FONT FACE="arial" SIZE="-1">
        <INPUT Name="CommitChanges"
            TYPE="submit"
            VALUE="Save Changes">
        </FONT></TD>
```

continues

Listing 10.7 Continued

```
                    </TR>
                </TABLE>    <!--- End FORM table. --->
                </CENTER>
            </TD>
        </TR>
    </TABLE> <!--- Outside table --->
    </CFFORM>
    </CFOUTPUT>
</CFIF>
</CFA_HANDLER>
```

The bottom half of the display section starts by calling <CFA_CONTENTOBJECTGETMULTIPLE> to get all the existing Author Content Items. We'll need them later.

Most of the rest of the form is similar to the one in Listing 10.5, until we get to the code that displays the PressRelease title. Rather than access `PressRelease.Title` as we would for a single-version property, we need to access the version of `Title` for the currently selected language. This is accomplished with the following:

```
<CFIF StructKeyExists(PressRelease.Title, SESSION.Language)>
    <CFSET MyTitle = Trim(PressRelease.Title[SESSION.Language])>
<CFELSE>
    <CFSET MyTitle = "">
</CFIF>
```

This checks for the existence of a key under `PressRelease.Title` that matches the current language (as contained in `Session.Language`). If it finds it, it sets a local variable to hold the title; if not, it sets the local variable to the empty string. We do the same thing with the `BodyText` property, except we use <CFA_HTMLEDITOR> to display an in-line WYSIWYG editor.

For the embedded Author object, we want to first check to see if the Content Item already has an embedded author. If not, we give the user the option of selecting an author; if it does, we display the author's name. This is accomplished with

```
<CFIF NOT IsStruct(PressRelease.RelatedAuthor)>
    <SELECT NAME="RelatedAuthor">
        <CFLOOP COLLECTION="#stAuthors#" ITEM="CurrAuthor">
            <OPTION VALUE="#stAuthors[CurrAuthor].ObjectID#">
                #stAuthors[CurrAuthor].Label#
        </CFLOOP>
    </SELECT>
<CFELSE>
    <B>#PressRelease.RelatedAuthor.Label#</B>
</CFIF>
```

If an author hasn't yet been embedded in the PressRelease, the `IsStruct()` function will fail, and we will show the user a drop-down box of available authors. If an object has been embedded, we just display the author's name (which was stored in the Content Item's `Label` property).

When the user clicks the Save Changes button, the form self-submits to `PressRelease.cfm` and is caught; the `PREdit` handler is invoked. This time, the handler section of `PREdit` runs.

To do the update we use the `<CFA_CONTENTOBJECTDATA>` tag and a series of `<CFA_CONTENTOBJECTPROPERTY>`. The only difference between updating an object with multilingual properties and without is the use of the `ISOLanguage` attribute. By specifying this attribute to `<CFA_CONTENTOBJECTDATA>`, we tell Spectra which version of the multilingual properties to update.

The only property we haven't updated is the `RelatedAuthors` property that contains the embedded object. That is done next. First, we check to see if `RelatedAuthors` already contains an embedded object by using the `IsStruct()` property to test whether it contains a structure. If it doesn't, we run the following:

```
<CFA_CONTENTOBJECTCREATEEMBEDDEDFROMORIGINAL
    DATASOURCE = "#request.cfa.a2zbooks.datasource#"
    OBJECTID="#ObjectID#.RelatedAuthor"
    ORIGINALOBJECTID="#FORM.RelatedAuthor#">
```

This tag creates an embedded object from what is called a *standalone original*—that is, a Content Item that already exists. In this case, we've chosen to embed a copy of the original object so that any changes to the original Author Content Item will be reflected in the PressReleases in which it is embedded.

The `<CFA_CONTENTOBJECTCREATEEMBEDDEDFROMORIGINAL>` tag uses the `ObjectID` attribute to tell it which object to embed into, as well as the property where the embedded object will live. It uses the `OriginalObjectID` attribute to determine which existing object to embed.

Fully Embedded Versus Shared Objects

Spectra supports two types of embedded objects, usually referred to as *fully embedded* and *shared embedded* objects. For you to understand the difference, I need to define a couple of words. Allaire uses the term *parent* to refer to a Content Item that has an embedded object. The word *child* refers to an object that's embedded in a Content Item.

A fully embedded object exists only within its parent Content Item. Updates to a fully embedded object affect only the data in the Content Item in which it is embedded.

In contrast, a shared embedded object exists as a standalone Content Item but has also been embedded into another Content Item. It's actually copied wholesale into a parent object. However, Spectra maintains synchronization data so that changes to the standalone Content Item are automatically propagated to all the child copies existing in parent Content Items.

Multilingual properties are extremely useful for sites that need to show different versions of the same content. Because they require special handling, it's best to implement them from the beginning of a project even if multilanguage versions won't be needed immediately.

Embedded objects are a powerful feature of Spectra, and we have only introduced the subject. Allaire provides additional tags for working with embedded objects; these are fully covered in Appendix A, "Allaire Spectra Tags."

Managing Core Object Types Through the Webtop

Core Object Types are specialized ContentObject Types that ship with Spectra. They are fully developed ContentObject Types for working with specialized objects such as files, images, RealMedia, and Flash animation files. Most often they are used as embedded objects—in other words, they are used as properties of a Content Item. See Chapter 6 for more information on embedded objects as properties of a ContentObject Type.

Although each Core Object Type is unique, all are handled in similar ways: Each is created in a similar way, and each has `Display` and `Edit` methods. Some types have additional methods appropriate to their uses. For example, the File Core Object Type has an `Upload` method to upload a file from a user's workstation to the Spectra server; the RealMedia Core Object Type has `Play` and `PlayBackground` methods.

Managing Core Object Types through the Webtop is almost identical to managing user-defined ContentObject Types. To manage Core Object Types, click Site Design and then Media Assets. To access a particular Core Object Type, click its link.

The following example will demonstrate how to create a File Core Object Type; the other Core Object Types are handled similarly.

If you haven't done so already, click the Files link under Media Assets in the Site Design section of the Webtop. This displays a grid containing any existing File Content Items. To create a new File Content Item, follow these steps:

1. In the Webtop, click Site Design.
2. Open Media Assets in the left column.
3. Click Files to display a list of existing files.
4. Click the Create button at the bottom of the page to create a File Content Item and open a new window with the familiar Object Viewer.
5. The Object Viewer opens with the Edit item highlighted. Enter the name to apply to the new file. This name will be assigned to the File Content Item's `label` property and displayed in the Webtop.
6. Select whether the new File Content Item should be active.
7. To upload a new file to associate with the new File Content Item, click Browse to open a Choose File dialog box. From this dialog box, which displays all local and networked drives on the user's workstation, choose the file to upload and click Open. Then click Upload to transfer the file from your local workstation to the Spectra server.

8. Choose the file to associate with the new Content Item in the Choose File drop-down box.
9. Click Apply to associate the chosen file with the new File Content Item (see Figure 10.18).

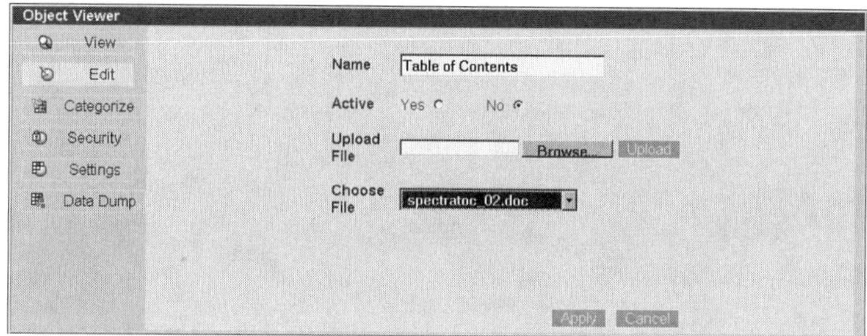

FIGURE 10.18
The Webtop provides an interface for selecting and uploading a file from your local workstation to the server.

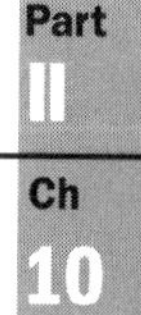

NOTE In Spectra 1.0, uploading a new file and associating it with a new File Content Item are separate steps. There has been some talk of changing this in future releases. For now, be sure to take the extra step of associating the uploaded file with the File Content Item.

Editing or deleting Core Object Types through the Webtop is done the same way as for user-defined ContentObject Types. See the section "Editing and Deleting Objects," earlier in this chapter.

Although Core Object Types can be used as standalone Content Items, most often they are used as embedded objects in other Content Items. Each Core Object Type has its own set of properties and methods that you use to interact with individual Content Items.

Advanced Spectra

CHAPTER 11

Working with Meta Data

In this chapter

Understanding Meta Data

Meta data is commonly described as "data about data." Less poetically, it's information that describes, summarizes, or categorizes another body of data.

To understand this, let's look at an example. The a2zBooks application stores information about individual books in Book Content Items. Each Book Content Item (an instance of the Book ContentObject Type) has properties that contain the book's title, author, ISBN, price, and so on. (See Chapter 6, "Introduction to Spectra Programming," for information on ContentObject Types, Content Items, and properties.) However, in addition to the basic book data, the site you're building might require that you classify books in different ways. For example, a book could be classified by its genre, by the audience it appeals to, by its distribution channel, or by its binding type.

One approach to this would be to create a new property in the Book ContentObject Type for each new classification scheme, but that would require a change in your object database for each new classification requirement. Fortunately, Spectra provides a more generic approach to classifying Content Items: meta data. The Spectra meta data service provides tools for you to define categories and keywords and then associate those categories and keywords with individual content items without having to change your object structure.

In Spectra, categories and keywords are stored in a familiar data structure that lends itself to intuitive user interfaces: a hierarchy.

Understanding Hierarchies

A *hierarchy* is a common, familiar data structure that presents information in a parent-child relationship. The Windows Explorer is a familiar example: a graphical representation of a hierarchy of directories and the files they contain. The organizational chart of most companies is another example. These typically contain hierarchical representations of the company's divisions, departments, and individuals. See Figure 11.1 for an example of a hierarchy. The Spectra meta data tools provide user and programmatic tools for creating, managing, and deleting hierarchies and the categories and keywords they contain.

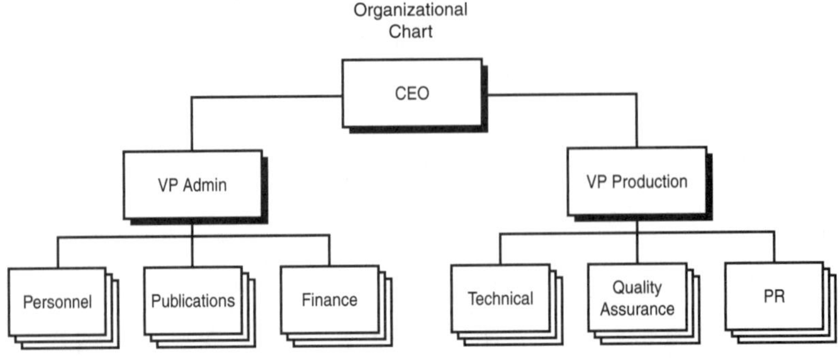

FIGURE 11.1
A hierarchy is a common, easy-to-understand way of presenting related data.

Hierarchy Terminology

Several sets of terms are used to describe hierarchies. The first two terms are generic technical terms:

- A *node* is a point where the connecting lines of a hierarchy intersect. Commonly, a node represents a piece of data or an object. For example, in the Windows Explorer, a node is an individual folder or file.
- *Edges* are the logical lines that connect the nodes. In Windows Explorer, the edges are the relationships between folders and files—in other words, which files are contained inside which folders.

Other common terms for hierarchies use family or tree metaphors:

- *Parent.* This node contains or is senior to at least one other node.
- *Child.* This node is contained in another node. The only node that isn't a child node is the top-level node of the hierarchy.
- *Branch node.* From a tree metaphor, this is another term for a node that has children.
- *Leaf node.* Also based on a tree metaphor, this node has no children; it is at the end of a branch of a hierarchy.

Spectra introduces its own names for branch and leaf nodes:

- *Keywords* are Spectra's leaf nodes. They may not contain other keywords or categories.
- *Categories* are Spectra's branch nodes. They may contain other categories or keywords.

This chapter uses the Spectra terms *category* and *keyword* to describe meta data that's created and maintained in Spectra. In some cases, we will also use the word *node* as a shortcut meaning both categories and keywords.

Creating and Managing Hierarchies via the Webtop

The Webtop provides two interrelated administrative interfaces for managing hierarchies and the categories/keywords associated with them:

- The Type Hierarchy Manager allows you to specify the ContentObject Types an individual hierarchy applies to and gives you the capability to create and manage new hierarchies.
- The Keyword Manager allows you to create and delete categories and keywords in an existing hierarchy.

You can access these interfaces from several places in the Webtop:

- The Business Center gives access to both Type Hierarchy Manager and the Keyword Manager. Click Business Center, and then Site Categories to access.
- Site Design gives access to the Keyword Manager.
- System Design gives access to the Keyword Manager and the Type Hierarchy Manager. Click System Design, and then Site Categories to access.

The Webtop also employs a user interface (UI) element that allows you to associate keywords with content items: the *Metadata Picker*. Figure 11.2 shows what the Metadata Picker looks like. The Metadata Picker is also available programmatically by coding the `CFA_METADATAPICKER` tag (discussed below).

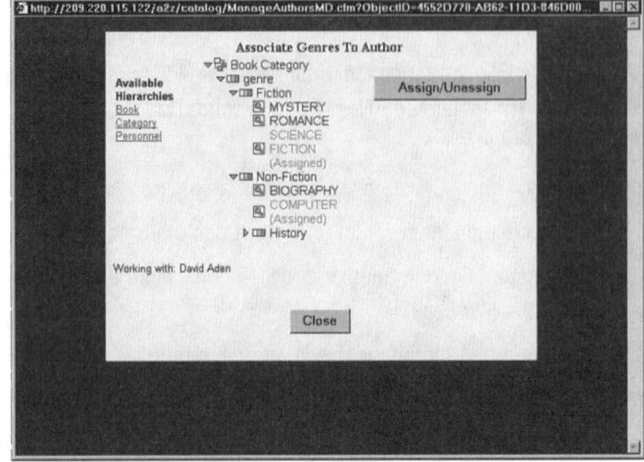

FIGURE 11.2
The Metadata Picker provides an interface for interacting with meta data and assigning it to Content Items.

Creating Meta Data Hierarchies Through the Webtop

After you and the other participants in the planning process work out what meta data hierarchies your application needs, you can use the Webtop to create them. To create a test hierarchy using the Webtop, follow these steps:

1. Click System Design.
2. Open Site Categories on the left.
3. Click Type Hierarchy Manager to display a list of existing user-defined hierarchies. You'll use this interface later to associate hierarchies with specific ContentObject Types.
4. Click Create Hierarchy at the bottom of the display. This opens a JavaScript box with a text area for entering the name of a new hierarchy. For test purposes, enter **`US Capitals`**, which will contain a list of U.S. state capitals and what they are known for. Figure 11.3 shows the Type Hierarchy Manager after entering the new hierarchy name.
5. Enter the new hierarchy name and click OK. Spectra opens the Keyword Manager with the new hierarchy displayed, ready for you to add categories or keywords. For an explanation of how to add categories and keywords, see the next section.

FIGURE 11.3
The Hierarchy Manager provides an interface for creating new hierarchies.

Adding and Editing Categories and Keywords

Adding categories and keywords to a hierarchy is straightforward, although Spectra provides two slightly different interfaces for accomplishing the same thing. You access the first through the System Design area. Follow these steps:

1. Click System Design.
2. Open Site Categories on the left.
3. Click Keyword Manager.
4. From the drop-down box, select US Capitals. The screen refreshes and displays the hierarchy's top level.
5. Begin adding a few categories to the hierarchy. Click US Capitals to select it, then click Add Category. In the JavaScript box, enter **`Massachusetts`** and click OK.
6. Use the same procedure to enter **`Virginia`** and **`Texas`**. Figure 11.4 shows the Keyword Manager after you've entered the states.

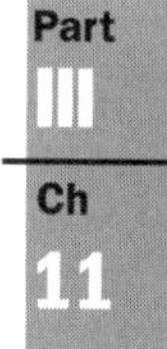

FIGURE 11.4
The Keyword Manager shows the current hierarchy and allows you to navigate through it.

7. Add `Boston` as a category under `Massachusetts`. When the screen refreshes, the hierarchy may display only the states. Click the triangular icon to the left of Massachusetts to open that category and display Boston underneath.
8. Add a keyword under Boston. Remember, keywords can be added only under categories. Click Boston to select it, then click Add Keyword. A JavaScript entry box opens.
9. Enter **`Chowder`** and click OK.
10. The Keyword Manager reappears. Unfortunately, in Spectra 1.0, whenever you add a keyword category, the hierarchy closes when it's refreshed. You need to reopen the hierarchy by clicking the triangular icons to the left of each category to see the changes you made. (Allaire has recognized this as a usability problem, so the behavior is likely to change in future releases.) Figure 11.5 shows the hierarchy, including the `Chowder` keyword.

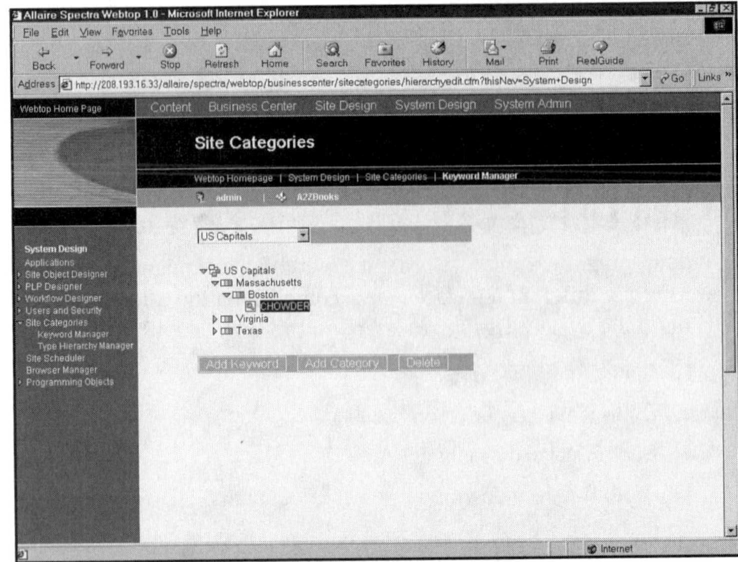

FIGURE 11.5
The hierarchy now includes the Chowder keyword.

The second way to add categories and keywords is through the Hierarchy Manager. Access it through the Type Hierarchy Manager, as follows:

1. Click System Design.
2. Open Site Categories in the left margin.
3. Click Type Hierarchy Manager.
4. Click the icon to the right of one of the ContentObject Type names. Although this icon is unlabeled, it opens an Edit Hierarchies form (see Figure 11.6).

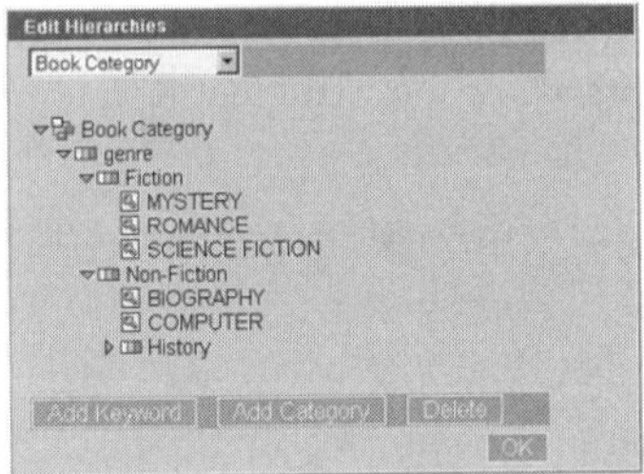

FIGURE 11.6
This window looks slightly different from the interface under the Keyword Manager, but it functions the same.

You can also use this interface for adding or deleting categories and keywords to a hierarchy.

Delete an Existing Hierarchy

Currently, there is no Webtop access for deleting a hierarchy—you can delete one only programmatically. See "Deleting Hierarchies Programmatically," later in this chapter, for information on how to do so.

Associating Keywords with Content Items Through the Webtop

The purpose of creating Spectra meta data is to associate it with Content Items. Once it's associated, you use meta data to find Content Items either in explicit searches or behind the scenes as part of site personalization.

Associating keywords with Content Items through the Webtop is straightforward:

1. Click Content.
2. Click Content Finder.
3. Select the Book ContentObject Type in the Filter By Type drop-down box. Spectra refreshes the screen to show the Book Content Items. Figure 11.7 shows a list of the Book Content Items.

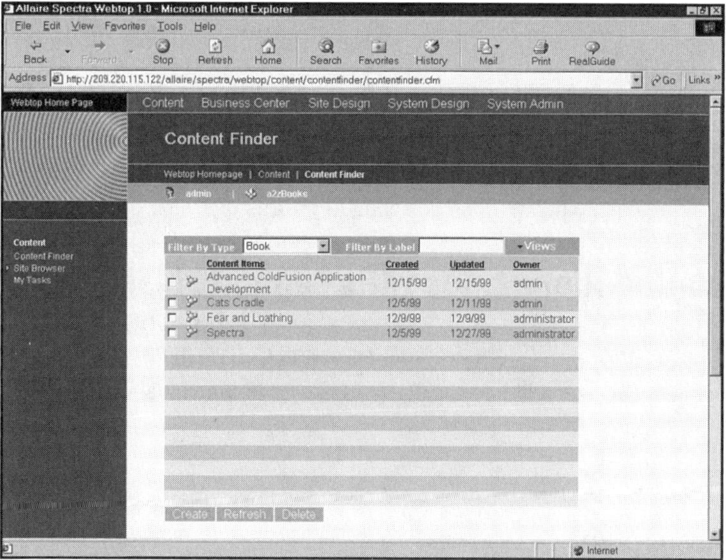

FIGURE 11.7
The Content Finder displays a list of existing Content Items of a particular type.

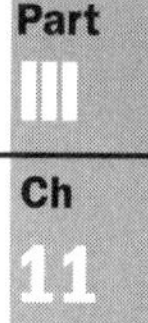

4. Click the Content Item icon next to the item you want to associate keywords with.
5. In the Object Viewer, click Categorize to open the Metadata Picker (see Figure 11.8).

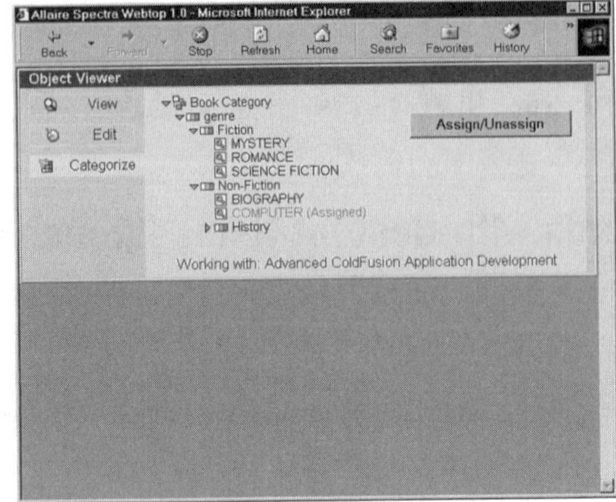

FIGURE 11.8
The Metadata Picker provides an interface for selecting categories and keywords to associate with your Content Items.

6. If Available Hierarchies is displayed, click the `Book Category` hierarchy containing the keywords you want to access. The Available Hierarchies section appears only if more than one hierarchy is available for the current Content Item. See "Associating Hierarchies with ContentObject Types" later in this chapter.
7. Open the hierarchy until you find the keywords you want to assign. Keywords already assigned are red.
8. Select the first keyword to assign by clicking it. To select additional keywords, Ctrl+click them.

   To unassign a keyword already assigned, click it.
9. When you are done selecting keywords to assign or unassign, click Assign/Unassign.

Associating Hierarchies with ContentObject Types

To restrict the hierarchies available through the Metadata Picker, you can associate individual hierarchies with specific ContentObject Types. By doing this, you can control which keywords the user will have available to assign to individual objects.

> **CAUTION**
>
> When you associate a hierarchy with a ContentObject Type, the association affects only the Metadata Picker display; it doesn't limit your ability to programmatically assign categories or keywords to Content Items.

To associate a ContentObject Type with specific hierarchies, follow these steps:

1. Click System Design.
2. Click Site Categories on the left.

3. Open Type Hierarchy Manager.
4. Click the Type icon to the left of the ContentObject Type. This displays the Assign Hierarchy to Type form (see Figure 11.9).

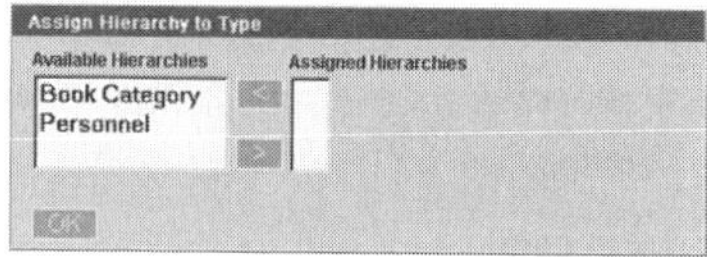

FIGURE 11.9
The Assign Hierarchy to Type form gives you a list of the available hierarchies that can be associated with the selected ContentObject Type.

5. Select the hierarchy you want to assign in the Available Hierarchies window. (Ctrl+click to select multiple hierarchies.)
6. Click > to move the selected hierarchies to Assigned Hierarchies (see Figure 11.10).

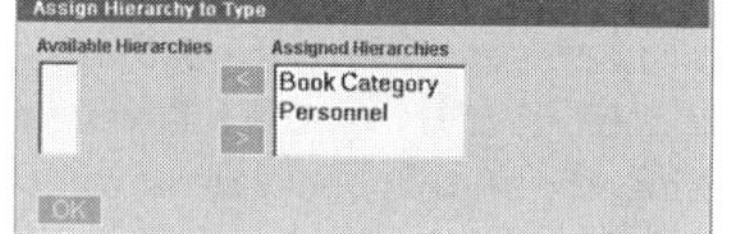

FIGURE 11.10
When you select an available hierarchy and click OK, Spectra associates it with the current ContentObject Type and updates the Assign Hierarchy to Type form.

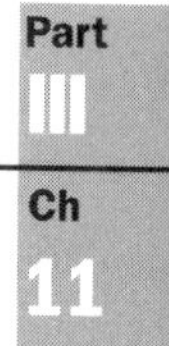

7. To unassign a hierarchy, click it in the Assigned Hierarchies window, then click < to move it into the Available Hierarchies window.
8. Click OK to save your changes.

Creating and Managing Hierarchies Programmatically

Spectra provides a wealth of tags that allow you to programmatically manage hierarchies, categories, and keywords. This section describes some basic meta data tags.

To Program or Not to Program

Although the Webtop is useful for learning about hierarchies or creating relatively small ones, it's recommended that you script the creation of any complex hierarchies. The advantages of scripting hierarchy creation—and their categories and keywords—include

continues

continued

- Once you understand the basic Spectra meta data tags, it will likely take you less time to script hierarchy creation than to use the Webtop interface for hierarchies of any appreciable size.
- During application prototyping, you may need to create, delete, and re-create your application's hierarchies several times, as business users and content owners revise them. By scripting hierarchy creation, these iterations will be faster and easier.
- The script can serve as a type of documentation for your hierarchies.
- After you create the script, you can use it to create the same hierarchy on multiple Spectra servers.

Creating Hierarchies Programmatically

You use the <CFA_METADATAHIERARCHYCREATE> tag to create hierarchies; the <CFA_METADATACATEGORYCREATE> tag to create categories for an existing Hierarchy; and the <CFA_METADATACATEGORYKEYWORDADD> tag to add a keyword to an existing category.

Listing 11.1 shows an example of how to create a hierarchy, add categories to it, and associate keywords with those categories. You don't need to run the following code, because the hierarchy already exists in the database shipped with this book. However, the following demonstrates how to create a hierarchy programmatically.

Listing 11.1 Tags to Create and Manage Hierarchies

```
<!---
File:        CreateHierarchy.cfm
Author:      david aden (david@wwstudios.com)
Date:        12/27/1999
Description: This template does not need to be run, but was used
             to create a hierarchy within the A2Z application.
Notes:
--->

<!--- Create the hiearchy --->
Create hierarchy....<br>
<CFA_metadataHierarchyCreate
    DATASOURCE="#REQUEST.CFA.A2Zbooks.datasource#"
    label="Audiences"
    r_ObjectID="NewHierarchy">

<!--- Output the UUID --->
<CFOUTPUT>
    New hierarchy ID: #NewHierarchy#<br>
</CFOUTPUT>

<!--- Create the categories --->
```

```
Create children category....<br>
<CFA_metadataCategoryCreate
    DATASOURCE="#REQUEST.CFA.A2Zbooks.datasource#"
    LABEL="Children"
    HIERARCHYID="#NewHierarchy#"
    r_OBJECTID="ChildrenID">

    <!--- Add some keywords --->
    <CFA_metadataCategoryKeywordAdd
        DATASOURCE="#REQUEST.CFA.A2Zbooks.datasource#"
        KEYWORD="Pokemon players"
CATEGORYID="#ChildrenID#">

    <CFA_metadataCategoryKeywordAdd
        DATASOURCE="#REQUEST.CFA.A2Zbooks.datasource#"
        KEYWORD="Soccer players"
        CATEGORYID="#ChildrenID#">

    <CFA_metadataCategoryKeywordAdd
        DATASOURCE="#REQUEST.CFA.A2Zbooks.datasource#"
        KEYWORD="Football players"
        CATEGORYID="#ChildrenID#">

Create teen category....<br>
<CFA_metadataCategoryCreate
    DATASOURCE="#REQUEST.CFA.A2Zbooks.datasource#"
    LABEL="Teens"
    HIERARCHYID="#NewHierarchy#"
    r_OBJECTID="TeenID">

    <!--- SubCats --->
    <CFA_metadataCategoryCreate
        DATASOURCE="#REQUEST.CFA.A2Zbooks.datasource#"
        LABEL="College"
        HIERARCHYID="#NewHierarchy#"
        PARENTID="#TeenID#"
        r_OBJECTID="CollegeID">

        <!--- Add some keywords --->
        <CFA_metadataCategoryKeywordAdd
            DATASOURCE="#REQUEST.CFA.A2Zbooks.datasource#"
            KEYWORD="Basketball players"
            CATEGORYID="#TeenID#">

        <CFA_metadataCategoryKeywordAdd
            DATASOURCE="#REQUEST.CFA.A2Zbooks.datasource#"
            KEYWORD="Frat members"
            CATEGORYID="#TeenID#">

    <CFA_metadataCategoryCreate
        DATASOURCE="#REQUEST.CFA.A2Zbooks.datasource#"
```


continues

Listing 11.1 Continued

```
        LABEL="High School"
        HIERARCHYID="#NewHierarchy#"
        PARENTID="#TeenID#"
        r_OBJECTID="HighSchoolID">

<!--- Categories --->
Create adult category....<br>
<CFA_metadataCategoryCreate
    DATASOURCE="#REQUEST.CFA.A2Zbooks.datasource#"
    LABEL="Adult"
    HIERARCHYID="#NewHierarchy#"
    r_OBJECTID="AdultID">

    <!--- SubCats --->
    <CFA_metadataCategoryCreate
        DATASOURCE="#REQUEST.CFA.A2Zbooks.datasource#"
        LABEL="20-30"
        HIERARCHYID="#NewHierarchy#"
        PARENTID="#AdultID#"
        r_OBJECTID="TwentyThirtyID">

        <!--- Add some keywords --->
        <CFA_metadataCategoryKeywordAdd
            DATASOURCE="#REQUEST.CFA.A2Zbooks.datasource#"
            KEYWORD="Lawyers"
            CATEGORYID="#TwentyThirtyID#">

        <CFA_metadataCategoryKeywordAdd
            DATASOURCE="#REQUEST.CFA.A2Zbooks.datasource#"
            KEYWORD="Engineers"
            CATEGORYID="#TwentyThirtyID#">

    <CFA_metadataCategoryCreate
        DATASOURCE="#REQUEST.CFA.A2Zbooks.datasource#"
        LABEL="31-55"
        HIERARCHYID="#NewHierarchy#"
        PARENTID="#AdultID#"
        r_OBJECTID="ThirtyOneFiftyFiveID">

    <CFA_metadataCategoryCreate
        DATASOURCE="#REQUEST.CFA.A2Zbooks.datasource#"
        LABEL="56-100"
        HIERARCHYID="#NewHierarchy#"
        PARENTID="#AdultID#"
        r_OBJECTID="FiftySixPlusID">
```

In Listing 11.1, `<CFA_METADATAHIERARCHYCREATE>` creates the hierarchy named `Audiences` and returns its ID in the variable `NewHierarchy`. The first `<CFA_METADATACATEGORYCREATE>` tag adds a category named `Children` to the new hierarchy and returns its ID in the variable `ChildrenID`.

The next Spectra tag, <CFA_METADATACATEGORYKEYWORDADD>, adds the keyword `Pokemon players` to the `Children` category. This tag doesn't return an ID because Spectra keywords aren't unique objects—they are stored as properties of their parent category.

A subsequent <CFA_METADATACATEGORYCREATE> tag creates the `Teens` category. Immediately following that is another <CFA_METADATACATEGORYCREATE> tag that creates the `College` category, but this instance of the tag has an additional attribute: `PARENTID`. This is set to `TeenID`, which tells Spectra to make `College` a subcategory to the `Teen` category.

Other <CFA_METADATACATEGORYCREATE> and <CFA_METADATACATEGORYKEYWORDADD> tags add categories and keywords to the hierarchy.

Figure 11.11 shows the hierarchy produced by the code in Listing 11.1.

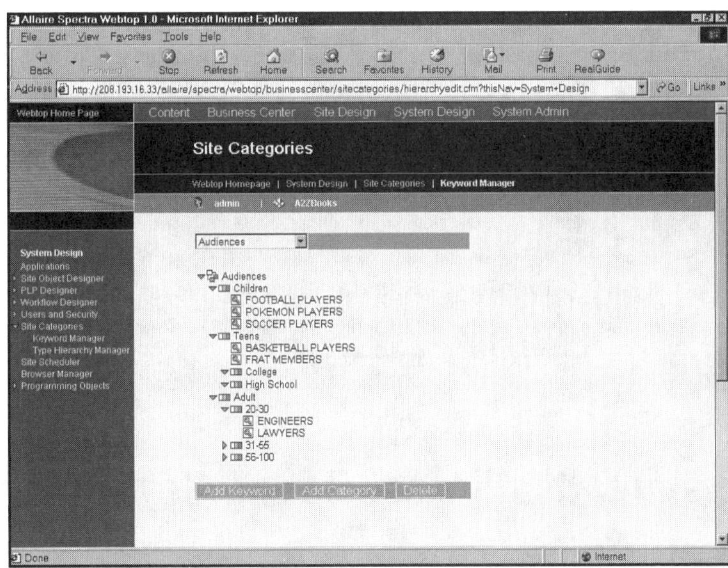

FIGURE 11.11
When you create a hierarchy programmatically, you can examine the results using the Keyword Manager.

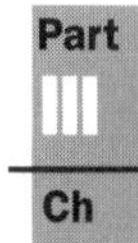

NOTE Spectra also provides a tag that encapsulates the Hierarchy Editor used in the Webtop. This lets you code the <CFA_METADATAHIERARCHYCREATE> tag and then call the Hierarchy Editor, so that your users can add and delete categories and keywords interactively. Invoke the Hierarchy Editor as follows:

```
<CFA_metadataHierarchyEditor
    DATASOURCE="#REQUEST.CFA.A2Zbooks.datasource#"
    HIERARCHYID="#NewHierarchy#"
    bNewwindow="FALSE">
```

Deleting Hierarchies Programmatically

If you need to delete a hierarchy, use the <CFA_METADATAHIERARCHYDELETE> tag. This deletes both the hierarchy and its subsidiary categories and keywords. It has a simple syntax, requiring only DATASOURCE and HIERARCHYID:

```
<CFA_METADATAHIERARCHYDELETE
    DATASOURCE="#REQUEST.CFA.A2Zbooks.datasource#"
    HIERARCHYID="EE10C854-BA06-11D3-847300E02C0708AF">
```

What this tag does *not* handle is keywords already assigned to Content Items.

> **CAUTION**
>
> Deleting a hierarchy whose keywords have been assigned to Content Items is a potentially complicated operation that may affect several areas of your application. As of Spectra 1.0, Allaire doesn't provide a tag to completely remove a hierarchy from the ContentObject Database. <CFA_METADATAHIERARCHYDELETE> deletes only the hierarchy and its categories; it doesn't remove keywords already assigned to Content Items.
>
> To remove a hierarchy after you assign its keywords to Content Items, you first need to remove all keyword assignments. You can do this through the Webtop or by writing a script that finds and unassigns the assigned keywords. (Later sections in this chapter explain how to find Content Items programmatically by keyword, as well as how to unassign keywords.) Only after you remove all the keyword assignments can you use <CFA_METADATAHIERARCHYDELETE> to delete the hierarchy and its categories.
>
> This limitation makes it particularly important to stabilize your application's hierarchies early in the design phase—and certainly before data is entered into the production system.

Programmatically Associating Keywords with Content Items

The primary use of meta data is to associate it with Content Items. After you associate keywords with Content Items, you use them to find those Content Items either through explicit searches or as part of site personalization.

Spectra provides the high-level <CFA_METADATAPICKER> tag that allows you to invoke the Metadata Picker from your code. This gives your users a ready-made graphical interface for assigning and unassigning keywords to Content Items (see Listing 11.2).

Listing 11.2 Encapsulating the Metadata Picker

```
<!---
File:       /catalog/ManageAuthorsMD.cfm
Author:     david aden (david@wwstudios.com)
```

```
Date:         12/15/1999
Description:  Associating Meta Data with an Author Object.
Notes:
--->

<CFPARAM NAME="URL.ObjectID">

<!--- Display the basic a2z formatting. --->
<CF_A2ZFORMATTING SUBTITLE="Assigning Meta Data" TABLEWIDTH="450">

    <CENTER>
        <b>Associate Genres To Author</b>
    </CENTER>

    <CFA_METADATAPICKER
        DATASOURCE="#request.cfa.a2zbooks.datasource#"
        OBJECTID="#URL.ObjectID#"
        BNEWWINDOW=FALSE>

    <br>
    <CENTER>
        <FORM NAME="CloseWin" METHOD="POST" ACTION="#">
            <INPUT
                TYPE="Button"
                NAME="Closeit"
                VALUE=" Close "
                onclick="self.close();">
        </FORM>
    </CENTER>

</CF_A2ZFORMATTING><!--- Close the page formatting --->
```

Part III Ch 11

Listing 11.2 is a simple template: It calls `CF_A2ZFORMATTING` to display the standard page format and then invokes the Metadata Picker with the `CFA_METADATAPICKER` tag, passing it the UUID of the Content Item you're going to associate keywords to. Figure 11.2, earlier in this chapter, shows what the Metadata Picker looks like.

This template isn't directly accessible; it expects to be passed the objectID of an Author Content Item. To access it, open the template `/a2z/catalog/ManageAuthors.cfm` in your installation of the a2zBooks application. Click an author name to open the Edit Existing Author screen. Click the Metadata Picker button at the bottom of the page to run the code in Listing 11.2.

NOTE To assign a keyword using the Metadata Picker, click the keyword you want to assign, and then click Assign/Unassign. The Metadata Picker refreshes. To verify that your selected keyword was assigned, reopen the hierarchy—all associated keywords are displayed in red.

continues

continued

Although the Metadata Picker allows you to select a category and click Assign/Unassign, this doesn't actually do anything. You can assign keywords only to Content Items; you can't assign entire categories. However, when you assign a keyword to a Content Item, Spectra can also record the keyword's category. Later, we will show you how to find Content Items by the categories their keywords are associated with.

This can be somewhat confusing, so it is important to remember that you can assign keywords only to Content Items. However, you can find Content Items by either keyword *or* category.

You can also assign keywords to Content Items programmatically. This may be useful if you want to build an alternative interface to the Metadata Picker or need to assign a keyword to a Content Item when it's created. For example, the `ManageAuthorsMD2.cfm` file gives an alternative way of selecting and associating keywords with a Content Item (see Listing 11.3).

Listing 11.3 Associating Categories and Keywords with a Content Item

```
<!---
File:         /catalog/ManageAuthorsMD2.cfm
Author:       david aden (david@wwstudios.com)
Date:         12/15/1999
Description:  Associating Meta Data with an Author Object without using
              the Metadata Picker.
Notes:
--->

<!--- Display the basic a2z formatting. --->
<CF_A2ZFORMATTING subtitle="Assigning Meta Data" TableWidth="400">

<!---  --->
<CFIF Not IsDefined("URL.ObjectID") OR Len(URL.ObjectID) EQUAL 0>
    Error! ObjectID is required!<br>
    <CFABORT>
</CFIF>

<!--- Get the object as we'll need this for the form and the handler. --->
<CFA_CONTENTOBJECTGET
    DATASOURCE="#REQUEST.CFA.a2zbooks.Datasource#"
    OBJECTID="#URL.ObjectID#"
    R_STOBJECT="stObject">

<!--- Check if the FORM was submitted. --->
<CFIF IsDefined("FORM.SaveCats")>

    <!--- Copy the Object's stKeywords structure to a local variable. --->
    <CFSET stKeywords = StructCopy(stObject.stKeywords)>

    <!--- Remove the LCategories key from the local version as that isn't
          a keyword to remove. --->
```

```
    <CFIF StructKeyExists(stKeywords,'LCATEGORIES')>
        <CFSET temp = StructDelete(stKeywords,'LCATEGORIES')>
    </CFIF>

    <!--- Delete the existing keywords. --->
    <CFA_METADATAOBJECTKEYWORDREMOVE
        DATASOURCE="#request.cfa.a2zbooks.datasource#"
        OBJECTID="#URL.ObjectID#"
        STKEYWORDS="#stKeywords#">

    <!--- If we selections were made of the Keywords, then associate them
          with the current object --->
    <CFIF IsDefined("FORM.Genres")>

        <!--- Initialize the structure we're going to put the chosen
              keywords into. --->
        <CFSET stKeywords = StructNew()>

        <!--- Loop through the choices and set the values into the
                structure. --->
        <CFLOOP LIST="#FORM.Genres#" index="CurrCat">
            <CFSET stKeywords[ListGetAt(CurrCat,1,":")] =
                ListGetAt(CurrCat,2,":")>
        </CFLOOP>

        <!--- Update the Object with the Keywords --->
        <CFA_METADATAOBJECTKEYWORDASSIGN
            DATASOURCE="#request.cfa.a2zbooks.datasource#"
            OBJECTID="#URL.ObjectID#"
            STKEYWORDS="#stKeywords#">
    </CFIF>

    <!--- Update the Verity indexes for the current object. --->
    <CFA_METADATAINDEXUPDATE
        DATASOURCE="#request.cfa.a2zbooks.datasource#"
        LOBJECTIDS="#URL.ObjectID#">

    <!--- Reload the original page --->
    <cflocation url="#CGI.SCRIPT_NAME#?#CGI.QUERY_STRING#" addtoken="No">

<!--- Otherwise display the form. --->
<CFELSE>

    <!--- Set the Hierarchy we're going to use --->
    <CFSET BookHierID = 'A4912F66-9EEB-11D3-846A00E02C0708AF'>

    <!--- Get the keywords structure into a local var --->
    <CFSET stKeywords = stObject.stKeywords>

    <CFOUTPUT>
    <CFFORM METHOD="Post" ACTION="#CGI.SCRIPT_NAME#?#CGI.QUERY_STRING#">
```

continues

Part III Ch 11

Listing 11.3 Continued

```
<CENTER>
<TABLE BORDER="0" WIDTH="350">
    <TR>
        <TH COLSPAN="11" align="center">Associate Genres To Author</th>
    </TR>

    <TR>
    <CFLOOP FROM="1" TO="10" INDEX="COUNTER">
        <TD WIDTH="10"> </TD>
    </CFLOOP>
        <TD width="250"> </TD>
    </TR>

    <TR>
        <TD COLSPAN="11"><b>Book Category</b></TD>
    </TR>

    <TR>
        <TD> </TD>
        <TD COLSPAN="10"><b>Genre</b></TD>
    </TR>

    <TR>
        <TD> </TD>
        <TD> </TD>
        <TD COLSPAN="9"><b>Fiction</b></TD>
    </TR>

    <!--- Set the Current CategoryID into a variable. --->
    <CFSET CurrCat = 'A4912F74-9EEB-11D3-846A00E02C0708AF'>

    <!--- Display the hierarchy --->
    <TR>
        <TD>
            <CFSET CurrGenre = "Mystery">
            <INPUT
                TYPE="Checkbox"
                NAME="Genres"
                VALUE="#CurrGenre#:#CurrCat#"
                <CFIF StructKeyExists(stKeywords,'#CurrGenre#') AND
                    stKeywords['#CurrGenre#'] EQUAL '#CurrCat#'>
                    CHECKED</CFIF>>
        </TD>
        <TD> </TD>
        <TD> </TD>
        <TD COLSPAN="8">#CurrGenre#</TD>
    </TR>

    <TR>
        <TD>
            <CFSET CurrGenre = "Romance">
```

```
        <INPUT
            TYPE="Checkbox"
            NAME="Genres"
            VALUE="#CurrGenre#:#CurrCat#"
            <CFIF StructKeyExists(stKeywords,'#CurrGenre#') AND
                stKeywords['#CurrGenre#'] EQUAL '#CurrCat#'>
                CHECKED</CFIF>>
    </TD>
    <TD> </TD>
    <TD> </TD>
    <TD COLSPAN="8">#CurrGenre#</TD>
</TR>

<TR>
    <TD>
        <CFSET CurrGenre = "Science Fiction">
        <INPUT
            TYPE="Checkbox"
            NAME="Genres"
            VALUE="#CurrGenre#:#CurrCat#"
            <CFIF StructKeyExists(stKeywords,'#CurrGenre#') AND
                stKeywords['#CurrGenre#'] EQUAL '#CurrCat#'>
                CHECKED</CFIF>>
    </TD>
    <TD> </TD>
    <TD> </TD>
    <TD COLSPAN="8">#CurrGenre#</TD>
</TR>

<TR>
    <TD> </TD>
    <TD> </TD>
    <TD COLSPAN="9"><b>Non-Fiction</b></TD>
</TR>

<!--- Current CategoryID --->
<CFSET CurrCat = 'A4912F78-9EEB-11D3-846A00E02C0708AF'>

<TR>
    <TD>
        <CFSET CurrGenre = "Biography">
        <INPUT
            TYPE="Checkbox"
            NAME="Genres"
            VALUE="#CurrGenre#:#CurrCat#"
            <CFIF StructKeyExists(stKeywords,'#CurrGenre#') AND
                stKeywords['#CurrGenre#'] EQUAL '#CurrCat#'>
                CHECKED</CFIF>>
    </TD>
    <TD> </TD>
    <TD> </TD>
```

Part III

Ch 11

continues

Listing 11.3 Continued

```
                <TD COLSPAN="8">#CurrGenre#</TD>
            </TR>

            <TR>
                <TD>
                    <CFSET CurrGenre = "Computer">
                    <CFSET CurrCat = 'A4912F78-9EEB-11D3-846A00E02C0708AF'>
                    <INPUT
                        TYPE="Checkbox"
                        NAME="Genres"
                        VALUE="#CurrGenre#:#CurrCat#"
                        <CFIF StructKeyExists(stKeywords,'#CurrGenre#') AND
                            stKeywords['#CurrGenre#'] EQUAL '#CurrCat#'>
                            CHECKED</CFIF>>
                </TD>
                <TD> </TD>
                <TD> </TD>
                <TD COLSPAN="8">#CurrGenre#</TD>
            </TR>

            <TR>
                <TD COLSPAN="11" align="center">
                    <INPUT TYPE="Submit" NAME="SaveCats" VALUE="Save"> 
                    <INPUT TYPE="Button" NAME="Closeit" VALUE=" Close "
                        onclick="self.close();">
                </TD>
            </TR>

        </TABLE>
        </CENTER>
        </CFFORM>
        </CFOUTPUT>
</CFIF>

</CF_A2ZFORMATTING><!--- Close the page formatting --->
```

This template is also not directly accessible, because it expects to be passed the object ID of an Author Content Item. To access it, open the template `/a2z/catalog/ManageAuthors.cfm` in your a2zBooks installation. Click an author name to open the Edit Existing Author screen. Click the Metadata button at the bottom of the page.

Listing 11.3 is a self-posting form that provides an interface for selecting and associating keywords with Content Items. It begins by setting the standard a2z formatting and verifying you've passed in the required object ID (for the Content Item we are going to be handling) as a URL variable. Figure 11.12 shows the interface created with Listing 11.3.

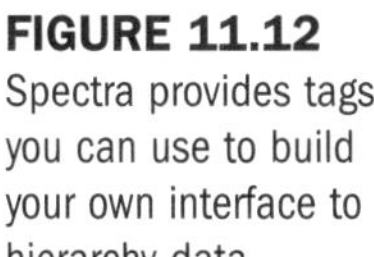

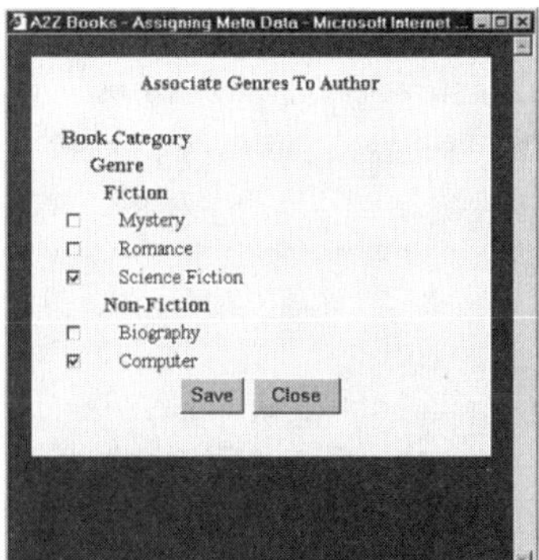

FIGURE 11.12
Spectra provides tags you can use to build your own interface to hierarchy data.

You call <CFA_CONTENTOBJECTGET> to get information on the current Content Item. Its data is returned in the stObject structure. The first time the user comes to the page, you want to display a form that allows him to select the keywords to assign to the current Content Item.

For purposes of demonstration, we set a local variables to hold the ID of the hierarchy we're using (normally this shouldn't be hard-coded into a template). We also create a local variable to hold the stKeywords structure that's in the current Content Item:


```
<!--- Set the Hierarchy we're going to use --->
<CFSET BookHierID = 'A4912F66-9EEB-11D3-846A00E02C0708AF'>

<!--- Get the keywords structure into a local var --->
<CFSET stKeywords = stObject.stKeywords>
```

The rest of the form is standard HTML and CFML. You use HTML check boxes so the user can select the keyword(s) to assign. The check box VALUE attribute contains both the keyword (CurrGenre) and the ID of the current category (CurrCat) in a semicolon-delimited string. We need both to make the assignment successfully when the form is submitted. In the browser, the VALUE attribute will look like the following:

```
VALUE="Mystery:A4912F74-9EEB-11D3-846A00E02C0708AF"
```

Each check box includes a CFIF that checks to see if the keyword was previously assigned to the current Content Item and, if so, places a check in the check box.

NOTE In this example, the categories and keywords are hardcoded because we don't anticipate the hierarchy will change much. You could also write code to build the interface dynamically based on the hierarchy definition. This more advanced task requires a thorough understanding of how hierarchies are defined and how keywords are stored in Content Items.

To see the structure of a hierarchy, use the <CFA_METADATAHIERARCHYGET> tag and then <CFA_DUMP> the structure it returns.

continues

continued

To understand how categories and keywords are stored in Content Items, use <CFA_CONTENTOBJECTGET> to get a Content Item that has keywords associated with it and <CFA_DUMP> the structure it returns.

Also see Appendix B, "Spectra Structures," for more information on the hierarchy and `stKeywords` structures.

When the user submits the form, the top half of the template runs. First, you need to clear the existing keyword associations by using the <CFA_METADATAOBJECTKEYWORDREMOVE> tag, which expects the attribute `STKEYWORDS` containing a structure of keywords to delete. In the code we take advantage of the Content Item itself containing a `stKeywords` structure that can be used, with slight modification, by the <CFA_METADATAOBJECTKEYWORDREMOVE> tag. First, copy the Content Item's `stKeywords` to a local structure:

```
<CFSET stKeywords = StructCopy(stObject.stKeywords)>
```

Then remove the `LCATEGORIES` key that exists in the Content Item but isn't needed to delete the existing keywords:

```
<CFSET temp = StructDelete(stKeywords,'LCATEGORIES')>
```

Now you're ready to call the <CFA_METADATAOBJECTKEYWORDREMOVE> tag to actually remove the assigned keywords.

```
<CFA_METADATAOBJECTKEYWORDREMOVE
     DATASOURCE="#request.cfa.a2zbooks.datasource#"
     OBJECTID="#URL.ObjectID#"
     STKEYWORDS="#stKeywords#">
```

After the existing keywords are removed from the Content Item, check to see if the user selected any keywords by testing to see if `FORM.Genres` exists. If so, it will contain a comma-delimited list of the selected keywords. Loop through the list and parse out the keyword and Category ID from each item and use these to build the `stKeywords` structure:

```
<CFLOOP LIST="#FORM.Genres#" index="CurrCat">
   <CFSET stKeywords[ListGetAt(CurrCat,1,":")] = ListGetAt(CurrCat,2,":")>
</CFLOOP>
```

Simply pass this structure to the <CFA_METADATAOBJECTKEYWORDASSIGN> tag through the `stKeywords` attribute, along with the current Content Item ID and datasource:

```
<CFA_METADATAOBJECTKEYWORDASSIGN
   DATASOURCE="#request.cfa.a2zbooks.datasource#"
   OBJECTID="#URL.ObjectID#"
   STKEYWORDS="#stKeywords#">
```

The chosen keywords are now associated with the Content Item.

NOTE You could write code to figure out which keywords need to be removed, which need to be maintained, and what new ones are being added and then use a combination of <CFA_METADATAOBJECTKEYWORDREMOVE> and <CFA_METADATAOBJECTKEYWORDASSIGN> to update the Content Item. However, it's easier programmatically to simply delete all the existing keywords and then associate all the new ones passed in from the form. In many cases, this means you'll delete a keyword and then reassociate it immediately, but this overhead is relatively minor given the coding simplicity it buys.

Behind the Scenes

Each Content Item has a system-generated `stKeywords` property that contains a key for each keyword associated with the Content Item. The value of the key is the Category ID to which the keyword belongs. For example, if a Content Item is associated with the keyword `Mystery`, which is in the category Fiction (whose Category ID is `A4912F74-9EEB-11D3-846A00E02C0708AF`), `stKeywords` would contain the following key-value pair:

```
stKeywords['Mystery'] = 'A4912F74-9EEB-11D3-846A00E02C0708AF'
```

`stKeywords` also has an `LCATEGORIES` key that contains a comma-delimited list of all the categories of its assigned keywords.

In the preceding example, Fiction is the only category associated with the Content Item. In this case, `LCATEGORIES` would contain only the ID for the Fiction category:

```
stKeywords['LCATEGORIES'] = 'A4912F74-9EEB-11D3-846A00E02C0708AF'
```

As keywords belonging to other categories are assigned to this Content Item, those other categories are added to the `LCATEGORIES` list.

The last thing you need to do after changing keyword assignments is update the Verity collections used for fast category and keyword lookup. Spectra maintains two collections for category and keyword searches:

- `cfa_metadata_categories`
- `cfa_metadata_keywords`

You virtually never interact directly with these collections—they are maintained and used behind the scenes by the Spectra meta data tags. However, any time you programmatically change the keywords assigned to a Content Item, you need to include code to do the update:

```
<CFA_METADATAINDEXUPDATE
    DATASOURCE="#request.cfa.a2zbooks.datasource#"
    LOBJECTIDS="#URL.ObjectID#">
```

It's possible for the Verity collections to become corrupt. If your code that depends on the meta data collections stops working, first try reindexing the meta data. Spectra encapsulates a "reindex all" function in the <CFA_METADATAINDEXALL> tag. It takes only one attribute:

```
<CFA_METADATAINDEXALL
    DATASOURCE="#REQUEST.CFA.a2zbooks.Datasource#">
```

Using Keywords and Categories to Find Content Items

Spectra provides two tags to search for items based on their meta data associations:

- `<CFA_METADATACATEGORYOBJECTFIND>`
- `<CFA_METADATAKEYWORDOBJECTFIND>`

Both tags can return the Content Items they find in either a CF Query or a CF Structure. Both tags take an attribute that specifies how much detailed information should be returned. See `DisplayAuthorByGenre.cfm` in Listing 11.4.

Listing 11.4 Locating Content Items Through Their Keyword Associations

```
<!---
File:         /catalog/DisplayAuthorByGenre.cfm
Author:       david aden (david@wwstudios.com)
Date:         12/27/1999
Description:  Displays authors by the Genres they are associated with.
Notes:
--->

<!--- Display the basic a2z formatting. --->
<CF_A2ZFORMATTING subtitle="Authors By Genre">

<!--- Log the page. --->
<CFA_PAGE
    datasource="#REQUEST.CFA.a2zBooks.DATASOURCE#"
    pagename="A2Z Author By Genres"
    sectionname="catalog"
    sitename="a2zBooks"
    cachepage="No"
    bpreloadpageobjects="No"
    logpage="No"
    logcachedobjects="No">

<!--- Set the list of lKeywords to search for --->
<CFSET lKeywords = "Mystery,Romance,Science Fiction,Biography,Computer">

<CFOUTPUT>
<!--- Outside table --->
<TABLE WIDTH="620" BORDER="0" CELLPADDING="0" CELLSPACING="0">
    <TR>
        <TD ALIGN="center" colspan="4">
        <FONT SIZE="+1">
            <B>Authors By Genre</B>
            <BR><BR>
        </FONT>
        </TD>
    <TR>

    <!--- Column headings --->
    <TR>
```

```
        <TH ALIGN="left">Name</TH>
        <TH ALIGN="left">Email</TH>
    </TR>

    <CFLOOP LIST="#lKeywords#" INDEX="CurrKeyword">
        <!--- Find any Content Items associated with this keyword. --->
        <CFA_METADATAKEYWORDOBJECTFIND
            DATASOURCE="#REQUEST.CFA.a2zbooks.Datasource#"
            KEYWORDS="#CurrKeyword#"
            RESULTSET="FULL"
            LTYPEIDS="#APPLICATION.AuthorTypeID#"
            R_QOBJECTS="qObjects">

        <!--- If we found something, then display info about it. --->
        <CFIF qObjects.RecordCount GREATER THAN 0>
            <TR>
                <TD><b>Category: #CurrKeyword#</b></TD>
            </TR>

            <CFLOOP QUERY="qObjects">
                <!--- Get the object Data into a structure we can use --->
                <CFWDDX ACTION="WDDX2CFML" INPUT="#qObjects.ObjectData#"
                    OUTPUT="stObject">
                <TR>
                  <TD>
                  <a href="ManageAuthors.cfm?ObjectID=#qObjects.ObjectID#">
                      #qObjects.Label#</a>
                  </TD>
                  <TD>#stObject.Email[1]#</td>
                </TR>
            </CFLOOP>

            <TR>
                <TD> </TD>
            </TR>
        </CFIF>
    </CFLOOP>

</TABLE>
</CFOUTPUT>

</CFA_PAGE>

</CF_A2ZFORMATTING><!--- Close the page formatting --->
```

This code is included on the CD, but there's no link with the a2zBooks application. However, you can run it directly by typing the URL `A2ZInstallDirectory/catalog/DisplayAuthorByGenre.cfm` into your browser. The code begins with the usual A2Z formatting and `<CFA_PAGE>` tags and then defines a list containing all the keywords to search:

```
<CFSET lKeywords = "Mystery,Romance,Science Fiction,Biography,Computer">
```

To find and display the appropriate Content Items, loop through the list of individual keywords and pass them to the Spectra <CFA_METADATAKEYWORDOBJECTFIND> tag in its KEYWORDS attribute:

```
<CFA_METADATAKEYWORDOBJECTFIND
    DATASOURCE="#REQUEST.CFA.a2zbooks.Datasource#"
    KEYWORDS="#CurrKeyword#"
    RESULTSET="FULL"
    LTYPEIDS="#APPLICATION.AuthorTypeID#"
    R_QOBJECTS="qObjects">
```

Set the RESULTSET attribute to either "FULL" (to return complete Content Item data) or "KEY" (to return a subset of the Content Item data, including the object ID). In this template, you want to request the FULL result set because you need detailed Content Item data to properly construct the display. Figure 11.13 shows the detailed Content Item data.

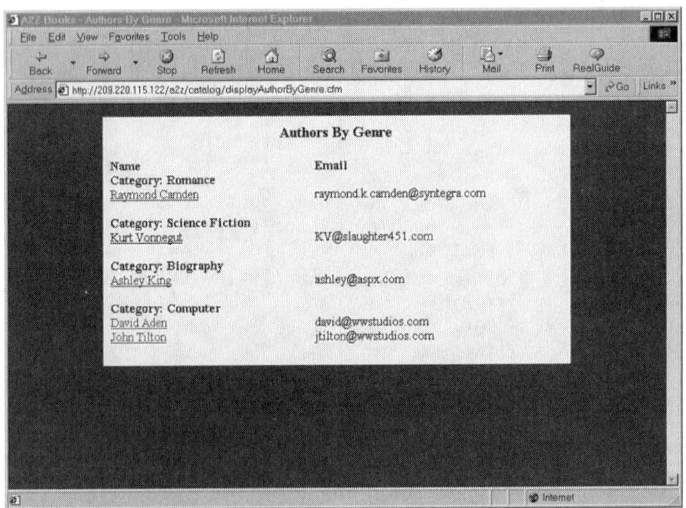

FIGURE 11.13
The detailed Content Item data.

Full Versus *Key* Result Sets

Setting the RESULTSET attribute of the <CFA_METADATAKEYWORDOBJECTFIND> and <CFA_METADATACATEGORYOBJECTFIND> tags controls how much information the tag returns. The KEY result set is smaller and should be used only when you need to use keys such as ObjectID. The FULL result set should be used when you need to work with the data in each found Content Item.

The KEY result set returns the following for each Content Item it finds:

- Label
- ObjectID

- TypeID
- Score

The FULL result set returns the same items, plus ObjectData, which contains the property values for the Content Item.

The found Content Items can be returned in either a query or a structure, depending on whether you specify the r_qObjects or r_stObjects attribute. According to Allaire's documentation, when you specify the query format (r_qObjects), the Content Item data is returned as a WDDX packet in a query field called ObjectData. You access the data by using <CFWDDX> to deserialize it.

The documentation also states that when you specify the structure return format (r_stobjects), the Content Item data is returned as a structure under a key named stProperties. However, testing showed that the Content Item data is actually returned in a key called ObjectData.

Because we used R_QOBJECTS as the return variable, the data is returned in a ColdFusion query rather than in a structure. ObjectData is one of the fields in the returned query—it holds a WDDX packet containing properties of the Content Item. To access this data, you deserialize it using <CFWDDX>:

```
<CFWDDX ACTION="WDDX2CFML" INPUT="#qObjects.ObjectData#" OUTPUT="stObject">
```

Choosing whether to return the <CFA_METADATAKEYWORDOBJECTFIND> results in a query or a structure depends on what you need to do with the data. The query version returns records in the same order they were returned from the Verity search–in order from highest to lowest by Verity score.

When you return the data in a ColdFusion structure, there's no guarantee of the order, because ColdFusion structures are unordered. However, you may want to display the returned data ordered by one of its subkeys, such as LastName or Title. In that case, the structure return would be more appropriate because you can use the <CFA_STRUCTSORTCOMMONSUBKEYS> tag to generate an array ordered by the subkey. See Appendix A, "Allaire Spectra Tags," for more information on the <CFA_STRUCTSORTCOMMONSUBKEYS> tag.

Finding Content Items by category works virtually the same way as finding Content Items by keyword, except that you use the <CFA_METADATACATEGORYOBJECTFIND> tag instead of the <CFA_METADATAKEYWORDOBJECTFIND> tag. The <CFA_METADATACATEGORYOBJECTFIND> tag expects a list of Category IDs instead of a list of keywords. For example, in Listing 11.4, we could have used

```
<!--- Set the list of categories to the 'Fiction' category --->
<CFSET lCategories = "A4912F74-9EEB-11D3-846A00E02C0708AF">

<CFA_METADATACATEGORYOBJECTFIND
    DATASOURCE="#REQUEST.CFA.a2zbooks.Datasource#"
    LCATEGORYIDS="#lCategories#"
    RESULTSET="FULL"
    LTYPEIDS="#APPLICATION.AuthorTypeID#"
    R_QOBJECTS="qObjects">
```

This finds all the Content Items that were assigned any keyword in the Fiction category.

Where Meta Data Is Used

In this chapter, you have seen the basics of creating category and keyword hierarchies and how to associate them to Content Items. You have also looked at how to search for Content Items based on their associated categories and keywords. But where is this functionality used in a real-world Spectra application?

The basic purpose of meta data is to "tag" individual Content Items as an additional means of classifying them. You can then search for Content Items based on these assignments. As seen in the template that displays authors by genre, you can use this functionality to find and display items according to their associated categories or keywords.

You can also use this search functionality for personalization. For example, you could provide a registration form in which a user selects keywords from a list that matches your site's meta data keywords. You stored these preferences in the user's profile. See Chapter 18, "Implementing Personalization," for more information on customizing the user's profile.

As users move through your site, the keywords they select affect the content they see. You can select the customized content by coding `<CFA_METADATAKEYWORDOBJECTFIND>` or `<CFA_METADATACATEGORYOBJECTFIND>` tags directly in your pages, as done in this chapter. Or, you can code publishing rules for use in containers. The publishing rules also select content according to the user's keyword preferences, but automate the process of presenting Content Items. For full data on how to use Spectra containers to customize content, see Chapter 19, "Rules-Based Publishing."

Application Design and Meta Data

Because meta data is fundamental to how content is categorized throughout your application, it is important to design your meta data hierarchies early in the development cycle.

Minimally, business users and content owners should be involved in the meta data planning process because they are affected the most by the results. It's important to work with these groups to establish what hierarchies will be needed and the individual category and keyword items in each. When you have a reasonably good list of the hierarchies and their categories, it's a good practice to produce them in Spectra and then let the users take another look. Iterate as needed to get a hierarchy that satisfies all the participants as much as possible. Although it's possible to change hierarchies after the application goes into production, it's much easier to get it right before loading in a lot of content.

Understanding Meta Data's Limitations

Although Spectra's meta data services are useful tools for designing applications, the current implementation has some important limitations that you'll want to keep in mind. Some of these have been touched on elsewhere in the chapter but are worth summarizing here:

- You can't edit a category or a keyword once it is entered—you can only delete and then create a new one.
- It's important to remember that keyword storage has been "denormalized" by keeping the keyword itself in individual Content Items. This speeds performance but puts limitations on how many changes can be or should be made to hierarchies after keywords have been associated with Content Items.
- You can't delete a hierarchy through the Webtop. You can delete a hierarchy programmatically by using the `<CFA_METADATAHIERARCHYDELETE>` tag, but this has limitations. (See the next item.)
- After you assign a hierarchy's keywords to Content Items, you can't cleanly delete the hierarchy without first unassigning the keywords. This is because the `<CFA_METADATAHIERARCHYDELETE>` tag deletes only the hierarchy and its categories; it does *not* unassign the hierarchy's keywords from any Content Items they have been assigned to.
- When you create a hierarchy through the Webtop, you need to assign at least one category or keyword to it or the hierarchy itself won't be saved.
- Although the `<CFA_METADATACATEGORYOBJECTFIND>` tag finds Content Items associated with specified categories, there's no direct way to associate a Content Item with a category. However, when you associate a Content Item with a keyword, the Content Item is also automatically associated with the keyword's category.

Hierarchies and ContentObject Types

Within Spectra, the definition of a hierarchy is stored in a Content Item of object type `metaDataHierarchy`. You can view the definition of the ContentObject Type through the Webtop if System Entities has been turned on in the Webtop Preferences. `metaDataHierarchy` has two properties and no methods:

- `hierarchyData` contains a WDDX packet that holds information on all the categories and subcategories within the hierarchy.
- `RelatedTypes` contains a list of the ContentObject Types the hierarchy can be used with. This list is used only to restrict access to a hierarchy within the Metadata Picker; it doesn't prevent the interactive developer from programmatically assigning keywords from any other hierarchy.

Similarly, categories are stored as Content Items of object type `metaDataCategory`. This ContentObject Type consists of a single property—`categoryData`—that contains a WDDX packet that holds all information concerning the category.

Because most hierarchy and category related data is stored in WDDX packets, it's almost always better to use Spectra's meta data tags to create, update, and delete hierarchy and category definitions than to try to directly update `metaDataHierarchy` or `metaDataCategory` Content Items.

CHAPTER 12

Using Process Logic Paths

In this chapter

Understanding PLPs

In this chapter, we will discuss how to use Spectra to create and work with PLPs, or Process Logic Paths. Spectra has a very robust system to handle processes, including automatic state management and rollback capabilities.

A *process* is any action that takes multiple steps. For example, when you water your plants, you first have to turn on the hose, then you bring the hose to the plants, and then you spray the plants with water. Every step has to be done in order; individual step details can vary based on prior steps, and some steps might have to be repeated or skipped. As Web developers, we face similar problems on the Internet.

Processes and Web Applications

Every action on a Web site involves a user requesting information and then waiting for that information to return. Between hits, nothing else is going on, and all requests are processed without knowledge or awareness of prior requests. From a Web server's perspective, every request stands on its own two feet. This is known as *statelessness*. This stateless behavior of the Web has been a common problem for Web developers over the years, and various solutions have been created to address it.

The problem of "state" is even more troublesome when presenting a multistep process to a user. Just what is a multistep process on the Web? A simple example might be the typical "check-out" routine on an e-commerce site:

1. Display shopping cart and allow user to modify items.
2. Ask user for shipping address.
3. Ask user for payment information.
4. Process order.
5. Thank the user.

Figure 12.1 displays a flowchart of this process.

Now imagine that the user has the ability to go back and forth among those steps. How do you handle the data so that if the user backs up a step, her data won't be lost when she returns to that step? What if the user closes her browser or loses her Internet connection? Should she have to begin the process all over again? Web developers have commonly had these kinds of problems when trying to re-create a process on the Web.

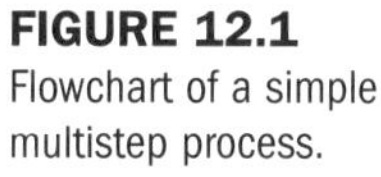

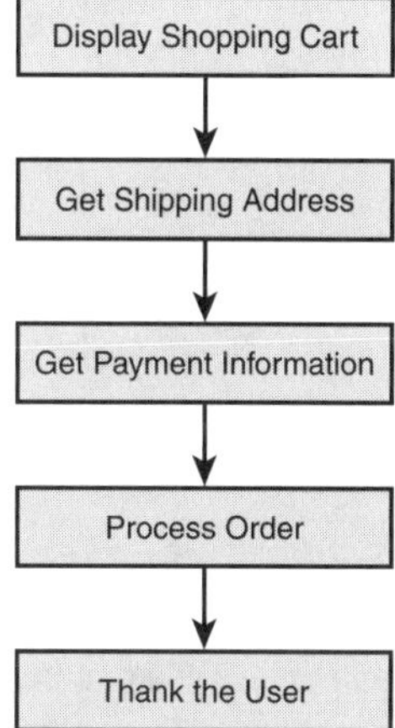

FIGURE 12.1
Flowchart of a simple multistep process.

Processes with Spectra

Luckily, Spectra provides a powerful service that allows you to design processes without having to worry about state management. In fact, Spectra handles almost every detail, leaving the programmer to worry about only how each step will be coded. He won't have to worry about remembering what step a user is in, what the next or previous step is, or whether the values saved in a step are available to the next step. Spectra will handle all of this for you!

The Spectra service used in this chapter is the PLP (Process Logic Path) service. This service allows you to

- Design a process path within the Webtop or via CFA tags.
- Design processes that run from step to step or branch and loop, depending on conditions.

Creating PLPs with Spectra

Designing PLPs in Spectra is very easy. Like with most other services in Spectra, you can design PLPs with the Webtop, in a nice, GUI type format, or you can use CFA tags. Your first problem is to identify the process that you want to develop for your system.

The sample Web site includes a catalog of books. A typical process may be the addition of a book to your catalog. This process might look something like Figure 12.2.

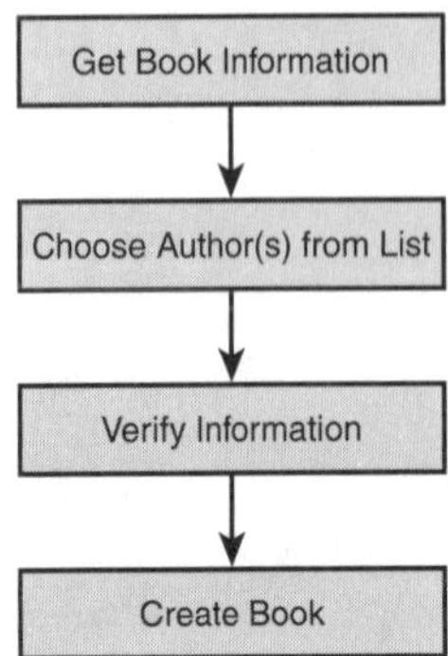

FIGURE 12.2
Flowchart for the book addition process.

Now that you have an idea of what the process will entail, you can begin to design the PLP with the Webtop. Open your Webtop (`http://localhost/allaire/spectra/webtop`) and navigate to the System Design area. Then, click the PLP Designer link and select the PLP Wizard. The screen shown in Figure 12.3 is what you should see.

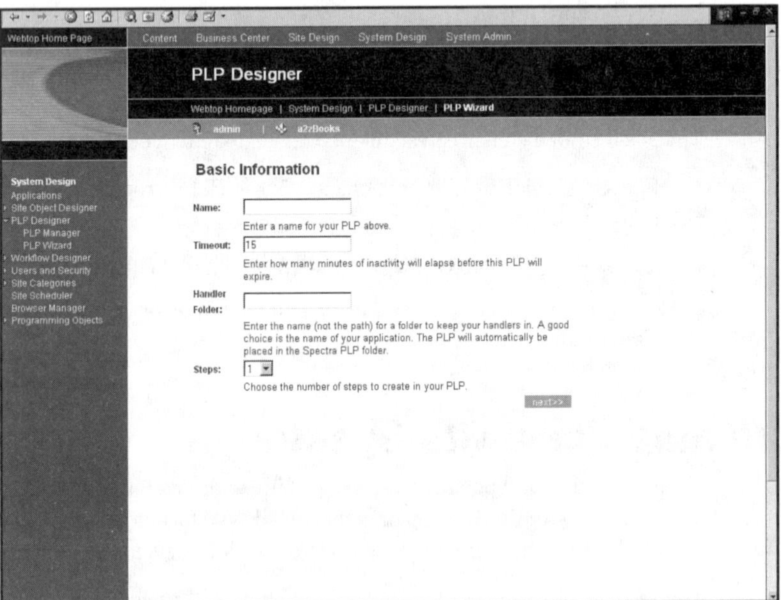

FIGURE 12.3
The Webtop PLP Wizard.

TIP If you are asked to log in, remember the username (`admin`) and password (also `admin`) set up in an earlier chapter.

The PLP Wizard is a simple, step-by-step guide that makes creating a PLP very easy. More importantly, it's a PLP itself! Later, you can examine the code and learn from it. Let's begin entering information about our PLP.

Entering the Basic Information

First, we need to give the PLP a name. Since we are creating a Book object, we will call this PLP `BookCreate`. The timeout value relates to the state management capabilities of PLPs in Spectra. By default, PLPs will remember what step of a PLP you are on. The timeout value simply sets how *long* it will remember what step you are on. For now, let's leave it at the default of 15 minutes.

Next, we need to pick a folder name for our PLP. By default, the PLP Wizard will create this folder under the *`spectra_install_root`*`/plp` folder. So, if your install root was `c:\program files\allaire\spectra`, PLPs will be saved under: `c:\program files\allaire\spectra\plp`. When we enter a name in this field, we are telling Spectra what folder to create under the above directory. Now, this is where things get interesting. Let's say we want to save our PLP under an A2ZBooks folder. What Spectra will do is create a folder called `a2zbooks` and then a folder called `BookCreate`. In other words, the `a2zbooks` folder will be the folder we use for all A2ZBooks PLPs. Think of it as a common PLP directory for our application.

The final question relates to the number of steps in our PLP. According to the flowchart in Figure 12.2, we will have four steps, but rather than choose 4 from the drop-down list, you will select 3. Why? Our PLP will handle only the first three steps of the flowchart. We will collect information about the book, choose the authors, and confirm. When that is done, the PLP will end, passing the information collected back to the template that called it. At that point we will actually create the Book object. After selecting 3 from the drop-down list, your screen will look like that in Figure 12.4.

Now that we have entered the basic information about the PLP, click the Next button to begin the second part of the PLP Wizard.

Creating the DDO

The next step of the PLP Wizard requires us to create a DDO, or Defined Data Object. What does this mean in plain English? In the shopping cart example, the DDO can be thought of as the shopping cart itself that travels along with the user at each step of the PLP. This cart will hold data and be available to each step of the PLP.

For our PLP, we want to create a DDO that will store the information about the book being created. Click the Build DDO button to launch the dataBuilder, a DHTML tree control where we can design our DDO. Figure 12.5 shows our initial (and empty) DDO.

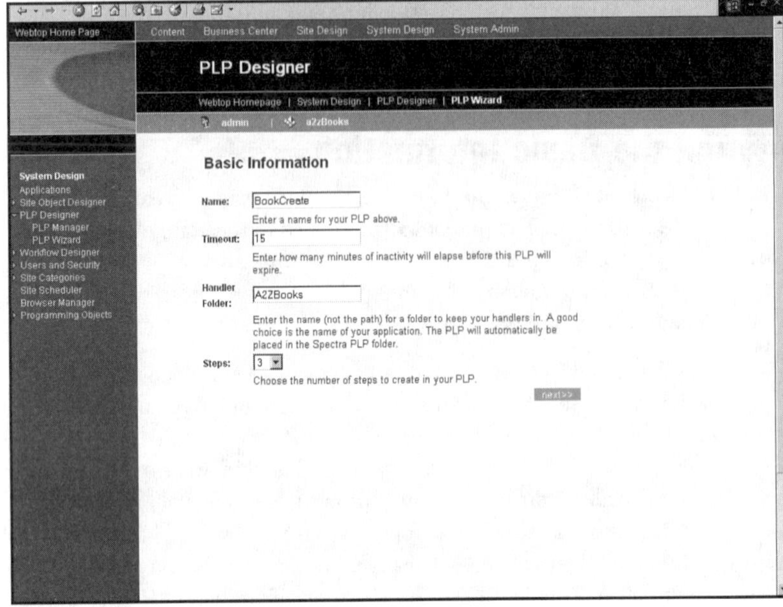

FIGURE 12.4
The first page of the PLP Wizard, with information inserted.

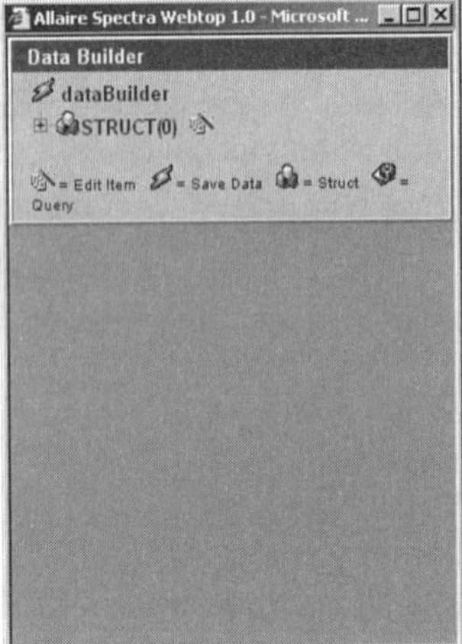

FIGURE 12.5
The Build DDO button launches a new window with the dataBuilder.

To begin adding properties to the DDO, click the Add icon to the right of `STRUCT(0)`. This launches a new window in which we can begin adding keys (or properties) to our DDO. Figure 12.6 shows this new window.

FIGURE 12.6
The dataBuilder with the Add window.

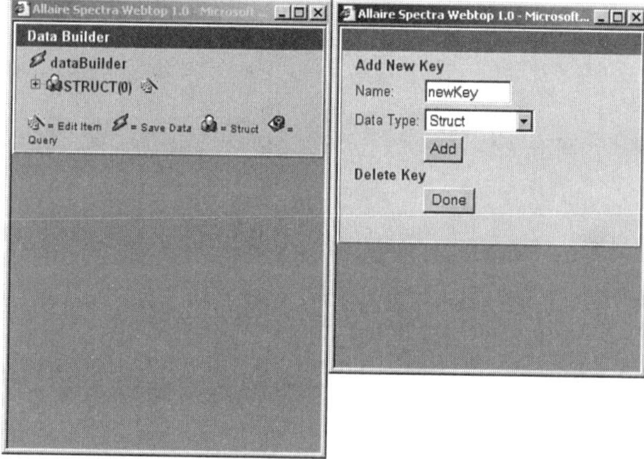

Each key we add to our DDO can be one of three types:

- A Simple Value is what it sounds like—the simplest key you can add to a DDO. It will hold one value. This is the only type we are going to use for our DDO.
- Struct is short for *structure*. If you want a structure for your DDO—perhaps to organize the DDO into sections—you would add a Struct value. Think of this as adding a subtree to the existing tree.
- The last type is the Query type. If you want part of your DDO to hold a query, create a key of this type.

Our DDO will be a direct copy of the properties of the Book type. We are going to add one key for each of the eight properties of the book. For each property, type in the name and be sure to select the Simple Value data type. Enter a key for each of the following properties:

```
author        price
edition       published
isbn          publisher
pages         title
```

As you add each property, it will become available in the Delete Key drop-down. If you make a mistake typing in the name of the key, simply delete it and reenter the property. After you finish creating the keys, click the Done button to reload the dataBuilder. Rather than `Struct(0)`, you should now see `Struct(8)`. This reflects the addition of eight keys to the DDO. If you click the plus symbol next to Struct, you can expand the tree and look at your DDO. Figure 12.7 shows the completed DDO.

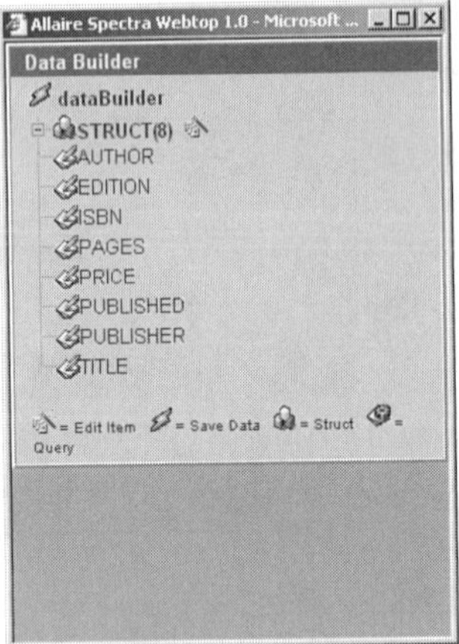

FIGURE 12.7
The dataBuilder with the completed DDO.

Now that we have created our DDO, we can click the lightning bolt icon to save the data. The window will close, and we can continue with the PLP Wizard by clicking the Next button.

Be sure to click the lightning bolt icon to save the DDO. If you aren't sure that you saved the DDO when the window is closed, simply click the Build DDO button again. You can examine your DDO to make sure that it saved your keys.

Entering the Step Information

The PLP Wizard is now going to ask us to enter information about each step of the PLP. Since we told the wizard we had three steps, this screen will be repeated three more times, once for each step. The first screen, Edit STEP1, presents a set of options we can use to describe the first step. The first question asked is what name we will use to describe the first step. To keep things simple (and obvious), name this step Step1.

The second thing the PLP Wizard wants to know is the name of the handler file. In the first part of the wizard we told Spectra what the handler folder for our PLP would be. Now we tell it what filename to use for this step. Spectra will automatically use the handler folder we set up when looking for the handler files. (Remember, the folder will be under the Spectra install root and will contain the handler folder, `a2zbooks`, and the name of the PLP: `<spectra install root>\allaire\spectra\plp\a2zbooks\bookcreate`.) We will name this file `step1.cfm`, so it will be similar to the name of the step itself. This makes debugging much easier. If I have a problem with step 2 or 3, I will know immediately what file to edit.

Let's leave everything else alone now and move on to the next step. Figure 12.8 shows what the form should look like before moving on to step 2. Table 12.1 describes the other settings. Although we are not going to modify them at this time, you should familiarize yourself with what they do.

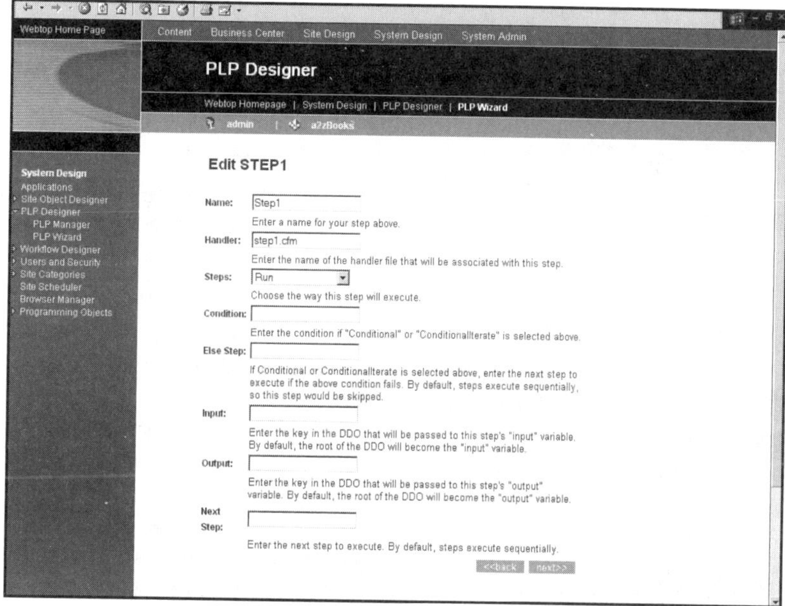

FIGURE 12.8
Information for Step1 has been entered.

Table 12.1 PLP Step Options

Option	Description
Name	We described this already, but the name of the step gives the PLP a way to uniquely identify each step in the process.
Handler	The filename for the particular step of the PLP. You should not specify a folder, just the filename (example: `step2.cfm`).
Steps	Determines how the step will execute. You have four options: *Run* simply means to run the step. *Conditional* means that the step will run only if a certain condition is true. (See the Condition option following.) *DataIterate* means to iterate over each key in the DDO. This is useful if you want to iterate over a set of questions or other items. *ConditionalIterate* means to loop over a step while a condition is true.
Condition	The condition to check for. This is used in both Conditional and ConditionalIterate type steps.
Else Step	If a step is marked as Conditional and that condition is false, specify the name of a step the PLP should execute instead of the current step. The same is true for ConditionalIterate. The PLP will repeat a step until the condition is false. At that point it will run the step specified in the Else Step section.

continues

Table 12.1 Continued

Option	Description
Input	The name of the input scope. This defaults to `input`.
Output	The name of the output scope. This defaults to `output`.
Next Step	By default, a PLP will run the step that comes next in order. In other words, when step 1 is done, step 2 will follow. If you want, you can specify the name of a step to run instead of the normal step that would follow.

NOTE The information in Table 12.1 covers all the options you are presented with in each iteration of the PLP Wizard step editor. The only piece of information missing is the ability to specify a step to call in case of an error. This option is available when you edit a PLP in the PLP Manager. The `Error Handler` attribute allows you to specify a handler file to call in case of a thrown error. The error must be of type CFA.

The PLP Wizard automatically moves us to the edit page for step 2. Let's fill in the same information for each step. For steps 2 and 3, name each step `Step`*`X`* and use `step`*`X`*`.cfm` as the handler name (both times, replace *`X`* with the number of the step). After you finish entering information for all three steps, the PLP Wizard displays the ID of the newly created PLP (see Figure 12.9).

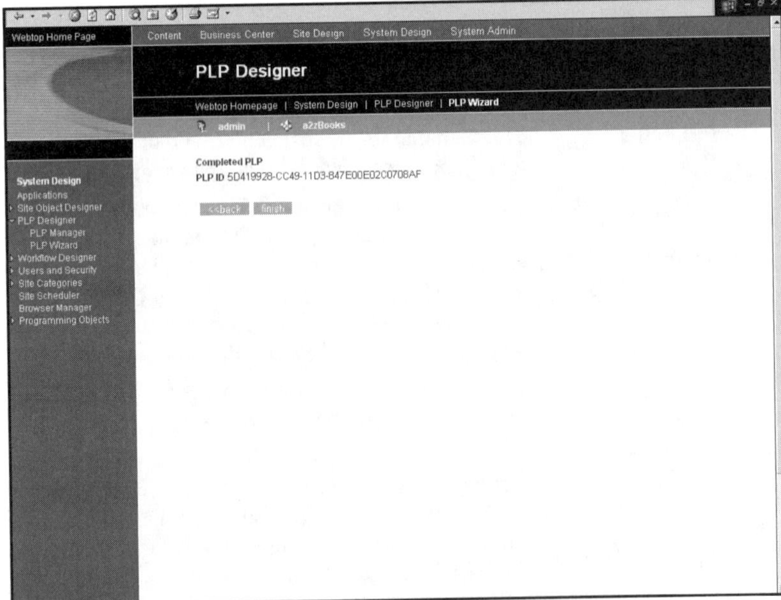

FIGURE 12.9
The completed PLP.

Once you click the Finish button, you will be brought to the PLP Manager. This section of the Webtop allows you to edit, view, export, and delete PLPs. To edit a PLP, simply click the PLP's name. To view a graphical representation of the PLP, click the icon to the left of the PLP's name. Figure 12.10 shows the layout of our PLP.

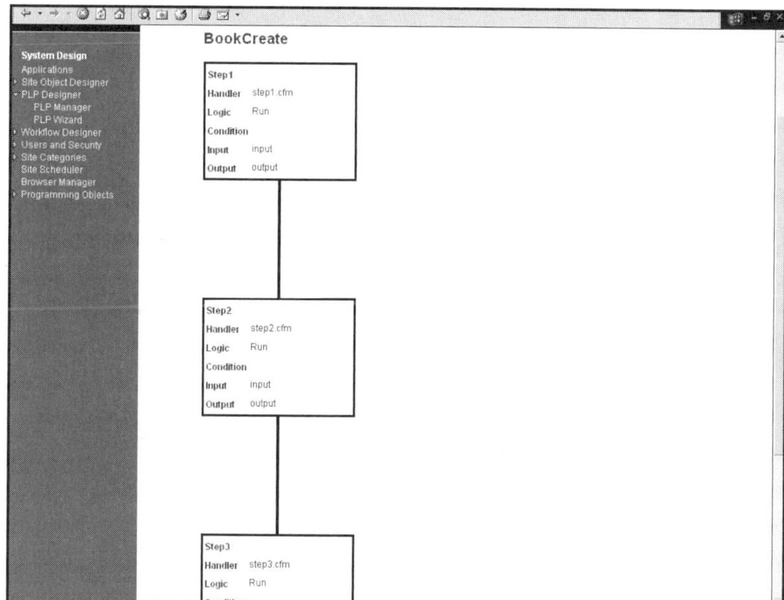

FIGURE 12.10
The first few steps of our PLP, represented graphically by the Webtop.

To delete the PLP, select the check box and click the Delete button. Be sure you know what you're doing because, once you delete it, there's no coming back!

To export the PLP, click the cube-shaped icon to the right of the PLP Manager. More information on exporting PLPs can be found later, in the section "Exporting PLPs."

Creating a PLP with the *<CFA_PLPCREATE>* Tag

Now thatwe have covered the basics of creating a PLP via the Webtop, we should also note that it's possible to create a PLP with code as well. This is not as easy as creating it via the Webtop, but it could be useful if you have to design a PLP on-the-fly or without user interaction. The Spectra tag for creating a PLP is `<CFA_PLPCREATE>`. The `<CFA_PLPCREATE>` tag is an example of a PITA tag. You normally don't use these tags in your day-to-day Spectra programming. Table 12.2 lists the attributes for `<CFA_PLPCREATE>`.

Table 12.2 <CFA_PLPCREATE> Arguments

Argument	Required?	Description
`datasource`	Yes	The datasource where the PLP will be stored.
`Name`	Yes	The name of the PLP.
`PLPID`	No	If you pass a UUID via the `PLPID` argument, the PLP will use the specified ID. Otherwise, a new UUID is created.
`stDDO`	No	If you've created a DDO (defined data object), pass in the name of the structure here.
`iTimeout`	No	The timeout value for the PLP. If a user doesn't perform an action within this limit, the PLP will be reset. The default is 15 minutes.
`bCreateStructure`	No	If set to true, the `<CFA_PLPCREATE>` tag will create the directory structure for your PLP.
`handlerRoot`	No	The root of the PLP. If you don't specify this, the `handlerRoot` will default to where you installed Spectra.
`handlerRelativePath`	No	The relative path to your PLP. If you don't specify this, the PLP will use the `handlerRoot` argument to determine where PLP files are. When Spectra searches for the PLP files, it will look in the mapping that matches the `handlerRelativePath` value as well as assume that a subfolder exists that's the same as the name of the PLP. For example, if we use a `handlerRelativePath` of `/work` and a PLP name of `BookCreate`, Spectra will assume the handler files exist in `/work/BookCreate`.
`r_stOutput`	No	The `<CFA_PLPCREATE>` tag will return the newly created PLP structure using the name you pass to this argument.
`r_objectID`	No	The `<CFA_PLPCREATE>` tag will return the ID of the newly created PLP using the variable name you pass to this argument.

Argument	Required?	Description
r_bStructureWasCreated	No	If you asked the <CFA_PLPCREATE> tag to create the directory structure for the PLP, the tag will return true if the action was a success, false if there was a problem. A returned false value doesn't mean the PLP wasn't created—it simply means that the directory specified in handlerRoot or handlerRelativePath wasn't set correctly.

Listing 12.1 shows an example of creating a simple PLP.

Listing 12.1 Sample of <*CFA_PLPCREATE*>

```
<!---
File:          /a2zTestScripts/createPLP.cfm
Author:        Raymond Camden (raymond.k.camden@syntegra.com)
Date:          12/1/1999
Description: Creates a PLP using the PITA cfa_plpCreate tag.
Notes:         Feel free to delete this plp in the webtop.
--->

<CFA_GlobalSettings>

<CFSET filmDDO = StructNew()>
<CFSET filmDDO.Name = "">
<CFSET filmDDO.DateCreated = "">
<CFSET flimDDO.Rating = "">


<cfa_PLPCreate
     dataSource = "CFAObjects"
     Name = "FilmPLP"
     stDDO = "#filmDDO#"
     iTimeout = "15"
     bCreateStructure = "True"
     handlerRelativePath = "Test1"
     r_stOutput = "myPLP"
     r_objectID="newID"
     r_bStructureWasCreated="dirMade">

<CFOUTPUT>
The new PLP's ID is: #newID#<BR>
Was the directory structure created? #dirMade#<BR>
Here is a dump of the new PLP:<BR>
</CFOUTPUT>

<CFA_DUMP VAR="#myPLP#">
```

Listing 12.1 shows a simple example of creating a PLP via code instead of the Webtop. We begin by calling `<CFA_GLOBALSETTINGS>`, which sets up some default variables that Spectra needs to work properly. We then create a new structure to store our DDO. We call this structure `filmDDO`, as I'm going to use it to hold a DDO for a film. I have keys for the film's name, `DateCreated`, and rating. Once I do that, I call `<CFA_PLPCREATE>` and pass in some of the arguments I described earlier. The name of my PLP is `FilmCreate`. The `stDDO` is the structure we just created, `filmDDO`. I set a timeout value of `15`, although that's unnecessary, as the PLP will default to `15` anyway. I used a `handlerRelativePath` of `Test1`. Lastly, I asked the tag to return a structure containing my PLP, the value of the ID of the PLP, and a Boolean value that will let me know if the directory structure was created.

The next few lines simply output the values I asked the tag to return. The last line calls a fabulous Spectra utility called `cfa_Dump`. This tag will dump any value, whether it's a structure, a query, or an array (or any combination thereof). I use this tag to dump the PLP structure that was created. Figure 12.11 shows the results in the browser.

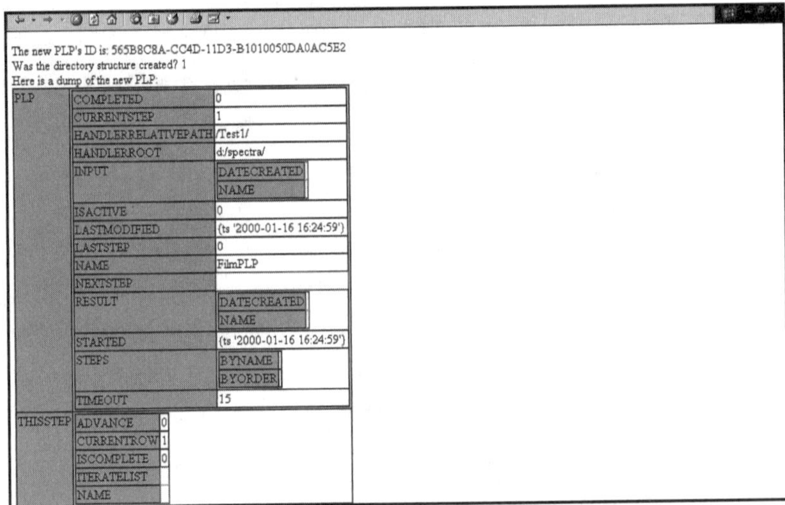

FIGURE 12.11
The result of creating a PLP with `<CFA_PLPCREATE>`.

At this point you may want to return to the Webtop and delete the PLP we just created.

Coding the Steps of a PLP

Now that we have designed our BookCreate PLP in the Webtop, we can begin working on the code that will make up the steps of the PLP.

Before creating the code behind the PLP, we need a way to begin the PLP. PLPs are started by using the `<CFA_PLP>` custom tag. Let's create a new page within the catalog folder of the A2Z Web site called `bookcreate.cfm`. If your Web server's root is `c:\inetpub\wwwroot`, the location of the file would be `c:\inetpub\wwwroot\a2z\catalog\bookcreate.cfm`. Listing 12.2 shows `bookcreate.cfm`.

Listing 12.2 *bookcreate.cfm*

```
<!---
File:          /a2z/catalog/bookcreate.cfm
Author:        Raymond Camden (raymond.k.camden@syntegra.com)
Date:          12/10/1999
Description:   launches the BookCreate PLP
Notes:         Change the PLP ID to match the ID created on your system.
--->

<CFSET PLPID = "59791C63-A8F1-11D3-B0FA0050DA0AC5E2">

<CF_a2zFormatting>

        <CFA_PLP PLPID="#PLPID#" DATASOURCE="#Request.CFA.DataSource.DSN#"
         R_BPLPISCOMPLETE="bComplete" r_stOutput="NewBook">
<CFIF bComplete>

            <!--- Create a label based on the Title --->
            <CFSET NewBook.Label = NewBook.Title>
            <!--- Get the author list... --->
            <CFSET AuthorList = NewBook.Author>
            <!--- The Author Property is an array. --->
            <CFSET NewBook.Author = ArrayNew(1)>
            <!--- We populate the Author array with the list we have. --->
            <CFSET NewBook.Author = ListToArray(AuthorList)>

            <!---
                Remove the publisher as well, it's an embedded object.
                We will repopulate it in a moment.
            --->
            <CFSET Publisher = NewBook.Publisher>
            <CFSET StructDelete(NewBook,"Publisher")>

            <!--- Create the object. --->
            <CFA_CONTENTOBJECTCREATE DATASOURCE="#Request.CFA.DataSource.DSN#"
             TYPEID="#Application.bookTypeID#" STPROPERTIES="#NewBook#"
             R_ID="NewID">

            <!--- Embed the Publisher object. --->
            <CFA_CONTENTOBJECTCREATEEMBEDDEDFROMORIGINAL
                    DATASOURCE="#Request.CFA.DataSource.DSN#"
                    ORIGINALOBJECTID="#Publisher#"
                    OBJECTID="#NewID#.publisher">

            <CFOUTPUT>
            The book #NewBook.Title# (#NewID#) has been created.
            </CFOUTPUT>
        </CFIF>

</cf_a2zFormatting>
```

This template is pretty simple. First we define our `PLPID` variable. This ID is the number that Spectra generated to identify our PLP. You should replace this number with the ID on your system. We then include our `<CF_A2ZFORMATTING>` custom tag, which simply outputs the layout of our site. Next, we call `<CFA_PLP>`, pass in the ID and datasource, and then ask it to create a variable that will store a Boolean value that lets us know whether the PLP has completed. If the PLP *is* done, we create a new Book object and output information about this new book. We can specify the name of the variable that will contain the output of the PLP by using the `R_BPLPISCOMPLETE` attribute. In our script, we specify the name `NewBook` for our output data. In other words, the information we enter in our PLP will be available in this structure. We will discuss what happens when the PLP is finished later in this chapter, in the section "The End of Our PLP."

This is all that is required to start off the PLP. If you want to test this in your browser, go ahead! The PLP Wizard actually creates a file for each step of your PLP. Spectra, of course, doesn't write the real code for you; it simply creates a default PLP step handler that shows off a Next button. You can run through the PLP, although you will get an error at the end when `bComplete` is true.

Listing 12.3 shows the default code that Spectra writes. You can find this file by navigating to your Spectra installation directory. Then pick the `PLP\a2zbooks\bookcreate` folder. You should see three files: `step1.cfm`, `step2.cfm`, and `step3.cfm`.

Listing 12.3 *step1.cfm*

```
<cfa_PLPHandler>
<!--- /// Change the form.submit in the following line to be
      'form.the name of your submit button' /// --->
<CFIF IsDefined('form.submit')>

    <!--- default form processing here --->
        <CFSET output[thisstep.name] = StructNew()>
        <CFLOOP index="formItem" list="#Form.Fieldnames#">
            <CFSET "output.#thisstep.name#.#FormItem#"
             = Evaluate("Form.#FormItem#")>
</cfloop>
    <cfset thisStep.isComplete = 1>
    <cfset thisStep.advance = 1>

<CFELSE>

<!--- the step code --->
    <cfoutput>
        <!--- /// Put your form Here /// --->
        Step1<p>
        <form action="#thisStep.url#" method="POST">
            <input type="Submit" name="submit" value="next&gt;&gt;">
        </form>
```

```
    </cfoutput>

</cfif>
</cfa_PLPHandler>
```

The file begins by using the `<CFA_PLPHANDLER>` tag. Like `<CFA_HANDLER>`, this tag handles most of the chores for us. We don't have to worry about creating the correct scope, we just work in our input and output scope. It also makes sure we have access to the `thisStep` scope as well.

The default PLP step handler is split into two main sections within the `<CFA_PLPHANDLER>` tag. The first section checks to see whether the form is submitted. We then create a scope based on the name of the step. This line

```
<CFSET output[thisstep.name] = StructNew()>
```

would create an `output.Step1` structure if the name of the step was `Step1`. The default handler doesn't do any kind of error checking; it simply moves all the form values into the `output.`*`StepName`* scope we created. It does this by looping through the special form variable, *`form.fieldnames`*. This value is available to any CFM page processing a form (as long as the form isn't a file upload form) and contains a list of all the form variables passed to the action page. Lastly, we mark the step as being complete and tell our PLP to advance. The `CFA_PLP` tag will automatically check for the `thisStep.isComplete` and `thisStep.advance` values.

The second part of the file contains the form, which in this case consists of a dynamic form tag and one simple button. This is where we will begin our editing.

Coding Step 1

The first step of our PLP will gather information about the book. We want to gather up every bit of information *except* the author name, which will come in step 2. We need to ask for the following values:

- `edition`
- `isbn`
- `pages`
- `price`
- `published`
- `publisher`
- `title`

Listing 12.4 shows the modified version of the `step1.cfm` file.

Listing 12.4 *step1.cfm*

```
<!---
File:           step1.cfm
Author:         raymond camden (raymond.k.camden@sytegra.com)
Date:           12/10/1999
Description:    step1 of the book create PLP
Notes:
--->

<cfa_PLPHandler>
<!--- /// Change the form.submit in the following line to be
      'form.the name of your submit button' /// --->
<CFIF IsDefined('form.submit')>
   <CFSET ERROR = "">
   <!--- default form processing here --->
   <!--- Our modifications begin --->
   <CFIF NOT Len(Trim(Form.Title))>
        <CFSET ERROR = ERROR & "You must include a title.<BR>">
   <CFELSE>
        <CFSET Output.Title = Form.Title>
   </CFIF>
   <CFIF NOT Len(Trim(Form.isbn))>
        <CFSET ERROR = ERROR & "You must include an ISBN.<BR>">
   <CFELSE>
        <CFSET Output.isbn = Form.isbn>
   </CFIF>
   <CFIF NOT Len(Trim(Form.price)) OR NOT IsNumeric(Form.price)>
        <CFSET ERROR = ERROR & "You must include a numeric price.<BR>">
   <CFELSE>
        <CFSET Output.price = Form.price>
   </CFIF>
   <CFIF NOT Len(Trim(Form.pages)) OR NOT IsNumeric(Form.pages)>
        <CFSET ERROR = ERROR & "You must include the number of pages.<BR>">
   <CFELSE>
        <CFSET Output.pages = Form.pages>
   </CFIF>
   <CFIF NOT Len(Trim(Form.published)) OR NOT IsDate(Trim(Form.published))>
        <CFSET ERROR = ERROR & "You must include a date of publication.<BR>">
   <CFELSE>
        <CFSET Output.published = Form.published>
   </CFIF>
   <CFSET Output.edition = Form.edition>
   <CFSET Output.publisher = Form.publisher>
   <CFIF NOT Len(ERROR)>
        <cfset thisStep.isComplete = 1>
        <cfset thisStep.advance = 1>
   </CFIF>

<CFIF NOT thisStep.isComplete>
```

```
<!--- End our modifications --->

<!--- the step code --->
   <cfoutput>
       <!--- /// Put your form Here /// --->
       Step1<p>
       <form action="#thisStep.url#" method="POST">
           <!--- Our modifications begin --->
           <CFIF IsDefined("ERROR")>
               <B>There is a problem with your submission.<BR>
               #ERROR#
               </B>
           </CFIF>
           <!--- gather all publishers --->
           <CFA_CONTENTOBJECTGETMULTIPLE DATASOURCE="A2ZAccess"
            TYPEID="#Application.publisherTypeID#"
            R_STOBJECTS="publishers">
Title:
           <INPUT TYPE="text" NAME="title" VALUE="#Output.title#">
           <BR>
           ISBN:
           <INPUT TYPE="text" NAME="isbn" VALUE="#Output.isbn#">
           <BR>
           Edition:
           <INPUT TYPE="text" NAME="edition" VALUE="#Output.edition#">
           <BR>
           Price:
           <INPUT TYPE="text" NAME="price" VALUE="#Output.price#">
           <BR>
           Pages:
           <INPUT TYPE="text" NAME="pages" VALUE="#Output.pages#">
           <BR>
           Published:
           <INPUT TYPE="text" NAME="published" VALUE="#Output.published#">
           <BR>
           Publisher:
           <SELECT NAME="publisher">
           <CFLOOP ITEM="publisherID" COLLECTION="#publishers#">
           <OPTION VALUE="#publisherID#"
           <CFIF publisherID IS Output.publisher>SELECTED</CFIF>>
           #publishers[publisherID].label#
           </CFLOOP>
           </SELECT>            <P>
           <!--- End our modifications --->
           <input type="Submit" name="submit" value="next&gt;&gt;">
       </form>
   </cfoutput>

</cfif>
</cfa_PLPHandler>
```

This is a big change from the default file Spectra created for us, so let's go through it step by step. The first change is the comment header at the top. The <CFA_PLPHANDLER> tag is still wrapping the bulk of the page. Again, the idea here is that the tag will set up our default values for us. Our next block of code does the error checking. I won't spend much time describing the error checking here, because it's rather simple. We check for every value but `edition` and `publisher`. `edition` isn't required, and since `publisher` is a drop-down, it will always contain a value. We do special checking for `pages` and `price`, both of which must be numbers. Lastly, we make sure `published` is a valid date string. For each error, we append an error message to a variable called `ERROR`.

For each correct value, we copy the form value to the output scope. Why do we do this? Do you see how we default the form fields to values from the output scope? We can do that because as soon as the PLP begins, our output scope contains one key for each key of the DDO we created earlier. By copying the form values into the output scope, we can redisplay some values in case an error was thrown. For example, if we enter a title but forget to enter the number of pages, the form will display the title for us and we will not be forced to re-enter everything simply because we had an error. Notice how we don't output to a scope called `output[thisStep.`*`name`*`]`. The default code created by the PLP Wizard wanted to save data from each step into an individual section of the output scope. This is unnecessary and is more work than we need to do. It's better to just save our values into the output scope directly.

Next, we check to see if we encountered an error. All we need to do is see if the `ERROR` variable has any data in it. The `Len` function is a quick way of doing that. If we have not encountered an error, we set `thisStep.isComplete` and `thisStep.advance` to `1`. This tells our PLP to move on to the next step.

NOTE The two variables, `thisStep.isComplete`, and `thisStep.advance`, must both be set to true. If they aren't, you won't advance to a different step.

Notice that we also changed the <CFIF> block. Previously we had a <CFIF> block, like so:

```
<CFIF isDefined("form.submit")>
    move form data to output scope and advance to next step
<CFELSE>
    show the form for the step
</CFIF>
```

We have modified this `CFIF` block by splitting it into two blocks. Our first block is still run only if the Submit button was clicked. The second block will fire only if the step hasn't been completed. Notice how I can use the value (`thisStep.isComplete`) even when I don't set it anywhere. This is an example of one of the values the <CFA_PLPHANDLER> sets up for you. You can see another example of this inside the form tag. Our action is `thisStep.url`. The nice thing about this value is that it allows us to start the PLP from any file at all. If we were to rename the `bookcreate.cfm` file to something else, it would continue to work, since our form tag has abstracted the value.

Next, we check for the `ERROR` variable. If it has been defined, there must have been an error. We output a simple message to that effect and display the error text.

Our form has been modified to include labels and inputs for each field we need to check for. The only really interesting field here is the `publisher`. In our Book object type, we have defined the `publisher` property as being an embedded type. This means the value is actually a pointer to another object. In this case, we have a pointer to an object of type `publisher`. I use the `<CFA_CONTENTOBJECTGETMULTIPLE>` tag to grab all our `publisher` objects and return them as a structure called `publishers`. I can then output `publishers` inside a select box. I use the ID of the publisher as the value of the option and the label as the text that is presented to the user. Figure 12.12 shows our PLP with form fields and error messages in action.

FIGURE 12.12
The first step of the PLP viewed in the browser.

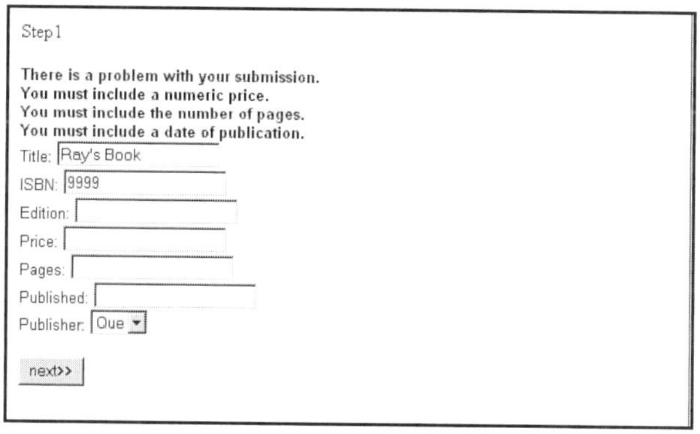

Step 1

There is a problem with your submission.
You must include a numeric price.
You must include the number of pages.
You must include a date of publication.

Title: Ray's Book
ISBN: 9999
Edition:
Price:
Pages:
Published:
Publisher: Que

next>>

Coding Step 2

In the first step of our PLP, we asked for information about the book being created. The only piece of information we didn't get was the author. The `author` property of the Book type has been defined as an array of UUIDs, where each UUID points to an Author object. The code in Listing 12.5 will allow us to pick and choose multiple authors for our new book.

Part III Ch 12

Like before, we have an existing piece of code for `step2.cfm`. We're not going to show the file again, but be aware that our code is a modification of the code Spectra generated for us. When you enter this file, you may just want to clear out all the code Spectra's PLP Wizard made.

Listing 12.5 *step2.cfm*

```
<!---
File:           step2.cfm
Author:         raymond camden (raymond.k.camden@sytegra.com)
Date:           12/10/1999
Description:    step2 of the book create PLP
Notes:
--->
```

continues

Listing 12.5 Continued

```
<cfa_PLPHandler>

<CFIF IsDefined('form.submit')>
    <CFSET ERROR = "">
    <CFIF NOT IsDefined("Form.Author")>
        <CFSET ERROR = ERROR & "You must include at least one author.<BR>">
    <CFELSE>
        <CFSET Output.Author = Form.Author>
    </CFIF>

    <CFIF NOT Len(ERROR)>
        <cfset thisStep.isComplete = 1>
        <cfset thisStep.advance = 1>
    </CFIF>

<CFELSEIF IsDefined("Form.Back")>

    <CFIF IsDefined("Form.Author")>
        <CFSET Output.Author = Form.Author>
    </CFIF>
    <CFSET thisStep.nextStep = "Step1">
    <CFSET thisStep.isComplete = 1>
    <CFSET thisStep.advance = 1>

</CFIF>

<CFIF NOT thisStep.isComplete>

    <!--- Get our Authors --->
    <CFA_CONTENTOBJECTGETMULTIPLE DATASOURCE="A2ZAccess"
     TYPEID="#Application.authorTypeID#" R_STOBJECTS="authors">

<!--- the step code --->
    <cfoutput>
        <!--- /// Put your form Here /// --->
        Step2<p>
        <CFIF IsDefined("ERROR")>
            <B>There is a problem with your submission.<BR>
            #ERROR#
            </B>
        </CFIF>

        <form action="#thisStep.url#" method="POST">
            <SELECT NAME="author" SIZE=5 MULTIPLE>
            <CFLOOP ITEM="Author" COLLECTION="#Authors#">
                <OPTION VALUE="#Author#"
                 <CFIF ListFind(Output.Author,Author)>SELECTED</CFIF>>
                 #Authors[Author].label#
            </CFLOOP>
            </SELECT>
            <P>
```

```
            <INPUT TYPE="Submit" NAME="Back" VALUE="Back &lt;&lt;">
            <input type="Submit" name="submit" value="next&gt;&gt;">
        </form>
    </cfoutput>

</cfif>
</cfa_PLPHandler>
```

This step is a bit more complex than last time, so let's carefully examine the script. Like we saw in `step1.cfm`, the step is separated into a section that checks for errors and a section that displays the form. This time, however, we have two sections that check for form information. We have added a Back button to this step so that the user can go back to step 1. For this to work, we have to provide some code that looks out for this event.

Let's begin by looking at the first block of code. As before, we check to see if `form.submit` is defined. If it is, we need to do some error checking. We create an `ERROR` variable that will store any possible error messages. Since this step is simple, we only have one field to check for. We use the `IsDefined()` function because our form field is a multi-select (we'll talk about the form later). If the user doesn't pick any authors, the field won't be blank, it simply won't exist. If the field doesn't exist, we add an error string to our `ERROR` variable. If the field does exist, we copy the value to our output scope. Next, we check to see if the `ERROR` variable has anything inside it. We do this with the `Len()` function, just like last time. If it's empty, we let the PLP know that the step is complete and that it's time to advance.

The next block handles the Back user action:

```
<CFELSEIF IsDefined("Form.Back")>

    <CFIF IsDefined("Form.Author")>
        <CFSET Output.Author = Form.Author>
    </CFIF>
    <CFSET thisStep.nextStep = "Step1">
    <CFSET thisStep.isComplete = 1>
    <CFSET thisStep.advance = 1>

</CFIF>
```

Part III Ch 12

We simply check to see if the Back button was clicked. If so, we first want to save any information the user entered. This means the user can change the information on this step *and* return to step 1 to make changes. In this case, we have only one form field and, like the code above, we save it only if the user entered something. This time we check to see if `Form.Author` is defined. In the previous block, our `<CFIF>` statement checked to see if it was *not* defined. Once we determine the user picked an author, we copy that information to our output scope. Now we have to actually move the user. This is not complex at all. We begin by changing the `nextStep` parameter of `thisStep`. At the beginning of this chapter we described how the Spectra PLP service takes care of a lot of the details of processes for you. This is one of those things that the `<CFA_PLP>` tag normally does for you—in other words, we don't normally have to specify what the next step is. In this case, however, we want to go backward to step 1. By setting the `nextStep` value to `"Step1"`, and by setting `isComplete` and `advance` to `1`, we tell the PLP to move past this step, but to go to `Step1` instead of `Step3`.

Our next block of code is enclosed by this `<CFIF>` statement:

```
<CFIF NOT thisStep.isComplete>
```

As described in step 1, we can use this variable to determine whether we should show the form. If it's false, we know that we need to display the form. In this step we will present a list of authors to choose from. To get these authors, we use the `<CFA_CONTENTOBJECTGETMULTIPLE>` tag. This is very similar to what we did in step 1 to get the publishers. We pass in the TypeID (`Application.authorTypeID`) and ask the tag to return the authors in a variable called `authors`. This will be a structure of Author objects in which each key of `authors` is an object ID. The value of the key is another structure containing the information about the author.

Next, we output any error that may exist. If you remember the code from step 1, we can check for the existence of our `ERROR` variable and, if it exists, display the error message. Immediately after this we output our form tag. Just as in step 1, our action is `thisStep.url`. We don't have to worry about setting it to anything. The `<CFA_PLP>` tag will set this value for us. As was said, this step has only one field in it, the Author field. Since our Book object uses an array of authors, we used a `<SELECT>` tag with `SIZE=4` and `MULTIPLE` to allow the user to select one or more authors. The next change we made was the addition of another button. This line of code

```
<INPUT TYPE="Submit" NAME="Back" VALUE="Back &lt;&lt;">
```

adds a Back button to our form. If you remember, we added a check for `IsDefined("Form.Back")` to look for this button. The rest of the template hasn't been modified from the code the Spectra PLP Wizard created for us. We include our Next button, end the form, and end the entire script with the ending tag `</CFA_PLP>`. Figure 12.13 shows the form displayed in step 2.

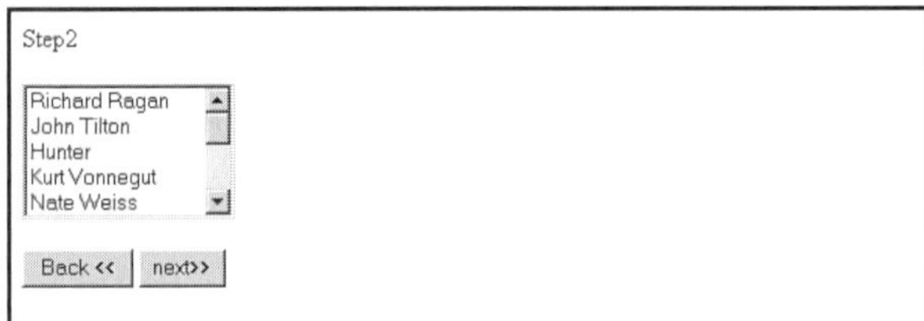

FIGURE 12.13
The second step of the PLP viewed in the browser.

Coding Step 3

Our last step is the simplest yet. All we want to do here is display the values the user entered. If the user notices a mistake, he can go back and correct it. Otherwise, he can end the PLP by clicking the Finish button. Listing 12.6 shows the code for `step3.cfm`.

Listing 12.6 *step3.cfm*

```
<!---
File:           step3.cfm
Author:         raymond camden (raymond.k.camden@sytegra.com)
Date:           12/10/1999
Description:    step3 of the book create PLP
Notes:
--->

<cfa_PLPHandler>
<!--- /// Change the form.submit in the following line to be
      'form.the name of your submit button' /// --->
<CFIF IsDefined('form.submit')>

    <cfset thisStep.isComplete = 1>
    <cfset thisStep.advance = 1>

<CFELSEIF isDefined("Form.Back")>

    <CFSET thisStep.nextStep = "Step2">
    <CFSET thisStep.isComplete = 1>
    <CFSET thisStep.advance = 1>

</CFIF>

<CFIF NOT thisStep.isComplete>
<!--- the step code --->
    <cfoutput>
        <!--- /// Put your form Here /// --->
        Step3<p>
        Please check the values below. If anything is wrong,
        click the Back button to make corrections.
        <P>
        <TABLE>
        <TR>
            <TD><B>Title:</B></TD>
            <TD>#output.title#</TD>
        </TR>
        <TR>
            <TD><B>ISBN:</B></TD>
            <TD>#output.isbn#</TD>
        </TR>
        <TR>
            <TD><B>Edition:</B></TD>
            <TD>#output.edition#</TD>
        </TR>
        <TR>
            <TD><B>Price:</B></TD>
            <TD>#DollarFormat(output.price)#</TD>
        </TR>
```

continues

Listing 12.6 Continued

```
        <TR>
            <TD><B>Pages:</B></TD>
            <TD>#output.pages#</TD>
        </TR>
        <TR>
            <TD><B>Published:</B></TD>
            <TD>#output.published#</TD>
        </TR>
        <!--- Get the object for the publisher --->
<CFA_CONTENTOBJECTGET DATASOURCE="A2ZAccess"
         OBJECTID="#output.publisher#" R_STOBJECT="publisherOb">
        <TR>
            <TD><B>Publisher:</B></TD>
            <!--- Display the label property of the publisher. --->
            <TD>#publisherOb.label#</TD>
        </TR>
        <!--- Get the author objects that correspond
              to our list of UUIDs --->
        <CFA_CONTENTOBJECTGETMULTIPLE DATASOURCE="A2ZAccess"
         LOBJECTIDS="#output.author#" R_STOBJECTS="Authors">
        <TR>
            <TD><B>Author:</B></TD>
            <!--- We have a struct of authors that match the UUIDs we
                  picked. Loop through and display the labels --->
            <TD>
            <CFLOOP ITEM="Author" COLLECTION="#Authors#">
                #Authors[Author].label#<BR>
            </CFLOOP>
            </TD>
        </TR>

        </TABLE>
        <form action="#thisStep.url#" method="POST">
            <INPUT TYPE="Submit" NAME="Back" VALUE="Back &lt;&lt;">
            <input type="Submit" name="submit" value="Finish&gt;&gt;">
        </form>
    </cfoutput>

</cfif>
</cfa_PLPHandler>
```

Like step 2 and step 1, step 3 has two major sections. The first section will check for the Submit or Back button. The second section will appear only if we haven't ended the step. Our first section checks to see if the Submit button has been clicked. Since we're not doing any form entering on this step, we don't need to do any error checking. We simply set `thisStep.isComplete` and `thisStep.advance` to `1`. The next `<CFELSEIF>` block checks for the Back button. If it was clicked, we move the user back to step 2. This is the same code we had in `step2.cfm`, except this time we set `nextStep` to `Step2`.

The second section of our script displays the user's data. We output the title, ISBN, edition, price, number of pages, and publication date. This leaves only the publisher and author. If you remember, however, both values are UUIDs. Since this wouldn't be very useful for the user, we translate these UUIDs into something more readable. To get the name of our publisher, we use `<CFA_CONTENTOBJECTGET>` to retrieve the object corresponding with the UUID value (`output.publisher`) we have. Once we have that object, we can output its label. Since we can have multiple authors, we need to use `<CFA_CONTENTOBJECTGETMULTIPLE>`. Again, we pass in the UUIDs we have (`output.author`) and retrieve a group of corresponding objects. For each Author object, we output the label, which in this case is the name of the author. As before, we output a form tag with a dynamic action attribute, as well as Back and Finish buttons. Figure 12.14 shows how this form looks in the browser.

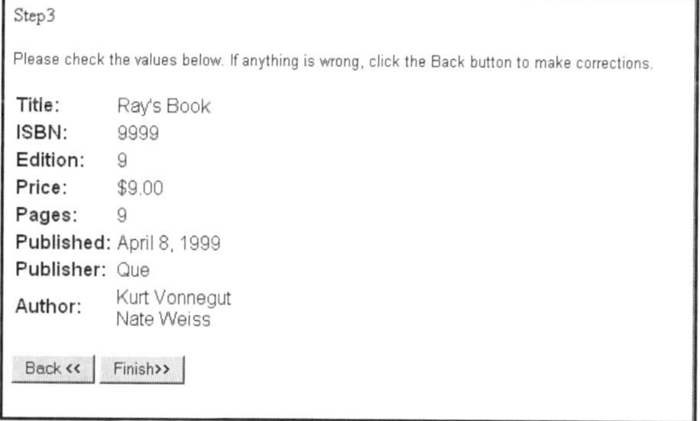

FIGURE 12.14
The third and final step of the PLP viewed in the browser.

The End of Our PLP

That ends the coding for the PLP. If you remember, we began our coding with the file `bookCreate.cfm` (refer to Listing 12.2). In this file, we started our PLP and added a check for the end of the PLP. The code that checks for the end of the PLP is this:

```
<CFIF bComplete>

    <!--- Create a label based on the Title --->
    <CFSET NewBook.Label = NewBook.Title>
    <!--- Get the author list... --->
    <CFSET AuthorList = NewBook.Author>
    <!--- The Author Property is an array. --->
    <CFSET NewBook.Author = ArrayNew(1)>
    <!--- We populate the Author array with the list we have. --->
    <CFSET NewBook.Author = ListToArray(AuthorList)>

    <!---
        Remove the publisher as well, it's an embedded object.
        We will repopulate it in a moment.
    --->
    <CFSET Publisher = NewBook.Publisher>
    <CFSET StructDelete(NewBook,"Publisher")>
```

```
    <!--- Create the object. --->
    <CFA_CONTENTOBJECTCREATE DATASOURCE="A2ZAccess"
     TYPEID="#Application.bookTypeID#" STPROPERTIES="#NewBook#"
     R_ID="NewID">

    <!--- Embed the Publisher object. --->
    <CFA_CONTENTOBJECTCREATEEMBEDDEDFROMORIGINAL
            DATASOURCE="#request.cfa.a2zbooks.datasource#"
            ORIGINALOBJECTID="#Publisher#"
            OBJECTID="#NewID#.publisher">

    <CFOUTPUT>
    The book #NewBook.Title# (#NewID#) has been created.
    </CFOUTPUT>
</CFIF>
```

The `<CFA_PLP>` will automatically set `bComplete` to true since we passed `bComplete` to the `R_BPLPISCOMPLETE` attribute. We are going to create a new Book object, but before we do that we have to massage the data a bit. First, we want to create a label for the new Book object. Labels are a quick way to identify an object and are useful within the Webtop. The title is a good label, so we create the `label` property simply by copying the `title` value from the NewBook structure. What is NewBook? Remember that within our `<CFA_PLP>` tag we asked that the output of the PLP be returned in a variable called `NewBook`. Since our PLP steps copied the bits and pieces of the book to this scope, we can access it in the NewBook structure.

The next problem we have is that the `author` property of the Book ContentObject Type is an array of UUIDs. Unfortunately, our value is a list. We can translate this to an array by first copying the value to `AuthorList`, a temporary value, creating a new array in `NewBook`, and then by using the `ListToArray()` function to populate the new array.

Lastly, the `publisher` property of the Book ContentObject Type is a shared embedded object. We will need to create the link between the embedded object and the new Book object *after* we create the book, so we copy the value of `publisher` and then delete the key from the NewBook structure.

Now we're ready to create the object. We call `<CFA_CONTENTOBJECTCREATE>` and pass in our datasource, type ID, and the structure containing our values, NewBook. We also ask the tag to return the new object ID in a variable called `NewID`. Since the object now exists, we can create a link to the shared embedded object. We use `<CFA_CONTENTOBJECTCREATEEMBEDDEDFROMORIGINAL>` to make this link. We pass in a datasource, the ID of the publisher (remember that we copied this from the NewBook scope a few lines earlier), and the ID of the link, which in this case is the ID of the new book and the name of the property that holds the embedded object, `publisher`.

▶ **See** Chapter 8, "Building the Site Structure," for more information on embedded objects.

Exporting PLPs

Spectra provides a simple tool that we can use to export PLPs from one database to another. To export a PLP, simply go to the PLP Manager in the Webtop. Here you will see a list of PLPs. To export a PLP, click the cube-like icon to the right side of each PLP. Your browser will prompt you to download the file. Figure 12.15 shows an example of this.

FIGURE 12.15
Exporting a PLP.

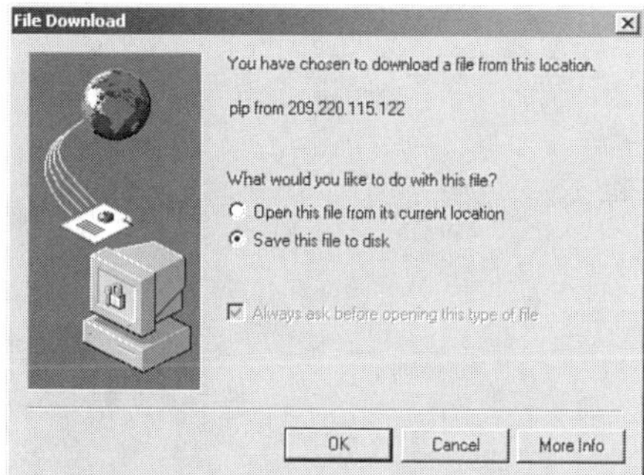

You can save this file anywhere on your computer, just don't forget where you saved it! You should also give it a new name. By default, the Save As dialog will want to use `plp` for the filename. Since you are saving a WDDX version of the PLP, you may want to give it a name like `MyPLP.xml`. The interesting side-effect of this is that Microsoft's Internet Explorer 5 can view this XML file in the browser! After you save the PLP, double-click it and it should open up in your browser. You can then examine the WDDX version of the PLP. You can also open the file in Studio to examine it.

Of course, if you can export PLPs, you can also import them. To import a PLP, go to the System Admin part of the Webtop and select the Database Manager. One option you will see is an Import PLP page. This utility is shown in Figure 12.16.

To use this utility, you must have already exported a PLP (of course) and must have access to that file. Simply use the Browse button to choose the file and then click the Import button. Your PLP will be imported and immediately available to your Spectra application.

NOTE Importing a PLP doesn't copy the scripts that make up the steps of the PLP. You will have to transfer those via FTP or some other mechanism.

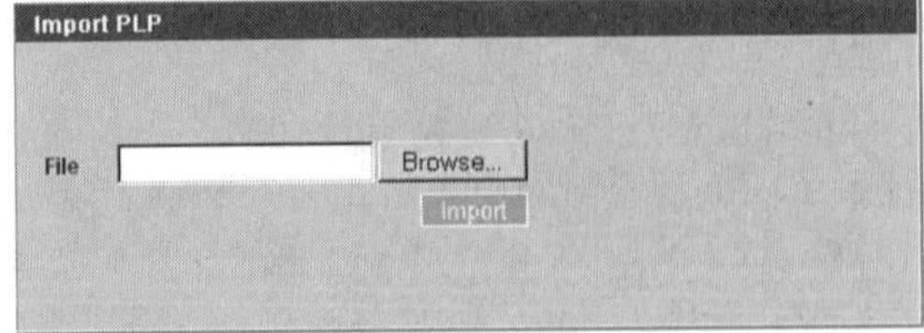

FIGURE 12.16
Importing a PLP.

CHAPTER 13

Working with Workflow

In this chapter

Understanding Workflows

The term *workflow* describes the collective established business processes by which work is accomplished. For example, in a magazine publishing business, an editor gets the idea for an article, assigns it to a writer, who returns the resulting story to an editor (perhaps the same person). The editor edits the story, then passes it on to production people to lay out and add graphics. At some point it probably passes back through the editor for a final okay and then is sent to the printer.

Each action performed as part of the workflow is a *task*. The product produced by the workflow is called an *artifact*. Each person involved in the workflow, whether he has been assigned a task or because he is overseeing the workflow to make sure it gets done, is termed a *participant*.

Some steps in a workflow may depend on other steps. For example, final editorial approval in the above example cannot be given until the story and graphics are complete and in place. In other words, some workflow tasks can happen concurrently with others, while some tasks must happen sequentially.

A workflow, then, is a series of business events that results in a product, large or small.

Spectra provides services you can use to define, create, and manage workflows. It also allows you to define tasks, assign them to individual participants, and establish precedence and relationships between those actions—that is, to identify which tasks need to be completed before a given task can be started.

This service includes a notification architecture that allows you to notify workflow participants using email, page, fax, or custom methods when they have outstanding tasks. Workflow oversight functions allow managers to track the progress of individual workflows and their tasks.

If a particular workflow results in a Content Item, Spectra allows you to associate the workflow with a ContentObject Type. For example, the article in the above publishing example is a Content Item that would be associated with a workflow. You can also define workflows that don't relate to Spectra-created products. Your company might build custom-made PCs. In that case, you could define a workflow of tasks that results in a completed computer. Here, you would use Spectra's notification services to tell each person in the workflow when he has an outstanding task.

Creating Workflows and Tasks Through the Webtop

The Webtop provides interfaces to create the basic elements of a workflow. You begin by planning the workflow, determining the artifact you want to create, the steps you need to do to create it, and the people that will be involved in the process. The design work isn't done in Spectra, only the subsequent implementation.

For the following, we're going to create a workflow for A2Z Books that results in a shipped order of books. This example doesn't involve a Spectra-based artifact but uses Spectra's notification system to let participants know when they have tasks to perform.

The high-level view of defining a workflow is pretty simple:

1. Define a type of workflow (also referred to as a *workflow specification*). At this step you name the workflow type, assign a default user and, if applicable, specify the artifact the workflow creates. This isn't a running workflow—it's the type from which a workflow instance is created.
2. Define types of tasks (also referred to as *task specifications*). At this step you name the task types, assign a default task owner and, if the workflow creates an artifact, specify the method the task invokes on the workflow artifact. This step results in task types from which Spectra will create task instances.
3. Associate task types with a workflow type.
4. Define the precedence of those tasks.

After you do the above, you will have defined a *type* of workflow, such as "Shipping an order of books," made up of *types* of tasks, such as "Package the books." At runtime, Spectra gives you tools to create an *instance* of the workflow *type,* which contains *instances* of the task *types*—you may run multiple instances of a single type at the same time.

Creating a Workflow Specification

First, let's define a workflow type called "Shipping a Book Order":

1. Click System Design, and then open Workflow Designer in the navigation area on the left.
2. Click Workflow Templates to display the Workflow Templates screen (see Figure 13.1).
3. Click Create at the bottom of the screen to bring up the Create Workflow Template form (see Figure 13.2).
4. In the Title field, enter **`Handling a book order`**.
5. In the User Name field, select the default owner for this workflow.
6. In the Artifact Type drop-down, select None, since we aren't going to create a Content Item with this workflow.
7. Enter a description in the Description field.
8. Click Apply to save the workflow specification.

After you click Apply, Spectra displays the Edit Workflow form. This contains the information you already entered in the Create Workflow Template form and provides a section to assign tasks with this workflow (see Figure 13.3). Since you just created the workflow, this section is empty.

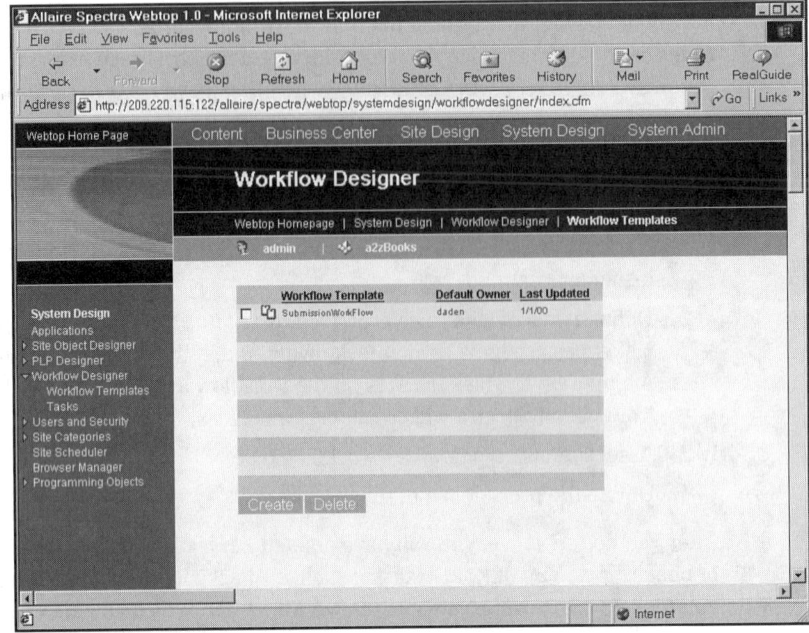

FIGURE 13.1
The Workflow Designer displays a list of all existing workflows.

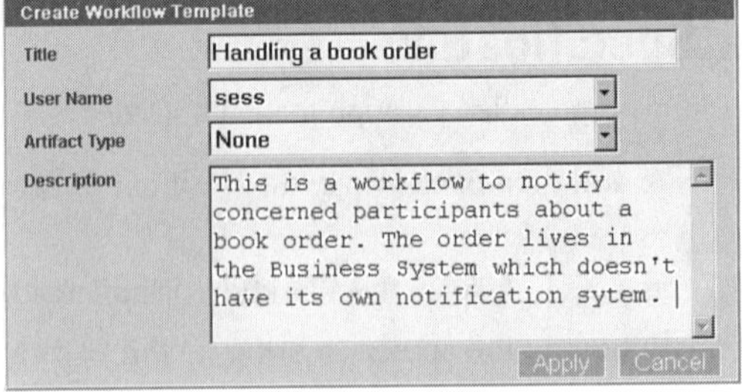

FIGURE 13.2
Use the Create Workflow Template form to enter basic information about your workflow.

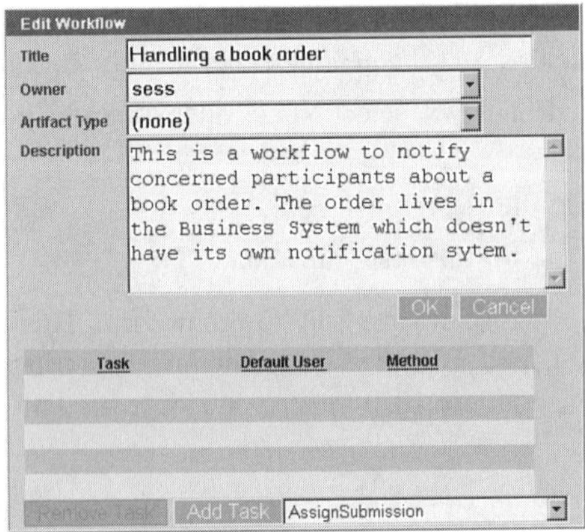

FIGURE 13.3
The Edit Workflow form provides an interface for adding tasks to a Workflow.

Before we can associate tasks with the workflow, we need to define some task types.

Creating Task Specifications

In the example, we are going to create a simple, four-step workflow. Remember that in this example we are using the workflow architecture only to notify participants of outstanding tasks; all the work is done outside Spectra. The following tasks will be defined for the workflow:

1. A sales representative starts a workflow that notifies the Fulfillment Department that an order exists in the business system.
2. The Fulfillment Department receives notification and accesses the business system to get the details of the order. When the order has been put together, the task is marked as complete. This sends notification to the Shipping Department that a package is ready for shipment.
3. The Shipping Department ships the order, then marks its task as done. This kicks off notification back to the Sales Department that the order has been sent.
4. The Sales Department receives notification that the order has been shipped and notifies the customer the order has been sent. The last task is marked as complete.

NOTE This workflow is purposely short and simple; in an actual production environment, you would probably want to create an order in Spectra that would be updated by each participant.

The first step of this workflow doesn't need a task—all the sales rep does is kick off the workflow. Each subsequent step does need a task, though, so let's create a task type for each:

1. Click System Design.
2. Open Workflow Designer in the navigation area.
3. Click Tasks to display a list of existing task types (see Figure 13.4).
4. Click Create at the bottom of the screen to display the Edit Task form.
5. For the task Title, enter **`Compile books`**; for User Name, enter a user who exists on your system; for Description, enter a description (or instruction) concerning this task (see Figure 13.5).
6. Click OK to save.
7. Repeat steps 1 through 6 to create tasks called "Ship book order" and "Notify customer."

Associating Tasks Types with Workflow Types

After creating some tasks, you associate them with the "Handling a book order" workflow type. Follow these steps:

1. Click System Design, open Workflow Designer on the left, and then click Workflow Templates.

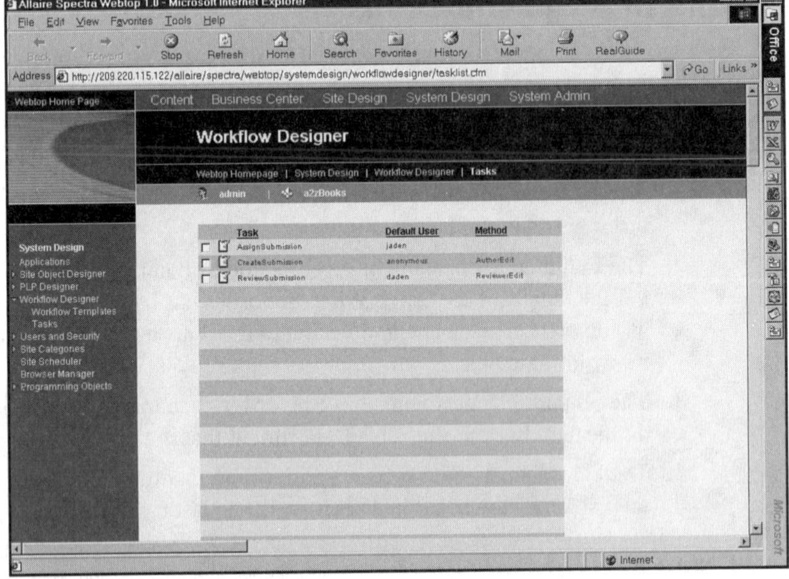

FIGURE 13.4
The Task List displays a list of available task types.

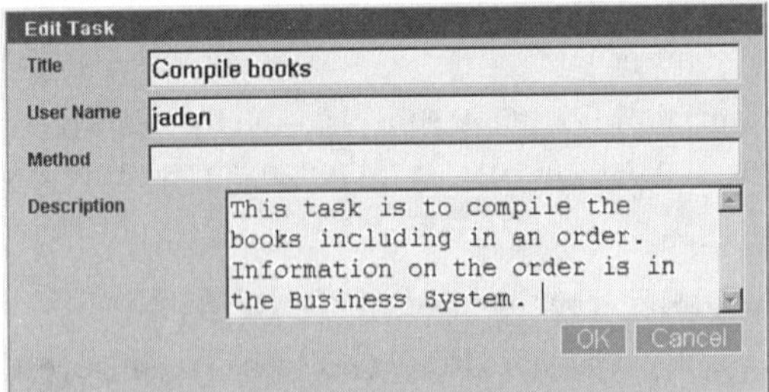

FIGURE 13.5
The Edit Task form allows you to edit basic data for a single task.

2. Click the "Handling a book order" workflow to open the Workflow Editor form.
3. In the Add Task drop-down box at the bottom of the form, select Compile Books, then click Add Task. Figure 13.6 shows an example of this form.
4. Repeat steps 1 through 3 to add the "Ship book order" and the "Notify customer" tasks. All three tasks should show up in the Task list.

Setting Task Precedence

Now, we assign precedence to the tasks. By doing this, we tell Spectra the order of task execution. A dependent task won't execute until a precedent task finishes. Defining precedence is easy to do:

1. Click System Design, open Workflow Designer, then click Workflow Templates.
2. Click the "Handling a book order" workflow to open the Edit Workflow dialogue.

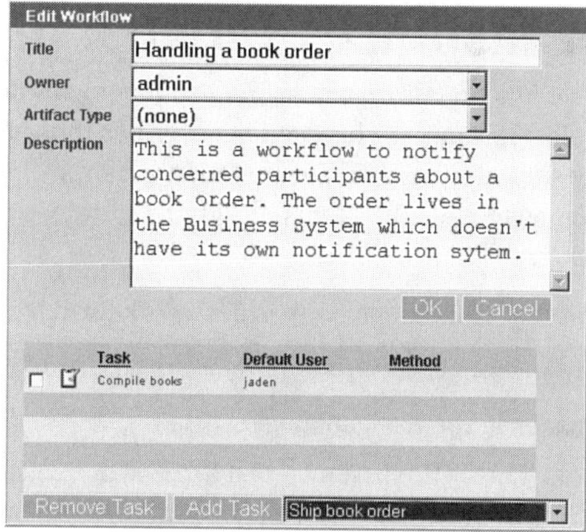

FIGURE 13.6
The Edit Workflow form displays the tasks as we add them to the workflow definition.

3. Click the icon next to the "Ship book order" task. This opens the Edit Task form.
4. In the Available Tasks list box, click "Compile books," then click the left arrow. This moves "Compile books" to the Task Predecessors list. Figure 13.7 shows an example of the Edit Task form after "Compile books" is added to the Task Predecessors list.
5. Return to the Edit Workflow form and click the "Notify customer" task. Make "Ship book order" a predecessor.

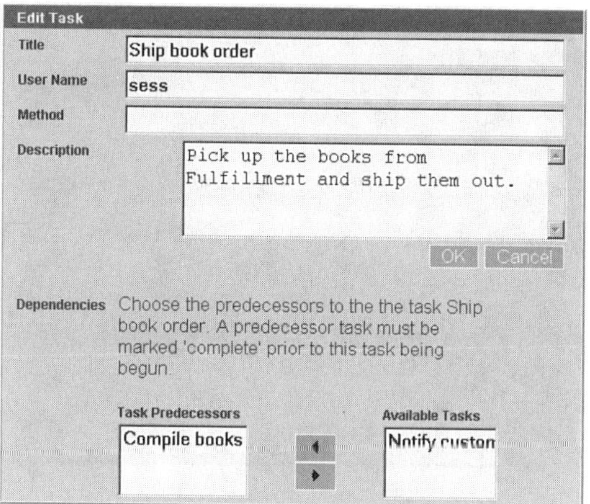

FIGURE 13.7
The Edit Task form allows you to define task predecessors.

This completes the definition of the "Handling a book order" workflow. We've defined the workflow, assigned tasks to it, and set the precedence for those tasks; in essence, we've created a template for a workflow instance. It's the workflow instance that actually runs.

Creating Workflow Instances Through the Webtop

The Webtop provides basic functionality for managing running workflows—that is, for creating and monitoring workflow instances. This section describes those functions. Although the Webtop functionality may serve for some implementations, it's very likely you will want to code your own workflow management functions. Programmatically controlling workflows is covered later in this chapter.

Let's create an instance of the "Handling a book order" workflow:

1. Click Business Center.
2. Open Process Manager in the navigation area.
3. Click Start Workflow. This is the first step of a three-step wizard to create a workflow. It displays Choose a Workflow Template, which lists all available workflow types.
4. Click the radio button to select "Handling a book order." Figure 13.8 shows an example of the Choose a Workflow template.

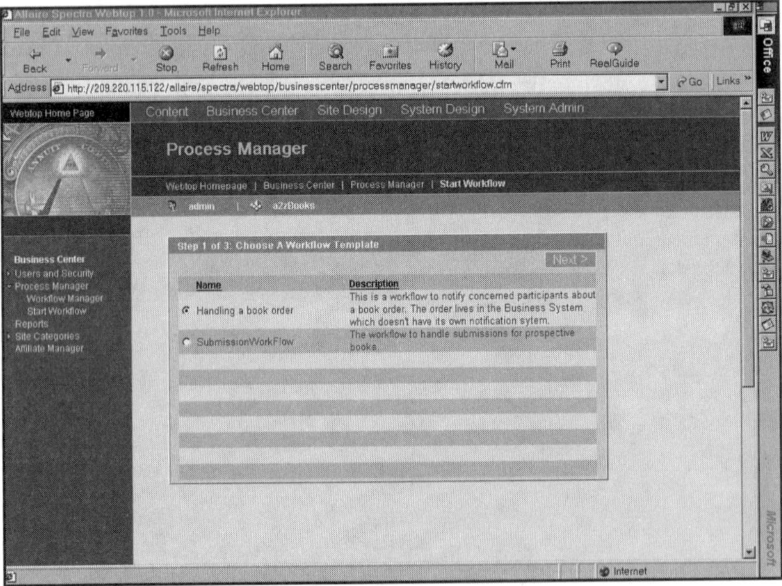

FIGURE 13.8
The first step of creating a workflow instance is to pick from a list of existing workflows.

5. Click Next. This displays step 2 of the wizard, in which you assign owners for each step of the workflow as well as a deadline for each step. Assign Admin as the owner of "Compile books," with an end date one day from the current date. Similarly, assign the other task to owners that exist on your system. See Figure 13.9 for an example of the window used to assign task owners and deadline dates.

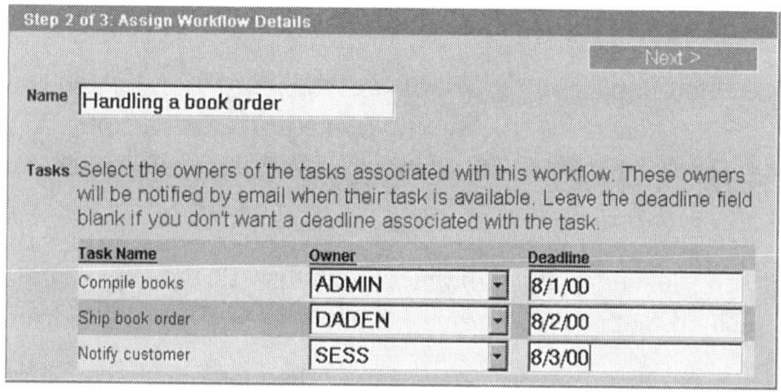

FIGURE 13.9
The second step of creating a workflow instance is to assign users and deadlines to workflow steps.

6. After you assign the task owners and deadlines, click Next. Spectra instantiates a new workflow, shows a success message (see Figure 13.10), and provides a link to a page that allows you to manage the new workflow.
7. Click the Manage This Workflow link to see the Workflow Detail (see Figure 13.11).

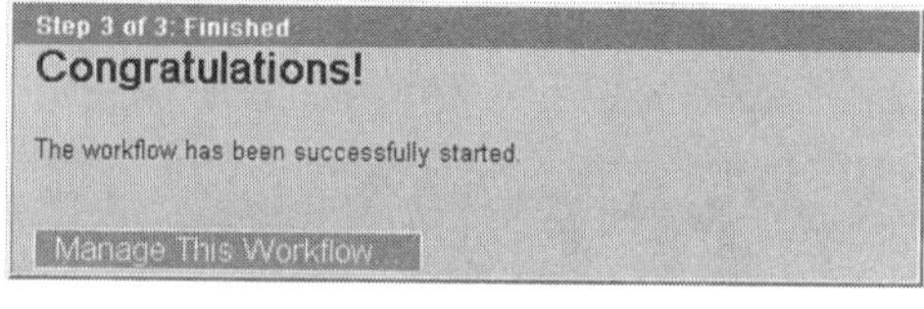

FIGURE 13.10
When you successfully create a workflow instance, Spectra gives you a link to manage it.

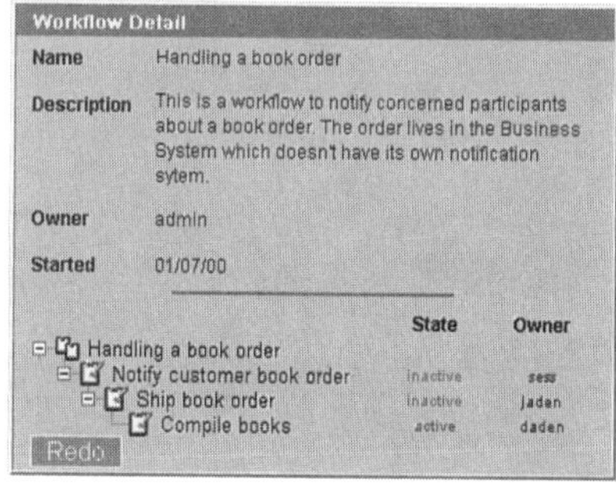

FIGURE 13.11
The Workflow Detail form shows the current state of a workflow instance.

Handling Tasks

When Spectra creates a new workflow, it analyzes all the workflow's tasks to see which ones require immediate notification. In our workflow, only the owner of the first task will receive notification, because the other tasks depend on the first task being complete. So, in this case, notification is sent via email (the default notification method) to the admin user.

Users can view a list of their outstanding tasks in two places in the Webtop:

- The Webtop home page, if Enable Personalized Home Page is checked in the Preferences section of the Webtop home page. See Chapter 5, "Navigating the Spectra Design Tools," for more information on Webtop preferences.
- In the Content section by clicking My Tasks in the navigation area.

Both areas show a list of outstanding tasks. Figure 13.12 shows an example of the My Tasks listing of outstanding tasks.

To manage a task, click the icon to the left of the task name. This displays the Task Detail interface (see Figure 13.13). From this screen you can

- Mark a task as started by clicking Start. This informs Spectra (and anyone monitoring this workflow instance) that you have begun work on the task.
- End a task. When you complete a task, return to the Task Detail screen and click End.

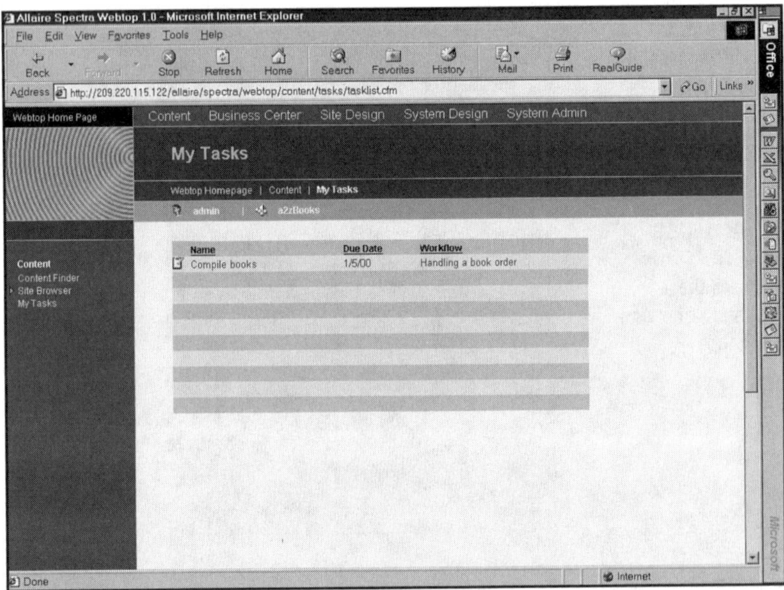

FIGURE 13.12
The My Tasks list shows the current user's tasks.

NOTE You can't short-circuit this process on the Webtop; you need to start a task before you are allowed to end it.

To end the "Compile books" task, click End. The causes two things to happen:

- The My Tasks list refreshes and no longer shows the "Compile books" task.
- Spectra updates the current workflow and sends mail to the owner of the next task.

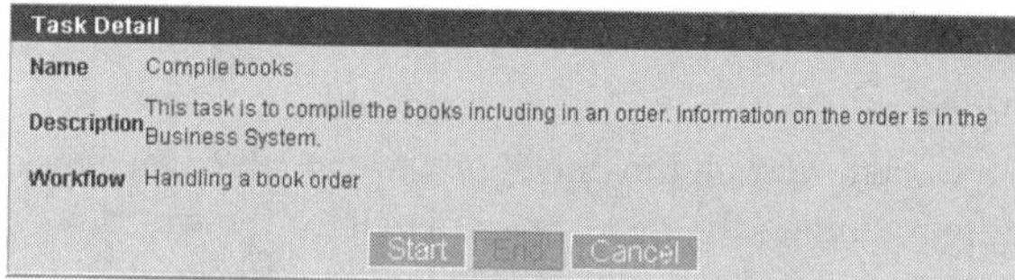

FIGURE 13.13
The Task Detail window allows you to start or end your tasks.

The Webtop doesn't give us the option of changing the notification method, so notification is sent using a default email message, which has a simple format:

```
The following task is ready for you to begin:
Name: Ship book order
Description: Pick up the books from Fulfillment and ship them out.
Deadline: The completion of this task is set for 06-Jan-00.
```

Later in this chapter we'll examine how to customize this message. If we reload the Workflow Manager and click the icon to the left of the "Handling a book order" workflow to open the Workflow Detail form, the "Compile books" task is now marked as completed and the "Ship book order" task is marked as active. Figure 13.14 shows an example of the Workflow Detail form.

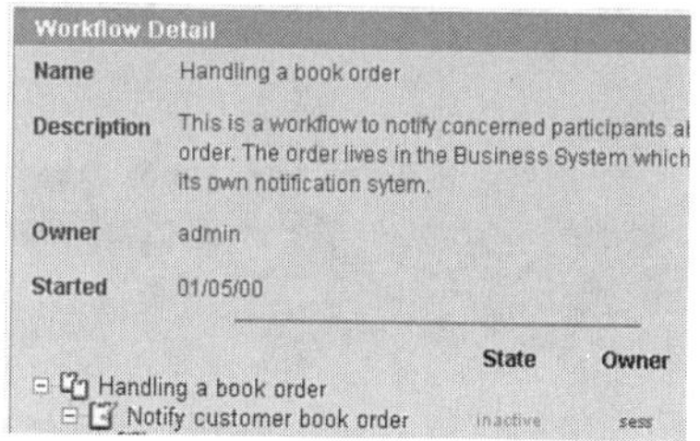

FIGURE 13.14
The Workflow Detail form is updated to show the current status of the workflow instance.

Similarly, when the Shipping department has completed its task, it would access its My Tasks section and mark the task as complete. This automatically sends notification to the Sales department that the order has been filled.

NOTE Spectra sends notifications to the email address stored in the user profile of the person assigned to the task. Spectra uses the email address stored in *`UserProfile`*`.home.electronicinfo.email`. For more information on user profiles, see Chapter 18, "Implementing Personalization."

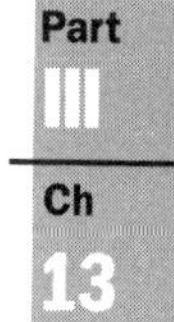

Managing Workflows with the Webtop

You can use the Webtop to perform basic management functions for existing workflows: deleting an existing workflow and setting a task within a workflow to be redone. You use the Workflow Manager to accomplish both of these:

1. Click Business Center.

2. Open Process Manager in the navigation area.
3. Click Workflow Manager.
4. To delete a workflow, click the check box to the left of the workflow's name, then click Delete at the bottom of the page. Spectra deletes the workflow and all the tasks under it. Figure 13.15 shows the Workflow Manager with a workflow selected for deletion.
5. To manage an existing workflow, click the one you'd like to manage. This opens the Workflow Detail window. To redo a task, click the task name, then click Redo.

Redoing a task resets the state of the task to active and sets any dependent tasks to inactive. Spectra also reissues the notification for the redone task.

CAUTION

Although this example doesn't involve an artifact, many workflows do. When you use the Webtop to delete a workflow, Spectra deletes the workflow instance and all related task instances. However, Spectra does *not* automatically delete workflow artifacts. To delete workflow artifacts, you need to either use the Object Finder to locate and manually delete them or write code that does the deletion.

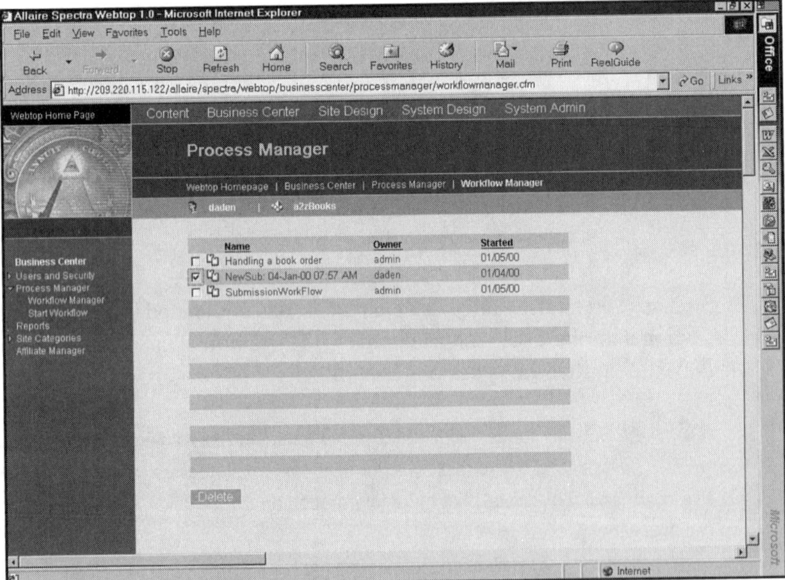

FIGURE 13.15
The Workflow Manager allows you to delete existing workflow instances.

After all the tasks of a workflow are completed, the workflow itself is complete and may be deleted.

Webtop Workflow Limitations

Although the Webtop is very useful for managing some kinds of workflows and for getting familiar with how workflows function in Spectra, it's likely that you will need to write code to manage your application's workflows. Some limitations of the Webtop interface are as follows:

- The Workflow Manager allows a manager to see only the state of the workflow and, if necessary, redo a particular task. The manager can't mark a task as complete; only the task owner can mark a task as started or completed.
- You can't change the notification method for a particular task through the Webtop. All notification is done using the default email method.
- The Webtop interface doesn't automatically delete workflow artifacts when a workflow instance is deleted.

Creating Workflows and Tasks Programmatically

Spectra provides a wealth of tags for creating and managing workflows and tasks. You can use these tags to define workflow and task types, create instances of workflows, and manage the instances.

These tags give you control over virtually every aspect of Spectra's workflow service—more granular control than you have through the Webtop.

We'll examine some of these tags through example templates.

See Appendix A, "Allaire Spectra Tags," for a full list of the workflow-related Spectra custom tags.

Creating Workflow Types Programmatically

A workflow type is stored in Spectra as a Workflow ContentObject Type. This ContentObject Type is created when you install the ContentObject Database.

Workflow Back End

Like almost everything else in Spectra, workflow, task definitions, and instances are stored in ContentObject Types. To get a full grasp of how to program the workflow service, it may be helpful to understand something about how Spectra stores workflow data. The first thing to know is that Spectra stores workflow information in two different ContentObject Types:

- The Workflow ContentObject Type contains a workflow's basic definition. Its properties include the UUID of the artifact created by the workflow (if any), a workflow description, a list of Task Types associated with the workflow, and a structure that defines task dependencies. (This structure is an associative array whose keys are the UUIDs for each of the workflow's tasks that have dependencies. The value associated with each key is a list of the UUIDs of the predecessor tasks.)

continues

continued

- The Workflow Instance ContentObject Type contains data about a workflow instance. Whenever you create a workflow instance, either through the Webtop or programmatically, Spectra creates an instance of this ContentObject Type that contains the same properties as the Workflow ContentObject Type, with additional properties:

Property	Description
`isActive`	Set to 1 if the workflow is active, 0 if not.
`lActiveTasks`	Lists the workflow's currently active tasks.
`ltargetTaskIDs`	Lists the tasks defined as "target" tasks—those tasks whose completion signals the completion of the workflow.
`lTaskIDs`	Lists the tasks associated with the workflow.
`parentSpecID`	The UUID of the workflow specification from which the instance was created.
`stTaskDependencies`	An associative array in which the key is the UUID of the dependent task and the value is a list of predecessor task UUIDs. This property is stored as a WDDX packet, so accessing it requires you to deserialize it with `<CFWDDX>`.
`stTasksFinished`	A structure containing a key for each task. The value of each element is 0 if the task is incomplete, 1 if it's complete. This property is stored as a WDDX packet.
`stTasksHaveNotified`	A similar structure to `stTasksFinished`, except that it's used to flag which tasks have received their notification. This property is stored as a WDDX packet.
`stWorkflowData`	Although this property exists in Spectra 1.0, it's a remnant of functionality that was removed before release. Don't use it for anything, because it might be removed from future releases.

These two ContentObject Types have different methods:

- The Workflow Type methods relate to creating the workflow definition, adding/removing tasks types, and defining task type dependencies.
- The Workflow Instance Type methods relate to a workflow instance—including marking a task to be redone and "refreshing" a workflow (checking for completed tasks and sending notifications of any dependent tasks as appropriate or deleting a workflow instance).

As you may have guessed, task-related data is also stored using two ContentObject Types:

- The Task ContentObject Type contains the task definition or specification.
- The Task Instance ContentObject Type contains information on a specific task. Task Instance Content Items are created by Spectra when a Workflow Instance Content Item is created.

If you're coding workflow service applications at a low level, it's important to keep the difference between these two sets of ContentObject Types in mind. To summarize:

- You deal with Workflow and Task ContentObject Types when defining workflows and tasks.
- You deal with Workflow Instance and Task Instance ContentObject Types when creating or managing a runtime workflow application.

You create workflows with the `<CFA_WORKFLOWTYPE>` tag, as shown in Listing 13.1.

Listing 13.1 Create a Workflow Type (*WorkflowMisc.cfm*)

```
<!--- Set a variable to hold the UUID of the BookSubmission Content
      Object Type --->
<CFSET SubmissionTypeID = "EE10D018-BA06-11D3-847300E02C0708AF">

<!--- Create a Workflow Type --->
<CFA_WORKFLOWTYPE
   DATASOURCE="#REQUEST.CFA.A2ZBooks.DATASOURCE#"
   ACTION="Create"
   NAME="SubmissionWorkFlow"
   DESCRIPTION="The workflow to handle submissions for prospective books."
   WORKFLOWDIRECTOR="daden"
   ARTIFACTTYPEID="#SubmissionTypeID#"
   R_WORKFLOWTYPEID="SubmissionWorkFlowID">
```

This creates a workflow type called `SubmissionWorkFlow`, assigns the user `daden` as the default owner, and associates the workflow type with an existing ContentObject Type. The latter means that when Spectra creates an instance of this workflow type, it will also create an artifact (an instance of the associated ContentObject Type). Spectra automatically associates the artifact and the workflow instance.

In this case, the artifact is an instance of the Book Submission ContentObject Type. This is a just a ContentObject Type that contains properties to hold data about a prospective book an author would like to write for A2Z. Table 13.1 summarizes its properties.

Table 13.1 The Book Submission Properties

Property	Description
`FirstName`	Author's first name
`LastName`	Author's last name
`Email`	Author's email address
`BookName`	The name of the prospective book
`Genre`	The genre of the book
`Description`	A description of the book

Part III Ch 13

continues

Table 13.1 Continued

Property	Description
`Outline`	An outline for the book
`AssignEditor`	The initial reviewing editor
`EditorComments`	The reviewing editor's comments

Creating Tasks Programmatically

Similarly, you can create task types programmatically by using the `<CFA_TASKTYPE>` tag shown in Listing 13.2.

Listing 13.2 Create a Task Type (*WorkflowMisc.cfm*)

```
<CFA_TASKTYPE
   DATASOURCE="#REQUEST.CFA.A2ZBooks.DATASOURCE#"
   ACTION="Create"
   NAME="CreateSubmission"
   DESCRIPTION="First step in the process -- used by anonymous users to
                  create a submission."
DA: OK.    METHOD="AuthorEdit"
   OWNER="anonymous"
   R_TASKTYPEID="CreateSubmissionId">

<CFA_TASKTYPE
   DATASOURCE="#REQUEST.CFA.A2ZBooks.DATASOURCE#"
   ACTION="Create"
   NAME="AssignSubmission"
   DESCRIPTION="A task to assign Submissions to authors."
   OWNER="jaden"
   R_TASKTYPEID="AssignSubmissionId">

<CFA_TASKTYPE
   DATASOURCE="#REQUEST.CFA.A2ZBooks.DATASOURCE#"
   ACTION="Create"
   NAME="ReviewSubmission"
   DESCRIPTION="A task to review Submissions and make a decision on them."
   METHOD="ReviewerEdit"
   OWNER="daden"
   R_TASKTYPEID="ReviewSubmissionId">
```

The code in this listing creates three task types: `CreateSubmission`, `AssignSubmission`, and `ReviewSubmission`. `CreateSubmission` and `ReviewSubmission` are each associated with a method: `AuthorEdit` and `ReviewerEdit`, respectively. These methods of the artifact are created by the workflow with which we will associate these tasks.

Each task is assigned an owner. Although these assignments serve as defaults, they can be changed when the task instances are created. We capture the UUID of each task type in a return variable specified with the <R_TASKTYPEID> attribute.

Associating Task Types with a Workflow Type

Now that we have some task types, we can associate them with our workflow type by using the <CFA_WORKFLOWTASKTYPEBIND> tag shown in Listing 13.3.

Listing 13.3 Associate Tasks with a Workflow (*WorkflowMisc.cfm*)

```
<CFA_WORKFLOWTASKTYPEBIND
     DATASOURCE="#REQUEST.CFA.A2ZBooks.DATASOURCE#"
     ACTION="Create"
     WORKFLOWTYPEID="#SubmissionWorkFlowID#"
     LTASKTYPEIDS="#CreateSubmissionID#,#AssignSubmissionID#,
     #ReviewSubmissionID#">
```

This tag passes the workflow type ID as well as a list of the task type IDs we want to associate with the workflow type.

Setting Task Precedence Programmatically

After tasks are assigned to a workflow, you set the precedence between the tasks by using the <CFA_TASKTYPEDEPENDENCY> tag, shown in Listing 13.4.

Listing 13.4 Assign Dependencies Between Tasks (*WorkflowMisc.cfm*)

```
<CFA_TASKTYPEDEPENDENCY
     DATASOURCE="#REQUEST.CFA.A2ZBooks.DATASOURCE#"
     ACTION="CREATE"
     WORKFLOWTYPEID="#SubmissionWorkFlowID#"
     TASKTYPEID="#AssignSubmissionID#"
     LPREDECESSORTASKTYPEIDS="#CreateSubmissionID#">

<CFA_TASKTYPEDEPENDENCY
     DATASOURCE="#REQUEST.CFA.A2ZBooks.DATASOURCE#"
     ACTION="CREATE"
     WORKFLOWTYPEID="#SubmissionWorkFlowID#"
     TASKTYPEID="#ReviewSubmissionID#"
     LPREDECESSORTASKTYPEIDS="#AssignSubmissionID#">
```

The code in Listing 13.4 defines precedence for two tasks within our workflow: the Assign Submission task and the Review Submission task. It sets the CreateSubmission task as a precedent for the AssignSubmission task and sets the AssignSubmission task as a precedent for the ReviewSubmission task.

The `<CFA_TASKDEPENDENCY>` tag requires the workflow type ID and the task type ID for the task whose predecessors you're setting. You pass the predecessor task type IDs in with the `lPredecessorTaskTypeIDs` attribute.

Programming Workflows

Now that the workflows and types are defined, let's actually do some work with them. We're going to build a template that allows an anonymous Web user to come to the site and create a book proposal. When this is submitted, our workflow notifies the person responsible for assigning submissions to a preliminary editor that a submission has been received. Once assignment is done, the initial review editor is notified. He then accesses the submission, reads it, and adds his comments. When completed, Spectra either routes the editor's comments back to the author or sends the complete submission to the Acquisitions Department.

This scaled-down workflow would undoubtedly include more steps in a production environment.

Initiating the Workflow

The first thing we need to do is provide a page for an anonymous user to enter the basic information about his proposed book (see Listing 13.5).

Listing 13.5 Create a New Submission and Kick Off the Workflow (*MakeSubmission.cfm*)

```
<!---
File:          /submission/MakeSubmission.cfm
Author:        david aden (david@wwstudios.com)
Date:          12/31/1999
Description:   Interface for creating and submitting a new book
                submission. Kicks off a workflow.
Notes:
--->

<!--- Display the basic a2z formatting. --->
<CF_A2ZFORMATTING SUBTITLE="Creating a New Book Submission">

<!--- Log the page. --->
<CFA_PAGE
    DATASOURCE="#REQUEST.CFA.a2zBooks.DATASOURCE#"
    PAGENAME="A2Z New Book Submission"
    SECTIONNAME="Submission"
    SITENAME="A2ZBooks"
    CACHEPAGE="No"
    BPRELOADPAGEOBJECTS="No"
    LOGPAGE="No"
    LOGCACHEDOBJECTS="No">
```

```
<!--- If the user submitted a new book submission, then call the edit
      handler. --->
<CFIF IsDefined("FORM.SubmitSubmission")>

    <!--- After the Edit form is submitted, we need to go back to the
          Edit handler to kick off the workflow.  --->
    <CFA_CONTENTOBJECTINVOKEMETHOD
         DATASOURCE = "#REQUEST.CFA.A2ZBOOKS.Datasource#"
         LOBJECTIDS="#FORM.NewSubmissionID#"
         METHOD="AuthorEdit">

<!--- If the user clicked the "Cancel" button, then delete the
      Submission Object that was made. --->
<CFELSEIF IsDefined("FORM.Cancel")>

    <!--- If the user cancels, then clean up the object --->
    <CFA_CONTENTOBJECTDELETE
         DATASOURCE = "#REQUEST.CFA.A2ZBOOKS.Datasource#"
         OBJECTID="#FORM.NewSubmissionID#">

<CFELSE>

    <!--- Create the Workflow. Keep the WorkFlowID in a SESSION var so
          we can get to it later. --->
    <CFA_WORKFLOWINSTANCECREATE
        DATASOURCE="#REQUEST.CFA.A2ZBOOKS.Datasource#"
        WORKFLOWTYPEID="#APPLICATION.SubmissionWorkFlowID#"
        NAME="NewSub: #DateFormat(Now())# #TimeFormat(Now())#"
        DESCRIPTION="A new book submission"
        R_WORKFLOWID="SESSION.WorkFlowID">

    <!--- Get info on the Workflow just created.
          NOTE: cfa_WorkFlowGetList gets both the workflow instance
          data and info on the workflow's tasks. --->
    <CFA_WORKFLOWGETLIST
        DATASOURCE="#REQUEST.CFA.A2ZBOOKS.Datasource#"
        WORKFLOWID="#SESSION.WorkFlowID#"
        R_STWORKFLOWAGENDA="stWorkFlowAgenda">

    <!--- Set the name of the created Submission to the name we're
          using for all newly-created objects. (This name is used
          to clean up orphaned Content Items that don't get
          completed for one reason or another.) --->
    <CFA_CONTENTOBJECTDATA
        DATASOURCE="#REQUEST.CFA.A2ZBOOKS.Datasource#"
        OBJECTID="#stWorkFlowAgenda.ARTIFACTINSTANCEID#">

        <CFA_CONTENTOBJECTPROPERTY
            NAME="Label"
            VALUE="#APPLICATION.NewObjectName#">
    </CFA_CONTENTOBJECTDATA>
```

continues

Listing 13.5 Continued

```
<!--- Need to set the notification method for the first task
      to "custom" with a NOTIFICATIONMETHOD of "DoNothing"
      which points to a cfm template that doesn't do anything.
      This is to work around the Spectra 1.0 bug in
      NotificationType of "none". --->
<CFLOOP COLLECTION="#stWorkFlowAgenda.Tasks#" ITEM="CurrTaskID">
    <!--- Customize the CreateSubmission Notification method --->
    <CFIF stWorkFlowAgenda.Tasks[CurrTaskID].Label EQ
        "CreateSubmission">
        <CFA_TASKUPDATE
            DATASOURCE="#REQUEST.CFA.A2ZBOOKS.Datasource#"
            TASKID="#CurrTaskID#"
            NOTIFICATIONTYPE="Custom"
            NOTIFICATIONMETHOD="DoNothing">

        <!--- Make a note of the CreateSubmission TaskID --->
        <CFSET CreateTaskID = CurrTaskID>
    </CFIF>

    <!--- Customize the AssignSubmission notification
            method --->
    <CFIF stWorkFlowAgenda.Tasks[CurrTaskID].Label EQ
        "ReviewSubmission">
        <CFA_TASKUPDATE
            DATASOURCE="#REQUEST.CFA.A2ZBOOKS.Datasource#"
            TASKID="#CurrTaskID#"
            NOTIFICATIONTYPE="Custom"
            NOTIFICATIONMETHOD="ReviewSubmissionEmail">

        <!--- Mark the ReviewSubmission task as being a
                Workflow target --->
        <CFA_WORKFLOWTARGET
            DATASOURCE="#REQUEST.CFA.A2ZBOOKS.Datasource#"
            ACTION="CREATE"
            WORKFLOWID="#SESSION.WorkFlowID#"
            TASKID="#CurrTaskID#">
    </CFIF>
</CFLOOP>

<!--- Execute the Workflow -- this instantiates the Tasks for
      this Workflow and sends notifications. --->
<CFA_WORKFLOWEXECUTE
    DATASOURCE="#REQUEST.CFA.A2ZBOOKS.Datasource#"
    WORKFLOWID="#stworkFlowAgenda.ObjectID#">

<!--- Execute the first task to let the user edit the
        Submission that is created by kicking off the
        workflow. --->
<CFA_TASKEXECUTE
    DATASOURCE="#REQUEST.CFA.A2ZBOOKS.Datasource#"
    TASKID="#CreateTaskID#">
```

```
    </CFIF>

</CFA_PAGE>

</CF_A2ZFORMATTING><!--- Close the page formatting --->
```

See Chapter 8, "Building the Site Structure," for more information on defining the Site Layout.

This page is implemented as a self-posting form. The first time a user comes to the page, we call the `<CFA_WORKFLOWINSTANCECREATE>` tag to instantiate an instance of the Book Submission workflow. We return the ID of the new instance into the `SESSION.WorkFlowID`. Because the parent workflow type is associated with the BookSubmission ContentObject Type, Spectra automatically creates a BookSubmission Content Item when the workflow is instantiated.

To get the specifics on the workflow instance, we call the `<CFA_WORKFLOWGETLIST>` tag. This returns a structure into `stWorkFlowAgenda`, whose keys are the properties of the workflow instance. It also includes a key named `Tasks`, which itself is a structure containing the current information on all the workflow's tasks. We'll use the data in `stWorkFlowAgenda` in subsequent tags.

Next, we relabel the Content Item created when the workflow was instantiated. Spectra gives a default label to Content Items it creates in association with a workflow ("Artifact Instance"). We use `<CFA_CONTENTOBJECTDATA>` and `<CFA_CONTENTOBJECTPROPERTY>` to change the label to `APPLICATION.NewObjectName`, which contains the name we're using to identify newly created objects.

See Chapter 10, "Creating and Managing Content," which covers giving a newly created object an easily identifiable label, so that those that are never populated with data can be found easily.

Next, we customize the notification method used by two of our tasks. To do this, we `<CFLOOP>` over `stWorkFlowAgenda.Tasks`, which contains a key for each of the tasks associated with this workflow. Within the `<CFLOOP>`, we look for the tasks labeled CreateSubmission and ReviewSubmission and use `<CFA_TASKUPDATE>` to update their notification types. See the sidebar "Customizing Notification Types" for more information on how to customize and control notification methods.

NOTE We've set the notification method of the CreateSubmission task to Custom and set `NOTIFICATIONMETHOD` to `DoNothing`. `DoNothing` is a custom notification method that doesn't do any notification. This is a workaround for a bug in Spectra 1.0 that prevents you from setting the notification type to none.

The code block that updates the CreateSubmission task also saves the CreateSubmission task ID in a local variable, because it's needed later.

The code block that updates the ReviewSubmission task also invokes `<CFA_WORKFLOWTARGET>` to identify the ReviewSubmission task as a target task, which means that its completion signals completion of the workflow.

Customizing Notification Types

Notification methods are implemented as CFML templates that Spectra includes into one of its handlers. Spectra determines which notification template to include based on the value of the `NOTIFICATIONTYPE` attribute passed to the <CFA_TASKUPDATE> tag.

Spectra ships with only a simple email notification template, but the `NOTIFICATIONTYPE` attribute of the <CFA_TASKUPDATE> custom tag accepts any of the following values:

```
email
pager
none
custom
```

If you set `NOTIFICATIONTYPE` to `custom`, you must also set the `NOTIFICATIONMETHOD` attribute. You set its value to the name of the custom notification template you write (minus the `cfm` extension). All notification methods are stored in the same directory. For example, you can see the email basic notification template in

```
SpectraInstallRoot/workflow/notifications/email.cfm
```

Spectra also ships with a `pager.cfm` file, but this is just a shell to which you need to add code.

The `email.cfm` template uses the following variables, which are available to your custom notification templates:

`wfdirEmailAddr` The email address of the workflow director as found in the director's user profile. (Spectra uses *`UserProfile`*`.emailaddr` for the director's email address.) If no email address is available in the workflow director's user profile, Spectra puts the string `Allaire Spectra Task Notification Service` in the email From line.

> **CAUTION**
>
> ColdFusion Server 4.5 has a bug in the `CFMAIL` code—if the `From` attribute has any spaces in it, it will not send email. This is an issue for Spectra 1.0 because the default email address used in the default notification handlers contains spaces.
>
> The ColdFusion 4.5 bug will be fixed in a maintenance release, but to be safe you should inspect the default notification templates in
>
> *`SpectraInstallDir`*`\allaire\spectra\workflow\notifications`
>
> If any of them use `Allaire Spectra Task Notification Service` as the `From` attribute, change the spaces to underscores as follows:
>
> `Allaire_Spectra_Task_Notification_Service`

`emailAddr` The email address of the task owner, as found in the owner's user profile. (Spectra uses *`UserProfile`*`.home.electronicinfo.email` for the user's email address.)

`workflowTitle` Contains the title given to the workflow.

`taskName`	The name of the task; comes from the name assigned to the Task Type.
`taskDescription`	The task's description.
`scheduleEnd`	The date the task is scheduled to end.

You also have access to several structures, although you should only read values from these structures; don't attempt to change any values in them:

`stObjectData`	A structure containing all the current task instances. For information on the task instance structure, see Appendix B, "Spectra Structures."
`stOwner`	A structure containing the task owner's user profile. For more information on the User Profile structure, see Appendix B.
`stWFDir`	A structure containing the workflow director's user profile.

Unfortunately, in Spectra 1.0, the `none` notification method throws an error, although this will be fixed in an interim or future release. You can work around this by defining a `custom` notification method that doesn't do anything. The example in this chapter uses this workaround.

Now that we have updated the workflow and its tasks, we call `<CFA_WORKFLOWEXECUTE>` to tell Spectra to refresh the workflow and its tasks and take any needed actions. Most importantly, `<CFA_WORKFLOWEXECUTE>` checks to see which tasks have finished. If it finds some, it marks them as done and then determines if they have any dependent tasks that should be notified.

`<CFA_WORKFLOWEXECUTE>` Details

`<CFA_WORKFLOWEXECUTE>` is a wrapper that invokes the `workflowinstrefresh` method of a workflow instance. `workflowinstrefresh` checks each workflow task and then

1. Sends out notifications for all tasks whose dependents are complete.
2. Sets the `isActive` attribute of the workflow instance to `1` (true).
3. Updates the `lActiveTasks` list of the workflow to include the currently active tasks.
4. Updates the `stTasksHaveNotified` structure to reflect any tasks for which notification was sent out.
5. Checks if any of the newly completed tasks are target tasks and, if so, returns `TRUE` in the variable named in the `R_BTARGETTASKEND` attribute. This can be used to determine if a workflow has been completed.

We now invoke the first task in the workflow: the CreateSubmission task using `<CFA_TASKEXECUTE>`. In many workflow applications, you will write code to instantiate the workflow, which sends notification for the first task. The owner of the first task then uses the Webtop or an interface you build to start the first task. In this case, however, we both instantiate the workflow and invoke the first task in the same template.

When we execute the first task, we're executing the CreateSubmission task. Spectra invokes the method we've associated with this task, which is the `AuthorEdit` method of the BookSubmission ContentObject Type. (See Listing 13.1 earlier in this chapter, which assigns the `AuthorEdit` method to the CreateSubmission task.) This handler displays a tabbed form the author uses to enter data about his proposed book. Figure 13.16 shows the OverView tab of the `AuthorEdit` handler.

`AuthorEdit` is a handler that uses some workflow-specific tags, as shown in Listing 13.6.

▶ **See** Chapter 10 for more information on writing handlers, and edit handlers in particular.

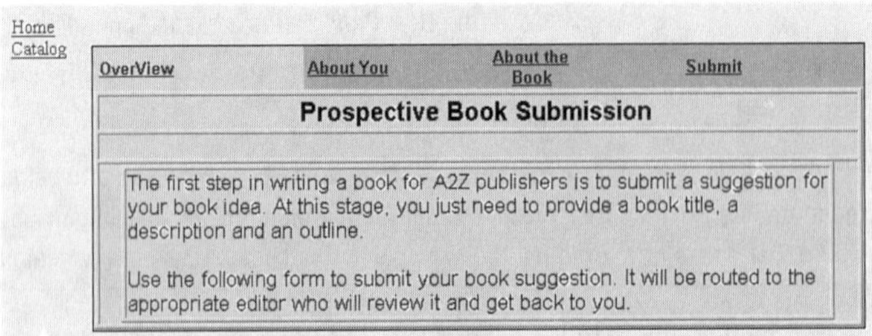

FIGURE 13.16
The `AuthorEdit` method of the Book Submission ContentObject Type uses a tabbed interface for suggesting a new book.

Listing 13.6 The *AuthorEdit* Method of the Book Submission ContentObject Type

```
<!---
File:          <Program Files>/allaire/spectra/handlers/a2z/
                submission/AuthorEdit.cfm
Author:        david aden (david@wwstudios.com)
Date:          12/31/1999
Description:   Handler for the Book Submission Object Type -- the
                handler that is called when the anonymous user creates
                a new Book Submission.
Notes:
Change History: 1/15/2000 (JT) - Added Tab Control to form
--->

<CFA_HANDLER
      OBJECT="NewSub" >

    <!--- Second time through (after we submitted) --->
    <CFIF ISDEFINED("FORM.SubmitSubmission")>

        <!--- Create a structure to use to update the
              submission object. --->
        <CFSCRIPT>
```

```
    // create the struct
    stProperties = StructNew();

    // Populate the Struct from the form
    stProperties.Label = FORM.BookName;
    stProperties.FirstName = FORM.FirstName;
    stProperties.LastName = FORM.LastName;
    stProperties.Email = FORM.Email;
    stProperties.BookName = FORM.BookName;

    stProperties.Description = FORM.Description;
    stProperties.Outline = FORM.Outline;
</CFSCRIPT>

<!--- Update the Content Item --->
<CFA_CONTENTOBJECTDATA
    DATASOURCE = "#REQUEST.CFA.A2ZBOOKS.Datasource#"
    OBJECTID="#NewSub.ObjectID#"
    STPROPERTIES="#stProperties#"/>

<!--- Get the current workflow data --->
<CFA_WORKFLOWGETLIST
    DATASOURCE="#REQUEST.CFA.A2ZBOOKS.Datasource#"
    WORKFLOWID="#SESSION.WorkFlowID#"
    R_STWORKFLOWAGENDA="stWorkFlowAgenda">

<!--- We need to get ID for the Task this was called from by
      checking for active tasks (there should only be 1). --->
<CFIF LISTLEN(STWORKFLOWAGENDA.LACTIVETASKS) NEQ 1>
    <CFOUTPUT>
        Error! Instead of one active task, there's
            #ListLen(SESSION.stworkFlowAgenda.lActiveTasks)#!<BR>
    </CFOUTPUT>
    <CFABORT>
<CFELSE>
    <CFSET ACTIVETASK = LISTFIRST(STWORKFLOWAGENDA.LACTIVETASKS)>
</CFIF>

<!--- Since this is being done as part of a Workflow, and so is
      called from a step, we need to mark the step as done. --->
<CFA_TASKEND
    DATASOURCE="#REQUEST.CFA.A2ZBOOKS.Datasource#"
    TASKID="#ActiveTask#"
    WORKFLOWID="#SESSION.WorkFlowID#">

<!--- Now update the Workflow (to kick off notification to
      the next step). --->
<CFA_WORKFLOWEXECUTE
    DATASOURCE="#REQUEST.CFA.A2ZBOOKS.Datasource#"
    WORKFLOWID="#SESSION.WorkFlowID#">

<CFOUTPUT>
    <!--- Show a success message --->
```


continues

Listing 13.6 Continued

```
            Submission successfully updated!<BR>
            <BR>
            Someone will get back to you concerning your submission.<BR>
            <BR>
        </CFOUTPUT>

    <!--- First time through we're going to display the object. --->
    <CFELSE>

        <CFOUTPUT>
        <!--- Get the query string --->
        <CFSET IIF( LEN(CGI.QUERY_STRING),
            "thisQueryString='?#cgi.query_string#'",
            "thisQueryString=''" )>

        <CFA_TABAREA WIDTH=400 HEIGHT=200 TABWIDTH=70>

        <CFA_TABPAGE NAME="OverView" SELECTED="Yes">

        <TABLE BORDER="1" WIDTH="620">
            <TR>
                <TD COLSPAN="2" ALIGN="CENTER">
                <FONT SIZE="+2">
                    <B>Prospective Book Submission</B>
                </FONT>
                </TD>
            </TR>
            <TR>
                <TD COLSPAN="2"> </TD>
            </TR>
            <TR>
                <TD COLSPAN="2" ALIGN="CENTER">
                <TABLE BORDER="1" WIDTH="575">
                    <TR>
                        <TD>
                <FONT SIZE="+1">
                    The first step in writing a book for A2Z publishers
                    is to submit a suggestion for your book idea. At
                    this stage, you just need to provide a book title, a
                    description and an outline.<BR>
                    <BR>
                    Use the following form to submit your book suggestion.
                    It will be routed to the appropriate editor who will
                    review it and get back to you.
                </FONT>
                        </TD>
                    </TR>
                </TABLE>
                </TD>
            </TR>
            </TABLE>
```

```
</CFA_TABPAGE>
<CFA_TABPAGE NAME="About You" SELECTED="No">
<FORM
    NAME="BookSubForm"
    ACTION="#cgi.script_name##thisQueryString#"
    METHOD="post">

<INPUT TYPE="Hidden" NAME="NewSubmissionID"
    VALUE="#NewSub.ObjectID#">
    <TABLE>
    <TR>
        <TD><B>First Name:</B></TD>
        <TD>
            <INPUT TYPE="Text" NAME="FirstName" SIZE="20" VALUE="">
         </TD>
    </TR>
    <TR>
        <TD><B>Last Name:</B></TD>
        <TD>
            <INPUT TYPE="Text" NAME="LastName" SIZE="20" VALUE="">
        </TD>
    </TR>
    <TR>
        <TD><B>Email Address:</B></TD>
        <TD>
            <INPUT TYPE="Text" NAME="Email" SIZE="20" VALUE="">
        </TD>
    </TR>
    </TABLE>
</CFA_TABPAGE>
<CFA_TABPAGE NAME="About the Book" SELECTED="No">
    <TABLE>
    <TR>
        <TD><B>Book Name:</B></TD>
        <TD>
            <INPUT TYPE="Text" NAME="BookName" SIZE="50" VALUE="">
        </TD>
    </TR>
    <TR>
        <TD><B>Description</B></TD>
        <TD>
          <TEXTAREA COLS=40 ROWS=5 NAME="Description"></TEXTAREA>
        </TD>
    </TR>
    <TR>
        <TD><B>Outline</B></TD>
        <TD>
            <TEXTAREA COLS=40 ROWS=5 NAME="Outline"></TEXTAREA>
         </TD>
    </TR>
    </TABLE>
 </CFA_TABPAGE>
<CFA_TABPAGE NAME="Submit">
```


continues

Listing 13.6 Continued

```
            <TABLE height="100%" width="100%">
            <TR><TD align="center">
                <FONT SIZE="+1">
                Click the Submit Button to complete the submission.
                </FONT>
            <TR>
                <TD ALIGN="CENTER">

                    <INPUT NAME="SubmitSubmission" TYPE="Submit"
                       VALUE="Submit">
                    <INPUT NAME="Cancel" TYPE="Submit" VALUE="Cancel">
                </TD>
            </TR>
            </TABLE>
                </form>
         </CFA_TABPAGE>
    </CFA_TABAREA>
    </CFOUTPUT>

    </CFIF>

</CFA_HANDLER>
DA: DONE.
```

This is implemented as a self-posting form. The bottom half displays a tabbed interface that allows a prospective author to enter information about the proposed book. This uses <CFA_TABAREA> to create the interface.

▶ **See** Chapter 9, "Building Display Components," for more information on building UI components in Spectra,

When the form is submitted, the top half runs and we create a structure, `stProperties`, to hold the information passed in from the form. This structure is passed to the <CFA_CONTENTOBJECTDATA> tag to update the Book Submission created when the workflow was instantiated.

Next, we use <CFA_WORKFLOWGETLIST> to return the data on the current workflow in the `stWorkFlowAgenda` structure and access the `lActiveTasks` property of the workflow to identify the currently active task. In this case, there will be only one active task.

We call the <CFA_TASKEND> tag to end the current task, followed by a <CFA_WORKFLOWEXECUTE> to refresh the workflow. <CFA_WORKFLOWEXECUTE> checks through all the workflow's tasks and discovers that the CreateSubmission task has been completed. Because that was the only predecessor for the AssignSubmission task, Spectra sends notification to the owner of the AssignSubmission task.

We then give an appropriately bland, non-committal success message.

Generating a List of Outstanding Tasks

The next task involves reviewing the Book Submissions and assigning them to appropriate initial editors to review. This is done through the `AssignSubmission.cfm` template, the code of which is shown in Listing 13.7.

Listing 13.7 Assign the Book Submissions to Appropriate Editors

```
<!---
File:          /Submission/AssignSubmission.cfm
Author:        david aden (david@wwstudios.com)
Date:          12/31/1999
Description:   Interface for reviewing the book submissions that have come
                in and then assigning them to the appropriate editor.
Notes:
--->

<!--- Display the basic a2z formatting. --->
<CF_A2ZFORMATTING SUBTITLE="Assigning a New Book Submissions">

<!--- Log the page. --->
<CFA_PAGE
     DATASOURCE="#REQUEST.CFA.a2zBooks.DATASOURCE#"
     PAGENAME="A2Z Book Submission Assignment"
     SECTIONNAME="Submission"
     SITENAME="A2ZBooks"
     CACHEPAGE="No"
     BPRELOADPAGEOBJECTS="No"
     LOGPAGE="No"
     LOGCACHEDOBJECTS="No">

     <CFIF IsDefined("FORM.AssignReviewer")>

          <!--- Loop through the list of fields passed in --->
          <CFLOOP LIST="#FORM.FieldNames#" INDEX="CurrField">

               <!--- If the FIELD name has 'WFID' in it, we need
                     to handle it as it is passing us the ID for a
                     Workflow for which the user MAY have made a Reviewer
                     selection --->
               <CFIF FindNoCase("WFID_", Currfield)>

                    <!--- Get the value of the field --->
                    <CFSET CurrValue = Trim (Evaluate( "FORM.#CurrField#" ) )>

                    <!--- If the length of the field value is greater than 0,
                          then a Reviewer was selected for that task --->
                    <CFIF Len( CurrValue ) GT 0>

                         <!--- Strip out the "WFID" to get the Workflow ID
                               and convert the underscores back into dashes --->
                         <CFSET CurrWFID =
```

continues

Listing 13.7 Continued

```
                    ReplaceNoCase(CurrField,"WFID_","","ALL")>
                <CFSET CurrWFID =
                    ReplaceNoCase(CurrWFID,'_','-','ALL')>

                <!--- Get the Workflow info --->
                <CFA_WORKFLOWGETLIST
                    DATASOURCE="#REQUEST.CFA.A2ZBOOKS.Datasource#"
                    WORKFLOWID="#CurrWFID#"
                    R_STWORKFLOWAGENDA="stWorkFlowAgenda">

                <!--- Find the Workflow's "AssignSubmission" task and
                      the "ReviewSubmission" task. --->
                <CFLOOP COLLECTION="#stWorkFlowAgenda.Tasks#"
                    ITEM="CurrTask">
                    <CFIF stWorkFlowAgenda.Tasks[CurrTask].Label EQ
                        'AssignSubmission'>
                        <CFSET AssignTaskID =
                            stWorkFlowAgenda.Tasks[CurrTask].ObjectID>
                    </CFIF>
                    <CFIF stWorkFlowAgenda.Tasks[CurrTask].Label EQ
                        'ReviewSubmission'>
                        <CFSET ReviewTaskID =
                            stWorkFlowAgenda.Tasks[CurrTask].ObjectID>
                    </CFIF>
                </CFLOOP>

                <!--- Mark the AssignSubmission task as ended --->
                <CFA_TASKEND
                    DATASOURCE="#REQUEST.CFA.A2ZBOOKS.Datasource#"
                    TASKID="#AssignTaskID#"
                    WORKFLOWID="#stWorkFlowAgenda.ObjectID#">

                <!--- Update the Owner for the next task to the one
                      chosen by the user.  --->
                <CFA_TASKUPDATE
                    DATASOURCE="#REQUEST.CFA.A2ZBOOKS.Datasource#"
                    TASKID="#ReviewTaskID#"
                    OWNER="#CurrValue#">

                <!--- Execute the Workflow to update it, send new
                      notifications, etc. --->
                <CFA_WORKFLOWEXECUTE
                    DATASOURCE="#REQUEST.CFA.A2ZBOOKS.Datasource#"
                    WORKFLOWID="#stWorkFlowAgenda.ObjectID#">
            </CFIF>  <!--- End Len(CurrValue) IF --->
        </CFIF>  <!--- End IF to check FORM Fields names. --->
</CFLOOP>

<!--- Reload this page to show remaining outstanding
        submissions (if any). --->
<CFLOCATION URL="AssignSubmission.cfm">
```

```
<!--- First time in, let's show the choices. --->
<CFELSE>

    <!--- Set the properties to search for in the Content Item --
            we're going to get the tasks by the label. --->
    <CFSET stFilter = StructNew()>
    <CFSET stFilter['label'] = "AssignSubmission">

    <!--- Get all the AssignSubmission Task instances. --->
    <CFA_CONTENTOBJECTFIND
        DATASOURCE="#REQUEST.CFA.A2ZBOOKS.Datasource#"
        TYPEID="#APPLICATION.TaskInstID#"
        STFILTER="#stFilter#"
        R_STOBJECTS="stTasks">

    <!--- Get the query string --->
    <cfset iif( Len(cgi.Query_string),
        "thisQueryString='?#cgi.query_string#'",
        "thisQueryString=''" )>

    <!--- Table for holding the outstanding workflows to handle --->
    <CFOUTPUT>
    <FORM NAME="AssignNewSubs"
        ACTION="#CGI.SCRIPT_NAME##thisQueryString#" METHOD="POST">
    <TABLE BORDER="1" WIDTH="620">
        <TR>
            <TD COLSPAN="4" ALIGN="CENTER">
            <FONT SIZE="4">
                <B>New Book Submissions to Assign</B>
            </FONT>
            </TD>
        </TR>

        <TR>
            <TD COLSPAN="4"> </TD>
        </TR>

        <TR>
            <TH ALIGN="CENTER">Author Name</TH>
            <TH ALIGN="CENTER">Book Title</TH>
            <TH ALIGN="CENTER">Reviewer</TH>
        </TR>

        <!--- Loop through the list of returned Tasks and get
              the Workflow in for each as long as we have
              been notified of each and it is not done. --->
        <CFLOOP COLLECTION="#stTasks#" ITEM="CurrTask">

            <!--- Make sure the user has been notified and the
                    step is NOT done. --->
            <CFIF stTasks[CurrTask].HasNotified AND
                NOT stTasks[CurrTask].IsDone>
```


continues

Listing 13.7 Continued

```
                        <!--- Get the workflow data --->
                        <CFA_WORKFLOWGETLIST
                            DATASOURCE="#REQUEST.CFA.A2ZBOOKS.Datasource#"
                            WORKFLOWID="#stTasks[CurrTask].WorkFlowID#"
                            R_STWORKFLOWAGENDA="stWorkFlowAgenda">

                        <CFSET CurrWorkFlow = stWorkFlowAgenda.ObjectID>

                        <!--- Get the workflow's artifact data --->
                        <CFA_CONTENTOBJECTGET
                           DATASOURCE="#REQUEST.CFA.A2ZBOOKS.Datasource#"
                           OBJECTID="#stWorkFlowAgenda.artifactInstanceID#"
                           R_STOBJECT="stArtifact">

                            <!--- Give the user a chance to see the whole
                                  thing or just to assign it to a Reviewer.
                                  NOTE: Currently just using the default
                                  display handler. --->
                            <TR>
                                <TD>
                                    #stArtifact.FirstName# #stArtifact.LastName#
                                </TD>
                                <TD>
  <a href="/a2z/invoke.cfm?ObjectID=#stArtifact.ObjectID#&Method=display">
        #stArtifact.BookName#</a>
                                </TD>
                                <TD>
   <SELECT NAME="WFID_#ReplaceNoCase(CurrWorkFlow,'-','_','ALL')#" SIZE="1">
        <OPTION VALUE="">Select Reviewer
        <OPTION VALUE="jaden">Jason Aden
        <OPTION VALUE="sess">Jesse Aden
        <OPTION VALUE="ahewitt">Andrew Hewitt
   </SELECT>
                                </TD>
                            </TR>
                    </CFIF>
                </CFLOOP>

                <TR>
                    <TD COLSPAN="4" ALIGN="CENTER">
                        <INPUT TYPE="Submit" NAME="AssignReviewer"
VALUE="Assign">
                    </TD>
                </TR>

                <!--- <TR>
                    <TD COLSPAN="4" ALIGN="RIGHT">
                        <A HREF="MakeSubmission.cfm">Create a submission</A>
                    </TD>
                </TR> --->

            </TABLE>
```

```
        </FORM>
        </CFOUTPUT>
    </CFIF>

</CFA_PAGE>

</CF_A2ZFORMATTING><!--- Close the page formatting --->
```

This is a self-posting form. As usual, the bottom half displays a form with which the user interacts; the top half contains the code for processing the form submission. Figure 13.17 shows the form it generates.

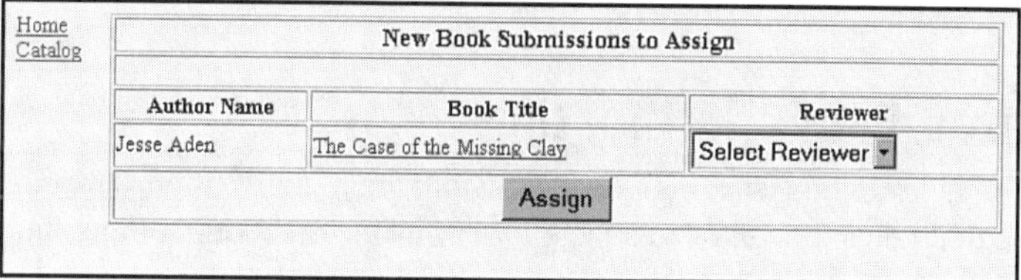

FIGURE 13.17
The Assign Submissions template lists the outstanding book submissions and allows the user to assign them to an editor.

In the bottom half, we create a `stFilter` structure and pass it to `<CFA_CONTENTOBJECTFIND>` to find all task instances with the label `AssignSubmission`. A structure of the found tasks is returned in `stTasks`.

Inside the HTML form, we loop through this structure but only display those tasks for which notification has been sent out and which aren't yet done. This is determined with

```
<CFIF stTasks[CurrTask].HasNotified AND NOT stTasks[CurrTask].IsDone>
```

We use `<CFA_WORKFLOWGETLIST>` to get the related workflow data (each task stores the ID of its parent workflow in the `WorkFlowID` property). From the workflow data, we use the `artifactInstanceID` property to get the BookSubmission Content Item so we can display basic data about the proposal.

The rest of the template displays a list of the book submissions that need to be assigned with a drop-down list of available editors. For the purposes of this example, we hard-coded the editors into the list; in a production version, this information should be stored in the ContentObject Database.

The book name is rendered as a hyperlink to `invoke.cfm`, a template that ships with Spectra that you can use to invoke a method on an object. In this case, we invoke the `display` method. Because we haven't coded our own display handler, Spectra uses its default display handler.

The `<SELECT>` box of editors encodes the current workflow's UUID into its name, replacing the dashes in the UUID with underscores, since the dashes would confuse a `<CFLOOP>` in the handler:

```
<SELECT NAME="WFID_#ReplaceNoCase(CurrWorkFlow,'-','_','ALL')#" SIZE="1">
```

When the form is self-submitted, the top half runs. We look through the submitted fields to find items from the <SELECT> box that include an encoded workflowID (their values have a length). When we find some, we use <CFA_WORKFLOWGETLIST> to return the workflow details into stWorkFlowAgenda. We then loop through the tasks associated with the workflow to find the AssignSubmission and ReviewSubmission task IDs:

```
<CFLOOP COLLECTION="#stWorkFlowAgenda.Tasks#" ITEM="CurrTask">
```

The AssignSubmission task is ended using <CFA_TASKEND>; the ReviewSubmission task is updated using <CFA_TASKUPDATE> to set the selected editor as the task owner. We then refresh the workflow using <CFA_WORKFLOWEXECUTE>. This checks the existing tasks and sends notification to the new owner of the ReviewSubmission task, since its predecessor, AssignSubmission, is now complete.

Customized Email Notification

The ReviewSubmission task uses a custom email notification. The custom email includes a link that takes the editor to a page for reviewing and commenting on the submission. Listing 13.8 contains the body of the custom notification template.

Listing 13.8 The Customized Email Notification Used to Pass a Link To the New Submission

```
<cfsetting enablecfoutputonly="yes">
<!---
File:          <install root>/allaire/spectra/workflow/
                notifications/ReviewSubmissionEmail.cfm
Author:        david aden (david@wwstudios.com)
Date:          12/31/1999
Description:  The customized email notification that provides a link
                to the Submission to be handled.
Notes:         Adapted from one of the default email handlers that
                ships with Spectra.
--->

<!--- 3/11/00: daden: Changed the default wfdirEmailAddr by replacing
        spaces with underscores due to a bug in CF 4.5 CFMAIL tag. --->
<cfif not len(trim(wfdirEmailAddr))>
    <cfset wfdirEmailAddr = "Allaire_Spectra_Task_Notification_Service">
</cfif>
<CFMAIL TO="#emailAddr#"
        FROM="#wfdirEmailAddr#"
        SUBJECT="Task Notification- #workflowTitle#"
        TYPE="HTML">
    <CFIF Len( Trim(stOwner.Name.FirstName) )>
    #stOwner.Name.FirstName#,</CFIF><BR>
    <BR>
    The following Book Submission is ready for you to review:<BR>
    <BR>
```

```
     Name: #taskName#<BR>
     Description:  #taskDescription#<BR>
     <cfif len(scheduleEnd)>
          Deadline: The completion of this task is set for
          #dateformat(scheduleEnd)#.<BR>
     <cfelse>
          Deadline: At this time there is no deadline for this task.<BR>
     </cfif>
     <BR>
     To access the submission, go to:<BR>
     <A HREF="http://#CGI.HTTP_HOST#/A2Z/Submission/
               ReviewSubmission.cfm?TaskID=#stObjectData.ObjectID#">
          Submission Review</A><BR>

     A2Z Books
</CFMAIL>
<cfsetting enablecfoutputonly="no">
```

The bulk of this template consists of a `<CFMAIL>` tag. (See the sidebar "Customizing Notification Types," earlier in this chapter for more information on custom notification templates.) The template uses many of the variables available to any notification template.

It includes a hyperlink to a template that displays the workflow's artifact and gives a `TEXTAREA` for the reviewer to enter comments.

Displaying and Finishing a Workflow

Reviewers get access to Book Submission data through the `ReviewSubmission.cfm` template, as shown in Listing 13.9. The Review Submission template invokes an edit handler so a reviewer can add comments and route a book submission.

Listing 13.9 The Review Submission Template

```
<!---
File:          /submission/ReviewSubmission.cfm
Author:        david aden (david@wwstudios.com)
Date:          12/31/1999
Description:  Invokes a task that displays a book submission for
               review.
Notes:
--->

<!--- Display the basic a2z formatting. --->
<CF_A2ZFORMATTING SUBTITLE="Review Book Submission">

<!--- Log the page. --->
<CFA_PAGE
     DATASOURCE="#REQUEST.CFA.a2zBooks.DATASOURCE#"
     PAGENAME="A2Z Review Book Submission"
     SECTIONNAME="Submission"
```


continues

Listing 13.9 Continued

```
    SITENAME="A2ZBooks"
    CACHEPAGE="No"
    BPRELOADPAGEOBJECTS="No"
    LOGPAGE="No"
    LOGCACHEDOBJECTS="No">

    <!--- If the ReviewerEdit handler form was submitted --->
    <CFIF IsDefined("FORM.SubmitSubmission")>

        <CFA_CONTENTOBJECTINVOKEMETHOD
            DATASOURCE="#REQUEST.CFA.A2ZBOOKS.Datasource#"
            LOBJECTSIDS="#FORM.ReviewSubmissionID#"
            METHOD="ReviewerEdit">

    <CFELSEIF IsDefined("FORM.Cancel")>

        <!--- Give a message about finishing it up some other time. --->
        <CFOUTPUT>
        <TABLE BORDER="1" WIDTH="620">
            <TR>
                <TD ALIGN="CENTER">
                <FONT SIZE="+2">
                    <b>Book Submission Review Cancelled</b><BR>
                    <BR>
                    Please return later to finish it up. To get back to this
                    Book Submission:<BR>
                    <BR>
                    <A HREF="http://#CGI.HTTP_HOST#/A2Z/Submission/
                        ReviewSubmission.cfm?TaskID=#URL.TaskID#">
                        Submission Review</A>
                </FONT>
                </TD>
            </TR>
        </TABLE>
        </CFOUTPUT>

        <CFABORT>

    <!--- First time through --->
    <CFELSE>

        <!--- Invoke the Task --->
        <CFA_TASKEXECUTE
            DATASOURCE="#REQUEST.CFA.A2ZBOOKS.Datasource#"
            TASKID="#URL.TaskID#">

    </CFIF>
</CFA_PAGE>

</CF_A2ZFORMATTING><!--- Close the page formatting --->
```

This template is simple and short because most of the work is done in the `ReviewEdit` handler of the Book Submission ContentObject Type (see Figure 13.18).

The template invokes the formatting custom tag, then the `<CFA_PAGE>` tag to include itself into the Site Layout. This is a self-posting form, although the bottom half includes very little code—all it does is call the `<CFA_TASKEXECUTE>` tag to execute the task ID that was passed to it as a URL variable.

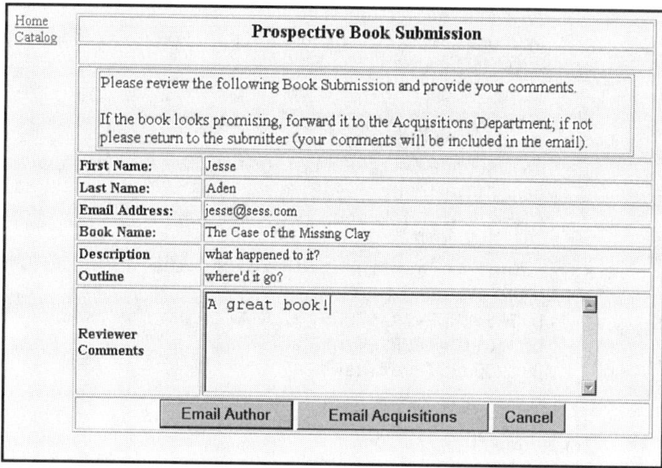

FIGURE 13.18 The `ReviewEdit` handler allows the reviewer to see all the data associated with the submission and enter his own comments.

This invokes the ReviewSubmission task, which is associated with the `ReviewerEdit` method of the Book Submission ContentObject Type. Listing 13.10 contains the `ReviewerEdit` handler.

Listing 13.10 The *ReviewerEdit* Handler for the BookSubmission ContentObject Type

```
<!---
File:          <Program Files>/allaire/spectra/handlers/
                a2z/submission/ReviewerEdit.cfm
Author:        david aden (david@wwstudios.com)
Date:          1/3/00
Description:   Edit handler called by a Book Submission reviewer.

Notes:
--->

<CFA_HANDLER
     OBJECT="ReviewSub" >

    <!--- Second time through (after we submitted) --->
    <CFIF IsDefined("FORM.EmailAuthor") OR
        IsDefined("FORM.EmailAcquisitions")>
```

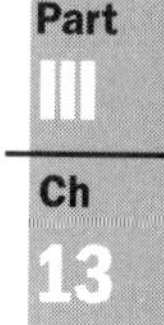

continues

Listing 13.10 Continued

```
<!--- Create a structure to use to update the
      submission object. --->
<CFSCRIPT>
    // create the struct
    stProperties = StructNew();

    // Populate the Struct from the form (only the EditorComents
    //  are being updated
    stProperties.EditorComments = FORM.EditorComments;
</CFSCRIPT>

<!--- Update the Content Item --->
<CFA_CONTENTOBJECTDATA
    DATASOURCE = "#REQUEST.CFA.A2ZBOOKS.Datasource#"
    OBJECTID="#ReviewSub.ObjectID#"
    STPROPERTIES="#stProperties#"/>

<!--- Need to get the task to get the WorkFlowID --->
<CFA_CONTENTOBJECTGET
    DATASOURCE="#REQUEST.CFA.A2ZBOOKS.Datasource#"
    OBJECTID="#URL.TaskID#"
    R_STOBJECT="stTask">

<!--- Mark the task as completed. --->
<CFA_TASKEND
    DATASOURCE="#REQUEST.CFA.A2ZBOOKS.Datasource#"
    TASKID="#URL.TaskID#"
    WORKFLOWID="#stTask.WorkFlowID#">

<!--- Now update the Workflow --->
<CFA_WORKFLOWEXECUTE
    DATASOURCE="#REQUEST.CFA.A2ZBOOKS.Datasource#"
    WORKFLOWID="#stTask.WorkFlowID#"
    R_BTARGETTASKEND="bTargetTaskEnd">

<!--- Get the artificate Content Item so we can send the info to
     either the author or the Acquisitions Department --->
<CFA_CONTENTOBJECTGET
    DATASOURCE="#REQUEST.CFA.A2ZBOOKS.Datasource#"
    OBJECTID="#ReviewSub.ObjectID#"
    R_STOBJECT="stObject">

<!--- If the Reviewer clicked EmailAuthor and we have an email
        address for the author, then send to the author. --->
<CFIF IsDefined("FORM.EmailAuthor") AND Len(stObject.email)>
    <!--- Email the submission and comments back to the
        author. --->
    <CFMAIL TO="#stObject.email#"
            FROM="A2Z_Book_Submission_Review"
            SUBJECT="Your recent submission"
            TYPE="HTML">
```

```
        <CFIF Len(stObject.email)>Dear #stObject.FirstName#,<BR>
        </CFIF>
        <BR>
        Your recent suggestion for a book entitled
        #stObject.BookName# was received.<BR>
        <BR>
        Following are the comments from our editor who reviewed
        your suggestion: <BR>
        <BR>
        #stObject.EditorComments#<BR>
        <BR>
        Please let us know if we can do anything else for you! <BR>
        <BR>
        Sincerely,<BR>
        <BR>
        A2Z Books<BR>
        </CFMAIL>

    </CFIF>

    <!--- If the Reviewer clicked EmailAcquisitions... --->
    <CFIF IsDefined("FORM.EmailAcquisitions")>
        <!--- Email the submission and comments to the Acquisitions
                Dept. --->
        <CFMAIL
            TO="AcquisitionsDept@A2ZBooks.com"
            FROM="A2Z_Book_Submission_Review"
            SUBJECT="Promising Book Submission"
            TYPE="HTML">
        Dear Sir/Madam,<BR>
        <BR>
        Following is a submission recently received from the web
        site. I think it has promise -- my comments are
        included.<BR>
        <BR>
        COMMENTS:<BR>
        #stObject.EditorComments#<BR>
        <BR>
        AUTHOR NAME: #stObject.FirstName# #stObject.LastName#<BR>
        <BR>
        BOOK NAME: #stObject.BookName#<BR>
        <BR>
        DESCRIPTION: #stObject.Description#<BR>
        <BR>
        OUTLINE: #stObject.Outline#<BR>
        <BR>
        Please let me know if you need anything else from me on
        this.<BR>
        <BR>
        Thanks!<BR>
        <BR>
        #stTask.Username#<BR>
        </CFMAIL>
```

continues

Listing 13.10 Continued

```
        </CFIF>

        <!--- Message --->
        <CFOUTPUT>
            <!--- Show a success message --->
            Submission successfully updated and mail sent as
            appropriate!<BR>
            <BR>
        </CFOUTPUT>

    <!--- First time through we're going to display the Submission with
          box for comments. --->
    <CFELSE>

        <CFOUTPUT>
        <!--- Get the query string --->
        <cfset iif( Len(cgi.Query_string),
            "thisQueryString='?#cgi.query_string#'",
            "thisQueryString=''" )>

        <CFFORM
            NAME="BookSubForm"
            ACTION="#cgi.script_name##thisQueryString#"
            METHOD="post">
        <INPUT
            TYPE="Hidden"
            NAME="ReviewSubmissionID"
            VALUE="#ReviewSub.ObjectID#">

        <TABLE BORDER="1" WIDTH="620">
            <TR>
                <TD COLSPAN="2" ALIGN="CENTER">
                <FONT SIZE="+2">
                    <b>Prospective Book Submission</b>
                </FONT>
                </TD>
            </TR>
            <TR>
                <TD COLSPAN="2"> </TD>
            </TR>
            <TR>
                <TD COLSPAN="2" ALIGN="CENTER">
                <TABLE BORDER="1" WIDTH="575">
                    <TR>
                        <TD>
                <FONT SIZE="+1">
                    Please review the following Book Submission and provide
                    your comments.<BR>
                    <BR>
                    If the book looks promising, forward it to the
                    Acquisitions Department; if not please return to
                    the submitter (your comments will be included in the
```

```
            email).<br>
        </FONT>
                </TD>
            </TR>
        </TABLE>
        </TD>
    </TR>
    <TR>
        <TD><B>First Name:</B></TD>
        <TD>#ReviewSub.FirstName#</TD>
    </TR>
    <TR>
        <TD><B>Last Name:</B></TD>
        <TD>#ReviewSub.LastName#</TD>
    </TR>
    <TR>
        <TD><B>Email Address:</B></TD>
        <TD>#ReviewSub.Email#</TD>
    </TR>
    <TR>
        <TD><B>Book Name:</B></TD>
        <TD>#ReviewSub.BookName#</TD>
    </TR>
    <TR>
        <TD><B>Description</B></TD>
        <TD>#ReviewSub.Description#</TD>
    </TR>
    <TR>
        <TD><B>Outline</B></TD>
        <TD>#ReviewSub.Outline#</TD>
    </TR>

    <TR>
        <TD><B>Reviewer Comments</B></TD>
        <TD>
            <TEXTAREA
                COLS=40
                ROWS=5
                NAME="EditorComments"></TEXTAREA></TD>
    </TR>

    <TR>
        <TD COLSPAN="2" ALIGN="CENTER">
            <INPUT
                NAME="EmailAuthor"
                TYPE="Submit"
                Value="Email Author">
            <INPUT
                NAME="EmailAcquisitions"
                TYPE="Submit"
                Value="Email Acquisitions">
            <INPUT
                NAME="Cancel"
                TYPE="Submit"
```

continues

Listing 13.10 Continued

```
                              Value="Cancel">
                      </TD>
                  </TR>
              </TABLE>
              </CFFORM>
              </CFOUTPUT>

      </CFIF>

  </CFA_HANDLER>
```

This self-posting form displays the proposal as well as a <TEXTAREA> for editor comments. When the form is posted, we create the `stProperties` structure and pass it to the <CFA_CONTENTOBJECTDATA> to update the Content Item with the reviewer's comments.

We use <CFA_CONTENTOBJECTGET> to return the task data into `stTask`. We need the full task data to get the task's parent workflow ID for subsequent steps.

We call <CFA_TASKEND> to end the task and <CFA_WORKFLOWEXECUTE> to refresh the workflow instance.

Next, we use <CFA_CONTENTOBJECTGET> to get the artifact into the structure `stObject`. The next two sections use the artifact data to construct an email to either the originating author or the Acquisitions department, depending on which button the reviewer selected.

In a real production environment, the workflow would likely not end here. For example, subsequent tasks could be created for the Acquisitions department. We might also assign a task to the originating author—for example, to cover the case when a reviewer wants to clarify something about the proposal. In this case, we'd need to create a user account and profile for the author, since workflows rely heavily on user accounts and profiles. However, to keep the example to a manageable size, we have ended it here.

▶ **See** Chapter 16, "Using Spectra Security Options," for information on user accounts and Chapter 18 for information on user profiles. ●

CHAPTER 14

Searching and Indexing

In this chapter

Using Spectra to Find Content

One of Spectra's greatest strengths is its capability to create and manage content. Unfortunately, having a large amount of content won't be very useful to your audience unless you can provide a quick and easy way for them to search your site. Spectra provides multiple search services for your content. This chapter investigates type searching, all-type searching, the `<CFA_CONTENTOBJECTFIND>` tag, and SQL style searching.

Before jumping into the details for the search services in Spectra, let's take a general look at the benefits of each form of searching we have available. In general, the search services can be broken into three types:

- *Verity-based.* This includes Type and AllType searching. In general, Verity allows for powerful, text-based searches. It's fast and searches with a powerful query language. It's also the easiest of the three types to use.
- *ContentObjectFind.* This Spectra custom tag allows you to search with a bit more precision. For example, you can combine a search for a certain value in a certain property as well as filter out objects in a certain date range. Because it's hitting the database, it won't be as fast as Verity-based searching, but it does allow for a more specific type of searching.
- *SQL-style.* Like `ContentObjectFind`, this search is not Verity based, so it won't be fast. However, whereas `ContentObjectFind` allows a complex search, this allows an even more complex search. It's harder to use, but when the other two options don't cover your needs, use this search mechanism.

▶ **See** Chapter 11, "Working with Meta Data," for more information on the other method Spectra uses for searching: meta data searching.

Searching Types

The first type of searching we will investigate is *type* searching. This means we will be searching for content within one particular content type. Searching for content involves two steps. First we have to look at creating and updating the Verity collections behind type searching, and then we can look at the actual custom tags used to search for content.

Understanding Verity

Most people don't realize the strength of Verity, a full-featured search engine packaged with ColdFusion Server. It allows you to add powerful searching capabilities to a static site (a site where the content never changes), a dynamic site, or a combination of both. By using the Verity tool (along with the corresponding ColdFusion custom tags), you can create indexes of dynamic and static text as well as database content. Think of the index as a shorthand version of your content. After you create the index, Verity allows you to search quickly against the content. This becomes even more important when your site has a lot of content. Verity has a powerful search language, allowing you to search for combinations of words, phrases, and sentences.

Indexing Content Object Types

First, let's look at how Spectra decides what information should be indexed. When content is added or updated, Spectra looks at the content object type being indexed and determines which properties are marked as indexed. Normally, you mark properties as indexed only if you feel they would be good candidates for searching. In other words, if you have a property for your content type that people do not normally see (like the URL of a Web site that relates to the object), you may not want to mark the property as being indexed. On the other hand, properties such as `Body` and `Title` are good candidates for indexing, because they normally describe the object and would be good values to search.

Once Spectra determines which properties of an object type need to be indexed, it grabs every object of that type and indexes the data corresponding to those properties.

NOTE The collections created by this indexing are named by using the format *propertyUUID_propertyname*. You should never need to work manually with the collections Spectra creates. We describe the naming format here so that you'll know what this collection is if ever you come across it.

The Spectra custom tag used to create an index from a type is `<CFA_TypeIndex>`. This custom tag takes only two attributes: the type ID you want to search and the datasource where the content can be found. Before we can search our content, we need to create a script that will index our content. Listing 14.1 shows an example of an indexing script.

Listing 14.1 ***indexContent.cfm***

```
<!---
File:                   /a2z/indexContent.cfm
Author:                 raymond camden (raymond.k.camden@syntegra.com)
Date:                   12/5/1999
Description:            indexes content of the Book type
Notes:
--->

<!--- Do the indexing! --->
<CFA_TYPEINDEX DATASOURCE="a2zAccess" TYPEID="#Application.BookTypeID#">

<CFOUTPUT>
Indexing for book type (#Application.BookTypeID#) is now complete.
</CFOUTPUT>
```

Listing 14.1 is pretty simple. The only CFA tag is `<CFA_TYPEINDEX>`. We pass it the name of our datasource (`a2zAccess`) and the application variable that represents our book type ID. After running this template (it's a bit slow, so don't worry if the browser doesn't respond immediately), we output a message to let the user know that indexing is complete. We also output the ID of our book so we know exactly what type we were indexing. Figure 14.1 shows the result of this simple script.

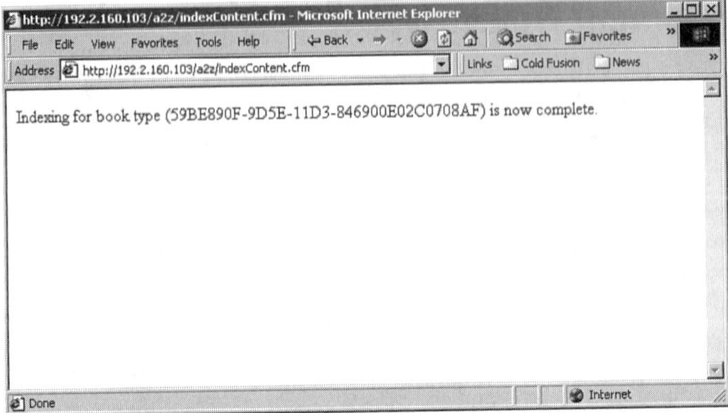

FIGURE 14.1
Result of our type index script.

Searching Types

Now that we have created our Verity collections, we can perform a search against them by using the <CFA_TYPESEARCH> tag. Before creating our script, let's look at the tag's arguments in Table 14.1.

Table 14.1 *<CFA_TYPESEARCH>* Arguments

Argument	Required?	Description
`Datasource`	Yes	The datasource that contains the type you are searching. This is required even though `<CFA_TYPESEARCH>` uses Verity for its searching.
`TypeID`	Yes if `lTypes` isn't passed	The UUID of the type to search against.
`lTypes`	Yes if `TypeID` isn't passed	A list of types to search against.
`SearchTerms`	Yes	The text to search for.
`lProperties`	No	A list of properties to search against. If specified, `<CFA_TYPESEARCH>` will return only matches that are within the specified properties. If not specified, `<CFA_TYPESEARCH>` will return a match in any (indexed) property.
`ResultSet`	No	Can be either `key` or `full`. This specifies how the matched objects are returned. If `key` is specified (default), the following values are returned: `Property`, `TypeID`, `ObjectID`, `Summary`,

Argument	Required?	Description
		Score, and Label. If full is passed, an additional value is returned for the object data. This data will either be a WDDX packet or a structure, depending on whether a query or a structure is returned.
BDistinctObject	No	Since a match can be found in multiple properties, this attribute allows you to specify whether multiple matches should be returned for one object. The default is FALSE.
r_qResults*	No	<CFA_TYPESEARCH> can return a query or a structure. To return a query, pass in the name of the query to r_qResults.
r_stResults*	No	Specifies the name of a structure to return containing the matches of the search.

** Although both r_qResults and r_stResults are optional arguments, it doesn't make sense not to pass a value to one of these attributes.*

Listing 14.2 shows the code for our search form.

Listing 14.2 *search.cfm*

```
<!---
File:            /a2z/catalog/search.cfm
Author:          raymond camden (raymond.k.camden@syntegra.com)
Date:            12/5/1999
Description:     searches books
Notes:
--->

<!--- Only search if a proper search term was passed. --->
<CFIF IsDefined("Form.searchTerms") AND Len(Trim(Form.searchTerms))>

     <!--- Perform the search. --->
     <CFA_TYPESEARCH DATASOURCE="a2zAccess"
      TYPEID="#Application.BookTypeID#"
      SEARCHTERMS="#Form.searchTerms#"
      BDISTINCTONLY="TRUE" RESULTSET="full"
      R_STRESULTS="matches">

</CFIF>
```

continues

Listing 14.2 Continued

```
<CF_a2zFormatting SubTitle="Search Books">

     <!--- Was a search done? --->
     <CFIF IsDefined("matches")>

          <!--- Did anything match? --->
          <CFIF Len(StructKeyList(matches))>

               <CFOUTPUT>
               Your search for <B>#Form.searchTerms#</B> returned the
       following match(es):<BR>
</CFOUTPUT>
               <TABLE WIDTH=100%>
               <TR>
               <TD><B>Score</B></TD>
               <TD><B>Title</B></TD>
               <TD><B>Price</B></TD>
               </TR>
               <!--- Loop through each matched object. --->
               <CFLOOP ITEM="bookID" COLLECTION="#matches#">
                    <CFOUTPUT>
                         <TR>
                         <TD>#matches[bookID].score#</TD>
                         <!--- invoke.cfm is a general purpose
                               'Do method Foo on object X' file. --->
<TD><A HREF =
                          "/a2z/invoke.cfm?objectID=#bookID#&method=Display">
                          #matches[bookID].label#</A></TD>
                         <TD>
                           #DollarFormat(matches[bookID].stProperties.price)#
                         </TD>
                         </TR>
                    </CFOUTPUT>
               </CFLOOP>
               </TABLE>

          <!--- Nothing matched. --->
          <CFELSE>

               <CFOUTPUT>
               Your search for <B>#Form.searchTerms#</B> did not match
               any book.
</CFOUTPUT>

          </CFIF>

     </CFIF>

     <P>
     Use the form below to search our book catalog:
```

```
        <P>
        <FORM ACTION="search.cfm" METHOD="POST">

            <INPUT TYPE="text" NAME="searchTerms" SIZE=30>
            <INPUT TYPE="submit" VALUE="Search">

        </FORM>

    </CF_a2zFormatting>
```

The code in Listing 14.2 displays a search form on the page and allows the user to enter a search term. The form is pretty simple (one text box and a Submit button), so let's focus on the actual search mechanics. We begin by checking to see whether a search term has been entered into the form. The line

```
<CFIF IsDefined("Form.searchTerms") AND Len(Trim(Form.searchTerms))>
```

checks for the existence of the `Form.searchTerms` variable and ensures that something (besides empty spaces) was entered. Once we have gotten past that, we run our search with this piece of code:

```
<CFA_TYPESEARCH DATASOURCE="a2zAccess" TYPEID="#Application.BookTypeID#"
 SEARCHTERMS="#Form.searchTerms#" BDISTINCTONLY="TRUE" RESULTSET="full"
 R_STRESULTS="matches">
```

We pass to `<CFA_TYPESEARCH>` the name of our datasource (`a2zAccess`) and the application variable that represents the UUID of the book type. Next we pass in our search terms (from the form variable `Form.searchTerms`) and ask `<CFA_SEARCH>` to return a distinct set of objects, a full result set, and a structure called `matches`. The reason we ask for a full result set instead of a key result set is so that we can display a bit of information about the matched books, specifically the price.

We check to see whether a search was performed by using the `IsDefined()` function to check for the existence of a variable name `matches`. If this variable exists, we must have performed a search. This search could have returned either a set of objects or an empty structure. We use this line

```
<CFIF NOT StructIsEmpty(matches)>
```

as a kind of shortcut to see if the search returned anything. If the structure is *not* empty, we must have a match. We loop through the structure, outputting the score (which represents how good the match was), the title, and the price. Let's examine this loop in detail:

```
<CFLOOP ITEM="bookID" COLLECTION="#matches#">
    <CFOUTPUT>
        <TR>
        <TD>#matches[bookID].score#</TD>
        <!--- invoke.cfm is a general purpose
              'Do method Foo on object X' file. --->
        <TD>
        <A HREF =
```

```
"/a2z/invoke.cfm?objectID=#bookID#&method=Display">#matches[bookID].label#</A>
          </TD>
<TD>#DollarFormat(matches[bookID].stProperties.price)#</TD>
          </TR>
     </CFOUTPUT>
</CFLOOP>
```

We begin by looping over each key of the structure by using the `ITEM` and `COLLECTION` attributes of the `<CFLOOP>` tag. The `<CFA_TYPESEARCH>` tag will create one key for each match (remember that we set `BDISTINCTONLY` to `TRUE`) where each key is the UUID of the object and is a structure itself, containing information about the object. To access information about each matched object, we simply use the `bookID` key of the `matches` structure, where `bookID` will represent the UUID of the object. Therefore, we can display the score of the match with this format:

```
#matches[bookID].score#
```

For the line that actually displays the label of the match, we create a link to `/a2z/invoke.cfm` and pass the UUID (`bookID`) and the method to use—in this case, `display`. Next, we want to display the price of the book. This is not normally returned by the search tag, which is why we specified the result set to be full. Once we have done that, we can access all the properties of the object by using the `stProperties` key of the structure returned by the search. We output the price of the book by using

```
#matches[bookID].stProperties.price#
```

We wrap this variable in the `DollarFormat()` function to nicely display the price of the book. Figure 14.2 displays the results of a successful search.

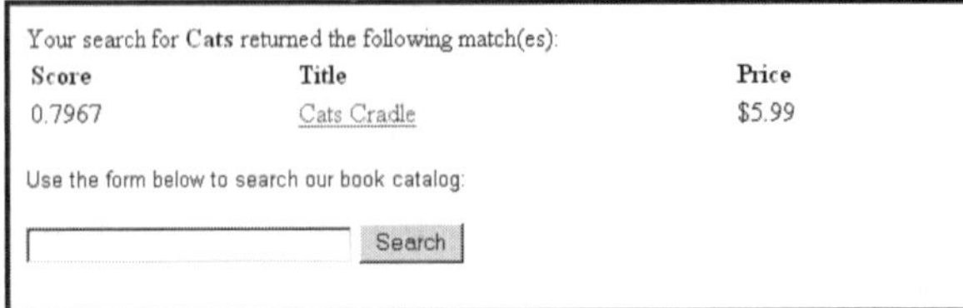

FIGURE 14.2
Results of a successful search.

If the search was not successful, we display a message to the user, letting him know there were no matches:

```
<CFELSE>

     <CFOUTPUT>
     Your search for <B>#Form.searchTerms#</B> did not match any book.
     </CFOUTPUT>

</CFIF>
```

Maintaining the Collection

Two support tags allow you to keep the collection created by <CFA_TYPEINDEX> up-to-date. They allow you to update and delete individual objects within the collection. The first tag, <CFA_TYPEINDEXKEYUPDATE>, allows you to update the information stored for a particular object. The following code snippet is an example:

```
<CFSET ObjectID = "85F57857-B0D7-11D3-847100E02C0708AF">
<CFA_TYPEINDEXKEYUPDATE
 DATASOURCE="a2zAccess"
 TYPEID="#Application.BookTypeID#"
 lObjectIDs="#ObjectID#">
```

In this example, we create a variable that defines which object ID we want to update in the collection. We then call <CFA_TYPEINDEXKEYUPDATE> and pass in the datasource, type ID, and lObjectIDs attribute. This tells Spectra what objects need to be updated in the collection. An excellent place for this tag would be in the edit handler for an object. You don't want to have to reindex the entire collection each time you make a small edit to a file. Since <CFA_TYPEINDEXKEYUPDATE> works with only one collection entry, it is much quicker and more efficient than performing a complete index operation on the database.

The tag we use to remove objects from the collection is <CFA_TYPEINDEXKEYDELETE>. This tag takes the same arguments as <CFA_TYPEINDEXKEYUPDATE> but, instead of updating the collection, it will remove the object, thus ensuring that it'll not show up in future search pages. When deleting an object, you should use this tag to ensure that the collections Verity uses are kept up to date.

Searching All Types in the Database

Spectra provides search mechanisms for specific types or all types. The difference is obvious: The first searches one type (or a list), whereas the latter searches against all types in a datasource. The custom tags we will use for these types of searches are <CFA_TYPEINDEXALL> and <CFA_ALLTYPESEARCH>. Let's begin by looking at how we index our data to be used for an all-type search.

Indexing All Types

To create an index of all the types in a datasource, we simply pass a datasource to the <CFA_TYPEINDEXALL> tag. Listing 14.3 shows a simple script that creates our index.

Listing 14.3 *indexAll.cfm*

```
<!---
File:                   /a2z/indexAll.cfm
Author:                 raymond camden (raymond.k.camden@syntegra.com)
Date:                   12/5/1999
Description:            indexes all the content in the database
Notes:
--->

<CFA_TYPEINDEXALL DATASOURCE="a2zAccess">

<CFOUTPUT>
Indexing for the database is complete.
</CFOUTPUT>
```

As we said, the `<CFA_TYPEINDEXALL>` tag is quite simple. The only argument it takes is the name of the datasource to index.

NOTE The name of the Verity collection created by this tag is based on the format `cfa_alltypes_`*`DSN`*, where *DSN* is the name of the datasource with spaces replaced by underscores. Like the collections created by `<CFA_TYPEINDEX>`, you should never need to work with them by hand.

Searching All Types

Once the script in Listing 14.3 is run, your browser should display the "complete" message, and we can then begin working with the search part of the AllType search service. The custom tag `<CFA_ALLTYPESEARCH>` has the same arguments as `<CFA_TYPESEARCH>`, except that there's no `TypeID` argument. Table 14.2 explains the arguments of this tag.

Table 14.2 *<CFA_ALLTYPESEARCH>* Arguments

Argument	Required?	Description
`Datasource`	Yes	The datasource that contains the type you are searching. This is required even though `<CFA_ALLTYPESEARCH>` uses Verity for its searching.
`lTypes`	No	A list of types to search against. If not specified, the tag will search against all types in the index.
`searchTerms`	Yes	The text to search for.
`lProperties`	No	A list of properties to search against. If specified, `<CFA_ALLTYPESEARCH>` will return matches that are only within the specified properties. If not specified, the tag will return a match in any (indexed) property.

Argument	Required?	Description
resultSet	No	Can be either key or full. This specifies how the matched objects are returned. If key is specified (default), the following values are returned: Property, TypeID, ObjectID, Summary, Score, and Label. If full is passed, an additional value is returned for the object data. This data will either be a WDDX packet or a structure, depending on whether a query or structure is returned.
bDistinctObject	No	Since a match can be found in multiple properties, this attribute allows you to specify whether multiple matches should be returned for one object. The default is FALSE.
r_qResults*	No	<CFA_ALLTYPESEARCH> can return either a query or a structure. To return a query, pass in the name of the query to r_qResults.
r_stResults*	No	Specifies the name of a structure to return containing the matches of the search.

** Whereas both r_qResults and r_stResults are optional arguments, it doesn't make sense not to pass a value to one of these attributes.*

As we can see, this tag is very similar to <CFA_TYPESEARCH>, the main difference being the lack of a necessary type ID to pass to the tag. Our search script, therefore, will also be very similar. Listing 14.4 modifies the script in Listing 14.2.

Listing 14.4 *searchAllTypes.cfm*

```
<!---
File:                /a2z/catalog/searchAllTypes.cfm
Author:              raymond camden (raymond.k.camden@syntegra.com)
Date:                12/5/1999
Description:         searches all content.
Notes:
--->

<!--- Only search if a proper search term was passed. --->
<CFIF IsDefined("Form.searchTerms") AND Len(Trim(Form.searchTerms))>

     <!--- Perform the search. --->
     <CFA_ALLTYPESEARCH
      DATASOURCE="a2zAccess"
      SEARCHTERMS="#Form.searchTerms#"
      BDISTINCTONLY="TRUE" RESULTSET="full"
      R_QRESULTS="matches">

</CFIF>
```


continues

Listing 14.4 Continued

```
<CF_a2zFormatting SubTitle="Search Books">

     <!--- Was a search done? --->
     <CFIF IsDefined("matches")>

          <!--- Did anything match? --->
          <CFIF matches.RecordCount>

               <CFOUTPUT>
               Your search for <B>#Form.searchTerms#</B>
               returned the following match(es):<BR>
</CFOUTPUT>
               <TABLE WIDTH=100%>
               <TR>
               <TD><B>Score</B></TD>
               <TD><B>Title</B></TD>
               <TD><B>Type</B></TD>
               </TR>
               <!--- Loop through each matched object. --->
               <CFLOOP QUERY="matches">
                    <CFWDDX ACTION="WDDX2CFML"
                     INPUT="#objectdata#"
                     OUTPUT="bookOb">
<CFOUTPUT>
                         <TR>
                         <TD>#score#</TD>
<!--- invoke.cfm is a general purpose
                                   'Do method Foo on object X' file. --->
                         <TD><A HREF=

"/a2z/invoke.cfm?objectID=#objectID#&method=Display">
                          #label#</A></TD>
                         <TD>
                         <CFIF typeID IS Application.BookTypeID>
                              Book (#DollarFormat(object.price)#)
                         <CFELSEIF typeID IS Application.AuthorTypeID>
                              Author
                         <CFELSEIF typeID IS Application.PublisherTypeID>
                              Publisher (#object.city#)
                         <CFELSE>
                              Unknown
                         </CFIF>
                         </TD>
                         </TR>
                    </CFOUTPUT>
               </CFLOOP>
               </TABLE>

          <!--- Nothing matched. --->
          <CFELSE>
```

```
                <CFOUTPUT>
                Your search for <B>#Form.searchTerms#</B>
                did not match any item.
</CFOUTPUT>

            </CFIF>

        </CFIF>

        <P>
        Use the form below to search our database:
        <P>
        <FORM ACTION="searchAllTypes.cfm" METHOD="POST">

            <INPUT TYPE="text" NAME="searchTerms" SIZE=30>
            <INPUT TYPE="submit" VALUE="Search">

        </FORM>

</CF_a2zFormatting>
```

Let's look at the part of this script that varies from the search script in Listing 14.2. The form is the same, so let's begin with the `<CFA_ALLTYPESEARCH>` tag in the top part of the page:

```
<CFA_ALLTYPESEARCH
 DATASOURCE="a2zAccess"
 SEARCHTERMS="#Form.searchTerms#"
 BDISTINCTONLY="TRUE" RESULTSET="full" R_QRESULTS="matches">
```

This tag performs the search against the `AllType` collection. Notice that we do not pass a type ID. We want to search against all types in the datasource. Also, this time we asked for a query back (`R_QRESULTS`) instead of a structure. There is no special reason for this, outside of wanting to work with something different this time.

To check if we performed a search, again we call `IsDefined()` on `matches`, but this time we use the `RecordCount` attribute to see if any matches were returned. The logic

```
<CFIF matches.RecordCount>
```

ensures that we display the results only if the search returned any hits. Since we request a query to be returned instead of a structure, our loop is a bit different this time. Let's examine it in detail:

```
<CFLOOP QUERY="matches">
      <CFWDDX ACTION="WDDX2CFML" INPUT="#objectdata#" OUTPUT="bookOb">
      <CFOUTPUT>
            <TR>
            <TD>#score#</TD>
            <!--- invoke.cfm is a general purpose
                  'Do method Foo on object X' file. --->
            <TD><A HREF=
            "/a2z/invoke.cfm?objectID=#objectID#&method=Display">#label#</A></TD>
```

```
            <TD>
            <CFIF typeID IS Application.BookTypeID>
                 Book (#DollarFormat(object.price)#)
            <CFELSEIF typeID IS Application.AuthorTypeID>
                 Author
            <CFELSEIF typeID IS Application.PublisherTypeID>
                 Publisher (#object.city#)
            <CFELSE>
                 Unknown
            </CFIF>
            </TD>
            </TR>
      </CFOUTPUT>
</CFLOOP>
```

Our `<CFLOOP>` tag begins by specifying the query to loop over. In this case, it's the same name passed to the `<CFA_ALLTYPESEARCH>` tag. Since we requested a full record set, we need to get access to the object data by using the `<CFWDDX>` tag to deserialize the packet. Once we have that, we begin by outputting the score. We need to refer only to `#score#` and not `#matches.score#` because we are looping over the query and have local access to all the properties of that query. The same is true when we output the object and label.

Since our search is being performed against every type in the database, we need some way to let the user know what kind of match was made. We examine the `typeID` of the match and compare it to static values we have for our book, author, and publisher types. If the match is a book, we output the price:

```
<CFIF typeID IS Application.BookTypeID>
     Book (#DollarFormat(object.price)#)
```

If the match is a publisher, we output the city of the publisher:

```
<CFELSEIF typeID IS Application.PublisherTypeID>
     Publisher (#object.city#)
```

This way, the user gets a bit more information then what type the match was. Figure 14.3 shows the result of a successful search.

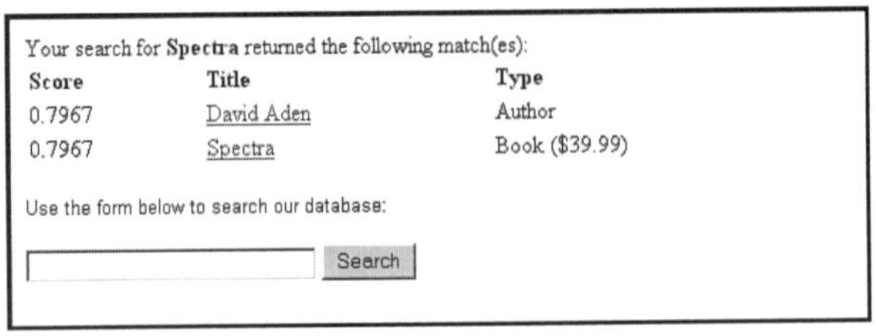

FIGURE 14.3
Result of a successful search.

Your search for **Spectra** returned the following match(es):

Score	Title	Type
0.7967	David Aden	Author
0.7967	Spectra	Book ($39.99)

Use the form below to search our database:

Search

Using <CFA_CONTENTOBJECTFIND>

Earlier, this chapter discussed Spectra's Verity-based searching techniques. Because of Verity's strengths, this powerful search service can be of great use to your site. We have two problems with Verity-based searching. First, the collections must be kept up-to-date. In other words, if you edit a particular article, you must be sure to update the Verity collection so that a search will return correct results. This isn't much of a problem, but it's still something to consider. The other problem is that Verity-based search works great for text type searches, but not for searches where you may want to filter content by date or some other property.

Spectra provides a non-Verity–based searching service with the `<CFA_CONTENTOBJECTFIND>` tag. This tag searches against any property that has been marked searchable in the Type Designer (as opposed to a property marked `Indexed`, which is searched by the `<CFA_TYPESEARCH>` tag using Verity). You can also use `<CFA_CONTENTOBJECTFIND>` to search by date and user parameters. For example, you can search for objects created before or after a certain date and for objects created by a specific user. Furthermore, the search terms can be applied to specific properties. In other words, you can search for an object that has a certain value for one property and another value for a separate property. This can't be done with `<CFA_TYPESEARCH>` unless you combine two searches. The tag goes even further in that it can natively call both the Meta data search service and the `<CFA_TYPESEARCH>` tag and combine those results with its own.

NOTE Remember that if you want to be able to use `<CFA_CONTENTOBJECTFIND>` to search a property, you must mark it `searchable`. If you want `<CFA_TYPESEARCH>` to search against a property, you must mark it `indexed`.

Let's begin by looking at the numerous arguments of the `<CFA_CONTENTOBJECTFIND>` tag. Table 14.3 displays all possible arguments for this tag.

Table 14.3 *CFA_CONTENTOBJECTFIND* Arguments

Argument	Required?	Description
`Datasource`	Yes	The datasource you are searching.
`typeID`	Yes	The type ID you will be searching against.
`lObjectIDs`	No	A list of object IDs to restrict the search to.
`stProperties`	No	A structure containing key-value pairs of properties and values to search for.

continues

Table 14.3 Continued

Argument	Required?	Description
`lPropertiesPrecedence`	Yes if `stProperties` is passed	A list of the keys of the structure passed to `stProperties`. This list should be ordered by importance or by whatever property has the greatest chance of having a match.
`dtCreatedBefore` and `dtCreatedAfter`	No	These two arguments allow you to specify a date range for the tag. An object will be returned only if it was created before or after (or between) the values passed to these arguments.
`dtUpdatedBefore` and `dtUpdatedAfter`	No	These two arguments allow you to specify a date range for the tag. An object will be returned only if it was updated before or after (or between) the values passed to these arguments.
`fullTextSearchCriteria`	No	If specified, the value of this argument will be passed to `<CFA_TYPESEARCH>`. If a match doesn't exist in this search, the object won't be returned.
`lFullTextSearchProperties`	No	A list of properties that will be used when performing a `<CFA_TYPESEARCH>` with the `fullTextSearchCriteria` argument.
`stKeywords`	No	A structure with key-value pairs of keywords and categories to restrict the search to. If passed, the structure is passed to the meta data keyword search. Each key of the structure represents a keyword to filter by. If a value is specified for the key, it should be a UUID of a category that the search should be restricted to.

Argument	Required?	Description
Label	No	Restricts the search to objects with a matching label.
CreatedBy	No	Filters the search to objects created by the username passed in this argument.
lastUpdatedBy	No	Filters the search to objects last updated by the username passed in this argument.
Bactive	No	Filters by whether an object is marked Active.
BActiveOnly	No	If TRUE, the tag will return only Active objects. Defaults to TRUE.
bPubishedOnly	No	If TRUE, the tag will return only objects marked as being published. Defaults to FALSE.
bNonArchivedOnly	No	If TRUE, the tag will return only objects not marked as being archived. Defaults to TRUE.
r_stObjects	No	If specified, the tag will return a structure of results with the name specified in the argument.
r_qObjects	No	If specified, the tag will return a query of results with the name specified in the argument.
r_lObjects	No	If specified, the tag will return a list of object IDs of the matched objects.
NmaxCount	No	If specified, the tag will return only a certain number of matches.
stFilter	No	Allows you to pass a structure containing *all* preceding attributes. This allows you to create a script where arguments passed to <CFA CONTENTOBJECTFIND> may not be known at runtime. Any argument passed to this attribute automatically becomes a "real" argument as if passed to the tag directly.

As you can see, the <CFA_CONTENTOBJECTFIND> tag is quite complex. It allows for granular, very specific, and complex style searches. You will use this tag whenever <CFA_TYPESEARCH> or <CFA_METADATAKEYWORDOBJECTFIND> doesn't meet your needs. Let's look at a few examples of this tag in action. Listing 14.5 shows a simple search using the stProperties attribute.

Listing 14.5 *finder.cfm*

```
<!---
File:                    /a2z/catalog/finder.cfm
Author:                  raymond camden (raymond.k.camden@syntegra.com)
Date:                    12/5/1999
Description:             searches books using the <CFA_CONTENTOBJECTFIND> tag.
Notes:
--->

<!---Create a structure to hold the properties we want to search for.--->
<CFSET Props = StructNew()>
<!--- Set a specific value. --->
<CFSET Props.Title = "Cats Cradle">
<!--- The list to pass to lPropertiesPrecedence --->
<CFSET PropList = StructKeyList(Props)>

<!--- Do the search. --->
<CFA_CONTENTOBJECTFIND
 DATASOURCE="a2zAccess" TYPEID="#Application.BookTypeID#"
STPROPERTIES="#Props#" LPROPERTIESPRECEDENCE="#PropList#"
 R_STOBJECTS="matches">

<!--- Display the results. --->
<CFOUTPUT>
The tag returned the following matches:
<UL>
      <CFLOOP ITEM="match" COLLECTION="#matches#">
            <LI>#matches[match].label#<BR>
      </CFLOOP>
</UL>
</CFOUTPUT>
```

We begin our script by creating `Props`, a structure that will hold our property-value combinations. In this script, we want to find objects that have a title with the value `Cats Cradle`. Be aware that this requires an *exact* match. Unlike `<CFA_TYPESEARCH>`, if I search for `Cats`, I will not find an object with the title `Cats Cradle`. Next, we create a list of keys of our `Props` structure. We used the `StructKeyList` function as a quick way of doing this. It also means we can tweak with the `Props` structure without having to worry about updating the `lPropertiesPrecedence` attribute.

The next step is to pass the filters we have set up to the `<CFA_CONTENTOBJECTFIND>` tag. We request a structure called `matches` back and then loop through the results, if any. This is a rather simple example, so let's take it a step farther and add a date filter to it. Let's say that we want only books that have been created in the last two months. Listing 14.6 shows an example of such a search.

Listing 14.6 finder2.cfm

```
<!---
File:         /a2z/catalog/finder2.cfm
Author:       raymond camden (raymond.k.camden@syntegra.com)
Date:         12/5/1999
Description:  searches books using the <CFA_CONTENTOBJECTFIND> tag.
Notes:
--->

<!--- Create a date object signifying two months ago. --->
<CFSET TwoMonthsAgo  = DateAdd("m",-2,Now())>

<!--- Do the search. --->
<CFA_CONTENTOBJECTFIND
 DATASOURCE="a2zAccess" TYPEID="#Application.BookTypeID#"
 DTCREATEDAFTER="#TwoMonthsAgo#"  R_STOBJECTS="matches">

<!--- Display the results. --->
<CFOUTPUT>
The tag returned the following matches:
<UL>
     <CFLOOP ITEM="match" COLLECTION="#matches#">
          <LI>#matches[match].label#<BR>
     </CFLOOP>
</UL>
</CFOUTPUT>
```

The only difference in this script is that we no longer pass a set of property-values to search for. Instead, we simply pass a date object to the DTCREATEDAFTER attribute. This script will always return objects created in the last two months, no matter what time it is run.

The real power of <CFA_CONTENTOBJECTFIND> begins when you combine various arguments to create a very specific filter. The code in Listing 14.7 shows an example that combines code from Listings 14.5 and 14.6.

Listing 14.7 finder3.cfm

```
<!---
File:         /a2z/catalog/finder3.cfm
Author:       raymond camden (raymond.k.camden@syntegra.com)
Date:         12/5/1999
Description:  searches books using the <CFA_CONTENTOBJECTFIND> tag.
Notes:
--->

<!---Create a structure to hold the properties we want to search for.--->
<CFSET Props = StructNew()>
<!--- Set a specific value. --->
<CFSET Props.Title = "Cats Cradle">
```


continues

Listing 14.7 Continued

```
<!--- The list to pass to lPropertiesPrecedence --->
<CFSET PropList = StructKeyList(Props)>

<!--- Create a date object signifying two months ago. --->
<CFSET TwoMonthsAgo = DateAdd("m",-2,Now())>

<!--- Do the search. --->
<CFA_CONTENTOBJECTFIND
 DATASOURCE="a2zAccess" TYPEID="#Application.BookTypeID#"
 STPROPERTIES="#Props#" LPROPERTIESPRECEDENCE="#PropList#"
 DTCREATEDAFTER="#TwoMonthsAgo#"  R_STOBJECTS="matches">

<!--- Display the results. --->
<CFOUTPUT>
The tag returned the following matches:
<UL>
      <CFLOOP ITEM="match" COLLECTION="#matches#">
            <LI>#matches[match].label#<BR>
      </CFLOOP>
</UL>
</CFOUTPUT>
```

This code simply combines `finder.cfm` and `finder2.cfm`. In this script, we combine both a property value search (using the `STPROPERTIES` attribute) and a date search (using the `DTCREATEDAFTER` attribute). This is just one example of how `<CFA_CONTENTOBJECTFIND>` can combine multiple search parameters to create a search filter.

Using SQL-Style Searches

As explained at the start of this book, part of Spectra's strength lies in the COAPI, an abstracted interface to the database that allows the developer the luxury of not having to write the complicated SQL statements necessary to get content objects. Sometimes, however, you may want to access the content object database directly with your own SQL. If you need to perform a complex search and `<CFA_CONTENTOBJECTFIND>` won't work, you can write your own SQL as a last resort.

CAUTION

The Spectra COAPI can change during revisions of the Spectra product. This means that while your Spectra code will always work no matter how much the database structure changes, a SQL statement may *not* work in the future. You should write your own SQL only if you can't accomplish what you want with a CFA tag, and you should be sure to check your code when installing the next version of Spectra.

Before writing any SQL, we need to understand how Spectra stores data. When we mark a property as being searchable, Spectra will automatically begin storing the value of that property in a table called `properties`. One row for each searchable property will exist for each content object created. Table 14.4 lists the columns of this table.

Table 14.4 The *properties* Table

Column	Description
`propertyname`	The name of the property.
`objectid`	The ID of the object where the data comes from.
`integerdata`	If the property is defined as `Integer`, the value will be stored here.
`numericdata`	If the property is defined as `Numeric`, the value will be stored here.
`chardata`	If the property is defined as `Char`, the value will be stored here.
`datetimedata`	If the property is defined as `DateTime`, the value will be stored here.
`longchardata`	If the property is defined as `LongChar`, the value will be stored here.

To perform a SQL-style search, you need to know the name and data type of the properties you want to search against. Listing 14.8 uses a SQL-style search to find matches in the database. We are modifying the code used in Listing 14.2.

Listing 14.8 *SQLsearch.cfm*

```
<!---
File:          /a2z/catalog/SQLsearch.cfm
Author:        raymond camden (raymond.k.camden@syntegra.com)
Date:          12/5/1999
Description:   searches books
Notes:
--->

<!--- Only search if a proper search term was passed. --->
<CFIF IsDefined("Form.searchTerms") AND Len(Trim(Form.searchTerms))>

      <!--- Perform the SQL search. --->
      <CFQUERY NAME="Search" DATASOURCE="a2zAccess">
            SELECT DISTINCT objectid
            FROM   properties
            WHERE  longchardata LIKE '%#Trim(Form.searchTerms)#%'
            OR     chardata         LIKE '%#Trim(Form.searchTerms)#%'
      </CFQUERY>

</CFIF>

<CF_a2zFormatting SubTitle="Search Database">
```

continues

Listing 14.8 Continued

```
     <!--- Was a search done? --->
     <CFIF IsDefined("Search")>

          <!--- Did anything match? --->
          <CFIF Search.RecordCount>

               <CFOUTPUT>
               Your search for <B>#Form.searchTerms#</B>
               returned the following match(es):<BR>
</CFOUTPUT>
               <TABLE WIDTH=100%>
               <TR>
               <TD><B>Object ID</B></TD>
               <TD><B>Label</B></TD>
               </TR>
               <!--- Loop through each matched object. --->
               <CFLOOP QUERY="Search">
                    <!--- Get the object data --->
                    <CFA_CONTENTOBJECTGET DATASOURCE="a2zAccess"
                     OBJECTID="#objectID#" R_STOBJECT="object">
<CFOUTPUT>
                         <TR>
                         <TD>#objectID#</TD>
                         <!--- invoke.cfm is a general purpose
                                'Do method Foo on object X' file. --->
                         <TD><A HREF =

"/a2z/invoke.cfm?objectID=#objectID#&method=Display">
                         #object.label#</A>
                         </TD>
</TR>
                    </CFOUTPUT>
               </CFLOOP>
               </TABLE>

          <!--- Nothing matched. --->
          <CFELSE>

               <CFOUTPUT>
               Your search for <B>#Form.searchTerms#</B>
               did not match any item.
</CFOUTPUT>

          </CFIF>

     </CFIF>

     <P>
     Use the form below to search our database:
```

```
        <P>
        <FORM ACTION="SQLsearch.cfm" METHOD="POST">

             <INPUT TYPE="text" NAME="searchTerms" SIZE=30>
             <INPUT TYPE="submit" VALUE="Search">

        </FORM>

</CF_a2zFormatting>
```

Like our other search scripts, we have a simple form that sends the search term to the real meat of our script within the

```
<CFIF IsDefined("Form.searchTerms") AND Len(Trim(Form.searchTerms))>
```

block. This time our search is performed by using the following `<CFQUERY>` statement:

```
<CFQUERY NAME="Search" DATASOURCE="a2zAccess">
     SELECT DISTINCT objectid
     FROM   properties
     WHERE  longchardata LIKE '%#Trim(Form.searchTerms)#%'
     OR     chardata     LIKE '%#Trim(Form.searchTerms)#%'
</CFQUERY>
```

We begin by selecting the `objectid` column. This is the only value we will need. We use the `DISTINCT` modifier to ensure that we get only one result per object. Our `WHERE` clause searches against the two text-based columns, `longchardata` and `chardata`. We modify the `Form.searchTerm` variable by wrapping it with `%` characters. This allows a search for `cat` to match `jedicat`, `catapult`, and `cats`.

It's important to remember that, unlike our other search services, when we do a SQL-style search, all we get back is the object ID. We could have more, like the property name, but what we really want is the complete object. When we output our results, we use the `<CFA_CONTENTOBJECTGET>` tag to grab the object and return it as the "object" structure. Once we have that, we can output the label or any other property of the object. Figure 14.4 shows the result of a search using the SQL-style method.

Your search for cat returned the following match(es):

Object ID	Label
4552D477-AB62-11D3-846D00E02C0708AF	Cats Cradle
7DCD84AD-AA6D-11D3-846D00E02C0708AF	Catalog Homepage
85F57857-B0D7-11D3-847100E02C0708AF	Advanced ColdFusion Application Development
A4913238-9EEB-11D3-846A00E02C0708AF	Catalog

Use the form below to search our database:

Search

FIGURE 14.4
Result of a SQL-style search.

Scheduling Indexing Operations

Both the <CFA_TYPESEARCH> and <CFA_ALLTYPESEARCH> tags use Verity collections on the back end to allow for quick searching of large amounts of information. Creating, repairing, and optimizing collections enable your Verity-based searches to run more quickly and efficiently. On the other hand, you probably don't want to do this by hand. It would be nice if Spectra would do this for you and, of course, it does. The Webtop provides an interface to the ColdFusion scheduler. It creates a simple way to schedule indexing, repairing, and optimizing of type and all-type collections.

To find the Indexing scheduler, follow these steps:

1. Open your Webtop to the System Admin section and click Indexing. Figure 14.5 shows what the Indexing screen looks like.

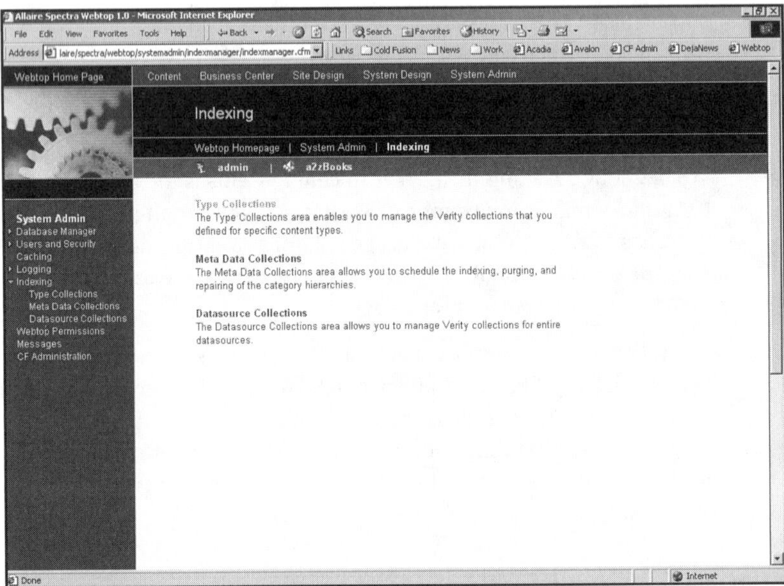

FIGURE 14.5
The main Indexing screen.

2. To create a schedule for repairing and optimizing the collection based on the Book object type, first click the Type Collections link. You will see a screen like Figure 14.6.
3. To create a scheduled time for repairing the Book collection, click the *unscheduled* link beneath Repair in the Book row. This will load a form that will allow you to specify the time and interval for the repair operation.
4. For this example, set up the scheduled event to run forever (use a date in the past for the `start` value and a date for enough in the future for the `end` value), once a day, at one minute past midnight (`00:01:00`). Figure 14.7 shows the completed form.

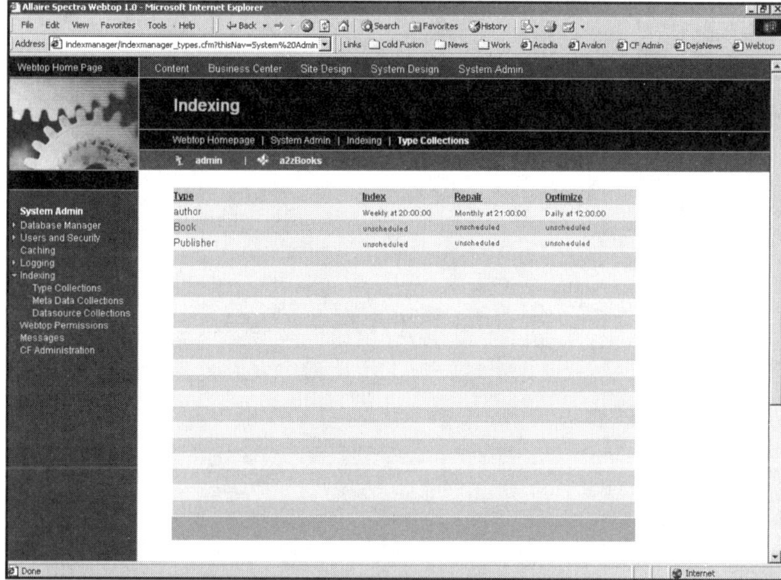

FIGURE 14.6
The Type Collections screen.

Schedule Repair for Book

Schedule Date

12/26/1998 start 12/26/3000 end

Schedule Time

00:01:00 start end

Repeat

Only Once

Daily

Weekly

Monthly

Every 1 minute(s)

Every 1 hour(s)

OK Cancel Clear Schedule Execute Now

FIGURE 14.7
The completed form to schedule the Repair operation.

5. After you enter the information, click OK. You should now see a scheduled event on the Type Collections page for the Repair operation on the Book type.

How often should you schedule these operations? That depends. Maybe your data changes so rarely that a scheduled event doesn't really make sense. Maybe it changes so often that you need to run an Optimize operation every hour. The nature and interval of what operations you perform will change case by case. The truly nice thing is that Spectra provides the tools for you to use as you see fit.

Indexing can take a lot of time and a lot of RAM. One solution you may want to consider is a dedicated machine for Verity indexing. You would need to install Spectra on that box and point it to your main database server. After you do that, all you need to do is set up scheduled indexing and then write a script that will move the files from the Verity machine to your Web server (or Web servers). This will lessen the impact of indexing on your Web site.

CHAPTER 15

Using Message Queuing

In this chapter

Understanding Message Queues in Spectra

This chapter discusses how to use Spectra to design message queues. A *queue* is defined as a list or a line. If you've ever spent any time at the DMV (or any other government office), you know what it means to wait in line.

It may seem relatively simple, but let's talk about *why* you wait in line when you go to an office, or stand in line to buy a movie ticket, or wait in line for anything. The basic reason is because the server (if you're waiting at the DMV, this is the person who will help you; if you're waiting to buy a movie ticket, this is the ticket agent) can handle only one process (think *person*) at a time. Even that's not completely true. Maybe the server can handle numerous processes (people) at one time but, when it does, the service begins to slip. Imagine the agent trying to sell tickets to four people at once. After a few minutes she gets confused and ends up handing out the wrong tickets. Also, it may not be that the server would get confused, but that it just doesn't make sense to handle more than one process at a time. Again, think of the line waiting to buy tickets. To be fair, the agent must sell in order of first come, first served. The idea here is that the first person in line should be the first person taken care of.

How can we apply this to the world of Web applications? In the Web world, we can have the same kind of problems that a clerk would. Imagine a program that had a backup routine. Once a month it decides, according to a set of rules, that certain objects (articles, user profiles, and so on) need to be saved to another database. The application can create a queue of items that need to be backed up. It can then tell another application to begin processing that queue. The other application would take the first task ("Back up article X"), process it, and then move on to the next job.

Spectra allows us to design queues for our applications. It handles the addition of new items at the end of the queue and provides easy methods to get the queue and process the items in it. Typically, we use this service for messages.

In this chapter we will design a message queue for the A2Z company's Web site. This message queue will consist of support messages visitors have written from the Web sites. For example, a user may want to know how he can return a book. We will use a message queue to store the user's message and create a way to deliver it to the support personnel at A2Z.

How is this better than simply sending email to a customer service agent? By using a queue, we can do several things. First, we can handle the task (helping a specific user with a specific problem) in more ways than simply with email. We can log the task. We can look at a group of customer service agents and see who has the shortest queue or, depending on what kind of task it is (a question about returning a book or a question about the Web site), send it to a specific person. If we just emailed the service request, we wouldn't be able to log it or do any "smart" redirections on it. Let's look at how we can create a queue in Spectra.

Creating Message Queues in Spectra

Like any other object in Spectra, we can create a message queue either in the Webtop or with a Spectra custom tag. Since there is no dedicated message queue area of the Webtop, we are going to create a message queue using a simple script. Once we have created the queue, we are going to copy the ID of our queue so we can use it later. The Spectra custom tag that creates a message queue is `<CFA_MESSAGEQUEUECREATE>`. Table 15.1 displays and explains this tag's arguments.

Table 15.1 *<CFA_MESSAGEQUEUECREATE>* Arguments

Argument	Required?	Description
`datasource`	Yes	The datasource where the message queue (and messages) will be stored.
`label`	Yes	The label of the message queue.
`objectID`	No	The ID of the message queue. If you don't provide one, Spectra will create a UUID for the object ID.
`handleRoot`	No	The folder where Spectra can find your message queue handlers. This should be defined as a mapping path, not an absolute path—for example, `/allaire/spectra/handlers/myqueue`.
`r_objectID`	No	If specified, Spectra will return the value of the ID as a variable with the name you specify here.

To create our message queue, we will write a simple CFM page that we will run one time. This will not be on the "real" A2Z site, since users don't need to hit it. Once we run it, we can delete the file or move it off the system. Listing 15.1 shows the code for `a2zQueueCreate.cfm`.

Listing 15.1 *a2zQueueCreate.cfm*

```
<!---
File:         /a2zTestScripts/a2zQueueCreate.cfm
Author:       Raymond Camden (raymond.k.camden@syntegra.com)
Date:         12/10/1999
Description: Creates a message queue for the A2ZSite.
Notes:        This is a 'one time only' script and should not be run more
               than once.
--->

<!--- Preset default things Spectra needs --->
<CFA_GLOBALSETTINGS>
<!--- Create the queue. --->
<CFA_MESSAGEQUEUECREATE
    DATASOURCE = "A2ZAcess"
    LABEL = "supportmessages"
```

continues

Listing 15.1 Continued

```
    HANDLERROOT = "/allaire/spectra/handlers/a2z/supportmessages/"
    R_OBJECTID = "queueID"
>
<!--- Display the ID of the new Queue. --->
<CFOUTPUT>
The ID of the new queue is #queueID#.
  </CFOUTPUT>
```

This template is pretty simple. We begin by calling `<CFA_GLOBALSETTINGS>`. By now you know that this tag is necessary when running Spectra code outside a Spectra application directory.

See Appendix A, "Allaire Spectra Tags," for more information on the `<CFA_GLOBALSETTINGS>` tag.

We then create the message queue using the parameters described in Table 15.1. I used the same datasource name as before, and I chose a label of `supportmessages` because this queue will contain messages for the A2Z Support team. As a handler root, I chose `/allaire/spectra/handlers/a2z/supportmessages/`, since we already have an `/allaire/spectra/handlers/a2z` folder that stores our display handlers.

TIP Grouping your handler files in the same root folder is good practice.

Lastly, we output the value of the message queue ID that was just created. It is important that you copy this number down, since we will be using it in later code examples. If you lose it, simply go to your Webtop and use the Object Finder to dig up the object ID. Figure 15.1 shows the script after it is run in a browser.

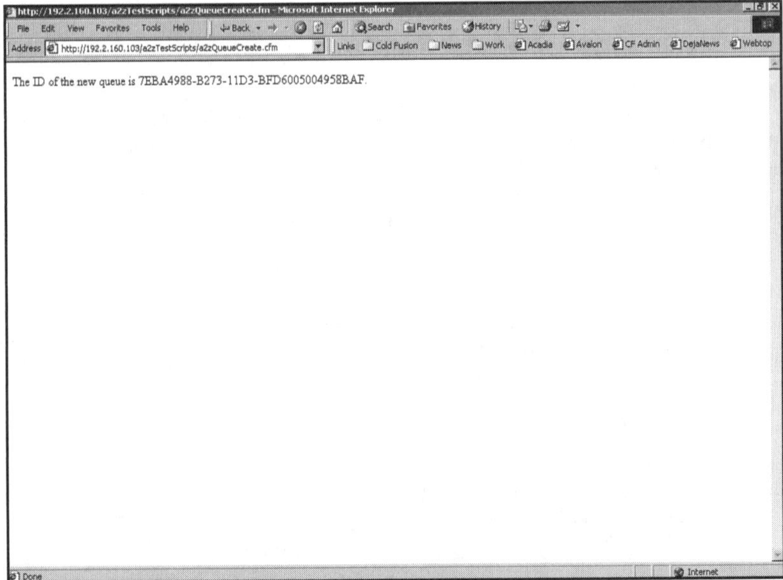

FIGURE 15.1 The result of our message queue creation.

NOTE The Object Finder may not give you an option to search for objects of the message queue type. This is because message queues are considered system objects. If you don't see `messageQueue` as one of the types you can filter by, go to your Webtop preferences and enable system entities.

Adding a Handler to Message Queues

Now that we have created an object queue, we need to add a method to it. This is similar to adding methods to content object types. It tells the system that we want to add a way in which the message queue can act upon itself. A typical method for a message queue would be `Send`. Since all messages will be processed by the handler, we can use the `Send` method to process the messages waiting for the A2Z Support team. We add methods to queues by using the `<CFA_MESSAGEQUEUEMETHODADD>` tag. Like the previous tag, we will create a one-time-only script that we will run in a browser and then not worry about again. Table 15.2 describes the attributes for `<CFA_MESSAGEQUEUEMETHODADD>`. None of the attributes are optional.

Table 15.2 Required *<CFA_MESSAGEQUEUEMETHODADD>* Arguments

Argument	Description
`datasource`	The datasource where the message queue is stored.
`method`	The name of the method.
`messageQueueID`	The ID of the message queue where the method will be added.
`handler`	The filename of the handler. Specify just the filename of the handler, not the full path. Spectra will use the `handlerRoot` of the message queue to determine what folder to look into.

Listing 15.2 shows the code for `a2zQueueMethodAdd.cfm`. Again, this is a template that we need to run only once. Be aware that you should replace the queue ID with the ID we created earlier.

Listing 15.2 *a2zQueueMethodAdd.cfm*

```
<!---
File:        /a2zTestScripts/a2zQueueMethodAdd.cfm
Author:      Raymond Camden (raymond.k.camden@syntegra.com)
Date:        12/10/1999
Description: Adds a handler to our queue.
Notes:       This is a 'one time only' script and should not be run more
              than once.
--->

<!--- Preset default things Spectra needs --->
<CFA_GLOBALSETTINGS>
```

```
<!---
You should replace this ID with the message queue ID created on your
     system. If you did not save the ID, use the Object Finder (with
     system entities turned on!) to find it.
--->
<CFSET QueueID = "7EBA4988-B273-11D3-BFD6005004958BAF">

<!--- Create the queue. --->
<CFA_MESSAGEQUEUEMETHODADD
     DATASOURCE = "A2ZAccess"
     METHOD = "send"
     MESSAGEQUEUEID = "#QueueID#"
     HANDLER = "send.cfm"
>
<CFOUTPUT>
The method has been added to the message queue.
<P>
</CFOUTPUT>

<!--- Get the queue --->
<CFA_MESSAGEQUEUEGET
     DATASOURCE="cfaobjects"
     MESSAGEQUEUEID="#QueueID#"
     R_STMESSAGEQUEUE="queue"
>
<!--- Display the queue. --->
  <CFA_DUMP VAR="#queue#">
```

Let's look at this simple script. We begin with a call to `<CFA_GLOBALSETTINGS>`. Again, the purpose of this tag is to set up some defaults that Spectra needs. Next, we create a variable for our message queue ID. This is the variable that you will want to change to match your system.

Next, we call the `<CFA_MESSAGEQUEUEMETHODADD>` custom tag. We pass in our datasource first. Then we pass in the name of the method—in this case, `Send`. Spectra needs to know the ID of the queue we are adding to, so we pass that in via the `messageQueueID` argument. Lastly, Spectra also needs to associate a filename with the handler called `send`. We used a filename of `send.cfm`.

After we add the method, we output some text to let us know everything worked out. To prove that the method was added, I threw in one of the message queue custom tags that Spectra provides—`<CFA_MESSAGEQUEUEGET>`. As you can imagine, this simple tag grabs a queue and returns it as a structure. I told the tag what datasource and ID to use to locate my queue and then what structure to return it as. Lastly, I used the `<CFA_DUMP>` tag to display the queue. Figure 15.2 shows how the queue looks after we have added the method.

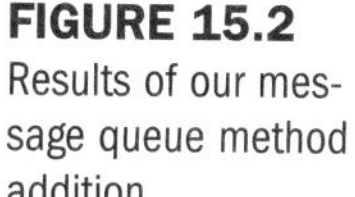

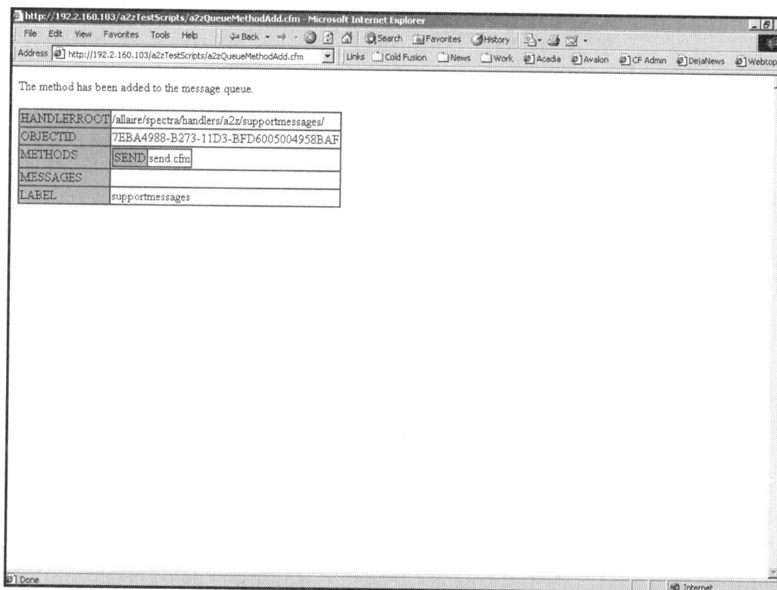

FIGURE 15.2
Results of our message queue method addition.

Adding Messages to Queues

Now that we have a message queue, we need a way to add messages to it. This is a two-fold process. First, we need some kind of simple form that will create the data for the message. Since we are building a support form, this page will be part of the A2Z Web site. After we create the form, we need a way to take that form data and create a message for it.

Let's start by building the template that will allow a user to send a message to the Support team. Listing 15.3 represents `customerHelp.cfm`, our support form that integrates with the message queue. Save it in the root of your Web server under the `a2z` folder you created earlier.

Listing 15.3 ***customerHelp.cfm***

```
<!---
File:        /a2z/customerHelp.cfm
Author:      Raymond Camden (raymond.k.camden@syntegra.com)
Date:        12/10/1999
Description: Sends a message to our queue.
```

continues

Listing 15.3 Continued

```
Notes:
--->

<CFSET QueueID = "7EBA4988-B273-11D3-BFD6005004958BAF">

<CF_A2ZFORMATTING SUBTITLE="Customer Help">

    <!--- The user has submitted the form. --->
    <CFIF IsDefined("Form.gogo")>

        <!--- Create the message structure --->
        <CFSET MessageData = StructNew()>
        <CFSET MessageData.Header = StructNew()>
        <CFSET MessageData.Header.To = "customersupport@a2zbooks.com">
        <CFSET MessageData.Header.Subject = "Request from #Form.Name#">
<CFSET MessageData.Header.From = Form.Email>
        <CFSET MessageData.Body = Form.Problem>

        <!--- Add the message to the queue. --->
        <CFA_MESSAGECREATE DATASOURCE="a2zAccess"
            STMESSAGEDATA="#MessageData#" ESSAGEQUEUEID="#QueueID#"
            R_OBJECTID="ID">
<FONT FACE="Arial" SIZE=2>
        <B>Customer Help</B>
        <P>
        Your request for help as been sent to our customer support team.
        It will be added to their queue and addressed in a first-come,
        first-served order.
<P>
        In any future correspondence, please include the tracking number:
        <CFOUTPUT>#ID#</CFOUTPUT>
        </FONT>

    <!--- Present the form to the user. --->
    <CFELSE>
        <FONT FACE="Arial" SIZE=2>
        <B>Customer Help</B>
        <P>
        Please use the form below to send your request for help to our
        customer support team. Try to describe your problem as completely
        as possible so that we can help you better.
</FONT>

        <P>

        <FORM ACTION="customerHelp.cfm" METHOD="POST">
            <TABLE>
            <TR>
                <TD><FONT FACE="Arial" SIZE=2>Your Name</FONT></TD>
                <TD><FONT FACE="Arial" SIZE=2>
```

```
                        <INPUT TYPE="text" NAME="name" VALUE="" SIZE=40>
                        </FONT></TD>
</TR>
            <TR>
                <TD><FONT FACE="Arial" SIZE=2>Email Address</FONT></TD>
                <TD><FONT FACE="Arial" SIZE=2>
                    <INPUT TYPE="text" NAME="email" VALUE="" SIZE=40>
                    </FONT></TD>
</TR>
            <TR>
                <TD COLSPAN=2><FONT FACE="Arial" SIZE=2>
                    Describe your problem:<BR>
<TEXTAREA NAME="Problem" COLS=50 ROWS=5></TEXTAREA>
                </FONT>
                </TD>
            </TR>
            <TR>
                <TD> </TD>
                <TD><FONT FACE="Arial" SIZE=2>
                    <INPUT TYPE="submit" NAME="gogo" VALUE="Send">
                    </FONT></TD>
</TR>
            </TABLE>
        </FORM>
    </CFIF>
 </CF_A2ZFORMATTING>
```

After you save this file, view it in your Web browser. Once filled in, it should look like Figure 15.3.

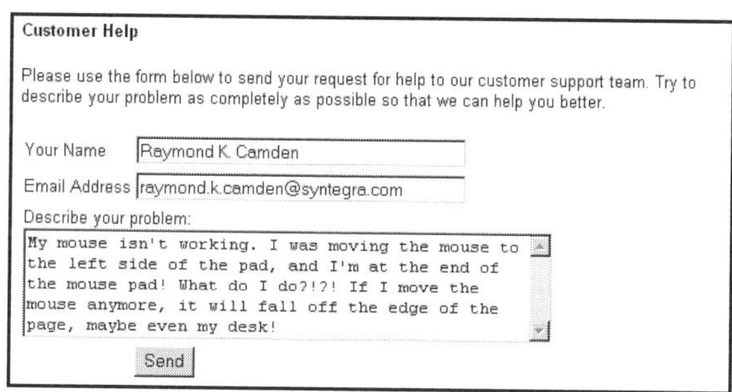

FIGURE 15.3
Our form to send a message to the support queue.

The code above is pretty simple. I have divided it into two sections:

- The first section processes the form. It's run after the user enters his information and clicks the Submit button. The `<CFIF IsDefined("Form.gogo")>` line checks the user's form information.
- The `<CFELSE>` block in the second half of the code displays the form to the user. We ask for his name, email address, and information about his problem. Since the problem may be quite complex, we use a `textarea` field that allows the user to type quite a bit.

The form doesn't need any explanation, so let's jump right into the first half of the code, the part that processes the form and sends a message to the support queue we created earlier.

The first thing we do is create a structure called `MessageData`. This is the structure that will be passed to our queue. Next, we create another structure as a part of the `MessageData` structure. This substructure is called Header and, like an email, will contain header information of the message. We include keys and values for the header's `To`, `From`, and `Subject` fields. We use the values from the form to populate these fields. Lastly, we store the user's problem in the body of the `MessageData` structure.

Now let's get to the interesting part. To add the message to the queue, use the `<CFA_MESSAGECREATE>` tag. Let's look at each attribute passed to the tag. The first thing we pass in is the datasource, which in our script is `a2zAccess`. Next we pass in the message via the `stMessageData` attribute. We use the `MessageData` structure we just created. Of course, Spectra needs to know into what queue to add the message, so we use the same queue ID we created earlier. If your queue has a different ID, change the `<CFSET QUEUEID = "7EBA4988-B273-11D3-BFD6005004958BAF">` line. The last attribute we pass to `<CFA_MESSAGECREATE>` is `R_OBJECTID`. We pass in the name of a variable to be created that will store the ID of the message added to the queue. A few lines later, after we output some text to the user, we output the ID number as a tracking number for the user. Many support systems use setups like this so that one particular problem can be tracked easier. Figure 15.4 shows the result of submitting our request form.

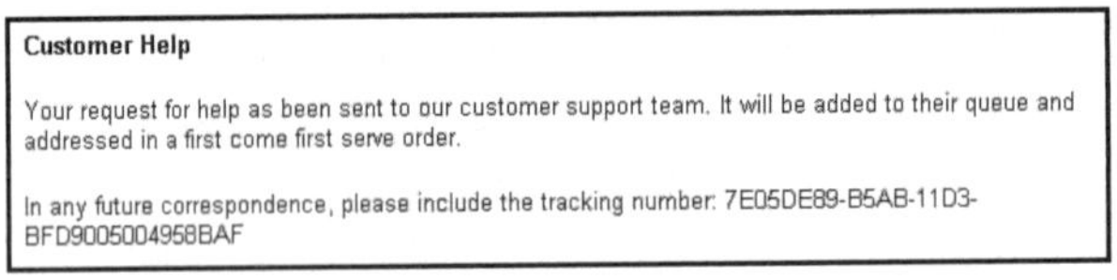

FIGURE 15.4
Our message has been sent to the Support system.

Customer Help

Your request for help as been sent to our customer support team. It will be added to their queue and addressed in a first come first serve order.

In any future correspondence, please include the tracking number: 7E05DE89-B5AB-11D3-BFD9005004958BAF

To verify that our message has been added to the queue, we can use the `<CFA_MESSAGEQUEUEGET>` tag we used earlier. Let's create a new file that will display the message queue. Listing 15.4 is a simple queue displayer.

Listing 15.4 *queueDisplay.cfm*

```
<!---
File:        /a2zTestScripts/queueDisplay.cfm
Author:      Raymond Camden (raymond.k.camden@syntegra.com)
Date:        12/10/1999
Description: Simply displays our queue.
Notes:
--->

<CFSET QueueID = "7EBA4988-B273-11D3-BFD6005004958BAF">

<!--- Get the queue --->
```

```
<CFA_MESSAGEQUEUEGET DATASOURCE="a2zAccess" MESSAGEQUEUEID="#QueueID#"
    R_STMESSAGEQUEUE="queue">

<!--- Display the queue. --->
 <CFA_DUMP VAR="#queue#">
```

This template simply gets the message queue and uses the `<CFA_DUMP>` tag to display it. Figure 15.5 shows the result of this script. As you can see, the message we created now exists in the queue.

FIGURE 15.5
Our queue with the message in it.

HANDLERROOT	/allaire/spectra/handlers/a2z/supportmessages/	
LABEL	supportmessages	
MESSAGES	7E05DE89-B5AB-11D3-BFD9005004958BAF	7EBA4988-B273-11D3-BFD6005004958BAF
METHODS	SEND	send.cfm
OBJECTID	7EBA4988-B273-11D3-BFD6005004958BAF	

Coding and Calling Message Queue Handlers

Now that our queue exists, we need to do something with it. Earlier we added a method to our queue called `Send`. This handler will process our queue, sending each email to the Support team. For this handler to work, of course, we need to actually code it. Listing 15.5 shows the code of our handler.

Listing 15.5 ***send.cfm***

```
<!---
File:        send.cfm
Author:      Raymond Camden (raymond.k.camden@syntegra.com)
Date:        12/10/1999
Description: Send handler for the queue.
Notes:
--->

<CFA_MESSAGINGHANDLER OBJECT="Message" SEPARATOR="<P>">

    <!--- Param our values in case any don't exist. --->
    <CFPARAM NAME = "Message.Header.To" DEFAULT="">
    <CFPARAM NAME = "Message.Header.From" DEFAULT="">
    <CFPARAM NAME = "Message.Header.CC" DEFAULT="">
    <CFPARAM NAME = "Message.Header.Subject" DEFAULT="">
    <CFPARAM NAME = "Message.Body" DEFAULT="">

    <!--- Send the message using the CFMAIL tag --->
    <CFMAIL TO="#Message.Header.To#" FROM="#Message.Header.From#"
        CC="#Message.Header.CC#" SUBJECT="#Message.Header.Subject#">
```

continues

Listing 15.5 Continued

```
#Message.Body#
    </CFMAIL>

    <CFOUTPUT>
    Message #Message.Header.Subject# sent.
    </CFOUTPUT>

    <!--- Delete the old message from the queue. --->
    <CFA_MESSAGEDELETE MESSAGEID="#Message.objectID#"
        MESSAGEQUEUEID="#Message.messageQueue#"
        DATASOURCE="#Attributes.datasource#">

</CFA_MESSAGINGHANDLER>
```

This file needs to be saved in the directory we set up as the handler root for the queue. If you examine Listing 15.1, you will see we used the `handlerRoot` attribute to set the handler folder as `/allaire/spectra/handlers/a2z/supportmessages`. This should be done under the installation folder for Spectra. Let's look at this script.

The first and last lines of code in `send.cfm` are the `<CFA_MESSAGINGHANDLER>` tag. As you can see, we wrap the entire meat of our handler with this, much like we do for display handlers. Just as the `<CFA_HANDLER>` tag makes it easier to work with handlers, the `<CFA_MESSAGINGHANDLER>` makes it easier to call a method on our queue. This tag will automatically loop for each message in the queue and will pass the message into a structure defined by the `OBJECT` parameter. In our case, we set this attribute to `Message`, which will copy the message data into a structure called `Message`. The `<CFA_MESSAGINGHANDLER>` tag has a `SEPARATOR` attribute just like the `<CFA_HANDLER>` tag. You can use the `SEPARATOR` attribute to automatically output HTML between each message. For each message we process, we want the handler to spit out a paragraph tag, so we pass `<P>` to the `SEPARATOR` attribute. Next, we use a set of `<CFPARAM>` tags to set up default variables for the message we will pass to the `<CFMAIL>` tag. We use `<CFPARAM>` in case certain parameters don't exist. For example, in the script we wrote in Listing 15.3, we don't pass a `CC` parameter to the queue. We may change this in the future, so we automatically `<CFPARAM>` it for now. Next, we pass these values to the `<CFMAIL>` tag. Between the beginning and closing `<CFMAIL>` tags we pass the body of the message. This will become the body of the email sent to the Support team. After sending the email, we output the value of the Subject line. The next important line is the `<CFA_MESSAGEDELETE>` tag. As you can probably guess, it deletes a message from a queue. We pass it the ID of the message, which in this case is in the message structure. (Remember that the `<CFA_MESSAGINGHANDLER>` tag will automatically loop for each message in the queue and will automatically repopulate the message structure.) We then tell the `<CFA_MESSAGEDELETE>` tag which queue to use. This exists in the message structure as well. Lastly, we pass in the datasource of the queue. For this, we pass in the value `ATTRIBUTES.DataSource`. This value will automatically be passed by the script that calls the handler. We end this script by closing the `<CFA_MESSAGINGHANDLER>` tag.

Now that we have coded the handler, let's write a script that will call the handler. Listing 15.6 displays a script that calls the handler for our queue.

Listing 15.6 *callQueueHandler.cfm*

```
<!---
File:        /a2zTestScripts/callQueueHandler.cfm
Author:      Raymond Camden (raymond.k.camden@syntegra.com)
Date:        12/10/1999
Description: Calls the handler for the queue.
Notes:
--->

<CFSET QueueID = "7EBA4988-B273-11D3-BFD6005004958BAF">

About to call the 'Send' method on our queue.
<P>

<CFA_MESSAGEQUEUE METHOD="send" MESSAGEQUEUEID="#QueueID#"
    DATASOURCE="a2zAccess">

<P>
 Done calling the 'Send' method.
```

As before, we start off by creating a variable to store our queue ID. After that, we use the `<CFA_MESSAGEQUEUE>` custom tag to call our method. Table 15.3 lists the attributes of the `<CFA_MESSAGEQUEUE>` custom tag.

Table 15.3 *<CFA_MESSAGEQUEUE>* Arguments

Argument	Required?	Description
`Datasource`	Yes	The datasource that stores the message queue. For our script, we used `a2zAccess`.
`Method`	Yes	The method you want to pass the queue to.
`MessageQueueID`	Yes	The ID of the message queue.
`OwnerObjectID`	No	If specified, the handler will process messages belonging to the user specified in this attribute.
`StMessageData`	No	Allows you to specify a message on-the-fly to pass to the handler. This object won't actually be added to the queue but will be processed as if it were.
`r_stObjects`	No	If specified, creates a structure with the same name that contains a structure containing the messages passed to the handler.
`r_stResultParams`	No	If the handler returns any data, this parameter specifies the name of the structure that will hold the results.

After you save this file, you can view it in your browser. Figure 15.6 displays the result of calling our method. As you can see, only one message was created.

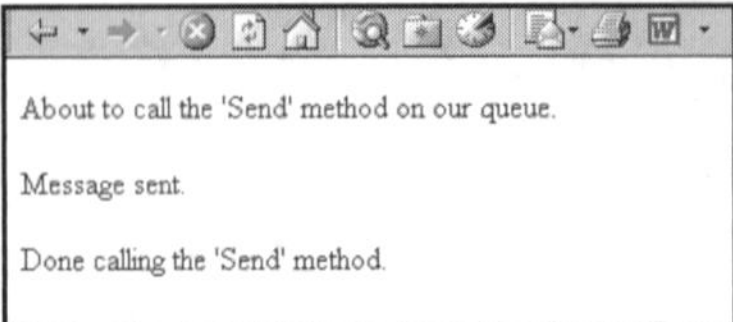

FIGURE 15.6
The `Send` method has been called on our queue.

We have shown only the simplest of possible message queues. Advanced users may wish to add more methods; for example, a `Table of Contents` method could display the title of each message without deleting it. Also, you may not want to delete messages from the queue automatically when you send them. Instead, you could create new Spectra objects for each object and store them in the COAPI. As always, Spectra gives you the tools to use this service in any way imaginable!

PART IV

Spectra Administration

CHAPTER 16

Using Spectra Security Options

In this chapter

Introduction to Security

All Web-based applications of any size have some security component. It may be as simple as providing secure access to administrative functions or as complicated as controlling the display of individual objects or GUI elements (such as buttons and drop-down lists) based on a user's security settings.

Advanced Security has been available in ColdFusion since ColdFusion Server 4.0 but hasn't been widely used, partly due to the complexity of its administrative interface. With Spectra, Allaire has simplified the interactions with ColdFusion Advanced Security by streamlining it to focus on the core functions needed to build robust Spectra applications.

Still, it's important to understand how ColdFusion handles Advanced Security and, in particular, the nomenclature Allaire uses to describe security concepts. Let's begin with some definitions:

- *Authentication.* The process of verifying that a user is who he says he is. In ColdFusion, this is accomplished by maintaining a list of usernames and passwords and requiring users to supply them when logging in.
- *Authorization.* The process of verifying that a user has sufficient authority or permission to perform a particular action or to access a particular Content Item.

One thing generally omitted from Allaire's Advanced Security documentation is an explanation of an application that's installed with ColdFusion 4.0—SiteMinder. SiteMinder, produced by Netegrity, Inc. (`www.netegrity.com`), is a prepackaged solution adopted by Allaire to handle authentication and authorization needs. In practice, this means that ColdFusion Server makes calls to SiteMinder to *authenticate* a user when the user logs in and to *authorize* him to access content or site functions. SiteMinder stores and manages the data needed to authenticate and authorize. It also provides an interface for ColdFusion to interact with the authentication and authorization data it holds. The ColdFusion Markup Language (CFML) and Spectra tags abstract interaction with SiteMinder into several tags and functions.

ColdFusion authentication is implemented with the `<CFAUTHENTICATE>` tag; this allows a developer to pass a username and password to SiteMinder to verify a login attempt. Basic ColdFusion authorization interaction is done through the `IsAuthorized()` function, which checks to see if whether a previously authenticated user has a particular permission.

Spectra includes a third component that is closely associated with user security: the User Profile. Whereas user authentication data (username and password) is stored in a datasource managed by SiteMinder, the User Profile is stored as a Content Item managed by Spectra. This is where detailed information about the user lives, such as full name, address, email address, and job title. The User Profile ContentObject Type can also be customized by the interactive developer to manage application-specific data.

▶ **See** Chapter 18, "Implementing Personalization," for more detailed information on the User Profile and how it's used in Spectra.

Although the primary use for the User Profile is to enable personalization, it's tightly integrated into the Security Service. For example, the main Spectra tag used to authenticate users will also return the user's profile when authentication succeeds.

Authentication Basics

The key pieces of data that are stored in the authentication datasource are

- Username
- Password
- Group definitions
- Associations between users and groups—that is, which users belong to which groups

As noted earlier, the authentication data includes group definitions and associations between individuals and defined groups. Administrators can assign group permissions to groups that are inherited by all members of the group. This lightens the administrator's burden, because he doesn't have to manage permissions for individual users. This common security practice is often referred to as *roles-based security.*

Allaire refers to the data repositories that hold authentication information as *user directories.* When Spectra installs, it creates and configures a default user directory with a potentially confusing name—`UserDirectory`. This default data repository is an Access database with tables designed to hold the authentication information described above. The Access database file is located in

```
SpectraInstallDirectory/database/UserDirectory.mdb
```

Again, ColdFusion Server and Spectra do *not* interact directly with this database—SiteMinder does. To set or get authentication information, ColdFusion calls to SiteMinder, which uses an ODBC connection to this user directory to get the requested data, which it then returns to ColdFusion. Some of the basic Spectra tags that abstract this interaction include the following:

- `<CFA_USERCREATE>` creates a new user in a specific user directory.
- `<CFA_USERDELETE>` deletes a user from a specific user directory.
- `<CFA_USERADDGROUPS>` associates a user with a specified group(s) in a specified user directory.
- `<CFA_GROUPCREATE>` creates a new group in a specified user directory.
- `<CFA_GROUPDELETE>` deletes a group in a specified user directory.

▶ **See** Appendix A, "Allaire Spectra Tags," for a complete list of security-related tags and a detailed description of how to use them.

The key advantage of using SiteMinder for the authentication service is that it understands how to talk to different kinds of user directories. As mentioned above, Spectra installs a default Access database user directory that SiteMinder talks to through an ODBC connection. However, SiteMinder also knows how to talk to Windows NT domains and Lightweight Directory Access Protocol (LDAP) servers. To SiteMinder, Windows NT domains and LDAP servers are just other possible sources of authentication information. Later in this chapter, we'll see how to configure SiteMinder to interact with various kinds of user directories. (For more information on LDAP directories and how ColdFusion Server interacts with them, see *The ColdFusion 4.0 Web Application Construction Kit* by Ben Forta.)

CAUTION

Spectra stores basic user information such as usernames and passwords in SiteMinder's authentication database. It stores additional user information in a User Profile Content Item. Taken together, these two datasources–SiteMinder's authentication database and Spectra's User Profile Content Items–contain all the basic information about an individual user. However, Spectra doesn't automatically keep these databases in sync. Therefore, if you create a user in the authentication database programmatically (using the `<CFA_USERCREATE>` tag), you also need to create a user profile programmatically by using the `<CFA_USERPROFILECREATE>` tag. Likewise, if you allow users to change their usernames in the user directory, you also need to make the change in their user profiles.

NOTE To use a Windows 2000 active directory as a user directory, you will need to address it as an LDAP directory. ■

Authorization Basics: Resources and Actions

Authorization data is also managed by SiteMinder. The basic building blocks it uses to store security information are as follows:

- *Resources* are the individual items we want to secure—that is, particular items to which we want to limit users' access.
- *Actions* are specific actions related to a resource. Different types of resources have different types of possible actions.

When programming in ColdFusion, the term *resources* can mean many things such as files, directories, pages, ODBC datasources, or CF tags; *actions* can include things like reading, writing, updating, or viewing. For example, we might want to control who can view (an action) the contents of a file (a resource). Or we might want to limit who can use (an action) the `<CFREGISTRY>` tag (a resource).

A key action within ColdFusion and Spectra security is to create a list of the resource-action pairs for which we want to limit access.

NOTE In the Allaire documentation about Advanced Security, a resource-action pair is referred to as a *rule*. For example, you might want to limit `write` access to the `C:\cfusion` directory. The Advanced Security interface allows you to define a rule called `CFUSION_Write`, which is just a user-assigned name for the resource-action pair made up of the `C:\cfusion` directory and the `write` action.

This nomenclature tends to be confusing because resource-action pairs don't intuitively seem like a "rule"—they just seem like a way of specifying a particular type of resource and a particular action to perform on it. And in fact, that's all they are.

In Spectra programming, the range of resources and actions has been simplified greatly. Resources are either ContentObject Types or Content Items. Actions are just the methods available for a particular ContentObject Type or a particular Content Item.

For example, we may want to limit the users who are allowed to invoke the edit handler (an action) for the Author ContentObject Type (a resource). Or, we might want to limit the users who are allowed to view (an action) the Content Item that holds a particular employee's personnel record (a resource).

See Chapter 6, "Introduction to Spectra Programming," for basic information on ContentObject Types and their methods. See Chapter 10, "Creating and Managing Content," for more information on Content Items.

NOTE Although Spectra programming relies on this streamlined view of resources and actions, "regular" ColdFusion security is also available to you when writing Spectra applications. In other words, nothing can prevent you from using non-Spectra ColdFusion Advanced Security even when building Spectra applications. From a practical standpoint, however, the Spectra view of security will likely cover all your application needs.

Authorization Basics: Policies

So far, we have defined users and the groups they belong to and we have named resources and the actions that can be performed on them. These two concepts—users and resource-action pairs—are combined in what Allaire refers to as *policies*. Put simply, policies associate users (or groups) with resource-action pairs ("rules").

In ColdFusion Advanced Security, you can include more than one resource-action pair in a single policy. However, to help simplify matters, Spectra assigns only one resource-action pair to any one policy. Of course, in Spectra you may still assign multiple users (or groups) to a single policy.

In Spectra, most of the interaction with the Security system can be performed through the Webtop, which tends to hide the details of creating policies.

Security Administrative Units: Security Contexts

ColdFusion organizes the preceding security elements into one administrative unit—what Allaire calls a *security context* or *Security Realm*. A security context is just a logical grouping of

- User Directories
- Resource-action pairs ("rules")
- Policies that associate resource-action pairs with users and groups

NOTE For more information on security contexts and managing them through the ColdFusion Administrator, see *Advanced ColdFusion 4.0 Application Development* by Ben Forta.

To determine whether a user has permission to perform a specific action on a specific resource, ColdFusion calls to SiteMinder's Authorization Service. SiteMinder checks to see if a resource-action pair is defined within the specified security context. If so, SiteMinder verifies that the specified user is associated with it.

SiteMinder returns a "user is authorized" message if either of the following is true:

- The resource-action pair is *not* defined in the SiteMinder database. This means there are no security limitations, so everyone has access.
- The resource-action pair *is* defined in the SiteMinder database *and* the user is associated with it in a policy.

For example, if Spectra needs to know if a user Jesse is authorized to invoke the edit handler of the Author ContentObject Type, it requests the data from the SiteMinder Authorization Service. SiteMinder checks for a policy covering that handler and, if it exists, verifies that the user Jesse is in the list of users associated with it. If so, it returns a "user is authorized" message to ColdFusion; if not, it returns a "user is not authorized" message.

SiteMinder handles all the actual storage and management of resource-action definitions, their association with users in a policy, and the mechanics of querying that database. Later, this chapter will cover some of the Spectra tags that encapsulate SiteMinder functions.

As with the authentication data, authorization data is stored by default in an Access database. This is installed when ColdFusion Advanced Security is installed and is located in

```
COLDFUSION_INSTALLATION_DIRECTORY/Database/smpolicy.mdb
```

In almost all cases, you should upgrade this to either an LDAP server or an enterprise-class database such as SQL Server or Oracle. We'll cover upgrading the policy database later in the chapter.

This has been a pretty extended introduction to ColdFusion security. It's important to understand the general concepts that underlie Spectra's security implementation. The following sections amplify on the basics described thus far to show how to implement security in your applications and how to use it to control access to the Webtop.

Using the Webtop to Manage Security

Most security functions can be accomplished through the Webtop. This section covers some basic Webtop functions to demonstrate the principles involved. From these descriptions, you should be able to perform most security functions. However, for additional data, refer to Allaire's *Programming with Allaire Spectra* book.

Securing the Webtop

First, let's see how to secure sections of the Webtop. As appropriate, we'll relate actions performed in the following sections to the basic definitions and concepts described earlier.

During the Spectra installation, Allaire suggests that you turn on authentication and authorization caching to improve performance. However, when this is turned on during development, you sometimes get confusing behavior, and changes to the security databases may not show up immediately.

For the examples in this chapter, it's suggested that you turn off security caching through the ColdFusion Administrator. To do so, follow these steps:

1. Open the ColdFusion Administrator.
2. Click the Advanced Security link in the navigation area on the left.
3. Deselect Load Security Server Policy Store Cache at Startup, Use Security Server Policy Store Cache, and Use Security Server Authorization Cache (see Figure 16.1).
4. Click Apply at the bottom of the page.
5. Restart the ColdFusion, SiteMinder Authentication, and SiteMinder Authorization services through the Services applet.

Before you go to production, remember to turn caching back on; otherwise Spectra will take a noticeable performance hit.

Controlling Webtop Access The following examples use a plain vanilla Spectra installation. First, let's create a new user and assign him to the Webtop Administrators group. This user will have unlimited access to the Webtop. Follow these steps:

1. In the Webtop, click System Admin.
2. In the navigation area, open Users and Security.
3. Click User Directories to display a list of available user Directories. Figure 16.2 shows the default `userDirectory`.
4. Click the icon in the Users column to list the current users.
5. Click Create at the bottom of the page to open the New User form.
6. Enter **`WebAdmin`** for the username, and then enter a password and a description (see Figure 16.3).

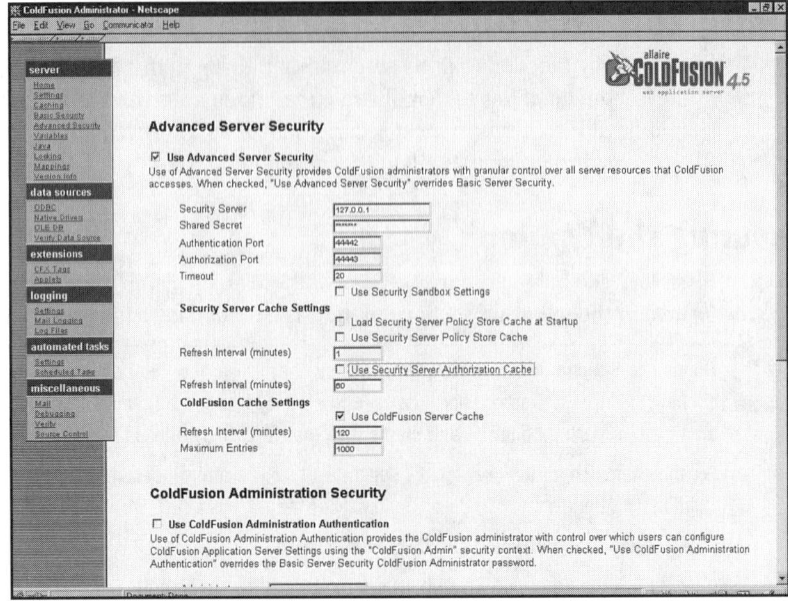

FIGURE 16.1
The Advanced Security page of the ColdFusion Administrator with the security cache settings disabled.

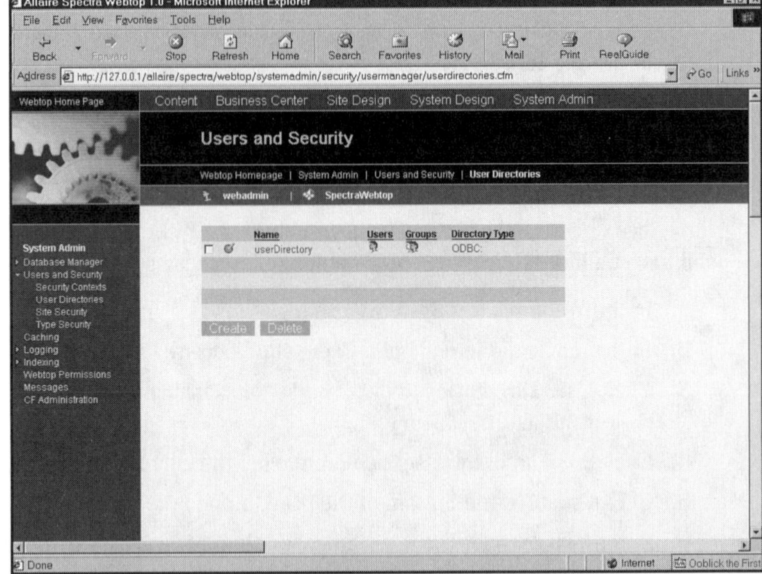

FIGURE 16.2
The User Directory list displays all user directories now in place. In this instance, the default `userDirectory` is the only directory in place.

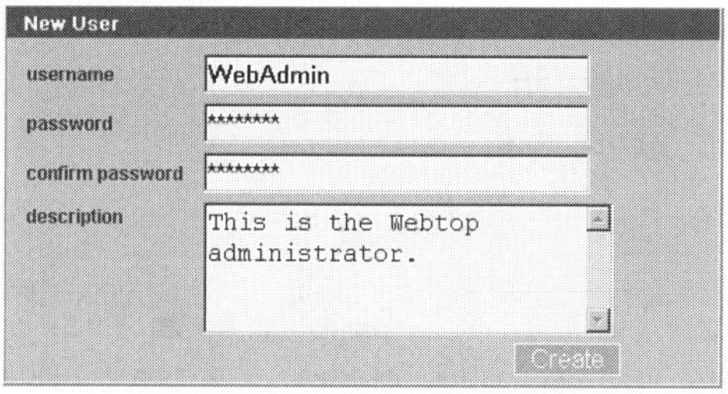

FIGURE 16.3
The `WebAdmin` user is created and is assigned a password and a description.

New User

username: WebAdmin
password: ********
confirm password: ********
description: This is the Webtop administrator.

Create

7. Click Create to create the new user. The current user directory updates to include the new user (see Figure 16.4).

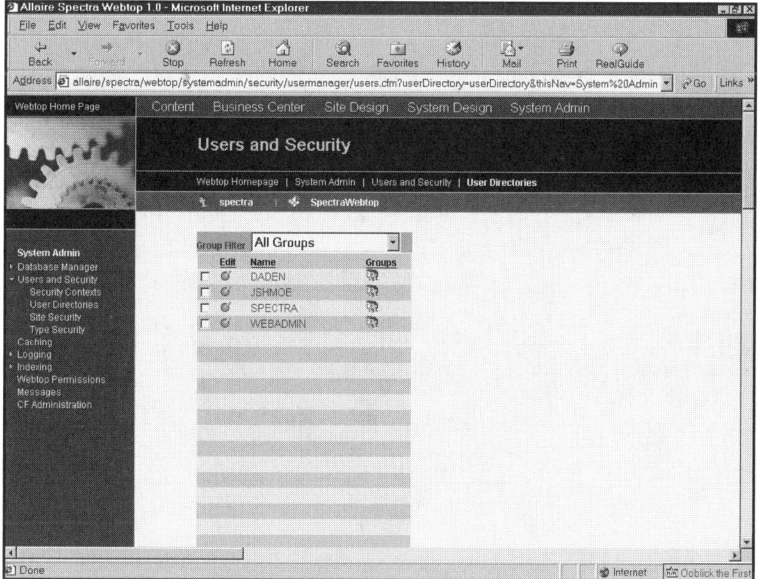

FIGURE 16.4
The user list of the current user directory now includes `WebAdmin`.

8. Click the faces icon in the Groups column next to the `WebAdmin` user. The Assign Groups window appears (see Figure 16.5).

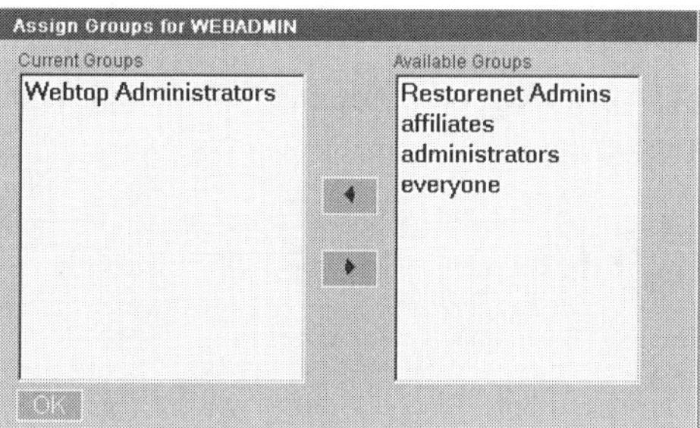

FIGURE 16.5
In the group assignment window, the user `WebAdmin` is assigned to the Webtop Administrators group.

9. Click Webtop Administrators in the right Available Groups list; then click the left arrow to move Webtop Administrators to the Current Groups list.
10. Click OK to save the association.

> **CAUTION**
>
> The next procedure limits access to the System Admin area of the Webtop to users assigned to the Webtop Administrators group. Make sure you have assigned all users who need System Admin access to the Webtop Administrators group before proceeding.

Now, use the same procedure to create a user `jshmoe`, except don't assign `jshmoe` to any groups. Follow these steps:

1. Click System Admin.
2. In the navigation area, click Webtop Permissions to display the Webtop Security Settings form.
3. In the drop-down box, select System Admin. For a new Spectra installation, no groups will be listed in the Granted column. (Remember that, because *no one* has been granted access, *everyone* is granted access.) See Figure 16.6.

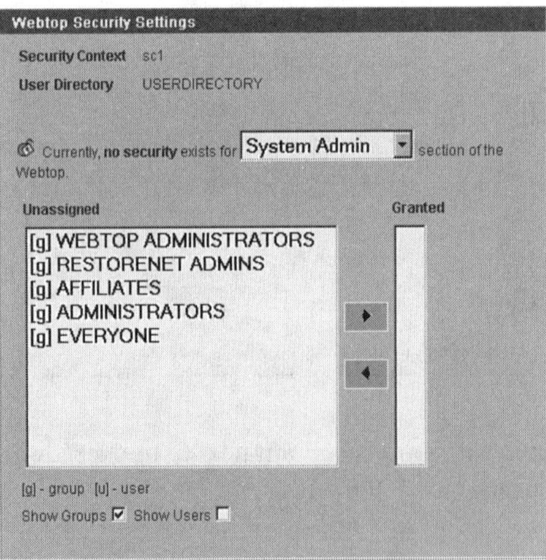

FIGURE 16.6
The Webtop Security Settings page will allow you to secure sections of the Webtop to individuals and groups.

4. In the Unassigned list, select Webtop Administrators, and then click the right arrow to move it into the Granted list (see Figure 16.7).

After performing these steps, you should be able to log in to the Webtop as `WebAdmin` and have full access to all areas of the Webtop. However, when you log in as `jshmoe`, the System Admin link won't appear.

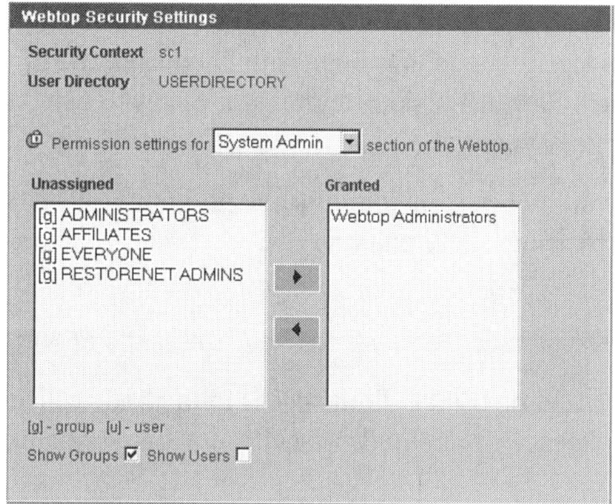

FIGURE 16.7
The System Admin section of the Webtop is now secured to only members of the Webtop Administrators group.

NOTE Spectra 1.0 has no "log out" function for the Webtop. Because your login is maintained in a cookie, you remain logged in until you close all browsers. To switch between the `WebAdmin` and `jshmoe` logins, close all instances of the browser you are using, and then reopen a new browser instance.

When you enter the Webtop, you will be presented with another login screen. Later, this chapter examines how to log out users programmatically.

It may also be necessary to cycle the CF and SiteMinder services in the Services Control Panel, to clear any security caching.

Behind the scenes, the preceding steps create a policy that associates members of the Webtop Administrators group with the ability to access the System Admin section of the Webtop. All other users are denied access.

CAUTION

Because ColdFusion Server and Spectra's security model operate on the basis of "full access unless restricted," it's important to set up policies to secure the Webtop immediately after installation. Until these policies are created, all users have access to all Webtop functions.

These steps describe how to create a new user. An example of how to create a new group is provided later in this chapter.

Controlling Site Access Through the Webtop Spectra provides a way to set Site Security in the System Admin area. You get to this interface by clicking System Admin, opening Users and Security in the left column, and then clicking Site Security to open a Site Layout interface. Unfortunately, the Site Layout interface didn't work properly at Spectra 1.0, the version available at press time, so a detailed description isn't presented here. However, these problems were reportedly scheduled to be fixed in a maintenance release. See your Allaire documentation for further information on how to use this feature.

Controlling ContentObject Type Access As covered earlier, in the section "Introduction to Security," the Spectra security model has been simplified from the model used in ColdFusion Advanced Security. The following sections demonstrate how to use the Webtop to set security for specific ContentObject Types.

Our goal is to specify which users can edit information in the Author ContentObject Type. We're going to do this by using the Webtop to define a policy that limits access to the `EditAuthor` method.

We'll use the `jshmoe` user created earlier, since he wasn't added to any groups.

The following method could be used to limit access to methods called by the Webtop, but it's typically used to control access to methods associated with user-defined ContentObject Types.

First, let's create an `AuthorAdmin` group that we'll assign permissions to. By using a group, we avoid the administrative overhead of having to individually assign permissions to all application users; instead, we assign appropriate users to the `AuthorAdmin` group and then assign the required permissions to the group. Follow these steps:

1. Click System Admin.
2. In the navigation area, open Users and Security.
3. Click User Directories.
4. Click the faces icon in the Groups column to open the Groups list.
5. Click Create at the bottom of the page to open the New Group form (see Figure 16.8).

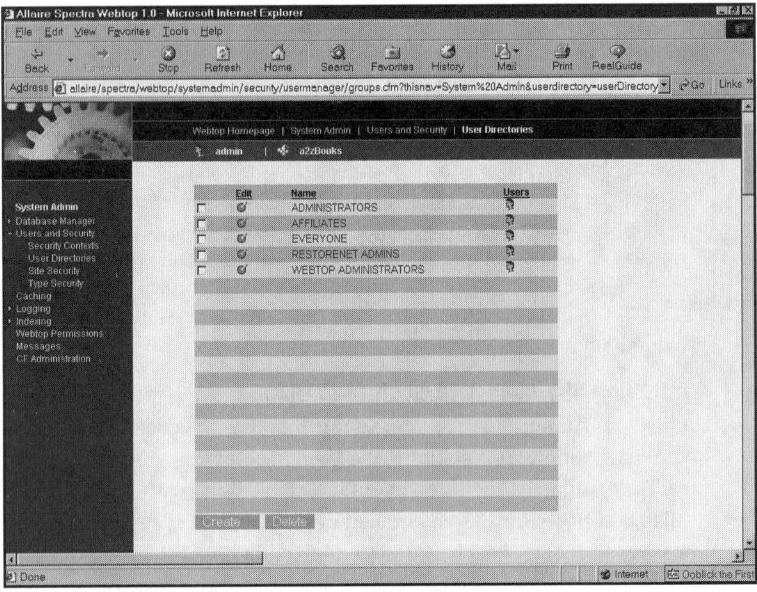

FIGURE 16.8
The groups screen will let you choose a group to edit or create a new group.

6. Enter **AuthorAdmin** in the Group Name field. Enter a description for this group (see Figure 16.9).

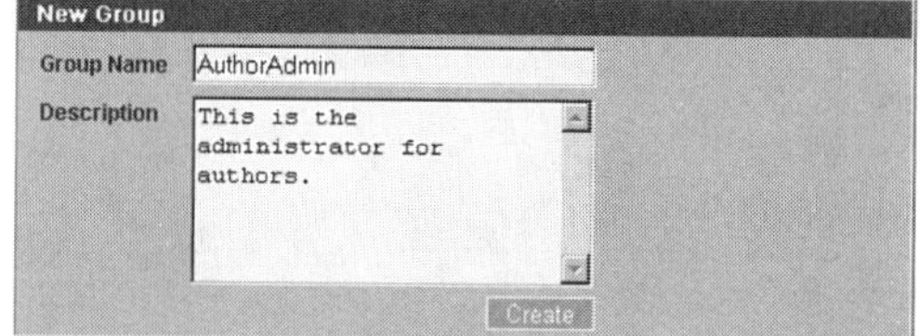

FIGURE 16.9
A new group, AuthorAdmin, is created, to encapsulate those who will administer the authors.

7. Click Create at the bottom of the page to create the group. This returns you to the Groups list.
8. Click the icon in the Users column to display a form for assigning users to a group.
9. Select the users who should have access to edit author information. Make sure that jshmoe is *not* selected.
10. Click the left arrow to move the selected users into the Members column.
11. Click OK to return to the Groups list.

Now, we're going to tell Spectra to restrict access to the EditAuthor method of the Author ContentObject Type to members of the AuthorAdmin group. Follow these steps:

1. Click System Admin.
2. In the navigation area, open Users and Security.
3. Click Type Security to open a list of available ContentObject Types.
4. To sort the list by name, click Name (see Figure 16.10).
5. Click the security icon to the left of Author. This opens the Types security edit form.
6. In the drop-down box, select the EditAuthor method. This refreshes the screen to show any policies already set for the method.
7. Select AuthorAdmin in the Unassigned list, and then click the right arrow to move AuthorAdmin into the Granted list (see Figure 16.11).

Use these steps to create polices that restrict access to ContentObject Type methods. This particular example creates a policy that we will use later to determine which users can invoke the EditAuthor method. This policy doesn't by itself limit access to the object; whether security is enforced is determined by how your application is coded, as examined in the next section.

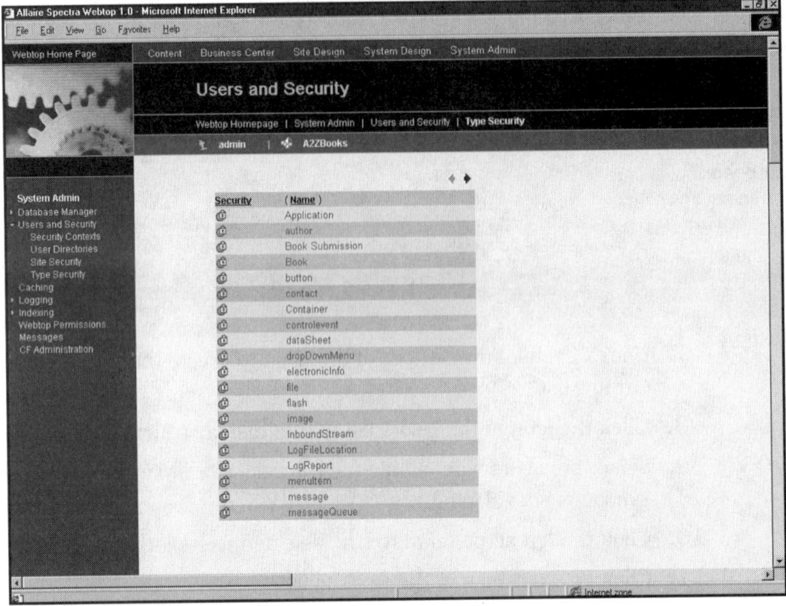

FIGURE 16.10
The Type Security list is sorted by the names of the types.

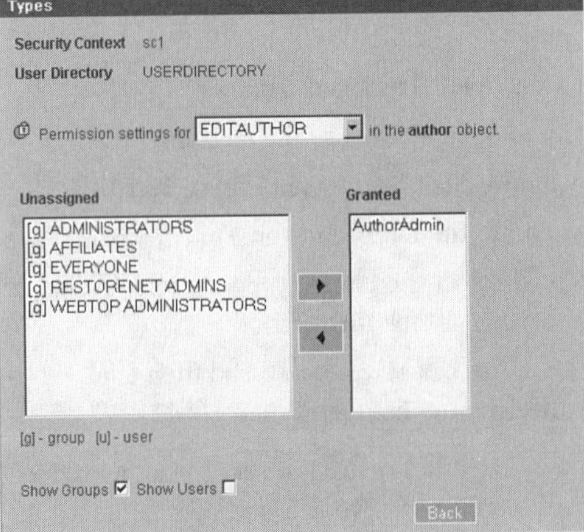

FIGURE 16.11
The `EditAuthor` method is secured to the `AuthorAdmin` group.

Programming Security

In the previous section, we used the Webtop to create a policy that defines which users can access a particular method. For that policy to take effect, we need to code our application pages to enforce security, as described in the following sections.

Authenticating Users

Within an application, the first step in implementing security is to authenticate the current user. Spectra provides two tags you can use to authenticate users:

- <CFA_SECURE> encapsulates several important functions including authentication.
- <CFA_AUTHENTICATE> encapsulates the <CFAUTHENTICATE> tag and is used to verify whether a user is authenticated in a particular security context. Using <CFA_AUTHENTICATE> instead of <CFA_SECURE> may be appropriate in some circumstances, although it requires the programmer to explicitly code more functions that are automatically handled by <CFA_SECURE>.

<CFA_SECURE> provides the most functionality, because it encapsulates several key functions. It's a somewhat complicated tag but is worth the time to understand how it works and how to use it. According to the Allaire documentation, <CFA_SECURE> encapsulates the following functionality:

- *Authentication.* It does this by calling the <CFA_AUTHENTICATE> tag.
- *Session management.* It does this by calling <CFA_SESSION>. The session it creates uses a temporary cookie that expires when the user closes all instances of his browser.
- *Login form display.* <CFA_SECURE> automatically invokes the template named in the AUTHENTICATEURL attribute when it needs user input to authenticate a user.
- *Accessing the user profile.* When <CFA_SECURE> successfully authenticates a user, it calls <CFA_USERPROFILEGET> to get the user's profile, which it returns in the variables specified with the R_STUSERPROFILE attribute.
- *Preserves user information.* It stores user login information, including the username and password in either cookie or session variables.

NOTE <CFA_SECURE> is one of the few encrypted tags that ship with Spectra. It's therefore not possible to look into the tag to evaluate its logic. It's encrypted because it uses an internal, undocumented ColdFusion function that cannot be used in general user applications.

Probably the best way to see how <CFA_SECURE> works is to provide an example of it in action. Before we look at a more complete example of its use, let's look at a relatively simple implementation of it. Listing 16.1 is a slightly edited version of the A2Z adminhome.cfm template.

Listing 16.1 The Admin Home Page

```
<!---
File:          admin/adminhome.cfm - Login form for administrators
Author:        david aden (david@wwstudios.com)
Date:          1/23/2000
```

continues

Listing 16.1 Continued

```
Description:  Admin users call this template to get access to restricted
              areas of the site.

Notes:      This uses the guts of the login form that is used by CFA_secure
            in the application.cfm file -- although that is used to
            prevent someone from going into design mode without being
            authenticated.

Change History:

--->

<!--- Log the page. --->
<CFA_PAGE
    datasource="#REQUEST.CFA.a2zBooks.DATASOURCE#"
    pagename="Admin Login Page"
    sectionname="Admin"
    sitename="A2ZBooks"
    cachepage="No"
    bpreloadpageobjects="No"
    logpage="No"
    logcachedobjects="No">

<CFPARAM NAME="username" DEFAULT="">
<CFPARAM NAME="password" DEFAULT="">
<CFPARAM NAME="loginSuccess" DEFAULT="FALSE">

<CFA_SECURE
      USERNAME="#username#"
      PASSWORD="#password#"
      SECURITYCONTEXT="#request.cfa.security.securitycontext#"
      AUTHENTICATIONURL="/allaire/spectra/handlers/a2z/loginform.cfm"
      STORAGETYPE="Cookie"
      R_BRESULT="loginSuccess"
      R_STUSERPROFILE="request.stUserProfile">

<!--- If CFA_Secure completed successfully, then show the list of available
      links. --->
<CFIF loginSuccess>

    <CF_A2ZFORMATTING>

    <CFOUTPUT>
    <TABLE BORDER="0" CELLPADDING="0" CELLSPACING="0" WIDTH="100%">
        <TR>
            <TD ALIGN="Center">
            <font face="arial" size="3">
                <B>Successfully logged in as:
                #request.stUserProfile.label#</B>
```

```
</TD>
        </TR>

        <TR>
            <TD> </TD>
        </TR>

        <!--- If the person is in the admin group, then show them a link
              to the Admin page --->
        <CFA_GROUPGET
            USERDIRECTORY="UserDirectory"
            GROUPNAME="AuthorAdmin"
            R_STGROUP="stGroup"
            R_LUSERNAMES="lUserNames">

        <CFIF ListFindNoCase(lUserNames,cfa_user)>
            <TR>
                <TD>
                    <A HREF="AdminLinks.cfm">Admin Links Page</A>
                </TD>
            </TR>
        </CFIF>


    </TABLE>
    <BR>
    </CFOUTPUT>
    </CF_A2ZFORMATTING>

</CFIF>
```

Let's examine what happens when a user requests this page:

1. After the opening `<CFA_PAGE>` call, default variable values that will be used later are set for `username`, `password`, and `loginSuccess`.
2. `<CFA_SECURE>` is invoked. The first time the user requests this page, `username` and `password` are empty, which causes `<CFA_SECURE>` to invoke the template named in the `AUTHENTICATIONURL` attribute.
3. Listing 16.2 contains the `loginform.cfm` template, a standard HTML form with input fields for `username` and `password`. When the user clicks the Login button, the form self-submits to the original page that contains the `<CFA_SECURE>` tag.

Listing 16.2 The A2Z Login Form

```
<!---
File:         \handlers\a2z\loginform.cfm
Author:       jeff tapper
Date:         1/19/2000
```

continues

Part IV Ch 16

Listing 16.2 Continued

```
Description:  Login page for A2ZBooks
Notes:

--->
<CFSETTING ENABLECFOUTPUTONLY="Yes">
<!--- Template that holds the default authentication form;
      this template will be called from cfa_secure. --->

<CFPARAM NAME="username" DEFAULT="">
<!--- Get the query string --->
<cfset iif( Len(cgi.Query_string),
    "thisQueryString='?#cgi.query_string#'",
    "thisQueryString=''" )>
<CFOUTPUT>
    <CF_A2ZFORMATTING ShowLinks="No" TableWidth="400">
        <FORM NAME="loginform"
          ACTION="#cgi.script_name##thisQueryString#"
          METHOD="post">
          <CENTER>
          <TABLE BORDER=0 CELLSPACING=0 CELLPADDING=20 BGCOLOR="##669966">
            <TR><TD>
              <CENTER>
                <FONT SIZE=4 FACE="arial">
                <B>Please Login</B>
                </FONT><BR>
                <P>
                Username:
                <INPUT TYPE="text" NAME="username" VALUE="#username#">
                </P>
                <P>
                Password:
                <INPUT TYPE="password" NAME="password">
                </P>
                <INPUT NAME="AdminLogin" TYPE="submit" VALUE="login">
              </CENTER>
            </TD></TR>
          </TABLE>
        </form>
    </CF_A2ZFORMATTING>
</CFOUTPUT>
<CFSETTING ENABLECFOUTPUTONLY="No">
```

4. This time, `username` and `password` *are* populated and `<CFA_SECURE>` uses them to authenticate the user within the security context named in the `SECURITYCONTEXT` attribute.
5. If the user does *not* authenticate in the named security context, `<CFA_SECURE>` reinvokes the template named in `AuthenticateURL`.

If the user *does* authenticate in the named security context, `<CFA_SECURE>` creates three variables:

- `CFA_USER` is set to the value of `username`.
- `CFA_PASSWORD` contains an encrypted version of the value of `password`.
- `CFAUTH` is populated with a security token that encodes session and user information into an encrypted string.

6. `<CFA_SECURE>` stores these three variables for later use:
   - `CFAUTH` is stored as a cookie in the user's browser.
   - `CFA_USER` and `CFA_PASSWORD` are stored by default as cookies on the user's system. Optionally, you can store these as session variables by setting the attribute `STORAGETYPE` to `Session`.
7. `<CFA_SECURE>` invokes `CFA_USERPROFILEGET` and returns the user's profile to the variable named in the `R_STUSERPROFILE` attribute.
8. `<CFA_SECURE>` returns a Boolean into the variable named in the `R_BRESULTS` attribute to indicate if authentication was successful.
9. The next time the user requests this page, `<CFA_SECURE>` automatically uses the `CFA_USER` and `CFA_PASSWORD` variables (whether stored as cookies or in session variables) to authenticate. The user therefore *won't* be given a login screen after he successfully logs in.

`<CFA_SECURE>` uses temporary cookies to store `CFA_USER` and `CFA_PASSWORD`, which expire when the user closes the last instance of his browser. This means that once the user closes his browser, he will need to log in again.

NOTE Although `<CFA_SECURE>` permits you to store `CFA_USER` and `CFA_PASSWORD` as session variables, it always stores `CFAUTH`, which is required for security to work properly, as a cookie.

The Webtop also uses cookie storage for `CFA_USER` and `CFA_PASSWORD`. Because of this, it may be advantageous to use the default cookie storage for your application. By doing this, you minimize the risk of conflicts that may arise by having Webtop authentication data stored in cookie variables and your application's authentication data stored in session variables.

The preceding template is a standalone use of `<CFA_SECURE>` that demonstrates how it works. In actual practice, you'll want to code `<CFA_SECURE>` into your `application.cfm` file. That way, you can ensure that all site users are authenticated, even if only as an `anonymous` user. Listing 16.3 contains part of the a2zBooks `application.cfm` file:

Part IV Ch 16

Listing 16.3 *application.cfm*—Global Variables for the Application and for Managing Authentication

```
<!---
File:         application.cfm
Author:       jeff tapperDate:        12/5/1999
Description:  Global Settings For a2zBooks
Notes:
Change History:
1/9/00: daden: CustomTag to workaround problem with setting REQUEST
      scope Log-related variables when the application datasource is
      different from the Webtop datasource.

1/10/00: daden: commented out -- it looks like we need to manually copy
      the Logfile definition from the cfaobjects database to the CODB for
      our app, in which case the following should NOT be necessary.

1/15/00 (JT)    Added call to cfa_browser if request.cfa.browser is not
                already populated.
1/19/00 (JT)    Added user profiling.
1/22/00 (RR)    Added secure login if trying to use designmode and cookie
                to remember mode.
1/25/00 (DA)    Revised to cause a CFA_SECURE to run for all users, if only
                using the "anonymous" user name. Also added some
                functionality to let it work with the "Admin" login
                template.
--->

<!--- If we're receiving a logout, then get rid of any mode and
      user cookies. --->
<CFIF IsDefined("URL.logout")>
    <CFCOOKIE NAME="Mode" VALUE="" EXPIRES="NOW">
</CFIF>

<!--- Default mode is "browse". If Cookie.mode exists, then that is
      used instead. --->
<CFPARAM NAME="mode" DEFAULT="Browse">

<CFA_APPLICATIONINITIALIZE
      NAME="a2zBooks"
      SESSIONMANAGEMENT="True"
      SESSIONTIMEOUT="#CreateTimeSpan(0,0,10,0)#"
      MODE="#mode#">


<!--- If we're at the Admin login page, then skip the authentication done
      here because we're goign to do it in the login page. --->
<CFIF FindNoCase("adminhome.cfm", CGI.CF_TEMPLATE_PATH)>

    <!--- Don't do anything --->

<CFELSE>

    <!--- If the user has requeted designmode... --->
    <CFSET DesignRequest = IsDefined("URL.designmode")
```

```
    OR (IsDefined("URL.mode") AND URL.Mode IS 'design')>
<CFIF DesignRequest>
    <!--- <CFIF IsDefined("URL.designmode")> --->
        <!--- If this is the first time through, i.e. username and password
              are not yet set (as FORM variables), then set a username and
              password that will fail, forcing a new login. --->
        <CFPARAM NAME="username" DEFAULT="#COOKIE.CFID#">
        <CFPARAM NAME="password" DEFAULT="#COOKIE.CFTOKEN#">

    <!--- If the user isn't already logged in, then we're going to log them
          in as the user "anonymous".  --->
    <CFELSEIF NOT IsDefined("Cookie.cfa_user")
    OR NOT IsDefined("Cookie.cfa_password")>
<CFSET username = "anonymous">
        <CFSET password = "anonymous">

    <!--- ELSE set username and password to empty strings which will force
          CFA_Secure to use the cookie data. --->
    <CFELSE>
        <CFPARAM NAME="username" DEFAULT="">
        <CFPARAM NAME="password" DEFAULT="">
    </CFIF>

    <!--- if username and password are empty, cfa_secure will authenticate
          the user or use its own authentication storage (cookies or
session) to authenticate the user.  --->
    <CFA_SECURE
        SECURITYCONTEXT="sc1"
        USERNAME="#username#"
        PASSWORD="#password#"
        AUTHENTICATIONURL="/a2z/a2zlogin.cfm"
        R_BRESULT="bResult"
        R_STUSERPROFILE="request.stUserProfile"
        >

    <!--- if the user wants to see the sight in design mode, we need to
          make sure they belong to the administrator group --->
    <!--- <CFIF IsDefined("URL.DesignMode") AND bResult> --->
    <CFIF DesignRequest AND bResult>
        <!--- If the user has passed a URL variable for Designmode and they
              successfully logged in, then check to ensure the user is
              part of the Administrators group. --->
        <CFA_GROUPGET
            USERDIRECTORY="UserDirectory"
            GROUPNAME="Administrators"
            R_STGROUP="stGroup"
            R_LUSERNAMES="lUserNames">

        <CFIF ListFindNoCase(lUserNames,cfa_user)>
            <!--- Set the mode to design --->
```

continues

Listing 16.3 Continued

```
            <CFSET request.cfa.a2zbooks.mode = "design">
            <CFSET request.cfa.activeMode = "design">

            <!--- Preserve the fact we're in design mode in the cookie
                  Mode --->
            <CFCOOKIE NAME="mode" VALUE="design">

            <!--- Setting security on when in design mode --->
            <CFSET request.cfa.security.bIsSecure = "TRUE">

        <!--- Otherwise, kill any cookie and set the mode to browser --->
        <CFELSE>
            <CFCOOKIE NAME="Mode" VALUE="" EXPIRES="NOW">
            <CFSET request.cfa.a2zbooks.mode = "browse">
            <CFSET request.cfa.activeMode = "browse">
        </CFIF>
    </CFIF>
</CFIF>
```

Listing 16.3 contains only the parts of `application.cfm` that relate directly to security. In the a2zBooks application, we need to control several things:

- Anonymous users coming to the site need to be logged in to the default `anonymous` user account.
- Users who request to see the site in Design mode need to be authenticated, and then we need to verify that they belong to the Administrators group, which has permission to see the site in Design mode.

▶ **See** Chapter 5, "Navigating the Spectra Design Tools," for more information on Design versus Browse mode.

- Users who have logged in as a2z administrators through the `adminhome.cfm` template described above need to retain their credentials.

The first thing we do is check to see if the user arrived at this page by clicking a link that passed a logout URL variable. If so, we kill any existing mode cookie that may have been set earlier. The `mode` variable is used to control whether the site is displayed in Browse or Display mode. Next, we set a default for `mode`.

`<CFA_APPLICATIONINITIALIZE>` initializes the application using the value in `mode`, which is either the default or the value in `cookie.mode`, if `Cookie.mode` does exist.

`CFIF` checks whether the user has requested the `adminhome.cfm` template, which contains its own `CFA_SECURE`. If so, we don't do anything. If not (for all the rest of the pages on the site), the body of the `<CFELSE>` executes.

First, we check for the URL variable `designmode` or `mode`, which would indicate the user wants to view the site in Design mode. If so, we set the username and password to values guaranteed not to authenticate. This forces <CFA_SECURE> to display the login form specified in the AUTHENTICATIONURL attribute.

Next, we check if either the CFA_USER or CFA_PASSWORD cookie is missing; if so, this means that the user hasn't logged in, so we set username and password to anonymous to log him in as the anonymous user. If neither condition exists, we default username and password to empty strings.

Next, we call <CFA_SECURE>, which uses either the values in username and password (as set in the previous steps) or the cookie or session values of CFA_USER and CFA_PASSWORD to authenticate the current user. In the latter case, whoever is the currently authenticated user will remain authenticated.

Although the user has now been authenticated, if he is requesting Design mode, we need to verify that he is authorized to do so. So, when the user requests Design mode, we use CFA_GroupGet to get a list of all the members of the Administrators group.

The next <CFIF> verifies that the user is a member of the Administrators group and, if so, sets the request scope variables that control the mode of the site:

- request.cfa.a2zbooks.mode
- request.cfa.activeMode

We also set a cookie variable holding mode so it will be used for subsequent page requests. Finally, we turn on security when in Design mode by setting request.cfa.security.bIsSecure to TRUE. (Later in this chapter there is an explanation of the variable request.cfa.security.bIsSecure.)

If the user isn't in the Administrators group, we set the request scope variables that control mode to browse and expire the mode cookie.

CAUTION

In Spectra 1.0, setting security on objects doesn't appear to have an effect *unless* you have used <CFA_SECURE> or <CFAUTHENTICATE> to authenticate the user. In other words, elements that should be secure won't be if users can go directly to the page without being required to run <CFA_SECURE>.

For this reason, it's advisable to put <CFA_SECURE> into the application.cfm file so it will always run before any pages in your application.

Logging Out a User

Although the Webtop doesn't include a logout function, it's easy to write one. Listing 16.4 shows an addition to the adminhome.cfm page with which you worked in Listing 16.1. This doesn't show the entire template, only the part until the <CFA_SECURE> tag.

Listing 16.4 The Administrators' Login Page

```
<!---
File:         admin/login.cfm - Login form for administrators
Author:       david aden (david@wwstudios.com)
Date:         1/23/2000
Description:  Admin users call this template to get access to restricted
              areas of the site.

Notes:      This uses the guts of the login form that is used by CFA_secure
            in the application.cfm file -- although that is used to
            prevent someone from going into design mode without being
            authenticated.

Change History:

--->

<!--- Log the page. --->
<CFA_PAGE
    datasource="#REQUEST.CFA.a2zBooks.DATASOURCE#"
    pagename="Admin Login Page"
    sectionname="Admin"
    sitename="A2ZBooks"
    cachepage="No"
    bpreloadpageobjects="No"
    logpage="No"
    logcachedobjects="No">

<CFPARAM NAME="username" DEFAULT="">
<CFPARAM NAME="password" DEFAULT="">
<CFPARAM NAME="loginSuccess" DEFAULT="FALSE">

<!--- If we're coming to this page newly, it's because we want to log in
      so we need to clear the username and password's that are stored
      to force CFA_SECURE to present the login form. --->
<CFIF NOT IsDefined("FORM.username")>
    <!--- Kill any security-related cookies --->
    <CFCOOKIE NAME="cfa_user" EXPIRES="NOW">
    <CFCOOKIE NAME="cfa_password" EXPIRES="NOW">
    <CFCOOKIE NAME="CFAUTH" EXPIRES="NOW">

    <!--- Get rid of design mode login --->
    <CFCOOKIE NAME="Mode" EXPIRES="NOW">
</CFIF>

<CFA_SECURE
     USERNAME="#username#"
     PASSWORD="#password#"
     SECURITYCONTEXT="#request.cfa.security.securitycontext#"
     AUTHENTICATIONURL="/allaire/spectra/handlers/a2z/loginform.cfm"
     STORAGETYPE="Cookie"
     R_BRESULT="loginSuccess"
     R_STUSERPROFILE="request.stUserProfile">
```

Notice the boldfaced <CFIF> block right before the <CFA_SECURE> tag. This runs the first time the user comes to this page, which removes any existing authentication, so the user is forced to log in again. In essence, this forces a logout.

Turning On Security: Using Authorization

In the preceding sections, we've created policies that associate users and resource-action pairs. We also have coded the <CFA_SECURE> tag to authenticate users coming to our site.

The only major remaining task is to tell Spectra to use security checking—in other words, that it should use the data in the policy database to verify at runtime that the authenticated user is authorized to carry out a particular action. By default, security is turned off to allow you to turn it on selectively in appropriate sections of your site.

Spectra allows you to turn on security at several levels. At the lowest level, you turn it on for a method call. This is done through the BSECURE attribute of the <CFA_CONTENTOBJECT> or <CFA_CONTENTOBJECTINVOKEMETHOD> tag, as follows:

```
<cfa_contentobject
    datasource="#REQUEST.CFA.a2zBooks.DATASOURCE#"
    objectid="#iif(IsDefined('URL.ObjectID'),'URL.ObjectID',
             'FORM.ObjectID')#"

method="EditAuthor"
    stParams="#stParams#"
    bSecure="Yes"
    bAbortOnUnauthorizedAccess="No"
    blogging="No"
    busecache="No"
    r_stparams="stParams" >
```

Notice the BSECURE attribute. When this is set to "Yes", Spectra will verify the currently authenticated user's permissions to invoke the EditAuthor method. If the user has permission, the method is invoked; if not, the method isn't. <CFA_CONTENTOBJECT>'s behavior is controlled by the BABORTONUNAUTHORIZEDACCESS attribute. If this is set to "Yes", Spectra throws an error if an unauthorized user attempts to invoke the method; if set to "No", Spectra simply doesn't invoke the method and no data is returned.

To review, Spectra's decision as to whether the user has sufficient permission involves the following steps:

1. Spectra checks to see if a policy exists covering the selected method of the selected object.
2. If no policy exists, all users are granted access.
3. If a policy exists but the user is *not* associated with it, the user is denied access.
4. If a policy exists and the user *is* associated with it, he is granted access.

You can also turn on security checking for an entire request by setting

```
request.cfa.security.bIsSecure="Yes"
```

This has the same effect as setting the `BSECURE` attribute to `"Yes"` for all `<CFA_CONTENTOBJECT>` and `<CFA_CONTENTOBJECTINVOKEMETHOD>` tags within the request.

NOTE If this is set to `"No"`, the `BSECURE` attribute of `<CFA_CONTENTOBJECT>` can override it for individual calls to `<CFA_CONTENTOBJECT>` and `<CFA_CONTENTOBJECTINVOKEMETHOD>`.

In most cases, it's advisable to use `request.cfa.security.bIsSecure` to control security. This ensures that any nested calls to `<CFA_CONTENTOBJECT>` use enforced authorization and also keeps security management simpler.

Another request scope variable disables all security checking:

```
request.cfa.security.bIsAdmin="Yes"
```

This is used only to allow site administrators access to all methods and content. To demonstrate how security works, do the following:

1. Open `/A2Z/Catalog/ManageAuthors.cfm`.
2. Find the comment `Invoke the EditAuthor handler on the selected object.`
3. In the `<CFA_CONTENTOBJECT>` tag under this comment, change the value of `BSECURE` to `"Yes"`.
4. Go to the A2ZBook Admin login page at `/A2Z/Admin/Adminhome.cfm`. This displays a login screen, as shown in Figure 16.12.

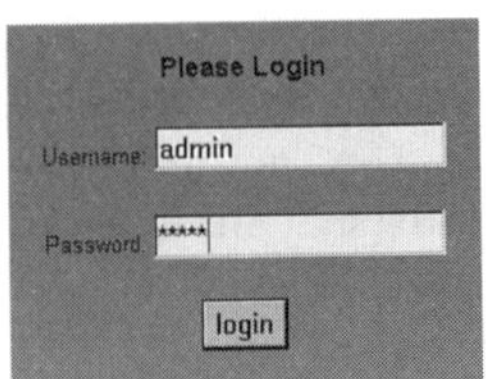

FIGURE 16.12
The administrator's login screen.

5. Enter the username **`admin`** and password **`admin`**. This tells `<CFA_SECURE>` to authenticate you as an administrative user.
6. On the success page, click Admin Links Page, which opens a window containing links used for administration purposes.
7. Click Manage Authors to open the template `/A2Z/catalog/ManageAuthors.cfm`.

8. Click an author's name to open a form for editing author information (see Figure 16.13).

FIGURE 16.13
The author editing form uses the edit handler for the Author object.

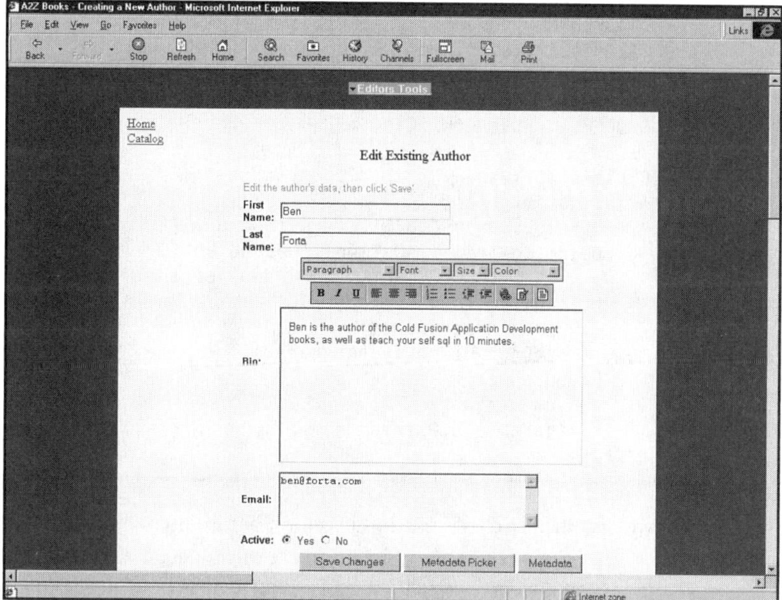

9. Now return to /A2Z/Admin/Adminhome.cfm and log in as anonymous with the password anonymous. The success page won't show the Admin Links Page link because you aren't logged in as an administrator.
10. In the browser Address line, enter **/A2Z/catalog/ManageAuthors.cfm**, and then click an author's name. The page will run, but the edit form won't be displayed because you are no longer authorized to invoke the EditAuthor method.

This example used the BSECURE attribute of <CFA_CONTENTOBJECT> to control access to the EditAuthor method. You could also turn on security for the entire ManageAuthor.cfm template by removing the BSECURE attribute from <CFA_CONTENTOBJECT> and placing the following at the top of the page:

```
<CFSET request.cfa.security.bIsSecure = "Yes">
```

Spectra also provides the <CFA_USERISAUTHORIZED> tag to explicitly check if the currently authenticated user is authorized to invoke a method. Rather than use the BSECURE attribute in the preceding example, we could have used the code in Listing 16.5.

Listing 16.5 The <CFA_USERISAUTHORIZED> tag

```
<!--- Invoke the EditAuthor handler on the selected object. --->
<CFA_USERISAUTHORIZED
    DATASOURCE="#REQUEST.CFA.a2zBooks.DATASOURCE#"
OBJECTID="#iif(IsDefined('URL.ObjectID'),'URL.ObjectID',
             'FORM.ObjectID')#"
    METHOD="EditAuthor"
    R_BRESULT="bIsAuthorized">

<CFIF bIsAuthorized>
    <cfa_contentobject
        datasource="#REQUEST.CFA.a2zBooks.DATASOURCE#"
        objectid="#iif(IsDefined('URL.ObjectID'),
                 'URL.ObjectID','FORM.ObjectID')#"
        method="EditAuthor"
        stParams="#stParams#"
        bAbortOnUnauthorizedAccess="No"
        blogging="No"
        busecache="No"
        r_stparams="stParams" >
    </CFIF>
```

Here we specifically check for authorization before invoking the `<CFA_CONTENTOBJECT>` tag. In this case, it's obviously more efficient to set the `BSECURE` attribute of `CFA_CONTENTOBJECT` or use `BISSECURE` instead of explicitly calling `<CFA_USERISAUTHORIZED>`. However, if you need to determine whether an entire block of code should be executed, you can use `<CFA_USERISAUTHORIZED>` and wrap the block in a `<CFIF>`.

Managing the Security Databases

As described earlier in this chapter, the security service uses several distinct datasources:

- *User directories.* By default, Spectra installs the `UserDirectory.mdb` Access database to hold user authentication, including group-association data.
- *Policy database.* By default, ColdFusion installs the `smspolicy.mdb` Access database to hold authorization information.
- *User Profile data.* By default, User Profile data is stored in the `cfaObjects` ContentObject Database. However, in most cases, your applications will use their own ContentObject Database that contains User Profile data.

In almost all cases, it's advisable that each of these databases be upsized as soon as possible. Upsizing the User Profile data occurs when upsizing `cfaObjects` or when you create an entirely new ContentObject Database.

▶ **See** Chapter 24, "Deploying Spectra Applications," for detailed instructions on how to create or migrate ContentObject Databases.

However, it's also advisable to upsize the authentication and authorization databases. Both of these can be upsized to either an enterprise-class database (such as SQL Server or Oracle) or to an LDAP server.

You can upsize `UserDirectory.mdb` to SQL Server with either the Access Upsizing Add-In, available for download from the Microsoft site, or by using SQL Server's import tools. For any other database, you need to use the database's own import tools. After you upsize the database, delete the existing `UserDirectory` ODBC datasource in the ColdFusion administrator and then re-create a new one with the same name that points to your new database. Be sure to include in the ODBC datasource definition the username and password needed to access the new database. Then, stop and start the SiteMinder services through the Windows NT services applet.

Upsizing the policy database, `smspolicy.mdb`, is similar but requires additional steps to reconfigure SiteMinder. The procedure is fully covered in an Allaire Knowledge Base article available at

`http://www.allaire.com/handlers/index.cfm?ID=14566&Method=Full`

Managing User Directories

User directories are simply datasources that contain username/password information, as well as a list of groups that individual users belong to. You can upsize the default user directory into either an ODBC datasource or an LDAP server. For example, to upsize the default `UserDirectory` into a SQL Server database, follow these steps:

1. In the Windows NT Services applet, stop the SiteMinder authentication and authorization services.
2. Upsize the Access database installed as `C:\Program Files\Allaire\Spectra\database\UserDirectory.mdb` (your path may vary) using Access's upsizing tool. (The Access upsizing tool is an add-in available as a free download from Microsoft.)
3. Using the ColdFusion Administrator, delete the existing `UserDirectory` datasource.
4. In the Administrator, create a new ODBC datasource called `UserDirectory` and point it at the new upsized database.
5. Restart the SiteMinder services.
6. Stop and start the ColdFusion server to ensure that it picks up the new ODBC DSN.

More often, however, you will need to configure Spectra to use an existing user directory, which may be an ODBC, LDAP, or Windows NT Domain datasource. In that case, the following steps are required:

- If you are using an SQL database, create an ODBC datasource through the ColdFusion administrator that points at the existing directory.
- If you are using an SQL datasource, create an entry in the SiteMinder initialization file that tells SiteMinder how to request data from the new user directory.
- Define the new user directory within Spectra and assign it to appropriate security contexts.

Configuring SiteMinder Query Files for ODBC and LDAP Directories

SiteMinder expects a certain structure in the user directories it manages. More accurately, it expects to be able to get certain data out of a user directory in specific formats.

To accommodate databases with different schemas, SiteMinder uses an `.ini` file that tells it how to get the specific data it needs from your particular database. The file is located under the ColdFusion installation directory as

```
C:\CFUSION\BIN\SmDSQuery.ini
```

Although it may look confusing at first, it's a relatively simple file of key/value pairs. The keys are a list of functions SiteMinder performs against a user directory; the values are the SQL commands it will use to request the data from your user directory. For example, the key/value pair for getting user properties from the default user directory is

```
Query_GetUserProp=select %s from Users where UserName = '%s'
```

The key, `Query_GetUserProp`, identifies the function defined by the entry. The value, `select %s from Users where UserName = '%s'`, tells SiteMinder how to get the data.

For each ODBC or LDAP user directory you define to Spectra, you need to create a section in the `SmDSQuery.ini` file. The easiest way to do this to copy an existing section and alter it to fit the new user directory.

To create a new user directory in Spectra, do the following:

1. In the Webtop, click System Admin.
2. In the left navigation, open Users and Security.
3. Click User Directories to display a list of user directories.
4. Click Create at the bottom of the list to open the User Directory form.
5. Enter a name and description for the user directory.
6. From the Namespace drop-down list, select the type of datasource. The choices are LDAP, ODBC, and Windows NT (see Figure 16.14).

FIGURE 16.14
This User Directory screen shows the settings of the default `userDirectory`.

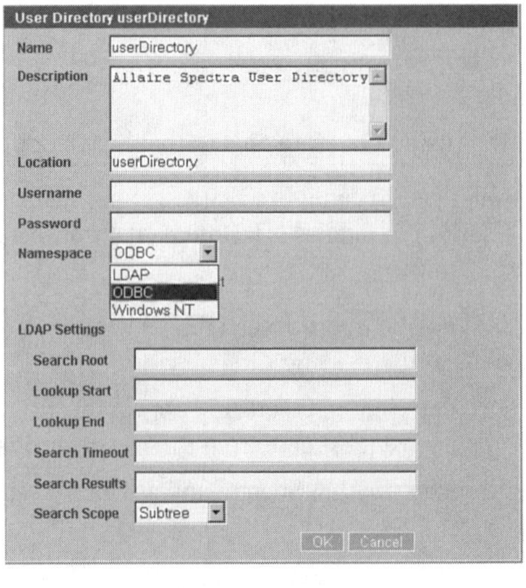

7. Depending on your choice in the Namespace field, enter any additional data needed to define your new user directory:
   - For an ODBC datasource, the Location field contains the name of the ODBC DSN.
   - For a Windows NT domain namespace, the location is the name of the domain controller or its IP address.
   - For an LDAP server, fill out the LDAP Settings section at the bottom of the form.

After you create the user directory, assign it to a security context. This is accomplished by following these steps:

1. In the Webtop, click System Admin.
2. In the left navigation area, open Users and Security.
3. Click Security Contexts to display a list of existing security contexts (see Figure 16.15).

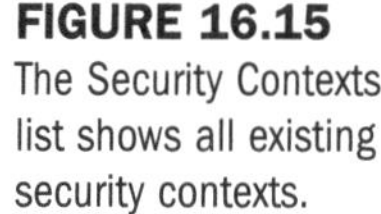

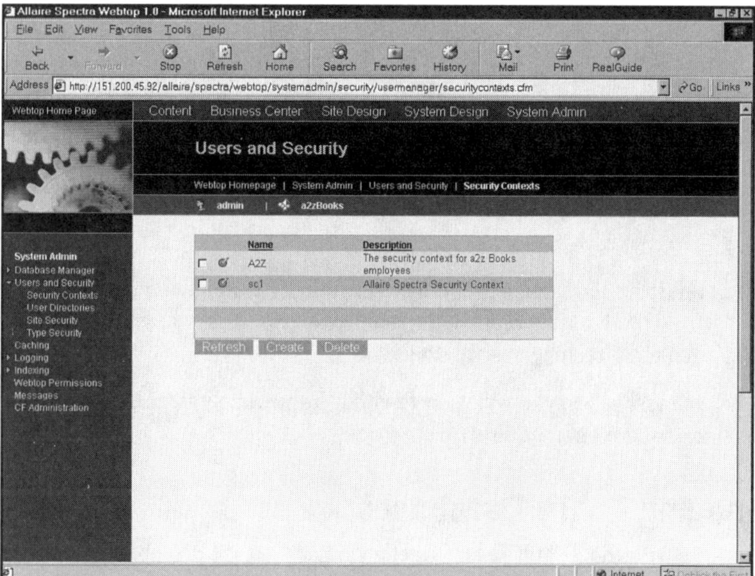

FIGURE 16.15
The Security Contexts list shows all existing security contexts.

4. Click the icon to the left of the security context name to edit the security context.
5. This opens a security context edit form. Click Directories to see the directories associated with the security context (see Figure 16.16).
6. To assign additional user directories to the current security context, select the user directory in the Available list, and then click the left arrow. Spectra associates the selected user directory with the current security context and the screen refreshes.

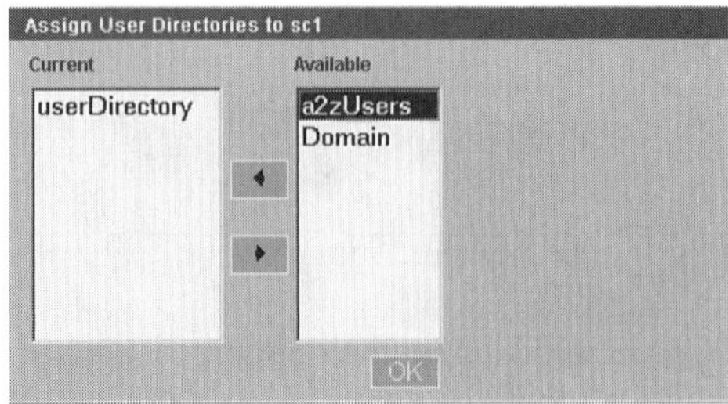

FIGURE 16.16
The `sc1` security context is now using the `userDirectory` directory.

> **CAUTION**
>
> Although it's possible to associate more than one user directory with a single security context, it's not advisable, because ColdFusion doesn't manage name collisions between multiple user directories assigned to a single security context.
>
> In other words, if the same username exists in two user directories assigned to the security context `sc1`, Spectra will behave unpredictably. Most likely, only one user will be able to log in. This is because when a user attempts to log in, Spectra searches in turn through all user directories associated with the named security context to find a match. As soon as it finds a matching username, it stops searching.
>
> Moreover, if a user is added to one of several user directories in a security context, Spectra doesn't automatically check to see if the user already exists in another user directory.
>
> Because of these problems, it's safer to limit all security contexts to one user directory.

Spectra allows you a great deal of flexibility when it comes to user directories. You can use the default user directory that ships with Spectra or any other ODBC, LDAP, or Windows NT domain directory-based services.

In most cases, you will want to either immediately upsize the default user directory or use an existing corporate directory service.

Managing Policy Databases

As with the default User Directory databases, it's possible to upsize the default policy database to an enterprise-class RDMS. For example, to upsize to SQL Server, follow these steps:

1. In the Windows NT Control Panel Services applet, stop the SiteMinder authentication and authorization services.
2. Upsize the Access database installed as `C:\Program Files\Allaire\Spectra\database\UserDirectory.mdb` (your path may vary) using Access's upsizing tool. (The Access upsizing tool is an add-in available as a free download from Microsoft at `http://www.microsoft.com/ACCESSDEV/ProdInfo/exe/wzcs97.ex`.)
3. Using Control Panel's ODBC applet, rename the SiteMinder Datasource DSN "SiteMinder Access Data Source."
4. Create a new SiteMinder datasource that points to your new `SQLServer` datastore.

5. Run `C:\cfusion\bin\smconsole.exe` (your directory may vary, depending on installation).
6. Click the ODBC tab.
7. In the Select a Database drop-down, select Policy Store.
8. In the Datasource Information section, enter the SiteMinder datasource, and then enter the SQL Server username and password used to connect to and access the database.
9. Click OK to save the changes.
10. Restart the SiteMinder services using Control Panel's Services applet.

You can also upsize the policy store to an LDAP server, but this requires a working knowledge of your individual LDAP server. For general guidelines, see Allaire's Knowledge Base article at `http://www.allaire.com/Handlers/index.cfm?ID=13335&Method=Full`.

Final Notes on Security

Security is an integral part of any large Web application. Spectra's security implementation is flexible enough to provide you with the tools to customize it to myriad applications. However, along with that flexibility comes some complexity. It's therefore important to master the basics of Spectra security and to plan its use early in your development process.

Part of this planning should entail how to distribute security responsibilities. Although substantial responsibility for Spectra security lies with the system administrator, some security functions can be delegated to other roles within Spectra's Spectrum of Participants.

Distributed Security Responsibilities

All Spectra security functions are available through the System Admin area, but some other functions are available elsewhere in the Webtop. This allows you to distribute security responsibilities to the people who should be managing them. The following Webtop sections include these security functions:

Webtop Section	Security Function(s) Available
Content	None
Business Center	User Manager (can manage users but not create new user directories), Site Security, and Type Security
Site Design	None
System Design	User Manager (can manage users but not create new user directories), Site Security, and Type Security
System Admin	Security Contexts, User Directories, Site Security, and Type Security

These roles should be part of any application security model.

NOTE For the latest information on Spectra security, be sure to visit the Allaire Security Zone at `http://allaire.com/developer/securityzone/` or subscribe to Allaire's security mailing list at `http://allaire.com/developer/securityzone/AlertUs.cfm`.

CHAPTER 17

Site Reporting

In this chapter

Introduction to Business Intelligence

The Spectra Business Intelligence service provides flexible architecture for defining and generating highly customized reports for your application. At the lowest level, it simply provides the infrastructure for logging application events in a simple text-file format. On top of this foundation, you can build rather sophisticated logging and analysis reports.

Tracking user interaction with your site is an important part of building any enterprise application. Various levels of your organization's management will *always* want to know more about how your site is being used, which includes data such as

- What are the most popular sections and pages?
- Are any bottlenecks affecting performance?
- From what pages or sections do people most often enter or leave the site?
- What are the most common paths people take through the site?

When working in a Spectra environment, you have access to at least three levels of logging:

- Logs generated by the Web server
- The ColdFusion server logs
- Log files generated by Spectra itself

NOTE This chapter covers only Spectra-specific logs; see documentation for your Web and ColdFusion servers to understand their logging and reporting capabilities.

Spectra's approach to logging is designed to be adaptable to many different application and system requirements. Although this flexibility makes it possible for the interactive developer to customize very specific log reports, it also means he needs to have a detailed understanding of how the Spectra logging service works.

Spectra Logging Terms

It's important to understand the basic terms Allaire uses to describe parts of the logging service:

- *Business Intelligence.* The general term used to describe Spectra's service that includes logging and report generation.
- *Observation architecture.* The logging part of the Business Intelligence infrastructure. It creates text files that contain entries describing user interaction with a Spectra site. It's implemented through the Log File ContentObject Type.
- *Analysis and reporting framework.* The set of services that processes raw log data into usable information. It includes the infrastructure used to generate reports from the processed data. It consists of the Log Report ContentObject Type, along with its properties and methods that allow the user to define new reports.

- *Log file.* A tab-delimited text file created by Spectra that contains logged information generated as a user moves through your application. These files contain the raw material from which you generate reports.
- *Log file directory.* A directory you specify in which Spectra creates log files. Usually, you will define a log file directory for each Spectra application.
- *Log (or report) datasource (or database).* A datasource that points to a database containing tables that are populated from the raw data contained in log files. This is referred to as a *Reports Database* in this chapter, although Allaire sometimes refers to it as the *Reporting Database*.
- *Report.* A display generated for a user that summarizes the data contained in the report datasource tables.

Following are the basic steps involved in turning on logging and generating default reports, each of which is covered in detail throughout this chapter:

1. Define a log file directory into which Spectra will write log files.
2. Use the Site Layout Model to adjust your application's logging settings to turn on logging for sites, sections, pages, or objects (Content Items).
3. Run the log file process handler to parse and move log file data into the Reports Database.
4. Run the Report Execute handler to query the Reports Database and build a report based on the returned recordset.

The reports that ship with Spectra will satisfy many user requirements. When they don't, Spectra allows an interactive developer to define highly customized reports.

▶ **See** "Designing and Programming Your Own Reports," later in this chapter, for coverage of how to design and write your own reports.

Using the Webtop to Manage Business Intelligence

Most logging management is done through the Webtop; we'll take up each part involved in setting up logging on your site in the following sections.

Defining a Log File

The first step in turning on application logging involves defining a log file directory so Spectra knows where to put the data. Although Allaire uses the terminology *log file* to refer to the following process, in fact we're defining a log file directory into which Spectra will write individual log files.

As part of defining a new log file directory, you need to assign the log file directory a Reports Database into which its data will be processed. The following example uses the installed `cfaObjects` ContentObject Database.

▶ **See** "Installing a Reports Database," later in this chapter for more information on creating a new Reports Database.

Let's create a new log file directory definition:

1. Click System Admin.
2. In the navigation area on the left, open Logging.
3. Click Log Files to open the Log Files form.
4. To create a new log file, click Create at the bottom of the list. This displays the Log Editor screen (see Figure 17.1).

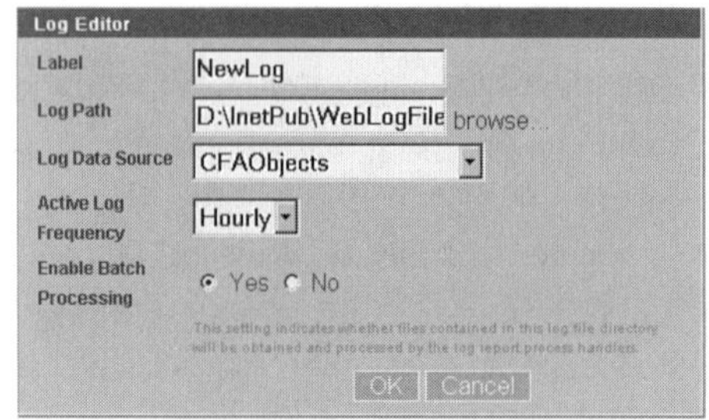

FIGURE 17.1
The Log Editor dialog allows you to define a new log file directory and associate a datasource with it.

TIP To edit an existing log file, click the icon to the left of the log file's name.

5. Enter **`NewLog`** in the Label field. This is the name that will appear in any lists of available log files.
6. Enter a directory into the Log Path field to specify the directory into which Spectra will write log files. This example uses `D:\InetPub\WebLogFiles`; the exact path will depend on your system configuration.
7. Select the ODBC datasource for the Reports Database that will house the processed data for this report. In this case, select `cfaObjects`, which we're going to use for our Reports Database.
8. Select Hourly for the Active Log Frequency field.
9. Leave Enable Batch Processing set to Yes. This is usually set to Yes unless you plan to process the log files outside Spectra using third-party software.
10. Click OK to save the log file definition.

Associating a Log File with an Application

Next, we need to associate the new log file directory with an application. Follow these steps:

1. Click System Design.
2. In the navigation area on the left, click Applications to display a list of existing applications.
3. Click the icon next to the iBuild application to display the Edit Application dialog.
4. In the Log File Object drop-down, select NewLog (the log file directory defined in the preceding section).
5. Click OK to save the changes.

CAUTION

In Spectra 1.0, a bug existed in the Edit Application dialog, so log files created in the System Admin area sometimes didn't show up in the drop-down box. This occurred when the Current Application setting in the Webtop Preferences window was set to an application that used its own ContentObject Database instead of the `cfaObjects` ContentObject Database. For example, the a2zBooks application example used throughout this book uses its own ContentObject Database accessed through the ODBC DSN `A2ZAccess`. In this case, log file directories you create won't show up in the Edit Application dialog box.

If this problem exists in your installation, it's easily fixed. Open this file:

```
Program Files\Allaire\Spectra\handlers\system\application\edit.cfm
```

At line 72, you need to change the `<CFA_CONTENTOBJECTGETMULTIPLE>` tag's datasource from `request.cfa.webtop.dsn` to `request.cfa.objectstore.dsn` so that it looks like the following:

```
<cfa_contentobjectGetMultiple
    typeID="2481659E-144C-11D3-AE340060B0EB4972"
    r_stObjects="stObjects"
    datasource="#request.cfa.objectstore.dsn#">
```

Turning on Logging for an Application

When an application is associated with a log file, you need to tell Spectra which events in the application should be logged. You do this by adjusting the site logging settings through the Site Layout Manager.

CAUTION

The link System Admin-Logging-Site Logging Settings opens a logging-specific version of the complete Site Layout Manager available through the Site Design area. You should be able to use this logging-specific interface to change the settings for your application.

However, a bug in Spectra 1.0 sometimes prevented this interface from working (this bug will be fixed in subsequent releases, including the maintenance release). If you don't have the fix available, you can change logging settings through the full Site Layout Manager available in the Site Design area, which is used in the examples in this chapter.

Spectra gives you the capability to control logging at the site, section, page, and object levels. Based on your reporting needs and site traffic, you will need to determine how much detail you want to capture. More granular reporting allows you to generate more detailed reports, but also involves more overhead—not only because Spectra has to generate more entries in the logs, but also due to the sheer physical size of the log files. Fortunately, it's easy to change logging settings for a particular site, section, page, or container. Let's adjust the logging settings for the iBuild application:

1. Click Site Design.
2. In the navigation area, open Site Layout Manager.
3. Click Site Layout Model. Figure 17.2 shows the current logging and caching settings for the available applications.

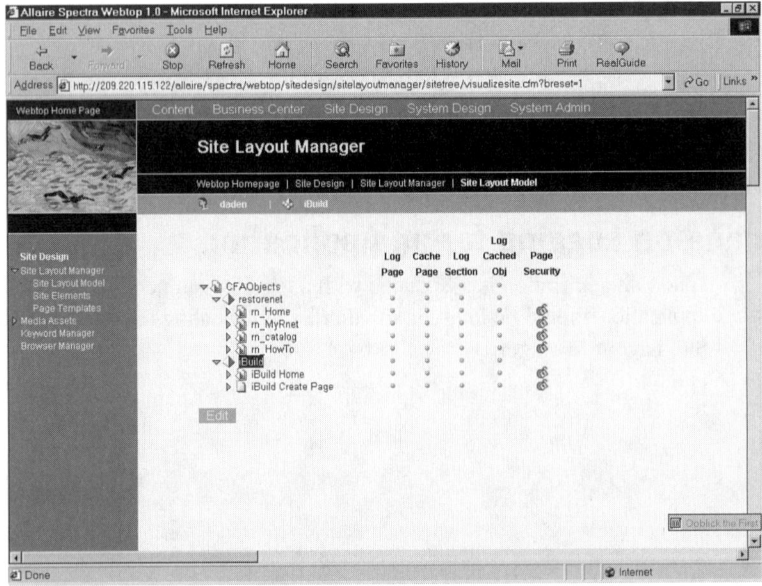

FIGURE 17.2
The Site Layout Manager provides an interface for viewing and setting your application's logging settings.

4. Click iBuild, the top level of the iBuild application.
5. Click Edit to open the Site Component Editor (see Figure 17.3).

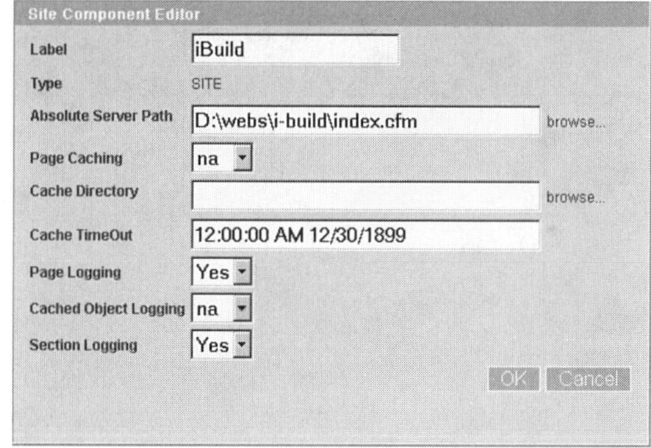

FIGURE 17.3
The Site Component Editor allows you to tune logging at the page and section levels.

6. To turn on page logging, select Yes in the Page Logging drop-down list.
7. To turn on section logging, select Yes in the Section Logging drop-down list.
8. Click OK to save your changes.

In this case, we've turned section and page logging on for the entire iBuild site because logging settings are inherited by lower levels of the site layout. Since we have set page and section logging on at the iBuild level, all page, section, and container access within our application will also be logged.

Container- and object-level logging settings are handled similarly, although the interface for adjusting a container's logging is somewhat different. To adjust the logging settings for a container, follow these steps:

1. Click Site Design.
2. In the navigation area, open Site Layout Manager.
3. Click Site Layout Model.
4. Open iBuild Home, the top level of the iBuild application.
5. Open the iBuild About page to display the containers on that page (see Figure 17.4).
6. Click Left Column to select the Left Column container in the iBuild About page.
7. Click the Edit button at the bottom of the Site Layout Manager. This opens a new window with the Container Editor, populated with the information on the Left Column container.
8. Click Settings in the left column to open a form for changing container-level settings, such as Caching and Logging (see Figure 17.5).
9. By default, a container uses the logging setting for the page in which it's located. To change this, make adjustments in the settings, and then click OK.

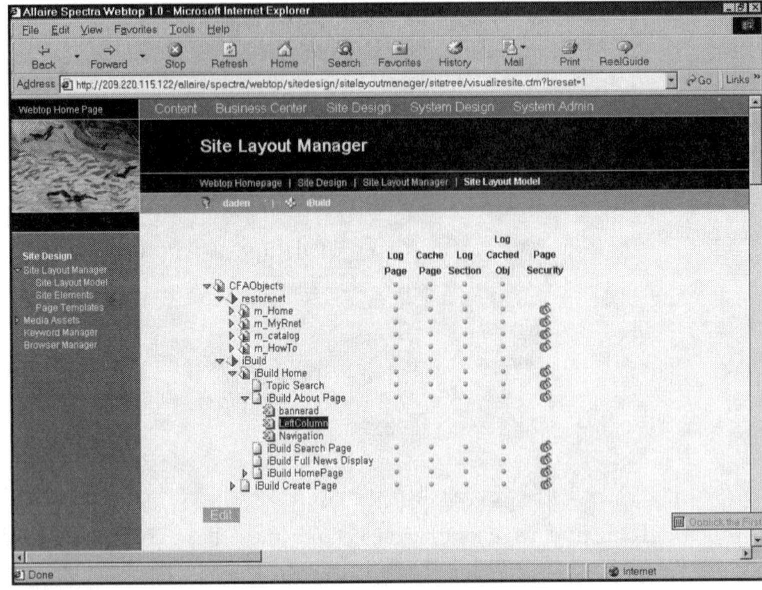

FIGURE 17.4
The Site Layout Manager allows you to select items down to the container level to manage logging settings.

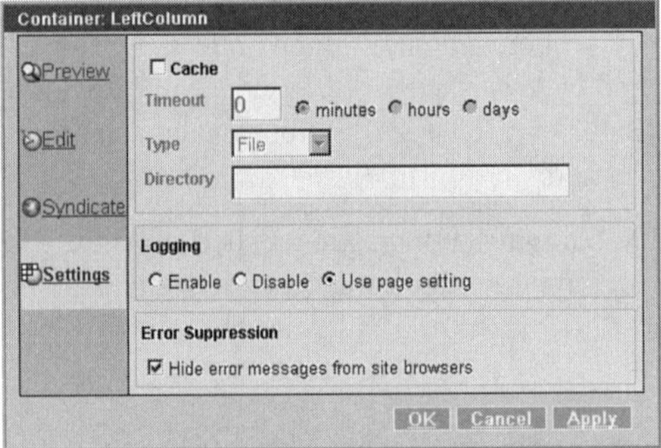

FIGURE 17.5
The Container Editor provides an interface for setting container-level logging.

Content Item logging is controlled through the `BLOGGING` attribute of the `<CFA_CONTENTOBJECT>` Spectra custom tag. It defaults to `No`, so to turn Content Item–level logging on, you need to set the `BLOGGING` attribute to `Yes`.

Because Spectra can generate a tremendous amount of log data, it's probably a good idea for large sites to begin with a relatively restrictive logging policy, increasing the scope of logging as needed. You may want to start with section and page logging turned on, but container and object logging turned off. Unfortunately, to do this under Spectra 1.0, you will need to turn off logging for each container individually in your site.

In summary, Spectra begins to collect log data and write it to log files once you have accomplished the steps described in the previous sections:

1. Create a datasource to contain the report tables (optional).
2. Define a log file directory.

3. Associate the log file directory with your application.
4. Turn on logging for your application at whatever level is appropriate.

However, to enhance performance, log data is buffered for several minutes and is written to the current log only when the next request for a page comes in after the buffer time period is exceeded. This means it may be several minutes before you see log files appearing in your log file directory.

Populating the Report Tables with Log Data

To generate reports from log data, you need to process the log files into SQL tables contained in the Reports Database. After the log files are processed, users can generate reports.

You can schedule the processing of log files off-hours or run the process handlers manually. To schedule the handlers, follow these steps:

1. Click System Admin.
2. In the navigation area, open Logging.
3. Click Reports to display a list of existing reports (see Figure 17.6).

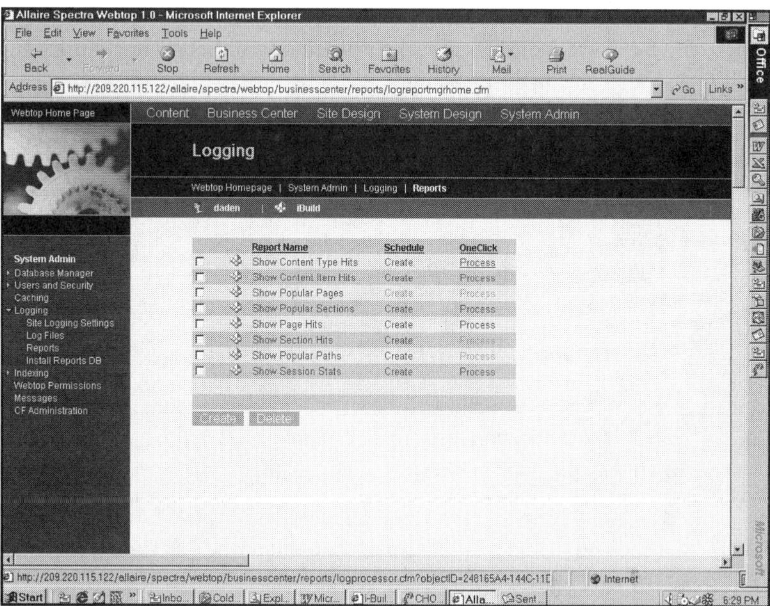

FIGURE 17.6
The Reports List displays a list of existing reports and provides an interface for processing the log files.

4. To define a schedule for the Show Popular Pages report, click Create in the Schedule column next to it in the list. This opens the Log Process Scheduler (see Figure 17.7).

FIGURE 17.7
The Log Process Scheduler allows you to schedule log file processing.

Log Process Scheduler - Show Popular Pages
Schedule Date
01/17/2000 Start End
Schedule Time
03:00:00 Start End
Repeat
Only Once
Daily
Weekly
Monthly
Every 1 minute(s)
Every 2 hour(s)
OK Cancel

5. In the first set of input fields, enter the date and time you'd like the handler to first run. This example uses 1/17/2000 as the start date and 03:00:00 as the start time. Adjust your date and times appropriately.
6. Optionally, in the second set of input fields, fill in the end date and time. For this example, leave this blank.
7. In the Repeat section, select whether you want to process the log files handler daily, weekly, monthly, or every few minutes or hours. For this example, set the process handler to run every 2 hours.
8. Click OK to save the schedule settings.

CAUTION

With Spectra 1.0, there appears to be problems with the Log Report Scheduler; schedule reports don't seem to run when expected. This might be fixed in Spectra 1.01.

You can also manually kick off log file processing by following these steps:

1. Click System Admin.
2. In the navigation area, open Logging.
3. Click Reports to display a list of existing reports (refer to Figure 17.6).
4. Click Process in the OneClick column next to Show Popular Pages. This starts the log file processing and displays a message when all unprocessed files have been processed (see Figure 17.8).
5. Click Back to return to the Reports list.

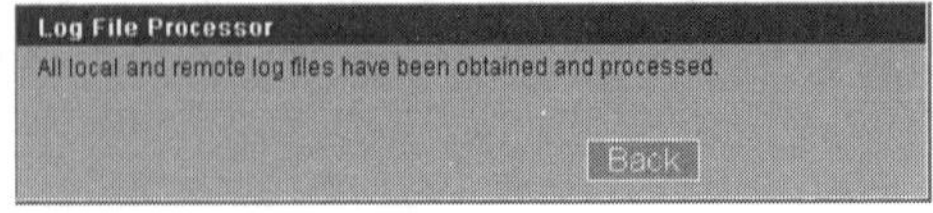

FIGURE 17.8
Spectra displays a completion message when it has processed all the log files.

Viewing Log Reports

The above sections describe the "back end" required to generate log files and populate the Reports Database used to generate reports that describe activity on your site. Once the above is in place, log processing happens behind the scenes for most Spectra applications.

After logging is set up as described, the most frequently used function of the Business Intelligence service is in the Business Center, where managers and others can access reports. To display reports, follow these steps:

1. Click Business Center.
2. Click Reports in the navigation area to display a list of the available reports (see Figure 17.9).

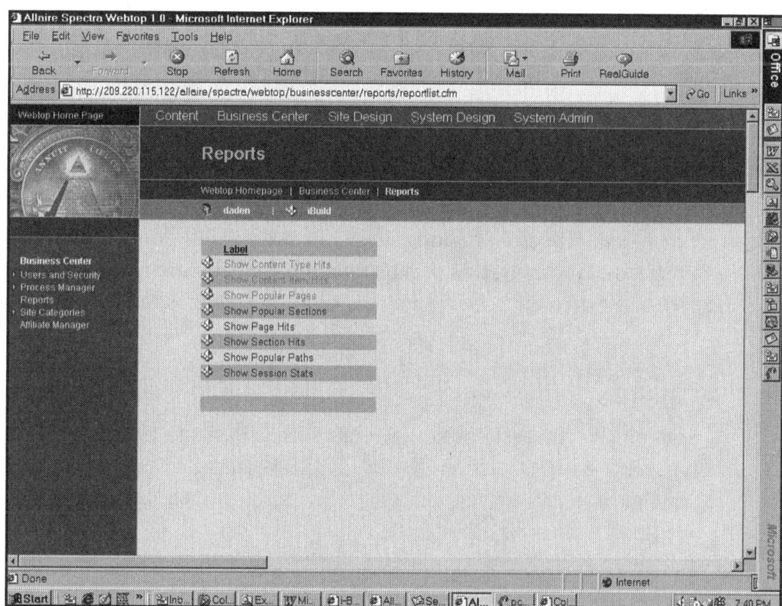

FIGURE 17.9
The Reports List shows you the available reports. Click a report icon to display the report.

3. Click the icon to the left of the Show Popular Pages report to display it (see Figure 17.10).

When the report runs, Spectra presents default report results, followed by a form for changing the search criteria. The customization options vary, depending on the specific report but typically might provide a way to limit the report by date, by objects reported, or by the number of items to display. In the Show Popular Pages report, you can specify how many pages to show and the date range to report on.

This report also includes a Reset button that allows you to rerun the report using the default criteria.

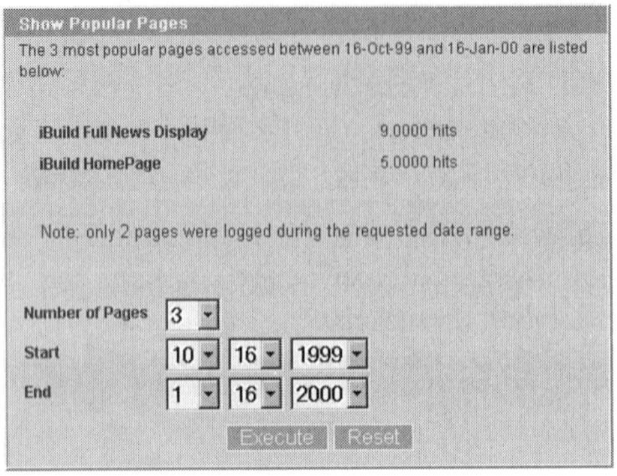

FIGURE 17.10
When you click a report, Spectra displays a default report result and gives you the option to configure it.

Show Popular Pages
The 3 most popular pages accessed between 16-Oct-99 and 16-Jan-00 are listed below:

iBuild Full News Display	9.0000 hits
iBuild HomePage	5.0000 hits

Note: only 2 pages were logged during the requested date range.

Number of Pages 3
Start 10 16 1999
End 1 16 2000
Execute Reset

NOTE Some default reports require the `CFX_J` to run properly. Make sure that this is properly installed and registered if, for example, you plan to use the Show Content Type Hits and Show Content Item Hits reports.

Installing a Reports Database

For most installations, it's recommended that you create a separate datasource for the Reports data. Spectra provides a way to create a set of default Reports tables in a datasource you specify. Normally, this section would have been included earlier in the chapter but, in Spectra 1.0, creating a new Reports Database caused some problems.

CAUTION

Although it's advisable to create a separate Reports Database for your application, this caused some problems with the default report in Spectra 1.0. As a result, the default report discussion is done using the iBuild example. Allaire reported that these problems would be fixed in a maintenance release, expected well before this book is published.

NOTE Before completing the following, you need to create an ODBC connection on your Spectra server. The following example uses an ODBC connection called A2ZSQLLog, which was defined through ColdFusion Administrator. For more information on how to set up a new ODBC datasource, see the ColdFusion Administrator manual. This datasource is shown for demonstration only and won't be available in your installation of the a2z application.

Use the following steps to create a new set of default Reports Database tables:

1. Click System Admin.
2. In the navigation area, open Logging.
3. Click Install Reports DB to open the Install Spectra Reporting Database window. Figure 17.11 shows the screen for selecting a datasource to install to.

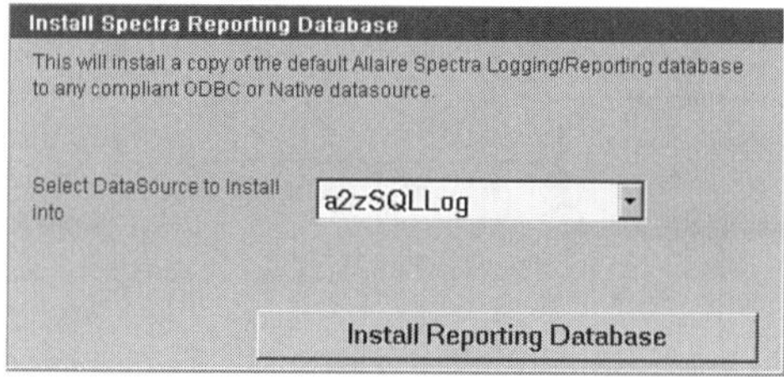
Install Spectra Reporting Database
This will install a copy of the default Allaire Spectra Logging/Reporting database to any compliant ODBC or Native datasource.
Select DataSource to Install into: a2zSQLLog
Install Reporting Database

FIGURE 17.11
The Install Spectra Reporting Database form allows you to install the tables necessary for the default reports.

4. Select the datasource you want to copy the Reports Database into. Here, we've selected the a2zSQLLog datasource.
5. Click Install Reporting Database.

This copies a set of three tables into the selected datasource. Data is written to these tables by the default handlers installed with Spectra, and the default reports access them to generate reports.

Designing and Programming Your Own Reports

Although the default reports provide a fair amount of information about your site, it's likely you will need to program your own templates to parse and analyze the log data and to customize reports to your needs.

The Spectra architecture for log analysis and reporting is intentionally flexible enough to accommodate the widest possible range of business needs. The cost of this flexibility is that the interactive developer will need to understand thoroughly how Spectra implements logging.

Programming the logging service entails actions performed through the Webtop as well as designing and writing CFML templates that analyze log files. Basic logging service administration, such as defining log file directories, associating them with your applications, and tuning the granularity of Spectra's logging all still need to be done when you start to write customized log analysis templates. See the previous sections of this chapter for full descriptions of how you set up the logging service.

The following sections describe the basics of coding the log handler and walk you through a typical example of what it takes to code handlers for a new report.

Logging ContentObject Types Overview

Before going into the particulars of a specific report, it might help to understand the underpinnings for the logging service, most of which is implemented through two ContentObject Types. It's important to understand the properties of these ContentObject Types and how they relate to the final product of a generated report. First, Figure 17.12 shows an overview of the Business Intelligence service.

FIGURE 17.12
The LogFile Content Item defines the location where Spectra will create the log files; the LogReport Content Item defines the handlers that are used to process the log files.

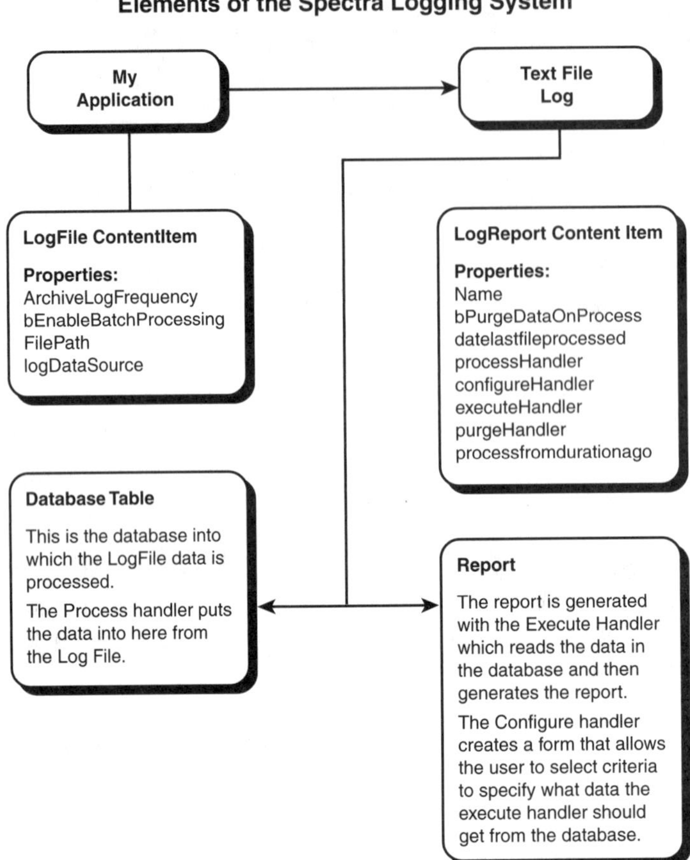

In Figure 17.12, the application (`MyApplication`) is associated with an instance of the LogFile ContentObject Type. Its properties include the following:

- `ActiveLogFrequency` specifies how often to create a new log file. The choices are `Daily` or `Hourly`.
- `bEnableBatchProcessing` is a Boolean that controls whether the log files should be included in the log file processing. This defaults to `yes`; generally, it's set to `no` only if you plan to use a third-party analysis tool.
- `FilePath` indicates the directory in which Spectra creates log files.
- `logDataSource` is the ODBC datasource associated with this log file. This is the Reports Database into which the raw log data will be processed.

The second object used in the logging service is a LogReport Content Item. This Content Item contains properties that define the location of the handler used to parse the log file, as well as the handlers used to generate the report. Its properties include the following:

- `Name` indicates the name of the report displayed in report lists.
- `bPurgeDataOnProcess` specifies whether the SQL tables that hold the report data should be purged before processing new log files.
- `DateLastFileProcessed` stores the date the log files were last processed. Spectra uses the data in this property to determine which log files need to be processed when the process handler is invoked.
- `processHandler` stores the name of the CFML template that reads the log file and processes the information into tables housed in the Reports Database specified in the `logDataSource` property of the LogFile Content Item.
- `configureHandler` indicates the name of the CFML template that presents a form from which the user can select criteria to customize the generated report.
- `executeHandler` indicates the name of the CFML template that queries the table(s) in the Reports Database and then generates a report.
- `purgeHandler` specifies the name of a CFML template that empties the tables used by the report. This template is called if the `bPurgeDataOnProcess` property is set to `yes`.
- `ProcessFromDurationAgo` stores a date indicating how far back the report should process log files. This is most important when a report is run for the first time, since it determines how many log files to process. After the process handler runs once, the `DateLastFileProcessed` property controls the files to process.

When you process log files, Spectra invokes the handler named in the `ProcessHandler` template once for each unprocessed log file, which it determines based on the value in the `DateLastFileProcessed` property.

CAUTION

Spectra determines which log files to process based on a date stamp embedded in the log files' names. Hence, you should never change the name of Spectra-created log files.

The process handler parses the log file, (optionally) summarizes or aggregates data in it, and then writes the results to the Reports Database specified in the `logDataSource` property of the LogFile Content Item. If you set the `bPurgeDataOnProcess` property of the LogReport Content Item to `Yes`, Spectra calls the Purge handler before calling the process handler to delete all the data in the Reports tables.

To display a report, Spectra invokes the Execute handler of the LogReport Content Item. This queries the Reports Database, then formats and displays the report. Usually, the Execute handler uses simple HTML tables to display a report, but it's also possible to pass the data to charting or graphing tags to produce more elaborate reports.

The Configure handler displays a form that allows the user to specify the search and other criteria used to generate the reports. When it's submitted, the Execute handler runs to display the report with selected criteria.

Defining a New Report

As with any reporting system, it's important for the developer to understand the business reporting requirements before coding starts. This is particularly true when working in Spectra, since creating a new Spectra report often involves creating a report-specific database table, writing code to appropriately analyze the log files, and then writing templates to generate the report itself.

Generally, the best way to design a new Spectra report is to "work backward," as follows:

1. In association with the business users who need the report, figure out what information the report needs to present and how it will look.
2. Work backward from there to determine the database structure you'll need to generate the report.
3. Work backward from there to determine how to extract the needed information from the raw log files into the Reports Database tables.
4. Work backward from there to determine what logging settings need to be enabled on your site.

For the example report, the business users have asked for a report that tells them how users move through the site—in particular, what are the most common section-to-section patterns. We need a report that segregates data by site and day and gives us a count of how often users went from one section of the site to another. To hold this data, we determine we need a database table that contains the following fields:

Field	Description
SiteID	The UUID of the site.
Day	An integer representing the day.
Month	The number of the month.
Year	The number of the year.
SectionPath	A two-element colon-delimited string. The first element is the section the person came from (the `FromSection`); the second element is the section the person went to (the `ToSection`).
HitCounter	An integer that holds the total number of times in any one day any user moved along a particular section-to-section path for a particular site.
SessionID	Used to temporarily hold SessionIDs while we are processing log files.

This table may already exist in your a2z installation, but if not, it can be created by running the template `CreateSectionReportTable.cfm` on the CD included with this book. This template simply runs the query in Listing 17.1.

Listing 17.1 Building the SectionReport Table

```
<CFQUERY NAme="CreateSectionTable" datasource="A2ZAccess">
    CREATE TABLE SectionReport (
        Day int NULL,
        Month smallint NULL,
        Year smallint NULL,
        SectionPath char (75) NULL,
        HitCounter int NULL,
        SiteID char (35) NULL,
        SessionID char (35) NULL)
</CFQUERY>
```

The next step is to work out how to get this data out of the log files.

Content of the Log Files

Spectra writes tab-delimited text log files with the following fields:

- DateTime contains a floating-point number that represents the date and time the entry was made. (This number can be formatted into a displayable date with ColdFusion's `DateFormat()` function.)
- Site ID shows the site UUID as contained in the Objects table of the ContentObject Database.
- Section ID indicates the section UUID as contained in the Objects table of the ContentObject Database.
- Page ID shows the page UUID as contained in the Objects table of the ContentObject Database.
- Object (Content Item) ID shows the Content Item UUID as contained in the Objects table of the ContentObject Database.
- Label indicates the label associated with the Content Item.
- Method indicates the method invoked on the Content Item. When Spectra records a page access, the value of this is set to `PageAccess`; when it records a section access, this is set to `SectionAccess`.
- Type(ContentObject Type) ID shows the ContentObject Type UUID as contained in the Types table of the ContentObject Database.
- Session ID indicates the unique session UUID associated with each user's session.
- User ID indicates the user's UUID as contained in the Objects table of the ContentObject Database.
- IP Address contains the value of the CGI variable `Remote_Addr`.
- HTTP User Agent contains the value of the CGI variable `HTTP_User_Agent`.

If a field doesn't contain a value, Spectra fills the field with the string `null`.

Creating a New Report

You define (and edit) reports in the System Admin section of the Webtop. If the a2zBooks application isn't already set up as the current application for the Webtop, set it as the current application now.

▶ **See** Chapter 5, "Navigating the Spectra Design Tools," for information on setting a current Webtop application.

Before you can generate reports for the a2z application, you need to use the steps described earlier in the chapter to

1. Define a log file.
2. Associate it with the a2z application.
3. Turn logging on for the a2z application through the Site Layout Manager.

After logging is turned on for the A2Z site, you need to visit the site to cause Spectra to generate some log entries. Spectra caches log entries for several minutes before writing the information to disk, so you may need to use the site for 5 or 10 minutes before the first records will be written to the log file you define.

To define the new SectionReport to the system, follow these steps:

1. Click System Admin.
2. In the navigation area, open Logging.
3. Click Reports to display a list of existing reports.
4. Click Create at the bottom of the list to create a new report. This displays the Report Editor.
5. Enter `Section Path Report` in the Label field.
6. Enter the Process, Purge, Configure, and Execute handler names as shown in Figure 17.13.

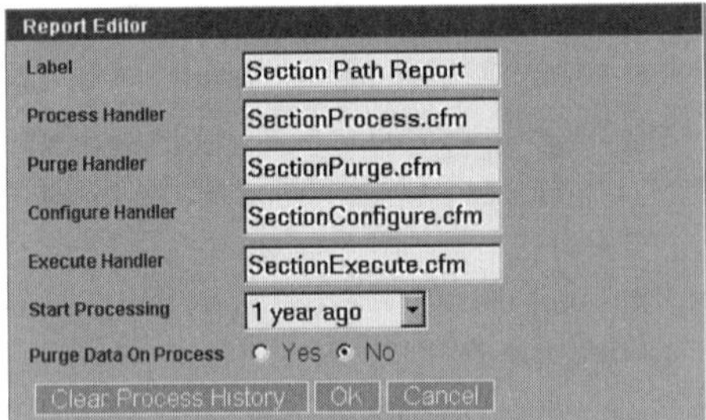

FIGURE 17.13
The Report Editor allows you to define a report to Spectra.

7. Leave the default in the Start Processing drop-down box.
8. Leave the default No for Purge Data On Process.
9. Click OK to save the report definition.

This defines Section Path Report to the system. The next step is to code the report's handlers.

To help understand what this form is doing, you might want to map its entries to the properties in the LogReport ContentObject Type described above.

Creating a Process Handler

WhenSpectra processes log files, it generates a list containing each log file that needs to be processed for a particular report. It then invokes the handler named in the LogFile's process handler property once for each log file in the list. Listing 17.1 shows the code for the Section Path Report Process handler. This handler reads and parses the raw data contained in each log file passed to it and then writes summarized information into the Reports Database.

Listing 17.2 Section Path Report Process Handler

```
<!---
File:         <SpectraInstallFile>/Allaire/Spectra/handlers/
                system/logreports/SectionProcess.cfm
Author:       david aden (david@wwstudios.com)
Date:         1/13/00
Description:  Process handler for the Section report. This will report on
              what are the most common section-to-section movements, i.e.
              how often users when from one section to another. A similar
              template could be used to find out what's the most common
              page someone goes to from the home page.

Notes:        Spectra passes the stParams structure in which is where all
              the attributes are.
--->

<!--- Set variables used throughout --->
<CFPARAM NAME="LogFile" DEFAULT="#ATTRIBUTES.stParams.logfile#">
<CFPARAM NAME="LogDataSource"
    DEFAULT="#ATTRIBUTES.stParams.LogDataSource#">

<!---Set a default for the maximum number of entries to handle. In this
     template, we're setting the value sufficiently high that it shouldn't
     limit file importing (if your logs have more a billion rows of data,
     the logs need to be created more often! --->
<CFPARAM NAME="logEntryMaxCount" DEFAULT="10000000">

<!--- Set the name of the Table we're going to go into --->
<CFSET TargetTable = "SectionReport">

<!--- Read the file in --->
<CFIF FileExists(LogFile)>
    <CFFILE
        ACTION="Read"
```

continues

Listing 17.2 Continued

```
        FILE="#LogFile#"
        VARIABLE="LogFileData">

    <!--- Rename the file so no one else does stuff with it while we're
          using it --->
<CFLOCK NAME="RenameLog" TIMEOUT="5">
        <CFFILE
            ACTION="Rename"
            SOURCE="#LogFile#"
            DESTINATION="#LogFile#.inuse">
    </CFLOCK>

<!--- Throw an error if the file doesn't exist --->
<CFELSE>
    <CFSET stDetail = StructNew()>
    <CFSET stDetail.file = LogFile>
    <CFA_THROW
        BABORT="1"
        ERRORCODE="filedoesnotexist"
        STDETAIL="#stDetail#">
</CFIF>

<!--- Set variables to hold the delimiters --->
<CFSET CR = "#Chr(13)##Chr(10)#">
<CFSET TAB = "#Chr(9)#">

<!--- List the fields in the LogFiles --->
<CFSET lLogFields="DateTime,SiteID,SectionID,PageID,ObjectID,
    Label,Method,TypeID,SessionID,UserID,IPAddress,UserAgent">

<!--- Set variables to identify the fields in the LogFile
      (for code clarity) --->
<CFSET Counter = 1>
<CFLOOP LIST="#lLogFields#" INDEX="CurrField">
    <CFSET Temp = SetVariable("#Trim(CurrField)#",Counter)>
    <CFSET Counter = IncrementValue(Counter)>
</CFLOOP>

<!-----------------------------------------------------------------
READ THE LOG FILE
Loop through the LogFile row-by-row, identify and count all the
      Section-to-Section combinations.

      NOTE: The stSession structure is going to hold the data from the
      LogFile. It has the following "structure":

      stSession[SessionID]["FromSection:ToSection"] = COUNT

      WHERE SessionID = the UUID of the session, gotten from the log.
            FromSection = the section the user started in
```

```
        ToSection = the section the user went to
        COUNT = the number of times the user went FROM the
          FromSection TO  the ToSection
----------------------------------------------------------------->

<CFSET stSessions = StructNew()>
<CFLOOP INDEX="CurrRow" LIST="#LogFileData#" DELIMITERS="#CR#">

    <CFIF ListGetAt(CurrRow,Method,TAB) EQUAL 'SectionAccess'>
        <!--- Get the data elements we need from the row --->
        <CFSCRIPT>
            // Date elements
            thisDayTime = ListGetAt(CurrRow,DateTime,TAB);
            thisDay = Fix(thisDayTime);    // Day (minus time)
            thisMonth = DateFormat(thisDay, "mm");
            thisYear = DateFormat(thisDay, "yyyy");

            // SessionID
            thisSession = ListGetAt(CurrRow,SessionID,TAB);

            // SectionID
            thisSection = ListGetAt(CurrRow,SectionID,TAB);

            // SiteID (I assume sessions are by Site, but we want to
            // record the site in the database.
            thisSite = ListGetAt(CurrRow,SiteID,TAB);
        </CFSCRIPT>

        <!--- Check if this is the first time we've seen
              this SessionID --->
        <CFIF NOT StructKeyExists(stSessions, thisSession)>
            <CFSET stSessions[thisSession] = StructNew()>

            <!--- Create a key to hold the previous section. (We can set it
                  to thisSection now because we don't use PreviousSection
                  until we handle the next row. --->
            <CFSET stSessions[thisSession].PreviousSection = thisSection>

            <!--- Record the SiteID for inserting --->
            <CFSET stSessions[thisSession].SiteID = thisSite>

            <!--- Set a marker to identify this as the first Section for
                  this session in this logfile.  --->
            <CFSET stSessions[thisSession]["null:#thisSection#"] = 1>
            <CFSET stSessions[thisSession].FirstSection = thisSection>

            <!--- Create a key for the First Section --->
            <CFSET stSessions[thisSession]["#thisSection#:null"] = 1>

        <!--- We've seen this session before and just need to add new keys
              or increment existing ones. --->
        <CFELSE>
```

continues

Listing 17.2 Continued

```
            <!--- Get the previous section --->
            <CFSET PrevSection = stSessions[thisSession].PreviousSection>

            <!--- Since we're going to set a ToSection for the Previous
                  Section, we need to delete the ":null" marker if it
                  exists. StructDelete() deletes the key if it finds it,
                  but doesn't fail if it isn't found. Added in the CFIF to
                  make the logic clearer. --->
            <CFIF StructKeyExists(stSessions[thisSession],
             "#PrevSection#:null")>
                <CFSET Temp = StructDelete( stSessions[thisSession],
                 "#PrevSection#:null" ) >
            </CFIF>

            <!--- Set a variable to hold the current PrevSection:thisSection
                  combo --->
            <CFSET CurrKey = "#PrevSection#:#thisSection#">

            <CFIF NOT StructKeyExists(stSessions[thisSession],CurrKey)>
                <!--- If not, then create it and initialize --->
                <CFSET stSessions[thisSession][CurrKey] = 1>
            <CFELSE>
                <!--- Otherwise, increment it --->
                <CFSET stSessions[thisSession][CurrKey] =
                 IncrementValue(stSessions[thisSession][CurrKey])>
            </CFIF>

            <!--- Update the Previous Section for this Session --->
            <CFSET stSessions[thisSession].PreviousSection = thisSection>
        </CFIF>
    </CFIF>  <!--- If to check for SectionAccess --->
</CFLOOP>

<!-------------------------------------------------------------
CREATE A KEY FOR THE LAST SECTION VISITED BY SESSION ID.
Let's loop through the structure and mark the last visited sections
      for each session -- the items left in "PreviousSection" are the last
      places a person was.

------------------------------------------------------------->

<CFLOOP COLLECTION="#stSessions#" ITEM="CurrSession">
    <!--- Get the PreviousSection --->
    <CFSET PrevSection = stSessions[CurrSession].PreviousSection>

    <CFSET stSessions[CurrSession]["#PrevSection#:null"] = 1>

</CFLOOP>

<!--- Create a Listing containing the SessionIDs --->
<CFSET lSessions = StructKeyList(stSessions, "|")>

<!-------------------------------------------------------------
```

```
GET ALL "LAST SECTIONS VISITED" ENTRIES IN THE TABLE -- ONLY GETTING THOSE
FOR THE SESSIONS WE FOUND IN THE CURRENT LOGFILE.
Let's get any existing items that have a SessionID because they should
      all be "UUID:null" in format -- they may be the previous items to
      ones in this log.
------------------------------------------------------------------->

<CFQUERY NAME="GetLastVisited" DATASOURCE="#LogDataSource#">
    SELECT *
    FROM #TargetTable#
    WHERE SessionID IN ( '#ReplaceNoCase(lSessions,"|",chr(39),"ALL")#' )
    AND SectionPath LIKE '%:null'
</CFQUERY>

<!--- Loop through the results --->
<CFLOOP QUERY="GetLastVisited">

    <!--- Set a var to hold the current SessionID --->
    <CFSET CurrSession = GetLastVisited.SessionID>

    <!--- Get the Section ID --->
    <CFSET EarlierBeginningID = ListFirst(GetLastVisited.SectionPath,":")>

    <!--- Get the Starting Section --->
    <CFSET FirstSection = stSessions[CurrSession].FirstSection>

    <!--- Construct the key for the first Section visited by the current
          session in this log --->
    <CFSET FirstSectionKey = "#EarlierBeginningID#:#FirstSection#">

    <CFIF NOT StructKeyExists( stSessions[CurrSession],FirstSectionKey )>
        <CFSET stSessions[CurrSession][FirstSectionKey] = 1>
    <CFELSE>
        <CFSET stSessions[CurrSession][FirstSectionKey] =
         IncrementValue(stSessions[CurrSession][FirstSectionKey])>
    </CFIF>

    <!--- Delete the item from the database --->
    <CFQUERY NAME="DeleteStartSection" DATASOURCE="#LogDataSource#">
        DELETE
        FROM #TargetTable#
        WHERE SessionID = '#CurrSession#'
        AND SectionPath = '#EarlierBeginningID#:null'
    </CFQUERY>

    <!--- Remove the FirstSection key --->
    <CFSET Temp = StructDelete(stSessions[CurrSession],FirstSection)>

    <!--- Delete the key from stSessions that shows the first Section for
          the current session (since we found an earlier beginning --->
    <CFSET Temp = StructDelete(stSessions[CurrSession],
```

continues

Listing 17.2 Continued

```
    "null:#FirstSection#") >
</CFLOOP>

<!-------------------------------------------------------------------
UPDATE the database section: This part puts the accummulated data
    into the database table for use with the reports.
-------------------------------------------------------------------->

<!---Get the existing data in there so we know whether to INSERT or UPDATE
     the data we got on this run. --->
<CFQUERY NAME="GetSectData" DATASOURCE="#LogDataSource#">
    SELECT *
    FROM #TargetTable#
</CFQUERY>

<!--- Create a structure to hold the existing data in the database
      This has the following structure:
          stExistingData[SITEID][SECTIONPATH] = HITCOUNT
        WHERE
            SITEID = The SiteID for the current site.
            SECTIONTPATH = The UUIDs of the "sectionpath", i.e
                a FromSection and a ToSection --->

<CFSET stPathData = StructNew()>
<CFLOOP QUERY="GetSectData">
    <CFSCRIPT>
        // If the SiteID doesn't already exist, create it and create the
        //  the key for the current SectionPath
        if ( NOT StructKeyExists( stPathData, GetSectData.SiteID ) ) {
            stPathData[GetSectData.SiteID] = StructNew();
        }

        // If the SectionPath doesn't exist already under the current Site,
        //  then create the key for it and set it to the HitCount.
        if ( NOT StructKeyExists( stPathData[GetSectData.SiteID],
            GetSectData.SectionPath )) {
            stPathData[GetSectData.SiteID][Trim(GetSectData.SectionPath)] =
                GetSectData.HitCounter;
        }
    </CFSCRIPT>
</CFLOOP>


<!--- Okay, now let's Loop through the data from the current log and add
      it into the data that was already in the table. --->
<CFLOOP COLLECTION="#stSessions#" ITEM="CurrSession">

    <!--- Note what the current siteID is --->
    <CFSET SiteID = Trim(stSessions[CurrSession].SiteID)>

    <!--- Remove the SiteID, PreviousSection and FirstSection keys as
          they would get in the way of the rest of this. --->
```

```
<CFSET Temp = StructDelete( stSessions[CurrSession], "SiteID" ) >
<CFSET Temp = StructDelete( stSessions[CurrSession],
 "PreviousSection" ) >
<CFSET Temp = StructDelete( stSessions[CurrSession],
 "FirstSection" ) >

<!--- Loop through the Session's info and gather  --->
<CFLOOP COLLECTION="#stSessions[CurrSession]#" ITEM="CurrPath">
    <!--- If CurrPath represents the last Section visited for this
          Session (in the current logfile), then we need to INSERT a
          record for it and include the SessionID. --->
    <CFIF REFindNoCase(".*:null",CurrPath)>
        <CFQUERY NAME="AddKey" DATASOURCE="#LogDataSource#">
            INSERT INTO #TargetTable# (Day,Month,Year,
                SectionPath,HitCounter,SiteID,SessionID)
            VALUES(
                #thisDay#,
                #thisMonth#,
                #thisYear#,
                '#CurrPath#',
                #Trim(stSessions[CurrSession][CurrPath])#,
                '#SiteID#',
                '#CurrSession#')
        </CFQUERY>

    <!--- Otherwise, if the current SiteID or the CurrPath keys don't
          exist in stPathData, then we need to INSERT a new
          record.  --->
    <CFELSEIF NOT StructKeyExists( stPathData,SiteID) OR
     NOT StructKeyExists( stPathData[SiteID],CurrPath)>
        <CFQUERY NAME="AddKey" DATASOURCE="#LogDataSource#">
            INSERT INTO #TargetTable# (Day,Month,Year,
                SectionPath,HitCounter,SiteID)
            VALUES(
                #thisDay#,
                #thisMonth#,
                #thisYear#,
                '#CurrPath#',
                #Trim(stSessions[CurrSession][CurrPath])#,
                '#SiteID#')
        </CFQUERY>
    <!--- Otherwise, we update the current path for the
          current site. --->
    <CFELSE>
        <CFSET NewTotal = stPathData[SiteID][CurrPath] +
         stSessions[CurrSession][CurrPath]>
        <CFQUERY NAME="UpdateKey" DATASOURCE="#LogDataSource#">
            UPDATE #TargetTable#
            SET HitCounter = #NewTotal#
            WHERE SectionPath = '#CurrPath#'
            AND SiteID = '#SiteID#'
        </CFQUERY>
    </CFIF>
```

continues

Listing 17.2 Continued

```
    </CFLOOP>
</CFLOOP>

<!--- Let's rename the current file to the original name. --->
<CFLOCK NAME="RenameLog" TIMEOUT="5">
    <CFFILE
        ACTION="Rename"
        SOURCE="#LogFile#.inuse"
        DESTINATION="#LogFile#">
</CFLOCK>
```

Listing 17.2 is a long and complicated example. However, the good news is that a report process handler is generally the most complicated report handler you need to write; the execute, configure, and purge templates tend to be much simpler.

The template begins by setting default variables. Allaire's documentation—and the Spectra 1.0 versions of the default process handler—all refer to or set attribute-scoped variables. However, because of the way Spectra invokes a report's handlers, it will never receive any attribute-scoped variables except for `stParams`, which contains keys for each variable the template can access.

By default, process handlers receive

- `stParams.LogDatasource`, which contains the Reports Database into which the process handler writes processed log data.
- `stParams.LogFile`, which contains the full path to the current log file that needs to be processed.

We set these to local variables and set a default for `logEntryMaxCount`, which we can use later to control how many log entries are processed per log file.

NOTE In Spectra 1.0, Allaire's default handlers set attribute-scoped variables because within the handlers the variables are used as one normally uses attribute-scoped variables. Conceptually, they fit into that scope. However, since log report handlers are invoked in such a way that they are unlikely to ever receive any attribute-scoped variables other than `stParams`, you can simplify the code by setting local, not attribute-scoped variables. It's likely the default report handlers will be revised in future versions to not use attribute-scoped variables.

Also, most of the default handlers use `CFPARAM` to set a value for the `logEntryMaxCount` variable and then limit the number of records they process for each log file by its value. However, in Spectra 1.0, you can't set this number from the Webtop. This is also likely to change in a future release.

The next section verifies the existence of the log file and, if found, reads it into a local variable. It renames the log file so no other processes will attempt to write or read to it while processing is occurring.

We then initialize variables to hold the row and field delimiters for the log file and do a `<CFLOOP>` over a list of the target table's field names to create variables named for each field. This is done to make later code easier to read.

The first major section of the template loops through the log file data, sequentially setting the variable `CurrRow` to the value of each row. We check if the Method field of the current row contains `SectionAccess`, since for this report we're interested only in section accesses. When we find such a row, we set several local variables that will be used to populate the `stSessions` structure we're using to accumulate the log data.

We then check to see if `stSessions` contains a key for the current session. If not, we create one and then create several keys under the current SessionID, including `SiteID` and `PreviousSection`.

The heart of the `stSessions` structure is keys made up of two SectionIDs, delimited with a colon. The first SectionID is `FromSection`, the second is `ToSection`. For example, if a user whose SessionID `= 100` starts in a section that has an ID of 3 (to simplify the example, we're using integer IDs rather than UUIDs) and then requests a page in section 2, we create an element that looks like this:

```
stSessions["100"]["3:2"]
```

The first time the user moves from section 3 to section 2, the value of this element is set to 1. Each subsequent time the user moves from section 3 to section 2, the value of `stSession["100"]["3:2"]` increments by 1.

What makes this a bit tricky is that whenever a user goes to a new section, the new section is both a `ToSection` and a potential `FromSection`.

So in the above example, if the user later leaves section 2 and goes to section 1, we'd also need a structure element that looks like this:

```
stSessions["100"]["2:1"]
```

To store the data when there isn't a predecessor (such as the section the user starts in) or an ancestor (such as the last section the user was in before leaving the site), we set the SectionID for the "missing" section to the string `null`:

```
stSessions["100"]["null:3"] (represents the first Section the user visted)
stSessions["100"]["1:null"] (represents the last Section the user visted)
```

Within the `CFELSE`, we look up the previous section for this particular session and then check to see if the `PreviousSection:null` key exists. If so, we delete it, since we now know the user did go someplace from the previous section.

We then check for the existence of the key PreviousSection:CurrSection. If we don't find it, we instantiate it and set its value to 1; if we do find it, we increment its value.

The next CFLOOP cycles through all the sessions contained in the stSessions structure and creates a key representing the last section the user visited:

```
<CFSET stSessions[CurrSession]["#PrevSection#:null"] = 1>
```

After this, we create a delimited list of the SessionIDs contained in stSessions:

```
<CFSET lSessions = "#lSessions#,|#CurrSession#|">
```

NOTE We use the pipe delimiter, |, and replace it later when lSessions is used in a SQL query. Originally, we tried using a comma to delimit the list but this caused problems with the SQL query in that case.

The GetLastVisited query gets any records from the table whose SessionID field is included in the list of SessionIDs we just created. We also limit the query to items that record the last section a user visited. We get this data to catch the situation in which a previous log file held data about a session that also has records in the current log file.

We loop through the recordset returned by GetLastVisited. First we set a local variable to hold the current SessionID, then we set a local variable to hold the SectionID at the beginning of the current session, that is, the last section visited under the current SessionID in the previous log file:

```
<CFSET EarlierBeginningID = ListFirst(GetLastVisited.SectionPath,":")>
```

From stSessions, we get the first section visited under the current SessionID in the current log file:

```
<CFSET FirstSection = stSessions[CurrSession].FirstSection>
```

We then construct a key made up of the EarlierBeginningID and the FirstSectionID and look for that key in stSessions. If it doesn't exist, we create it; if it does, we increment it.

We then do some cleanup, as follows:

- We use a <CFQUERY> to delete the Earlier Beginning row from the Reports Database table.
- We use StructDelete() to remove the key that holds the ID of the FirstSection in stSessions.
- We use StructDelete() to remove the null:FirstSection key.

The next step is to retrieve the data already stored in the Reports Database table because we'll need to integrate the data from the current log into it. We get the existing data with a simple query:

```
<CFQUERY NAME="GetSectData" DATASOURCE="#LogDataSource#">
    SELECT *
    FROM #TargetTable#
</CFQUERY>
```

We <CFLOOP> through the returned recordset and construct another structure, `stPathData`, to hold the data from the Reports Database. This is a "structure of structures." The first level structure contains a key for each SiteID; the second level structure contains keys for each SectionPath (that is, `FromSection:ToSection` combinations). In summary, this structure has the following schema:

```
stPathData["#SiteID#"]["#FromSectionUUID#:#ToSectionUUID#"] = #HitCounter#
```

Having now created the `stSessions` structure to hold the data from the current log file and the `stPathData` structure to hold the data already in the Report table, we combine the two. We do this by looping through `stSessions`:

```
<CFLOOP COLLECTION="#stSessions#" ITEM="CurrSession">
```

First we set a local variable to hold the SiteID and then delete the `SiteID`, `PreviousSection`, and `FirstSection` keys from `stSessions`, since we only want to examine the `FromSection:ToSection` combinations.

Part IV Ch 17

We loop through the keys associated with the current session:

```
<CFLOOP COLLECTION="#stSessions[CurrSession]#" ITEM="CurrPath">
```

If we find a key that identifies the last section the user visited—in other words, it looks like `#SectionID#:null`—we insert it into the database and include the SessionID (since we'll need this later to link it to records in the next log file). Otherwise, if we find a `FromSection:ToSection` combination in `stSessions[CurrSession]` that does *not* exist in the data contained in `stPathData`, we insert the new key into the Report table.

Finally, if the `FromSection:ToSection` key does exist, we add the `HitCounter` value in `stSessions` into the `HitCounter` value in `stPathData` and update the database.

The last step is to rename the log file.

As mentioned, this process handler is rather long and complicated. However, its sections are typical of the work you need to do in a process handler:

1. Read the log file and rename it to prevent contention.
2. Parse and aggregate the log file data as appropriate for the report you want to generate.
3. Integrate the parsed and aggregated data from the current log into the data that already exists in the Reports Database. This may involve inserting some new records while updating existing ones.
4. Rename the log file back to its original.

Coding a Configure Handler

The configure handler specified in the LogReport ContentObject Type gives the user an interface for selecting which records from the Reports Database to include in the report. The options you build into the configure handler are customized to fit the exact report you are building. Listing 17.3 shows the configure handler for the Section Path Report.

Listing 17.3 The Section Path Report's Configure Handler

```
<!---
File:        <SpectraInstallFile>/Allaire/Spectra/handlers/system/
                 logreports/SectionConfigure.cfm
Author:      david aden (david@wwstudios.com)
Date:        1/10/00
Description: Process handler for the Test Report

Notes:
--->

<!--- Set variables used throughout --->
<CFPARAM NAME="LogDatasource"
 DEFAULT="#ATTRIBUTES.stParams.LogDatasource#">
<CFPARAM NAME="ReportObjectID"
 DEFAULT="#ATTRIBUTES.stParams.ReportObjectID#">

<!--- Set the name of the table to look into --->
<CFSET Table = "SectionReport">

<!--- Set the SiteTypeID --->
<CFSET SiteTypeID = '6482A0A5-F75C-11D2-AE2E0060B0EB4972'>

<!--- Get the available Sites from the Report table --->
<CFQUERY NAME="GetExistingSites" DATASOURCE="#LogDatasource#">
    SELECT Distinct SiteID
    FROM #Table#
</CFQUERY>

<!--- Make a list of the sites found --->
<CFSET lSiteIDs = ValueList(GetExistingSites.SiteID)>

<!--- Get details on the sites --->
<CFA_CONTENTOBJECTGETMULTIPLE
    DATASOURCE="#REQUEST.CFA.A2ZBOOKS.Datasource#"
    LOBJECTIDS="#lSiteIDs#"
    TYPEID="#SiteTypeID#"
    R_STOBJECTS="stObjects">

<!--- Get a Range of dates available in the log --->
<CFQUERY NAME="GetDateRange" DATASOURCE="#LogDatasource#">
    SELECT Max(Day) AS MaxDate,
        Min(Day) AS MinDate
    FROM #Table#
</CFQUERY>

<!--- Get the query string --->
<cfset iif( Len(cgi.Query_string), "thisQueryString='?#cgi.query_string#'",
    "thisQueryString=''" )>

<CFOUTPUT>
<CFFORM
```

```
    NAME="SelectCriteria"
    METHOD="Post"
    ACTION="#thisQueryString#">
<TABLE BORDER="0">
    <TR>
        <TD COLSPAN="2" ALIGN="Center">
            <B>Configure Usage Report</B>
        </TD>
    </TR>

    <TR>
        <TD COLSPAN="2">
           Click "Submit" to generate a report of the most common paths --
           optionally, you can define a date range, pick a Site to report
           on or specify how many paths to show.<BR>
        </TD>
    </TR>

    <!--- Spacer --->
    <TR>
        <TD COLSPAN="2"> </TD>
    </TR>

    <!--- Show the sites --->
    <TR>
        <TD VALIGN="Middle" WIDTH="50">
            <B>Sites:</B>
        </TD>
        <TD WIDTH="250">
            <SELECT NAME="SelectSite">
                <OPTION VALUE="All">All
                <CFLOOP QUERY="GetExistingSites">
                    <OPTION VALUE="#GetExistingSites.SiteID#">
                        #stObjects[GetExistingSites.SiteID].label#
                </CFLOOP>
            </SELECT>
        </TD>
    </TR>

        <!--- Spacer --->
    <TR>
        <TD COLSPAN="2"> </TD>
    </TR>

    <!--- Pick a date range --->
    <TR>
        <TD VALIGN="Middle">
            <B>Date Range:</B>
        </TD>
        <TD>
            <INPUT
                TYPE="Text"
                SIZE="10"
```

continues

Listing 17.3 Continued

```
                NAME="MinDate"
                VALUE="#DateFormat(GetDateRange.MinDate,'m/d/yy')#">
                    <B>Start</B><BR>
            <INPUT
                TYPE="Text"
                SIZE="10"
                NAME="MaxDate"
                VALUE="#DateFormat(GetDateRange.MaxDate,'m/d/yy')#">
                    <B>End</B><BR>
        </TD>
    </TR>

        <!--- Spacer --->
    <TR>
        <TD COLSPAN="2"> </TD>
    </TR>

    <!--- Pick a date range --->
    <TR>
        <TD VALIGN="Middle">
            <B>Number to Display:</B>
        </TD>
        <TD>
            <INPUT TYPE="Radio" NAME="NumToDisplay"
                VALUE="All" CHECKED>All 
            <INPUT TYPE="Radio" NAME="NumToDisplay" VALUE="3">3 
            <INPUT TYPE="Radio" NAME="NumToDisplay" VALUE="5">5 
            <INPUT TYPE="Radio" NAME="NumToDisplay" VALUE="10">10 
        </TD>
    </TR>

    <!--- Spacer --->
    <TR>
        <TD COLSPAN="2"> </TD>
    </TR>

    <!--- Submit --->
    <TR>
        <TD COLSPAN="2" ALIGN="Center">
            <INPUT TYPE="Submit" NAME="ShowReport" VALUE="Submit">
        </TD>
    </TR>
</TABLE>
</CFFORM>
</CFOUTPUT>
```

Listing 17.3 is obviously much shorter and simpler than Listing 17.2. See Figure 17.14 for an image of what the configure handler generates.

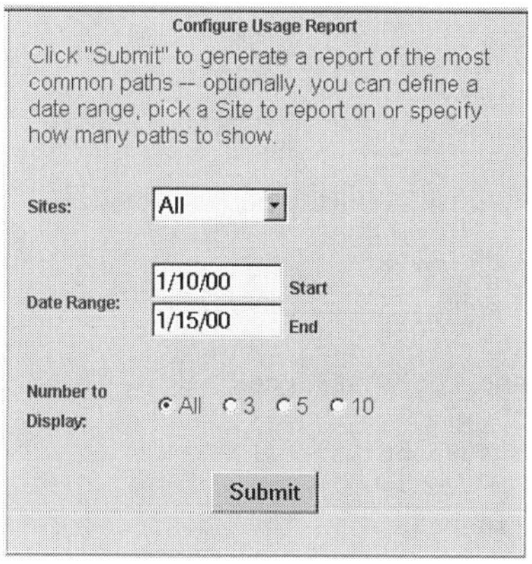

FIGURE 17.14
The Configure handler generates an interface that allows users to customize the data displayed by the report.

The template begins by setting into local variables the values passed in through `stParams`, then sets the name of the table that contains the data, and finally sets the UUID of the Site ContentObject Type (which is needed in the `CFA_CONTENTOBJECTGETMULTIPLE` we run later).

We then do three "queries" to get data we'll need to construct the HTML form:

- A simple `<CFQUERY>` on the Reports Database to list all the distinct sites it contains.
- `<CFA_CONTENTOBJECTGETMULTIPLE>` to get details about each site we found.
- Another simple `<CFQUERY>` to get the maximum and minimum dates available in the Reports Database.

The rest of the template creates an HTML form that allows users to specify the site they want to report on, the date range the report should cover, and the number of path combinations to display for each site.

Coding an Execute Handler

The execute handler can receive a submission from the configure handler to determine which records to display in the report, but it also must be written to stand on its own—that is, it must include default values sufficient to run the report without any information from the configure handler. See Listing 17.4.

Listing 17.4 The Section Report Execute Handler

```
<!---
File:         <SpectraInstallFile>/Allaire/Spectra/handlers/system/
                  logreports/SectionExecute.cfm
Author:       david aden (david@wwstudios.com)
Date:         1/10/00
Description:  Process handler for the Test Report

Notes:         This is the handler to display
--->

<!--- Set variables used throughout --->
<CFPARAM NAME="LogDatasource"
 DEFAULT="#ATTRIBUTES.stParams.LogDatasource#">
<CFPARAM NAME="ReportObjectID"
 DEFAULT="#ATTRIBUTES.stParams.ReportObjectID#">

<!--- The stColor structure is passed in that contains button
      and menu info --->
<CFPARAM NAME="stColor" DEFAULT=ATTRIBUTES.stParams.stColor>

<!--- Set the name of the table to look into --->
<CFSET Table = "SectionReport">

<!--- Default the variables that might be passed in --->
<CFPARAM NAME="FORM.SelectSite" DEFAULT="All">
<CFPARAM NAME="FORM.MinDate" DEFAULT="11/20/1984">
<CFPARAM NAME="FORM.MaxDate" DEFAULT="#DateFormat(Now(),'m/d/yyyy')#">
<CFPARAM NAME="FORM.NumToDisplay" DEFAULT="5">

<CFIF NOT IsDate(FORM.MinDate)>
    <CFSET FORM.MinDate = "11/20/1984">
</CFIF>

<!--- Convert the Min data to an integer --->
<CFSET numMinDate = Evaluate("FORM.MinDate * 1")>

<CFIF NOT IsDate(FORM.MaxDate)>
    <CFSET FORM.MaxDate = "#DateFormat(Now(),'m/d/yyyy')#">
</CFIF>

<!--- Convert the Max data to an integer --->
<CFSET numMaxDate = Evaluate("FORM.MaxDate * 1")>

<!--- Verify NumTodisplay is numeric --->
<CFIF NOT IsNumeric(FORM.NumToDisplay)>
    <CFSET FORM.NumToDisplay = 5>
</CFIF>

<!--- Get the data based on the criteria passed in --->
<CFQUERY NAME="GetData" DATASOURCE="#LogDataSource#">
```

```
    SELECT
        SiteID,
        SectionPath,
        Sum(HitCounter) AS MyHitCounter
    FROM #Table#
    WHERE 1 = 1
    AND Day >= #numMinDate#
    AND Day <= #numMaxDate#
    <CFIF FORM.SelectSite NOT EQUAL "All">
        AND SiteID = '#FORM.SelectSite#'
    </CFIF>
    GROUP BY SiteID,SectionPath
    ORDER BY SiteID,Sum(HitCounter) DESC
</CFQUERY>

<!--- Create lists for the SiteIDs and the SectionIDs
      we got with the query --->
<CFSET lSiteIDs = ValueList(GetData.SiteID)>

<!--- Create a structure to hold the Sections for which
      we need to get details --->
<CFSET stSections = StructNew()>

<!--- Loop through the SectionPaths we got from the query and create a
      structure element for each Section. This will likely make
      items more than one time, but we don't save much by wrapping it
      in a CFIF --->
<CFLOOP LIST="#ValueList(GetData.SectionPath)#" INDEX="CurrPath">
    <CFSET stSections[ListFirst(CurrPath,":")] = 1>
    <CFSET stSections[ListLast(CurrPath,":")] = 1>
</CFLOOP>

<!--- Create a list of the keys --->
<CFSET lSectionIDS = StructKeyList(stSections)>

<!--- Get the Site and Section objects --->
<CFA_CONTENTOBJECTGETMULTIPLE
    DATASOURCE="#REQUEST.CFA.A2ZBOOKS.Datasource#"
    LOBJECTSIDS="#lSiteIDs#"
    R_STOBJECTS="stSites">

<CFA_CONTENTOBJECTGETMULTIPLE
    DATASOURCE="#REQUEST.CFA.A2ZBOOKS.Datasource#"
    LOBJECTSIDS="#lSectionIDs#"
    R_STOBJECTS="stSections">

<!--- Display the results (Note: Since this is inside a handler, we need
      to wrap anything to display in CFOUTPUT tags for it to show up. --->
<CFOUTPUT>
<CENTER>
<TABLE BORDER="1">
    <TR>
        <TD COLSPAN="4" ALIGN="Center">
            <B>Section-to-Section Report</B>
```

continues

Part IV Ch 17

Listing 17.4 Continued

```
        </TD>
    </TR>

    <TR>
        <TD COLSPAN="2" ALIGN="Center">From: #FORM.MinDate#</TD>
        <TD COLSPAN="2" ALIGN="Center">To: #FORM.MaxDate#</TD>
    </TR>

    <TR>
        <TD ALIGN="CENTER"><B>Site</B></TD>
        <TD ALIGN="CENTER"><B>Source Section</B></TD>
        <TD ALIGN="CENTER"><B>Target Section</B></TD>
        <TD ALIGN="CENTER"><B>Hit Count</B></TD>
    </TR>
</CFOUTPUT>
    <CFSET PreviousSiteID = "">

    <!--- Loop through the GetData recordset --->
    <CFOUTPUT QUERY="GetData">
        <!--- If the current SiteID doesn't equal the current SiteID, set
              some variables that are used to govern the display. --->
        <CFIF GetData.SiteID NOT EQUAL PreviousSiteID>
            <CFSET PreviousSiteID = GetData.SiteID>
            <CFSET CurrSite = stSites[GetData.SiteID].label>
            <CFSET CountBySite = 1>
        </CFIF>

        <!--- If we've exceeded the number of items we're supposed to show
              per Site, then don't display anything... --->
        <CFIF CountBySite GREATER THAN FORM.NumToDisplay>
            <!--- Do nothing --->

        <!--- ...otherwise, display some info. --->
        <CFELSE>
            <TR>
                <TD>
                    <!--- If we're at the first row for a site, then
                          display the name of the site; otherwise, put
                          an empty cell. --->
                    <CFIF CountBySite EQUAL 1>
                        <B>#CurrSite#</B>
                    <CFELSE>
                         
                    </CFIF>
                </TD>

                <TD>
                    <!--- Display either the name of the FromSection or
                          "None" if the FromSection is set to "null" --->
                    <CFSET SourceSection =
                       Trim( ListFirst(GetData.SectionPath,":") )>
```

```
                    <CFIF SourceSection NOT EQUAL 'null'>
                        #stSections[SourceSection].label#
                    <CFELSE>
                        None
                    </CFIF>
                </TD>
                <TD>
                    <!--- Display either the name of the ToSection or
                          "None" if the ToSection is set to "null" --->
                    <CFSET TargetSection =
                      Trim( ListLast(GetData.SectionPath,":") )>
                    <CFIF TargetSection NOT EQUAL 'null'>
                        #stSections[TargetSection].label#
                    <CFELSE>
                        None
                    </CFIF>
                </TD>
                <TD>#GetData.MyHitCounter#</TD>
            </TR>
        </CFIF>
        <!--- Increment the Counter --->
        <CFSET CountBySite = IncrementValue(CountBySite)>
    </CFOUTPUT>

<CFOUTPUT>
    </TABLE>
    </CENTER>
</CFOUTPUT>
```


Although this handler is more complicated than the Configure handler, it's still far simpler than the process handler. Figure 17.15 shows what the Execute handler generates.

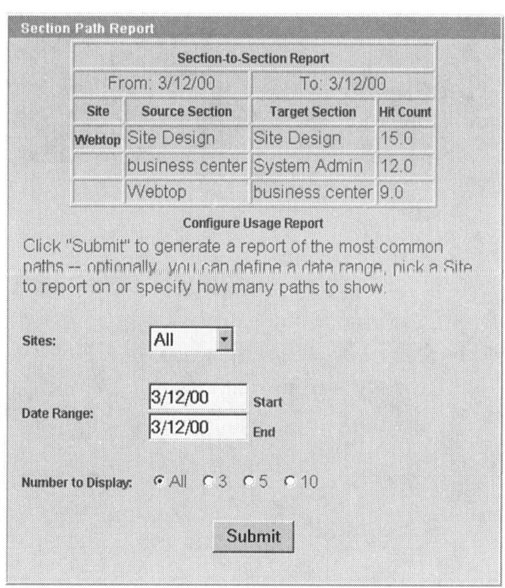

FIGURE 17.15
The Execute handler generates a report from the data stored in the Reports Database. The top half is generated by the Execute handler; the bottom half is generated by the Configure handler to allow the user to customize the report.

We begin by setting local variables for the values passed in through `stParams` and then use `<CFPARAM>` to set defaults for the `FORM` variables passed by the configure handler. We also do some type checking to make sure the values in the `FORM` variables match the types we need.

The `GetData` query retrieves the records, as specified by the `FORM` variables. Using the returned recordset, we create a list of the sites:

```
<CFSET lSiteIDs = ValueList(GetData.SiteID)>
```

We then create the `stSections` structure and create a key for each section about which we'll need to display information. Then, we generate a list of sections:

```
<CFSET lSectionIDS = StructKeyList(stSections)>
```

We then invoke `<CFA_CONTENTOBJECTGETMULTIPLE>` twice: once to retrieve details on all the sites, and again to retrieve details on all the sections.

The remainder of the template displays an HTML form that displays the requested information.

Running the Configure and Execute Handlers

You run user-defined reports from the Reports section of the Business Center just as you would for default reports (see Figure 17.16). To run the Section Path Report, click the icon to the left of the report name. Spectra invokes the Execute handler (which runs with default settings) and displays the report results. It then invokes the Configure handler at the bottom of the report to allow users to specify criteria and rerun the report.

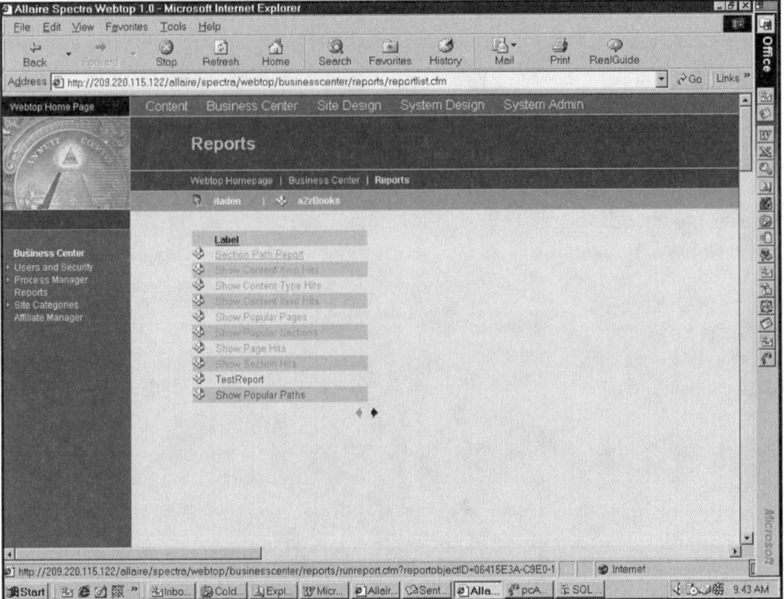

FIGURE 17.16
You generate a report by clicking its icon in the Report List.

Coding Purge Handlers

The Purge handler is run only if the Purge Data On Process option is set to `Yes` in the report definition (refer to Figure 17.13). When you set it to `Yes`, Spectra invokes the Purge handler before it invokes the process handler for any new files (see Listing 17.5).

Listing 17.5 The Section Report Purge Handler

```
<!---
File:          <SpectraInstallFile>/Allaire/Spectra/handlers/system/
                   logreports/SectionPurge.cfm
Author:        david aden (david@wwstudios.com)
Date:          1/17/00
Description:   Deletes all records from the Reports database prior to running
               the Process Handler.

Notes:
--->

<!--- Set the name of the table to look into --->
<CFSET Table = "SectionReport">

<!--- Delete the data in the Reports table --->
<CFQUERY NAME="DeleteData" DATASOURCE="#LogDataSource#">
    DELETE
    FROM #Table#
</CFQUERY>
```

This extremely simple template just runs a `<CFQUERY>` to delete all rows in the Reports table.

Listing 17.4—and the examples provided by Allaire—use the SQL `DELETE` command to remove data from Report tables. However, in SQL Server, it would be much more efficient to use the `TRUNCATE` command. `TRUNCATE` doesn't log the changes to the database, so it's much faster than `DELETE`. The only problem, of course, is that `TRUNCATE` isn't reversible, whereas `DELETE` is.

Although Allaire refers to this as the Purge handler, you aren't limited to using it only to delete records. It's just a template that runs before running the process handler when Purge Data On Process is set to `Yes`. So, in some circumstances, you could use it to do some pre-processing actions before running the process handler.

Offloading Processing to the Database

Although all the Allaire documentation examples and the default process handlers shipped with Spectra include CFML code to parse and summarize log file data, in many cases it may be advisable to offload this processing to your database server.

In installations of any size, you should set up a log server dedicated to analyzing log files and generating reports. Part of the process you'll need to establish in this case is to move the log files to

continues

continued

this separate machine (alternatively, you could have Spectra write its log files directly to the log server). Once the log files are there, you can use a relatively simple CFML template to import all the log file data into a single Reports Database table without doing any summarization. You then write logic within the database to summarize the data.

This approach promises several advantages:

- Process handlers tend to be complicated, which makes them more difficult to write and maintain. If you move just the log file data into the database without any transformation, the process handler becomes very simple.
- In most cases, databases should be more efficient and flexible about analyzing and presenting different views of the same data than you can be when writing ColdFusion code.

For example, in SQL Server 7.0, you could use the Data Transformation Service (DTS) to massage the raw log data into a data warehouse. This approach would enable you to use SQL Server's advanced OnLine Analytic Processing (OLAP) capabilities and multi-dimensional cubes, thereby minimizing the load on ColdFusion servers and maximizing the number and types of reports you could generate.

Since SQL Server includes efficient utilities for importing data, you may even want to dispense with the CFML parsing template altogether and just use native database tools to import the data.

Even under this scenario, you could still write Execute and Configure handlers the user would call to display the data, but those handlers would call into a database-generated view or multidimensional *cube* (a data structure that facilitates ad hoc queries along many *dimensions* or slices).

CHAPTER 18

Implementing Personalization

In this chapter

Setting Up Your Own Private Web

What do you see when you open your Web browser? Chances are you see one of the major portal sites, such as `My.Netscape.com` or `My.Yahoo.com`. What makes these sites so popular? You could say it's the information, news, and links they provide. But what really makes these sites interesting is the way that you can customize them. These sites, and many others, allow you to customize the news and information you see. For example, when I open my Web browser, I see technology, entertainment, and world news. I also see weather for my hometown and NFL sports scores. I set up these preferences with a customization tool.

This chapter discusses how you can use Spectra to add customization and user profiling to your Web site. We'll talk about the User Profile object and how you can save preferences and track user behavior. We will then discuss how you can take that information and provide a personalized Web site to the user.

Establishing Spectra User Profiles

Before we can begin creating a customizable Web site, we need a way to store information about the user. This can be biographical information (name, gender, age) or personal preferences (tech news, specific stock symbols). To store this information, Spectra provides a ContentObject Type specifically tailored for profile information.

The UserProfile ContentObject Type

One core system type that ships with Spectra is the UserProfile ContentObject Type. This type contains a set of keys that describe, in general terms, the facets of a profile. For example, keys exist for `JobTitle`, `BirthDate`, and `Gender`. The following list details the keys of the UserProfile type:

- `JobTitle`
- `Gender`
- `Department`
- `BirthDate`
- `EmailAddr`
- `Employer`
- `Name.firstName`, `Name.middle`, `Name.lastName`
- `Home`, `Business`, and `BillTo`
- `Preferences`

The `Home`, `Business`, and `BillTo` keys are all address sections. They each contain the following keys:

- `telecomm.mobile.intCode` (the international code for the mobile phone number)
- `telecomm.mobile.areaCode`
- `telecomm.mobile.number`
- `telecomm.mobile.ext`
- `telecomm.fax.intCode` (the international code for the fax phone number)
- `telecomm.fax.areaCode`
- `telecomm.fax.number`
- `telecomm.fax.ext`
- `telecomm.phone.intCode` (the international code for the phone number)
- `telecomm.phone.areaCode`
- `telecomm.phone.number`
- `telecomm.phone.ext`
- `telecomm.pager.intCode` (the international code for a pager number)
- `telecomm.pager.areaCode`
- `telecomm.pager.number`
- `telecomm.pager.ext`
- `electronicInfo.email`
- `electronicInfo.homepage`
- `postal.streetAddress`
- `postal.statProv` (state or province)
- `postal.city`
- `postal.countryCode`
- `postal.postalCode`
- `postal.postalName.firstName`, `postal.postalName.middleName`, `postal.postalName.lastName`

Each key can be populated with relevant data. For example, you may want to add a user survey that asks for some of the information listed above. When you have this information stored in a user profile, Spectra provides an easy way to retrieve it.v

NOTE The UserProfile ContentObject doesn't have any methods. It has only properties that you can store information in.

NOTE Spectra's implementation of user profiles is based on W3C's P3P base data set. This set of information is still being developed, and it's expected that Spectra's User Profile will be updated to match the final profile decided upon by the W3C. For more information, go to `http://www.w3c.org/p3p`.

Creating User Profiles

So now that we know what kind of information can be stored in user profiles, how do we start using them? Like many other aspects of Spectra, we can define user profiles in either the Webtop or via custom tags. Creating a user profile in the Webtop isn't very interesting, because the Webtop actually does it in the background when you edit the profile. Since we will be looking at that later in the chapter, let's take a look at how we can create a user profile with <CFA> tags. Listing 18.1 creates a user profile for a new user.

Listing 18.1 *createUserProfile.cfm*—Creating a User Profile for a New User

```
<!---
File:        /a2zTestScripts/createUserProfile.cfm
Author:      Raymond Camden (raymond.k.camden@syntegra.com)
Date:        12/1/1999
Description: Creates a user and a user profile.
Notes:
--->

<!--- Sets up some default variables Spectra needs --->
<CFA_GLOBALSETTINGS>

<!--- The name of our new User. --->
<CFSET User="TestUser">

<!--- The password. --->
<CFSET Password="Foo">

<!--- The description of the user. --->
<CFSET Description="This is a temporary user.">

<!--- Use cfa_userget to check to see if the user already exists --->
<CFA_USERGET USERDIRECTORY="UserDirectory" USERNAME="#User#"
        r_stuser="myuser">

<!--- If the user does not exist then create the user --->
<cfif not isdefined("myuser.username")>

        <!--- Create a new user in the UserDirectory user directory. --->
        <CFA_USERCREATE USERDIRECTORY="UserDirectory" USERNAME="#User#"
         PASSWORD="#Password#" DESCRIPTION="#Description#">

        <CFOUTPUT>
        The user, #User#, has been created.
        <P>
        </CFOUTPUT>

        <!--- Create the userProfile --->
        <CFA_USERPROFILECREATE DATASOURCE="a2zAccess" USERNAME="#User#"
        R_STUSERPROFILE="myProfile">
```

```
        I have created a profile. Here it is...
        <P>

        <CFA_DUMP VAR="#myProfile#">

<CFELSE>

      The user is already defined.

</CFIF>
```

Let's look at this script and see what's going on. Listing 18.1 begins with <CFA_GLOBALSETTINGS>. We have described this tag before but, in case you forgot, it's kind of a "setup" tag for Spectra files that are run outside of a <CFA_APPLICATIONINITIALIZE> scope. After that tag, we then set up a few variables for the username, password, and description.

NOTE Since we are creating a user on your Spectra system, it may be in your best interest to remove this user as soon as you are done with this chapter. Conversely, you may alter the line that sets the name of the user or the password.

Our second Spectra tag is <CFA_USERGET>. This tag checks for the existence of the user. The first attribute we pass is USERDIRECTORY. This tells Spectra in what user directory we are looking for the user. The second is the USERNAME we are checking. The third is the r_stUser attribute, which allows you to specify the structure's name. We then check to see whether the variable exists. If a user is found, the structure returned will contain the user's username, password, and description. I cut out the table and rewrote the text in one sentence.

Now we can call <CFA_USERCREATE>. As you can guess, this creates a new user. The first attribute we pass is the USERDIRECTORY, which tells Spectra what user directory will store the user.

▶ **See** Chapter 16, "Using Spectra Security Options," for more information on user directories.

After passing in the USERDIRECTORY, we then pass in the USERNAME, PASSWORD, and DESCRIPTION attributes. We will use the values we created earlier in the script. After we create the user, we output a simple message stating so.

After creating the user, we next call <CFA_USERPROFILECREATE>. This tag will create a copy of the UserProfile object. We assign it to the user by passing the USERNAME attribute. User profiles are stored in the ContentObject Database, so we have to pass in a DATASOURCE attribute as well. Last but not least, we can optionally pass in an attribute and ask for a copy of the user profile to be returned to us. As you can imagine, this user profile will be empty, since we haven't saved any information about this user. We end the script by <CFA_DUMP>ing the user profile we created. You can see keys (with no values) for the parts of the user profile we described earlier in this chapter. Figure 18.1 shows the results of this script as seen in the browser.

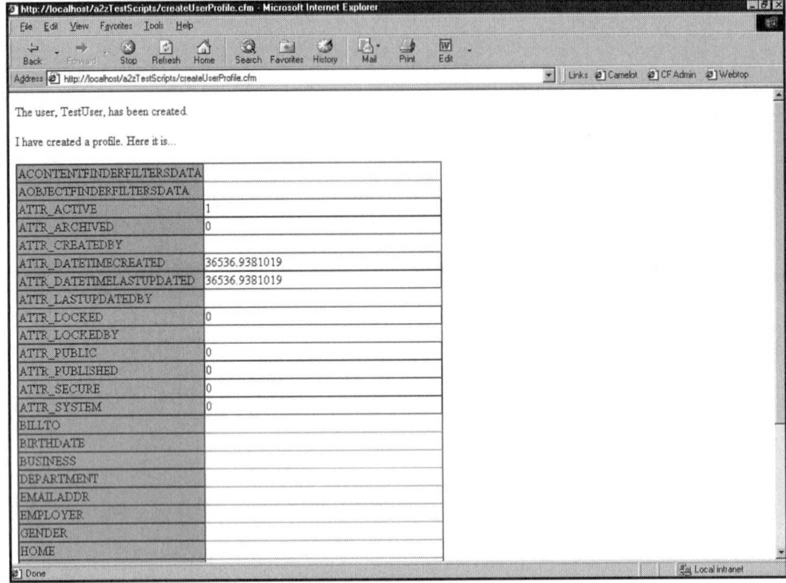

FIGURE 18.1
The results of creating a user and a profile and dumping the profile.

NOTE Don't forget that the `UserProfile` object is stored in the ContentObject Database, *not* the User Directory Database. The actual user (and password) is stored in the user directory called `UserDirectory`. This is created by the Spectra installation program and is an Access database. If you are familiar with ColdFusion's Advanced Security service, you know that user directories can be databases, LDAP servers, or Windows NT users. The important thing to remember here is that the user is stored in the user directory and the profile in the ContentObject Database. This means that although there may be one username `jedimaster`, the username may have multiple user profiles, one in each of several ContentObject Databases.

Defining User Profiles

Now that we have created a user profile, let's see how we can insert information into it. As you can imagine, we can edit user profiles with either the Webtop or a CFA custom tag. Let's look at editing profiles via the Webtop first.

To call up a user's profile so you can edit it, follow these steps:

1. In the Business Center, click the Users and Security section and then the User Manager.

NOTE You can also access the User Manager via the System Admin section of the Webtop.

The User Manager displays all known user directories on the system. For each user directory, you can view the users and groups or edit information about the user directory. Figure 18.2 shows the User Manager.

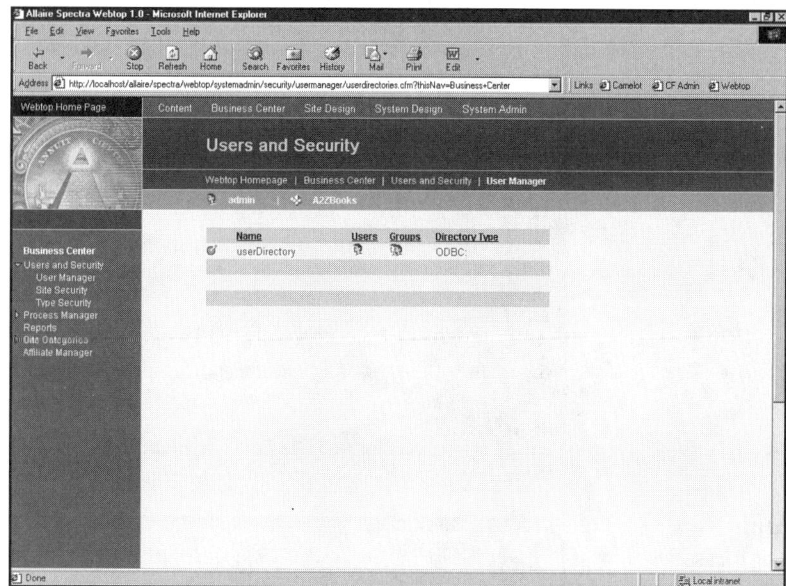

FIGURE 18.2
The Webtop's User Manager.

2. To get to a user profile, click the face icon beneath the Users column. Be sure to click the icon in the same row as the `UserDirectory` user directory.

   The next screen lists users in the user directory. You should see the user we just created, `TestUser`. Figure 18.3 shows the users in the user directory.

3. Click the icon beneath the Edit column next to the user you want to edit. Click the icon in the same row as `TestUser`, the user we just created.

The next screen displays the user profile for `TestUser`. A few tabs across the top of the screen split the user profile's numerous keys into appropriate sections. Figure 18.4 shows the Personal tab of the User Directory screen.

Feel free to play around with the profile. Give `TestUser` a name or a job title. When you want to save a preference, be sure to click the Apply button at the bottom of the form. The tab that may be most interesting is the Preferences screen. When you first examine it, there will (most likely) be no preferences at all on this tag. The Spectra Webtop allows you to add specific keys *and* values with this form. To test this, add a new preference by using the following values:

- New Preference Name: `FavoriteMovie`
- New Preference Value: `Star Wars`

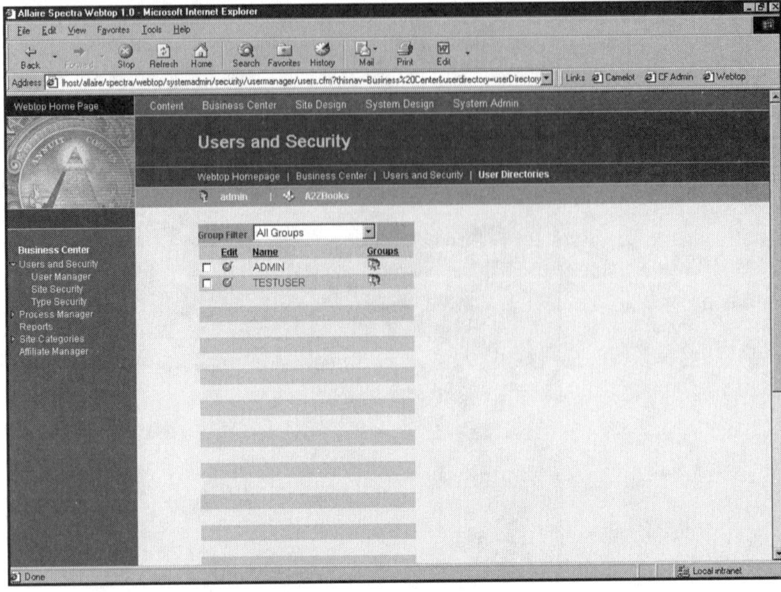

FIGURE 18.3
The `UserDirectory` user directory.

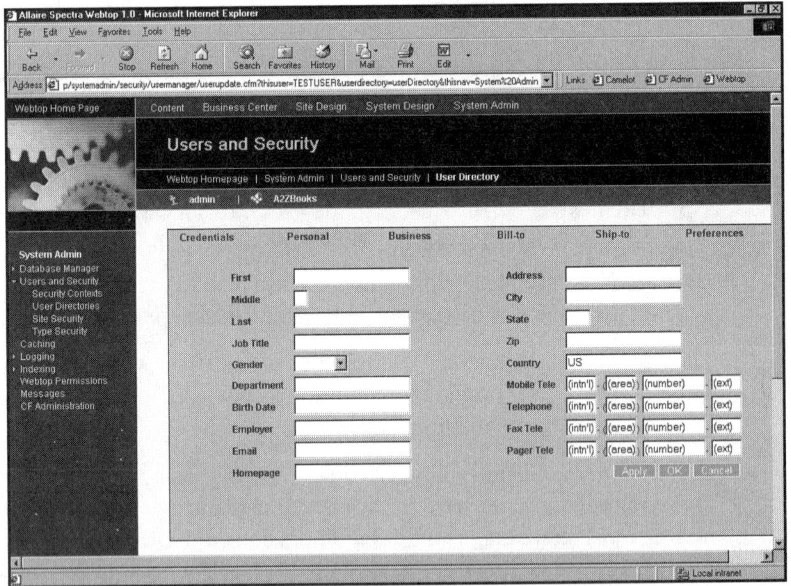

FIGURE 18.4
Editing the user profile.

Next, click the Apply button. Spectra will add a new key to the Preferences section of the user profile. The name of this key will be `FavoriteMovie`, and the value will be `Star Wars`. Figure 18.5 shows the user profile after this key is added.

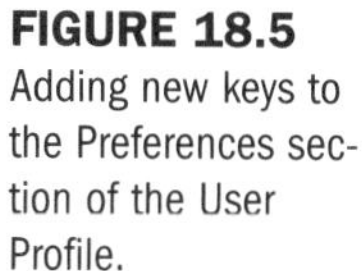

FIGURE 18.5
Adding new keys to the Preferences section of the User Profile.

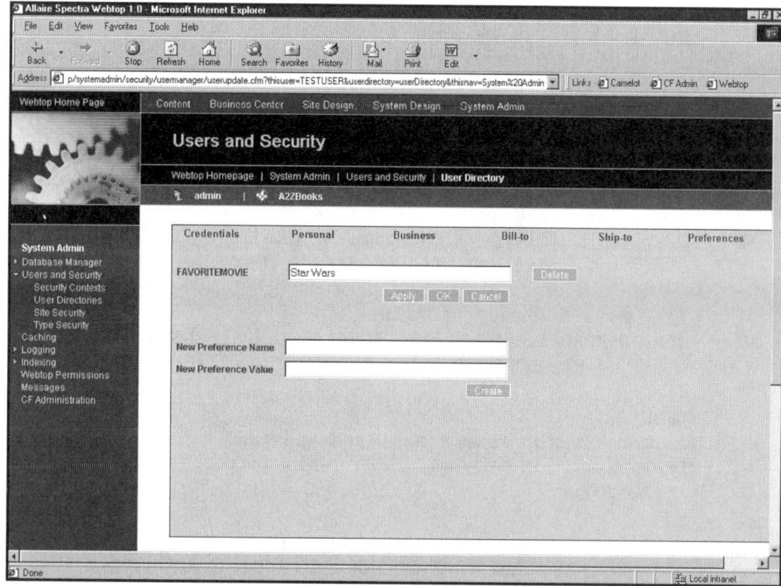

After you add a new key to the Preferences section, you can edit the value of that key or remove it all together. The Preferences section is the part of the User Profile we will use to store personal preferences and other settings for our application. For example, if we wanted to store a user's favorite band, we would store it in the Preferences section. Let's see how we would do this outside the Webtop. Listing 18.2 shows how we edit user profile information with CFA tags.

Listing 18.2 ***editUserProfile.cfm***

```
<!---
File:        /a2zTestScripts/editUserProfile.cfm
Author:      Raymond Camden (raymond.k.camden@syntegra.com)
Date:        12/1/1999
Description: Edits a use profile.
Notes:
--->

<!--- Sets up some default variables Spectra needs --->
<CFA_GLOBALSETTINGS>

<!--- The name of our User. --->
<CFSET User="TestUser">

<!--- Get the userProfile --->
<CFA_USERPROFILEGET DATASOURCE="a2zAccess" USERNAME="#User#"
          R_STUSERPROFILE="myProfile">
```

continues

Listing 18.2 Continued

```
<!--- Save our name and job title. --->
<!--- The name part of the profile is a structure.
       I need to create a blank struct first. --->
<CFSET myProfile.name = StructNew()>
<CFSET myProfile.name.firstName = "Raymond">
<CFSET myProfile.name.middle = "K">
<CFSET myProfile.name.lastName = "Camden">
<CFSET myProfile.JobTitle = "Senior Developer">

<!--- Save the user profile. --->
<CFA_USERPROFILESET DATASOURCE="a2zAccess" USERNAME="#User#"
          STUSERPROFILE="#myProfile#">

<CFOUTPUT>
The profile for #User# has been updated.
<P>
</CFOUTPUT>

<!--- Get the user profile, just to prove us right... --->
<CFA_USERPROFILEGET DATASOURCE="a2zAccess" USERNAME="#User#"
          R_STUSERPROFILE="myNewProfile">

<CFOUTPUT>
Here is the edited profile.
<P>
</CFOUTPUT>

<CFA_DUMP VAR="#myNewProfile#">
```

We begin this script like our others, with a call to the `<CFA_GLOBALSETTINGS>` tag. Next, we create a variable to store the name of the user we are playing with. In this case, our username is `TestUser`. We begin by getting the current user profile using the `<CFA_USERPROFILEGET>` tag in Listing 18.1. Now that we have the profile, we can begin putting information in. The first thing we want to add is the name. The `name` property of the UserProfile ContentObject Type is actually an embedded type. Before we can set this information, we need to create a struct with the `StructNew()` function. Then, we add a key for `firstName`, `middle`, and `lastName`. (Feel free to edit the code and use your own name.) After setting the name, we then enter a `JobTitle` value. After we update the profile, we need to save it. We use the `<CFA_USERPROFILESET>` custom tag. First we pass it a datasource, then the user, and lastly a structure containing the updated profile.

After we save the user profile, we output some text to let the user know what's going on. Then we use `<CFA_USERPROFILEGET>` again to grab the user profile for `TestUser`. We use `<CFA_DUMP>` to display the edited profile. Figure 18.6 shows the results displayed in the browser.

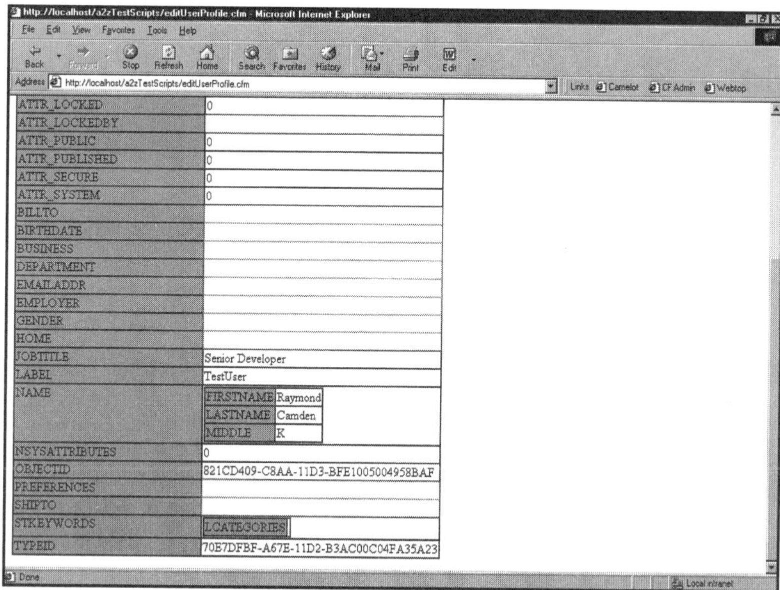

FIGURE 18.6
The dump of an edited user profile.

As a last test, you can return to the Webtop and re-examine the `TestUser` user. You should see entries now for `firstName`, `middle`, and `lastName`, as well as `JobTitle`. Figure 18.7 shows the Personal tab of the `TestUser` user profile after running the `editUserProfile.cfm` script.

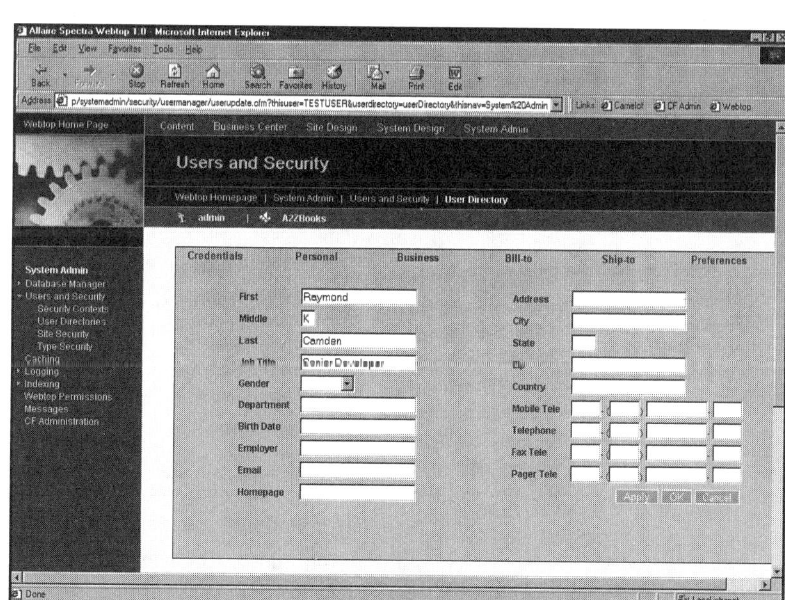

FIGURE 18.7
The Spectra User Profile editor reflects the changes implemented in the script.

Along with <CFA_USERPROFILEGET>, Spectra has a <CFA_USERPROFILEGETMULTIPLE> tag. Unlike <CFA_USERPROFILEGET>, this tag allows you to get any or all of the user profiles in a datasource.

Implementing the User Profile

We've discussed the facets of the UserProfile ContentObject Type and how we can edit the user profile, but we haven't actually used the profile yet. Personalization involves implementing the user profile. This can be as simple as explicit choices (a user picks what types of news she wants to read) or implicit (content appears based on previous actions the user has taken). Let's see how we can start using personalization on our Web site.

Loading the User Profile

Earlier in the chapter, we showed how you can load a user profile with <CFA_USERPROFILEGET>. This works fine, but it isn't the primary way we will load a profile. We have two Spectra custom tags we can use to load a user profile. The first, <CFA_PROFILE>, allows you to load a user profile without explicitly passing a username. The tag defaults to a value set in a cookie (CFA_USER) on the user's browser. The other tag we can use is <CFA_SECURE>. This tag handles login authentication and can also return a user profile. We will deal with <CFA_PROFILE> in this chapter; <CFA_SECURE> is discussed elsewhere.

Let's begin by looking at the <CFA_PROFILE> tag, which takes the arguments defined in Table 18.1.

Table 18.1 *<CFA_PROFILE>* Arguments

Argument	Description
`Datasource`	The datasource that stores the user profile. This is the only required attribute.
`Username`	The name of the user profile to retrieve. If you leave this blank, the tag will default to a cookie named `CFA_USER`.
`StorageType`	Specifies how the username will be stored on the user's browser. The options are `cookie` and `session`. By default, the username will be stored as a permanent cookie on the user's browser. This means that you won't need to pass in a `USERNAME` attribute to the `<CFA_PROFILE>` tag.
`Expires`	The number of days the `CFA_USER` cookie will last. This will be set automatically if you pass in a `USERNAME` attribute.
`SessionExpires`	The number of minutes the username will be stored on the browser if `StorageType` is `session`.
`r_stUserProfile`	Gives a name to the user profile returned by the tag.

Now that we have described the tag, examine Listing 18.3 for an example of `<CFA_PROFILE>` in action.

Listing 18.3 ***profileLoad.cfm—<CFA_PROFILE> at Work***

```
<!---
File:           /a2z/profileLoad.cfm
Author:         Raymond Camden (raymond.k.camden@syntegra.com)
Date:           12/1/1999
Description:
Notes:
--->

<!--- Has the user logged on before? --->
<CFIF IsDefined("Cookie.CFA_USER")>
    <!--- Load their profile --->
    <CFA_PROFILE DATASOURCE="a2zAccess" R_STUSERPROFILE="myProfile">
<CFELSE>
    <!--- Load the anonymous profile. --->
    <CFA_PROFILE DATASOURCE="a2zAccess" USERNAME="anonymous"
    R_STUSERPROFILE="myProfile">
</CFIF>

<CF_a2zFormatting>

    <CFIF Cookie.CFA_USER IS NOT "anonymous">
        <CFOUTPUT>
            Welcome back, #myProfile.label#.
        </CFOUTPUT>
    <CFELSE>
        Welcome to our site. To add to your enjoyment, we recommend that
        you create a user account.
</CFIF>

</CF_a2zFormatting>
```

We begin this script by checking for the `CFA_USER` cookie. As mentioned earlier, this cookie will store the current username. If it exists, we load the profile into a variable named `myProfile`. If the cookie doesn't exist, we load the `anonymous` user profile into a variable with the same name.

After loading the user profile into the `myProfile` variable, we call our `a2zFormatting` custom tag. Then, we examine the cookie `CFA_USER`. We know it exists at this time because, if it doesn't, it will be created when we load the `anonymous` user profile. Depending on the value in this cookie, we either welcome the user by name or let him know that he is `unknown` to our system.

So what will happen when you run this script in your browser? One of two things:

- If you've recently logged in to the Webtop with the `admin` account, you will still have a `CFA_USER` cookie on your browser. The cookie will have `admin` as its value and the `admin` user profile will be loaded.
- If you haven't logged in to the Webtop yet, the script won't know who you are.

Figure 18.8 shows how this script is displayed in the browser.

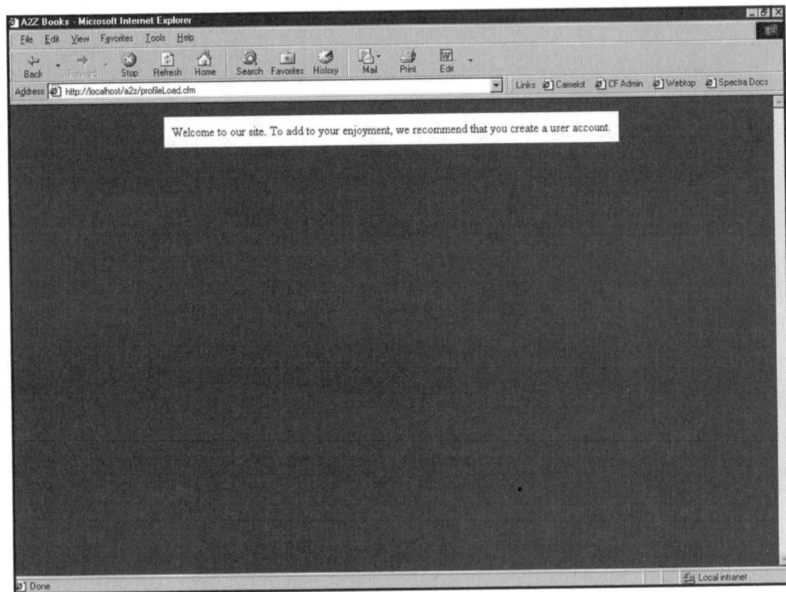

FIGURE 18.8
The site doesn't know who we are, so we are prompted to create a user account.

Saving and Using Preferences

Now that we have retrieved the user profile, we can begin saving data to it. As described earlier in the chapter, we have two different ways we can save user preferences. The first way is to explicitly ask for it. The code in Listing 18.4 presents a form to users that allows them to save personal preferences.

Listing 18.4 ***customizeSite.cfm*—Allowing Users to Save Their Preferences**

```
<!---
File:        /a2z/customizeSite.cfm
Author:      Raymond Camden (raymond.k.camden@syntegra.com)
Date:        12/1/1999
Description:
Notes:
--->
```

```
<!--- cheat and pretend we are TestUser --->
<CFSET Cookie.CFA_USER = "TestUser">

<!--- Has the user logged on before? --->
<CFIF IsDefined("Cookie.CFA_USER")>
     <!--- Load their profile --->
     <CFA_PROFILE DATASOURCE="a2zAccess" R_STUSERPROFILE="myProfile">
<CFELSE>
     <!--- Load the anonymous profile. --->
     <CFA_PROFILE DATASOURCE="a2zAccess" USERNAME="anonymous"
     R_STUSERPROFILE="myProfile">
</CFIF>

<!--- Set defaults --->
<CFIF NOT IsStruct(myProfile.Preferences)>
     <CFSET myProfile.Preferences = StructNew()>
</CFIF>
<CFPARAM NAME="myProfile.Preferences.TextColor" DEFAULT="Black">

<!--- Update the user profile? --->
<CFIF IsDefined("Form.textcolor") AND Cookie.CFA_USER IS NOT "anonymous">
     <CFSET myProfile.Preferences.TextColor = Form.textcolor>
     <CFA_USERPROFILESET DATASOURCE="a2zAccess"
     USERNAME="#Cookie.CFA_USER#" STUSERPROFILE="#myProfile#">
</CFIF>

<CF_a2zFormatting>

     <CFIF Cookie.CFA_USER IS NOT "anonymous">
          <CFOUTPUT>
               <FONT FACE="Arial" SIZE=2
               COLOR="#myProfile.Preferences.TextColor#">
Personalize the site:
               <BR>
               <FORM ACTION="customizeSite.cfm" METHOD="POST">
               Change Font Color:
               <SELECT NAME="textcolor">
               <OPTION <CFIF myProfile.Preferences.TextColor IS "Black">
                        SELECTED</CFIF>>Black
               <OPTION <CFIF myProfile.Preferences.TextColor IS "Red">
                        SELECTED</CFIF>>Red
               <OPTION <CFIF myProfile.Preferences.TextColor IS "Blue">
                        SELECTED</CFIF>>Blue
</SELECT>
               <P>
               <INPUT TYPE="Submit" VALUE="Save Preferences">
               </FORM>
               </FONT>
          </CFOUTPUT>
     <CFELSE>
          Before you can customize the site, you must create a user account.
</CFIF>

</CF_a2zFormatting>
```

This is a complex script, so let's look at it in detail. We begin by overriding the cookie value in your browser. For testing purposes, assume that we are `TestUser`, the same user created earlier in this chapter. This line

```
<CFSET Cookie.CFA_USER = "TestUser">
```

overrides any other value you may currently have in your cookies. Once we have done that, the script thinks we are the `TestUser` user.

Next, we have the same `<CFIF>` logic used in Listing 18.3. If the cookie value exists (which it will, since we just set it), we load the user profile. Otherwise we load the `anonymous` user profile.

Our next block of code checks to see if the `Preferences` key of our user profile exists as a structure. This may seem a bit confusing, so let's examine what's going on. When a user profile is created, we are creating an instance of the UserProfile object. This automatically creates an object with a certain set of keys, one of which is `Preferences`. Unfortunately, this key is *not* created as a structure. The very first time we want to set a value in this key, we need to see if it's a structure; if not, we must create it as such with the `StructNew()` function. Once we have done that, we can use the `<CFPARAM>` tag to define the preference we are going to play with, `TextColor`. This line

```
<CFPARAM NAME="myProfile.Preferences.TextColor" DEFAULT="Black">
```

essentially says, "If a `TextColor` key doesn't exist in the user's `Preferences` structure, define one with the value of `Black`."

Now that we have set up some default values, we have a `<CFIF>` block that checks to see if the users are updating their preferences. Our form only has one field (we will get to that later), called `TextColor`. By using the `IsDefined()` function on this field, we can check to see if the form is currently being submitted by the user. If so, we update `myProfile`, and then we save the user profile through the `<CFA_USERPROFILESET>` tag we used earlier.

NOTE Why both update `myProfile` and use the `<CFA_USERPROFILESET>` tag? Remember that `myProfile` comes from the `<CFA_PROFILE>` tag. This means that Spectra is going to make a database call to retrieve the user profile into a structure. What we have, then, is a *copy* of the user profile, not the user profile itself. We update our copy and then update the master copy in the database. Otherwise, the user profile wouldn't stick.

The next code block is wrapped in our `<CF_A2ZFORMATTING>` custom tag. Remember that this tag simply abstracts the look-and-feel of the A2Z Company Web site. Next, we have a large `<CFIF>` block that does one of two things. If the user is `anonymous`, again we present some text to urge him to create a user account. Normally we would have a link to a page that does just that, but creating and managing users are covered in Chapter 16. This code is handled in the `<CFELSE>` part of the `<CFIF>` block.

The first block of the `<CFIF>` block is run only if a "real" user is on the site (which we will be since we are pretending to be `TestUser`). The next line of code, `<CFOUTPUT>`, simply tells the user that we are about to output dynamic content. Immediately after this line of code we have our first use of personalization. This line

```
<FONT FACE="Arial" SIZE=2 COLOR="#myProfile.Preferences.TextColor#">
```

simply outputs the value stored in our user profile. Depending on what our `TextColor` value is, the color of the text on the page will change. This isn't exactly rocket science here, and if it seems overly simple, it is. It's one of the great strengths of Spectra that using personalization is this simple. After the `<FONT>` tag we output the form that allows the user to pick his text color. We present the user with a drop-down that defaults to the current value of `myProfile.Preferences.TextColor`. We do this by checking the value of `TextColor` against the value of the option tag:

```
<OPTION <CFIF myProfile.Preferences.TextColor IS "Black">
         SELECTED</CFIF>>Black
<OPTION <CFIF myProfile.Preferences.TextColor IS "Red">
         SELECTED</CFIF>>Red
<OPTION <CFIF myProfile.Preferences.TextColor IS "Blue">
         SELECTED</CFIF>>Blue
```

These three lines simply output three different `<OPTION>` tags. If the user has chosen black, red, or blue, that color will show up automatically selected. Figure 18.9 shows a site that has been customized to use red as the `TextColor`.

FIGURE 18.9
A site customized to use red as the color of the body text.

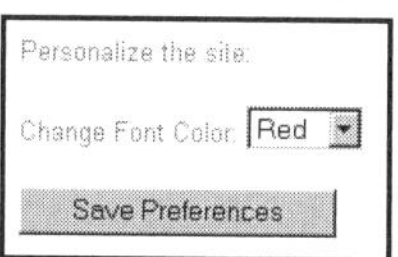

This site is pretty simple and doesn't allow for much customization, but it would be trivial to add additional levels of customization. Listing 18.5 is an edited version of Listing 18.4.

Listing 18.5 *customizeSite2.cfm*—A Different Way to Allow Users to Save Their Preferences

```
<!---
File:         /a2z/customizeSite2.cfm
Author:       Raymond Camden (raymond.k.camden@syntegra.com)
Date:         12/1/1999
Description:
Notes:
--->

<!--- cheat and pretend we are TestUser --->
<CFSET Cookie.CFA_USER = "TestUser">
```

continues

Listing 18.5 Continued

```
<!--- Has the user logged on before? --->
<CFIF IsDefined("Cookie.CFA_USER")>
    <!--- Load their profile --->
    <CFA_PROFILE DATASOURCE="a2zAccess" R_STUSERPROFILE="myProfile">
<CFELSE>
    <!--- Load the anonymous profile. --->
    <CFA_PROFILE DATASOURCE="a2zAccess" USERNAME="anonymous"
    R_STUSERPROFILE="myProfile">
</CFIF>

<!--- Set defaults --->
<CFIF NOT IsStruct(myProfile.Preferences)>
    <CFSET myProfile.Preferences = StructNew()>
</CFIF>
<CFPARAM NAME="myProfile.Preferences.TextColor" DEFAULT="Black">
<CFPARAM NAME="myProfile.Preferences.TextFont" DEFAULT="Arial">

<!--- Update the user profile? --->
<CFIF IsDefined("Form.textcolor") AND Cookie.CFA_USER IS NOT "anonymous">
    <CFSET myProfile.Preferences.TextColor = Form.textcolor>
    <CFSET myProfile.Preferences.TextFont = Form.textfont>
    <CFA_USERPROFILESET DATASOURCE="a2zAccess"
    USERNAME="#Cookie.CFA_USER#" STUSERPROFILE="#myProfile#">
</CFIF>

<CF_a2zFormatting>


    <CFIF Cookie.CFA_USER IS NOT "anonymous">
        <CFOUTPUT>
            <FONT FACE="#myProfile.Preferences.TextFont#"
            SIZE=2 COLOR="#myProfile.Preferences.TextColor#">
Personalize the site:
            <BR>
            <FORM ACTION="customizeSite2.cfm" METHOD="POST">
            Change Font Color:
            <SELECT NAME="textcolor">
            <OPTION <CFIF myProfile.Preferences.TextColor IS "Black">
            SELECTED</CFIF>>Black
            <OPTION <CFIF myProfile.Preferences.TextColor IS "Red">
            SELECTED</CFIF>>Red
            <OPTION <CFIF myProfile.Preferences.TextColor IS "Blue">
            SELECTED</CFIF>>Blue
</SELECT>
            <BR>
            Change Font:
            <SELECT NAME="textfont">
            <OPTION <CFIF myProfile.Preferences.TextFont IS "Arial">
            SELECTED</CFIF>>Arial
            <OPTION <CFIF myProfile.Preferences.TextFont IS "Verdana">
            SELECTED</CFIF>>Verdana
```

```
                <OPTION <CFIF myProfile.Preferences.TextFont IS "Courier">
                SELECTED</CFIF>>Courier
</SELECT>
                <P>

                <INPUT TYPE="Submit" VALUE="Save Preferences">
                </FORM>
                </FONT>
            </CFOUTPUT>
        <CFELSE>
            Before you can customize the site, you must create a user account.
</CFIF>

</CF_a2zFormatting>
```

Since this script is similar to Listing 18.4, let's focus on what's different. First, we add a new default value to our `myProfile` structure:

```
<CFPARAM NAME="myProfile.Preferences.TextFont" DEFAULT="Arial">
```

The `TextFont` key will store the user's preferred text font. If it doesn't exist, we default to Arial. The next change is in the section where we save the user preferences:

```
<CFSET myProfile.Preferences.TextFont = Form.textfont>
```

This line ensures that the user's choice (from the changes we made to the form) will be correctly displayed. We need only one `<CFA_USERPROFILESET>`, since the tag passes in the entire `myProfile` structure.

Since our script now assumes we have a `TextFont` form field, we added a new drop-down. This time, instead of color choices we have font choices: Arial, Verdana, and Courier. In Figure 18.10, we see this Web page form in action. The user has chosen a red text color and the Courier font.

Part IV Ch 18

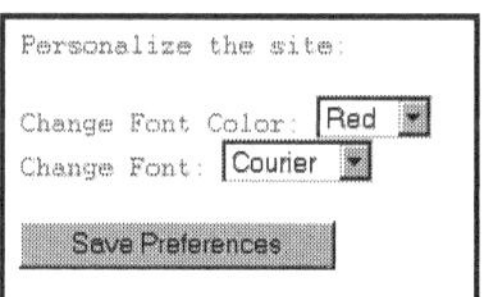

FIGURE 18.10
A site customized to use red as the color of the body text and Courier as the font.

Implicit (Behind-the-Scenes) Profiling

The previous scripts employed personalization based on explicit options the user picked. This works for some settings, but sometimes you want to save user profile information without the user's knowledge. As an example, imagine a site that remembers that you searched for action films. Next time you come to the site, it may present you with films in the action genre that are on sale. The idea here is that the site made the assumption that, since you were browsing for action films last time you were at the site, you must have some kind of interest in films of that type. This doesn't work well all the time. You may want to remember only the things a user searches for more than once.

▶ **See** Chapter 19, "Rules-Based Publishing," for more information on using implicit profiling to alter the content that shows up on Web pages.

NOTE One more utility Spectra gives us is the capability to search for user profiles with specific values. The tag to use is `<CFA_USERPROFILEFIND>`. Unfortunately, this tag is simply a wrapper for `<CFA_CONTENTOBJECTFIND>`, which means you can search only for "top level" properties of the user profile, such as the label. You can't search for a particular value in the preference.

Taking Personalization to the Next Level

When you begin working with personalization, you will quickly grasp how easy it is to implement on your site. To help you further enable personalization, Allaire has announced support from major personalization engines that will greatly increase the power of personalization. These personalization engines are Net Perceptions (`http://www.netperceptions.com`), Andromedia LikeMinds (`http://www.andromedia.com`), and Bowne OpenSesame.

CHAPTER 19

Rules-Based Publishing

In this chapter

Using Rules-Based Publishing

One success indicator for a Web site is *stickiness.* This means that visitors to the site return often. One thing that creates return visits is changing content on the site. After all, nobody reads Wednesday's newspaper day after day. So site developers are always pursuing ways to make the site appear dynamic and regularly serve up content that's new as well as relevant to the visitor. This is often referred to as *dynamic content publishing* and *personalization.*

Dynamic content publishing is the first reason most people turn to Spectra. Static Web sites are totally passé. Some sites offer dynamic content, but at a price—there's some poor devil in the Web group who has the task of perpetually "freshening" the site by adding new content and removing content whose "best by" date has come and gone. This poor fellow, like Sisyphus pushing the rock, will never get done with his labors.

People have been publishing dynamic content with ColdFusion for a long time. In each case, however, they had to build, from the ground up, a database-driven publishing system with rules. This is a bit like saying, "Here are all the parts—build a car and then go someplace interesting." Spectra removes the hurdle to dynamic content publishing. You are given "the car" and all you have to do is make a few adjustments to be ready to "go someplace interesting."

You will want to develop rules for your Spectra application that implement dynamic content selection for your site. Rules can provide time-sensitive content. That is, some content may appear only on Monday to Friday, whereas other content might appear on the weekend. Another important reason to use rules is to show users of your site content that's personalized for them.

This chapter shows how to use Spectra rules to select content for dynamic publication. You will see how to make your rules customizable so that content managers and business managers can tweak the behavior of the rules to suit their daily needs and customize the appearance of the site, all without you having to get involved. Finally, you will learn how to use rules to support personalization of content.

Let's start with a quick review of a couple of key terms that we will use a lot in this chapter and then add a few new terms.

- *Container* is a Spectra site element with associated rules that select content for publication by the Container object. (Containers were introduced in Chapter 8, "Building the Site Structure.") A container is defined with the `<CFA_CONTAINER>` tag. Although colloquially called a container, you might rightly guess that it's a really a Container object. The Container object holds all the information and parameters associated with the container as properties of the object.
- *Container Editor* is a user interface object provided by Spectra. The Container Editor lets authorized users choose content to be published in a container. In Chapter 8, "Building the Site Structure," when you did scheduled publication, you were using the Container Editor interface.

- *Publishing rule* is a specification of parameter values stored with the Container object and associated ColdFusion code called the *rule execute handler*. The publishing rule determines what content will be published.
- *Rule edit handler* is the user interface where you can set the parameters that govern rule behavior. This is the first of the three handlers that make up a rule.
- *Rule update handler* is the second handler making up a rule. It receives the parameters from the rule edit handler and stores them for use by the rule execute handler.
- *Rule execute handler* is the third and most interesting handler of a rule. This ColdFusion code receives the parameters gathered and stored by the edit and update handlers and uses them to select content for publication in the container.

A2Z Books wants to add a new feature to its home page for book shoppers, a list of new books that will be published soon. By doing this, the store will encourage shoppers to place orders for the books, which will then be shipped when they are published.

Let's summarize the steps we will take to add this capability:

1. Define the rule using the Webtop.
2. Code the rule edit handler.
3. Code the rule update handler.
4. Code the rule execute handler.
5. Add the Upcoming Books container to the home page.
6. Add the new rule to the Upcoming Books container.

So let's get started. First you need to start the Webtop and click the System Design link in the Webtop menu bar, open Programming Objects and click the Rules command. You will see a screen like that in Figure 19.1.

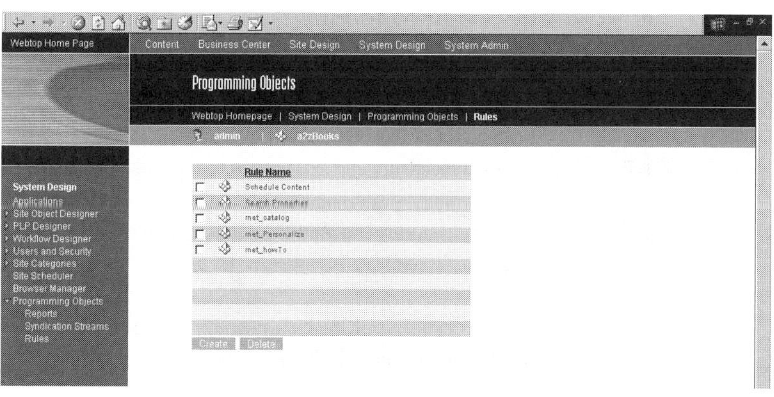

FIGURE 19.1
You used the Schedule Content rule in Chapter 8, but you may not have realized that it's just another rule supplied as part of Spectra.

Now click the Create button at the bottom of the screen to start the creation of your own new rule. You will see a display like that seen in Figure 19.2.

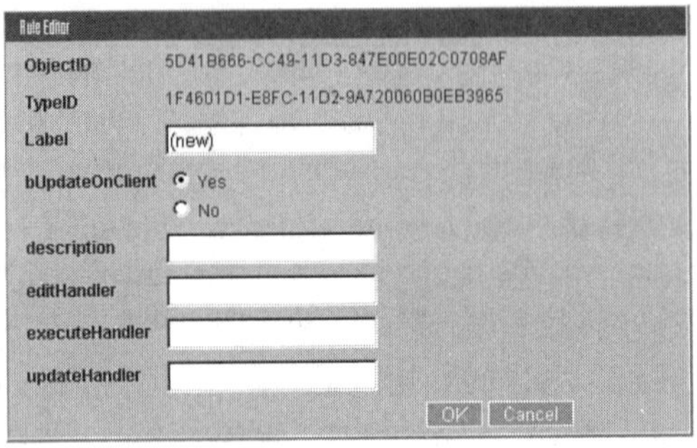

FIGURE 19.2
The Rule Editor dialog box is where you create a new rule definition. All the information needed to find your rule code is specified here.

The Label field provides a name for your rule that will be seen when the rule is chosen for use in a container, so be sure it makes sense in that context. Type **`Show Upcoming Books`** in the Label field. This is a nice description of what the rule does that the person selecting the rule will understand.

Click the No radio button for `bUpdateOnClient`. You can eliminate the need for a rule update handler if you write some JavaScript and perform the `update` function on the client, but for now, you will be using an update handler that runs on the server.

In the Description field, enter **`Shows Soon-to-Be-Published Books`**.

In the editHandler field, enter the path

`/allaire/spectra/rules/a2z/showupcomingedit.cfmv`

In the executeHandler field, enter

`/allaire/spectra/rules/a2z/showupcomingexecute.cfm`

In the updateHandler field, enter

`/allaire/spectra/rules/a2z/showupcomingupdate.cfm`

NOTE All three of the preceding paths are relative to the place where Spectra is installed on your system. The naming convention I use is root name + `edit`, `execute`, or `update`. So here the root name is `showupcoming`, and the name for the execute handler becomes `showupcomingexecute.cfm`.

Click the OK button to create your new rule definition. You should now see the new Show Upcoming Books rule onscreen (see Figure 19.3).

Now you need to start ColdFusion Studio and navigate to where Spectra rules are stored (typically `Program Files/Allaire/Spectra/rules`). Under the `rules` directory, make a new directory named `a2z` that will hold the rules you are going to write. When you are done, it should look like Figure 19.4.

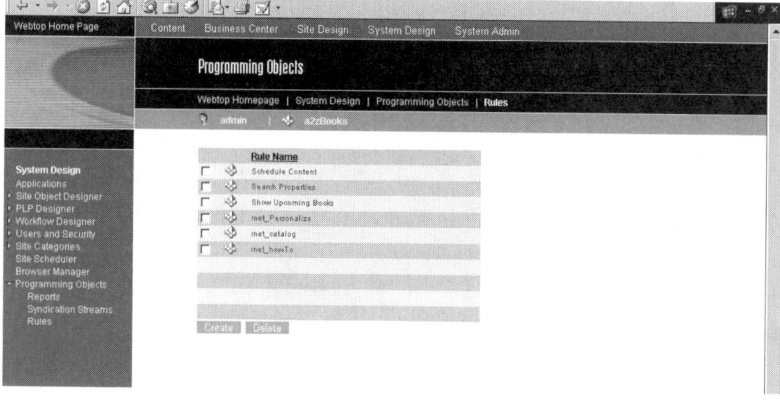

FIGURE 19.3
The Show Upcoming Books rule is now created and you are ready to begin coding it.

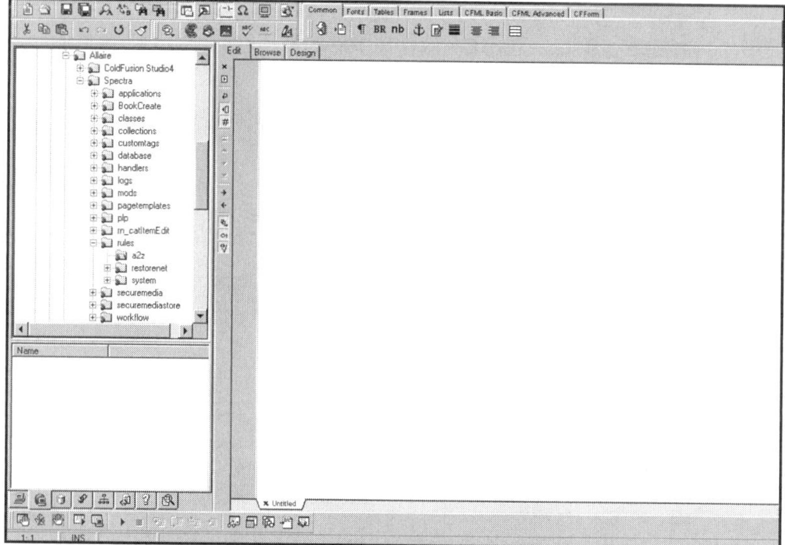

FIGURE 19.4
The `rules` directory under the installed Allaire Spectra root part of the file system holds all the rules defined for a Spectra system.

Coding a Rule Edit Hander

A rule edit handler is run whenever a user adds a rule to a container for the first time or chooses the rule and clicks the Edit button to change its settings.

The Container Editor is a standard user interface part of the Webtop. It provides a wrapper around the code of your edit handler. In particular, the Container Editor wraps your code in `<FORM></FORM>` tags. This means your code must be written as though it's inside a `<FORM>`, because it is. You don't need to write a `<FORM>` tag yourself.

What options do we want to provide the business manager at A2Z Books when it comes to placing new books into the Upcoming A2Z Books container? It seems likely that A2Z Books doesn't want to promote books that won't be published until six months from now. The more likely limit is maybe three months, but let's be flexible.

We will make the rule edit handler accept a value that determines the cutoff date for future publications to be shown. In this way, if three months is the wrong number, it can be changed without our help. We might also want to put a limit on how many books show up in the promotion box. If A2Z Books becomes wildly successful and is publishing 500 books in the next three months, that could overload the home page and overwhelm the visitor. Let's add a parameter that sets a maximum number of books that we will publish. We aren't going to tackle the trickier problem of deciding which ones to choose in this example.

Now what we need to do is write some ColdFusion and HTML to draw a form to collect these two values—something that's really pretty easy. Listing 19.1 shows how it's done.

Listing 19.1 The Edit Rule for Show Upcoming Books

```
<!---
File:        /allaire/spectra/rules/a2z/showupcomingedit.cfm
              - User Interface Rule for choosing upcoming books to show
Author:      rich ragan
Date:        1/20/2000
Description: showUpcomingEdit is the edit rule handler for the Show
              Upcoming Books rule. It collects two parameters, DaysAhead
              and MaximumNumber. Books with publish dates more than
              DaysAhead in the future will not be shown. More than
              MaximumNumber books will not be shown.
Notes:
--->

<!--- attributes.stParams holds the parameter values we are letting the
user edit. They may already have values if the rule is being edited rather
than just being added to the container. Default DaysAhead to 90 days
and MaximumNumber to publish to 5 books --->

<CFPARAM NAME=attributes.stParams.DaysAhead DEFAULT="90">
<CFPARAM NAME=attributes.stParams.MaximumNumber DEFAULT="5">

<CFOUTPUT>
    <H4>Select Display Criteria for Upcoming Books and click OK.</H4>
    <FONT SIZE="2">
    If the publication date is more than
    <INPUT TYPE="textbox" NAME="DaysAhead" SIZE=3
     VALUE=#attributes.stParams.DaysAhead#>
    days in the future, don't show the book.<p>
    </FONT>
    <FONT SIZE="2">
    Specify the maximum number of books to be shown.
    </FONT>
```

```
    <INPUT TYPE="textbox" NAME="MaximumNumber" SIZE=3
     VALUE=#attributes.stParams.MaximumNumber#>
</CFOUTPUT>
```

In Listing 19.1, first we make sure that we have default values set for the `DaysAhead` and `MaximumNumber` parameters, the values we expect the user to fill in on our form. Next we display a title giving the user some instructions on what to do and how to finish the process (click OK). Finally, we provide two textbox fields to collect the parameter values we use to control the Publishing rule. Remember that the Container Editor has wrapped the above code in a form that has an OK button, a Cancel button, and an Apply button. When OK is clicked, the form will be posted to the update handler shown in Listing 19.2.

Listing 19.2 The Update Rule for Show Upcoming Books

```
<!---
File:          /allaire/spectra/rules/a2z/showupcomingupdate.cfm
                - Handler for storing parameters for Show Upcoming Books rule
Author:        rich ragan
Date:          1/20/2000
Description: showUpcomingUpdate is the update rule handler for the Show
               Upcoming Books rule. It saves the two parameters, DaysAhead
               and MaximumNumber.
Notes:
--->

<!--- Set defaults in case the user cleared the form fields --->
<CFPARAM NAME="FORM.DaysAhead" DEFAULT="90">
<CFPARAM NAME="FORM.MaximumNumber" DEFAULT="5">

<!--- Place the values we got into the stParams structure of stRule
 so they are saved for the execute handler --->
<CFSET stTemp = attributes.stRule>
<CFSET stTemp.stParams.DaysAhead = "#FORM.DaysAhead#">
<CFSET stTemp.stParams.MaximumNumber = "#FORM.MaximumNumber#">

<!--- Send the updated stRule structure back to the caller --->
<CFSET CALLER.stRule = stTemp>
```

There's not much to the update handler, and later you will learn how to get rid of it completely. Again, we force our defaults in case the user cleared out the values on the form. The `stRule` structure is passed to us by the Container Editor. We store the values we want saved with the container and passed to our execute rule handler into the `stParams` structure. Finally, we send the update structure back to our caller.

Now that the user interface and parameter-gathering code are done, let's move on to the code that implements the dynamic publishing—the execute rule handler. Look at Listing 19.3.

Listing 19.3 The Execute Rule for Show Upcoming Books

```
<!---
File:         /allaire/spectra/rules/a2z/showupcomingexecute.cfm
               - Execute handler for Show Upcoming Books rule
Author:       rich ragan
Date:         1/27/2000
Description: showUpcomingExecute is the execute rule handler for the Show
               Upcoming Books rule. It uses the two parameters, DaysAhead
               and MaximumNumber to dynamically choose books being published
               with DaysAhead days to be shown in the Upcoming Books
               promotional container. No more than MaximumNumber will
               be shown.
Notes:
--->

<CFPARAM NAME="attributes.stParams.DaysAhead" DEFAULT="90">
<CFPARAM NAME="attributes.stParams.MaximumNumber" DEFAULT="5">

<!--- Get the current time information --->
<CFSET dtNow = ParseDateTime(Now())+ 0 >

<!--- Retrieve Book objects not yet published using the properties
     DB table built by Spectra when properties are marked "searchable"
     Order the objects by date --->
<CFQUERY DATASOURCE="#request.cfa.objectstore.dsn#"
     NAME="qFoundBooks">
     SELECT *  FROM properties
     WHERE propertyname = 'PUBLISHED'
     AND datetimedata > #dtNow#
     ORDER by datetimedata
     </CFQUERY>

<!--- If there are any books, scan them to see if they should be
      published. --->
<CFIF qFoundBooks.RecordCount>
<!--- Initialize number published and get length of container objects array
      holding objects published by rules run prior to our rule --->
     <CFSET numPublished = 0>
     <CFSET arrLen = arrayLen(request.cfaContainer.aObjects)>

<!--- Loop through the records outputting Books that meet the
      criteria . --->
     <CFLOOP QUERY="qFoundBooks">
        <!--- Compute how manys days until the book is published. --->
        <CFSET daysToGo=DateDiff("y",  dtNow, #qFoundBooks.datetimedata#)>
        <!--- Only publish if we have published less than MaximumNumber
         and the publish date is within the DaysAhead limit --->
```

```
        <CFIF (numPublished LESS THAN attributes.stParams.MaximumNumber)
            AND (daysToGo LESS THAN attributes.stParams.DaysAhead)>
            <CFSCRIPT>
                // Append an empty array element to hold our Book object
                tmp = arrayAppend(request.cfaContainer.aObjects,
                      structNew());
                // Keep arrlen accurate for length of aObjects
                arrLen = arrLen + 1;
                // Make a variable pointing to the new element
                stPoolObject = request.cfaContainer.aObjects[arrLen];
                // Add the objectID of the book to be published
                stPoolObject.objectID = qFoundBooks.objectID;
                // Add the method to use when publishing the book.
                // Use teaser by default.
                stPoolObject.containerMethod = "teaser";
                // Increment the count of books published
                numPublished = numPublished + 1;
            </CFSCRIPT>
          </CFIF>
    </CFLOOP>
<CFELSE>
    Keep watching for new books from A2Z Books.<br>
</CFIF>
```

Okay, let's take this bit by bit, because there's a lot more going on here. First, we set up our default values again and snapshot the current time and date. The date is needed to see if the publication date of a book is within, let's say, 90 days of now. Next is a `<CFQUERY>`:

```
<CFQUERY DATASOURCE="#request.cfa.objectstore.dsn#"
    NAME="qFoundBooks">
    SELECT *  FROM properties
    WHERE propertyname = 'PUBLISHED'
    AND datetimedata > #dtNow#
    ORDER by datetimedata
</CFQUERY>
```

Part IV Ch 19

We find books to be published using the properties database table that Spectra creates when you mark a property as searchable. We must select on the `propertyname` of `PUBLISHED`, since this is the name of the property in the Book type that holds the publication date. We also select only records that have `datetimedata` values in the future and sort the records so that we can list the books with the closest to publication appearing first.

Next, we put a `<CFIF>` around the rest of the code in case we get no books at all and initialize the number published so far and the size of the `request.cfaContainer.aObjects` array. This array is passed to us as input from the Container Manager. It contains an array entry for each object already selected for publication in this container by rules that ran before our rule. We will add objects to the end of the container to provide the items to publish.

NOTE Unless you have good reasons to do so and knowledge of the other rules associated with the container, you shouldn't change the existing data in the aObjects array that's passed into your rule. Just add your objects at the end.

In some cases you will want to see what's already selected for publication. For example, if an earlier rule already chose the book your rule would select, you probably don't want to publish it twice. Another thing you might want to do, as the last rule to be run on the container, would be to sort all the objects contributed by all the rules. The second example will show something like this.

A <CFLOOP> iterates over each book record in the query. First, we compute how many days until the book is published. We will use this value to decide if the book is too far in the future to be shown.

```
<CFSET daysToGo=DateDiff("y", dtNow, #qFoundBooks.datetimedata#)>
```

The real publishing selection takes place in the next piece of code. The <CFIF> makes two tests, and both have to pass before the book is published. First, the total number of books published to the container cannot have exceeded the MaximumNumber configured by the business manager. Second, the book's publication date must be within the DaysAhead limit set by the business manager. If both tests are met, then the book will be added to the aObjects container for publishing.

```
<!--- Only publish if we have published less than MaximumNumber
      and the publish date is within the DaysAhead limit --->
<CFIF (numPublished LESS THAN attributes.stParams.MaximumNumber)
 AND (daysToGo LESS THAN attributes.stParams.DaysAhead)>
```

The first five lines of code (not counting the comments) are almost boilerplate. For just adding an item to a container you will always use code like this. All it does is add an empty element at the end of the array, increment the array length, get a pointer to the new element, and put the object ID and method to be used for publishing it into the element. The increment of numPublished is particular to this rule and just keeps track of the total number published, so that we can stop when we hit the number set by the business manager.

```
// Append an empty array element to put our Book object in
tmp = arrayAppend(request.cfaContainer.aObjects, structNew());
// Keep arrlen accurate with respect to length of aObjects
arrLen = arrLen + 1;
// Make a variable pointing to the new element
stPoolObject = request.cfaContainer.aObjects[arrLen];
// Add the objectID of the book to be published
stPoolObject.objectID = qFoundBooks.objectID;
// Add the method to use when publishing the book. Use teaser by default.
stPoolObject.containerMethod = "teaser";
// Increment the count of books we have published to the container
numPublished = numPublished + 1;
```

Okay, having coded all this, let's see how it works. First you will need to add a button to the A2Z home page to link to the Show Upcoming Books page. Open the `a2z/index.cfm` home page of A2Z Books. Immediately after the `<CFA_BUTTON>` tag, add two more `<CFA_BUTTON>` tags to link to the two code samples you will use in this chapter. The resulting code section for all three buttons on the home page should look like this.

```
<cfa_button
            dataSource = "REQUEST.CFA.a2zBooks.DATASOURCE"
            id = "D3E48F89-FE2A-11e2-B6300060B0fB4967"
            label = "Browse our Catalog"
            action="url"
            actionData="/a2z/catalog/index.cfm"
            description="Browse the a2zBooks catalog"
            state="normal">
</td><td>
        <cfa_button
            dataSource = "REQUEST.CFA.a2zBooks.DATASOURCE"
            id = "AAA48F89-FE2A-11e2-B6300060B0fB4000"
            label = "See Upcoming Books"
            action="url"
            actionData="/a2z/catalog/upcoming.cfm"
            description="See books being published soon"
            state="normal">
</td><td>
        <cfa_button
            dataSource = "REQUEST.CFA.a2zBooks.DATASOURCE"
            id = "ABB48F89-FE2A-11e2-B6300060B0fB4000"
            label = "See Book Promotions"
            action="url"
            actionData="/a2z/catalog/promotion.cfm"
            description="See books on promotion"
            state="normal">
</td>
</tr></table>
```

Save the home page file and reload the home page to see the two new buttons you have created.

From the home page of A2Z Books, click the Show Upcoming Books button. The page you go to is already set up and has an empty container for publishing upcoming books. Add **`?designmode=1`** to the end of your URL in the browser and press Enter. You will be prompted for a password to enter Administration mode. Enter the Administrator username and password. Now you will see the page with the editing controls in addition to what was there before. Click the Edit Container icon that has the container name Upcoming next to it to bring up the Container Editor. Now click the Edit link. In the upper-right corner, use the pull-down to change the Edit mode from Simple to Advanced. This lets you see the rules associated with the container, add new rules, or remove old ones.

You should see one rule, Schedule Content. Select it and remove it with the Delete button below the Publishing Rules list box. Using the pull-down at the bottom of the dialog box, choose Show Upcoming Books and click the Add button next to it. This adds Show Upcoming Books to the rules and puts you in Edit mode immediately so that you can configure the rule. The display should look like Figure 19.5. Let's leave the settings as they are for now. Just click the OK button.

FIGURE 19.5
The Edit Rule interface to Show Upcoming Books lets the business manager adjust the criteria controlling publication of books in the container.

If all has been done correctly, you should see some books published in the container, provided you have some books defined with publication dates within 90 days. If you don't have any books that will be published in the next 90 days, create some as you learned in Chapter 8 and then return here and see if they show up.

Feel free to play around some with the parameters on the rule. Try increasing or reducing the default 90 days to add or eliminate books from your list. Try reducing the total number of books shown to, say, just 1. See how the parameterized rule implements publishing in accordance with the settings.

CAUTION

If you have any ColdFusion errors in your rule edit handler script or rule update script, of course you need to fix them and refresh the browser on the Container Editor window to apply the fix. However, each repair/retry cycle will add an extra copy of the rule to the list of publishing rules for the container. Once you get the rule correct, go back to Edit mode and remove all but one copy of the rule from the Publishing Rules list.

You don't need a rule update handler if you store the values you collect in the form into the `stParams` directly by using JavaScript. Let's see the changes to the previous example needed to do this. The changes are confined to the two `<INPUT>` tags and are shown in Listing 19.4. Both tags now include an `onChange` attribute that stores any change in the value immediately.

Listing 19.4 Modified Rule for Showing Upcoming Books

```
<CFOUTPUT>
    <H4>Select Display Criteria for Upcoming Books and click OK.</H4>
    <FONT SIZE="2">
```

```
      If the publication date is more than
      <INPUT TYPE="textbox" NAME="DaysAhead" SIZE=3
       VALUE=#attributes.stParams.DaysAhead#
       onChange="strule.stparams.DaysAhead = this.value">
      days in the future, don't show the book.<p>
      </FONT>
      <FONT SIZE="2">
      Specify the maximum number of books to be shown.
      </FONT>
      <INPUT TYPE="textbox" NAME="MaximumNumber" SIZE=3
       VALUE=#attributes.stParams.MaximumNumber#
       onChange="strule.stparams.MaximumNumber = this.value">
</CFOUTPUT>
```

NOTE When you eliminate the update handler, you must also be sure to set the `bUpdateOnClient` check box to Yes in the rule definition and omit the `updateHandler` path specification in the same dialog.

Now that you have a general idea of how rules interact with the container object, let's fill in all the details. Every rule associated with a container is called, in turn, by the Container Manager. The order in which rules are called is the order in which they are listed when you look at the container and have Edit mode set to Advanced, as described previously. Each rule is invoked by the Container Manager and passed the `request.cfacontainer.aObjects` array. This array contains one array element (a structure) for each object to be published. When a rule is called, the `aObjects` array contains any published items placed there by container rules that were run before it. It may then add items to the `aObjects` array. After all rules associated with the container have run, the Container Manager uses the `aObjects` array to invoke each method with the associated object. Usually this means the method will use the object to produce some visible content in the container.

An `aObjects` element has the following structure:

Field	Required?	Description
`objectID`	Yes	Object ID of the content item.
`containerMethod`	Yes	Method to be used with the content item.
`typeID`	No	Type ID of the content item. Supplying this can help performance because the Container Manager can group actions by type.
`stContainerParams`	No	Structure of parameters to be passed to the specified method.

The Container Manager provides a second structure: `request.cfacontainer.aRuleSet`, an array of rule structures. There's one element for every rule associated with the container. You won't normally need to work with the `aRuleSet` array unless your rules need to know what other rules are associated with the container. An `aRuleSet` element has the following structure:

Field	Description
`ruleID`	Identifier of the rule
`stParams`	Structure holding the parameters passed to the rule's execute handler

Finally, let's pull it all together with an annotated picture that's worth a thousand words. Figure 19.6 shows all the steps in the process of publishing a container. It doesn't show the edit and update rule handler processes. The process begins with the `<CFA_CONTAINER>` tag being called during the rendering of the page where it resides. It gets the container information (rules list and parameters for the rules) and then starts the process described here and shown in Figure 19.6:

1. The empty `aObjects` array is passed to the first rule in the container, Schedule Content. The parameter stored in the container with Schedule Content is a list of all the books manually scheduled for publication.
2. The Schedule Content rule runs and, using its stored parameters from its edit rule, adds two objects of Type X to the `aObjects` array, to be invoked later with the `display` method.
3. The Container Manager calls the next rule in the container and passes it the partially filled `aObjects` array.
4. The second rule, Personalize Content, runs and, using its parameters, contributes one more object of Type Y to the container with the `display` method. When it finishes, the Container Manager gets the fully filled `aObjects` array. Since there are no more rules, it moves into the next phase of its work.
5. It begins processing the `aObjects` array and calling the designated handler with the specified object. `typeID`, if present, allows multiple objects to be passed in one call to the handler, which is more efficient. So, the display method handler for Type X objects is invoked with the first two objects in the `aObjects` array. The display handler runs and generates some HTML as output.
6. The last element in `aObjects` is processed by the Container Manager. It invokes the `display` method for objects of Type Y and passes it the object, which is processed, yielding more HTML.

FIGURE 19.6
The container goes through all these steps in transforming rules to HTML output.

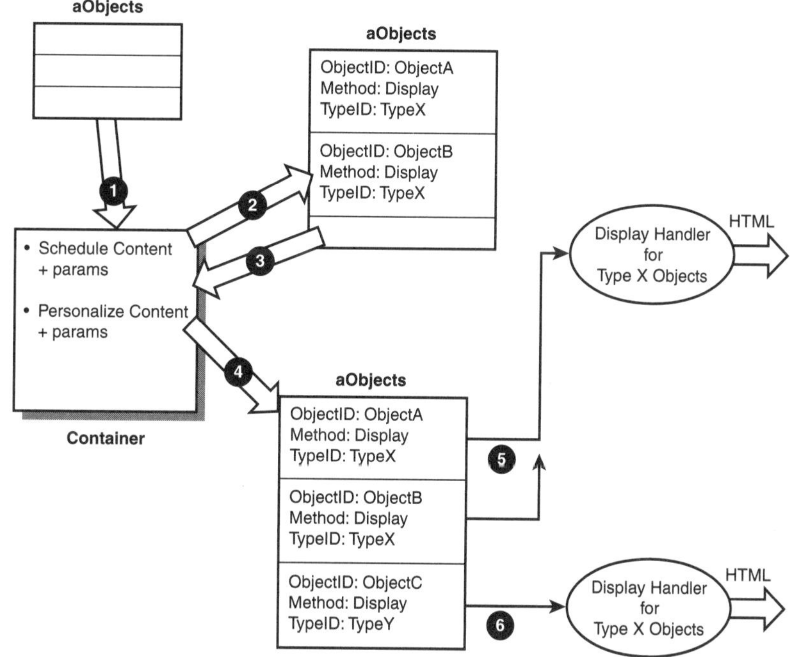

Client-Side Array Manipulation Methods

If you find yourself needing to manipulate the `aObjects` array on the client side from JavaScript, as Schedule Content does to implement the Up and Down buttons to rearrange objects, you will want to use the `<CFA_JSARRAYEXTENSIONS>` tag. Just code the tag with no parameters at the end of your rule handler. It adds the following methods to arrays:

- *`arrayname`*`.DeleteAt(`*`index`*`)` deletes data from the array at the specified index position.
- *`arrayname`*`.InsertAt(`*`index, value`*`)` inserts data into the array at the specified index position.
- *`arrayname`*`.Swap(`*`index1, index2`*`)` swaps the elements at *`index1`* and *`index2`*.
- *`arrayname`*`.ToList(`*`delimiter`*`)` converts a one-dimensional array to a list, delimited by the specified character.
- *`arrayname`*`.ToArray(`*`delimiter`*`)` converts a list, delimited by the specified character, into a one-dimensional array.

Integrating with Personalization

A very important use of rules-based publishing is to implement personalization. As you learned in the previous chapter, personalization is the process of tailoring the user's experience on a site so that it feels as if the site is especially for him. Rules and containers allow that process to be extended to include selecting content with his interests and preferences in mind.

We will be adding some personalization to A2Z Books to provide a Promotional Books container. The container will use two rules:

- The first rule will be the basic Schedule Content rule that comes with Spectra. The promotions manager will use this to select the promotional books for the month and add them to the container. The manager will pick a couple of books from each genre.
- The second rule looks at the user's profile to determine his favorite genre. Then the rule will rearrange the order of the promotional books being displayed by the container so that the books favored by the user will appear first.

Notice that this second rule will have no real interface for the edit handler part, since there are no parameters to control its behavior. You still need to have an edit rule, because it's always called when the rule is first added to the container. But all it will do is explain what's going on and remind the person adding it to the container that it must follow Schedule Content in the list of rules. It has to be after Schedule Content so it can rearrange the books put there by Schedule Content.

Since it does no updating of the `stParams` values, you won't need an update handler. As before, the first thing to do is define the rule in the Webtop. Go to System Design, Programming Objects, Rules, and click Create. Enter **`Rearrange Promotions`** for the label, leave `bUpdateOnClient` set to Yes, enter **`Personalize Promotions`** for the description, enter **`/allaire/spectra/rules/a2z/promotionedit.cfm`** for the edit handler and **`/allaire/spectra/rules/a2z/promotionexecute.cfm`** for the execute handler. Leave the update handler field empty. It should look something like Figure 19.7. If all looks good, click OK to finish defining the rule.

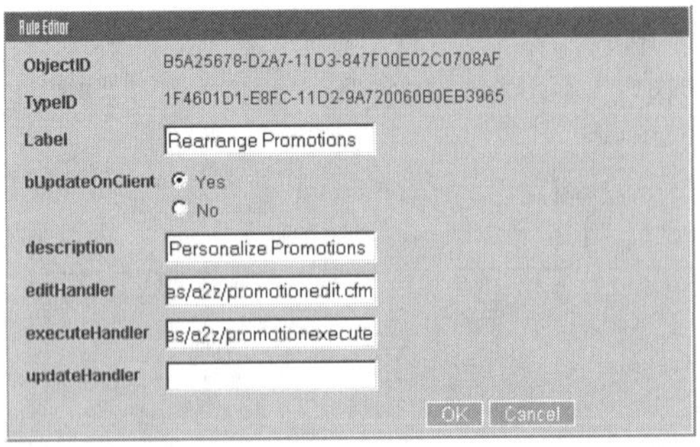

FIGURE 19.7
Define the Rearrange Promotions rule in the Webtop. It needs only an edit handler and an execute handler.

Now, using ColdFusion Studio, create the `promotionedit.cfm` file as shown in Listing 19.5.

Listing 19.5 The Edit Rule for the Promotions Container

```
<!---
File:        /allaire/spectra/rules/a2z/promotionedit.cfm
              - Empty user interface rule for personalized Promotions.
Author:      rich ragan
Date:        1/24/2000
Description: This rule has no user interface but we need some display
              because when it is added to the container, this rule is always
              run. Therefore, just explain what the rule does.
Notes:
--->

<CFOUTPUT>
<H4>Rearrange Promotional Books</H4>

This rule automatically takes the list of promotion books
published using Schedule Content and moves one or more of
them to the top of the display based on the user's genre
preferences. Be sure it is placed after the Schedule Content Rule.

</CFOUTPUT>
```

Now let's create the Execute rule for the Promotions container. It should look like Listing 19.6.

Listing 19.6 The Execute Rule for the Promotions Container

```
<!---
File:        /allaire/spectra/rules/a2z/promotionexecute.cfm
              - Execute handler for Promotion Rearrangement Rule
Author:      rich ragan
Date:        1/24/2000
Description: promotionExecute is the execute rule handler for the
              Promotion Rearrangement rule. It has no parameters. What it
              does is look up the user's favorite genre from the user
              profile and move any books of that genre to the top of the
              published item list as it is when this rule is called.
Notes:
--->

<!--- Get the user's favorite genre from the Preferences part of
    their profile. If there is no favorite, the rule does nothing. --->
<CFIF isDefined("request.stUserProfile.preferences.favoriteGenre")>
    <CFSET genre = request.stUserProfile.preferences.favoriteGenre>
```

continues

Listing 19.6 Continued

```
    <!--- Setup a temp structure for swapping elements and set the
        top index to point to the top of the list of books. It will
        be used as the place to promote a book to if one is found. --->
    <CFSET stTemp = StructNew()>
    <CFSET top=1>

   <!--- Now iterate over all the books in scheduled to be published. --->
    <CFLOOP INDEX="i" FROM="1"
     TO="#arraylen(request.cfaContainer.aObjects)#">
       <!--- Make references shorter --->
       <CFSET stAObject = request.cfaContainer.aObjects[i]>
       <!--- Get the current object so we can check its genre --->
       <cfa_contentObjectGet
        DATASOURCE="#REQUEST.CFA.a2zBooks.DATASOURCE#"
        OBJECTID="#stAObject.objectID#"
        R_STOBJECT="stObj">

      <!--- See if the user's favorite genre is associated with this book.
            If the genre is in the metadata, swap the entry at location
            "top" with the current location "i" and advance "top". This
            moves the genre entries to the top of the list. --->
       <CFIF structKeyExists(stObj.stKeywords, genre)>
           <CFSCRIPT>
               stTemp =  request.cfaContainer.aObjects[top];
               request.cfaContainer.aObjects[top] = stAObject;
               request.cfaContainer.aObjects[i] = stTemp;
               top=top+1;
           </CFSCRIPT>
       </CFIF>
    </CFLOOP>
</CFIF>
```

Okay, let's discuss what's going on in the rule execute handler and then we can see how it all works for real:

```
<CFIF isDefined("request.stUserProfile.preferences.favoriteGenre")>
    <CFSET genre = request.stUserProfile.preferences.favoriteGenre>
```

The rule begins by checking to see if the user has a favorite genre specified in his Preferences. If none is defined, the entire body of the rule is skipped and the ordering in the `aObjects` array is left untouched. The `request.stUserProfile` structure is set up in `Application.cfm`, where the user is identified. If the user has specified Preferences, they are kept in the `preferences` part of the structure. For this example, we assume that the user selects a favorite genre when he registers and that it's saved in his profile.

Our strategy is to keep an index pointing to the highest spot in the `aObjects` array, where we could place an entry matching the user's favorite genre. In fact, what we will do is swap the genre entry with the entry at the `top` index, which will put the entry of interest to the user at the top of the list. We also create a `stTemp` structure for use in swapping the two entries.

Now we create a <CFLOOP> that iterates over every entry in the aObjects array of published content:

```
<CFSET stAObject = request.cfaContainer.aObjects[i]>
        <!--- Get the current object so we can check its genre --->
        <cfa_contentObjectGet
         DATASOURCE="#REQUEST.CFA.a2zBooks.DATASOURCE#"
         OBJECTID="#stAObject.objectID#"
         R_STOBJECT="stObj">
```

We do a <CFA_CONTENTOBJECTGET> to retrieve the meta data information for the current book:

```
<CFIF structKeyExists(stObj.stKeywords, genre)>
    <CFSCRIPT>
        stTemp =  request.cfaContainer.aObjects[top];
        request.cfaContainer.aObjects[top] = stAObject;
        request.cfaContainer.aObjects[i] = stTemp;
        top=top+1;
    </CFSCRIPT>
</CFIF>
```

If the keyword in the user's favorite genre exists as a key in the object's meta data keywords, we want to swap this entry with the one at the `top` index location. Save the `top` entry in `stTemp`, replace it with the current one, and then put the entry that was at `top` in the current spot. Lastly, bump `top` so the next one we find will also move up to the top part of the list.

Now let's try it all out. First you need to be in Administration mode so that you can add the rule to the container. Go to the site home page (`http://localhost/a2z/index.cfm`) and click the See Book Promotions button. This will show a heading and nothing else. Add **`?designmode=1`** to the end of the URL and press Enter to go into Design mode. Click the icon for the Promotions container. Click the Edit command. You will see a list of all the books that have been manually selected by the promotions manager. If there are no books in the list, go ahead and add a couple via the Schedule Content rule. In the upper-right corner, use the Edit Mode pull-down to switch to Advanced mode so that we can add our new rule.

NOTE If the only rule in the container is Schedule Content, the Container Editor automatically sets Edit mode to Simple. To add more rules to the container, you must switch to Advanced mode. Once there is any rule other than Schedule Content in the rules list, the Container Editor will always come up in Advanced mode.

At the bottom, select the new rule, Rearrange Promotions (as shown in Figure 19.8), and click the Add button next to the rule selection pull-down. The rule edit handler now runs and puts up its explanation. Click OK.

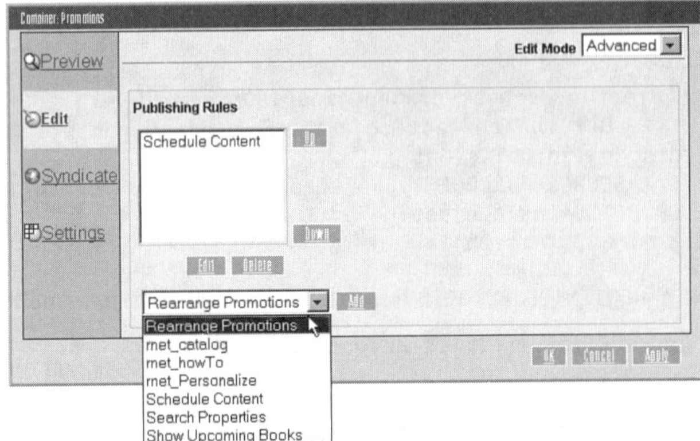

FIGURE 19.8
Add the rule Rearrange Promotions to the container. Schedule Content was already present and had some promotional books scheduled. Of course, you could add some promotional books if you want to.

Nothing should have happened to the order of the books in the container yet, because there is no favorite genre established for our user yet. Let's fix that. Open another window to the Webtop and go to Business Center, Users and Security, User Manager. Click the single user head icon under the Users title to bring up the list of users. Click the Edit icon to the left of the username you are logged in with. Click the rightmost tab, labeled Preferences. At the bottom of the dialog box, in the New Preference Name field, enter **`favoriteGenre`**. In the New Preference Value field, enter **`American`** to specify American history. Your screen should look like Figure 19.9. Then click the Create button to make the new user preference in the user profile. Leave the Webtop window open, because you will be changing the preference to see how it affects the Promotions container.

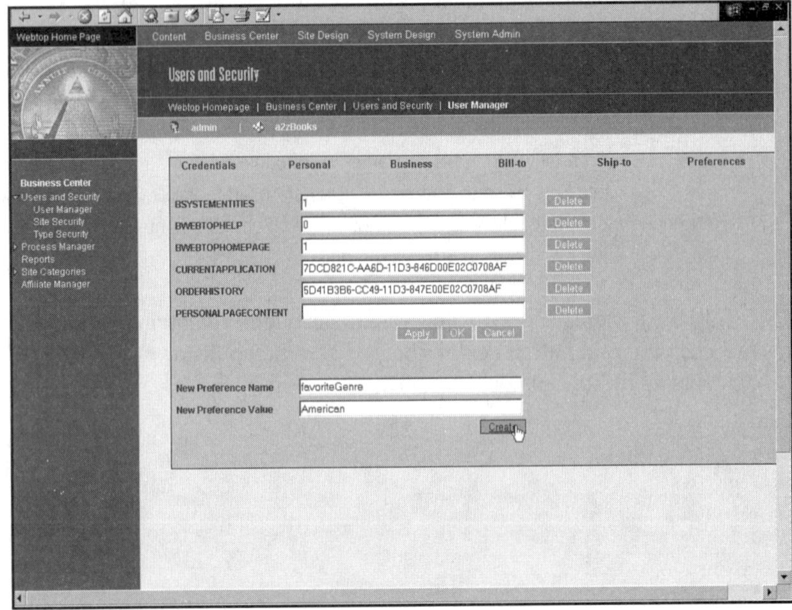

FIGURE 19.9
Add the user preference `favoriteGenre`, which is used by the Rearrange Promotions rule to personalize the Promotions container. Give it the value `American`, indicating the user is interested in American history.

Switch back to the Design Mode window on the site. If you have any books with the genre American, they may have already moved to the top of the list. If you haven't specified a meta data genre, use the Webtop and go to System Design, Site Object Designer, and Object Finder. Select a book, click Categorize, and specify a genre. For this example, make sure that at least one book has the genre American and another one has the genre Computer. Reload the page, and the genre American book will move to the top. Now flip back to the User Profile Preferences in Webtop. Change the `favorite Genre` value to `Computer` and click the Apply button. Now switch back to the Promotions page and reload the page. You should see the computer book move to the top and the American history books fall down the list.

With these two examples of rules-based publishing, you should have a good feel for how to make your own rules for dynamic publishing as well as personalization. ●

CHAPTER 20

Syndication

In this chapter

Syndication and Affiliation

We constantly read about the Internet's explosive growth. We are bombarded with figures and graphs showing that more and more people sign up and log on every day to surf the Web. What's becoming more and more apparent, however, is that people aren't the only ones cruising the Internet. What most people think of as the "Internet experience" is a person sitting in front of a computer requesting documents from Web sites. At the same time, however, another computer may be requesting Web documents as well. Typically, this is another business requesting information from a Web site. The business visitor requires a different set of information than the casual user. In fact, the information a business requires may have to be packaged and prepared for easy data transfer. Unlike the person who sees a site with pretty graphics and maybe even multimedia, normally the business will hit a Web site requesting just the content, plain text wrapped up in such a way so that it can be parsed by a computer program and reused.

This, in a nutshell, is what we call *syndication*. Think of syndication as a Web site's capability to share its information with business partners. This could be as simple as a news site sharing articles with a partner site. The partner gets the articles and can display them on its own site using its particular kind of formatting and display. This is what is referred to as *content syndication*. Along with content syndication, we have what's called *application syndication*. Imagine an auto parts distributor with a database of all its parts. It has a partnership with a company that sells its products. When a user hits the Web site of the company that sells the products, it can search for particular items. What the user doesn't realize is that when she searches for auto parts, the Web site makes a Web request against the distributor's Web site. The sales company doesn't have to worry about keeping a copy of the distributor's database. It just fires off any search request on its site to the distributor's site. We will look at this in detail later in the chapter. Let's begin by looking at content syndication.

Content Syndication

Content syndication involves the sharing of text, graphics, and other parts of what makes up a Web site. This syndication can happen in two ways:

- A site can send its content to its partners, also known as *affiliates*. This is known as *outbound syndication*.
- A site can *import*, or download, information from other sites. This is known as *inbound syndication*.

We will discuss how Spectra handles both forms of syndication. Before we go any further, let's cover a few basics of how content syndication works in Spectra.

Content syndication is tied directly to containers. This means that your site will syndicate content directly from containers, or content published via Spectra's publishing system.

▶ **See** Chapter 10, "Creating and Managing Content," for more information on containers and Spectra publishing techniques.

Since syndication is container based, we will be using the same container editors used to edit containers to set up syndication subscriptions. A *subscription* is simply a timed delivery of information, like a daily newspaper. We can say, "Deliver this container's information once a day at 7:30 a.m." We will get into the specifics of how this works later in the chapter.

Creating an Affiliate

Before we can begin working with syndication, we need to have someone to share information with. For this chapter, we are going to create a fake "dot com" company that will be our affiliate. The name of this company is WeOnlySellBooks.com. Since you probably don't have multiple servers, we are going to place its Web site on the same one you have worked on before.

NOTE The CD accompanying this book contains all the files for this Web site. Copy the `WeOnlySellBooks` folder from the CD to your Web server's root document folder. You should *not* put this folder inside the `a2z` folder used for a2zBooks.

To begin this process, we need to define WeOnlySellBooks.com as an affiliate. This is quite easy to do using the User Management tools in the Webtop. Open up your Webtop and navigate to the System Admin section. Next, click the Users and Security section, and then the User Directories link. Once there, click the Users icon next to the user directory called `userDirectory`. This is the user directory we are using for our Spectra server. At this point, you should see a list of users like that in Figure 20.1.

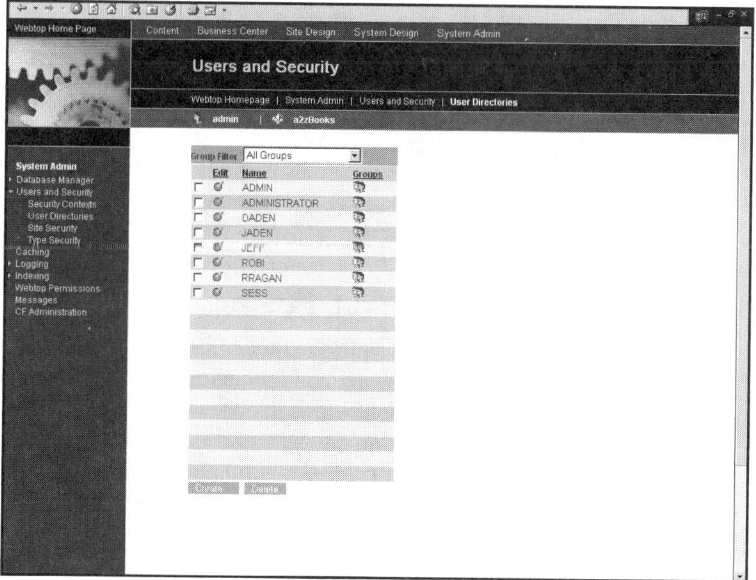

FIGURE 20.1
The users in `userDirectory`. Your listing might look different.

We need to create a user for the WeOnlySellBooks.com company. Click the Create button to start the user-creation process. The username should be `weonlysellbooks`. We will keep the password simple, just enter **`foo`** and be sure to enter the same thing in the Confirm Password text box. As for the description, enter **`The WeOnlySellBooks affiliate`**. Figure 20.2 shows what the final form should look like.

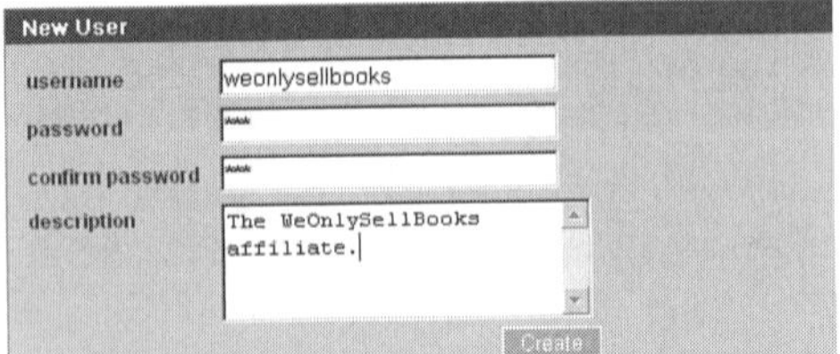

FIGURE 20.2
The completed form for the `weonlysellbooks` user.

Now that you've entered the relevant information for the user, click the Create button to finish the process. You will return to the same screen you saw in Figure 20.1, except this time you will see the `weonlysellbooks` user.

After creating the user, we need to let Spectra know that this user is an affiliate. This is rather easy, since Spectra creates an Affiliates group in the `userDirectory` user directory. To put our new user in that group, click the Groups icon (it looks like two faces) to the right of the `weonlysellbooks` user. This allows you to edit the groups that the user is in. All we want to do is put the user in the Affiliates group. To do that, select that group and click the arrow pointing to the left. This will move the entry from Available Groups to the Current Groups section. Figure 20.3 shows how this listing should look after the group is added. After you add the group to the user, be sure to click `OK`.

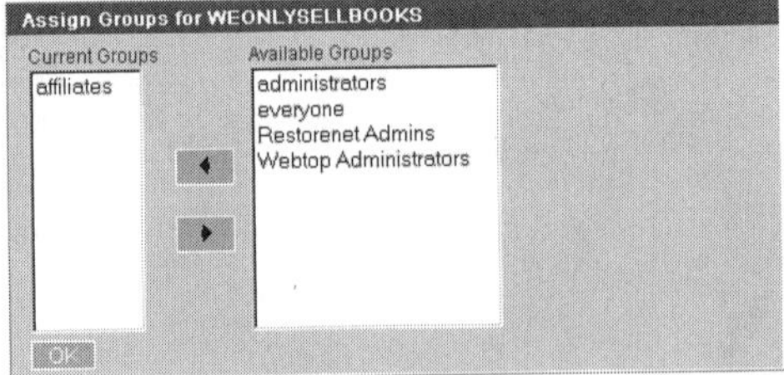

FIGURE 20.3
The Affiliates group has been added to the WeOnlySellBooks user. The user is now in the Affiliates group.

Outbound Syndication: Server Push

Now that we have created an affiliate, it's time to begin syndicating content. As described earlier, content syndication can be separated into outbound and inbound syndication. We will now discuss outbound syndication, which in our case involves the Spectra server sharing its content (or pushing it out) to its affiliates. We have a variety of ways to handle this and, in fact, can either push the content (server push) or allow the client to pull (client pull). When we set up the subscription for WeOnlySellBooks.com, we can choose to either push the content to them (and do it in multiple ways) or have them pull the content from us. Each method has its benefits and drawbacks.

Let's begin by creating the subscription. First, we need to pick what content we will share with our affiliate. Let's share the book Catalog. Browse to the Catalog page of the a2z site by opening your browser to `http://localhost/a2z/catalog/index.cfm`. To set up the subscription for the content on this page, we need to view the a2zBooks site as an admin would—in Design mode. To do so, append `?designmode=1` to the URL. You should see this URL in your browser's location bar:

```
http://localhost/a2z/catalog/index.cfm?designmode=1
```

If you're prompted to log on, use the username of the admin user we created. The username is `admin` and the password is `admin` as well. Since you just recently came from the Webtop, however, you probably won't be prompted to log on. Figure 20.4 shows the catalog page in Design mode.

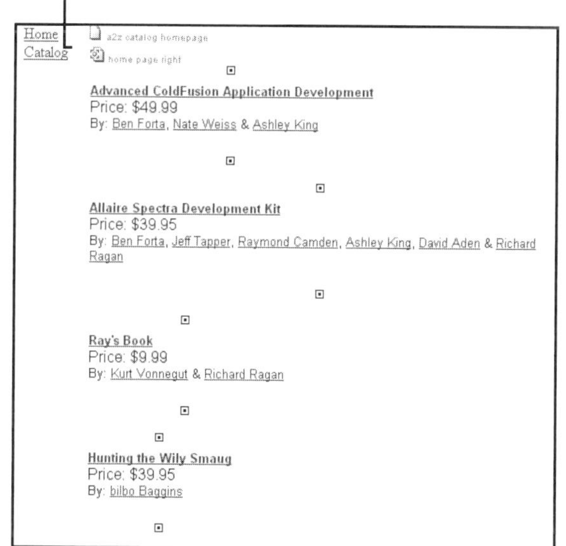

FIGURE 20.4
The Catalog page in Design mode.

Now that we see the edit controls on the page, click the Container Editor icon right above the first book title to bring up the Container Editor.

▶ **See** Chapter 10 for more information on containers and how they work.

When you worked with containers earlier in the book, you primarily worked with the Preview and Edit sections of the Container Editor. Now we are going to work in the Syndicate area. Click that link to bring up the Subscriptions and Schedule Editor. Figure 20.5 shows what this editor should look like.

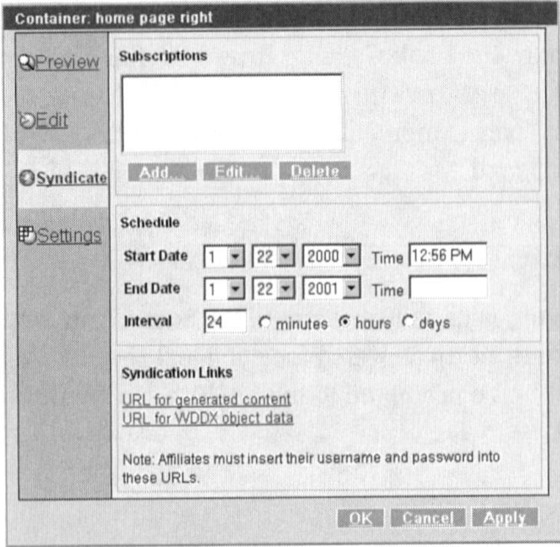

FIGURE 20.5
The Subscriptions and Schedule Editor for syndication.

As you can see, there are no subscriptions set up for this container. Let's create one by clicking the Add button. The first thing we have to do is pick a user. Why? Well, Spectra automatically ties in security to syndication. This allows you to restrict who can syndicate your content. Also, your container may publish different content, depending on the user viewing the container. In this respect, we are telling the container, "When you publish this content, pretend that a certain user is viewing it." We have two options here:

- The `unspecified` user is the same as the `anonymous` Web user, the person who hits your site without logging on.
- The other option is the user we just created. We see the description we entered earlier, the WeOnlySellBooks.com affiliate.

Now, our site has more users than what we see listed here. What Spectra is doing, however, is restricting the output to the `anonymous` user and any user in the Affiliates group.

TIP Notice that the users here are displayed by description rather than username. You may want to use short descriptions when creating affiliate users.

Select the WeOnlySellBooks.com affiliate for the user. Don't change the Security Context or User Directory values; they allow you to pick users from other security contexts or user directories, something you don't need to do now. Figure 20.6 shows the form with the correct user selected.

Click the Continue button to begin the next phase of the subscription editor. We are now asked to choose what format to syndicate the content in: Generated Content or WDDX Object Data. This allows us to either send to the affiliate simple text (HTML) or a WDDX packet. What we choose depends on what system the affiliate has. If we send the HTML, the affiliate can simply include that data on a page. They don't need to do anything with it. To see how this looks, click the Preview link next to the Generated Content option. Figure 20.7 shows what this option does.

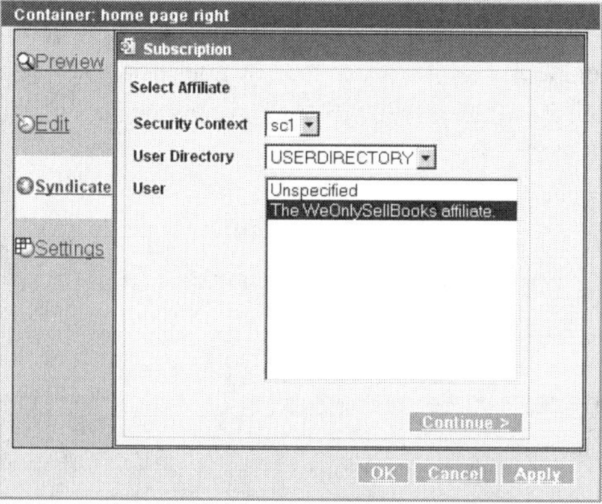

FIGURE 20.6
Here, we have chosen the user who "owns" the subscription.

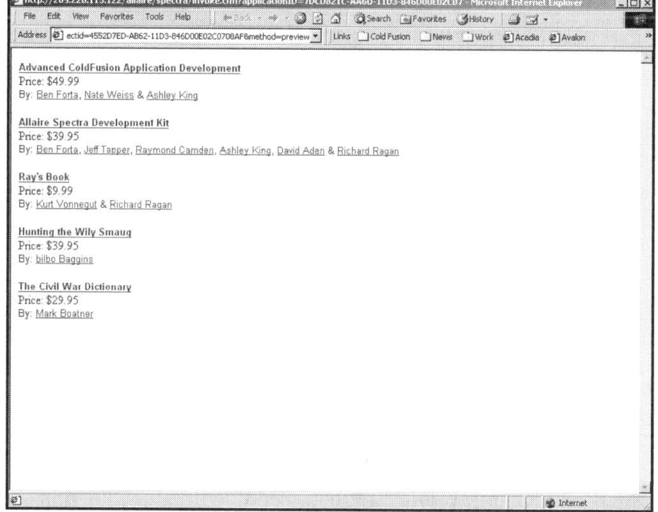

FIGURE 20.7
The Generated Content view of the subscription.

If you view the source of this page, you will see it's the exact same HTML that the container displays. Again, this makes it easy to use for the affiliate. The affiliate can save this HTML and then use a simple `<CFINCLUDE>` to display it on its site. But this prevents the affiliate from *rebranding* or changing the look-and-feel of the content. What if the affiliate didn't want the authors listed? What if they want the price to come first and then the title? They could certainly attempt to reformat the HTML, but it would be complex and hard to implement. Instead, it would be much easier to simply send the WDDX data. WDDX, or Web Distributed Data eXchange, is a way to package data so that it can be easily transferred to other systems. In our syndication model, we can send the WDDX packets that represent these books. If the affiliate supports WDDX, it can reformat the output any way it wants.

NOTE WDDX is supported on multiple systems. The affiliate doesn't need to be running Spectra or even ColdFusion. WDDX can be understood by ColdFusion, ASP, Perl, and other languages. More support is added for WDDX every day. For more information, visit the WDDX home page at `http://www.wddx.org`.

To see the WDDX output, click the Preview link to the right of that option. (You may want to close the window that was created to show the Generated Content preview.) Figure 20.8 shows this preview.

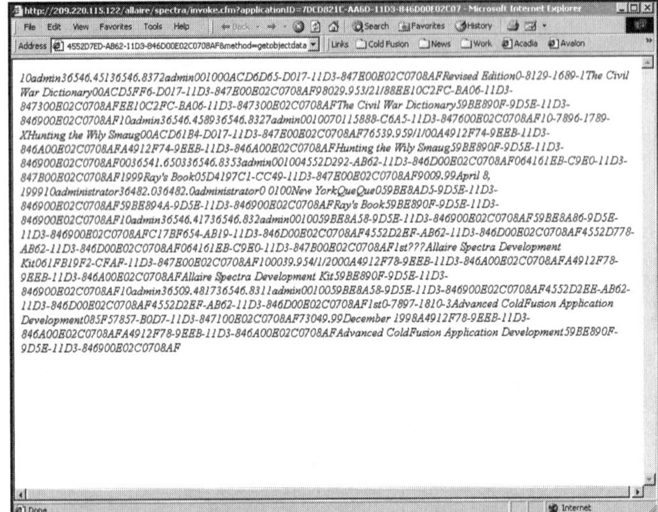

FIGURE 20.8
The WDDX Object Data view of the subscription.

This version of the data is almost impossible to read, but the point is that you (the user) don't need to be able to read it. The affiliate will take this WDDX packet, deserialize it, and use it on its site. Our affiliate, WeOnlySellBooks.com, uses a ColdFusion server and has told us that they prefer the WDDX Object Data version so that they can reformat the look-and-feel of the content. Select that option and click the Continue button.

Now we are asked to choose the delivery mode of the subscription. We have three options for pushing the content to the affiliate:

- *HTTP Post.* This method is the same as a Web "hit" on the affiliate's site. In this form of push, the Spectra server will make an HTTP Post to the affiliate's server. For this to work, the affiliate must have a Web page whose sole purpose is to wait to be hit by the Spectra server. Think of it as a dedicated "receiver" of the syndicated content. You will notice that the options for HTTP Post relate directly to the kinds of things we need to know. We have options for URL, Username, and Password (the receiver file may be protected by the Web server), Port, and Timeout. The only required value here is the URL. The username and password are required only if the URL is secured. The port is required only if the affiliate site uses a nonstandard port. (The standard port for Web servers is 80.) The timeout value allows us to terminate the attempt if it takes too long to finish.

HTTP is the best method of syndicating to another Web server because the connection is direct—that is, from one Web server to another. Unlike FTP and email syndication, this method has the best possibility of not failing.

- *FTP.* This option means that the Spectra server will use the FTP protocol to send the content to the affiliate. For this to work right, of course, the affiliate must have an FTP server set up. Like the HTTP Post method, the options here are specific for FTP connections. We need the server, the username and password, the directory to store the information, the filename to use, the port of the server, and a timeout value. The only required fields here are Server, Username, Password, and File. The Directory option will make the FTP connection switch to a new directory on connection. We can also make the filename dynamic by telling the Spectra server to append the date and time when the connection was made. This could be useful for the affiliate. It may want to store multiple versions of the syndicated content.
- *Email.* As you can imagine, this method sends an email to the affiliate. Our options are standard for emails: To, From, CC, and Subject. As with FTP, we can append the date and time to the subject. How could you use this option? The affiliate may create a special email address to receive the email with the content. It would then write a program that, according to a certain schedule, checks the email account for deliveries from A2Z. It could download the email and use it in whatever manner it wanted. Email would probably be best for syndication to a user rather than a computer. With the possibility of something going wrong on one of two email servers (the one that sends and the one that receives), as well as the wait between the time your server sends and the email is downloaded, this may not be the optimal way to syndicate to another Web site.

Email server push is a great way to allow people to subscribe to your site. Imagine that your site allowed people to sign up to receive content from your site. If your mail server has an alias for that group—let's say `subscribes@a2zbooks.com`—you could use the email syndication method to send them the content of your site once a week. Of course, you would probably want to use the Generated Content format instead of WDDX packets.

Now that we have described the three different ways we can push to our affiliate, let's choose the HTTP Post method as our way of sending content to WeOnlySellBooks.com. We need to enter the URL of the receiver file, so enter

```
http://localhost/weonlysellbooks/receiver.cfm
```

Don't enter anything for the Username, Password, Port, and Timeout values. Figure 20.9 shows how this form should look.

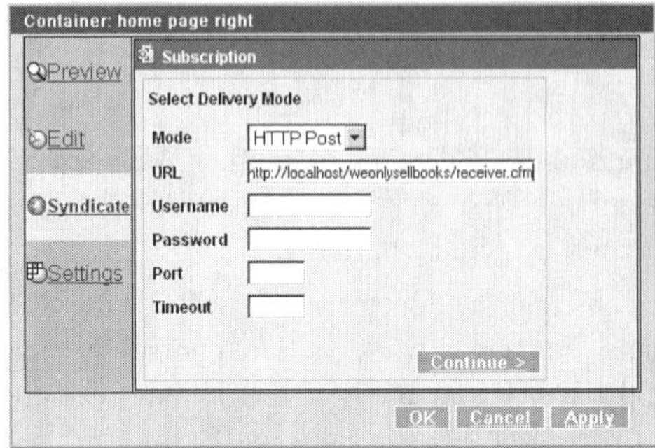

FIGURE 20.9
The information required for our HTTP Post to the affiliate.

After you enter the URL, click the Continue button to finish the Subscription Editor. We are now back to the beginning of the editor, and you should see your subscription listed in the Subscriptions box. The name of the subscription is the same as the username of the affiliate. If you want, you can create new subscriptions or edit and delete existing ones.

Beneath the list of subscriptions is the Schedule section. This allows you to specify when content will be pushed. The content will be pushed to *all* subscriptions according to the schedule you set up. To set up a schedule, first choose the date range of the subscription. We have values for the start date and time and for the end date and time. We want the schedule to start now and end far in the future. In the End Date section, pick the year 2010. This subscription is a permanent one, so we chose 2010 so that we don't have to worry about it (at least for a few more years!). Don't worry about setting the time. Now we need to signify how often the push will happen. What you choose will depend on your site. Does your site update itself quite often? Then maybe you will want to push content out every two hours. How often you push content will also depend on what the affiliate wants. Maybe your site updates quite often, but the affiliate wants content only once a week. In that case, you would enter **7** for the Interval and choose `days` as the unit.

Our affiliate has told us they want the content once a day, so enter **1** for the Interval and select `days` as the unit. Now we are ready to finalize the syndication. Click the Apply button and the syndication will be set up. Figure 20.10 shows us the syndication editor in its final state.

Now that we have created the subscription, we need to create the file that WeOnlySellBooks.com will use to intercept and parse the data. Listing 20.1 shows the code for the receiver file.

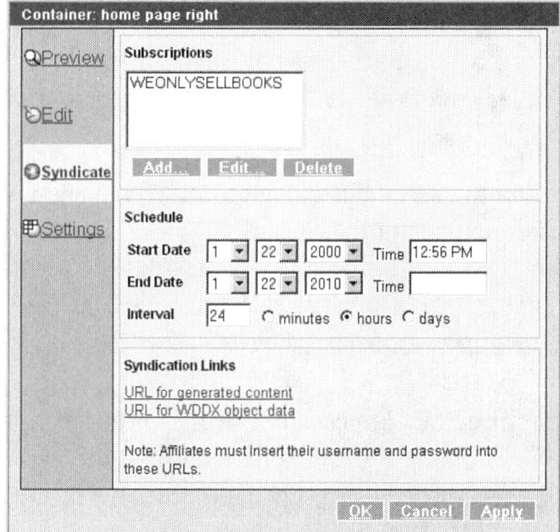

FIGURE 20.10
The syndication editor with our subscription and schedule set up. Notice how Spectra changed 1 day to 24 hours. Don't worry, this is just a reflection of how ColdFusion handles scheduled events.

Listing 20.1 ***receiver.cfm*—The Receiver File**

```
<!---
File:          /weonlysellbooks/receiver.cfm
Author:        Raymond Camden (raymond.k.camden@syntegra.com)
Date:          1/20/2000
Description:   Receives the syndicated content and
               saves it to the file system.
Notes:
--->

<!---
    This page is called by the A2Z Spectra system. It is not meant
    to be viewed by the general public. Therefore the page won't
    have any HTML or graphics in it.
--->

<!--- Spectra sends the content in a form field called "Payload." --->
<!--- If the variable doesn't exist, exit the template. --->
<CFIF NOT IsDefined("Form.Payload")>
    <CFABORT>
</CFIF>
<CFSET Content = Form.Payload>

<!--- Get the directory --->
<CFSET ThisDir = ExpandPath(".")>

<!--- FileName is packet.txt + directory. --->
<CFSET FileName = ThisDir & "\catalog_packet.txt">

<!--- Save the packet. --->
<CFFILE ACTION="WRITE" FILE="#FileName#" OUTPUT="#Content#">
```

Listing 20.1 is pretty simple. We begin by making sure that `Form.Payload` exists. As the comment in the code states, when Spectra sends syndicated content, it uses a form field called Payload. If there is no `Form.Payload`, we `<CFABORT>` and exit the template. If it does exist, we copy it to a local variable called `Packet`.

We want to save the packet in the same directory as our Web site, so we use the `ExpandDir()` function to find out our current directory.

NOTE Calling `ExpandDir(".")` simply tells ColdFusion to expand the current directory. The . simply represents the current working directory.

When we know the current directory, we create a string to represent the filename. We do this by starting with the directory, adding a \ character, and then the name of the file. We will name the file `catalog_packet.txt`, a descriptive name for what we are saving.

When we have the filename, all we need is one simple `<CFFILE>` tag to copy the contents of the packet to our file.

If you run this script in your browser, you won't see anything, because we set up our script to abort if it wasn't passed the `Form.Payload` variable. You have two options: wait for the scheduled event to fire or force it to happen now. We have two ways to force the scheduled event to run.

The first way is to open your ColdFusion Administrator (`http://localhost/cfide/Administrator`) and go to the Scheduled Tasks section. You should see an event with the word `syndicate` in it. It will probably look something like this:

```
cfa_4552D7ED-AB62-11D3-846D00E02C0708AF_syndicate_7DCD821C-AA6D-11D3-
➥846D00E02C0708AF
```

It's a complex name, and yours may be slightly different, but you should have only one task with the word `syndicate` in it.

The second way to force the scheduled event to run varies depending on the version of ColdFusion Server you're using. If you're running ColdFusion Server 4.5. On the right side of the task will be a link marked Run. This forces the event to run immediately. If you're running ColdFusion Server 4.01, you can follow these steps to run the event:

1. Begin by clicking the task name. This brings you to the details page for the event.
2. The value in the URL form field is a long URL that passes a lot of information to Spectra. Copy and paste this URL into the location bar of your browser.
3. Press Enter to load the URL.

   When you run this in your browser, you won't see anything. Remember that all of this is meant to happen without user interaction. By hitting this special URL on your server, you told Spectra to fire off the syndication. That in turn made the server do a HTTP push to WeOnlySellBooks.com, which in our case is on the same server.

4. To see if this worked, open the `weonlysellbooks` folder and see if there is a file called `catalog_packet.txt`. If not, an error occurred, and you should check your log files to see what happened.

Now that we have forced the scheduled event to run, we need to write a script that will work with the syndicated content. Listing 20.2 shows a script that parses the text file (`catalog_packet.txt`) created in Listing 20.1.

CAUTION

A bug exists with ColdFusion 4.5 that makes the HTTP Push method not work as expected. This bug is fixed in ColdFusion 4.5.1, a free upgrade of the 4.5 server.

Listing 20.2 ***catalog.cfm*—Parsing the Text File Created in Listing 20.1**

```
<!---
File:          /weonlysellbooks/catalog.cfm
Author:        Raymond Camden (raymond.k.camden@syntegra.com)
Date:          1/20/2000
Description:
Notes:
--->


<!--- Introduction Text --->
Welcome to the WeOnlySellBooks.com Catalog. Below is a listing of the
books we currently have for sale.
<P>

<!--- Load Packet --->
<CFFILE ACTION="Read" FILE="#ExpandPath("catalog_packet.txt")#"
      VARIABLE="ResultsPacket">

<!--- Convert packet into objects --->
<CFWDDX ACTION="WDDX2CFML" INPUT="#ResultsPacket#" OUTPUT="Books">

<!--- Loop through each book. --->
<CFLOOP ITEM="Book" COLLECTION="#Books#">
    <!--- We hike up the price a bit. --->
    <CFSET NewPrice = Books[Book].Price * 1.3>
    <!--- Add five bucks for the programmers swiss bank account --->
    <CFSET NewPrice = NewPrice + 5>
    <CFOUTPUT>
        <B><I>#Books[Book].Title#</I></B><BR>
        #DollarFormat(NewPrice)#
        <P>
    </CFOUTPUT>
</CFLOOP>
```

We begin this script with some simple text letting the user know what page he is on. Next, we use the `<CFFILE>` tag to read the file that A2ZBooks pushed to our site. The filename was `catalog_packet.txt`, but we need to supply the full pathname so we use the `ExpandPath()` function. This translates `catalog_packet.txt` into the full path and filename. We read this file into a variable called `ResultsPacket`. Next, we used the `<CFWDDX>` tag to convert the WDDX packet into a CFML structure.

Once we have the structure of book objects, we loop through each one using the `ITEM` and `COLLECTION` attributes of `<CFLOOP>`. For each book we grab the price and inflate it a bit, and then output the title and the new price. It's as simple as that. WeOnlySellBooks.com never needs to worry about the content. Once each day A2ZBooks will push the content to its server; WeOnlySellBooks.com doesn't need to do any work to update its content. As you can see already, this is quite simple to use!

Outbound Syndication: Client Pull

In the previous example, we set up our syndication to work via server push. In other words, our server sent the information to the affiliate. We can also allow our affiliate to pull information directly from the container. How is this done? If you closed the Container Editor we used earlier, return to the catalog page on the A2Z site and click the Container Editor icon again. Return to the Syndicate section and look at the section on the bottom called Syndication Links. These two links can be given to our affiliate and can then be used to pull content from the container. If you click either link, you will see a preview, just like we saw when setting up the server push subscription. Our affiliate likes the WDDX packet, so we need to give them the URL for WDDX object data. You can do this by right-clicking the link and selecting Copy Shortcut. (If you're using Netscape as your browser, right-click the link and select Copy Link Location.) After you do that, paste it into a blank, new document in Studio or in Notepad. You're going to need the URL in a few minutes.

Once we have the URL needed to pull the content from the container, we need to write a script that can grab it. Listing 20.3 displays the ColdFusion script WeOnlySellBooks.com uses to perform a client pull.

Listing 20.3 *catalog2.cfm*—Displaying the Script Used to Perform a Client Pull

```
<!---
File:          /weonlysellbooks/catalog2.cfm
Author:        Raymond Camden (raymond.k.camden@syntegra.com)
Date:          1/20/2000
Description:
Notes:
--->

<!--- Introduction Text --->
```

```
Welcome to the WeOnlySellBooks.com Catalog. Below is a listing of the
books we currently have for sale.
<P>

<!---
    URL to perform client pull on A2Z
    This is the URL that you will change to match
    your system

    notice that we entered the username and password
--->

<CFSET A2ZLink = "http://localhost/allaire/spectra/invoke.cfm?" &
"method=getobjectdata&objectID=4552D7ED-AB62-11D3-846D00E02C0708AF" &
"&applicationID=7DCD821C-AA6D-11D3-846D00E02C0708AF" &

<!--- Perform the 'pull' --->
<CFHTTP URL="#A2ZLink#" METHOD="GET">

<!--- Get ResultsPacket --->
<CFSET ResultsPacket = CFHTTP.FileContent>

<!--- Convert packet into objects --->
<CFWDDX ACTION="WDDX2CFML" INPUT="#ResultsPacket#" OUTPUT="Books">

<!--- Loop through each book. --->
<CFLOOP ITEM="Book" COLLECTION="#Books#">
    <!--- We hike up the price a bit. --->
    <CFSET NewPrice = Books[Book].Price * 1.3>
    <!--- Add five bucks for the programmer's swiss bank account --->
    <CFSET NewPrice = NewPrice + 5>
    <CFOUTPUT>
        <B><I>#Books[Book].Title#</I></B><BR>
        #DollarFormat(NewPrice)#
        <P>
    </CFOUTPUT>
</CFLOOP>
```

Our code begins with some simple text telling the user that this page is our book catalog. The next link is copied from the Container Editor. We have made one change to it. At the end, we changed `username=&password=` to `username=weonlysellbooks&password=foo`. This is the username and password for our affiliate. If we don't pass a valid username and password, Spectra will force us to log on. We would end up with a logon form onscreen instead of the syndicated content.

Part IV Ch 20

Next, we use the `<CFHTTP>` tag to perform the client pull. We pass in the `A2ZLink` variable and use the `Get` method. The result of this operation is available in the `CFHTTP.FileContent` variable. We save this into a local variable called `ResultsPacket` and then use the `<CFWDDX>` tag to convert it from WDDX into objects. Once we have the objects, we use the `<CFLOOP>` tag to iterate over each item. In this case we know we're getting a bunch of books, so we use the

`ITEM` attribute of `<CFLOOP>` to store the object ID. Once we have it, we can get values out of the `Books` structure by using the ID that is set in the `Book` variable. For each book, we want to create a new price. We take the price, `Books[Book].Price`, and up it by 30%. We then output the title and the price using the `DollarFormat()` tag. Pretty simple? As in Listing 20.2, we could modify the look and feel of the books to match our site. If I wanted to, I could have taken the title and used a third-party CFX tag and performed a translation on it. Figure 20.11 shows the result of the client pull.

As you can imagine, this is pretty powerful stuff. The second the A2Z site changes the contents of the container, it will be immediately reflected on the WeOnlySellBooks.com site. Unlike the server push content syndication, changes are reflected as soon as they happen. This can be both good and bad. If A2ZBooks had a large number of affiliates, and those affiliates got a lot of traffic, A2ZBooks may find its servers being pushed too hard. You have to find the balance between getting the most up-to-date information and managing server traffic.

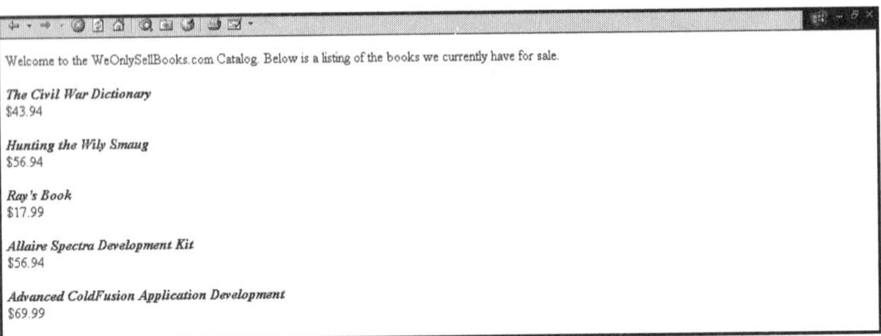

FIGURE 20.11
The syndicated catalog on the affiliate site.

NOTE We've said this already, but it bears repeating. There is *nothing* inherent about content syndication that requires the affiliate to have either Spectra or ColdFusion. The ColdFusion script we used to perform the client pull could have been written in ASP or Perl, or any language that can translate WDDX. If we didn't care about getting a nice WDDX packet, we could have used *any* language as long as it had a mechanism to perform a Web hit, like the `<CFHTTP>` tag.

Inbound Syndication

So far we have talked about how a Spectra server can share its content with other servers on the Internet. Now it's time to talk about how a Spectra server can import data from other sites. Imagine that A2Z wants to grab news headlines from a major news agency. A2Z can set up a relationship with the agency in which it is allowed to import news articles that deal with books, authors, and the publishing industry. A2Z could bring these articles in and automatically create Spectra objects out of them.

Spectra supports inbound syndication using what it calls *syndication streams*. A syndication stream is made up of two simple components:

- The first part is a *handler*. This tells the Spectra server what file to call to handle the stream. The handler will take care of grabbing the content from the affiliate and doing whatever needs to be done. For example, the handler could use the `<CFHTTP>` tag to hit the remote site, download content, and create new objects out of it.
- The second part of the stream is the *schedule*. This simply dictates how often the server will call the handler. This may be dictated by the affiliate (they may allow you to "call" them only once a day) or be totally up to your server's needs.

Spectra sets up syndication streams in the Webtop. Open your Webtop to the System Design area. Click the Programming Objects link in the navigation area and then select the Syndication Streams link. Figure 20.12 shows this section of the Webtop.

We're going to set up a syndication stream for the A2Z site. This syndication stream will grab content from the affiliate, WeOnlySellBooks.com. WeOnlySellBooks.com stores a list of new authors. We will take this list of authors and add them as new Author objects in our database. To begin this process, we need to create the stream in the Webtop. Click the Create link to begin. For the label, enter **`Import Authors from WeOnlySellBooks.com`** and use `/a2z/importAuthors.cfm` as the handler.

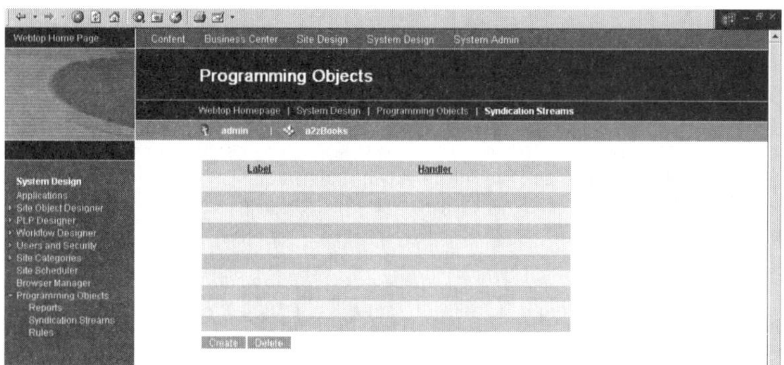

FIGURE 20.12 The Syndication Streams section of the Webtop.

For the schedule, let's set it up to run "forever." Leave the Start Date as is and change the year on the End Date to 2010. We want the import to run once a day, so leave the interval as it is. Figure 20.13 shows the completed form.

FIGURE 20.13 The `importAuthors` syndication stream.

After you enter all the data, click OK to complete the process. You should now see the stream listed and can either edit or delete the stream at a later time.

Now that we've set up the syndication stream, it would be a good idea to actually code the handler; otherwise, nothing will happen when the server fires off the scheduled event. Listing 20.4 shows how we import data from WeOnlySellBooks.com.

Listing 20.4 *importAuthors.cfm*—Importing Data

```
<!---
File:         /a2z/importAuthors.cfm
Author:       Raymond Camden (raymond.k.camden@syntegra.com)
Date:         1/20/2000
Description:  Hits our affiliate site and imports new authors
Notes:
--->

<!--- This is where we get our stuff. --->
<CFSET RemoteLink = "http://localhost/weonlysellbooks/authors.txt">

<!--- Perform the CFHTTP --->
<CFHTTP URL="#RemoteLink#" METHOD="Get">

<!--- Get the content --->
<CFSET Results = CFHTTP.FileContent>

<!---
    The text file we get from WeOnlySellBooks.com is in a special format.
    Each line is the name of an author.
    However, if the line begins with a #, it's a comment line.
--->

<!---
    To parse each line, we need to CFLOOP over Results. We
    can treat the new line character ( Chr(10) ) as a delimiter.
--->

<!--- Chr(10) is a new line character --->
<CFSET Delimiter = Chr(10)>

<!--- Loop over each line --->
<CFLOOP INDEX="Line" LIST="#Results#" DELIMITERS="#Delimiter#">
    <!--- If a line starts with #, it's a comment. --->
    <!--- We only want to do something if it DOESN'T start like that. --->
    <!---
        We use 2 #'s since # is a special character to CF. Using
        2 # characters really means just one.

        We also check Len(Line) to make sure the line isn't empty.
    --->
    <CFIF NOT Left(Line,1) IS "##" AND Len(Trim(Line))>
```

```
        <!---
            The string is FirstName Lastname.
            We split it to get first name and last name.
        --->
        <CFSET FirstName = ListFirst(Line," ")>
        <CFSET LastName = ListLast(Line," ")>

        <!--- Create a new Author object. --->
        <CFSET NewAuthor = StructNew()>
        <CFSET NewAuthor.firstname = FirstName>
        <CFSET NewAuthor.lastname = LastName>
        <CFSET NewAuthor.label = Line>

        <!--- Do we already have an author like this? --->
        <CFA_CONTENTOBJECTFIND DATASOURCE="a2zAccess"
            TYPEID="#Application.AuthorTypeID#" STPROPERTIES="#NewAuthor#"
            LPROPERTIESPRECEDENCE="label,firstname,lastname"
            r_lObjects="matchList">
        <!--- If matchList has ANYTHING, then we already have this
            author... --->
<CFIF NOT Len(matchList)>
            <!--- Mark the object 'active' --->
            <CFSET NewAuthor.ATTR_ACTIVE = 1>
            <!--- Since we didn't have a match, make the new author. --->
            <CFA_CONTENTOBJECTCREATE DATASOURCE="a2zAccess"
                TYPEID="#Application.AuthorTypeID#"
                STPROPERTIES="#NewAuthor#">
</CFIF>
    </CFIF>
</CFLOOP>
```

Let's see how this handler imports data. We begin by creating a variable, `RemoteLink`, to store the URL of the page we hit to import data. This is similar to the way our affiliate was given a URL to do a client pull on our site. This time, however, the affiliate gave us the URL to use. Once we have the URL, we use the `<CFHTTP>` tag to grab the content. We copy this into a variable called `Results`.

Now comes the important part. When we set up this syndication stream with WeOnlySellBooks.com, they told us what format their data was in. Again, this is just like outbound syndication. The party receiving the data needs to know what format the data is in. While we provided WeOnlySellBooks.com with a nice WDDX wrapped format, they aren't quite as nice. They are providing us a simple text file. In this text file, some lines begin with the `#` character and are considered comments. Every other line is the name of an author.

To begin parsing the data, we need to iterate over each line of the text file. We can do this easily by treating the file as though it were a list. The delimiter for our file is the new line character. This invisible character is entered when you press Enter or Return on your keyboard. We can access this character by using the `Chr()` function. This returns the character specified by the code passed to the function. (`Chr(10)` is the same as the new line character.)

Now that we know how to read our file, we use the `<CFLOOP>` tag to loop over the list using our new line character. For each iteration of the loop, we stuff the current line into a variable called `Line`. Next, we need to make sure that the line we are examining isn't a comment or a blank line. This piece of code

```
<CFIF NOT Left(Line,1) IS "##" AND Len(Trim(Line))>
```

checks to make sure the first character isn't a `#` character and the line isn't blank. Notice that we had to escape the `#` character, since ColdFusion treats this as a special character.

Once we are sure we have a good line, we need to parse it to find the author's first and last names. Each line with an author on it will have this format:

FirstName LastName

So, we can treat the line like one more list. This time, the space character (`" "`) is our delimiter.

NOTE Using the space character as a delimiter isn't the best way to split up the line. An author's last name could have a space in it. We have to make some assumptions here, since we don't have control over the format. In the real world, you often can't dictate the format of the data you import.

We grab the first name by using the `ListFirst()` function, which grabs the first element of a list. We pass in the list (which, remember, is our `Line` variable) and use a space character as the delimiter. We use the `ListLast()` function to grab the last name. As you can guess, this function gets the last element of a list.

Once we have the first and last names, we are about ready to create a new Author object. We begin by creating a structure called `NewAuthor` that will store the values of a new object. These lines create the structure and pass in our data.

```
<CFSET NewAuthor = StructNew()>
<CFSET NewAuthor.firstname = FirstName>
<CFSET NewAuthor.lastname = LastName>
<CFSET NewAuthor.label = Line>
```

We use the `Line` variable, which is the first and last names, as the label of our object.

Before creating the author, however, we should check to see if we don't already have an author with the same first and last names. To do this, we use the `<CFA_CONTENTOBJECTFIND>` tag to search for objects with the same name. This line

```
<CFA_CONTENTOBJECTFIND DATASOURCE="a2zAccess"
    TYPEID="#Application.AuthorTypeID#" STPROPERTIES="#NewAuthor#"
    LPROPERTIESPRECEDENCE="label,firstname,lastname"
    r_lObjects="matchList">
```

performs a search against our database.

▶ **See** Chapter 14, "Searching and Indexing," for more information on searching Spectra content.

We tell `<CFA_CONTENTOBJECTFIND>` to return any matches as a list of objects in a variable called `matchList`. We can then check the variable to see if we had a match. If there is *anything* in the variable, we shouldn't add the author. This line performs that check:

```
<CFIF NOT Len(matchList)>
```

Once we are sure that the author doesn't already exist on our system, we can create the new object. Before calling the tag that will create the author, we add one more property, `ATTR_ACTIVE`, to our structure. This will mark the new object as active and make it ready to be used by the system. The last line inside our `<CFIF>` block calls `<CFA_CONTENTOBJECTCREATE>` and passes in the new author information.

Now that we have the handler, how do we test it? Remember that Spectra has set up a scheduled event to call the handler. You can either wait around for it to run by itself, or you can use the methods described earlier in the chapter to force the event to fire. Forcing is actually a bit easier, since we saved the handler in the Web root. You can open your browser and manually enter

`http://localhost/a2z/importAuthors.cfm`

If everything worked right, you should see nothing onscreen. To see if the new authors were added, go to your Webtop and select the System Design area. Then choose the Site Object Designer. Next, select the Object Finder and in the Filter by Type drop-down, choose Author. Once the objects load, you should see the new authors.

NOTE If you don't know who the new authors are, just open the `authors.txt` file from the `weonlysellbooks` directory.

Figure 20.14 shows the author list with the new authors added.

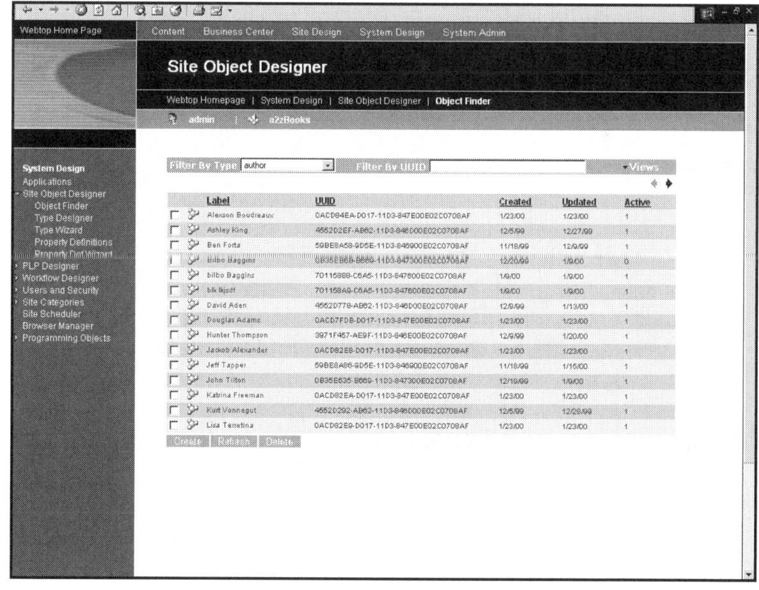

FIGURE 20.14
The authors on our system. Notice the new authors listed, including Alexson Boudreaux.

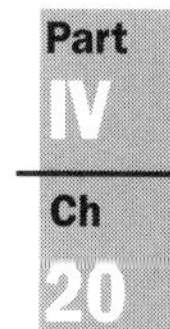

Application Syndication

The first half of this chapter discussed content syndication. This involves sharing ContentObjects such as articles, authors, or other bits of content. Spectra also supports the idea of application syndication. In this form of syndication, we actually share the application, not just the content. Imagine a site that allows its affiliates to search against its database. Another example might be a site that allows an affiliate to pass certain parameters to a special page. That page returns data according to what was passed. Imagine a site that could provide weather information according to the ZIP code sent to it.

There are two methods of application syndication:

- In direct remote access, the remote server calls a method on one object. For example, if the object ID for a certain book is 1, a direct remote access could be `Call the teaser method on object ID = 1`. The result of that operation is then returned to the remote server.
- In remote content searching, the Spectra server allows a remote server to search for content. The search mechanism is based on the same search services Spectra provides to the local server.

Direct Remote Access

Direct remote access allows a remote server to call a method on an object. For this to work, all requests from remote servers will come in to the same URL:

`http://your_server/allaire/spectra/invoke.cfm`

The file `invoke.cfm` must be passed certain parameters to work correctly. Table 20.1 shows the parameters that can be passed to `invoke.cfm`.

Table 20.1 *invoke.cfm* Parameters

Parameter	Required?	Description
`objectID`	Yes	The UUID of the object that the method will be called on. This can be one object or a list of objects.
`Method`	Yes	The method to call on the object.
`Username`	No, but is functionally required for security reasons	A valid username. This can be either an Administrator account of a member of the Affiliates group.
`Password`	No, but see `Username`	The password for the username.

Parameter	Required?	Description
applicationID	No	The UUID of the application ID that the object belongs to. This attribute lets the Spectra server know what datasource the object exists in. If this parameter and `applicationName` aren't passed, `invoke.cfm` assumes that the object exists in the `cfaobjects` database.
applicationName	No	The name of the application the object belongs to. You can use this instead of the ID value for the application.
bWDDXWrapper	No	If true, the object returned will be WDDX encoded. The default is false. Unlike the WDDX mode of content syndication, this does *not* return true objects. It returns the HTML of the method in WDDX format. This is really useful only when passing a list of object IDs. When you do that and use `bWDDXWrapper=true`, `invoke.cfm` will return the results of the operation in a WDDX structure where the result of each method call on an object is separated into multiple keys. In other words, if you passed two object IDs and told `invoke.cfm` to call the teaser method on them, the result of that call would be placed in a structure where the key is equal to the object ID. The resulting structure would have two keys, one for each object.

As an example of application syndication, if WeOnlySellBooks.com knew the UUID of a certain book, it could call the `display` method on the object, take the results, and display it on its own site. If you remember Listing 20.3, we used an example of client pull to grab the contents of a container. We could take that output and call a method on it remotely. Listing 20.5 shows a modified version of the catalog page that adds a link to invoke the teaser method.

Listing 20.5 *catalog3.cfm*—A Modified Catalog Page

```
<!---
File:          /weonlysellbooks/catalog3.cfm
Author:        Raymond Camden (raymond.k.camden@syntegra.com)
Date:          1/20/2000
Description:
Notes:
--->

<!--- Introduction Text --->
Welcome to the WeOnlySellBooks.com Catalog. Below is a listing of the
books we currently have for sale.
```

continues

Listing 20.5 Continued

```
<P>

<!---
    URL to perform client pull on A2Z
    This is the URL that you will change to match
    your system

    notice that we entered the username and password
--->

<CFSET A2ZLink =
"http://localhost/allaire/spectra/invoke.cfm?" &
"method=getobjectdata&objectID=4552D7ED-AB62-11D3-846D00E02C0708AF" &
"&applicationID=7DCD821C-AA6D-11D3-846D00E02C0708AF" &

<!--- Perform the 'pull' --->
<CFHTTP URL="#A2ZLink#" METHOD="GET">

<!--- Get ResultsPacket --->
<CFSET ResultsPacket = CFHTTP.FileContent>

<!--- Convert packet into objects --->
<CFWDDX ACTION="WDDX2CFML" INPUT="#ResultsPacket#" OUTPUT="Books">

<!--- Loop through each book. --->
<CFLOOP ITEM="Book" COLLECTION="#Books#">
    <!--- We hike up the price a bit. --->
    <CFSET NewPrice = Books[Book].Price * 1.3>
    <!--- Add five bucks for the programmers swiss bank account --->
    <CFSET NewPrice = NewPrice + 5>
    <CFOUTPUT>
        <A HREF="bookview.cfm?ObjectID=#Book#"><B><I>
                  #Books[Book].Title#</I></B></A><BR>
#DollarFormat(NewPrice)#
        <P>
    </CFOUTPUT>
</CFLOOP>
```

This listing is extremely similar to Listing 20.3. We made only one change, so let's look at it. In Listing 20.3, we simply output the title of the book like so:

```
<B><I>#Books[Book].Title#</I></B><BR>
```

In Listing 20.5, we have modified the title to make it a hyperlink:

```
<A HREF="bookview.cfm?ObjectID=#Book#"><B><I>
         #Books[Book].Title#</I></B></A><BR>
```

We wrap the title with a link to `bookview.cfm` and pass along the UUID of the book. Remember that the `<CFLOOP>` we used puts the UUID into the `Book` variable. `bookview.cfm` doesn't exist yet, so let's look at the code for this file in Listing 20.6.

Listing 20.6 *bookview.cfm*—A File for the Hyperlink

```
<!---
File:        /weonlysellbooks/bookview.cfm
Author:      Raymond Camden (raymond.k.camden@syntegra.com)
Date:        1/20/2000
Description:
Notes:
--->

<!---
    Attribute validation
    If URL.objectID doesn't exist, move user to home page.
--->

<CFIF NOT IsDefined("URL.objectID")>
    <CFLOCATION URL="index.cfm">
</CFIF>

<CFSET InvokeURL = "http://localhost/allaire/spectra/invoke.cfm?">

<!--- Add the object ID that was passed in via the URL parameter. --->
<CFSET InvokeURL = InvokeURL & "objectID=#URL.objectID#">
<!--- Add the method --->
<CFSET InvokeURL = InvokeURL & "&method=display">
<!--- Add the username --->
<CFSET InvokeURL = InvokeURL & "&username=WeOnlySellBooks">
<!--- Add the password --->
<CFSET InvokeURL = InvokeURL & "&password=foo">
<!--- Add the application name --->
<CFSET InvokeURL = InvokeURL & "&applicationName=A2ZBooks">

<!--- Now call the invoke.cfm file. --->
<CFHTTP URL="#InvokeURL#" METHOD="get">

<!--- Copy results --->
<CFSET Results = CFHTTP.FileContent>

<!--- Remove the price. --->
<CFSET Results = REReplace(Results,"\$[0-9]*\.[0-9]*","","ALL")>

<!--- Display the results. --->
<CFOUTPUT>#Results#</CFOUTPUT>

<P>
<A HREF="catalog3.cfm"><FONT COLOR="#FFFFFF">
Return to our catalog.</FONT></A>
```


We begin this script by doing a check for `URL.objectID`. If it doesn't exist, we push the user back to the index page using the `<CFLOCATION>` tag. Once we know we have an object ID, we begin to build the URL that we are going to hit to perform our remote method call. First, note that the URL (`http://localhost/allaire/spectra/invoke.cfm`) would normally point to another server. As we said at the beginning of this chapter, we have to fake remote servers by hitting separate folders on our own machine.

After initializing the URL, we begin to add pieces to it, starting with the object ID (`URL.objectID`) and then the method (`display`). Then we pass the username and password. The last thing we add to the URL is the name of the application, `a2zBooks`.

Once we have a URL, all we need to do is use `<CFHTTP>` again to call the remote server. Since we don't have access to the object directly, we can't suppress the output of the price. Therefore, we use the following regular expression to remove the price from the output.

```
<!--- Remove the price. --->
<CFSET Results = REReplace(Results,"\$[0-9]*\.[0-9]*","","ALL")>
```

After we clean up the results, we output it. Now we have a small problem. Because we are calling a `display` method on the A2Z Web site, we don't have control over the look-and-feel. We need to add a way to get the user back to our catalog. The last few lines of our script output a link back to `catalog3.cfm`. Because of the HTML generated by the A2Z book display handler, we need to color the link white so it stands out.

Just because we were stuck with the A2Z layout doesn't mean you have to be. The A2Z Company can create a handler just for the WeOnlySellBooks.com Company. This handler could either return the output of the book as A2Z would like it or return a packet. This could be a premium service that A2Z provides for its best affiliates or for those who pay extra. The only thing that WeOnlySellBooks.com would have to do is change the name of the method from `display` to whatever the new name is, like `affiliateDisplay`.

Figure 20.15 shows the result of clicking one of the links from `catalog3.cfm`.

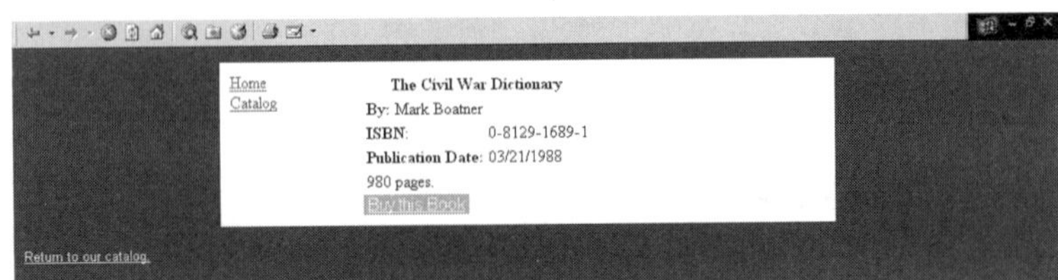

FIGURE 20.15
The result of calling the `teaser` method on the remote server. The content is displayed within the context of WeOnlySellBooks.com.

In the previous example, we passed in parameters to `invoke.cfm` by using URL variables. We did this by appending the values to the URL. We could have passed them in as form examples. In the following code snippet, the URL variables from Listing 20.6 have been rewritten to use form variables:

```
<CFHTTP URL="#InvokeURL#" METHOD="Post">
    <CFHTTPPARAM TYPE="FORMFIELD" NAME="objectID" VALUE="#URL.objectID#">
```

```
    <CFHTTPPARAM TYPE="FORMFIELD" NAME="method" VALUE="display">
    <CFHTTPPARAM TYPE="FORMFIELD"
        NAME="username" VALUE="weonlysellbooks">
    <CFHTTPPARAM TYPE="FORMFIELD" NAME="password" VALUE="foo">
    <CFHTTPPARAM TYPE="FORMFIELD" NAME="applicationName" VALUE="A2ZBooks">
</CFHTTP>
```

This time, rather than append values to a URL, we passed them as form fields. Also note that we changed the `METHOD` in the `<CFHTTP>` tag from `Get` to `Post`. Once we run this, we have the exact same output. One way in which this method is better than using URL parameters is that you can pass in additional values by just adding `<CFHTTPPARAM>` tags. One more advantage is that you can pass all the data along as one WDDX packet. This allows you to pass the items we described above (`objectID`, `method`, `applicationName`, and so forth) as well as complex structures. Here is one more code snippet that uses a WDDX packet instead of a bunch of `<CFHTTPPARAM>` tags:

```
<CFSET Data = StructNew()>
<CFSET Data.objectID = URL.objectID>
<CFSET Data.method = "display">
<CFSET Data.username = "weonlysellbooks">
<CFSET Data.password = "foo">
<CFSET Data.applicationName="A2ZBooks">
<CFSET Data.extraStuff = StructNew()>
<CFSET Data.extraStuff.mode = "Special">
<CFWDDX ACTION="CFML2WDDX" INPUT="#Data#" OUTPUT="wstPacket">

<CFSET InvokeURL = "http://localhost/allaire/spectra/invoke.cfm">
<CFHTTP URL="#InvokeURL#" METHOD="Post">
    <CFHTTPPARAM TYPE="FORMFIELD" NAME="wstPacket" VALUE="#wstPacket#">
</CFHTTP>
```

In this code snippet, we set all the variables inside a structure called `Data`. We then add extra information in a structure called `extraStuff`. This is all WDDX encoded and then passed in one form field. How could we use this? Imagine if the `display` method looked for the values passed in `extraStuff`. If it's detected that a value called `mode` was passed and it was `"Special"`, the handler could choose not to display the price. Handlers can take attributes when called locally and, as we can see, they can even be passed attributes by remote systems.

Remote Content Searching

Application syndication via the direct remote access method works fine if you know the object ID of a particular ContentObject. But what happens if you don't know? We could get IDs in our previous examples by using the content syndicated from the catalog container, but what if we didn't have access to those IDs?

Luckily, Spectra allows remote servers to search for content via the Remote Content Searching service. What's really nice about this capability is that remote servers have access to the exact same kind of searches that are local to the server. In all, four kinds of searching are available:

- `SQLSearch` is the same as using `<CFA_CONTENTOBJECTFIND>` to search for content.
- `FullTextSearch` is the same as using `<CFA_TYPESEARCH>` to search for content.
- `KeywordSearch` is the same as using `<CFA_METADATAKEYWORDOBJECTFIND>` to search for content.
- `CategorySearch` is the same as using `<CFA_METADATACATEGORYOBJECTFIND>` to search for content.

▶ **See** Chapter 14 for more information on search techniques using `<CFA_CONTENTOBJECTFIND>` and `<CFA_TYPESEARCH>`. See Chapter 11, "Working with Meta Data," for information on searching with `<CFA_METADATAKEYWORDOBJECTFIND>` and `<CFA_METADATACATEGORYOBJECTFIND>`.

Just like direct remote access, we have a specific URL that we will use when performing remote searching:

```
http://your_server/allaire/spectra/remote.cfm
```

Table 20.2 shows the parameters that `remote.cfm` can take.

Table 20.2 *remote.cfm* Parameters

Name	Required?	Description
`Method`	Yes	The kind of search to perform. This can be `SQLSearch`, `FullTextSearch`, `KeywordSearch`, or `CategorySearch`.
`Username`	No, but is functionally required for security reasons	A valid username. This can be either an Administrator account of a member of the Affiliates group.
`Password`	No, but see `Username`	The password for the username.
`applicationID`	No	The UUID of the application ID that the object belongs to. This attribute lets the Spectra server know what datasource the object exists in. If this parameter and `applicationName` aren't passed, `invoke.cfm` will assume that the object exists in the `cfaobjects` database.
`applicationName`	No	The name of the application the object belongs to. You can use this instead of the ID value for the application.

Name	Required?	Description
stParams	No	A structure of parameters. The keys of this structure will change according to the kind of search you are doing, but in general they are exactly the same as the parameters you would pass to the corresponding Spectra tag. In other words, since SQLSearch is the same as using <CFA_CONTENTOBJECTFIND>, the parameters you pass to stParams would be the same as what you pass to the <CFA> tag. The most important key, and the one all four types of searching will use, is the Method value. This tells the Spectra server what method should be called on whatever objects match the search. If you leave this parameter blank, Spectra returns a WDDX packet containing the object IDs of the matched records.

Let's look at an example of the first kind of search, SQLSearch. The code in Listing 20.7 is an example of remote content searching.

Listing 20.7 *search1.cfm*—Remote Content Searching

```
<!---
File:         /weonlysellbooks/search1.cfm
Author:       Raymond Camden (raymond.k.camden@syntegra.com)
Date:         1/20/2000
Description:  Performs a SQLSearch
Notes:
--->

<!--- Only perform a search if the form has been submitted. --->
<CFIF IsDefined("Form.searchTerms") AND Len(Trim(Form.searchTerms))>

    <!--- The structure we will send to the remote server. --->
    <CFSET stPacket = StructNew()>
    <!---
        The type of search we want to do.
        This is the same as using <CFA_ContentObjectFind>
    --->
    <CFSET stPacket.method = "SQLSearch">
    <!--- The username and password for our affiliate account. --->
    <CFSET stPacket.username = "weonlysellbooks">
    <CFSET stPacket.password = "foo">
    <!--- The application name. --->
    <CFSET stPacket.applicationName = "a2zBooks">

    <!---
        stParams contains the parameters we want
        sent to <CFA_ContentObjectFind>
    --->
```

Part IV Ch 20

continues

Listing 20.7 Continued

```
    <CFSET stPacket.stParams = StructNew()>
    <CFSET stPacket.stParams.method = "teaser">
    <!---
        The UUID of the Book Type
        You may have to change this to make it match the
        UUID of the Book type on your system.
    --->
    <CFSET stPacket.stParams.typeID = "59BE890F-9D5E-11D3-846900E02C0708AF">
    <!--- We specify the property and value to search for. --->
    <CFSET stPacket.stParams.stProperties = StructNew()>
    <CFSET stPacket.stParams.stProperties.title = "#Form.SearchTerms#">
    <CFSET stPacket.stParams.lPropertiesPrecedence = "title">
    <CFSET stPacket.stParams.dataSource = "a2zAccess">
    <CFSET stPacket.stParams.nMaxCount = "250">

    <!--- Create a WDDX packet out of the structure. --->
    <CFWDDX ACTION="CFML2WDDX" INPUT="#stPacket#" OUTPUT="wstPacket">

    <!--- Hit the remote server... --->
    <CFHTTP URL="http://localhost/allaire/spectra/remote.cfm" METHOD="Post">
      <CFHTTPPARAM TYPE="FORMFIELD" NAME="wstPacket" VALUE="#wstPacket#">
    </CFHTTP>

    <!--- Save the results. --->
    <CFSET Results = CFHTTP.FileContent>

    <!--- Output the results --->
    <CFOUTPUT>
        Here are the results of your search:
        <P>
        #Results#
    </CFOUTPUT>

</CFIF>

<P>
<FORM ACTION="search1.cfm" METHOD="post">
Search our catalog: <INPUT TYPE="text" NAME="searchTerms">
<INPUT TYPE="submit" VALUE="Search">
</FORM>
```

We begin this script by checking to see if the form variable `searchTerms` exists. If so, that means the user has entered a search phrase and hit the Search button on the form.

We will pass our information to `remote.cfm` as one big packet, so we begin by creating the `stPacket` structure. The first value we specify is the method, which tells `remote.cfm` what kind of search we want to do. In this case, we are demonstrating the `SQLSearch` style of remote searching, so we pass that value into the `Method` key. Next, we pass in the username and password for the WeOnlySellBooks.com affiliate. Lastly, we pass in the name of the application that A2Z uses. This tells Spectra what datasource to use when searching.

At this point, we've set up all the things that `remote.cfm` needs to know. Now we have to pass in the values that will be used for the search. Since we are using `SQLSearch`, and that is the same as `<CFA_CONTENTOBJECTFIND>`, we need to pass in the properties and values we want to search for. In our example, we say that we want to search the `title` property for an exact match of the value the user types in the form box. This is set up in these lines:

```
<CFSET stPacket.stParams.stProperties = StructNew()>
<CFSET stPacket.stParams.stProperties.title = "#Form.SearchTerms#">
<CFSET stPacket.stParams.lPropertiesPrecedence = "title">
```

We also pass in the UUID of the Book type and the datasource to search against. In case you're wondering, this *is* necessary even though we passed in an `applicationName` value. Why? The `applicationName` value does more then just tell Spectra what datasource to use—it also runs `<CFA_APPLICATIONINITIALIZE>` on the A2Z site. This sets up certain variables that the handlers need to run correctly. The last value we pass into `stParams` is the `nMaxCount` variable, which protects us from getting too many results back.

Now that the structure is complete, we use the `<CFWDDX>` tag to convert it into a WDDX packet. We then use the `<CFHTTP>` tag to hit `remote.cfm` and pass along the packet we just created. Once we've done that, we can copy the results of the `<CFHTTP>` tag to a local variable and then output it.

That's the meat of the script. The only part we didn't cover is the actual form at the bottom of the script, but as you can tell, it's an extremely simple form. If we wanted, we could add more form fields to allow for a better search. Since `<CFA_CONTENTOBJECTFIND>` allows us to do some complex searching, we could add many more fields to the form here.

The important thing to realize here is that we have just added a search interface on one site that uses a database on a different server. WeOnlySellBooks.com never needs to worry about keeping a copy of the A2ZBooks database. Even better, the user browsing WeOnlySellBooks.com has no idea what's going on behind the scenes. As far as she is concerned, her search is being performed on WeOnlySellBooks.com.

The `SQLSearch` method used above is a bit hard for the user to play with since the exact name of the book must be known for the search to work. Listing 20.8 switches to `FullTextSearch`, which is a bit looser in its search results.

Listing 20.8 *search2.cfm*—Switching Search Methods

```
<!---
File:         /weonlysellbooks/search2.cfm
Author:       Raymond Camden (raymond.k.camden@syntegra.com)
Date:         1/20/2000
Description:  Performs a FullTextSearch
Notes:
--->

<!--- Only perform a search if the form has been submitted. --->
```

continues

Listing 20.8 Continued

```
<CFIF IsDefined("Form.searchTerms") AND Len(Trim(Form.searchTerms))>

    <!--- The structure we will send to the remote server. --->
    <CFSET stPacket = StructNew()>
    <!---
        The type of search we want to do.
        This is the same as using <CFA_TypeSearch>
    --->
    <CFSET stPacket.method = "FullTextSearch">
    <!--- The username and password for our affiliate account. --->
    <CFSET stPacket.username = "weonlysellbooks">
    <CFSET stPacket.password = "foo">
    <!--- The application name. --->
    <CFSET stPacket.applicationName = "a2zBooks">

    <!---
        stParams contains the parameters we want
        sent to <CFA_ContentObjectFind>
    --->
    <CFSET stPacket.stParams = StructNew()>
    <CFSET stPacket.stParams.method = "teaser">
    <!---
        The UUID of the Book Type
        You may have to change this to make it match the
        UUID of the Book type on your system.
    --->
    <CFSET stPacket.stParams.typeID = "59BE890F-9D5E-11D3-846900E02C0708AF">
    <!--- We specify the SearchTerms to search for. --->
    <CFSET stPacket.stParams.SearchTerms = "#Form.SearchTerms#">
    <CFSET stPacket.stParams.dataSource = "a2zAccess">
    <CFSET stPacket.stParams.nMaxCount = "250">

    <!--- Create a WDDX packet out of the structure. --->
    <CFWDDX ACTION="CFML2WDDX" INPUT="#stPacket#" OUTPUT="wstPacket">

    <!--- Hit the remote server... --->
    <CFHTTP URL="http://localhost/allaire/spectra/remote.cfm" METHOD="Post">
      <CFHTTPPARAM TYPE="FORMFIELD" NAME="wstPacket" VALUE="#wstPacket#">
    </CFHTTP>

    <!--- Save the results. --->
    <CFSET Results = CFHTTP.FileContent>

    <!--- Output the results --->
    <CFOUTPUT>
        Here are the results of your search:
        <P>
        #Results#
    </CFOUTPUT>
```

```
</CFIF>

<P>
<FORM ACTION="search2.cfm" METHOD="post">
Search our catalog: <INPUT TYPE="text" NAME="searchTerms">
<INPUT TYPE="submit" VALUE="Search">
</FORM>
```

This script is similar to Listing 20.7 in that we perform the remote search only if `Form.searchTerms` is defined. As before, we create a structure, `stPacket`, that will store the values we pass to `remote.cfm`. This time our method is `FullTextSearch`, which as we said earlier is the same as using `<CFA_TYPESEARCH>`, a Verity-based search service. The username, password, and `applicationName` are the same as in Listing 20.7. The values in `stParams`, however, are different since were using a different kind of search. This time we specify the type ID and method again, but our search term is passed to a key called `searchTerms`. This will be passed to the `<CFA_TYPESEARCH>` tag. We pass in the datasource again as well as a maximum number of objects to return. Like our other example, this is a simple form of the search. `<CFA_TYPESEARCH>` allows us to specify what properties to search against when we perform the search. If we wanted to do something like that, we would simply add one more property to the `stParams` structure like so:

```
<stPacket.stParams.lProperties="body">
```

This would tell `<CFA_TYPESEARCH>` to restrict its search to values in the `body` property. The rest of the script is the same as Listing 20.7. We serialize the structure, pass it to `remote.cfm`, and output the results. Figure 20.16 shows the result of searching for `*`, which is the same as "match anything."

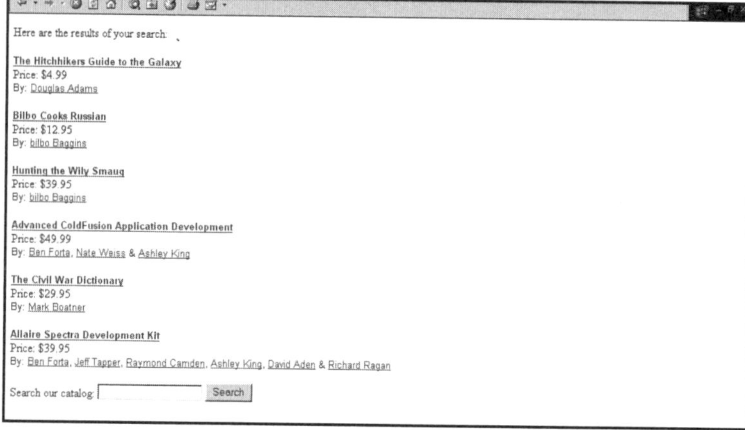

FIGURE 20.16
The result of searching for * on WeOnlySellBooks.com.

Our next example of remote searching is a keyword search. This uses <CFA_METADATAKEYWORDOBJECTFIND> as its back end.

See Chapter 11 for information on searching with <CFA_METADATAKEYWORDOBJECTFIND> and <CFA_METADATACATEGORYOBJECTFIND>.

Again we will modify the previous listing to use the new search type. Listing 20.9 shows this form of remote searching in action.

Listing 20.9 *search3.cfm*

```
<!---
File:         /weonlysellbooks/search3.cfm
Author:       Raymond Camden (raymond.k.camden@syntegra.com)
Date:         1/20/2000
Description:  Performs a KeywordSearch
Notes:
--->

<!--- Only perform a search if the form has been submitted. --->
<CFIF IsDefined("Form.searchTerms") AND Len(Trim(Form.searchTerms))>

    <!--- The structure we will send to the remote server. --->
    <CFSET stPacket = StructNew()>
    <!---
        The type of search we want to do.
        This is the same as using <CFA_MetaDataKeywordObjectFind>
        --->
    <CFSET stPacket.method = "KeywordSearch">
    <!--- The username and password for our affiliate account. --->
    <CFSET stPacket.username = "weonlysellbooks">
    <CFSET stPacket.password = "foo">
    <!--- The application name. --->
    <CFSET stPacket.applicationName = "a2zBooks">

    <!---
        stParams contains the parameters we want
        sent to <CFA_MetaDataKeywordObjectFind>
    --->
    <CFSET stPacket.stParams = StructNew()>
    <CFSET stPacket.stParams.method = "teaser">
    <!---
        The UUID of the Book Type
        You may have to change this to make it match the
        UUID of the Book type on your system.
    --->
    <CFSET stPacket.stParams.ltypeIDs =
    "59BE890F-9D5E-11D3-846900E02C0708AF">
<!--- We specify the keywords to search for. --->
```

```
    <CFSET stPacket.stParams.keywords = "#Form.SearchTerms#">
    <CFSET stPacket.stParams.dataSource = "a2zAccess">
    <CFSET stPacket.stParams.nMaxCount = "250">

    <!--- Create a WDDX packet out of the structure. --->
    <CFWDDX ACTION="CFML2WDDX" INPUT="#stPacket#" OUTPUT="wstPacket">

    <!--- Hit the remote server... --->
    <CFHTTP URL="http://localhost/allaire/spectra/remote.cfm" METHOD="Post">
      <CFHTTPPARAM TYPE="FORMFIELD" NAME="wstPacket" VALUE="#wstPacket#">
    </CFHTTP>

    <!--- Save the results. --->
    <CFSET Results = CFHTTP.FileContent>

    <!--- Output the results --->
    <CFOUTPUT>
        Here are the results of your search:
        <P>
        #Results#
    </CFOUTPUT>

</CFIF>

<P>
<FORM ACTION="search3.cfm" METHOD="post">
Search our catalog: <INPUT TYPE="text" NAME="searchTerms">
<INPUT TYPE="submit" VALUE="Search">
</FORM>
```

Again, not much has changed from the previous script. Let's focus on where things are different. The first difference is the method parameter we pass to `remote.cfm`. To run a keyword search, we pass `KeywordSearch` to `stPacket.method`. The username, password, and `applicationName` are the same as before, as is the method we want to call on the matched objects, `teaser`.

This time we pass a value called `lTypeIDs`, because `<CFA_METADATAKEYWORDOBJECTFIND>` uses it instead of one simple type ID. The search terms this time are passed to a value called `keywords` and, as before, we pass in the datasource and `nMaxCount` values. This script works just like the previous two, except this time it attempts to find a meta data keyword match. You may want to consider updating your meta data index to ensure that your collections are fresh.

As a last example of remote searching, we will use `CategorySearch`. Also, we won't call a method on the remote system. Instead, we will get the data back as a WDDX packet and perform some operations on it. Listing 20.10 shows this script.

Listing 20.10 *search4.cfm*—Getting the Data as a WDDX Packet

```
<!---
File:        /weonlysellbooks/search4.cfm
Author:      Raymond Camden (raymond.k.camden@syntegra.com)
Date:        1/20/2000
Description: Performs a CategorySearch
Notes:
--->

<!--- Only perform a search if the form has been submitted. --->
<CFIF IsDefined("Form.searchTerms") AND Len(Trim(Form.searchTerms))>

    <!--- The structure we will send to the remote server. --->
    <CFSET stPacket = StructNew()>
    <!---
        The type of search we want to do.
        This is the same as using <CFA_MetaDatCategoryObjectFind>
    --->
    <CFSET stPacket.method = "CategorySearch">
    <!--- The username and password for our affiliate account. --->
    <CFSET stPacket.username = "weonlysellbooks">
    <CFSET stPacket.password = "foo">
    <!--- The application name. --->
    <CFSET stPacket.applicationName = "a2zBooks">

    <!---
        stParams contains the parameters we want
        sent to <CFA_MetaDataContentObjectFind>
    --->
    <CFSET stPacket.stParams = StructNew()>
    <!---
        The UUID of the Book Type
        You may have to change this to make it match the
        UUID of the Book type on your system.
    --->
    <CFSET stPacket.stParams.ltypeIDs =
    "59BE890F-9D5E-11D3-846900E02C0708AF">
    <!--- We specify the keywords to search for. --->
    <CFSET stPacket.stParams.lCategoryIDs = "#Form.SearchTerms#">
    <CFSET stPacket.stParams.dataSource = "a2zAccess">
    <CFSET stPacket.stParams.nMaxCount = "250">

    <!--- Create a WDDX packet out of the structure. --->
    <CFWDDX ACTION="CFML2WDDX" INPUT="#stPacket#" OUTPUT="wstPacket">

    <!--- Hit the remote server... --->
    <CFHTTP URL="http://localhost/allaire/spectra/remote.cfm" METHOD="Post">
      <CFHTTPPARAM TYPE="FORMFIELD" NAME="wstPacket" VALUE="#wstPacket#">
    </CFHTTP>

    <!--- Save the results. --->
```

```
        <CFSET Results = CFHTTP.FileContent>

        <!--- The result is a WDDX encoded query. --->
        <CFWDDX ACTION="WDDX2CFML" INPUT="#Results#" OUTPUT="ResultsQuery">

        <!--- Output the results --->
        Here are the results of your search:
        <P>
        <CFOUTPUT QUERY="ResultsQuery">
            <A HREF="bookView.cfm?ObjectID=#ObjectID#">#label#</A><BR>
        </CFOUTPUT>

</CFIF>

<!--- Categories --->
<CFSET Cats = StructNew()>
<CFSET Cats["A4912F74-9EEB-11D3-846A00E02C0708AF"] = "Fiction">
<CFSET Cats["A4912F78-9EEB-11D3-846A00E02C0708AF"] = "Non-Fiction">
<CFSET Cats["CC10C2FC-BA06-11D3-847300E02C0708AF"] = "History">

<P>
<FORM ACTION="search4.cfm" METHOD="post">
Search our catalog:
<!--- Loop through cats --->
<SELECT NAME="SearchTerms" SIZE=3 MULTIPLE="Yes">
<CFLOOP ITEM="Cat" COLLECTION="#Cats#">
    <CFOUTPUT><OPTION VALUE="#Cat#">#Cats[Cat]#</CFOUTPUT>
</CFLOOP>
</SELECT>
<INPUT TYPE="submit" VALUE="Search">
</FORM>
```

This script works a bit differently from the rest, so let's focus on what makes this script special. Like the other scripts, we perform the remote search only if the form variable `searchTerms` was passed. Again we create a structure to hold our data, and this time our method is `CategorySearch`. As discussed earlier, this tells the remote service to use `<CFA_METADATACATEGORYOBJECTFIND>` to perform the search. Again we pass the username, password, and application name.

This time, notice that we don't pass in a method to `stParams`. We want to get the results back as a query, not as the output of some method. Since `<CFA_METADATACATEGORYOBJECTFIND>` requires a list of category IDs as its search terms, we pass the `Form.Search` term variable into that key. As before, we convert `stPacket` into a WDDX packet and pass it to `remote.cfm`. This time, however, when the result comes back we need to deserialize it using the `<CFWDDX>` tag. The deserialized data is a query, so we can use `<CFOUTPUT>` to iterate over the result. All we use in this script is the object ID and the label. For each result, we create a link to `bookView.cfm`, which, if you remember, uses direct remote access to call the `display` method on an object.

The code beneath the main `<CFIF>` block is a bit different this time. Since the remote search service needs a category UUID passed to it, we can't work with simple user input. We need to pass the UUIDs of the categories. We manually entered them into the script by creating a new structure called `Cats`. In this structure we used the category UUIDs as the keys and the names of the categories as the values. Later in the form, rather than use a simple text box, we iterate over each category and output an `<OPTION>` tag for it. Here is the code that handles that part of the form:

```
<SELECT NAME="SearchTerms" SIZE=3 MULTIPLE="Yes">
<CFLOOP ITEM="Cat" COLLECTION="#Cats#">
    <CFOUTPUT><OPTION VALUE="#Cat#">#Cats[Cat]#</CFOUTPUT>
</CFLOOP>
</SELECT>
```

As you can see, we pass the UUID into the value of the `<OPTION>` tag and use the value of `Cats[Cat]` for the display portion. We set up the `<SELECT>` tag to allow for multiple options to be selected. This allows the user to choose multiple categories. When the search is performed, any object that has been marked as being in one of the categories selected will be returned.

As you can imagine, a remote site wouldn't normally want to enter a list of category UUIDs. In fact, it normally wouldn't even have a way of knowing what the UUIDs are. There are a variety of ways around this. First, the category UUIDs, as well as the type UUID, could all be part of a "Affiliates Package" that WeOnlySellBooks.com could download. This package would tell the affiliate all it needed to know to set up its CFM script (or Perl, PHP, ASP, and so on) to perform various actions against A2ZBooks. You could even develop custom tags that a remote site could download. This would allow the site to add a search engine for your site with just one line of code!

CHAPTER 21

Creating e-Commerce Sites

In this chapter

What Is e-Commerce?

One of the most commonly required features of a Web site today is an e-commerce component. By allowing users to purchase items online, millions of businesses have been able to expand the scope of their sales from local to global. The online catalog allows users to see what items are offered by the store. Within the store, a user chooses items and puts them in his shopping cart. In this way, users can add or remove items from their shopping carts while they are in the store. The basic components of any e-commerce application are a catalog, which allows the user to see the items offered for sale; a shopping cart, which allows the user to purchase items, and a transaction history, so a user can browse all of his past purchases.

Figure 21.1 shows the flow of an e-commerce application, from browsing through available items to the completion of the purchase.

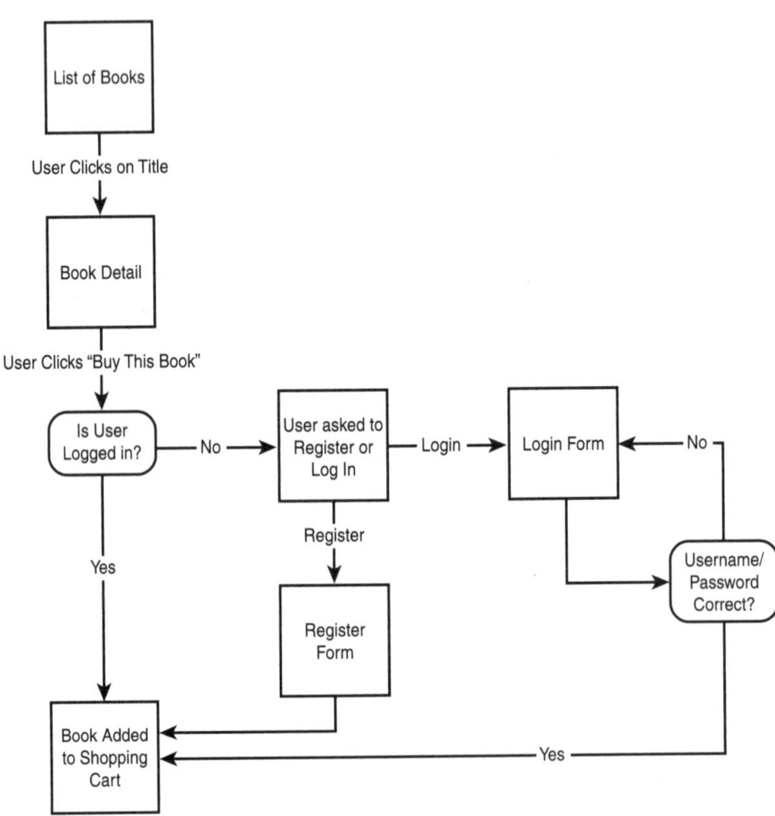

FIGURE 21.1
This flowchart shows the application flow for the a2zBooks application.

e-Commerce applications in Spectra involve the same principles. The a2zBooks application uses the `teaser` method to display a list of books and the `display` method to drill down to the detail level of the book. Figure 21.2 shows the `teaser` method.

▶ **See** Chapter 8, "Building the Site Structure," for the details on creating the `teaser` and `display` methods for the Book object type.

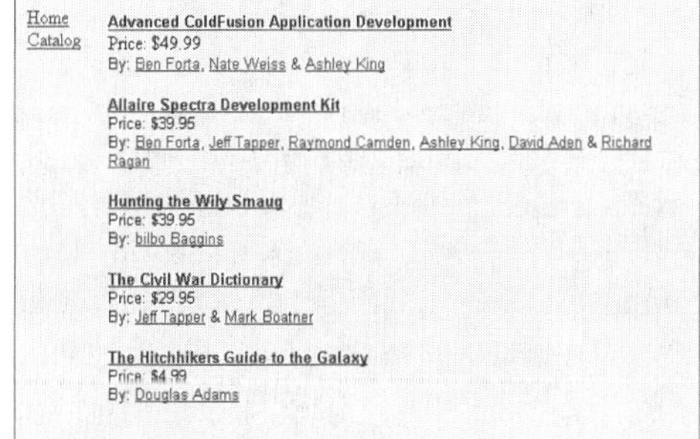

FIGURE 21.2
The A2ZBooks Catalog is shown as a container displaying the `teaser` handler of a number of Book objects.

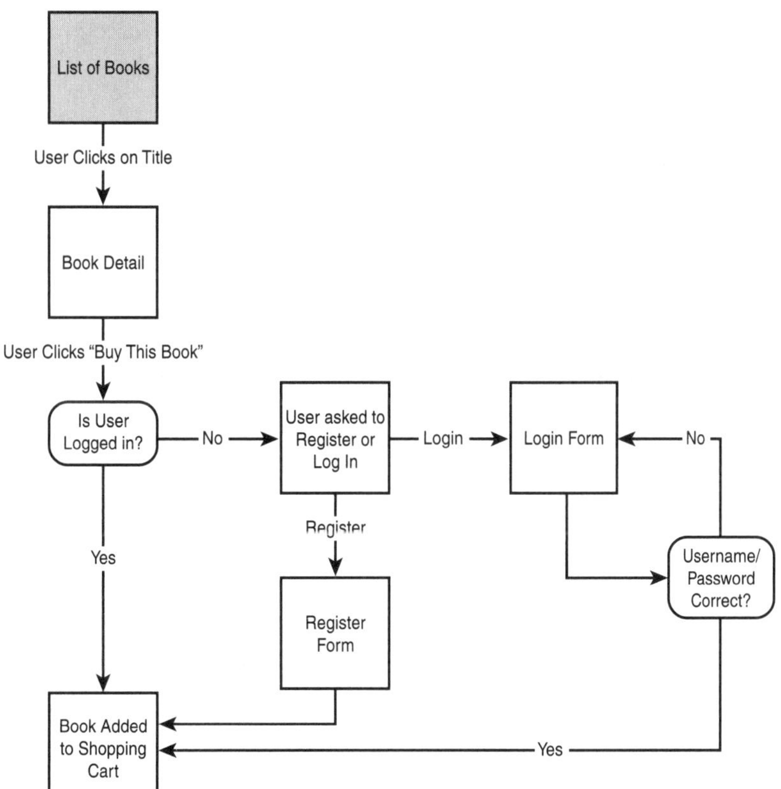

FIGURE 21.3
The application flowchart shows that the user is currently in the List of Books section.

Building Shopping Carts in Spectra

As discussed above, the shopping cart is the heart of an e-commerce application. It exists as a storage facility for items a user is interested in buying. Several different methodologies can be used to build a shopping cart in Spectra, one of which is in the following section.

Storing the Shopping Cart as a User Profile

A Shopping Cart is a collection of items that a user is purchasing. A Shopping Cart is related to a single user for a brief period of time and isn't persistent, such as a Book or an Author. It makes the most sense to store the Shopping Cart directly with the user. To create a Shopping Cart in Spectra, you can create a user preference that will hold it. That way, you can avoid the hassle of creating a Shopping Cart object for each user, securing it to that user, and deleting it when the transaction is complete. Also, if the Shopping Cart is stored as a preference instead of as a session variable, it will persist across several visits to the store, and the user can leave items in the cart until he chooses to remove or purchase them.

▶ **See** Chapter 16, "Using Spectra Security Options," to learn about logging in as a security measure.

In a typical e-commerce application, a user will browse through a catalog of items, find an item of interest, and click it for more details. Figure 21.4 shows where the Book detail falls in the application flowchart. From the detail page, there is usually a button that allows the user to add an item to his Shopping Cart. The code in Listing 21.1 shows a Spectra button that can be used to add a book to the user's Shopping Cart. Figure 21.5 shows the button displayed in the book's `display` handler.

Listing 21.1 *display.cfm*—A Button to Put a Book into the User's Shopping Cart

```
<CFA_BUTTON
    DATASOURCE = "REQUEST.CFA.a2zBooks.DATASOURCE"
    ID = "D3E48F89-FE2A-11e2-B6300060B0fB4967"
    LABEL = "Buy this Book"
    ACTION = "url"
    ACTIONDATA="/a2z/invoke.cfm?method=addToCart&objectID=#book.objectID#"
>
```

Listing 21.1 shows a `<CFA_BUTTON>` tag, which should be added to the `display` handler for a Book object. It defines the datasource for the application, the button's ID (which needs to be unique for the page), the label to display to the user, the URL action, and the `actionData`, which defines the URL that will be called when the button is clicked.

▶ **See** Chapter 9, "Building Display Components," for details on using the `<CFA_BUTTON>` tag.

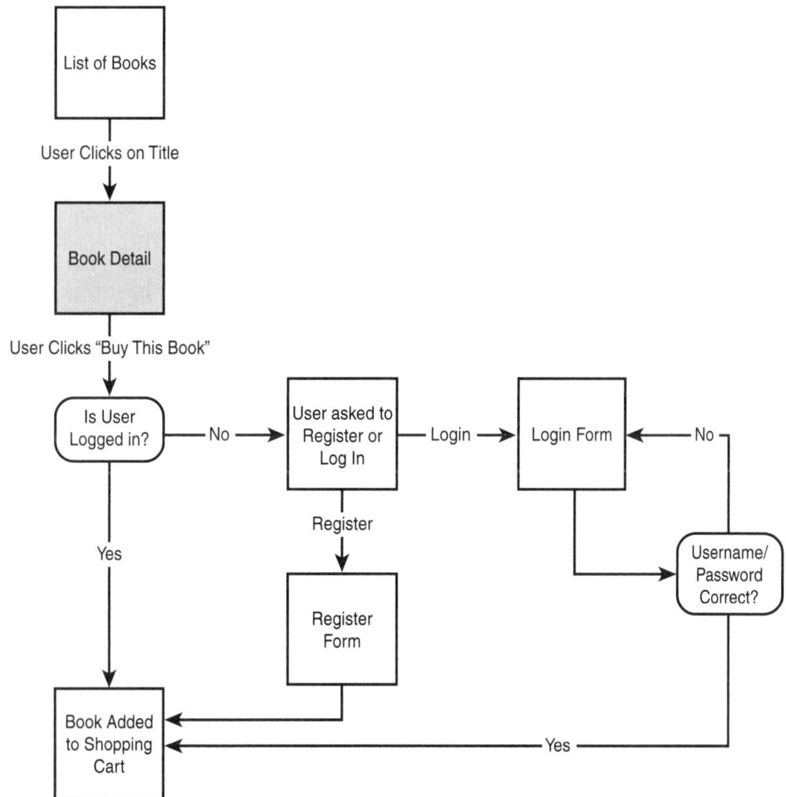

FIGURE 21.4
The application flowchart, highlighting the book detail page.

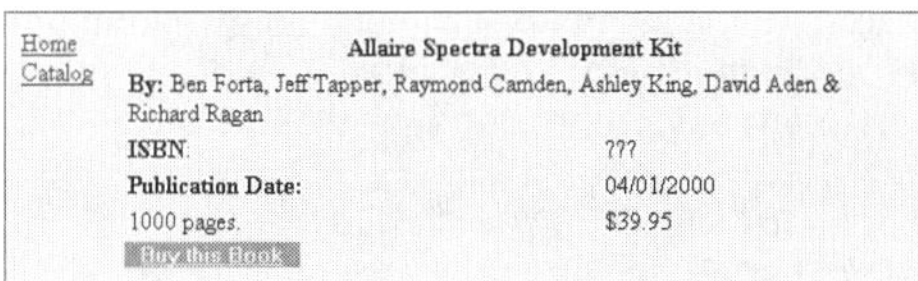

FIGURE 21.5
A Spectra button is displayed to entice users to buy the book.

Listing 21.2 shows an `addToCart` method for the Book object type, which will add the current book to the user's Shopping Cart.

Listing 21.2 A Book Object Method That Allows a Book to Be Added to a User's Shopping Cart

```
<!---
File:           /handlers/a2z/book/addToCart.cfm
Author:         jeff tapper (jeff@tapper.net)
Date:           1/19/2000
Description:   this handler will add an item to the current shopping cart,
                given that the user is logged in
Notes:          This handler was modified from the restorenet sample
                application which shipped with Spectra.

                Restorenet was developed by David An (david.an@mindseye.com)
                Senior Developer, Mindseye Inc.
--->

<CFPARAM NAME="request.cfa.activeUser" DEFAULT="anonymous">
<CFA_HANDLER OBJECT="book">

<CFIF REQUEST.CFA.ACTIVEUSER IS "anonymous">

    <CF_A2ZFORMATTING>
        <CFOUTPUT>
        Please <A HREF="/a2z/Register/">register</A>
        before purchasing any items.
<P>
        <A HREF="/a2z/login.cfm?returnTo=
         #URLENCODEDFORMAT('/a2z/invoke.cfm?objectID=#url.objectID#
         &method=addToCart')#">log in</A>.

        </CFOUTPUT>
    </CF_A2ZFORMATTING>

<CFELSE>
    <!--- okay, user is logged in; add item to
    the stProfile.preferences.shoppingcart structure--->

    <CFPARAM NAME="book.objectID" TYPE="UUID">
    <CFPARAM NAME="attributes.stParams.quantity"
     TYPE="numeric" DEFAULT="1">

    <CFSET QUANTITY = ATTRIBUTES.STPARAMS.QUANTITY>

    <!--- get userprofile info from Application.cfm --->
    <CFSET STPROFILE = STRUCTCOPY(REQUEST.STUSERPROFILE)>

    <CFSCRIPT>
    // make sure preference is a structure
    if (NOT IsStruct(stProfile.preferences)) {
        stProfile.preferences = StructNew();
    }
```

```
    // make sure shoppingcart exists
    if (NOT StructKeyExists(stProfile.preferences, "shoppingcart")) {
        stProfile.preferences.shoppingcart = StructNew();
    }

    // set shopping cart to a local var for easy coding
    cart = stProfile.preferences.shoppingcart;

    // does this object exist in the cart already?
    if (StructKeyExists(cart,book.objectID)) {
        // object exists; are we deleting this item
        // (changing quantity to 0)?
        if ((cart[book.objectID].quantity + quantity) eq 0) {
            // delete the key
            temp = StructDelete(cart,book.objectID);
        } else {
            // update the key's quantity
            cart[book.objectID].quantity =
            cart[book.objectID].quantity + quantity;
        }
    } else {
        // object does not exist in cart;
        // create the key and assign properties
        cart[book.objectID] = StructNew();
        cart[book.objectID].objectID = book.objectID;
        cart[book.objectID].quantity = quantity;
        cart[book.objectID].description = book.title;
    }

    // re-append cart to original profile structure
    stProfile.preferences.shoppingcart = cart;
    </CFSCRIPT>

    <!--- finally save the user profile --->
    <CFA_USERPROFILESET
        DATASOURCE="#request.cfa['a2zBooks'].datasource#"
        USERNAME="#request.cfa.activeuser#"
        STUSERPROFILE = "#stProfile#">

    <!--- cart has been updated; go to it. --->
    <CFLOCATION URL="/a2z/invoke.cfm?objectID=#book.objectID#
     &method=showcart&keepid=1" ADDTOKEN="No">
</CFIF>

</CFA_HANDLER>
```

This handler begins by setting a default value for the `REQUEST.CFA.ACTIVEUSER` variable. If the user has already been authenticated to the application, this variable will be populated with his username. If he hasn't yet logged in, he will have a default username of `anonymous`.

Next, a `<CFA_HANDLER>` tag is used to set a scope for the Book object that will be referenced throughout this handler.

Then, the REQUEST.CFA.ACTIVEUSER variable is checked to see if this user is authenticated or anonymous. An anonymous user will be prompted to register or to log in if he has registered previously.

Figure 21.6 shows this choice in the application flowchart.

FIGURE 21.6
A user who's not logged in must register or log in before continuing.

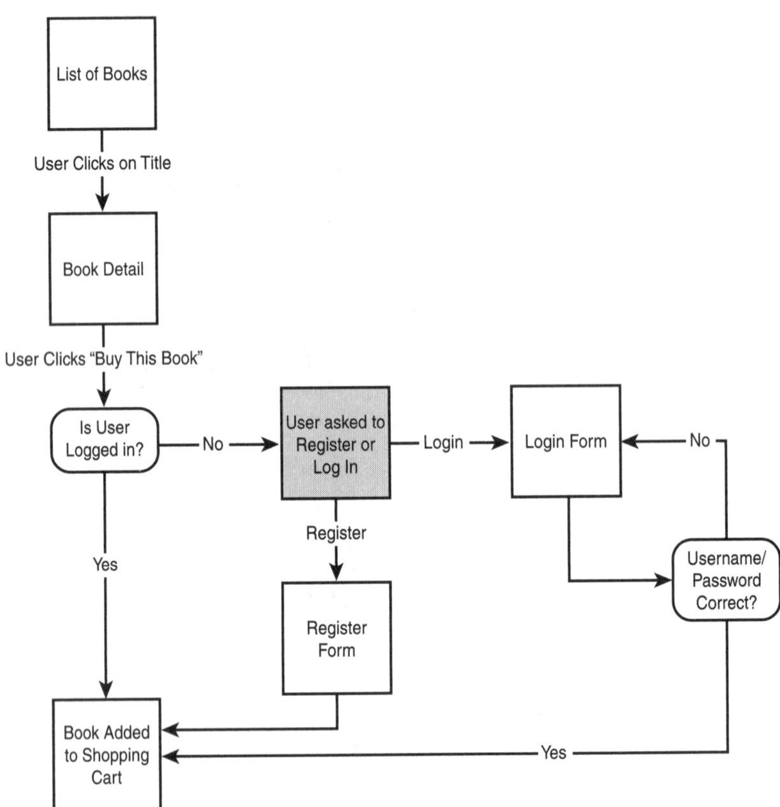

If he has been authenticated, a check is done to ensure that a BOOK.OBJECTID was passed to the handler as a UUID. A default value for ATTRIBUTES.STPARAMS.QUANTITY, which represents the quantity of the book being purchased, is set to 1. Then the variable is set to local variable QUANTITY for ease of coding.

The user profile structure, REQUEST.STUSERPROFILE, is copied into a local variable, so it can be modified without affecting the original. A check is then made to see if PREFERENCES is a structure within the user profile. If it's not, it's initialized as a structure with STRUCTNEW(). If the preference SHOPPINGCART doesn't yet exist as a key in the STPROFILE.PREFERENCES structure, it too is initialized as a structure with STRUCTNEW(). A local variable CART is set to point to the STPROFILE.PREFERENCES.SHOPPINGCART structure, to aid in coding.

Now that you have a Shopping Cart as part of the user's profile, you can add books to it. First, a check is made to see if the book being purchased is already in the cart; if so, the quantity is added to the quantity already in the cart. Should this total zero, the book is removed from the cart. If the item doesn't yet appear in the cart, a new structure is added to the Shopping Cart structure to hold the object ID of the book, its title, and its price. Then the local variable `CART`, into which the book was added, is written back to the user profile structure `STPROFILE.PREFERENCES.SHOPPINGCART`.

Using `CFA_USERPROFILESET`, this structure is set into the user profile in the database.

Finally, the `showCart` method is invoked, to show the user the current contents of his Shopping Cart. Listing 21.3 shows the handler for this method, as does Figure 21.7.

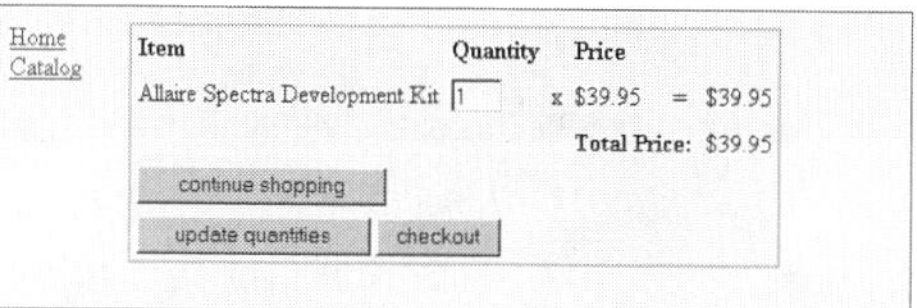

FIGURE 21.7
The `showCart` method displays all the items currently in the user's Shopping Cart.

Listing 21.3 Showing All Items Now in User's Shopping Cart

```
<!---
File:           /handlers/a2z/book/showCart.cfm
Author:         jeff tapper (jeff@tapper.net)
Date:           1/19/2000
Description:   this handler will show all of the items currently in the
                user's shopping cart.
Notes:          This handler was modified from the restorenet sample
                application which shipped with Spectra.

        Restorenet was developed by David An (david.an@mindseye.com)
        Senior Developer, Mindseye Inc.
--->
<CFSETTING ENABLECFOUTPUTONLY="Yes">

<CFA_HANDLER OBJECT="book">

    <!--- get the shopping cart (part of user profile preferences) --->

    <CFSCRIPT>
        if (NOT IsDefined("request.stUserProfile") OR
            NOT IsStruct(request.stUserProfile)) {
            request.stUserProfile = StructNew();
        }
        if (NOT StructKeyExists(request.stUserProfile,"preferences") OR
            NOT IsStruct(request.stUserProfile.preferences)) {
```

continues

Listing 21.3 Continued

```
          request.stUserProfile.preferences = StructNew();
     }
     if (NOT StructKeyExists(request.stUserProfile.preferences,
               "shoppingcart")) {
          request.stUserProfile.preferences.shoppingcart = StructNew();
     }

     // set to a local var for easier coding
     cart = request.stUserProfile.preferences.shoppingcart;

     if (IsDefined("FORM.btnSubmit")) {
          // form was submitted, update quantities
          for (objectID in cart) {
               // did user change quantity to zero,
               //which means we need to delete the key?
               if (Evaluate("FORM.quantity" & Replace(objectID,"-","_",
                    "ALL")) eq 0) {
                    // delete the key
                    temp = StructDelete(cart,objectID);
               } else {
                    // otherwise, update the quantity
                    cart[objectID].quantity = Evaluate("FORM.quantity" &
                       Replace(objectID,"-","_","ALL"));
               }
          } // end loop
     } // end if

     // reappend to profile structure
     request.stUserProfile.preferences.shoppingcart = cart;

</CFSCRIPT>

<CFIF ISDEFINED("FORM.btnSubmit")>
     <!--- update the user profile --->
     <CFA_USERPROFILESET
          DATASOURCE="#request.cfa['a2zBooks'].datasource#"
          USERNAME="#request.cfa.activeuser#"
          STUSERPROFILE="#request.stUserProfile#"
     >
</CFIF>

<CF_A2ZFORMATTING>
     <CFOUTPUT>
          <FORM NAME="shoppingcart" ACTION="/a2z/invoke.cfm?
           objectID=#book.objectID#&method=showcart" METHOD="post">
     </CFOUTPUT>

     <CFA_CONTENTOBJECTGETMULTIPLE
          DATASOURCE="#request.cfa['a2zBooks'].datasource#"
          LOBJECTIDS="#StructKeyList(cart)#"
          R_STOBJECTS="stObjects"
     >
```

```
<CFOUTPUT>
<TABLE BORDER=0 CELLSPACING=0 CELLPADDING=2 BGCOLOR="##f0b57b">
     <TR><TD>
     <TABLE BORDER=0 CELLSPACING=0 CELLPADDING=4 BGCOLOR="##fcfcde">
     <TR>
          <TD>
               <B>Item</B>
          </TD>
          <TD>
               <B>Quantity</B>
          </TD>
          <TD>
                
          </TD>
          <TD>
               <B>Price</B>
          </TD>
          <TD>
                
          </TD>
          <TD>
                
          </TD>
     </TR>
     <CFSET TOTALPRICE = 0>
     <CFLOOP COLLECTION="#cart#" ITEM="objectID">
          <TR>
               <TD>
                    #stObjects[objectID].title#
               </TD>
               <TD>
                    <INPUT TYPE="text"
                    NAME="quantity#Replace(objectID,"-","_","ALL")#"
                    SIZE="3" MAXLENGTH="3"
                    VALUE="#cart[objectID].quantity#">
               </TD>
               <TD>
                    x
               </TD>
               <TD>
                    #DollarFormat(stObjects[objectID].price)#
               </TD>
               <TD>
                    =
               </TD>
               <TD>
                    #DollarFormat(stObjects[objectID].price *
                        cart[objectID].quantity)#
               </TD>
          </TR>
          <CFSET TOTALPRICE = TOTALPRICE +
           (STOBJECTS[OBJECTID].PRICE * CART[OBJECTID].QUANTITY)>
     </CFLOOP>
```

Part IV Ch 21

continues

Listing 21.3 Continued

```
            <TR>
                <TD>
                     
                </TD>
                <TD>
                     
                </TD>
                <TD>
                     
                </TD>
                <TD ALIGN=RIGHT COLSPAN=2>
                    <B>Total Price:</B>
                </TD>
                <TD>
                    #Dollarformat(totalPrice)#
                </TD>
            </TR>
            <TR>
                <TD COLSPAN=6>
                 <INPUT TYPE="button" NAME="btnContinue"
VALUE="continue shopping" onClick="location='/a2z/catalog/index.cfm'">
                </TD>
            </TR>
            <TR>
                <TD COLSPAN=6>
                    <INPUT TYPE="submit" NAME="btnSubmit"
                    VALUE="update quantities">
                    <INPUT TYPE="button" NAME="btnCheckout"
                    VALUE="checkout" onClick="location='/a2z/invoke.cfm?
                          objectID=#book.objectID#&method=checkout'">
                </TD>
            </TR>

            </TABLE>

        </TD></TR></TABLE>
        </FORM>

        </CFOUTPUT>
    </CF_A2ZFORMATTING>
</CFA_HANDLER>
```

After using the CFA_HANDLER tag to declare a scope for the Book object, the user's Shopping Cart is retrieved from his user preferences. A number of checks are made to verify that STUSERPROFILE, PREFERENCES, and SHOPPINGCART exist and are structures. The structure REQUEST.STUSERPROFILE.PREFERENCES.SHOPPINGCART is set to the local variable CART to help simplify coding.

When the Shopping Cart is available for easy editing, a check is made to see if FORM.BTNSUBMIT exists; if it does, it indicates that the user has clicked the Update Quantity button. In that case, loop through each object ID in the Shopping Cart. The form field that holds the quantity of each item in the cart is named with the book's object ID appended to the word QUANTITY. The hyphens in the object IDs are all passed as underscores. To check the quantity for each item, the function

```
EVALUATE("FORM.QUANTITY" & REPLACE(OBJECTID,"-","_","ALL"))
```

is used. Hyphens are replaced as underscores to prevent the EVALUATE() function from interpreting hyphens as minus signs, indicating the values should be subtracted from each other. If this value equals zero, the item is removed from the cart; otherwise, the quantity for that item in the cart is set to the value passed in the form. The value of the variable CART is then set back into the variable

```
REQUEST.STUSERPROFILE.PREFERENCES.SHOPPINGCART
```

which is written back into the database with the <CFA_USERPROFILESET> tag.

Next, the form to display the Shopping Cart's contents starts. The form is coded to invoke the SHOWCART method of the book on submission. The <CFA_CONTENTOBJECTGETMULTIPLE> tag is called to get the details of each item in the Shopping Cart and to retrieve the details into a structure STOBJECTS.

An HTML table is then laid out, with the headings for the columns: Item, Quantity, and Price. A variable TOTALPRICE is then initialized with a value of zero. The items in the Shopping Cart are looped over, displaying each book's title, the quantity of the book currently in the cart, and the price per book. The total cost for this book is derived by multiplying the number of requested copies by the cost per copy.

NOTE The quantity form element is named as was described earlier, with the word QUANTITY concatenated with the object ID of the book, where the object ID has all its hyphens replaced with underscores.

At the end of each iteration of the loop, the total for each book is added to the TOTALPRICE variable. Once all the books are displayed, the TOTALPRICE variable will display the sum of all the books in the Shopping Cart.

The bottom of the form displays three buttons. The Continue Shopping button has a JavaScript onClick event that sends the user back to the Catalog. The Update Quantity button submits the form, running it through the routine at the beginning of the handler, and the Checkout button will invoke the checkout method (shown later in Listing 21.4, later in this chapter).

Building Order Histories

Each user who has purchased any items from A2ZBooks will have a single object representing his Order History. Each history will have a label with the appropriate username and a WDDX packet that contains the details of the user's history, such as the date of the purchase, the items purchased, and the quantity of each item.

The Checkout Process

After a user logs in to the application, browses the Catalog, selects the items he wants to purchase, and adds them to his Shopping Cart, the next logical step is to finalize his purchase and check out. This checkout process is handled by a method named `checkout`, the code for which is shown in Listing 21.4.

Listing 21.4 Allowing the User to Commit to the Purchase of Items in His Shopping Cart

```
<!---
File:          /handlers/a2z/book/checkout.cfm
Author:        jeff tapper (jeff@tapper.net)
Date:          1/19/2000
Description:  Checks out all items in the users shopping cart.
Notes:         This handler was modified from the restorenet sample
                application which shipped with Spectra.

                Restorenet was developed by David An (david.an@mindseye.com)
                Senior Developer, Mindseye Inc.
--->
<CF_A2ZFORMATTING>

    <!--- get shopping cart (part of user profile preferences) --->
    <CFA_USERPROFILEGET
        DATASOURCE="#request.cfa['a2zBooks'].datasource#"
        USERNAME="#request.cfa.activeuser#"
        R_STUSERPROFILE="stProfile"
    >

    <!--- assign to local variable for easier coding --->
    <CFSET CART = STPROFILE.PREFERENCES.SHOPPINGCART>

    <!--- payment processing goes here --->
        <!--- To simulate a successful transation, we return a payment
                successful flag. --->
<CFSET BPAYMENTSUCCESSFUL = 1>
    <!--- end payment processing --->

        <!--- If payment was successfully received, process the order --->
        <CFIF BPAYMENTSUCCESSFUL>
            <CFLOOP COLLECTION="#cart#" ITEM="objectID">
```

```
            <!--- order fulfillment goes here --->
                <!--- To simulate a successfully fulfilled order, we set
                      this item's status as shipped. --->
<CFSET CART[OBJECTID].STATUS = "shipped">
            <!--- end order fulfillment --->

                <CFOUTPUT>#cart[objectID].description# quantity
                          #cart[objectID].quantity# <FONT COLOR="##FF0000">
                          #cart[objectID].status#</FONT><BR></CFOUTPUT>
            </CFLOOP>
    <!--- if the order is successful, archive the cart and clear it. --->

            <!--- first, does archive exist for this user? --->
            <CFIF STRUCTKEYEXISTS(STPROFILE.PREFERENCES,"orderhistory")>
                <!--- archive exists --->
                <CFSET HISTORYOBJECTID =
                 STPROFILE.PREFERENCES.ORDERHISTORY>
            <CFELSE>
                <!--- archive did not exist; create it here --->
                <CFLOCK TIMEOUT="3" THROWONTIMEOUT="No"
                 NAME="SetAppVars" TYPE="readonly">
                <CFA_CONTENTOBJECTCREATE
                    DATASOURCE="#request.cfa['a2zBooks'].datasource#"
                    TYPEID="#Application.ORDERHISTORYTYPEID#"
                    LABEL="#request.cfa.activeuser#"
                    R_ID="historyObjectID">
                </CFLOCK>
            </CFIF>

            <!--- get the archive --->
            <CFA_CONTENTOBJECTGET
                DATASOURCE="#request.cfa['a2zBooks'].datasource#"
                OBJECTID="#historyObjectID#"
                R_STOBJECT="orderhistory"
            >

            <!--- convert the packet to a structure --->
            <CFA_ISWDDX
                INPUT = "#orderhistory.wHistory#"
                R_OUTPUT = "stHistory"
                R_BISWDDX = "isWDDX"
            >

            <CFSCRIPT>
                // if order history does not contain anything,
                //initialize the structure
                if (NOT isWDDX) {
                    stHistory = StructNew();
                }

                // create entries in the archive,
                // and copy the information to those keys
                for (objectID in cart) {
```

Part IV

Ch 21

continues

Listing 21.4 Continued

```
                historykey = objectID & "." & DateFormat(Now(),
                "yyyymmdd") & TimeFormat(Now(), "HHmmss");
                 stHistory[historykey] = cart[objectID];
                 stHistory[historykey].dateprocessed = Now();
            }

            // clear the active shopping cart
            stProfile.preferences.shoppingcart = StructNew();

            // link to the history
            stProfile.preferences.orderhistory = historyObjectID;
        </CFSCRIPT>

        <!--- translate back to WDDX --->
        <CFWDDX ACTION="CFML2WDDX" INPUT="#stHistory#"
         OUTPUT="wstHistory">

        <!--- update the archive object --->
        <CFA_CONTENTOBJECTDATA
            DATASOURCE="#request.cfa['a2zBooks'].datasource#"
            OBJECTID="#historyObjectID#"
        >
            <CFA_CONTENTOBJECTPROPERTY NAME="wHistory"
             VALUE="#wstHistory#">
            <CFA_CONTENTOBJECTPROPERTY NAME="attr_active" VALUE="1">
            <CFA_CONTENTOBJECTPROPERTY NAME="attr_published" VALUE="1">

        </CFA_CONTENTOBJECTDATA>

        <!--- now update the user profile with the cleared cart --->
        <CFA_USERPROFILESET
            DATASOURCE="#request.cfa['a2zBooks'].datasource#"
            USERNAME="#request.cfa.activeuser#"
            STUSERPROFILE="#stProfile#">
    <CFELSE>

            Sorry, there has been a problem processing your payment.
            Would you care to try an alternate form of payment?

    </CFIF>

  <CFOUTPUT>
      <A HREF="/a2z/invoke.cfm?objectID=#historyObjectID#
       &method=displayHistory">View Order History</A>
  </CFOUTPUT>
</CF_A2ZFORMATTING>
```

The checkout process begins by using the `<CFA_USERPROFILEGET>` tag to retrieve the user's profile into a variable named `STPROFILE`. Since the Shopping Cart is stored as a preference in the profile, this will make this user's cart available to us. To simplify coding, the `STPROFILE.PREFERENCES.SHOPPINGCART` is then set into a local variable named `CART`.

Next comes the payment process. Endless payment processing systems are available to merchants today, so the handler leaves out any vendor-specific processing, so that the merchant can plug in any payment processing system he favors. For demonstration purposes, the variable `BPAYMENTSUCCESSFUL` is set to true to simulate a successful transaction.

NOTE More than a dozen custom tags are available from the Allaire Developer Gallery (`http://www.allaire.com/developer/gallery`) for integrating with third-party engines for verifying credit cards, such as ICVerify, Cybercash, and Cybersource.

Next, a check is done to see whether the payment was successfully processed and, if so, the order fulfillment routine is executed, which will result in each book receiving a status of `SHIPPED` or `BACKORDER`. You should loop through each item in the cart so that you can properly determine the status of each item. Again, since every company's order fulfillment process varies, this section is left to the merchant's discretion. It's very possible that a workflow to fulfill the order could be executed here. For demonstration purposes, each item in the cart has its status set to `SHIPPED`.

Next, the customer's order needs to be archived into an Order History object. If this user has an existing Order History, the object ID of his Order History object will be stored in his user profile. If the history does exist, the variable is copied into a local variable named `HISTORYOBJECTID`. If it doesn't, the `<CFA_CONTENTOBJECTCREATE>` tag is used to create a new object of the `orderHistory` type and is labeled with this user's username. The object ID of the new Order History object is returned in a variable named `HISTORYOBJECTID`.

Then, the `<CFA_CONTENTOBJECTGET>` tag is used to retrieve the user's Order History, whether it has just been created or previously existed. This is returned in a structure named `ORDERHISTORY`. The `CFA_ISWDDX` is run on the `WHISTORY` key of the `ORDERHISTORY` structure, to determine if its value is a WDDX-encoded variable. This tag returns two variables. `ISWDDX` indicates whether the string was WDDX encoded; if it is, the structure `STHISTORY` is returned as a decoded version of the WDDX packet.

If this is a new Order History object, the `WHISTORY` key won't have been a WDDX packet, and a new structure needs to be created, which will hold this user's Order History. Then, the object ID of each book in the Shopping Cart is looped over, and a key made up of a concatenation of the object ID and the current date/time stamp is added to the structure. This key will hold the structure as it appeared in the Shopping Cart (which had the book's ID, its title, and its price). A fourth key is added to the structure, indicating the date the order was processed. The new structure is appended to the `STPROFILE.PREFERENCES` structure, and the user's `SHOPPINGCART` structure is emptied using the `STRUCTNEW()` function.

The `orderHistory` structure is processed through the `<CFWDDX>` tag to convert it to a WDDX packet in a variable named `WSTHISTORY`. The `<CFA_CONTENTOBJECTDATA>` tag is used to update the data in the `Order History` object to include the latest purchases. Then the `<CFA_USERPROFILESET>` tag is used to set the Order History and the empty Shopping Cart back into the database for this user. Finally, the user is presented with a link that will invoke the `display` handler of his Order History object when clicked. This handler can be seen in Listing 21.5.

Listing 21.5 Displaying the Order History for a User

```
<!---
File:          /handlers/a2z/orderHistory/displayHistory.cfm
Author:        jeff tapper (jeff@tapper.net)
Date:          1/19/2000
Description:  displays the transaction history for a user
Notes:         This handler was modified from the restorenet sample
                application which shipped with Spectra.

                Restorenet was developed by David An (david.an@mindseye.com)
                Senior Developer, Mindseye Inc.
--->
<CFA_HANDLER OBJECT="OrdHistory">

<CFPARAM NAME="URL.commonsubkey" DEFAULT="dateprocessed">
<CFPARAM NAME="URL.sortorder" DEFAULT="asc">
<CFPARAM NAME="URL.clearHistory" DEFAULT="0">

<CFWDDX ACTION="WDDX2CFML" INPUT="#OrdHistory.wHistory#"
 OUTPUT="stOrderHistory">

<CFIF URL.CLEARHISTORY>

     <CFSET STORDERHISTORY = STRUCTNEW()>
     <CFWDDX ACTION="CFML2WDDX" INPUT="#stOrderHistory#" OUTPUT="wstHistory">

     <!--- update the archive object --->
     <CFA_CONTENTOBJECTDATA
          DATASOURCE="#request.cfa['a2zBooks'].datasource#"
          OBJECTID="#OrdHistory.objectID#"
     >
          <CFA_CONTENTOBJECTPROPERTY NAME="wHistory" VALUE="#wstHistory#">
          <CFA_CONTENTOBJECTPROPERTY NAME="attr_active" VALUE="1">
          <CFA_CONTENTOBJECTPROPERTY NAME="attr_published" VALUE="1">

     </CFA_CONTENTOBJECTDATA>

</CFIF>

<CFIF URL.COMMONSUBKEY EQ "dateprocessed"
 OR URL.COMMONSUBKEY EQ "quantity">
     <CFSET SORTTYPE = "numeric">
<CFELSE>
     <CFSET SORTTYPE = "textnocase">
</CFIF>

<!--- Sort the Structure based on the sort field chosen --->
<CFA_STRUCTSORTCOMMONSUBKEYS
     STRUCT = "#stOrderHistory#"
     COMMONSUBKEY = "#URL.commonsubkey#"
     SORTTYPE = "#sorttype#"
```

```
    SORTORDER = "#URL.sortorder#"
    R_ASORTEDKEYS = "aKeys"
>

<CFOUTPUT>
<cf_a2zFormatting>
<TABLE BORDER=0 CELLSPACING=0 CELLPADDING=2 BGCOLOR="##669966"><TR><TD>
    <TABLE BORDER=0 CELLSPACING=0 CELLPADDING=4 BGCOLOR="##fcfcde">
    <TR>
        <TD>
            <CFSET THISSORTORDER = IIF((URL.COMMONSUBKEY EQ "dateprocessed"
             AND URL.SORTORDER EQ "ASC"),DE("DESC"),DE("ASC"))>
            <B><A HREF="/a2z/invoke.cfm?objectID=#OrdHistory.objectID#
&method=displayHistory&commonsubkey=dateprocessed&sortorder=#thissortorder#">
            Date</A></B>
        </TD>
        <TD>
            <CFSET THISSORTORDER = IIF((URL.COMMONSUBKEY EQ "description"
             AND URL.SORTORDER EQ "ASC"),DE("DESC"),DE("ASC"))>
            <B><A HREF="/a2z/invoke.cfm?objectID=#OrdHistory.objectID#
&method=displayHistory&commonsubkey=description&sortorder=#thissortorder#">
            Item</A></B>
        </TD>
        <TD>
            <CFSET THISSORTORDER = IIF((URL.COMMONSUBKEY EQ "quantity" AND
             URL.SORTORDER EQ "ASC"),DE("DESC"),DE("ASC"))>
            <B><A HREF="/a2z/invoke.cfm?objectID=#OrdHistory.objectID#&
method=displayHistory&commonsubkey=quantity&sortorder=#thissortorder#">
            Quantity</A></B>
        </TD>
        <TD>
            <CFSET THISSORTORDER = IIF((URL.COMMONSUBKEY EQ "status" AND
             URL.SORTORDER EQ "ASC"),DE("DESC"),DE("ASC"))>
            <B><A HREF="/a2z/invoke.cfm?objectID=#OrdHistory.objectID#
&method=displayHistory&commonsubkey=status&sortorder=#thissortorder#">
            Status</A></B>
        </TD>
    </TR>

    <!--- rather than looping through the structure,
          this loops through the list of keys returned from
          cfa_structsortcommonsubkeys.    --->
    <CFLOOP LIST="#ArrayToList(aKeys)#" INDEX="key">
        <TR>
            <TD>
              #DateFormat(stOrderHistory[key].dateprocessed,"mmm-dd-yyyy")#
            </TD>
            <TD>
              #stOrderHistory[key].description#
            </TD>
            <TD>
              #stOrderHistory[key].quantity#
```


continues

Listing 21.5 Continued

```
                </TD>
                <TD>
                    #stOrderHistory[key].status#
                </TD>
            </TR>
        </CFLOOP>

        </TABLE>

        <B><A HREF="/a2z/invoke.cfm?objectID=#OrdHistory.objectID#&
            method=displayHistory&clearhistory=1">Clear History</A></B>

    </TD></TR></TABLE>
    </cf_a2zFormatting>
    </CFOUTPUT>

    </CFA_HANDLER>
```

After using `<CFA_HANDLER>` to set a scope for the Order History object, default values are set for the variables `URL.COMMONSUBKEY`, `URL.SORTORDER`, and `URL.CLEARHISTORY`. `COMMONSUBKEY` and `SORTORDER` will be used to allow the user to sort the display of his Order History, whereas `CLEARHISTORY` is a flag that will be used to determine whether to empty the user's history.

Next, the `CFWDDX` translates the WDDX packet in the `WHISTORY` field of the object into a ColdFusion structure named `STORDERHISTORY`.

If the `CLEARHISTORY` attribute was passed in the `URL`, the next block of code is executed. This will create a new structure named `STORDERHISTORY`, use `CFWDDX` to encode that structure into a WDDX packet, and then set that new empty packet as the `WHISTORY` field of the object with `<CFA_CONTENTOBJECTDATA>` and `<CFA_CONTENTOBJECTPROPERTY>` tags.

Next is some logic to determine whether the structure is to be sorted as a text or numeric field. The field on which to sort is passed through the URL as a variable named `COMMONSUBKEY`. If the field is `DATEPROCESSED` or `QUANTITY`, the sort type is set to `NUMERIC`. Otherwise, the sort type is `TEXTNOCASE` (indicating a case-insensitive sorting on the text). The `<CFA_STRUCTSORTCOMMONSUBKEYS>` tag is then called, which will return the object IDs sorted by the property specified and return these in an array. Among the optional attributes of this tag are `SORTTYPE` and `SORTORDER`. `SORTTYPE` can be `TEXT` (case-sensitive sorting), `TEXTNOCASE` (case-insensitive sorting), and numeric. The `SORTORDER` can be `asc` (ascending) or `desc` (descending); ascending is the default if the attribute isn't provided.

Then, the table to hold the Order History is created, with column headers that allow you to sort by column. This is done by making each header a link, to invoke the `display` handler for the `Order History` object, with attributes to indicate which column is to be used for sorting. For each column, the variable `THISSORTORDER` is set to determine the sort order. With this variable, if a column is clicked once, it will be sorted in ascending order. If it's clicked again, it will be sorted in descending order.

The array returned by `<CFA_STRUCTSORTCOMMONSUBKEYS>`, which contains the object IDs sorted in the specified manner, is then looped over. This is used to output each book the user has purchased.

Finally, a link is offered to the user to allow him to clear his Order History. Figure 21.8 shows the Order History of a particular user.

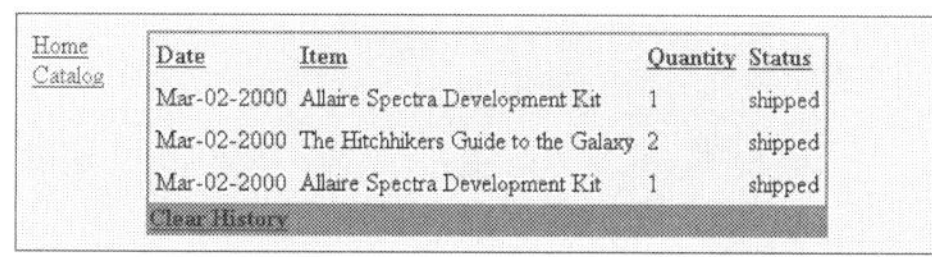

Date	Item	Quantity	Status
Mar-02-2000	Allaire Spectra Development Kit	1	shipped
Mar-02-2000	The Hitchhikers Guide to the Galaxy	2	shipped
Mar-02-2000	Allaire Spectra Development Kit	1	shipped
Clear History			

FIGURE 21.8
The Order History `display` handler shows all of the books this user has purchased.

CHAPTER 22

Extending Spectra

In this chapter

Using PITA Tags to Extend Spectra

A number of tags provided with Spectra are labeled PITA (Partner Integration Technology Architecture) tags. These tags behave just like any other Spectra tag, the only difference being that they exist to create functionality otherwise available only through the Webtop.

What Are PITA Tags?

PITA tags tend to fall into one of four categories, based on their function—security, PLP, logging, and object:

- Through the use of the security tags, you can create and manage all aspects of Spectra security. Tags are available for tasks from managing security contexts and user directories to securing individual methods of an object type.
- PLP tags allow you to create, update, and delete PLP definitions and steps without requiring the Webtop.
- Spectra provides a series of logging tags that allow system designers to customize what data Spectra logs and how these log files are processed.
- Spectra allows you to create your own tools for editing Content Objects, including creating and administering Property Definitions, ContentObject Types, individual objects, and meta data hierarchies.

More information is available about the PITA architecture in the *PITA Developer's Guide*, included with Spectra's documentation.

NOTE The Allaire Spectra documentation separates the Spectra tags into two types: Spectra tags and PITA tags. The PITA tags are primarily the lesser-used tags (for example, those used by the Webtop itself), but that distinction is arbitrary. The truth is that at some point, all the tags are useful.

Building a Custom Webtop

Spectra's Webtop provides so much functionality that many applications won't require all that it offers. One liability incurred with all this functionality is slower performance. What's more, specific applications might require the use of features not offered in the standard Webtop.

It's possible to build your own interface, to provide only the functionality of the Webtop that your application will require, and therefore not burden the system with managing functions you won't need. In the following sections, you will learn how to create your own version of the Site Object Designer, which can offer vast performance increases over the one with which Spectra ships.

Objects

The content object tags of the PITA architecture are used here to re-create a slimmer, faster version of the Webtop's Site Object Designer. Among the functionality that will be included is the capability to find, display, and edit objects.

Finding Objects Interactive developers will spend much of their time in the Site Object Designer and will soon find that there's no easily accessible interface to quickly find an individual object. Spectra does allow you to create views to build and save detailed searches of objects, but this method can be burdensome. Listing 22.1 shows a simplified version of the site object finder, which allows the developer to find and manage an object by its label and type.

Listing 22.1 Simplified Object Finder

```
<!---
File:          admin/webtop/objFind.cfm
Author:        jeff tapper
Date:          1/26/2000
Description:   Intended as a replacement for the object finder in the
                Spectra Webtop. This provides a search interface, to allow
                Users to search for objects by their label, as well as
                their type. This also provides an interface to create
                or delete instances of objects.
Notes:
Change History:
--->

<CFIF ISDEFINED("form.objFnd")>
   <!--- Get object Data --->
   <CFA_CONTENTOBJECTFIND
      DATASOURCE="#request.cfa['a2zBooks'].datasource#"
      TYPEID="#form.objectType#"
      R_STOBJECTS="stObjects"
      LABEL="%#form.objLabel#%"
   >

   <!--- Get object type data --->
   <CFA_OBJECTTYPEGET
      DATASOURCE="#request.cfa['a2zBooks'].datasource#"
      TYPEID="#form.objectType#"
      R_STTYPE="stType"
   >

      <CF_A2ZFORMATTING ADMINLINKS=1>
         <TABLE BORDER="1">
         <!--- display returned objects --->
            <CFLOOP COLLECTION="#stObjects#" ITEM="objID">
               <CFOUTPUT>
```

continues

Listing 22.1 Continued

```
                  <TR>
                      <TD WIDTH="15%">
                          <A HREF="objEdit.cfm?objectID=#objID#&method=edit">
                          Edit</A>
                      </TD>
                      <TD WIDTH="15%">
                        <A HREF="objEdit.cfm?objectID=#objID#&method=display">
                        Display</A>
                      </TD>
                      <TD WIDTH="15%">
                        <A HREF="objFind.cfm?objectID=#objID#&method=delete">
                        Delete</A>
                      </TD>
                      <TD WIDTH="55%">
                          #stObjects[objID].label#</A>
                      </TD>
                  </TR>
                  </CFOUTPUT>
              </CFLOOP>
              <TR>
                  <TD COLSPAN="3">
                      <CFOUTPUT>
                      <A href="objFind.cfm?typeID=#stType.typeID#&create=1">
                      Create a new #stType['label']#</A>
                      </CFOUTPUT>
                  </TD>
              </TR>
          </TABLE>
      </CF_A2ZFORMATTING>

<!--- creating new object? --->
<CFELSEIF ISDEFINED("url.create")>

    <CFA_CONTENTOBJECTCREATE
        DATASOURCE="#request.cfa.a2zBooks.datasource#"
        TYPEID="#url.typeID#"
        R_ID="objectID">

    <CFLOCATION URL="objEdit.cfm?objectID=#objectID#&method=edit">

<CFELSEIF ISDEFINED("url.method")>

    <CFIF URL.METHOD IS 'DELETE'>
    <!--- Ask for completion before deleting --->

    <CF_A2ZFORMATTING ADMINLINKS="1">
        <CFPARAM NAME="url.objectID">
        Are you sure you want to delete this object?<BR>
        <CFOUTPUT>
        <A HREF="objFind.cfm?objectID=#url.objectID#&method=confirmDelete">
        Yes</A>
        |
```

```
        <A HREF="objFind.cfm">No</A><BR>
        </CFOUTPUT>
    </CF_A2ZFORMATTING>

    <CFELSEIF URL.METHOD IS 'CONFIRMDELETE'>
    <!--- Delete confirmed, remove the item --->
        <CFPARAM NAME="url.objectID">

        <CFA_CONTENTOBJECTDELETE
            DATASOURCE="#request.cfa.a2zBooks.datasource#"
            OBJECTID="#url.objectID#">

        <CF_A2ZFORMATTING ADMINLINKS=1>
            <CFOUTPUT>Object Deleted!</CFOUTPUT>
        </CF_A2ZFORMATTING>

    </CFIF>

<!--- show the form --->
<CFELSE>
    <CFA_CONTROLHANDLER NAME="objectFinder">
    <CF_A2ZFORMATTING ADMINLINKS="yes">
    <TABLE>
        <TR>
            <TD>Object Label:</TD>
            <TD><INPUT TYPE="text" NAME="objLabel"></TD>
        </TR>
        <TR>
            <TD>Object Type:</TD>
            <TD>
                <CFA_OBJECTTYPEGETMULTIPLE
                    DATASOURCE = "#request.cfa.a2zBooks.datasource#"
                    R_STTYPES = "stTypes"
                >
                <SELECT NAME="objectType">
                    <CFLOOP COLLECTION="#STTYPES#" ITEM="objID">
                        <CFIF NOT STTYPES[OBJID].NSYSATTRIBUTES>
                            <CFOUTPUT>
                            <OPTION VALUE="#objID#">#stTypes[objID].label#
                            </CFOUTPUT>
                        </CFIF>
                    </CFLOOP>
                </SELECT>
            </TD>
        </TR>
        <TR>
            <TD COLSPAN="2">
                <INPUT TYPE="submit" NAME="objFnd" VALUE="find the objects">
            </TD>

        </TR>
    </TABLE>
    </CF_A2ZFORMATTING>
</CFIF>
```

This Object Finder begins by determining whether it has been passed a request to find specified objects. If it has, it uses the <CFA_CONTENTOBJECTFIND> tag to return all objects of the specified type, whose Label field contains the specified text. The label search executes a LIKE clause in the SQL; for this reason, you can use % signs around the value passed here to allow it to find this string anywhere within the field. This will also allow for you to leave this field blank and return all items of the specified type.

Data about the object type specified is also retrieved, to allow for the object type label to be used in the Create a New button at the bottom of the results.

The matched objects are then looped through, displaying each with a link to edit, view, or delete that object. The Delete link points back to this same file, with a different set of URL parameters. The Edit and View links point to objEdit.cfm (detailed later, in Listing 22.2). After all the items are displayed, a link appears to allow users to create a new object of this type.

Figure 22.1 shows the result list of one such search.

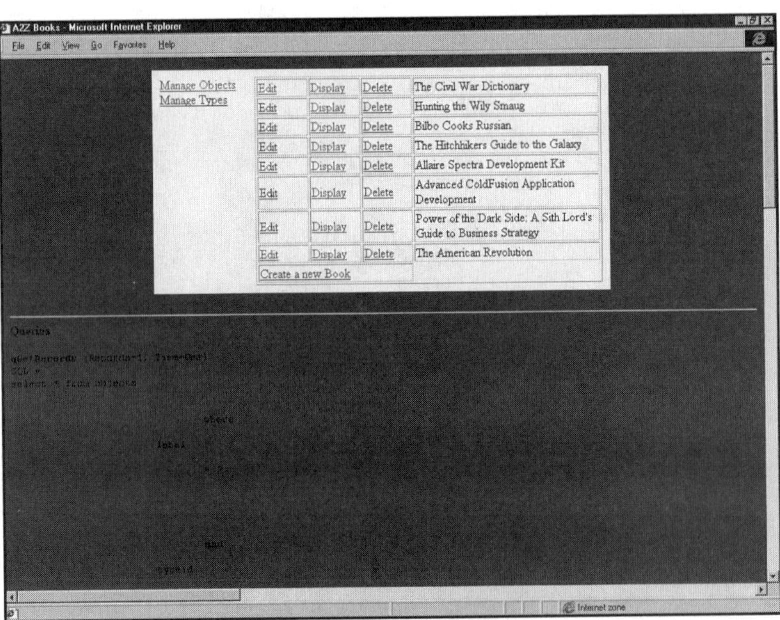

FIGURE 22.1
After submitting a search in the Object Finder, all matching objects are returned, with the options to edit, display, or delete them.

Next, a <CFIF> statement determines whether a request has been made to create a new object; if so, the OBJECTTYPEID passed in the URL is used with a <CFA_CONTENTOBJECTCREATE> tag to create a new object of that type. The new object ID is then passed into the Object Editor with a <CFLOCATION> tag.

This is followed by a conditional to determine whether a method attribute was passed in the URL to indicate that a particular object should be deleted. If there is a request to delete an object, the user is asked to confirm that they intend to remove this object entirely from the ContentObject Database (see Figure 22.2). If they confirm, the object is deleted. If not, they are returned to the Object Finder.

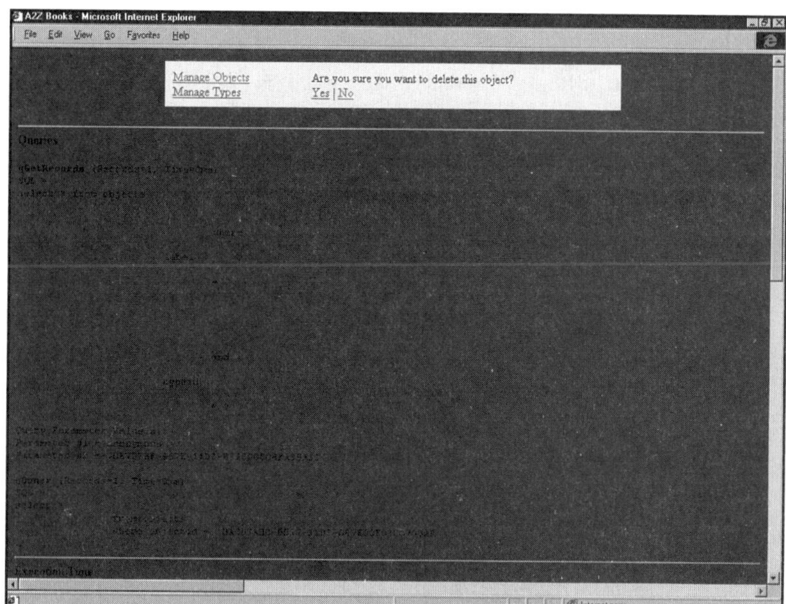

FIGURE 22.2
The Object Finder asks for confirmation before allowing users to delete an object.

If no `FORM` or `URL` variables are present to indicate that a different action should occur, the object search engine is displayed, prompting the user for a label and object type. Note that the Object Type menu is populated by the `<CFA_OBJECTTYPEGETMULTIPLE>` tag to return all available object types in that specified datasource. These types are looped over, inside of a select box, using their object type ID as the value, and the type label as the name displayed to the user.

Figure 22.3 shows the object search engine.

Editing Objects In the case that a user wanted to view, edit, or create an object, he would be directed to `objEdit.cfm`. The source of this can be seen in Listing 22.2.

Listing 22.2 A Simplified Object Editor

```
<!—-
File:         admin/webtop/objEdit.cfm
Author:       jeff tapper
Date:         1/26/2000
```

continues

Listing 22.2 Continued

```
Description:  Instantiates the specified method for object provided.

Notes:

Change History:

--->
<CFPARAM NAME="url.objectID">
<CFPARAM NAME="url.method">
<CF_A2ZFORMATTING ADMINLINKS="yes">
    <CFA_CONTENTOBJECT
      DATASOURCE="#request.cfa.a2zBooks.datasource#"
      OBJECTID="#url.objectID#"
      METHOD="#url.method#"
    >
</CF_A2ZFORMATTING>
```

This page is provided with a method and an object ID. By using a `<CFA_CONTENTOBJECT>` tag, the method indicated is executed on the specified object ID. With this simple interface, the same page can be used to edit or delete any object in the system. Figure 22.4 shows the edit handler being invoked for a Book object, whereas Figure 22.5 shows the `display` handler for the same object.

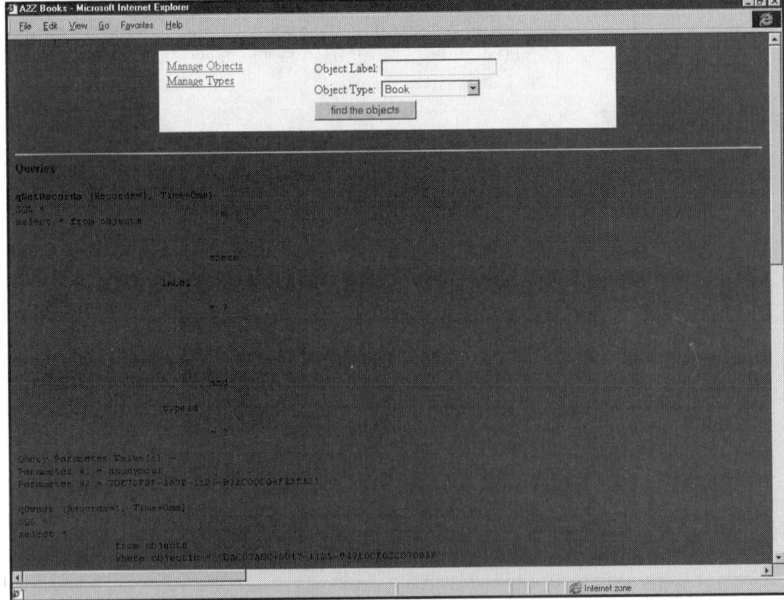

FIGURE 22.3
This Object Finder allows you to search for objects by their label, a feature the Webtop doesn't offer.

FIGURE 22.4
To edit an object, the Object Finder invokes the object type's `edit` handler.

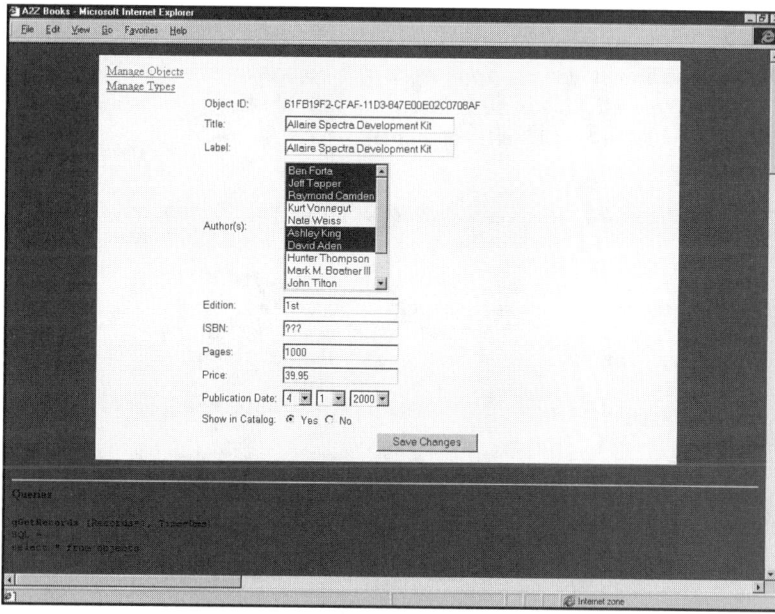

FIGURE 22.5
To display an object, the object finder invokes the object type's `display` handler.

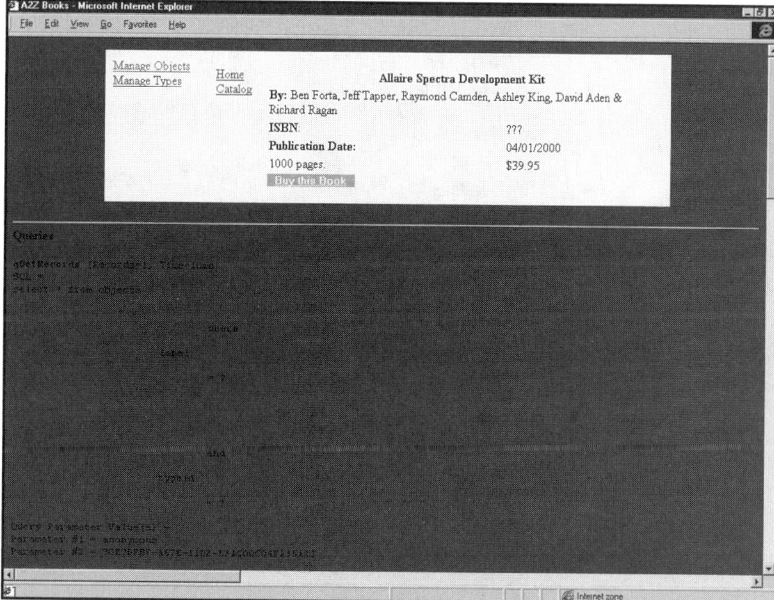

Types

In addition to being able to work with objects outside the Webtop, it may also be useful for system designers to be able to work with object types. Listing 22.3 shows the code for a slimmed down Object Type Finder.

Listing 22.3 A Simplified Object Type Finder

```
<!---
File:          admin/webtop/typeFind.cfm
Author:        jeff tapper
Date:          1/26/2000
Description:   Intended as a replacement for the object type editor in the
                Spectra Webtop. This provides an interface to allow
users to choose, edit, display and delete an objectType.

Notes:

Change History:

--->

<CFPARAM NAME="showForm" DEFAULT="1">

<CF_A2ZFORMATTING ADMINLINKS="1">

     <CFIF ISDEFINED("editType")>
          <CFIF ISDEFINED("url.TypeID")>
               <CFSET FORM.OBJECTTYPE = URL.TYPEID>
          </CFIF>

          <CFPARAM NAME="form.objectType">

          <CFIF ISDEFINED("updateSettings")>

               <CFA_OBJECTTYPE
                DATASOURCE="#request.cfa.a2zBooks.datasource#"
                ACTION="update"
                TYPEID="#form.OBJECTTYPE#"
                LABEL="#form.label#"
                DESCRIPTION="#form.description#"
                HANDLERROOT="#form.root#"
               >

          <CFELSEIF ISDEFINED("form.newProp")>

               <CFA_OBJECTTYPEPROPERTY
                ACTION="create"
                DATASOURCE="#request.cfa.a2zBooks.datasource#"
                TYPEID="#form.OBJECTTYPE#"
                PROPERTYNAME="#form.propName#"
```

```
        PROPERTYDEFINITIONID="#form.propType#"
       >
       <CFLOCATION URL="editProp.cfm?typeID=#form.OBJECTTYPE#
                       ➥&propName=#form.propName#">
<CFELSEIF ISDEFINED("form.newMethod")>

       <CFIF NOT ISDEFINED ("form.createMethod")>

         <CFSET SHOWFORM = 0>
         <CFA_CONTROLHANDLER NAME="methodCreate">
           <CFOUTPUT>
           <TABLE>
             <TR>
               <TD>Method:</TD>
               <TD>#form.methodName#
               <INPUT TYPE="hidden" NAME="methodName"
                      VALUE="#form.methodName#">
               </TD>
             </TR>
             <TR>
               <TD>Description:</TD>
               <TD><TEXTAREA NAME="description"></TEXTAREA></TD>
             </TR>
             <TR>
               <TD>Handler Name:</TD>
               <TD><INPUT TYPE="text" NAME="handlerName"></TD>
             </TR>
             <TR>
               <TD COLSPAN="2">
               <INPUT TYPE="submit" NAME="createMethod"
                      VALUE="Create">
               </TD>
             </TR>
             <INPUT TYPE="hidden" NAME="newMethod" VALUE="1">
             <INPUT TYPE="hidden" NAME="OBJECTTYPE"
                    VALUE="#form.OBJECTTYPE#">
             <INPUT TYPE="hidden" NAME="editType" VALUE="1">
           </TABLE>
           </CFOUTPUT>
         </CFA_CONTROLHANDLER>

       <CFELSE>
           <CFA_OBJECTTYPEMETHOD
            DATASOURCE="#request.cfa.a2zBooks.datasource#"
            ACTION="create"
            TYPEID="#form.OBJECTTYPE#"
            METHOD="#form.methodName#"
            DESCRIPTION="#form.description#"
            HANDLERURL="#form.handlerName#"
           >

       </CFIF>
```

continues

Listing 22.3 Continued

```
</CFIF>

<CFA_OBJECTTYPEGET
 DATASOURCE="#request.cfa.a2zBooks.datasource#"
 TYPEID="#form.objectType#"
 R_STTYPE="stType"
>

<CFIF SHOWFORM>
  <CFA_TABAREA WIDTH=400 HEIGHT=200 TABWIDTH=70>

    <!--- Settings Tab Page --->
    <CFA_TABPAGE NAME="Type Settings" SELECTED="Yes">
      <CFA_CONTROLHANDLER NAME="TypeEdit">
        <CFOUTPUT>
          <TABLE>
            <TR>
              <TD>Label:</TD>
              <TD>
              <INPUT TYPE="text" NAME="label"
              VALUE="#stType.label#">
              </TD>
            </TR>
            <TR>
              <TD>Description:</TD>
              <TD>
              <TEXTAREA COLS=45 ROWS=4 NAME="description">
                  #stType.description#
              </TEXTAREA>
              </TD>
            </TR>
            <TR>
              <TD>Handler Root:</TD>
              <TD>
              <INPUT TYPE="text" NAME="root"
                     VALUE="#stType.HANDLERROOT#" SIZE="50">
              </TD>
            </TR>
            <TR>
              <TD COLSPAN="2">
              <INPUT TYPE="submit" NAME="updateSettings"
                     VALUE="Update">
              </TD>
              <INPUT TYPE="hidden" NAME="editType">
              <INPUT TYPE="hidden" NAME="OBJECTTYPE"
                     VALUE="#form.OBJECTTYPE#">
            </TR>
          </TABLE>

        </CFOUTPUT>
      </CFA_CONTROLHANDLER>
```

```
              </CFA_TABPAGE>

              <!-- Properties Tab Page -->
              <CFA_TABPAGE NAME="Properties">

                <CFLOOP
                COLLECTION="#STTYPE['STTYPEPROPERTYDEFINITIONS']#"
                      ITEM="property">
                  <CFOUTPUT>
                  <A HREF="editProp.cfm?typeID=#stType.TypeID#
                        ➥&propName=#property#">#property#</A><BR>
                  </CFOUTPUT>
                </CFLOOP>

                <CFA_CONTROLHANDLER NAME="newProp">

                <CFA_PROPERTYDEFINITIONGETMULTIPLE
                 DATASOURCE="#request.cfa.a2zBooks.datasource#"
                 R_STDEFINITIONS="stProps"
                >
                <CFA_STRUCTSORTCOMMONSUBKEYS
                 STRUCT="#stProps#"
                 COMMONSUBKEY="label"
                 R_ASORTEDKEYS="aProps"
                >

                    <TABLE>
                      <TR>
                        <TD>New Property:</TD>
                        <TD><INPUT TYPE="text" NAME="propName"></TD>
                        <TD>
                          <SELECT NAME="propType">
                          <CFLOOP FROM="1" TO="#arrayLen(aProps)#"
                          INDEX="property">
                            <CFSET THISPROP = APROPS[PROPERTY]>
                            <CFOUTPUT>
                            <OPTION
VALUE="#thisProp#">#stProps[thisProp].label#
                             </CFOUTPUT>
                          </CFLOOP>
                          </SELECT>
                        </TD>
                      </TR>
                      <TR>
                        <TD COLSPAN="2">
                        <INPUT TYPE="submit" NAME="newProp" VALUE="Add">
                        </TD>
                        <INPUT TYPE="hidden" NAME="editType">
<CFOUTPUT>
                          <INPUT TYPE="hidden"
                                 NAME="OBJECTTYPE"
```

continues

Listing 22.3 Continued

```
                                VALUE="#form.OBJECTTYPE#">
                        </CFOUTPUT>
                      </TR>
                    </TABLE>

                </CFA_CONTROLHANDLER>
              </CFA_TABPAGE>

              <!—- Method Tab Page —->
              <CFA_TABPAGE NAME="Methods">

                <CFLOOP
                COLLECTION="#STTYPE['STTYPEMETHODDEFINITIONS']#"
                      ITEM="method">
                  <CFOUTPUT>
                  <A HREF="editMethod.cfm?typeID=#stType.TypeID#
                          ➥&methodName=#method#">#method#</A> <BR>
                  </CFOUTPUT>
                </CFLOOP>

                <CFA_CONTROLHANDLER NAME="newMethod">
                <TABLE>
                  <TR>
                    <TD>New Method:</TD>
                    <TD><INPUT TYPE="text" NAME="methodName"></TD>
                  </TR>
                  <TR>
                    <TD COLSPAN="2">
                    <INPUT TYPE="submit" NAME="newMethod" VALUE="Add">
                    </TD>
                    <INPUT TYPE="hidden" NAME="editType">
                    <CFOUTPUT>
                      <INPUT TYPE="hidden"
                             NAME="OBJECTTYPE"
                            VALUE="#form.OBJECTTYPE#">
                    </CFOUTPUT>
                  </TR>
                </TABLE>
                </CFA_CONTROLHANDLER>
              </CFA_TABPAGE>

            </CFA_TABAREA>
          </CFIF>

      <CFELSEIF ISDEFINED("form.AddType")>
          <CFA_OBJECTTYPE
           DATASOURCE="#request.cfa.a2zBooks.datasource#"
           ACTION="Create"
           LABEL="(new)"
           R_TYPEID="typeID"
          >
```

```
        <CFLOCATION URL="typeFind.cfm?typeID=#typeID#&EDITTYPE=1">
    <CFELSE>

        <CFA_CONTROLHANDLER NAME="objectFinder">

          <TABLE>
            <TR>
            <TD COLSPAN="2">
            Choose a object type to edit from the pull-down menu, or click
            "Create a new type" to add a new object type.

           </TD>
           </TR>
            <TR>
              <TD>Object Type:</TD>
              <TD>
                <CFA_OBJECTTYPEGETMULTIPLE
                 DATASOURCE = "#request.cfa.a2zBooks.datasource#"
                 R_STTYPES = "stTypes"
                >
                <SELECT NAME="objectType">
                  <CFLOOP COLLECTION="#STTYPES#" ITEM="objID">

                    <CFIF NOT STTYPES[OBJID].NSYSATTRIBUTES>
                      <CFOUTPUT>
                      <OPTION VALUE="#objID#">#stTypes[objID].label#
                      </CFOUTPUT>
                    </CFIF>

                  </CFLOOP>
                </SELECT>
              </TD>
            </TR>
            <TR>
              <TD>
                <INPUT
                TYPE="submit"
                NAME="editType"
                VALUE="Edit this type">
              </TD>
              <TD>
                <INPUT
                TYPE="submit"
                NAME="addType"
                VALUE="Create a new type">
              </TD>
            </TR>
          </TABLE>

        </CFA_CONTROLHANDLER>
    </CFIF>

</CF_A2ZFORMATTING>
```

Listing 22.3 begins by setting a default value for the Boolean flag indicating whether to display the Type editing form. This is on by default and is turned off only if a user is creating a new method for the object type, in which case a different form is displayed.

Next is a check to determine if the variable EDITTYPE is present. Its presence indicates that the object type form has been submitted, and there are actions to take place. If this is present and the URL variable TYPEID is also present, the value passed in the URL variable is set into the variable FORM.OBJECTTYPE, which is required to update the object type, to add a property or method, or to display the object type.

If the UPDATESETTINGS flag is present, the passed form variables are updated into the object type, using the <CFA_OBJECTTYPE> tag, with the action set to UPDATE.

If the FORM.NEWPROP variable is present, the <CFA_OBJECTTYPEPROPERTY> tag is used to create the property with the specified name and type, and a CFLOCATION tag is used to redirect the user to the page to edit the newly created property.

If the FORM.NEWMETHOD variable is present, the variable FORM.CREATEMETHOD is tested for existence. If it fails this test, you then know that the method creation form hasn't yet been submitted, and the form is displayed. If the variable does exist, the <CFA_OBJECTTYPEMETHOD> tag is used with the action CREATE. This will add the new method to the object type, with the name, description, and handler filename specified in the form.

NOTE When the method creation form is displayed, the variable SHOWFORM is set to 0 to suppress the display of the object type form as well.

Next, the object type details are retrieved with the <CFA_OBJECTTYPEGET> tag, using the TYPEID specified in the variable FORM.OBJECTTYPE. If SHOWFORM is set to true, the object type form is displayed, with all the information known about the object type.

To help make browsing and editing the object type easier, a TABAREA display control is used, defining an area 400 pixels wide and 200 pixels tall, with 75 pixels of width set aside for each link on each tab.

▶ **See** Chapter 9, "Building Display Components," for details on using the TABAREA and TABPAGE controls.

The first tab page, Type Settings, is selected by default. Within this page, a form is created to allow users to see and edit the label, description, and handler root for this object type. The object type ID is embedded into a hidden form field, and the EDITTYPE flag is set in a hidden field as well, to indicate that these values are to be updated when the page is submitted. Figure 22.6 shows the Type Settings tab page.

Next, the Properties tab page is defined. This page starts by looping through all the properties currently associated with this object type and displaying their labels, along with a link to a page to allow users to edit the details of the property. Below this list is a property creation form. This form allows users to choose a name for a new property or choose from the property definitions already available.

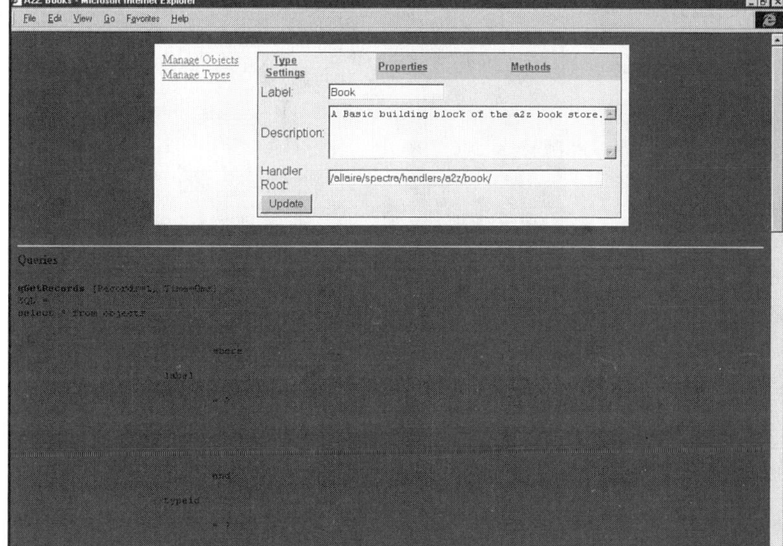

FIGURE 22.6
Here you can see the Type Settings tab page of the object type editor.

To generate the list of available property definitions, the <CFA_PROPERTYDEFINITIONGETMULTIPLE> tag is used to return all properties in the datasource. The returned properties are run through the <CFA_STRUCTSORTCOMMONSUBKEYS> tag with parameters to indicate that the structure's keys are to be sorted by the LABEL. The resulting array is looped over and used as a key to output PROPERTYDEFINITIONID and PROPERTYNAME of all available properties in a pull-down menu. Figure 22.7 shows the Properties tab page.

The Methods tab page is then defined. This starts by looping over the STTYPEMETHODDEFINITIONS key of the object type structure to display all the available methods, with links to edit them. Below this, a form is presented to allow a user to create a new method. Figure 22.8 shows the Methods tab page.

After the close of the TABAREA, the conditional at the beginning of the file testing for the variable EDITTYPE is ended with a CFELSEIF statement testing for the existence of FORM.ADDTYPE. The presence of ADDTYPE indicates that the user has chosen to add a new object type. In this case, a <CFA_OBJECTTYPE> tag is used with the action CREATE and a label (NEW). A <CFLOCATION> tag is then used to redirect the user to a page to edit the newly created object type.

If neither the EDITTYPE nor the ADDTYPE flag is available, the assumption is that the user has just arrived and needs to choose with which object type he wants to work. To help facilitate this choice, the <CFA_OBJECTTYPEGETMULTIPLE> tag is used to return all the object types in the datasource. These are looped over and tested to see if they are system object types, with the line

```
<CFIF NOT STTYPES[OBJID].NSYSATTRIBUTES>
```

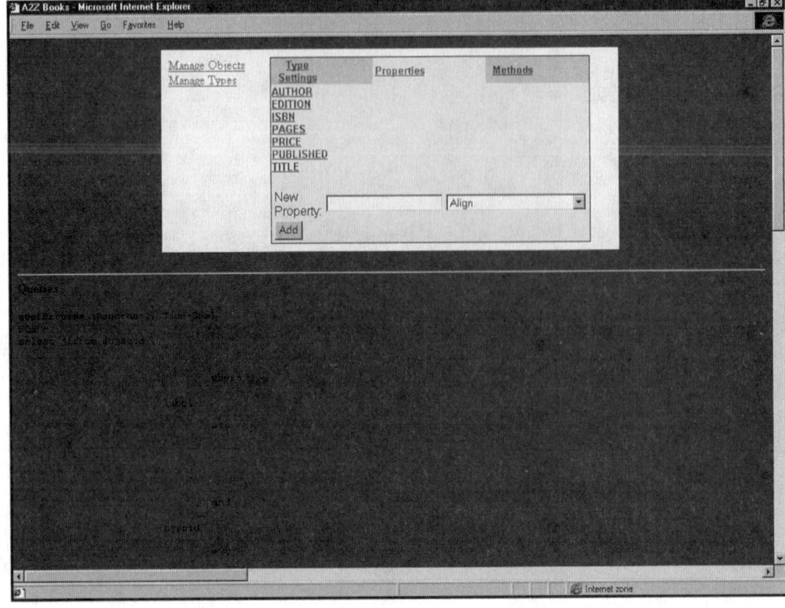

FIGURE 22.7
The Properties tab page of the object type editor allows you to create a new property for this type or edit an existing property. Align appears in the pull-down menu, as it is alphabetically the first available property.

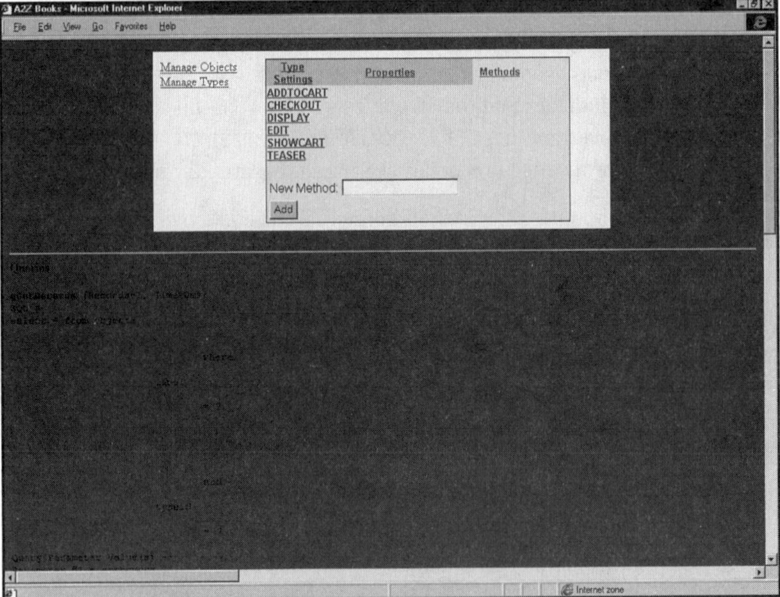

FIGURE 22.8
The Methods tab page of the object type editor allows you to create a new method or edit an existing one.

If they are system object types, the value of the NSYSATTRIBUTES key will be 6; if not, it will be 0. Using this test, only non-system objects are included in the pull-down menu.

This form ends with two submit buttons: one soliciting the user to edit the chosen type, the other to allow the user to add a new type. The object type chooser is shown in Figure 22.9.

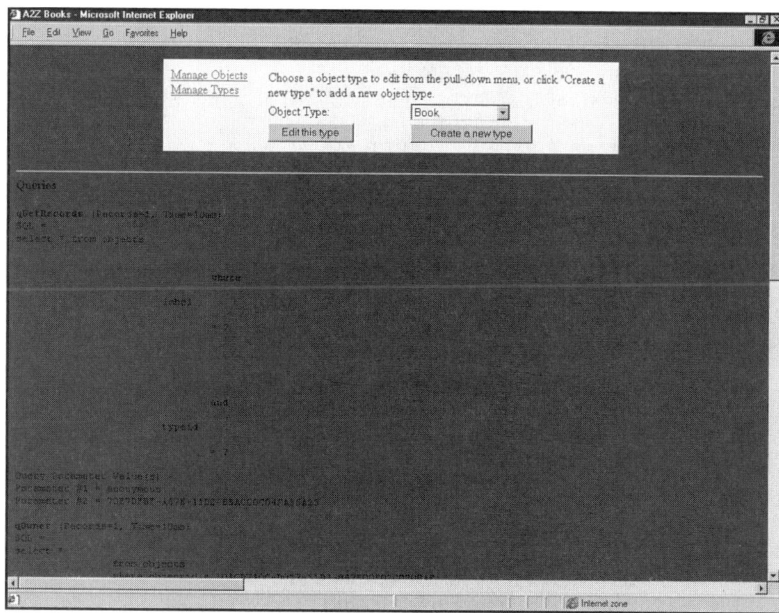

FIGURE 22.9
Before a user is allowed to work with an object type, he must first identify which type he wants to use or that he is creating a new type.

Editing Properties From the Properties tab page of the object type form, links are available to edit the object type's properties. The page, which allows users to make these edits, can be seen in Listing 22.4.

Listing 22.4 A Simplified Property Editor

```
<!---
File:          admin/webtop/editProp.cfm
Author:        jeff tapper
Date:          1/26/2000
Description:   Given an object type and a property name, this will display
                the details of the property, and allow users to update them,
                or to remove this property from the objectType

Notes:
```

continues

Listing 22.4 Continued

```
Change History:

--->

<CF_A2ZFORMATTING ADMINLINKS=1>

<CFIF ISDEFINED("form.update")>
    <CFIF TYPE IS 'ARRAY'>
        <CFSET ARRAY = 1>
        <CFSET MULTILINGUAL = 0>
    <CFELSEIF TYPE IS 'MULTILINGUAL'>
        <CFSET ARRAY = 0>
        <CFSET MULTILINGUAL = 1>
    <CFELSE>
        <CFSET ARRAY = 0>
        <CFSET MULTILINGUAL = 0>
    </CFIF>
    <CFPARAM NAME="form.indexed" default="0">
    <CFPARAM NAME="form.required" default="0">
    <CFPARAM NAME="form.searchable" default="0">

    <CFA_OBJECTTYPEPROPERTY
     ACTION="UPDATE"
     DATASOURCE="#request.cfa.a2zBooks.datasource#"
     TYPEID="#form.typeID#"
     PROPERTYNAME="#form.propname#"
     DEFAULTVALUE="#form.default#"
     BSEARCHABLE="#form.searchable#"
     BREQUIRED="#form.required#"
     BINDEXED="#form.Indexed#"
     BARRAY="#variables.array#"
     BMULTILINGUAL="#variables.multilingual#"
    >
    <CFLOCATION URL="typeFind.cfm?editType=1&TypeID=#form.typeID#">
<CFELSEIF ISDEFINED("form.delete")>
    <CFA_OBJECTTYPEPROPERTY
     ACTION="DELETE"
     DATASOURCE="#request.cfa.a2zBooks.datasource#"
     TYPEID="#form.typeID#"
     PROPERTYNAME="#form.propname#"
    >
    <CFLOCATION URL="typeFind.cfm?editType=1&TypeID=#form.typeID#">
</CFIF>
    <CFPARAM NAME="typeID">
    <CFPARAM NAME="propName">
        <CFA_OBJECTTYPEGET
            DATASOURCE="#request.cfa.a2zBooks.datasource#"
            TYPEID="#url.typeID#"
            R_STTYPE="stType"
        >

    <CFA_CONTROLHANDLER NAME="updateProperty">
```

```
<CFOUTPUT>
<TABLE>
    <TR>
      <TD>Property Name:
      </TD>
      <TD>
      #url.PropName#
      <INPUT TYPE="hidden" NAME="propname" VALUE="#url.propname#">
      <INPUT TYPE="hidden" NAME="typeID" VALUE="#url.typeID#">

      </TD>
    </TR>
    <TR>
      <TD>Alias:
      </TD>
      <TD>
      <INPUT
      TYPE="text"
      NAME="alias"
      VALUE="#sttype.STTYPEPROPERTYDEFINITIONS[url.propname].alias#">
      </TD>
    </TR>
    <TR>
      <TD>Default Value
      </TD>
      <TD>
      <INPUT TYPE="text"
      NAME="default"
      VALUE="#sttype.STTYPEPROPERTYDEFINITIONS[url.propname]
            ➥.defaultvalue#">

      </TD>
    </TR>
    <TR>
      <TD> </TD>
<TD>

      <INPUT TYPE="radio" NAME="type" VALUE="simple"
      <CFIF NOT STTYPE.STTYPEPROPERTYDEFINITIONS[URL.PROPNAME].BARRAY
      AND
      NOT STTYPE.STTYPEPROPERTYDEFINITIONS[URL.PROPNAME]
          ➥.BMULTILINGUAL>
      CHECKED
      </CFIF>
      >Simple<BR>
      <INPUT TYPE="radio" NAME="type" VALUE="array"
      <CFIF STTYPE.STTYPEPROPERTYDEFINITIONS[URL.PROPNAME].BARRAY>
      CHECKED
      </CFIF>
      >Array<BR>
      <INPUT TYPE="radio" NAME="type" VALUE="multilingual"
      <CFIF STTYPE.STTYPEPROPERTYDEFINITIONS[URL.PROPNAME]
          ➥.BMULTILINGUAL>
```

continues

Listing 22.4 Continued

```
                CHECKED
                </CFIF>
                >Multilingual<BR>
                </TD>

            </TR>
            <TR>
                <TD> </TD>

<TD>
                <INPUT TYPE="checkbox" NAME="required" VALUE="1"
                <CFIF STTYPE.STTYPEPROPERTYDEFINITIONS[URL.PROPNAME]
                    ➥.BREQUIRED>
                CHECKED
                </CFIF>
                >Required<BR>
                <INPUT TYPE="checkbox" NAME="searchable" VALUE="1"
                <CFIF STTYPE.STTYPEPROPERTYDEFINITIONS[URL.PROPNAME]
                    ➥.BSEARCHABLE>
                CHECKED
                </CFIF>
                >Searchable
                <BR>
                <INPUT TYPE="checkbox" NAME="Indexed" VALUE="1"
                <CFIF STTYPE.STTYPEPROPERTYDEFINITIONS[URL.PROPNAME]
                    ➥.BINDEXED>
                CHECKED
                </CFIF>
                >Indexed<BR>
                </TD>
            </TR>
            <TR>
                <TD><INPUT TYPE="submit" NAME="Update" VALUE="Update"></TD>
                <TD><INPUT TYPE="submit" NAME="delete" VALUE="Delete"></TD>
            </TR>
        </TABLE>
        </CFOUTPUT>
    </CFA_CONTROLHANDLER>

</CF_A2ZFORMATTING>
```

The property edit page begins by looking for the FORM variable UPDATE. If this is present, it indicates the property editing form has been submitted. Boolean values are set for the ARRAY and MULTILINGUAL attributes of the property, to allow no more than one of those two to be set to true. Next, default values of 0 are provided for the REQUIRED, SEARCHABLE, and INDEXED fields. The <CFA_OBJECTTYPEPROPERTY> tag is then used with an action of UPDATE to pass all the submitted data into the database for this object. The user is then redirected back to the object type editing form with a <CFLOCATION> tag.

If FORM.UPDATE doesn't exist, the page next checks for FORM.DELETE, indicating that a user has specified that the property should be removed from the object. If that is the case, the <CFA_OBJECTTYPEPROPERTY> tag is used with an action of DELETE, to remove the property from the object type. The user is then redirected back to the object type editing form with a <CFLOCATION> tag.

The property definition form is displayed if neither the UPDATE nor the DELETE form variable is present. <CFA_OBJECTTYPEGET> is used to retrieve the current values for the property, and these are populated into the form. The form ends with two submit buttons, allowing the user to update or delete the property. Figure 22.10 shows the property editing page.

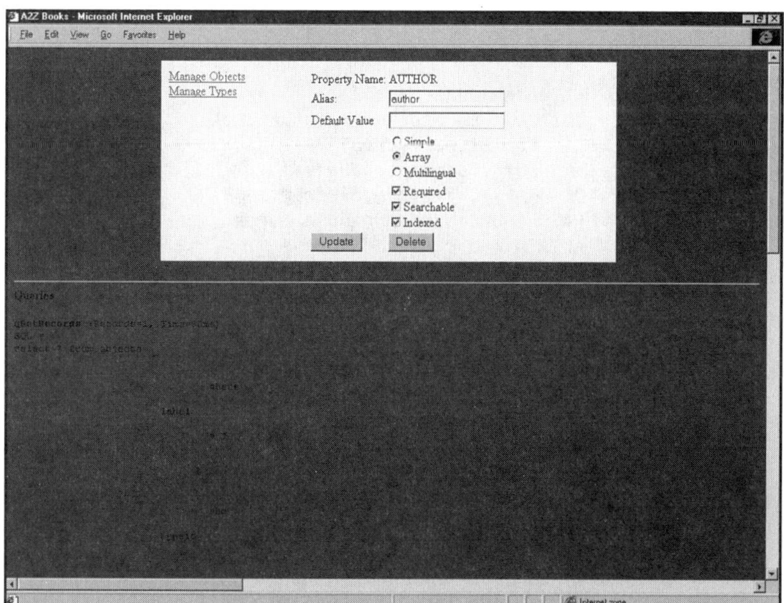

FIGURE 22.10
From the property editing page, you can change any of the settings for the property. You can also remove properties from an object type here.

Editing Methods The Methods tab page of the object type form presents users with links to edit the object type's methods. The page can be seen in Listing 22.5.

Listing 22.5 A Simplified Method Editor

```
<!—-
File:          admin/webtop/editMethod.cfm
Author:        jeff tapper
Date:          1/26/2000
Description:  Given an object type and a method name, this will display the
               details of the method, and allow users to update them, or to
```

continues

Listing 22.5 Continued

```
                remove this method from the objectType

Notes:

Change History:

--->
<!--- display the formatting, including the administrative links --->
<CF_A2ZFORMATTING ADMINLINKS=1>

    <!--- update the method--->
    <CFIF ISDEFINED("form.update")>

        <CFA_OBJECTTYPEMETHOD
         ACTION="update"
         DATASOURCE="#request.cfa.a2zBooks.datasource#"
         TYPEID="#form.typeID#"
         METHOD="#form.methodName#"
         DESCRIPTION="#form.description#"
         HANDLERURL="#form.handlerName#"
         ALIAS="#form.methodName#"
        >
        <CFLOCATION URL="typeFind.cfm?editType=1&TypeID=#form.typeID#">

        <!--- delete the method--->
    <CFELSEIF ISDEFINED("form.delete")>

        <CFA_OBJECTTYPEMETHOD
            ACTION="delete"
            DATASOURCE="#request.cfa.a2zBooks.datasource#"
            TYPEID="#form.typeID#"
            METHOD="#form.methodName#"
        >

        <CFLOCATION URL="typeFind.cfm?editType=1&TypeID=#form.typeID#">

        <CFOUTPUT>#form.methodName# deleted.</CFOUTPUT>

<!--- Display data about this method --->
    <CFELSE>

    <!--- retreive settings of the type --->
        <CFA_OBJECTTYPEGET
            DATASOURCE="#request.cfa.a2zBooks.datasource#"
            TYPEID="#url.typeID#"
            R_STTYPE="stType"
        >

        <!--- display the settings --->
        <CFA_CONTROLHANDLER NAME="UpdateMethod">
        <CFOUTPUT>
```

```
        <TABLE>
            <TR>
                <TD>Method:</TD>
                <TD>#url.methodName#
                <INPUT
                    TYPE="hidden"
                    NAME="methodName"
                    VALUE="#url.methodName#">
                 <INPUT
                    TYPE="hidden"
                    NAME="typeID"
                    VALUE="#url.typeID#">


                </TD>
            </TR>
            <TR>
                <TD>Description:</TD>
                 <TD>
                <TEXTAREA NAME="description">
                #sttype.STTYPEMETHODDEFINITIONS[url.methodName].Description#
                </TEXTAREA>
                </TD>
            </TR>
            <TR>
                <TD>Handler Name:</TD>
                <TD>
                <INPUT
                   TYPE="text"
                   NAME="handlerName"
                   VALUE="#sttype.STTYPEMETHODDEFINITIONS[url.methodName]
                         ➥.handlerURL#">
                </TD>
            </TR>
            <TR>
                <TD><INPUT TYPE="submit" NAME="update" VALUE="Update"></TD>
                <TD><INPUT TYPE="submit" NAME="delete" VALUE="delete"></TD>
            </TR>
            <INPUT TYPE="hidden" NAME="newMethod" VALUE="1">
            <INPUT TYPE="hidden" NAME="editType" VALUE="1">
        </TABLE>
        </CFOUTPUT>
        </CFA_CONTROLHANDLER>
    </CFIF>
</CF_A2ZFORMATTING>
```

The Methods editing page begins by checking to see if the FROM.UPDATE variable exists. Much like the property editing page above, FORM.UPDATE indicates that the update method form has been submitted, and there are values that should be updated for this method of the object type. <CFA_OBJECTTYPEMETHOD> is used with an action of UPDATE to set these new values. The user is then redirected back to the object type editing form with a <CFLOCATION> tag.

If FORM.UPDATE isn't present, FORM.DELETE is tested for existence. The presence of this parameter indicates the user wants to remove this method from the object type. This is done with the <CFA_OBJECTTYPEMETHOD> tag, with its action set to DELETE. The user is then redirected to the object type editing form with a <CFLOCATION> tag.

If neither form variable is passed, the <CFA_OBJECTTYPEGET> tag retrieves all known information about this method. This information is populated into a form, to allow users to update the data. Figure 22.11 shows the update method form. The form ends with two submit buttons, allowing the user to update or delete the property.

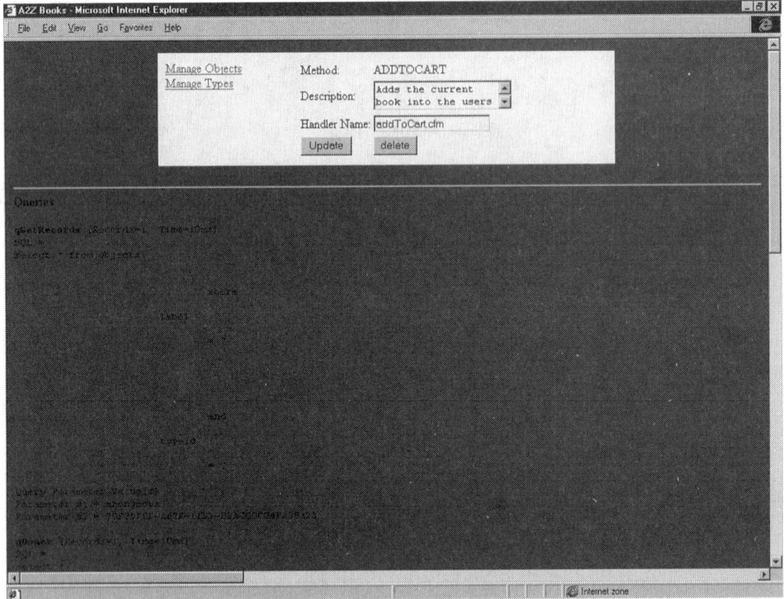

FIGURE 22.11
From the method editing page, you can change the handler file, alias, or description of this method. You can also use this page to remove a method from an object.

CHAPTER 23

Administering Spectra

In this chapter

Administering Applications

As a system administrator, your job begins with the installation and Webtop configuration of Spectra. You will also be responsible for installing and maintaining the ContentObject Databases, managing users and system security, managing the Verity indexes, maintaining the relationship between the ColdFusion Administrator and the Webtop, and overseeing application logging and cache settings.

See Chapter 4, "Installing and Configuring Spectra," for complete details on installing and configuring Spectra.

Overlapping Jobs

Spectra was designed as an open, flexible system to meet the needs of a large variety of businesses. As such, many tasks available to the system administrator are also available to other members of the development team. For example, users and security can be managed from both the Business Center and the Webtop's System Admin section. This allows for individual businesses to decide for themselves who best can make these decisions. You will also find overlap in the caching and logging sections of the System Admin and Site Designer sections.

By leaving the model flexible like this, you can apply your own personnel to tasks most appropriate for them and help facilitate communication among all the participants of the site.

System Administrator Webtop Overview

You will administer Spectra applications from the System Admin section of the Webtop (see Figure 23.1). The areas contained within it are as follows:

- With the Database Manager, you can create, import, export, and migrate a ContentObject Database. The Database Manager also includes tools for installing content types and PLPs.
- The Users and Security area allows for managing all users, whether they are internal, site members, or end users. In addition to adding, editing, and deleting users, you can integrate directly with your existing user directories, including Windows NT domains, LDAP, and pre-existing ODBC-compliant user directories.
- The Caching section is a set of tools for managing Spectra's caching system. You can control caching of data access, method execution, container rendering, and page rendering.
- The Logging section allows for managing site logging. Business managers use these logs to create reports and customize the site.
- The Indexing area allows for scheduled indexing, repairs, and optimizations of the Type Collections, Meta Data Collections, and Datasource Collections.

- Webtop Permissions allows you to control access to the various sections of the Webtop.
- In the Messages area, you can send a message site wide, to appear on the custom home page of every user.
- The CF Administration section links to the ColdFusion Application Server Administrator.

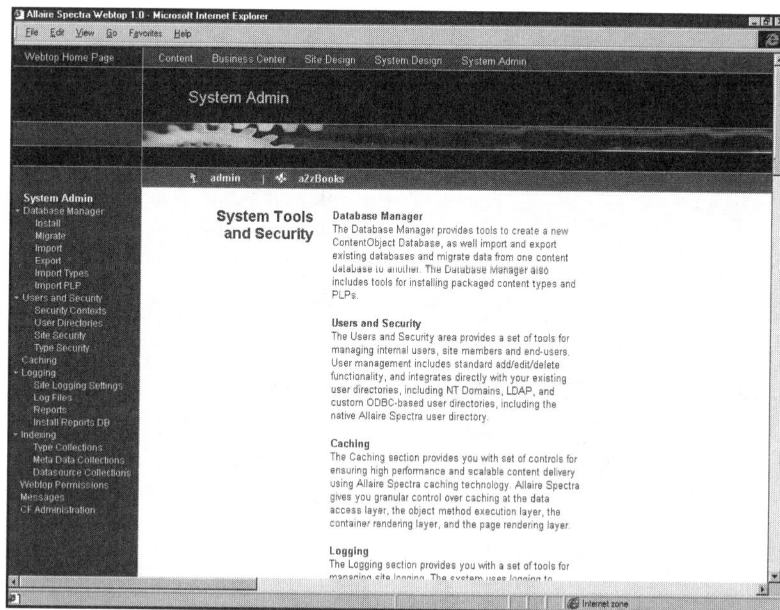

FIGURE 23.1
The navigation on the left of the System Admin's Webtop section will bring you to each function available to the system administrator.

Managing Data

As you've already learned, Spectra stores its data in an object store, which is stored in a database. Before Spectra objects can be stored in an existing database, the infrastructure for the object store must first be installed there. This infrastructure consists of the tables in Table 23.1.

Table 23.1 Table Definitions for a Spectra Object Store

Table Name	Description
`containerdescriptors`	Holds publishing rules and container-specific data
`logreports`	Holds data to be used in Log Reports
`objects`	Holds data on all objects used in the datasource
`pathreports`	Holds data for default reports
`plpinstances`	Holds data on all active PLPs

continues

Table 23.1 Continued

Table Name	Description
`plpprototypes`	Holds data on each PLP in the system
`plptransactionlog`	Holds data to be used for reporting on PLP activity
`properties`	Indexes data for optimized SQL searches
`propertydefinitions`	Holds data on each custom property definition
`sessionreports`	Holds aggregate data on individual user sessions
`sharedobjectsynchronization`	Synchronizes embedded objects with the objects from which they are created
`sitecomposition`	Holds data on the Site Layout Model
`types`	Holds data about each ContentObject type
`wddxdata`	Holds WDDX packets that are pointed to foreign keys in the `PLPTransactionLog`, `PLPPrototype`, and `PLPInstances` tables

Installing ContentObject Databases

To install a Spectra object store, go to the System Admin section of the Webtop, expand the Database Manager menu, and click the Install link. Figure 23.2 shows the ContentObject Database installation menu. Choose a datasource into which you will install the ContentObject Database.

CAUTION

If there is an existing ContentObject Database in the datasource into which you are attempting to install, the previous data will be erased.

FIGURE 23.2
Choose the datasource to which you want to install the ContentObject Database, and click the Install ContentObject Database button.

NOTE Before a ContentObject Database can be installed to a database, you must first set a datasource to point to the database. This is done through the ColdFusion Administrator. These datasources can consist of either an ODBC or a native connection to a database. While ODBC connections work across a greater set of databases, native connections are faster and more efficient.

After you click the Install ContentObject Database button, the installation process is automated. The screen will refresh itself several times during the process, informing you how far along it is. When the process is complete, you will see a form such as Figure 23.3, telling you that the install was successful.

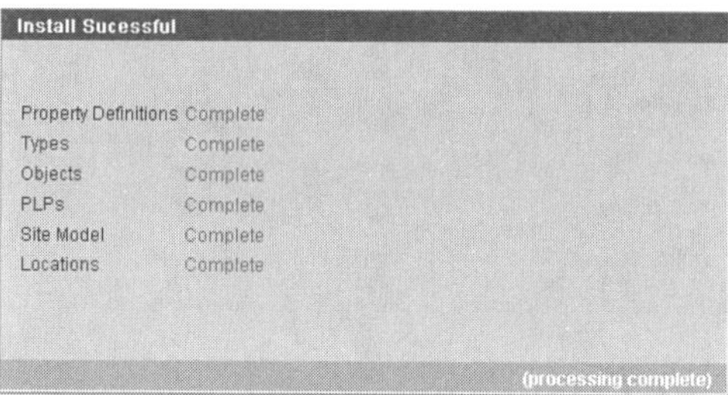

FIGURE 23.3
The ContentObject data store has been installed successfully.

Migrating ContentObject Databases

Spectra ships its object store in a Sybase SQL Anywhere database. While this is adequate for very low-traffic sites, you should consider moving this to a more robust database such as Oracle or SQL Server for any application that you expect will have much traffic. To do this, you need to migrate Spectra's object store to a new database.

To migrate a datasource, follow these steps:

1. Click the orange triangle next to Database Manager to expand the Database Manager choices.
2. Click Migrate. Figure 23.4 shows the database migration form that appears.
3. Choose the datasource from which you want to migrate, the datasource to which you want to migrate, and a directory where temporary files can be created.

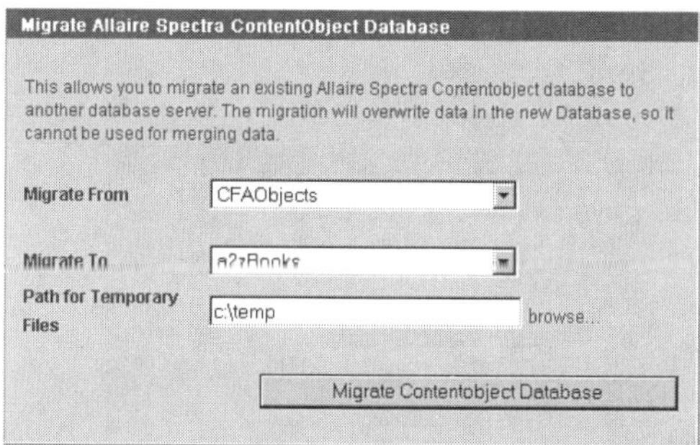

FIGURE 23.4
The `CFAObjects` datasource is being migrated to the a2zBooks datasource. The directory `c:\temp` will be used on the server to temporarily store the WDDX files during the transfer.

NOTE Spectra may not remove all the files created to facilitate the transfer. Be sure to check the directory you specified as the path for temporary files to be sure that all files created have been removed.

During migration, the screen will frequently update itself, informing you as to the current state of its progress. When it is complete, you will see a screen like that in Figure 23.5, informing you that the migration is complete.

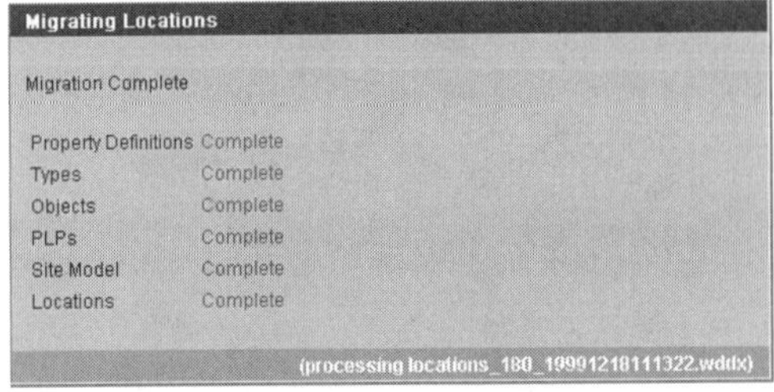

FIGURE 23.5
The ContentObject Database has been successfully migrated.

Exporting ContentObject Databases

Spectra will allow you to export your data, so it can be shared (imported) to another Spectra ContentObject Database. While Migrating Data is used to move data between two datasources of the same server, exporting is used to package the data to be sent to another server.

To move an application from a development server to a production server, exporting the development database will make it available to be imported into the production server.

To export a ContentObject Database, follow these steps:

1. Expand the Database Manager menu by clicking the orange triangle to the left of it.
2. Click the link that reads Export.
3. Choose the datasource to be exported and the path to which the export files will be written.
4. Click the Export button.

Figure 23.6 shows the ContentObject Database that has been chosen for export and the path to which the exported files will be saved.

FIGURE 23.6
The a2zBooks ContentObject Database is to be exported. The files generated will be stored in the `C:\Winnt\` directory on the server.

Export Allaire Spectra Contentobject Database

This allows you to export an Allaire Spectra Contentobject Database. It will generate a directory and file structure of WDDX (xml) files that can be imported into another database using the import tool included with Allaire Spectra. This process will only work with Allaire Spectra Contentobject Databases.

Select DataSource to Export: a2zBooks

Export File Path: c:\temp browse...

Export Contentobject Database

When you click the Export ContentObject Database button, the screen will frequently update itself, informing you of its progress. When it is complete, you will see a screen like that in Figure 23.7, informing you that the export is complete.

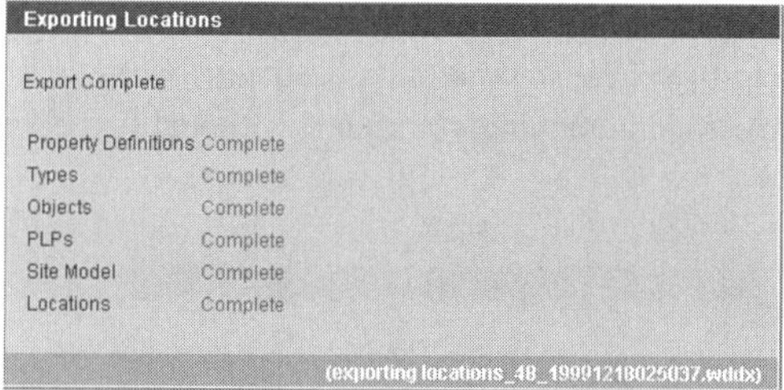

FIGURE 23.7
The ContentObject Database has been successfully exported.

Browse the `C:\Winnt\` directory of the server to find that the following directories have been created and populated:

```
locations      propertydefinitions
objects        sitecomposition
plps           types
```

You can now add these folders to a `.zip` or `.tar` file and send it to another Spectra site to be imported.

Importing ContentObject Databases

Spectra will allow you to import ContentObject Databases, which have been exported from other Spectra installations. This can be useful for importing data from a development server into a production server.

To import a ContentObject Database, follow these steps:

1. Expand the Database Manager menu by clicking the orange triangle to the left of it.
2. Click the link that reads Import.
3. You will be asked for the datasource into which you want to import the data and the path in which the exported data is located and whether you want the install to create data structures. If you choose to have the importer create the data structures, any existing Spectra data in the datasource will be destroyed before the new data is inserted. Figure 23.8 shows the data import screen.
4. Click the Import Content Object Database link.

FIGURE 23.8
The files in `c:\temp` on the server will be imported into the a2zBooks ContentObject Database.

Import Allaire Spectra Contentobject Database

This allows you to import a previously exported Contentobject database into another database.

Select DataSource to Import into: a2zBooks

Create Data Structures (this will drop existing tables)

Path to exported files: c:\temp
browse...

Import Contentobject Database

When you click the Import ContentObject Database button, the screen will frequently update itself, informing you as to the current state of its progress. When it is complete, you will see a screen like that in Figure 23.9, informing you that the import has been successfully completed.

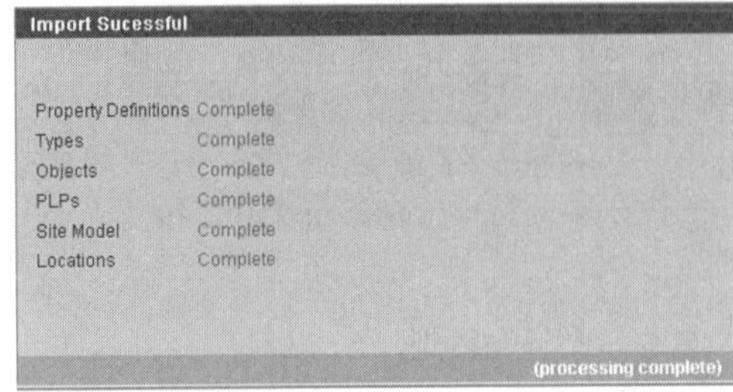

FIGURE 23.9
The ContentObject Database has been successfully imported.

Importing Types

After you develop a new object type on your development server and are ready to introduce it to the production environment, you will want to import the Type, so you don't need to re-create it on the production server.

Interactive developers on Spectra projects have the option to export ContentObject Types and to distribute them to other Spectra applications.

To import a ContentObject Type into the active application's ContentObject Database, follow these steps:

1. Expand the Database Manager menu by clicking the triangle to the left of it.
2. Click the Import Types link. Figure 23.10 shows the Import Type form.

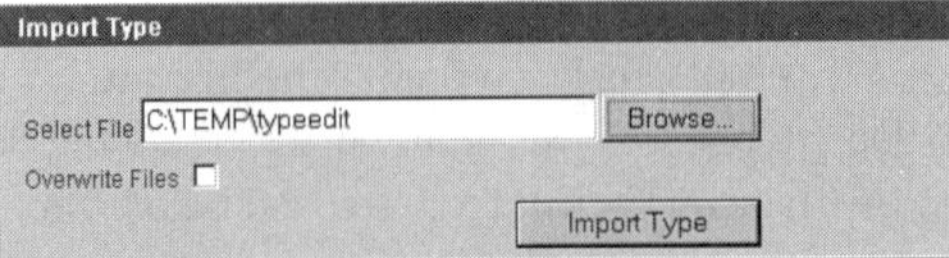

FIGURE 23.10
The object type import screen.

3. Select the file that contains the exported object type data (the default name of the field for the export is Typeedit).
4. Choose whether you want to overwrite an existing object type with the new data.
5. Click the Import Type button.

Unlike the paths specified in the ContentObject Database import, export, and migration above, the path specified here is the path of the file on your local workstation. This file will be uploaded to the server, where it will be imported into the current ContentObject Database.

When the type is done importing, a JavaScript alert box will appear to inform you the type has been successfully imported.

Importing PLPs

Just as developers may need to move object types from a development to a production server, it may also be necessary to move process logic paths. To accomplish this, PLPs should be exported from the development server and imported onto the production server.

Interactive developers on Spectra projects have the option to export process logic paths so they can distribute them to other Spectra applications. The export file created will contain all the files referenced within the PLP as well as the data about the PLP itself.

▶ **See** Chapter 12, "Using Process Logic Paths," for information on exporting process logic paths.

To import a process logic path into the active application's ContentObject Database, follow these steps:

1. Expand the Database Manager menu by clicking the triangle to the left of it.
2. Click the link that reads Import PLP. Figure 23.11 shows the Import PLP form.

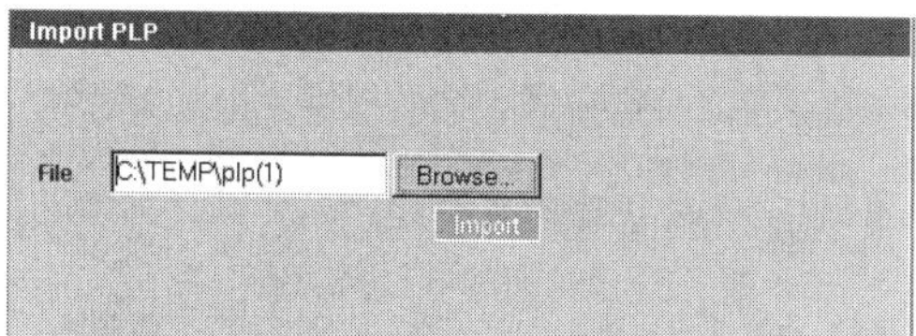

FIGURE 23.11
The file `plp(1)` is a previously exported PLP. Here, it is to be imported into the a2zBooks application.

Unlike importing object types, there is no confirmation screen if the PLP is imported successfully. Should you need confirmation, go to the PLP Manager in the System Design section of the Webtop to see if the PLP appears there.

Managing Security

Spectra application security is based on security contexts, user directories, groups, and users. Before you can implement security on any Spectra application, you must first have a security context in place. Spectra ships with a default security context, sc1, into which the administrative account you created during the Webtop configuration was registered.

Security Contexts

The Security Contexts area allows you to create new security contexts for applications and assign user directories to existing security contexts. Security contexts are the groups of policies that govern user access to site assets and activities.

Creating Security Contexts To create a new security context, follow these steps:

1. Expand the Users and Security navigation tool in the left column of the page.
2. Click the Create button at the bottom of the Security Contexts page. Figure 23.12 shows the security context creation form that appears.
3. Give the security context a name and description, and then click OK.

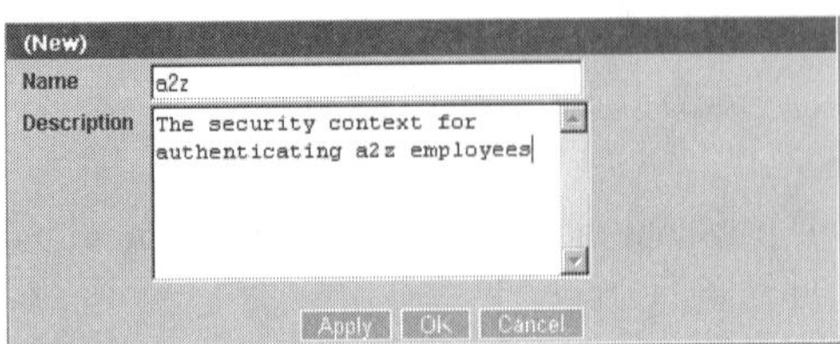

FIGURE 23.12
A new security context for the a2zBooks application is being created.

You are then returned to the main Security Contexts page (see Figure 23.13), from which you can edit or delete any existing security contexts.

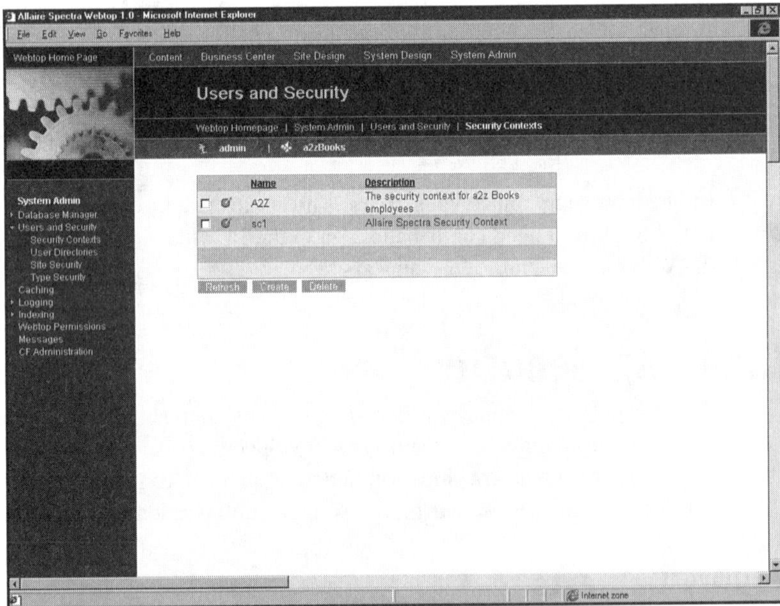

FIGURE 23.13
The new A2Z security context is now visible on the Security Contexts page.

Editing Security Contexts To edit a security context, follow these steps:

1. Go to the Security Contexts page.
2. Click the Edit icon next to the name of the security context you want to edit. This will bring you to a form (see Figure 23.14) that's much like the security context creation form, with the addition of a Directories button.

3. Click the Directories button to assign an existing user directory to this security context.

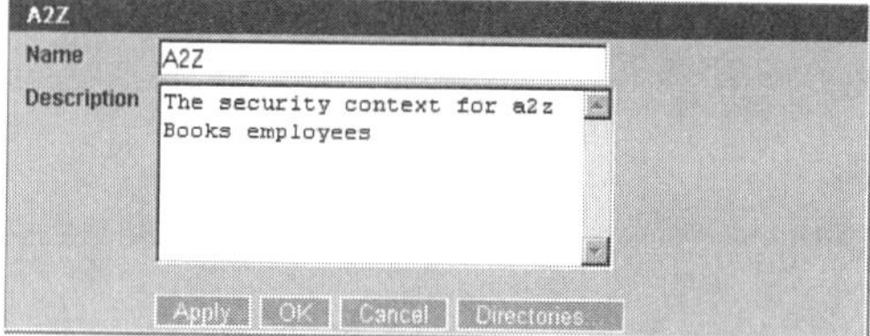

FIGURE 23.14
You can't change the name of the security context on this form, but you can edit the description.

User Directories

The user directories allow you to add, edit, and delete user information, browse user profile information, and assign users to groups. The User Directories option also allows you to access and edit settings for your existing user directories. Spectra creates a default user directory named `UserDirectory` during Webtop configuration.

Making a User Directory of an Existing Datasource Most businesses already have an existing user directory in a database or an LDAP server. To make this existing directory available as a Spectra user directory, you need to define several queries detailing how user and group information is to be pulled from the existing user directory. These queries are defined in a file named `smdsquery.ini`, which you can find in the `\cfusion\bin` directory on your server. Figure 23.15 shows the database layout of a simple user directory in an access database.

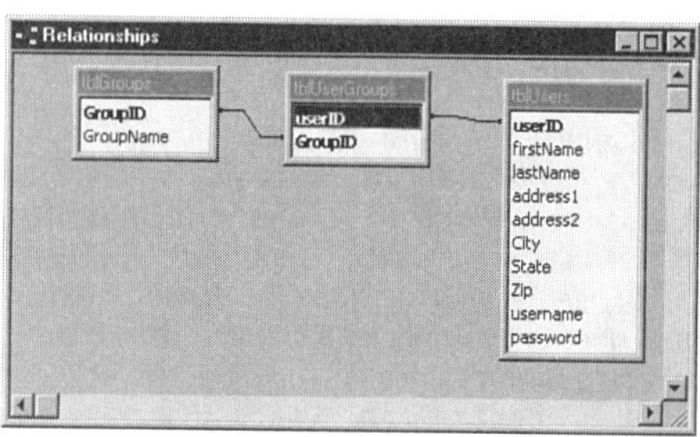

FIGURE 23.15
The Access Relationships window of the a2zUsers database shows three tables: one with users, one with groups, and one maintaining the relationship between them.

To make this database available to Spectra as a user directory, follow these steps:

1. Add the database as a ColdFusion datasource in the CF Administrator.
2. Create a Spectra user directory to point to this database (see Figure 23.16).
3. Modify the `smdsquery.ini` file, as shown in Listing 23.1.

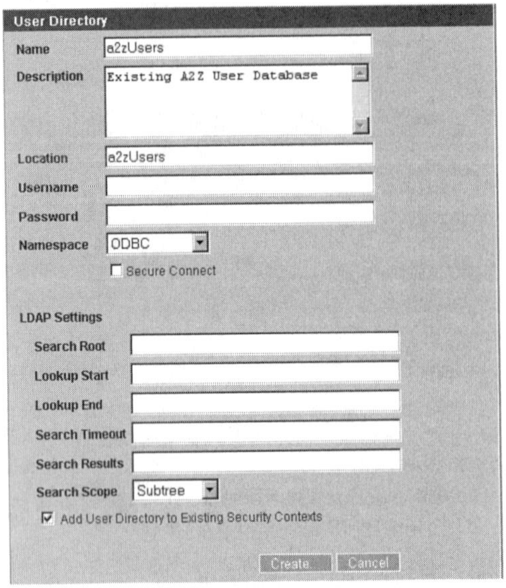

FIGURE 23.16
A new user directory is created. As this is a user directory in the ODBC namespace, the Location field reflects the ColdFusion data-source name.

Listing 23.1 The *smdsquery.ini* File

```
[UserDirectory]
Query_Enumerate=select UserName as Name, 'User' as Class from Users Union
    ➥select GroupName as Name, 'Group' as Class from Groups order by Class
Query_InitUser=select UserName as Name from Users where UserName = '%s'
Query_AuthenticateUser=select UserName as Name from Users where
    ➥UserName = '%s' and Password = '%s'
Query_GetGroups=select Groups.GroupName as Name from Groups, Users_Groups
    ➥where Users_Groups.UserName = '%s' and
    ➥Groups.GroupName = Users_Groups.GroupName
Query_GetUserProp=select %s from Users where UserName = '%s'
Query_SetUserProp=update Users set %s = %s where UserName = '%s'
Query_GetObjInfo=select UserName as Name, 'User' from Users where
    ➥UserName = '%s' Union select GroupName as Name,
    ➥'Group' from Groups where GroupName = '%s'
Query_GetUserProps=UserName, Description
Query_IsGroupMember=select GroupName from Users_Groups where
    ➥UserName = '%s' and GroupName = '%s'
[a2zUsers]
Query_Enumerate=select UserName as Name, 'User' as Class from tblUsers
    ➥Union select GroupName as Name, 'Group' as Class
    ➥from tblGroups order by Class
Query_InitUser=select UserName as Name from tblUsers where UserName = '%s'
Query_AuthenticateUser=select UserName as Name from tblUsers
    ➥where UserName = '%s' and Password = '%s'
Query_GetGroups=select tblGroups.GroupName as Name from tblGroups,
    ➥tblUserGroups, tblUsers
    ➥where tblUserGroups.userid = tblUsers.userid
```

```
    ➥and tblUsers.username = '%s'
    ➥and tblGroups.groupID = tblUserGroups.groupID
Query_GetUserProp=select %s from tblUsers where UserName = '%s'
Query_SetUserProp=update tblUsers set %s = %s where UserName = '%s'
Query_GetObjInfo=select UserName as Name, 'User' from tblUsers
    ➥where UserName = '%s' Union select GroupName as Name,
    ➥'Group' from tblGroups where GroupName = '%s'
Query_GetUserProps=UserName, password, firstname, lastname, address1,
    ➥address2, city, state, zip
Query_IsGroupMember=select GroupName from tblUsers, tblGroups, tblUserGroups
    ➥where tblUsers.userid = tblUserGroups.userid
    ➥and tblGroups.groupid = tblUserGroups.groupID
    ➥and tblUSers.UserName = '%s' and tblGroups.GroupName = '%s'
```


In Listing 23.1, you will find entries for two separate user directories. The first is `UserDirectory`, which ships with Spectra; the second is the custom `A2ZUSERS` directory, which integrates the `a2zUsers` database into Spectra. Each user directory requires 10 lines, as shown in Table 23.2.

Table 23.2 *smdsquery.ini* Field Enumeration

Line	Description
`[a2zUsers]`	The name of the user directory whose attributes are defined in the nine following queries. This needs to match the name as entered into the User Directory Creation Page. Here, the name a2zUsers matches the name a2zUsers entered in Figure 23.17.
`Query_Enumerate=`	A SQL query that will return all the users and groups in the database. Notice the similarities between this line in the `UserDirectory` definition and in the `a2zUsers` definition. The only discernable difference is the names of the tables being referenced. This query needs to select its fields into the names `NAME` and `CLASS` for Spectra.
`Query_InitUser=`	Determines whether a given username exists in the system. `%s` represents a variable passed into the query—in this case, the username.
`Query_AuthenticateUser=`	Passes a username and password; if there is a match, it returns the matching username. This is used to authenticate a user to the system. Again, `%s` represents the variables passed in—in this case, the first is the username, and the second is the password.
`Query_GetGroups=`	Returns all the groups of which the specified user is a member. The `%s` is the username passed. Notice that in the a2zUsers definitions, to accommodate the layout of the database, an extra join is required in the queries.

continues

Table 23.2 Continued

Line	Description
`Query_GetUserProp=`	Returns the value of a specific property of the user table. In the case of the a2zUsers database, `firstname`, `lastname`, `address`, `city`, `state`, and `zip` are all considered properties. This too has two `%s` in the query. The first represents the name of the field to be retrieved, the second the username whose properties you are returning.
`Query_SetUserProp=`	Updates user properties. This takes in three variables, all represented as `%s` in the file. The first is the field name, the second the value for that field, and the third the username whose properties you are updating.
`Query_GetObjectInfo=`	Determines the class (user or group) of a given object. This query treats both users and groups equally as objects. This query takes the object's name as `%s`.
`Query_GetUserProps=`	Not really a query, but a list of user properties stored in the user table. Notice that the UserDirectory definitions have only `username` and `description`, whereas a2zUsers has `UserName`, `password`, `firstname`, `lastname`, `address1`, `address2`, `city`, `state`, and `zip`.
`Query_isGroupMember=`	Given a username and group name, this query will determine if the user is a member of the specified group.

Making a User Directory of a Windows NT Domain On Windows NT installations of Spectra, you can use the Servers domain as a user directory. If you choose to do this, you will be able to administer only groups, users, and security policies through the Windows NT User Manager for domains. In the Location field of the User Directory Creation form, you need to enter the Primary Domain Control's machine name. You also need to enter the username and password of an administrative account into the appropriate fields.

Making a User Directory of an LDAP Server LDAP is the only option available to Solaris installations of Spectra for user directories. To create a new user directory in LDAP, you need to enter the LDAP host server name in the Location field and the administrative user's common name in the Username field, and then choose LDAP from the Datasource Type pull-down menu. You will also need to enter a number of LDAP-specific fields, such as

- *Search Root.* The beginning point of a user namespace, usually the organization unit (`ou`) or organization (`o`)
- *Lookup Start.* The beginning of the DN string, such as `uid=`
- *Lookup End.* The branch of the search following the user ID, such as `ou=customer,o=a2zBooks`

- *Search Timeout.* The maximum number of seconds the search should run before quitting
- *Search Results.* The maximum number of results the search should return
- *Search Scope.* Set to `Subtree` to search the entire LDAP tree, or to `One Level` to restrict the search

The following example allows you to use an LDAP server as your user directory. The start and end scripts allow LDAP to grab the userID and objects without having to know them in advance.

NameSpace	LDAP location, `ldap_server_name`
Search Root	`o=airius.com`
Lookup Start	`(&(objectclass=*)(uid=`
Lookup End	`))`
Search Timeout	10
Search Results	100
Search Scope	Sub Tree

NOTE See `http://home.netscape.com/directory/v4.0/index.html` for more information on using the Netscape directory server included on the Spectra CD-ROM. See `http://www.umich.edu/%7Edirsvcs/ldap/` for general information about LDAP.

Site Security

You can enter the Site Security Administrator by expanding the Users and Security menu. Click the orange triangle next to the Users and Security link, then click the Site Security link. This section will allow you to view and control access to the site-by-site layout. Here, you will find a page very similar to the Site Layout Model of the Site Designer and Business Center sections of the Webtop (see Figure 23.17).

To secure a page or section, follow these steps:

1. Click the lock image to the right of the page or section name. This will bring you to a Security Settings form for that item.
2. Choose a specific method to secure.
3. Choose a user directory from which users can be chosen.
4. Choose whether to display groups, users, or both.

Figure 23.18 shows the settings for the News section, which currently has no security, as no group has been specifically granted access. As soon as a group is granted access, the section won't allow others outside that group to access the specified method.

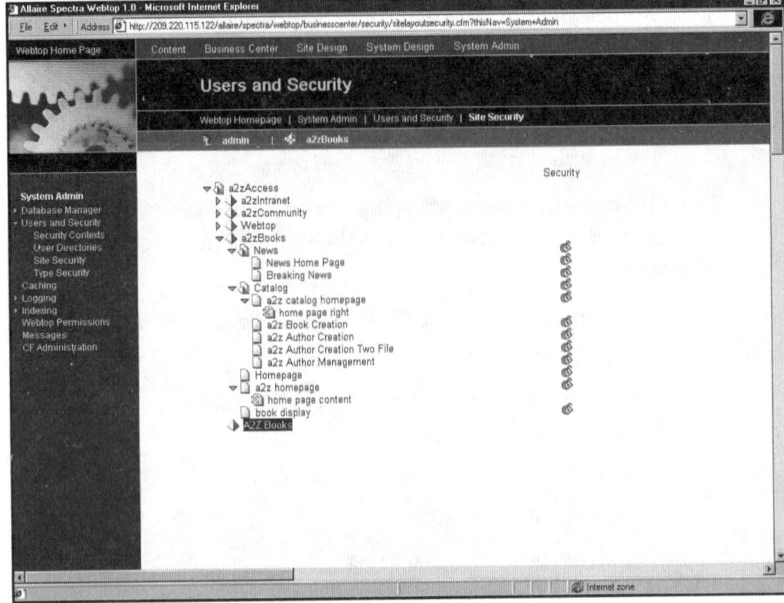

FIGURE 23.17
The Site Security Manager allows you to add security details to sections and pages of the application.

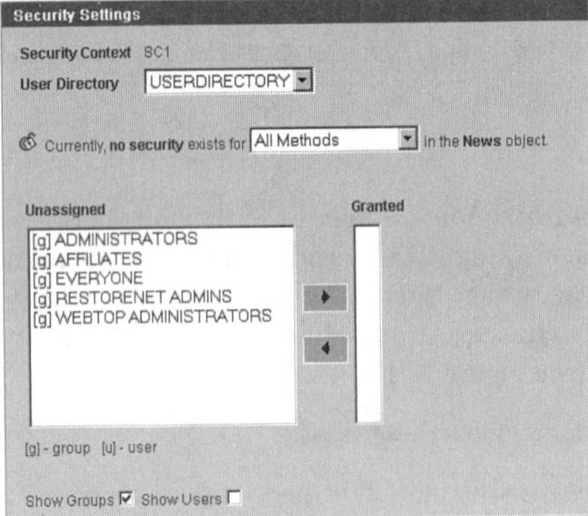

FIGURE 23.18
The Security Settings page for the News section of the application.

To secure all or some methods of a section or page, first choose the user directory that contains the users or groups who will be allowed to access the resources. Next, choose the method (or All Methods) from the pull-down menu to indicate exactly which resource you are securing. Finally, select the groups or users from the Unassigned column that you want to allow to access the resources and click the right arrow button to send them to the Granted column. Figure 23.19 shows the `delete` method of the News object restricted to administrators only.

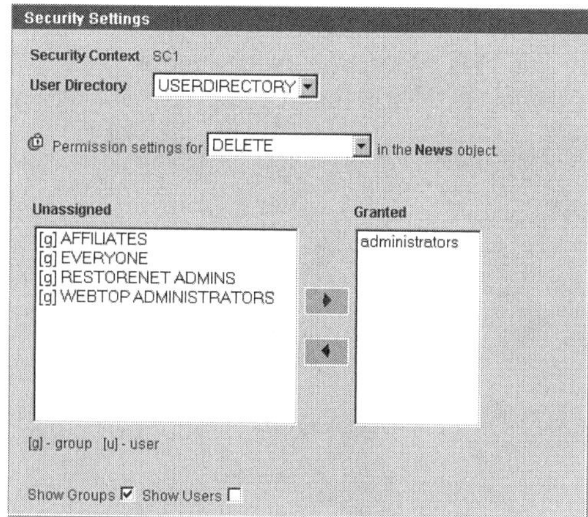

FIGURE 23.19
The `delete` method in the News section has been secured to Administrators only.

Type Security

To secure an object type, follow these steps:

1. Click the orange triangle next to the Users and Security link to expand the Users and Security menu.
2. Click the Type Security link. This will allow you to view and control access to the site by the Site Object Model. Figure 23.20 shows the Type Security page.

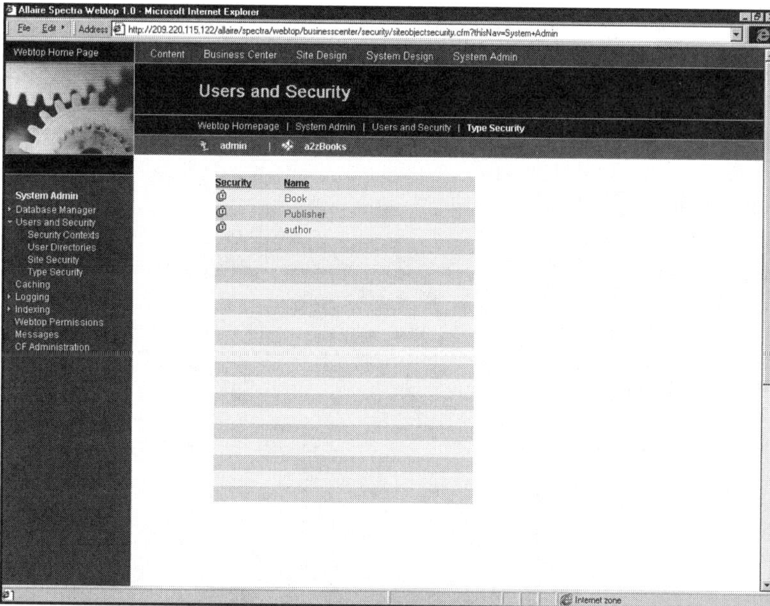

FIGURE 23.20
Here is the Type Security page, listing all the object types in the system.

3. Choose an object type to be secured by clicking the lock icon next to the object type. This will bring you to a Types form, as seen in Figure 23.21.

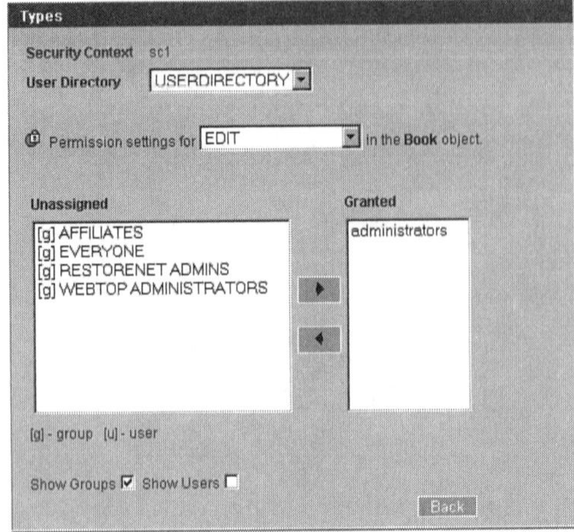

FIGURE 23.21
The Book object's `edit` method is being restricted to members of the Administrators group.

4. Choose a method of the object type to be secured from the drop-down menu. You also can choose to secure all methods.
5. Choose the user directory that contains the users or groups who will be accessing this object type. Click the right arrow to add them to the Granted column.

Webtop Security

As a system administrator, you can choose which groups and users can access particular sections of the Webtop. To do this, go to the System Admin section of the Webtop and click the Webtop Permissions link in the left column. Figure 23.22 shows the Webtop Security Settings form.

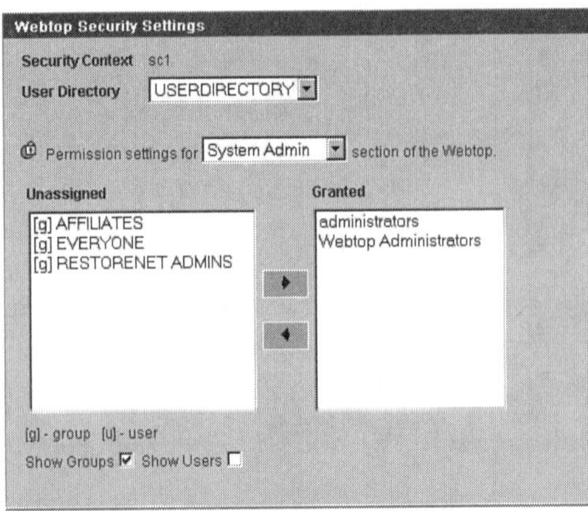

FIGURE 23.22
The Webtop's System Admin section is being restricted to members of the Administrators and Webtop Administrators groups.

CAUTION

Spectra ships with minimal Webtop security. By default, any user who can log in can access any section of the Webtop. It is strongly recommended that the first thing you do after adding users to the user directory is restrict access to the System Admin section.

Caching

A key component in creating scalable Web applications is to minimize the amount of processing required for each page. To help reduce page processing time, Spectra allows for caching at the Site Section and Page levels. To administer caching, click the Caching link in the System Administrator section of the Webtop. Here, you will be presented with a screen similar to the Site Layout Model of the Page Design and Business Center of the Webtop. Figure 23.23 shows the Caching editing page. A red dot in the Cache Page column indicates that the page is explicitly not cached; a green dot means it's cached. A gray dot indicates that the caching settings will be inherited from the parent section or site, if available.

FIGURE 23.23
On the System Administrator Caching page, you can see that the News homepage is set to be cached, whereas the Catalog homepage is set not to be cached.

To change the caching settings for a section or page, click the name of the item and then click the Edit button below. This will bring you to a Caching Edit Settings page (see Figure 23.24).

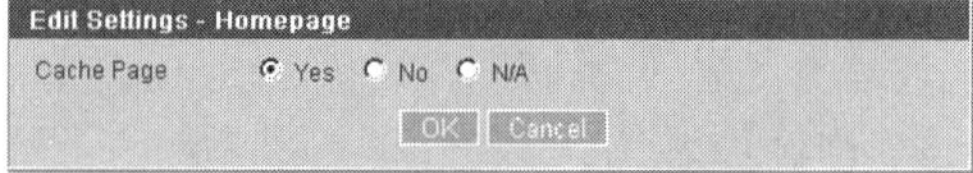

FIGURE 23.24
The homepage is currently set to be cached.

▶ **See** Chapter 24, "Deploying Spectra Applications," for more information on specific caching options.

Logging

The Spectra system administrator's role in logging and reporting involves overseeing the site logging settings, ensuring that the logging database is installed, creating and deleting log files, and creating or editing reports. The data from logs files can be used to create detailed reports on the usage patterns of visitors to the site.

▶ **See** Chapter 17, "Site Reporting," for more information on creating reports and to see examples of reports for the a2zBooks application.

Installing the Reports Database

To install a reports database follow these steps:

1. Expand the Logging menu of the System Administrators section by clicking the triangle next to the Logging link.
2. Click Install Reports DB. This will take you to the Install Reports DB page (see Figure 23.25).

FIGURE 23.25
To install a reports database, all you need do is choose a datasource into which the database will be installed.

3. Click the Install Reporting Database button to create the tables `logreports`, `sessionreports`, and `pathreports` in the selected datasource. Figure 23.26 shows the feedback after a successful installation.

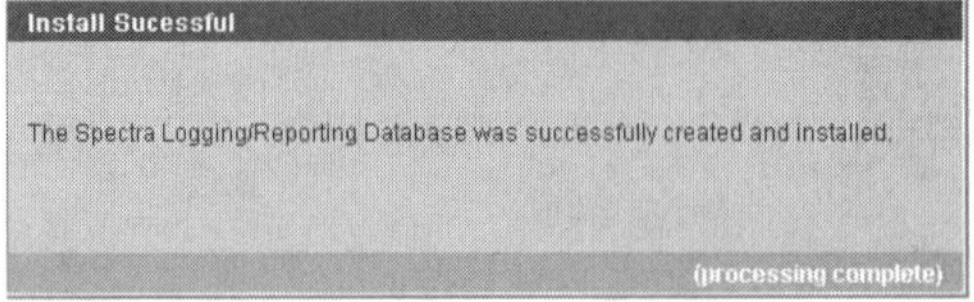

FIGURE 23.26
The Reporting database has been successfully installed.

> **CAUTION**
>
> If you choose to install a reports database into a datasource that already has reports, the old reports will be lost. If the tables already exist, Spectra drops them first before creating them again. Spectra offers no warnings about this in the process.

Site Logging Settings

To access Site Logging Settings, expand the Logging menu of the System Admin section of the Webtop, and click Site Logging Settings. Here, you will see a view similar to the Site Layout Model of the System Design section. Three columns next to each site element indicate whether the page is logged, if the section is logged, and whether cached objects should be logged. In Figure 23.27, you can see that the home page is logging the page, section, and cached objects.

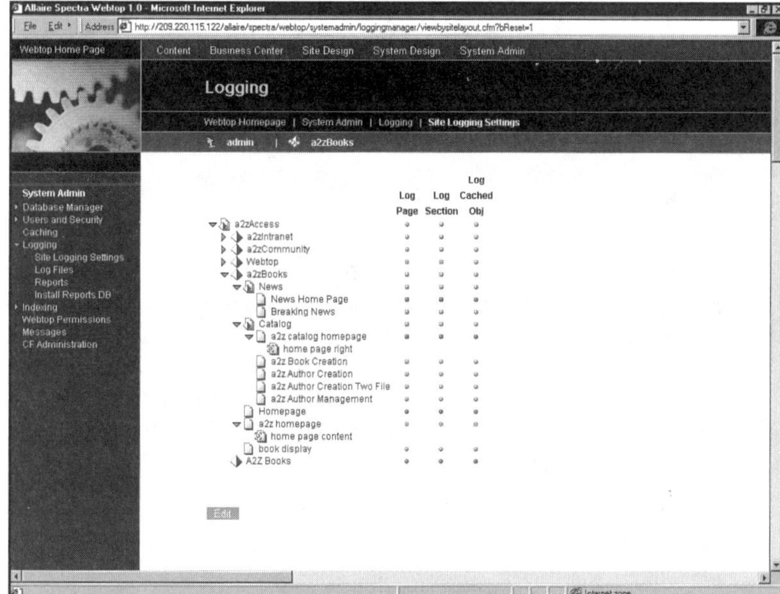

FIGURE 23.27
This is the System Admin site Logging view.

To edit the logging settings of any site, section, or page, click the element's name, and click the Edit button at the bottom of the page. This will open the form shown in Figure 23.28, which will allow you to choose the logging of the page, section, and cached objects of the selected site element.

FIGURE 23.28
The home page is set to log the page, section, and any cached objects that are accessed.

Edit Settings - a2z homepage

Log Page	(•) Yes	( ) No	( ) N/A
Log Sections	(•) Yes	( ) No	( ) N/A
Log Cached Objects	(•) Yes	( ) No	( ) N/A

OK Cancel

Log Files

Clicking the Log Files link of the System Admin section's Logging menu displays a list of all current log files. From here, you can add, edit, or delete new log files. To add a new log file, click the Create button at the bottom of the page. You will be presented with a form, as seen in Figure 23.29.

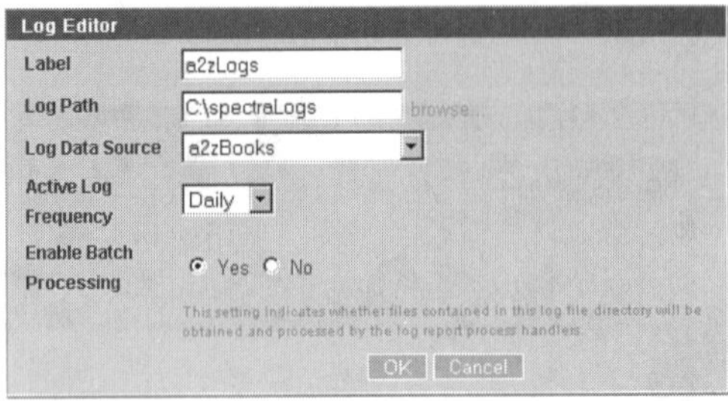

FIGURE 23.29
The a2zLogs file is being created. It will reside in the `c:\spectraLogs` directory of the server, archive itself daily, and be batch processed into the a2zBooks Logging database.

While creating a new log file, you will be asked for details about the file. First, provide a name, which will be used to refer to the file in the Webtop. Next supply a directory into which the logs will be written. You will also need to decide whether the log files should be archived hourly or daily. If you expect the site to have a lot of traffic, you should probably archive the files hourly, so that they are not unmanageably large and can be processed more easily. You will also need to choose the Logging database to which the processed log data will be written when processed, as well as whether the logs should be processed automatically or manually.

A unique filename is automatically created for each new log file. As these names contain a time stamp that Spectra uses for report generation, it is important not to rename these files manually.

Make sure that there is plenty of room on the drive you specify for the log file path. If you are logging aggressively on a high-traffic site, you will find the log files occupying a lot of disk space.

You can toggle a log file object between Active and Inactive by clicking the Active dot, next to the filename. A green dot indicates the file is active; a red dot indicates that it is not.

Reports

Creating new reports is often a collaborative effort among the business manager, the system designer, and the system administrator. The business manager requests a new report, specifying the details he would like to see in the report. Interactive developers will code process, purge, configure, and execute handlers for the new report. System administrators will add the report to the system and schedule the processing of log files for the new report.

When the handlers are created, as the system administrator you will need to add the report to the system. Give the new report a label, which will be used to identify the report within the Webtop. Enter the names of the handler files that the interactive developers have created in their appropriate areas, and select a time frame for how far back the report should begin in processing the data. Finally, decide if existing data should be purged as the report is created or if previously aggregated data should be maintained. Clicking OK will add the new report.

▶ **See** Chapter 17 for full information on creating reports and handlers.

Scheduling Log File Processing Data from the log files needs to be processed into the database for the data to be accessible for reporting. Spectra allows you to schedule the processing of these files, so that the data can be processed automatically, without the need for user intervention.

Process handlers for each report will parse through the archived log files and insert the data into the Logging database.

To schedule log processing, follow these steps:

1. Open the Logging menu of the System Admin section by clicking the triangle next to the Logging link.
2. Click the Reports link.
3. Click the Create link in the Schedule column opposite the appropriate report. This will open a Log Process Scheduler (see Figure 23.30).

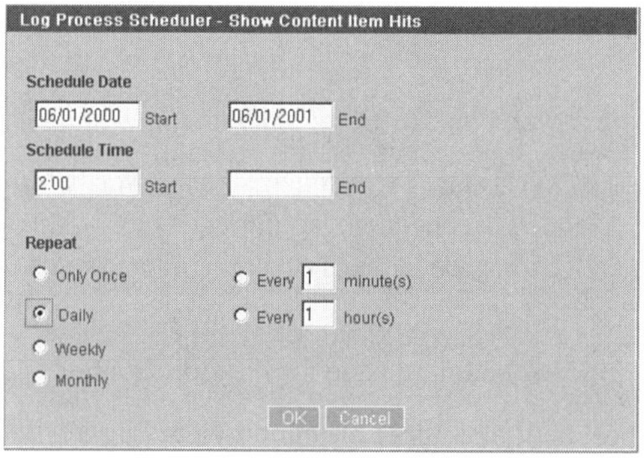

FIGURE 23.30
The Show Content Item Hits report is scheduled to process log files daily at 2 a.m. starting June 1, 2000, and ending June 1, 2001.

4. Choose a start date, end date, start time, end time, and frequency with which this report should process the files.

A low-volume site may be able to get away with weekly or monthly processing, whereas a high-volume site may need to process log files every few minutes to keep them from getting too large. You can also process the report logs manually by clicking the Process link in the OneClick column. These can be seen in Figure 23.31.

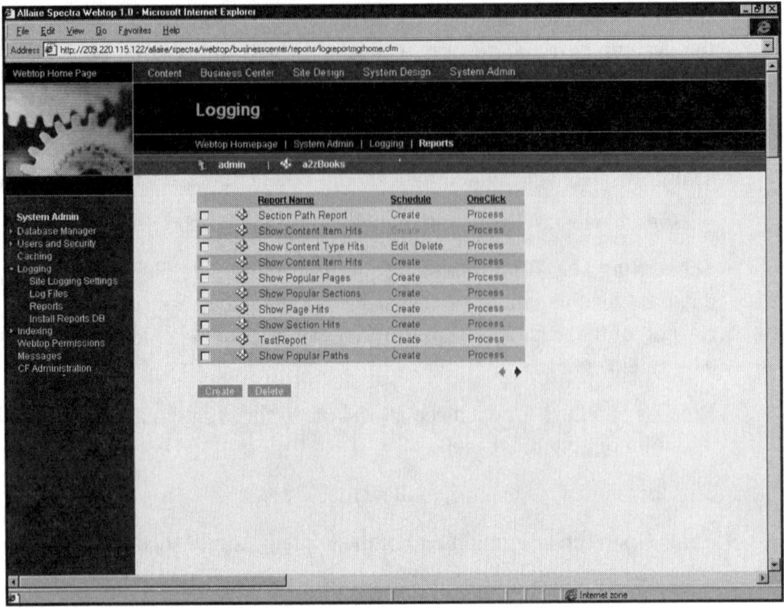

FIGURE 23.31
The Report menu allows you to schedule the processing of reports, as well as process them manually.

Indexing

Spectra indexes data in Verity collections. Although the collections are created programmatically through Spectra, the administrator has the responsibility for collection maintenance and scheduling.

▶ **See** Chapter 14, "Searching and Indexing," for more information on indexing data.

Spectra uses three types of collections. Type collections are Verity indexes of all the object types in the application. Meta Data collections are indexes of the Meta Data hierarchies of the application. Datasource collections are indexes of all the datasources of which Spectra is aware.

Figure 23.32 shows the index scheduling page for the Author object.

Collection indexing will rebuild the entire collection by reading all the data into the collection. This is a time-consuming process, which should be scheduled for low-traffic hours. The frequency with which collections need to be indexed varies, depending on how frequently new data is added to the system. A new book will not be available to a search until the collection is indexed. Figure 23.33 shows the collection indexing scheduling form.

TIP Determine your reindexing schedule based on how often data in that particular collection is updated.

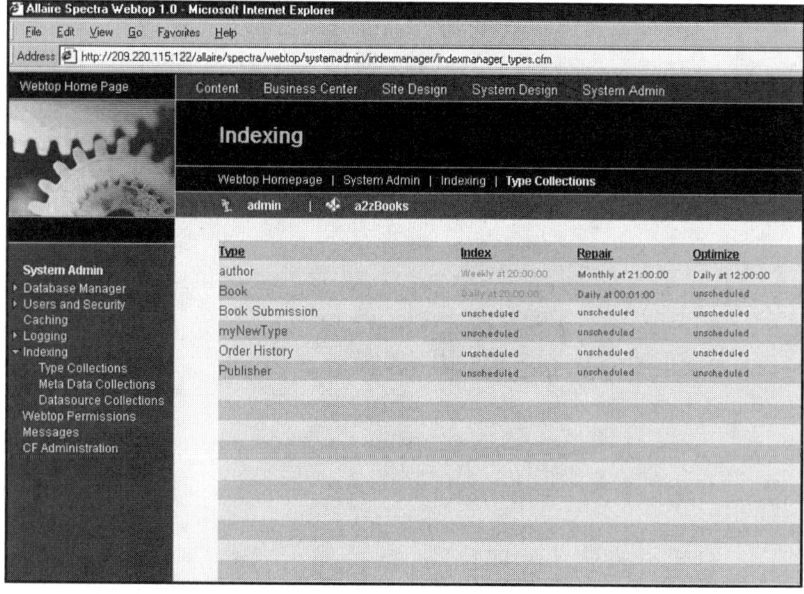

FIGURE 23.32
Here you can see all the indexed object types of the application, as well as any collection maintenance tasks scheduled for them.

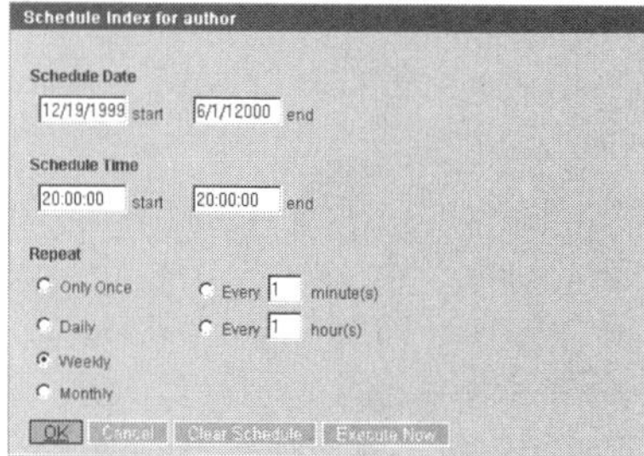

FIGURE 23.33
The Author object type collection is re-indexed weekly at 8 p.m.

Optimizing collections will reorganize the data already contained in the collection, without rebuilding the entire collection from the source data. Although optimizing data will not make new data available to the collection, it will help improve performance of slow collections. Figure 23.34 shows the optimization schedule of the Author object type.

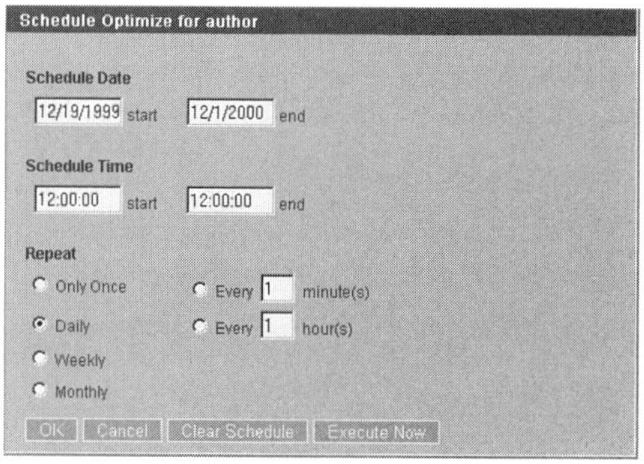

Schedule Optimize for author

Schedule Date

12/19/1999 start 12/1/2000 end

Schedule Time

12:00:00 start 12:00:00 end

Repeat

Only Once
Every 1 minute(s)
Daily
Every 1 hour(s)
Weekly
Monthly

OK Cancel Clear Schedule Execute Now

FIGURE 23.34
The Author object type collection is optimized daily at noon.

Repairing a collection will fix any corrupted data contained within the collection. Although this usually happens in response to feedback indicating a corrupted collection, it is not a bad idea to run an infrequent repair against collections to help catch corrupted data before your users do. Figure 23.35 shows the Author object type collection repair schedule.

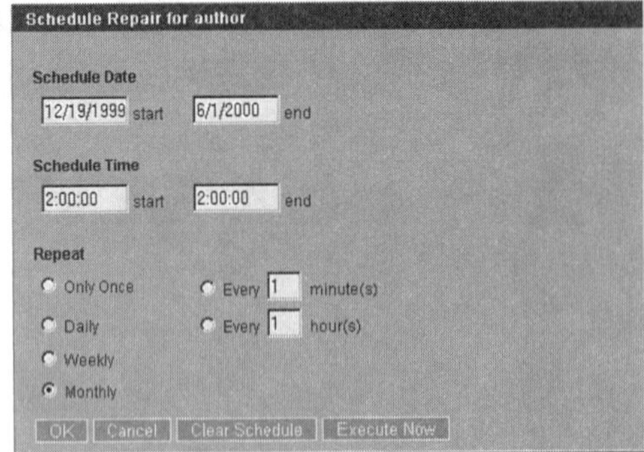

FIGURE 23.35
The Author object type collection is repaired on the 19th of each month at 2 a.m.

Through experience, you will find indexing, optimization, and repair schedules that work for you. ●

CHAPTER 24

Deploying Spectra Applications

In this chapter

Understanding Deployment

When we talk about *deploying* an application, we're talking about putting the application into a position that will advance or accomplish an objective. In this case, the objectives include

- Meeting or exceeding the application's performance requirements
- Making the application scalable to accommodate traffic increases
- Making the application easier to maintain and upgrade
- Accommodating changes to Spectra itself in subsequent versions

Most of the other chapters in this book cover issues that directly affect the above goals, but it's important to bring these key issues to one place. Moreover, we need to examine from a high level various ways to design a Spectra installation, since the architecture will have a major impact on how the site performs and how easy (or difficult) it will be to scale.

Setting Up a New Spectra Environment

Setting up a new Spectra environment is different from simply migrating pieces of an existing environment from one platform or server to another (such as when you need to move fixes to your application from a development environment into production). Nonetheless, how you set up your original Spectra environment will affect all later work.

A Spectra application consists of three fundamental elements, each with its own subdivisions, that must be taken into account in any deployment strategy:

- Application files
    - ColdFusion Web root templates
    - Object handlers
    - Application-specific custom tags
- Databases
    - Webtop database
    - Your application database
    - User directory database
    - Security policy database
- Logging service
    - Log files
    - The report database into which you process log data

As a guiding principle, you should establish an environment that allows you to manage each of the top-level elements independently. As your site grows, you may also want to begin managing some of the subdivisions independently. The more independence you achieve between these elements, the greater control you have over site performance and scalability.

Server Configurations

The low end server configuration for a Spectra site involves three servers (see Figure 24.1):

- Two clustered Spectra servers
- A database server

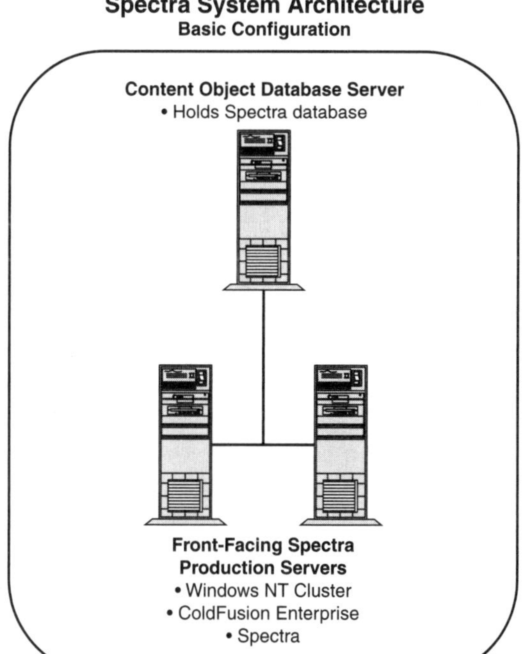

FIGURE 24.1
The basic Spectra installation consists of two clustered Spectra servers and a backend database server.

In this arrangement, two servers are clustered using the Cluster Cats software that ships with CF Enterprise. These may also be referred to as *front-facing* servers because they are the ones your users will access. For an Internet site, these face outward to the world.

If you use session management in your application, you should configure Cluster Cats to use *sticky sessions*—that is, when a user first requests a page, he is routed to a particular server in the cluster and remains there for all subsequent requests during that session. This is needed to ensure proper session management.

CAUTION

All front-facing servers in a cluster must be set up and configured identically. Minimally, make sure that ColdFusion and Spectra are installed to the same drives and directories on each machine. Creating

continues

continued

identical machines includes the placement of your application's templates. As your site grows, you will save yourself untold hours by establishing and using standards for how your machines are set up. Not doing this will make application and cluster configuration and maintenance much more difficult.

The Spectra databases live on the third server. For more information on the databases Spectra uses, see the following sidebar, "Spectra Databases."

Spectra usually writes its log files to the machine it's installed on, and each Spectra machine processes its own log files. However, the data is combined into one set of tables living on the database server. To accommodate this, make sure that each Spectra server processes its logs at a different time of day.

Spectra Databases

Spectra uses several databases. It's important to understand the role of each when configuring a new Spectra installation or migrating an existing installation:

- `cfaObjects`. Spectra installs this default database into a limited license version of Sybase SQLAnywhere. Initially, it holds data needed by the Webtop and the i-Build demonstration application. It's also used to hold basic data on any other applications you create.

  All Spectra applications–including the Webtop–store their data in a ContentObject Database, which is Allaire's object-based data storage scheme built within a standard relational database. To see how to create a new, empty ContentObject Database, see Chapter 23, "Administering Spectra."

- *Userdirectory*. SiteMinder, the program used by ColdFusion advanced security to manage authentication and authorization datasources, stores its authentication information in what it terms *User Directories*. SiteMinder knows how to use various datasources, including ODBC databases, LDAP servers, and Windows NT Domain servers, as User Directories. ColdFusion accesses SiteMinder-managed User Directories through a name you can create in the ColdFusion Administrator.

  One file installed with Spectra is an Access database that's used as Spectra's default User Directory. Spectra names this User Directory datasource, somewhat confusingly, `UserDirectory`. This database is used by SiteMinder for authenticating Spectra users, but it can be upsized to an enterprise-class relational database management system (RDBMS) or an LDAP server. See Chapter 16, "Using Spectra Security Options," for more information on this database.

- *Policy database*. SiteMinder uses this database for storing authorization information. By default, it's installed as an Access database, but it can be upsized to an enterprise-class RDBMS or an LDAP server. The Access database file is named `smpolicy.mdb`, and the ODBC datasource that points to it is called SiteMinder Data Source. In ColdFusion 4.0, this ODBC datasource doesn't show up in the ODBC section of the ColdFusion Administrator but is available through the Windows NT ODBC applet. See Chapter 16 for more information on this database.

- *Log tables.* The `cfaObjects` database includes several tables Spectra uses to store processed log data that are used to generate the default reports. These default tables can be upsized with the rest of the `cfaObjects` database or installed into a separate database entirely. You also may need to create other tables to support the reporting requirements for your application. These can be stored in any accessible database. For more information on logging and reports, see Chapter 17, "Site Reporting."

Even for the basic configuration of two Spectra servers and one database server, you should upsize these databases to an enterprise-class database on the third server.

Although the configuration discussed in the preceding sidebar may serve for relatively small installations, Allaire suggests using a two-tier production architecture, as shown in Figure 24.2.

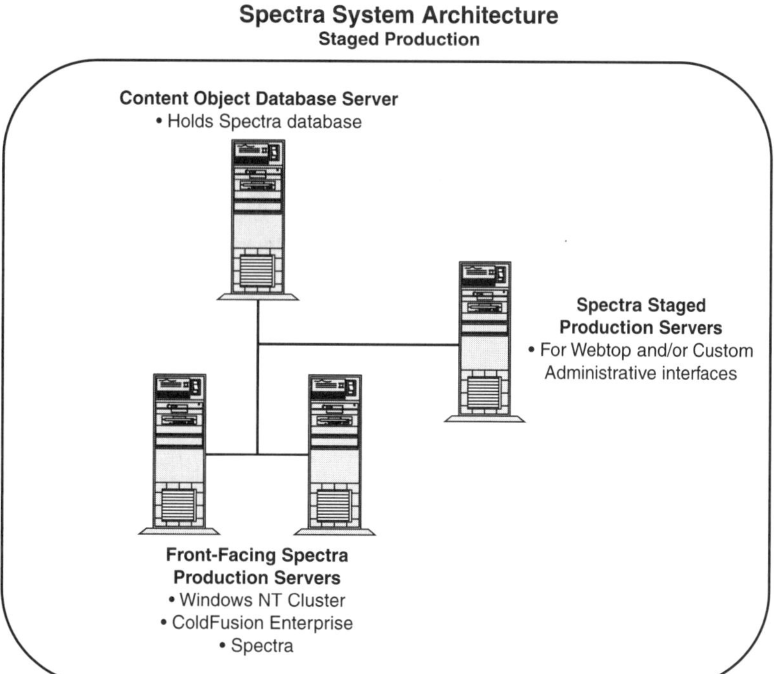

FIGURE 24.2
To the basic architecture we've added an administrative server—a *staged production server*—on which admin users manage content.

This shows the same basic setup as the basic Spectra installation in Figure 24.1, except with the addition of an administrative Spectra server. Allaire calls this a *staged production server,* which is used to administer the data on the site. In this architecture, no administration occurs on the front-facing clustered machines. (Front-facing servers are accessed only by end users of the site.) The primary reason for adding the staged production server is to offload administrative duties to a separate machine, thereby decreasing load on the servers accessed by your users. Keeping the relatively high overhead of administrative work off the front-facing cluster helps keep end-user performance high.

For businesses that use the Webtop to administer content, it's accessed by editors and administrators on the staged production server. They log in to the Webtop on the staged production server (which has access to the application data residing in the database back end) and carry out their work such as creating or editing content or managing workflows. For more information on managing content, see Chapter 10, "Creating and Managing Content." For more information on workflow, see Chapter 13, "Working with Workflow."

In many cases, however, you will create your own administrative interface. In that case, your editors and administrative users access your administrative interfaces on the staged production server to manage the application and its data.

Another possible next step for distributing functions is to set up a log server with an optional log database server (see Figure 24.3). Under this scheme, we've added a log server to hold the log files and do the log processing. By using this architecture, Spectra continues to write log files to the local front-facing machines, but during off-hours they are copied to the log server, where they are processed. As the handler digests the raw log data, it writes the results to an RDBMS that either lives on the log server itself or, for large sites with high-volume log files, to a database on an additional log database machine.

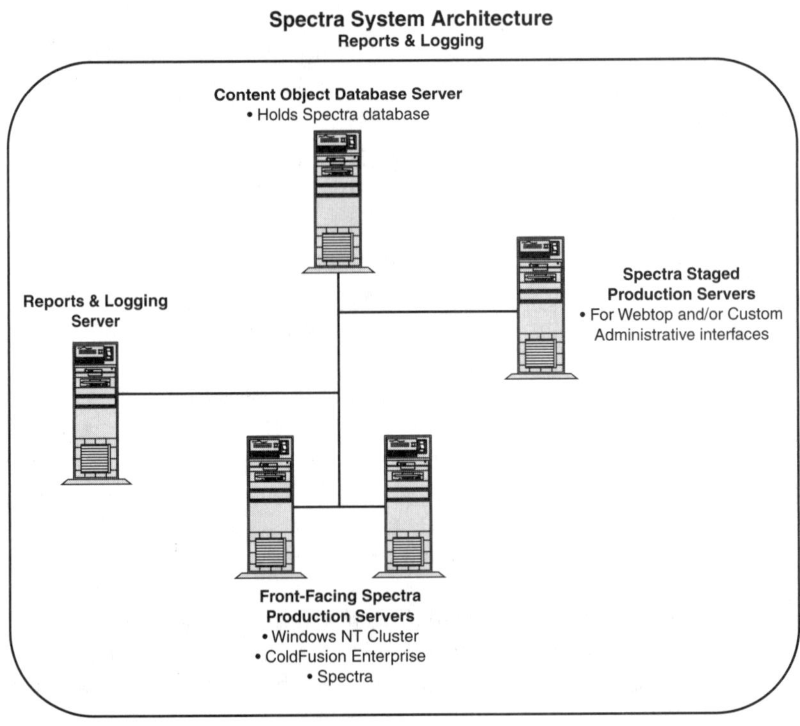

FIGURE 24.3
Log processing and report generation can be moved off front-facing and administrative servers to a separate log processing server.

When a business user wants to view report results, he logs onto the log server and views the reports there. This generates and displays the report without affecting either the front-facing servers or the production database.

All this helps keep process-intensive operations off the front-facing servers.

See Chapter 17 for more information on log files and how to create reports.

Another common way to distribute Spectra load is to use a separate server for user authentication and security authorization (see Figure 24.4).

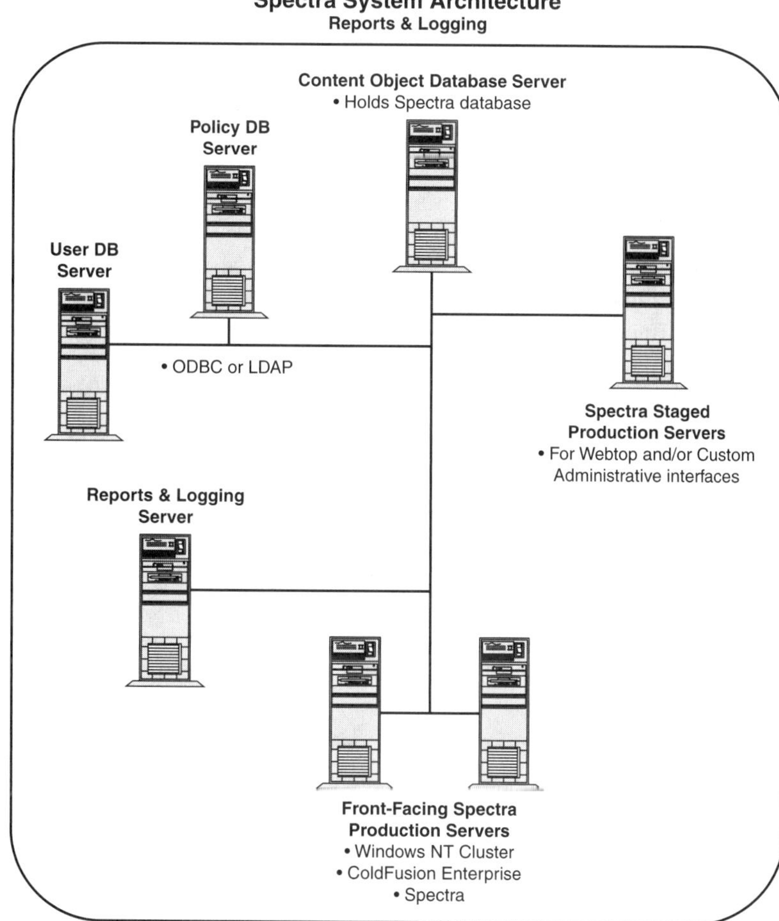

FIGURE 24.4
It's possible to distribute Spectra security functions to separate security servers.

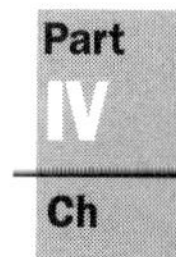

Although the previous examples assumed you were using the default user directory—or an upsized version of it—in most cases, Spectra will need to integrate with an existing corporate user directory. One key advantage of Spectra is that it makes it unnecessary for developers to continually write homegrown security mechanisms, since it can talk to most legacy systems.

In Figure 24.4, we've added separate LDAP or ODBC database servers to hold the user directory and the policy database for authentication and authorization. In this case, the templates you use to administer the user directory would live on the staged production server to avoid administrative overhead on the front-facing servers.

The separate policy database server can be either an LDAP server or an RDBMS to which you migrate the policy database. In either case, the security load has been removed from the production database server.

See Chapter 16 for more information on authentication, authorization, and general security issues.

The above shows a possible scaling path for Spectra installations. Most likely, while you are distributing user security and logging, you will also be adding machines to the original cluster, thereby directly boosting application performance as you offload processing from the front-facing machines.

Allaire suggests an upper-limit size of eight machines to a cluster. When that limit is reached, you will need to begin a new cluster that may use the same back-end resources as the first cluster or, more likely, will use its own replicated database servers. As the site grows, the pattern will remain the same. Instead of two front-facing servers, as shown in Figure 24.4, the cluster will include eight front-facing servers. When the first cluster reaches capacity, you can create another identical cluster, thereby enlarging the site in repeatable stages.

In the Windows NT environment, it's also possible to create a two-machine database cluster to manage the ContentObject Database. Allaire has used Compaq's Distributed Internet Server Array (DISA) architecture with Windows NT Enterprise Edition and Microsoft SQL Server Enterprise Edition. Although Spectra doesn't tend to place a heavy load on the database server, you may want to create a database cluster if only for failover. Of course, you can also increase performance by running two virtual instances of the database in parallel. In that case, you may find that one database cluster is sufficient to feed more than one Spectra cluster.

The preceding provides some specific suggestions for how to scale your Spectra site, but the more important point is the general concept that Spectra supports a distributed architecture. It's a good idea to plan your architecture from the beginning so that pieces of it can be offloaded to their own processors. Another prospect for offloading might be any Verity indexing used by your site.

Sizing Spectra Servers

Many factors affect the performance of Spectra applications, including the following:

- The quality of the Spectra code itself
- ColdFusion server configuration

- Web server configuration
- How well caching is used
- The complexity of the queries needed to generate pages
- Network and bandwidth issues
- The speed of the servers (which itself is affected by many factors)
- Database considerations such as the size of the Spectra database
- The amount of traffic at any given time

It's not uncommon in development environments for different groups—networking, application development, DBAs, and hardware—to end up pointing fingers at each other when it comes to performance problems or application failures. Because of this—and the many issues that can affect Spectra application performance—it's important to do a thorough and effective testing phase on any application before it goes live.

Testing Performance

Allaire offers a five-day testing service in which Allaire engineers put your application through its paces and help isolate and resolve coding, network, configuration, or hardware problems–in short, any performance bottlenecks that may affect your application's performance.

Experience has shown that the most effective way to test performance is to begin it early in the development cycle and continue throughout development. This can even start as early as initial application prototypes. Although positive results at this stage don't guarantee a high-performing app, they may help isolate major problems early on. It's therefore recommended that you invest in a testing environment and the software necessary to continually test your application software as it evolves. There are no small Spectra applications; in most cases, if you're building a Spectra application, it's worth investing in the tools to properly test it. Load-testing tools such as Segue Silk Performer or log reporting tools such as Webtrends all help make potential problems visible before your customers find them for you.

Although performance testing is usually considered in a prelaunch period, it's actually appropriate on an ongoing basis. Even well-designed applications may become overburdened with traffic. Load testing can help determine how much more capacity will be needed in the short and long terms so that scaling can be done before it becomes a crisis.

Having said that, it's still useful to look at performance figures for a known application. Based on such results, it's possible to estimate how many servers you may need for your application.

Allaire has done some performance tests on the i-Build application; the most recent and accurate results should be available at Allaire's site. However, based on the results available at press time, we can provide some guidelines to help size installations for Spectra 1.0 applications.

Spectra Test Bed Configuration

The i-Build testing front-facing servers consist of

- 1, 2, 4, and 8 Compaq 1850R dual-500MHz 512MB machines running Microsoft Windows NT 4.0, SP4, and IIS 4.0
- ColdFusion 4.5 NT Enterprise
- Spectra 1.0

The database server consisted of

- Two (1 active, 1 passive) Compaq 6400R, quad-500MHz Xeon Intel processors, 1GB machines configured in a Compaq Distributed Internet Server Array (DISA) architecture running Microsoft Windows NT Enterprise Edition
- Microsoft SQL Server 7.0 SP1 Enterprise Edition

The operating system and Web servers were configured according to Allaire's Knowledge Base articles #11772, "Platform-Specific Performance Settings," and #11773, "Performance-Related Resources," both available through the Allaire Web site at `http://www.allaire.com/Support/KnowledgeBase/SearchForm.cfm`.

The ColdFusion Administrator settings were as follows:

Setting	Value
Limit Simultaneous Requests	6
Suppress Whitespace by Default	OFF
Enforce Strict Attribute Validation	ON
Template Cache Size	40960
Trusted Cache	ON
Load Security Server Policy Store Cache at Startup	ON
Use Security Server Policy Store Cache	ON
Security Server Cache Refresh Interval	60 (minutes)
Use Security Server Authorization Cache	ON
Use ColdFusion Server Security Cache	ON
ColdFusion Security Cache Refresh Interval	120 (minutes)
ColdFusion Security Cache Maximum Entries	9999
Default Client Variable Storage	Cookie
Session Variable Default Timeout	20 min
Application Variable Default Timeout	1 day
Automatic Shared Variable Checking and Locking	NONE for All
Data Source Maintain Database Connections	ON for All

The test itself consisted of requests for eight different i-Build pages, including performing two searches.

Several important adjustments were made to the Spectra configurations and the i-Build code:

- Page caching was turned on through the Site Model so that cached pages could be served up rather than re-rendered for each request.
- Several code lines in the `application.cfm` page were replaced to eliminate getting the user profile with each request. By default i-Build's `application.cfm` file queries the ContentObject Database for the current user's user profile at the beginning of every page and places the data into a request scope variable. Moving away from using the user profile is an important change from the typical Spectra application, since the user profile is needed for any personalization. An alternative to the default i-Build approach is to request the user profile at the beginning of a session, store it in the session scope, and have your application access it from there.
- Object caching was turned on by setting `bUseCache=1` for the first ContentObject call. This causes Spectra to get the Content Item once and use the cached version for subsequent calls. This change was made in the `invoke.cfm`, `search.cfm`, and `topicsearch.cfm` templates.
- The calls to `<CFA_GLOBALSETTINGS>` in lines 141 and 170 of `/customtags/system/tier1/application/cfa_applicationinitialize.cfm` were moved to line 138.
- The `<FORM>` action attributes were changed from `post` to `get` in `/customtags/system/i-build/ibuildsearchbox.cfm` and `/customtags/system/i-build/ibuildtopicbox.cfm`.
- The search templates were changed to disable logging.

This information was taken from an version of the "Allaire Spectra Performance Fact Sheet," published by Allaire.

The first graph (see Figure 24.5) shows the response time for a single Windows NT server running the i-Build test as the number of simultaneous users increases. In this case, *simultaneous users* doesn't mean that each user is making a request at exactly the same moment. It means that the load-testing software simulated some number of users moving through the site, including users pausing between page requests.

In Figure 24.5, the response time stays below 1 second up to 200 simultaneous users, rising to 3 seconds as the number of users increases to approximately 225. From there, response times rise steadily to 8 seconds for approximately 260 users. Although 8 seconds may be an acceptable response time in some circumstances, you should size your infrastructure so that even during extreme traffic spikes your response times don't exceed this.

Despite the limitations of how this data might apply to any given application, it still provides a good rule of thumb that a single Windows NT server configured similarly should support approximately 200 simultaneous users with acceptable response times.

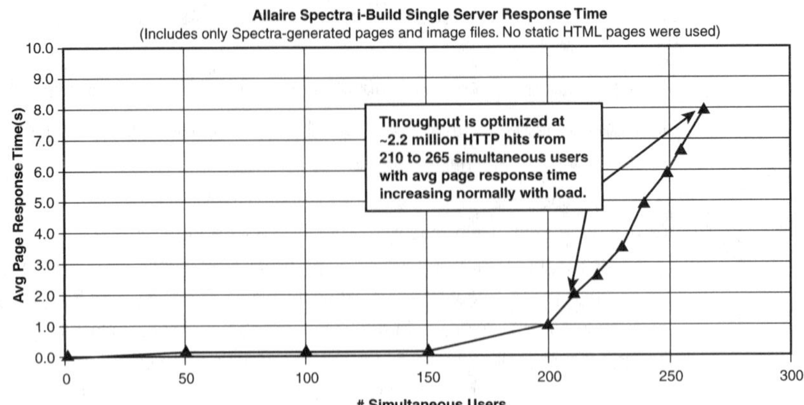

FIGURE 24.5
The average page response time for a single Windows NT server running the i-Build application.

The graph in Figure 24.6 demonstrates Spectra's ability to scale linearly—a desirable trait when scaling an installation, because you don't want to have random performance spikes.

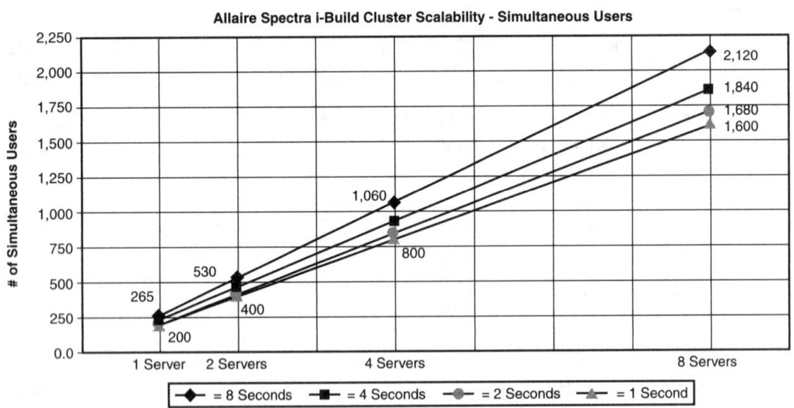

FIGURE 24.6
Testing data indicates that Spectra performance increases linearly as servers are added to the cluster.

Figure 24.6 shows the number of simultaneous users served with 1-, 2-, 4-, and 8-second response times as the Spectra cluster grows. As has already been said, your application's performance will vary, but it's important to note that performance increased linearly as servers were added to the cluster. This is a tremendous plus because once you know how your application performs under load, you can accurately predict the impact of adding servers to your cluster.

Based on the results from the single-server test for applications with a similar profile to i-Build, you can estimate approximately 200 users per server. This should scale to approximately 1,600 users for an eight-server cluster. However, to help you arrive at more accurate estimates, Allaire provides a detailed methodology based on both the i-Build tests and tests done with the Webtop to estimate the number of servers your application will need. (As of this writing, Allaire is also working to add testing data from third-party–developed applications.)

This methodology doesn't substitute for real load testing, but it can help with initial sizing. The methodology factors in circumstances that may raise or lower your application's performance, such as site complexity, how much caching and logging you use, or the degree of personalization. Heavy-load sites may get only a quarter of the performance, as demonstrated in the preceding i-Build examples. Because the test figures will continue to change as Spectra evolves, the best source of current information for sizing your site is available from Allaire's Web site. Look for Allaire's white paper, "Allaire Spectra Windows NT Performance Fact Sheet and Sizing Guide," for the latest figures and a thorough breakdown of the recommended sizing methodology.

Again, these estimates are extremely rough, and your mileage will definitely vary.

Development, Testing, and Production

The previous sections describe what's involved in setting up a production environment. However, once an application goes live, you will most likely need to maintain three Spectra environments:

- *Production*. This is the environment end users and administrators access to run your application.
- *Testing*. This environment should mirror the production code. Ideally, it will also mirror the physical architecture of the production environment, even if scaled down. If your production environment consists of a cluster and separate database server, your testing environment should as well, if possible. Post-launch, this environment is kept in sync with production and is used to test fixes or incremental enhancements before they are put into production.
- *Development*. You use this environment to push forward subsequent phases of the application after the initial launch. The code in this environment starts out looking like production but rapidly diverges as development continues.

Very often, for new Spectra applications, developers end up using what is slated to become the production environment for development. But sometime before launch it's important to set up the additional two environments.

Deploying Applications

The production, testing, and development environments establish the playing field in which your application and developers operate. We now need to examine the mechanics of how you move applications and databases around.

Spectra provides ways through the Webtop to install and migrate ContentObject Databases. Some of these tools can be used only to migrate an entire ContentObject Database from one server to another as they wipe out the destination database; others are used to migrate parts of an application.

The following sections explore the tools available for copying or migrating databases.

▶ **See** Chapter 23 for information on how to install a new ContentObject Database to a datasource you've created.

Moving an Entire Application

Let's begin with the easy task—moving an entire application from a source platform to a destination platform. To migrate any application, you must take into account at least three elements:

- Databases
- Application templates
- ColdFusion Server configurations such as ColdFusion mappings

In light of the above, let's examine the steps to move your application from a development environment to the final production environment.

Migrating the Databases Spectra provides tools for migrating a ContentObject Database from one server to another. You can use these tools as long as you have set up a datasource for the new database through the ColdFusion Administrator.

▶ **See** Chapter 23 for details on how to migrate a ContentObject Database from one server to another.

Although this method for transferring the ContentObject Database works for any supported database accessible through an ODBC or native connection, it can be time consuming, especially as the ContentObject Database grows. This is because it must serialize all the data in the source database into WDDX packets and then deserialized it into the new datasource.

In many cases, you will be able to transfer a ContentObject Database much more quickly by using native RDBMS tools. For example, in SQL Server 7.0, you can use the Data Transformation Services to copy a database into or out of SQL Server databases rapidly. See the documentation for your RDMS to understand its data migration tools.

Spectra doesn't provide any built-in tools for migrating or upsizing the existing user directory or policy databases. To move these, you will need to use the native tools for the RDBMS or LDAP server you are migrating from or to.

▶ **See** Chapter 16 for more information on upsizing or migrating user directories or policy databases.

When migrating or copying databases, no matter the application, you often run into the problem of how to balance the need to keep the databases in sync with the need to minimize down time for your users. In some cases, you may have to have some down time for some users. A key point to analyze is which users are involved in dynamic processes that are updating the Spectra database. If you are using Spectra to update user profiles dynamically as users move through your site, even seemingly mundane visitor interaction results in database updates.

Such constant database updating may provide rich data but can complicate required system administration tasks. Therefore, a good strategy always is to include plans for system admin time early in the design phase. This may be as simple as providing an administrative switch that allows you to turn dynamic personalization off for your site. Although you may lose some data you'd otherwise capture, this is preferable to jeopardizing your database integrity.

By building in control over database updates, you make it easier to get admin tasks done without having to bring the site down entirely.

Migrating the Templates In addition to your application's templates located in the server's Web root, you also need to transfer the ColdFusion templates you've written that are located elsewhere on the server. The following summarizes the most common templates types and where they live:

Template Type	**Usual location**
App Web Files	`Webroot/AppRoot`
Custom Tags	`Spectra_Install/CustomTags/AppDirectory` or `ColdFusion_Install/CustomTags/`
Handlers	`Spectra_Install/Handlers/AppDirectory`
PLP handlers	`Spectra_Install/PLP/AppDirectory`
Report handlers	`Spectra_Install/handlers/system/logreports/`
Page Templates	`Spectra_Install/pagetemplates/AppDirectory`

Spectra doesn't provide tools to migrate these automatically; you must copy them manually or, as needed, write a short script to move them.

NOTE Spectra also produces log files. The location of these is configured when you define a Log File ContentObject Type, so it may be anywhere on the system. For more information on log files and their location, see Chapter 17.

Specialized ColdFusion Settings If you've defined things such as ColdFusion mappings through the ColdFusion Administrator, you will also need to migrate these to your new system manually. Other examples of items you may need to migrate manually to the new server are

- Specialized ODBC definitions for non-Spectra datasources accessed by your application
- Any specialized Verity collections you use

- Any CFX tag or applet registrations
- The mail server setting
- Any scheduled tasks

These items aren't Spectra specific but are worth mentioning because overlooking migrating this information may cause your application not to work in the new environment.

Selective Migration

Perhaps the more involved type of migration involves selectively migrating items from a development or testing environment into your active production environment. In this case, you can't simply copy over the entire database, and you probably don't want to blindly copy the full set of development templates into your production environment.

Ideally, you should use the source control integration possible with ColdFusion Studio to manage your templates. As projects grow in scope, so too does the need for disciplined source control. For more information on this, see Que's *The ColdFusion 4.0 Web Application Construction Kit* by Ben Forta.

In other words, you want to be selective about what's copied and when. We'll examine how to copy selected items such as Spectra definitions and objects from a development environment into production. For the most part, these discussions will focus on copying definition-level items, such as ContentObject Types, instead of copying specific instances, such as individual Content Items. However, in some cases you will need to copy individual instances. For example, workflow definitions are actually instances of the WorkFlow ContentObject Type. If you create a new workflow definition in development, you will need to copy the Workflow Content Item that contains its definition into production.

Migrating New ContentObject Types If you create a new ContentObject Type in your development environment, Spectra provides a utility that allows you to easily migrate that new type to production. Let's see how to use the Webtop to migrate the Author ContentObject Type from the a2zBooks application to another Spectra system:

1. Log in to the Webtop in the source environment.
2. Click System Design.
3. Open Site Object Designer in the navigation area on the left.
4. Click Type Designer for a list of available ContentObject Types (see Figure 24.7).
5. Click the ContentObject Type icon to the left of Author. This displays an Edit Type interface (see Figure 24.8).
6. Click Utils to display the Utilities screen for this ContentObject Type (see Figure 24.9).

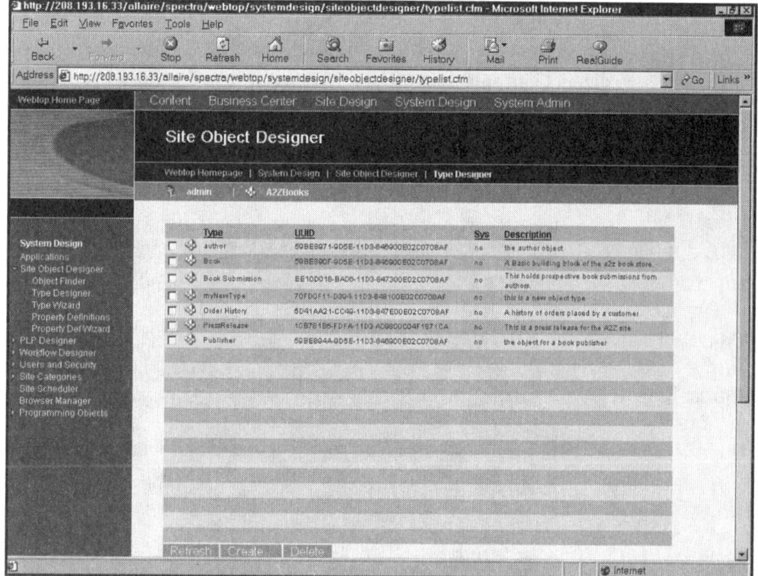

FIGURE 24.7
The list of ContentObject Types available in the a2zBooks application.

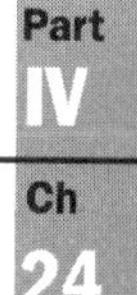

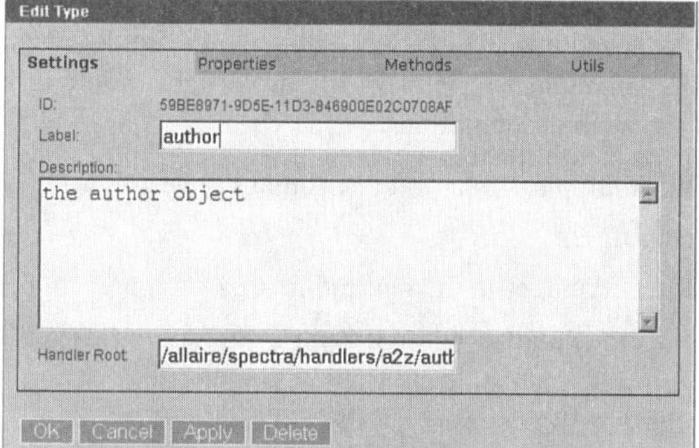

FIGURE 24.8
The Edit Type interface after clicking the Author ContentObject Type in the previous screen.

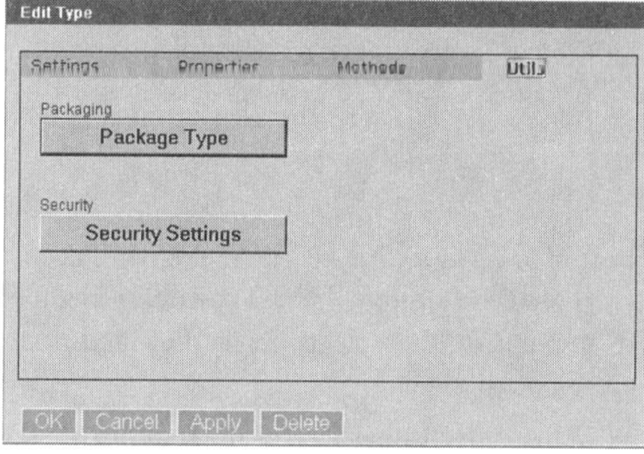

FIGURE 24.9
The Utils tab of the Edit Type form that gives you access to the Package Type functionality.

7. Click Package Type to kick off a process to serialize the definition of the Author ContentObject Type. This brings up a dialog box from which you can elect to open the serialized ContentObject Type or save it to a file on your local system (see Figure 24.10).
8. Click OK to save the definition. This leads to a standard Windows Save As dialog box that allows you to select the exact location.

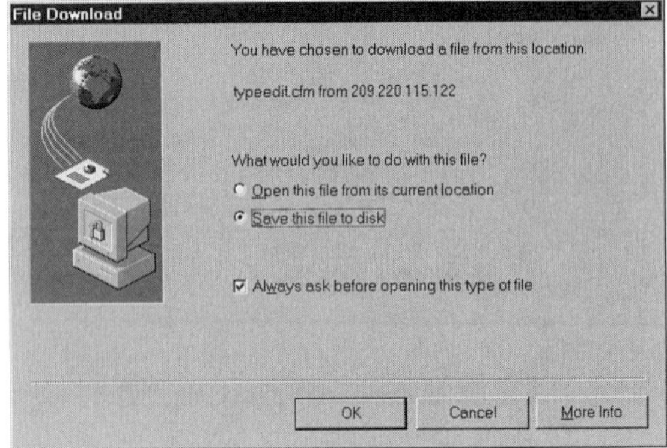

FIGURE 24.10
From here, you can elect to either open the WDDX packet containing the ContentObject Type definition or save it to a disk file.

At this point, you've saved a WDDX packet that contains the definition for the Author object. It also contains all the handlers defined for it. Through the Webtop, you can now migrate this ContentObject Type to your application.

1. Log in to the Webtop in the target environment.
2. Click System Admin.
3. Open Database Manager in the navigation area.
4. Click Import Types to display the Import Type form (see Figure 24.11).

FIGURE 24.11
The Import Type form provides an interface for uploading and importing a ContentObject Type definition to a target system.

5. Use the Browse button to open a Choose File dialog with access to all local files on your system. Navigate to the ContentObject Type definition file you saved in the previous step. Click OK to populate the Select File field of the Import Type form with the path to the file you selected.
6. Click Import Type. When Spectra has successfully imported the type, you'll receive a success message.

This process does the following:

- Creates the ContentObject Type in the new system.
- Optionally creates any Property definitions required by the ContentObject Type.
- Creates the handler files for the ContentObject Type's methods. These are installed in the same directory, relative to the Spectra installation directory, on the target machine.

The new ContentObject Type is installed using the same UUID as the original, so any hard references to the type in your code should continue to work.

Upgrading ContentObject Types The above technique works when you need to migrate a brand-new ContentObject Type from one environment to another. However, if you need to update an existing ContentObject Type by adding or removing a property, there may be additional steps, depending on the circumstances.

If you use the above method with a ContentObject Type that already exists, the existing definition is deleted first and then replaced with the new definition. In some cases, this may be more than is needed.

For example, if you've added or removed a property from a ContentObject Type and need to migrate that change to another server, you would just write a template that updates the existing definition rather than create an entirely new one. In this case you would also need to write a script to cycle through the existing Content Items of that type to update them to include the new property. This is done by calling `<CFA_CONTENTOBJECTDATA>` to update each Content Item.

Making fundamental changes to ContentObject Types, when Content Items already exist, must be done carefully. The exact procedure will depend on the circumstances. Therefore, be sure to test your scripts thoroughly in a development or testing environment before attempting to convert production data.

See Chapter 10 for additional information on ContentObject Types, see Chapter 6, "Introduction to Spectra Programming." For further information on managing Content Items.

Migrating PLPs The Webtop includes an interface for exporting PLPs that operates much the same as does the interface for exporting a ContentObject Type. Use the following procedure to export PLP definitions:

1. Log in to the Webtop for the source application.
2. Click System Design.
3. Open PLP Designer in the navigation area.
4. Click PLP Manager to display a list of the PLPs defined within the application (see Figure 24.12).
5. Click the package icon to the right of the UUID of the PLP you'd like to export. This displays a dialog for deciding whether to open the download directly or save it to disk. You are then asked to specify the filename and where to place it on your local machine.

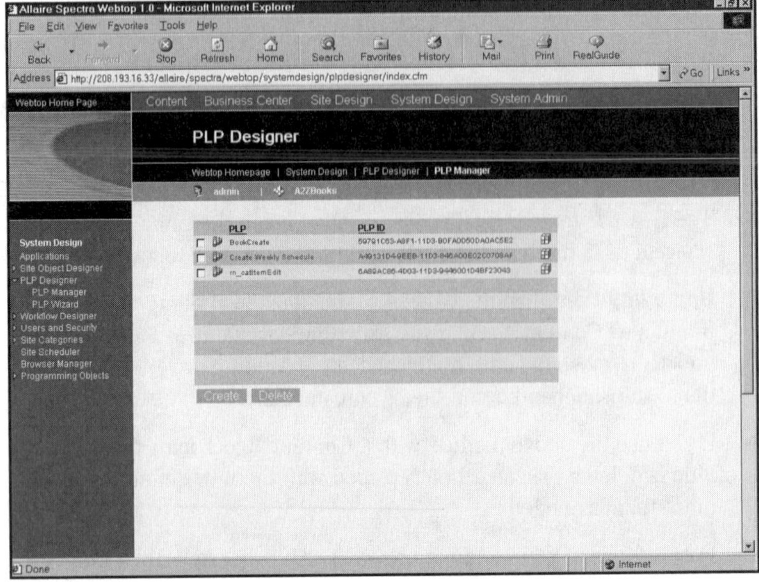

FIGURE 24.12
This displays a list of the PLPs defined on the system that are available for export.

After you export the PLP definition, use the same method as described earlier for importing a ContentObject Type, except choose Import PLP in the Database Manager section.

Spectra copies the PLP definition as well as all the PLP templates to the target machine.

Programmatically Migrating ContentObject Types and PLPs The underlying Spectra functionality that packages ContentObject Types and PLPs so they can be transferred from one environment to another is available to the interactive developer using the `<CFA_OBJECTPACKAGER>` and `<CFA_OBJECTINSTALLER>` tags. These tags are straightforward to use. For example, to package the Author object, use the following:

```
<!--- Set the Author ObjectID --->
<CFSET AuthorTypeID = '59BE8971-9D5E-11D3-846900E02C0708AF'>

<cfa_objectPackager
    DATASOURCE="#REQUEST.CFA.a2zBooks.DATASOURCE#"
    DATATYPE="COAPI"
    ID="#AuthorTypeID#"
    R_WSTOBJECT="wstObject">
```

This creates a WDDX packet containing the ContentObject Type definition as well as the handlers that implement its methods. You use the same tag to package a PLP by setting the `DataType` attribute to `PLP`.

You import the ContentObject Type into the target environment by using the `<CFA_OBJECTINSTALLER>` tag:

```
<cfa_objectInstaller
    DATASOURCE="#REQUEST.CFA.a2zBooks.DATASOURCE#"
    WSTOBJECT="wstObject"
    R_BSUCCESSFUL="bSuccessful">
```

Migrating Content Items The most common type of Content Item migration you will likely have to do involves migrating things such as Workflow Content Items that contain workflow definitions. Whatever the type of Content Item, you can use the same method for migrating it from one environment to another:

1. In the source environment, create an ODBC datasource that points to the ContentObject Database in the target environment.
2. Generate a list of the Content Items to be transferred.
3. Loop through that list and use `<CFA_CONTENTOBJECTCREATE>` to create a new Content Item in the target environment.

Listing 24.1 shows a specific example of how this can be done.

Listing 24.1 ***CopyContentItems.cfm*—Migrating Content Items**

```
<!---
File:          SpectraBookTestscripts/CopyContentItems.cfm
Author:        david aden (david@wwstudios.com)
Date:          1/30/2000
Description:   Used to copy Content Items from one environment to another,
               such such as development to production.

Notes:         This checks to see if the Content Items already exist in the
               target before copying them so only creates the ones that
               do NOT exist.

Change History:

--->

<!--- Set the Author Content Object ContentObject Type ID into a
variable. --->
<CFSET AuthorTypeID = '59BE8971-9D5E-11D3-846900E02C0708AF'>

<!--- Get a list of all the author objects from the source CODB --->
<CFA_CONTENTOBJECTGETMULTIPLE
    DATASOURCE="#REQUEST.cfa.A2ZBooks.Datasource#"
    TYPEID="#AuthorTypeID#"
    R_STOBJECTS="stSourceAuthors">

<!--- Get a list of all the author objects in the target CODB --->
<CFA_CONTENTOBJECTGETMULTIPLE
    DATASOURCE="YOUR TARGET DATASOURCE HERE"
    TYPEID="#AuthorTypeID#"
```

continues

Listing 24.1 Continued

```
    R_STOBJECTS="stTargetAuthors">

<!--- Loop through the author objects --->
<CFLOOP COLLECTION="#stSourceAuthors#" ITEM="CurrAuthor">

    <!--- Only transfer objects that don't exist in the target database
          already --->
    <CFIF Not StructKeyExists(stTargetAuthors,CurrAuthor)>

      <!--- Grab the Object ID and the label --->
      <CFSET thisObjectID = stSourceAuthors[CurrAuthor].ObjectID>
      <CFSET thisLabel = stSourceAuthors[CurrAuthor].Label>

      <!--- Strip out items we don't need to pass into the Create tag --->
      <CFSET temp = StructDelete(stSourceAuthors[CurrAuthor], "objectID")>
      <CFSET temp = StructDelete(stSourceAuthors[CurrAuthor], "typeID")>
      <CFSET temp = StructDelete(stSourceAuthors[CurrAuthor], "Label")>

      <!--- Okay, now let's create the new objects in the target
            database --->
      <CFA_CONTENTOBJECTCREATE
            DATASOURCE="TargetEnv"
            TYPEID="#AuthorTypeID#"
            OBJECTID="#thisObjectID#"
            STPROPERTIES="#stSourceAuthors[CurrAuthor]#"
            LABEL="stSourceAuthors[CurrAuthor].#thisLlabel#" >
    </CFIF>

</CFLOOP>
```

This begins by setting the UUID for the Author ContentObject Type into a local variable we can use throughout the script.

Then we use <CFA_CONTENTOBJECTGETMULTIPLE> to get all the Author Content Items from the source ContentObject Database. The second <CFA_CONTENTOBJECTGETMULTIPLE> gets any Author Content Items that already exist in the target ContentObject Database.

Next, we loop through the source Author Content Items. The <CFIF> checks to see if the current Author already exists in the target ContentObject Database. If it doesn't, we need to create a new Content Item.

First, we set the object ID of the current Author Content Item into a local variable and then remove the `ObjectID`, `TypeID`, and `Label` keys from the `stSourceAuthors` structure, since we pass these to <CFA_CONTENTOBJECTCREATE> separately.

Finally, we call the <CFA_CONTENTOBJECTCREATE> tag, which creates the new Object and populates it with the data passed through the `stProperties` structure.

Although the example in Listing 24.1 copies only the Author Content Items from the source to the target environments, it's possible to use the same basic template to copy several types of Content Items to a target environment. The simplest way to do this would be to replace `AuthorTypeID` with a list of ContentObject Types to copy—for example

```
<CFSET lObjectTypesToCopy = '59BE8971-9D5E-11D3-846900E02C0708AF,
                            59BE8972-9D5E-11D3-846900E02C0708AF'>
```

Then enclose the balance of the template with a `<CFLOOP>` that loops over this list. For each ContentObject Type in the list, the template will get all source and target instances and create new instances in the target environment for all those source instances that don't already exist.

If you are regularly adding Content Items in the development environment that need to be transferred to the production environment, it makes sense to build such a template and run it as needed. This template is intended to demonstrate how Content Items can be copied, but it won't necessarily work in all cases. In particular, you may need to take additional steps to copy ContentObject Types that have multilingual properties or embedded objects.

You could also use such a template if you use staged Content Item management in your application. In this scenario, Content Items are processed into an independent Spectra installation and subsequently transferred to production once authorized.

Using staged content management like this keeps all online entry, editing, and related actions off the front-facing servers, thereby lessening their load. After all approvals are secured, a workflow step could call a template similar to the one in Listing 24.1 to move the approved Content Items onto the production server.

Not until the Content Items have been moved to the production server would end users be able to access them.

Scripted Deployment By creating templates that combine the `<CFA_OBJECTPACKAGER>` and `<CFA_OBJECTINSTALLER>` tags with the Content Item–copying template described above, you can create a comprehensive script customized for your application that copies your application from a development environment into a production environment.

As your loads increase to the point where you need multiple clusters to handle the traffic, such a script could become an important administrative tool to help keep the development and production environments in sync.

Performance and Configuration

As mentioned earlier in the chapter, the way an application is written certainly has an impact on how it performs. But even after your application code is optimized, some items still need particular attention, specifically because of their effect on performance.

To reiterate, though, the only way to truly isolate performance bottlenecks for your application is to do official load testing. This should begin as early as possible in the development cycle and continue until your application is ready to be deployed.

One key result of load testing should be to determine the correct settings for your ColdFusion server. In particular, this applies to the `Limit simultaneous requests` setting in the ColdFusion Administrator (which controls the number of active threads ColdFusion will use to process requests). There has been a great deal of debate—and sometimes mixed messages from Allaire—over the last several years about the correct setting for this parameter. Although you often hear recommendations that it should be set at three to five simultaneous requests per processor, the current best answer is that the correct setting is determined by load testing your application and seeing which setting works best.

This leads to a general guideline that should be part of any effort to improve the performance of any Spectra application: Don't ignore the basics. In particular, use Allaire's online ColdFusion server-tuning guidelines. Also, make sure that your Web server is properly tuned and that the Spectra and database servers are performing optimally.

Problems with any of these items can greatly affect Spectra applications—there's no sense spending lots of time trying to improve your application's performance until you're sure of the platform it's running on.

Tuning Performance

Two areas of every Spectra application deserve special attention when you are trying to increase performance. Although the following list isn't complete, it should provide a place to start.

Logging Considerations Spectra permits you to log actions at a very granular level—down to individual actions on individual objects. If you log every user action, your application's performance will suffer. Moreover, the generated log files could become unmanageably large—both in terms of physical size and in terms of the amount of processing required to produce meaningful and timely reports.

Because of this, it's best to begin by turning on essential logging only, gradually adding items to the list of logged objects as needed. The key caution to remember is that when you use the Site Layout Model to turn on logging, settings higher in the hierarchy are inherited by lower levels. So if you turn logging on at the site level, all pages in the site will be logged unless you specifically turn off logging for each page.

Although it involves more work to turn on granularly only the logging you need, in the long run it's the safer approach.

▶ **See** Chapter 17 for detailed information on logging and how to configure logging for your site.

Caching One of the most attractive features of Spectra is its capability to cache content at many levels, thereby helping boost performance.

In most cases, during development you will want to have caching turned off, so you will have no problem seeing changes made in your templates or the content. Before going live, however, you should spend some time reviewing and setting caching policy for your site.

Caching has become an important feature in Allaire products in recent releases. For example, ColdFusion Server 4.0 added query caching directly to the `<CFQUERY>` tag, which is also available to you within Spectra if you're interacting with legacy or non-Spectra datasources. (For more information on caching in ColdFusion, see Que's *The ColdFusion 4.0 Web Application Construction Kit* by Ben Forta.)

Spectra takes this a step further by giving you control over caching for virtually every Spectra element: sites, pages, sections, containers, and accesses to individual Content Items. When you turn on caching for any of these elements, which is described below, you can also decide where the data will be cached. Your choices are

- Caching to a disk file. When you select this option, you need to specify the path where the file will be stored.
- Caching in the `SERVER` scope.
- Caching in the `SESSION` scope.
- Caching in the `REQUEST` scope.

Having these choices gives you granular control over caching's use of system resources, as well as a way to specify the extent or visibility of your caches. You can also control how often the cache is refreshed, so you can cache information that changes somewhat regularly but doesn't need to be changed in real time.

Just as it's important to be able to cache objects for performance, it's also important to be able to flush a cache on demand. You can do that programmatically by using the `<CFA_PAGECACHEFLUSH>` tag, which takes a page name as an attribute. This is useful when you've made database changes and want to force them to show up immediately in pages that are normally cached. It's also possible to force `<CFA_PAGE>` to flush a page cache by setting `request.cfa.sitemodel.flushpagecache` to `Yes` and requesting the page in a browser.

The security services managed by SiteMinder also include their own cache settings. During development, especially of login or security aspects of the site, it's useful to turn off security caching. However, security caching should be turned on in the development environment through the ColdFusion administrator. For more information on this, see Chapter 16.

In short, Spectra provides you a level of control over what and how items are cached that wasn't previously available in ColdFusion. By studying your site to determine what data does *not* need to be refreshed in real time (which for many sites is the majority of it) and appropriately turning on caching, you can get a significant performance boost.

Caching Pages You use the Site Layout Model to turn caching on at the site, page, or section level. To do this, follow these steps:

1. Click Site Design.
2. Open Site Layout Manager in the navigation area.
3. Click Site Layout Model.
4. Navigate to the site, page, or section for which you want to turn on caching.
5. Click the element you want to cache (see Figure 24.13).

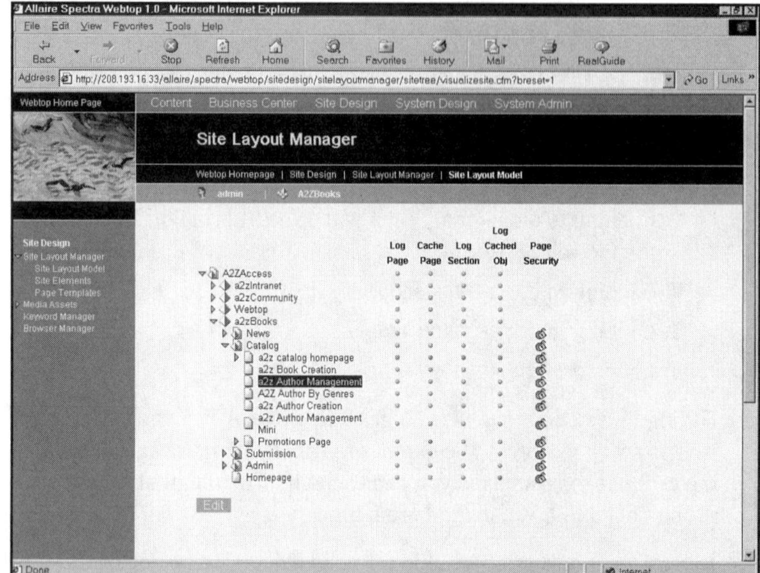

FIGURE 24.13
The Site Layout Manager provides an interface for managing caching at the site, section, and page levels.

6. Click Edit at the bottom of the list to open the Site Component Editor.
7. Adjust the cache setting by selecting from the Page Caching drop-down list. Choose Yes.
8. If you turn on caching, enter a directory in the Cache Directory text box. This is where Spectra will store the cached version of the page (see Figure 24.14).

These steps turn on caching for this page. The next time the page is requested, Spectra creates a file on disk in the directory specified in the Cache Directory text box. Subsequent calls to the page will use the disk file to return the page to the user more quickly.

FIGURE 24.14
The Site Component Editor allows you to define how the site, section, or page will be cached.

Site Component Editor

Label	a2z Author Managemer
Type	PAGE
Parent	[SECTION] Catalog
Absolute Server Path	C:\Inetpub\wwwroot\a2z\catalog\manag browse...
Page Caching	Yes
Cache Directory	C:\InetPub\wwwroot\a2z\catalog\ browse...
Cache TimeOut	12:00:00 AM 12/30/1899
Page Logging	na
Cached Object Logging	na
Section Logging	na

OK Cancel

Container and Content Item Caching You can also turn on caching for containers. This is controlled through the Container Editor. To see how this works in the a2zBooks application, follow these steps:

1. Log into the a2zBooks site in Design mode. You can do this by requesting `http://YOUR_A2Z_MACHINE/A2Z/index.cfm?designmode=1` and then logging in as `admin` with password `admin`.
2. Click Browse Our Catalog to open the main catalog page in Design mode (see Figure 24.15).

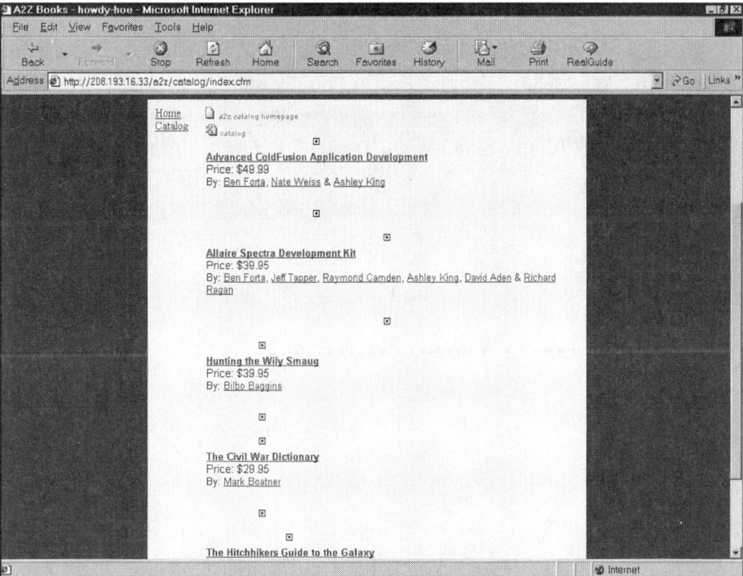

FIGURE 24.15
This shows the main catalog page in Design mode—which makes the editing widgets available.

3. Click Home Page Right to open the Container Editor.
4. Click Settings.
5. Enter **3** in the Timeout text box to set the cache to expire every 3 hours.
6. From the Type drop-down box, select Server (see Figure 24.16). This tells Spectra to cache the information in the server scope. You can also select File, Request, or Session. If you select File, provide a directory in which the cached information will be stored.

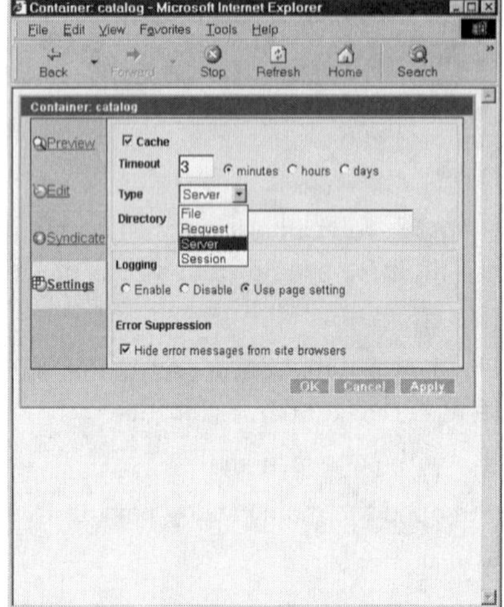

FIGURE 24.16
The Container Editor gives you access to set caching for the container. The cache can be stored as a file or in the server, session, or request scope.

You can also control Content Item caching with the `BUSECACHE` attribute of the `<CFA_CONTENTOBJECT>` tag. You additionally specify whether the Content Item should be cached in a file or the server, session, or request scope. For details on syntax and usage, see Appendix A, "Allaire Spectra Tags." ●

PART V

Appendixes

APPENDIX A

Allaire Spectra Tags

In this appendix

A Quick Reference to Spectra's Tags

Allaire Spectra is a massive collection of tags—more than 200 of them. Effective Spectra development requires an understanding of, and access to, all these tags. To facilitate this, even if you are unsure of tag names, the tags listed in this appendix are divided by service. The notable exceptions to this are the user interface and general utility tags, which aren't truly tied to any service, but are categorized under User Interface and Utilities for organizational purposes.

This appendix isn't a substitute for the Spectra documentation. It's intended to provide rapid access to basic tag information, syntax, and attributes only. Refer to the documentation for additional information and for usage examples.

NOTE The Allaire Spectra documentation separates the Spectra Tags into two types: Spectra tags and PITA tags. The PITA tags are primarily the lesser used tags (for example, tags used by the WebTop itself), but that distinction is arbitrary, and the truth is that all the tags are useful at some point. For this reason, this appendix doesn't make any distinction between these tags and groups them together for easier reference.

Browser Binding Tags

These tags are used to perform browser detection operations and to maintain a browser capabilities database.

<cfa_browser>

`<cfa_browser>` uses a maintainable browser capabilities database to provide information about a specific browser. This tag is used in implementing browser-aware interfaces. Calling this tag populates the `request.cfa.browser` structure with client-specific browser capabilities. If the client browser is unknown to Spectra, the structure is populated with options that Spectra deems most probably accurate.

Syntax:

```
<cfa_browser>
```

`<cfa_browser>` takes no attributes.

<cfa_browserCacheRefresh>

`<cfa_browserCacheRefresh>` is used to force a refresh of the browser definition cache. This is only needed if browser definitions are changed, in which case, it must be used.

Syntax:

```
<cfa_browserCacheRefresh>
```

<cfa_browserCacheRefresh> takes no attributes.

<cfa_browserDelete>

<cfa_browserDelete> is used to remove a browser definition from the browser capabilities database. Generally, this should never be used; browser definitions should always be kept (even for older infrequently used browsers).

Syntax:

```
<cfa_browserDelete userAgent="">
```

Attribute:

Attribute	Description
userAgent	Required browser to be deleted

<cfa_browserUpdate>

<cfa_browserUpdate> is used to update (or insert) a browser definition into the browser capabilities database. These are then returned by <cfa_browser> calls.

Syntax:

```
<cfa_browserUpdate bActiveXControls=""
                   bBackgroundSounds=""
                   bCookies=""
                   bCrawler=""
                   bDHTML=""
                   bFrames=""
                   bJavaApplets=""
                   bJavascript=""
                   browser=""
                   bStyleSheets=""
                   bTables=""
                   bVBScript=""
                   javascriptVer=""
                   majorversion=""
                   minorVersion=""
                   name=""
                   parentAgent=""
                   userAgent=""
>
```

Attributes:

Attribute	Description
`bActiveXControls`	Optional flag specifying whether this browser supports the use of client-side ActiveX controls
`bBackgroundSounds`	Optional flag specifying whether this browser supports the use of background sounds
`bCookies`	Optional flag specifying whether this browser supports the use of persistent client-side cookies
`bCrawler`	Optional flag specifying whether this browser is actually a search engine
`bDHTML`	Optional flag specifying whether this browser supports the use of dynamic HTML (DHTML)
`bFrames`	Optional flag specifying whether this browser supports the use of frames
`bJavaApplets`	Optional flag specifying whether this browser supports the use of embedded client-side Java applets
`bJavascript`	Optional flag specifying whether this browser supports the use of client-side JavaScript
`browser`	Optional browser information
`bStyleSheets`	Optional flag specifying whether this browser supports the use of cascading style sheets (CSS)
`bTables`	Optional flag specifying whether this browser supports the use of tables
`bVBScript`	Optional flag specifying whether this browser supports the use of client-side VBScript
`javascriptVer`	Optional JavaScript version supported
`majorVer`	Optional browser major version number
`minorVer`	Optional browser minor version number
`name`	Optional browser name (used for display purposes)
`parentAgent`	Optional browser parent (used to identify child browsers)
`userAgent`	Required browser to be updated

Content Management Tags

These tags provide the basic building blocks for all content management operations.

<cfa_contentObject>

`<cfa_contentObject>` invokes a specified method for one or more content objects. Multiple objects can be passed to this tag, as long as they are of the same object type. The object itself can be specified using any one of the attributes `lObjectIDs`, `objectID`, `stObject`, or `stObjects`.

Syntax:

```
<cfa_contentObject bAbortOnUnauthorizedAccess=""
                   bLogging=""
                   bSecure=""
                   bUseCache=""
                   cacheDir=""
                   cacheType=""
                   dataSource=""
                   dtCacheTimeout=""
                   lObjectIDs=""
                   method=""
                   objectID=""
                   r_stObjects=""
                   r_stParams=""
                   stObject=""
                   stObjects=""
                   stParams=""
>
```

Attributes:

Attribute	Description
bAbortOnUnauthorizedAccess	Optional flag specifying behavior upon security error. The default is global request.cfa.security.bAbortOnUnauthorizedAccess value.
bLogging	Optional logging flag. The default is NO.
bSecure	Optional flag to specify whether to check user permission to perform requested task. The default is NO.
bUseCache	Optional flag to specify whether to used cached copy of object if it exists (if not, create one). The default is NO.
cacheDir	Required only if cacheType is FILE. Path for cache files.
cacheType	Optional cache type (only used if bUseCache is YES). Options are SESSION, REQUEST, SERVER, and FILE. The default is SESSION.
dataSource	Required datasource of ContentObject Database.
dtCacheTimeout	Optional cache reset time used if cacheType is SESSION. The default is 0.

continues

continued

Attribute	Description
lObjectIDs	List of object IDs to invoke. Required if no other ID is specified.
method	Required name of method to invoke.
objectID	ID of object to invoke. Required if no other ID is specified.
r_stObjects	Optional name of variable into which content item structures are stored.
r_stParams	Optional name of variable into which content item parameters are stored.
stObject	Content object structure using objectID as the key. Required if no other ID is specified.
stObjects	Array of content object structures using objectID as the key. Required if no other ID is specified.
stParams	Optional structure containing method parameters.

<cfa_contentObjectCreate>

`<cfa_contentObjectCreate>` creates an instance of an object. This tag is used in create handlers.

Syntax:

```
<cfa_contentObjectCreate dataSource=""
                         label=""
                         method=""
                         objectID=""
                         r_id=""
                         stParams=""
                         stProperties=""
                         typeID=""
>
```

Attributes:

Attribute	Description
dataSource	Required datasource of ContentObject Database.
label	Optional name of the content item.
method	Optional name of the initialization method to invoke. The default is `CREATE`.
objectID	Optional ID of the content item. If not specified, ID will be created and returned in `r_id`.

Attribute	Description
r_id	Optional name of variable into which the tag places the object ID for the content item.
stParams	Name of variable into which content item parameters are stored. Required only if method is specified.
stProperties	Optional object properties structure.
typeID	Required ID of the content type to create.

<cfa_contentObjectCreateEmbeddedFromOriginal>

<cfa_contentObjectCreateEmbeddedFromOriginal> creates an embedded object from a standalone object. Either originalObjectID or stOriginalObject must be specified.

Syntax:

```
<cfa_contentObjectCreateEmbeddedFromOriginal dataSource=""
                                             objectID=""
                                             originalObjectID=""
                                             stOriginalObject=""
>
```

Attributes:

Attribute	Description
dataSource	Required datasource of ContentObject Database.
objectID	Optional pointer to the embedded object.
originalObjectID	ID of original object. Required if stOriginalObject not specified.
stOriginalObject	Structure containing original object. Required if originalObjectID not specified.

<cfa_contentObjectCreateOriginalFromEmbedded>

<cfa_contentObjectCreateOriginalFromEmbedded> creates a standalone object from an embedded object. Either embeddedObjectID or stEmbeddedObject must be specified.

Syntax:

```
<cfa_contentObjectCreateOriginalFromEmbedded dataSource=""
                                             embeddedObjectID=""
                                             objectID=""
                                             r_objectID=""
                                             stEmbeddedObject=""
>
```

Attributes:

Attribute	Description
`dataSource`	Required datasource of ContentObject Database.
`embeddedObjectID`	ID of embedded object. Required if `stEmbeddedObject` not specified.
`objectID`	Optional pointer to the standalone object.
`r_objectID`	Optional string containing variable to store the object ID of the standalone object.
`stEmbeddedObject`	Structure containing embedded object. Required if `embeddedObjectID` is not specified.

<cfa_contentObjectData>

`<cfa_contentObjectData>` is used to manage an object's properties.

Syntax:

```
<cfa_contentObjectData bSystemEnabled=""
                       dataSource=""
                       ISOLanguage=""
                       objectID=""
                       stObject=""
                       stProperties=""
>
  ...
</cfa_contentObjectData>
```

or

```
<cfa_contentObjectData bSystemEnabled=""
                       dataSource=""
                       ISOLanguage=""
                       objectID=""
                       stObject=""
                       stProperties=""
/>
```

Attributes:

Attribute	Description
`bSystemEnabled`	Optional flag used to prevent system objects from being overwritten. If `NO`, an error will throw if an overwrite is attempted. The default is `NO`.
`dataSource`	Required datasource of ContentObject Database.
`ISOLanguage`	Optional two-character ISO language code. The default is `en` (English).

Attribute	Description
objectID	Required object ID.
stObject	Optional structure containing content item data.
stProperties	Optional structure containing property name-value pairs.

<cfa_contentObjectDelete>

<cfa_contentObjectDelete> is used to delete a content object.

Syntax:

```
<cfa_contentObjectDelete bSystemEnabled=""
                         dataSource=""
                         method=""
                         objectID=""
                         stParams=""
>
```

Attributes:

Attribute	Description
bSystemEnabled	Optional flag used to prevent system objects from being deleted. If NO, an error will throw if a delete is attempted. The default is NO.
dataSource	Required datasource of ContentObject Database.
method	Optional method to invoke prior to deletion.
objectID	Required object ID.
stParams	Optional structure passed to method.

<cfa_contentObjectFind>

<cfa_contentObjectFind> is used to retrieve objects based on properties or meta data. Other than dataSource, all of this tag's non-return attributes are used to filter search results.

Syntax:

```
<cfa_contentObjectFind bActiveOnly=""
                       bNonArchivedOnly=""
                       createdBy=""
                       dataSource=""
                       dtCreatedAfter=""
                       dtCreatedBefore=""
                       dtUpdatedAfter=""
                       dtUpdatedBefore=""
                       fullTextSearchCriteria=""
                       label=""
```

```
                              lastUpdatedBy=""
                              lFullTextSearch=""
                              lPropertiesPrecedence=""
                              nMaxCount=""
                              r_lObjects=""
                              r_qObjects=""
                              r_stObjects=""
                              stFilter=""
                              stProperties=""
                              typeID=""
>
```

Attributes:

Attribute	Description
`bActiveOnly`	Optional flag specifying whether to search only active objects. The default is `YES`.
`bNonArchivedOnly`	Optional flag specifying whether to search only non-archived objects. The default is `YES`.
`createdBy`	Optional string containing name of user who created an object.
`dataSource`	Required datasource of ContentObject Database.
`dtCreatedAfter`	Optional created after date.
`dtCreatedBefore`	Optional created before date.
`dtUpdatedAfter`	Optional updated after date.
`dtUpdatedBefore`	Optional updated before date.
`fullTextSearchCriteria`	Optional Verity search string.
`label`	Optional label name.
`lastUpdatedBy`	Optional string containing name of user who last updated an object.
`lFullTextSearch`	Optional list of search properties for string specified in `fullTextSearchCriteria`.
`lPropertiesPrecedence`	List of properties in `stProperties` in order of search priority. Required if `stProperties` is used.
`nMaxCount`	Optional maximum number of items to retrieve. The default is `10000`.
`r_lObjects`	Optional string containing name of variable to store object ID.
`r_qObjects`	Optional string containing name of query to store object data.
`r_stObjects`	Optional string containing name of query to store object structures.

Attribute	Description
stFilter	Optional filter structure containing the name value pairs of the filters to be used.
stProperties	Optional structure containing property name value pairs.
typeID	Required content type ID.

<cfa_contentObjectGet>

<cfa_contentObjectGet> is used to retrieve an item's properties.

Syntax:

```
<cfa_contentObjectGet dataSource=""
                      objectID=""
                      r_stObject=""
>
```

<cfa_contentObjectGet> Attributes

Attributes:

Attribute	Description
dataSource	Required datasource of ContentObject Database
objectID	Required object ID
r_stObject	Required name of the structure to store object data

<cfa_contentObjectGetMultiple>

<cfa_contentObjectGetMultiple> returns properties for multiple objects.

Syntax:

```
<cfa_contentObjectGetMultiple bActiveOnly=""
                              bNonArchivedOnly=""
                              createdBy=""
                              dataSource=""
                              lastUpdatedBy=""
                              lObjectIDs=""
                              nMaxCount=""
                              r_qObjects=""
                              r_stObjects=""
                              typeID=""
>
```

Attributes:

Attribute	Description
bActiveOnly	Optional flag specifying whether to search only active objects. The default is YES.
bNonArchivedOnly	Optional flag specifying whether to search only non-archived objects. The default is YES.
createdBy	Optional string containing name of user who created an object.
dataSource	Required datasource of ContentObject Database.
lastUpdatedBy	Optional string containing name of user who last updated an object.
lObjectIDs	Optional list of desired object IDs.
nMaxCount	Optional maximum number of items to retrieve. The default is 10000.
r_qObjects	Optional string containing name of query to store object data.
r_stObjects	Optional string containing name of query to store object structures.
typeID	Required content type ID.

<cfa_contentObjectGetType>

<cfa_contentObjectGetType> is used to return type information for an object. Either r_stType or r_typeID is required.

Syntax:

```
<cfa_contentObjectGetType dataSource=""
                          objectID=""
                          r_stType=""
                          r_typeID=""
                          stOwnerObject=""
>
```

Attributes:

Attribute	Description
dataSource	Required datasource of ContentObject Database.
objectID	Required object ID.
r_stType	String containing the variable to store retrieved type structure. Required if r_typeID isn't specified.

Attribute	Description
r_typeID	String containing the variable to store the retrieved type ID. Required if r_stType isn't specified.
stOwnerObject	Required object structure of owning object.

<cfa_contentObjectIsLocked>

<cfa_contentObjectIsLocked> returns a flag indicating whether an object is currently locked. Possible return values are LOCKED (if locked by another user), LOCKEDBYUSER (if locked by current user), or FREE (if not locked).

Syntax:

```
<cfa_contentObjectIsLocked dataSource=""
                           objectID=""
                           r_status=""
>
```

Attributes:

Attribute	Description
dataSource	Required datasource of ContentObject Database
objectID	Required object ID
r_status	Required string containing the variable to store the lock status

<cfa_contentObjectLock>

<cfa_contentObjectLock> attempts to lock an object and returns the status of the lock operation.

Syntax:

```
<cfa_contentObjectLock dataSource=""
                       objectID=""
                       r_bSuccess=""
>
```

Attributes:

Attribute	Description
dataSource	Required datasource of ContentObject Database
objectID	Required object ID
r_bSuccess	Optional string containing variable to store lock success or failure flag

<cfa_contentObjectProperty>

`<cfa_contentObjectProperty>` is used within a `<cfa_contentObjectData>` tag to set individual object properties. No `datasource` or `objectID` is passed to this tag; the values passed to `<cfa_contentObjectData>` will be used.

Syntax:

```
<cfa_contentObjectLock name=""
                       value=""
>
```

Attributes:

Attribute	Description
`name`	Required property name
`value`	Required property value

<cfa_contentObjectUnlock>

`<cfa_contentObjectUnlock>` attempts to unlock an object and returns the status of the unlock operation.

Syntax:

```
<cfa_contentObjectUnlock dataSource=""
                         objectID=""
                         r_bSuccess=""
>
```

Attributes:

Attribute	Description
`dataSource`	Required datasource of ContentObject Database
`objectID`	Required object ID
`r_bSuccess`	Optional string containing variable to store unlock success or failure flag

Exception Handling Tags

These tags are used to throw and display errors.

<cfa_reThrow>

<cfa_reThrow> rethrows a ColdFusion exception as a Spectra exception.

Syntax:

```
<cfa_reThrow>
```

<cfa_reThrow> takes no attributes.

<cfa_showError>

<cfa_showError> displays Spectra exception text.

Syntax:

```
<cfa_showError displayTemplate="">
```

Attribute:

Attribute	Description
displayTemplate	Optional name of template to use to display error text

<cfa_throw>

<cfa_throw> throws a Spectra exception. Use this tag to handle occasional exceptions when success is expected. This tag isn't designed to be used to test the results of operations that are expected to fail; in that scenario, standard conditional processing is recommended.

Syntax:

```
<cfa_throw bAbort=""
           errorCode=""
           ISOLanguage=""
           stErrorData=""
>
```

Attributes:

Attribute	Description
bAbort	Flag indicating whether to abort processing after throwing the error. The default is NO.
errorCode	Required five-digit error code number.
ISOLanguage	Optional two-character ISO language code. The default is en (English).
stErrorData	Optional name of the structure to contain error data.

Logging Tags

These tags are used to interact with Spectra log data.

<cfa_log>

`<cfa_log>` is used to log server activity.

Syntax:

```
<cfa_log method=""
        stObjects=""
>
```

Attributes:

Attribute	Description
method	Required name of the method being logged
stObjects	Required structure containing information to be logged

<cfa_logFileConvertToStructure>

`<cfa_logFileConvertToStructure>` converts internal log file information into a useable structure containing the following keys: `Method`, `SessionID`, `UserID`, `TypeID`, `ObjectID`, `UserAgent`, `DtTimeStamp`, `RemoteAddr`, and `Label`.

Syntax:

```
<cfa_logFileConvertToStructure logEntryMaxCount=""
                               logFile=""
                               r_stLogFile=""
>
```

Attributes:

Attribute	Description
logEntryMaxCount	Optional maximum number of rows to return. The default is `1000`.
logFile	Optional name of log file to read. The default is `c:\cfalog.txt`.
r_stLogFile	Required name of the structure in which to store the retrieved log information.

<cfa_processLogFile>

`<cfa_processLogFile>` writes the current scope log to the log file.

Syntax:

```
<cfa_processLogFile bEnableNativeAndCustomHandler=""
                    customHandler=""
                    logFile=""
>
```

Attributes:

Attribute	Description
`bEnableNativeAndCustomHandler`	Optional flag used to specify whether to use custom log file processing. The default is `NO`.
`customHandler`	Optional path of custom handler.
`logFile`	Optional name of log file to read. The default is file referred to in `request.cfa.serverlogFilePath`.

Messaging Tags

These tags are used to create and manage message queues and to send messages to objects.

<cfa_messageCreate>

`<cfa_messageCreate>` is used to create a new message for submission to a message queue.

Syntax:

```
<cfa_messageCreate dataSource=""
                   messageQueueID=""
                   objectID=""
                   ownerObjectID=""
                   r_objectID=""
                   stMessageData=""
>
```

Attributes:

Attribute	Description
`dataSource`	Required datasource of ContentObject Database.
`messageQueueID`	Required ID of queue to process message.
`objectID`	Optional ID of new message. ID will be generated automatically if not specified.

continues

continued

Attribute	Description
ownerObjectID	Optional ID of message recipient.
r_objectID	Optional string containing variable to store the object ID of the created message.
stMessageData	Required structure containing the message.

<cfa_messageDelete>

<cfa_messageDelete> is used to delete a message.

Syntax:

```
<cfa_messageDelete dataSource=""
                   messageID=""
                   messageQueueID=""
>
```

Attributes:

Attribute	Description
dataSource	Required datasource of ContentObject Database
messageID	Required ID of message to delete
messageQueueID	Required ID of queue containing the message

<cfa_messageQueue>

<cfa_messageQueue> invokes the messaging service specifying a method to be executed.

Syntax:

```
<cfa_messageQueue dataSource=""
                  messageQueueID=""
                  method=""
                  ownerObjectID=""
                  r_stObjects=""
                  r_stResultsParam=""
                  stMessageData=""
>
```

Attributes:

Attribute	Description
dataSource	Required datasource of ContentObject Database
messageQueueID	Required ID of the message queue

Attribute	Description
method	Required name of method to invoke
ownerObjectID	Optional ID of associated messages
r_stObjects	Optional name of the structure to store objects matching ownerObjectID
r_stResultsParams	Optional name of variable to store results parameter populated by the handler
stMessageData	Optional message header and body structure

<cfa_messageQueueCreate>

<cfa_messageQueueCreate> creates a new message queue.

Syntax:

```
<cfa_messageQueueCreate dataSource=""
                        handlerRoot=""
                        label=""
                        objectID=""
                        r_objectID=""
>
```

Attributes:

Attribute	Description
dataSource	Required datasource of ContentObject Database.
handlerRoot	Optional directory containing message queue handlers.
label	Required queue name.
objectID	Optional ID for new message queue. If not provided, one will be assigned automatically.
r_objectID	Optional string containing variable to store the object ID of the created message queue.

<cfa_messageQueueDelete>

<cfa_messageQueueDelete> deletes a message queue.

Syntax:

```
<cfa_messageQueueDelete dataSource=""
                        handlerRoot=""
                        messageQueueID=""
>
```

Attributes:

Attribute	Description
dataSource	Required datasource of ContentObject Database
handlerRoot	Optional directory containing message queue handlers
messageQueueID	Required ID of queue to be deleted

<cfa_messageQueueGet>

<cfa_messageQueueGet> retrieves the contents of a message queue.

Syntax:

```
<cfa_messageQueueGet dataSource=""
                     messageQueueID=""
                     r_stMessageQueue=""
>
```

Attributes:

Attribute	Description
dataSource	Required datasource of ContentObject Database
messageQueueID	Required ID of queue to be retrieved
r_stMessageQueue	Optional name of variable to store the message queue

<cfa_messageQueueMethodAdd>

<cfa_messageQueueMethodAdd> adds a new method to a queue specification.

Syntax:

```
<cfa_messageQueueMethodAdd dataSource=""
                           handler=""
                           messageQueueID=""
                           method=""
>
```

Attributes:

Attribute	Description
dataSource	Required datasource of ContentObject Database
handler	Required name of handler file
messageQueueID	Required ID of queue to which method is to be added
method	Required method name

<cfa_messageQueueMethodDelete>

`<cfa_messageQueueMethodDelete>` deletes a method from a queue specification.

Syntax:

```
<cfa_messageQueueMethodDelete dataSource=""
                              messageQueueID=""
                              method=""
>
```

Attributes:

Attribute	Description
dataSource	Required datasource of ContentObject Database
messageQueueID	Required ID of queue from which method is to be deleted
method	Required method name

<cfa_messageQueueMethodUpdate>

`<cfa_messageQueueMethodUpdate>` updates an existing method in a queue specification.

Syntax:

```
<cfa_messageQueueMethodUpdate dataSource=""
                              handler=""
                              messageQueueID=""
                              method=""
>
```

Attributes:

Attribute	Description
dataSource	Required datasource of ContentObject Database
handler	Required name of handler file
messageQueueID	Required ID of queue in which method is to be updated
method	Required method name

<cfa_messageQueueUpdate>

`<cfa_messageQueueUpdate>` updates an existing message queue.

Syntax:

```
<cfa_messageQueueUpdate dataSource=""
                        handlerRoot=""
                        label=""
                        messageQueueID=""
>
```

Attributes:

Attribute	Description
dataSource	Required datasource of ContentObject Database
handlerRoot	Optional directory containing message queue handlers
label	Optional new queue name
messageQueueID	Required ID of message queue to be updated

<cfa_messagingHandler>

<cfa_messagingHandler> creates a scope name for the handled object and loops through the queued messages. Before using this tag, the queue must have been created, and one or more messages must have been queued.

Syntax:

```
<cfa_messagingHandler ISOLanguage=""
                      object=""
                      result=""
                      separator=""
>
...
</cfa_messagingHandler>
```

Attributes:

Attribute	Description
ISOLanguage	Optional two character ISO language code. The default is en (English).
object	Optional name for variable to contain object data.
result	Optional name for variable for result handle.
separator	Optional text to insert between loop iterations.

Meta Data Tags

These tags are used to create and manage meta data and meta data hierarchies.

<cfa_metadataCategoryCreate>

<cfa_metadataCategoryCreate> creates a meta data category and adds it to a hierarchy.

Syntax:

```
<cfa_metadataCategoryCreate categoryID=""
                            dataSource=""
                            hierarchyID=""
```

```
                                  label=""
                                  parentID=""
                                  r_objectID=""
>
```

Attributes:

Attribute	Description
categoryID	Optional category ID. Will be automatically assigned if not specified.
dataSource	Required datasource of ContentObject Database.
hierchary_id	Required meta data hierarchy ID.
label	Required category name.
parentID	Optional ID of parent associated with this category.
r_objectID	Optional name of variable to store new category ID.

<cfa_metadataCategoryDelete>

<cfa_metadataCategoryDelete> deletes a meta data category and removes it to a hierarchy.

Syntax:

```
<cfa_metadataCategoryDelete categoryID=""
                             dataSource=""
>
```

Attributes:

Attribute	Description
categoryID	Required ID of category to delete
dataSource	Required datasource of ContentObject Database

<cfa_metadataCategoryGet>

<cfa_metadataCategoryGet> creates a meta data category.

Syntax:

```
<cfa_metadataCategoryGet categoryID=""
                          dataSource=""
                          r_stCategory=""
>
```

Attributes:

Attribute	Description
categoryID	Optional ID of category
dataSource	Required datasource of ContentObject Database
r_stCategory	Optional variable to contain structure of category

<cfa_metadataCategoryKeywordAdd>

<cfa_metadataCategoryKeywordAdd> associates a keyword with a specified category.

Syntax:

```
<cfa_metadataCategoryKeywordAdd dataSource=""
                                categoryID=""
                                keyword=""
>
```

Attributes:

Attribute	Description
dataSource	Required datasource of ContentObject Database
categoryID	Required ID of category to which to associate keyword
keyword	Required keyword

<cfa_metadataCategoryKeywordDelete>

<cfa_metadataCategoryKeywordDelete> deletes a keyword association from a specified category.

Syntax:

```
<cfa_metadataCategoryKeywordDelete dataSource=""
                                   categoryID=""
                                   keyword=""
>
```

Attributes:

Attribute	Description
dataSource	Required datasource of ContentObject Database
categoryID	Required ID of category from which to delete keyword
keyword	Required keyword

<cfa_metadataCategoryObjectFind>

`<cfa_metadataCategoryObjectFind>` retrieves content items associated with meta data categories.

Syntax:

```
<cfa_metadataCategoryObjectFind dataSource=""
                                lCategoryIDs=""
                                lTypeIDs=""
                                r_qObjects=""
                                r_stObjects=""
                                resultSet=""
>
```

Attributes:

Attribute	Description
dataSource	Required datasource of ContentObject Database.
lCategoryIDs	Required comma-delimited list of category IDs.
lTypeIDs	Optional list of type IDs for which to search.
r_qObjects	Optional name of query to store retrieved items.
r_stObjects	Optional name of the structure to store retrieved items.
resultSet	Optional result desired specifier, either FULL (for all data) or KEY (for object IDs). The default is KEY.

<cfa_metadataCategoryUpdate>

`<cfa_metadataCategoryUpdate>` updates a meta data category.

Syntax:

```
<cfa_metadataCategoryUpdate categoryID=""
                            dataSource=""
                            stCategory=""
>
```

Attributes:

Attribute	Description
categoryID	Required ID of category to update
dataSource	Required datasource of ContentObject Database
stCategory	Required category structure

<cfa_metadataHierarchyAssignRelatedType>

`<cfa_metadataHierarchyAssignRelatedType>` assigns a list of object types related to the meta data hierarchy.

Syntax:

```
<cfa_metadataHierarchyAssignRelatedType dataSource=""
                                        hierarchyID=""
                                        lRelatedTypes=""
>
```

Attributes:

Attribute	Description
`dataSource`	Required datasource of ContentObject Database
`hierarchyID`	Required hierarchy ID
`lRelatedTypes`	Required list of object types to be assigned to specified hierarchy

<cfa_metadataHierarchyCategoryAdd>

`<cfa_metadataHierarchyCategoryAdd>` is used to add a category to a hierarchy.

Syntax:

```
<cfa_metadataHierarchyCategoryAdd categoryID=""
                                  dataSource=""
                                  hierarchyID=""
                                  label=""
                                  stParents=""
>
```

Attributes:

Attribute	Description
`categoryID`	Required ID of category to add.
`dataSource`	Required datasource of ContentObject Database.
`hierarchyID`	Required hierarchy ID.
`label`	Required category name to add.
`stParents`	Optional structure listing category parents. Defaults to `root` level.

<cfa_metadataHierarchyCategoryUpdate>

<cfa_metadataHierarchyCategoryUpdate> is used to update a category in a hierarchy.

Syntax:

```
<cfa_metadataHierarchyCategoryUpdate categoryID=""
                                     dataSource=""
                                     hierarchyID=""
                                     label=""
                                     stParents=""
>
```

Attributes:

Attribute	Description
categoryID	Required ID of category to update.
dataSource	Required datasource of ContentObject Database.
hierarchyID	Required hierarchy ID.
label	Required category name.
stParents	Optional structure listing category parents. Defaults to root level.

<cfa_metadataHierarchyCreate>

<cfa_metadataHierarchyCreate> creates a new meta data hierarchy.

Syntax:

```
<cfa_metadataHierarchyCreate dataSource=""
                             hierarchyID=""
                             label=""
                             lRelatedTypes=""
                             r_objectID=""
>
```

Attributes:

Attribute	Description
dataSource	Required datasource of ContentObject Database.
hierarchyID	Optional hierarchy ID. Will be assigned automatically if not specified.
label	Required hierarchy name.
lRelatedTypes	Optional list of object IDs to be assigned to specified hierarchy.
r_objectID	Optional variable to store new hierarchy ID.

<cfa_metadataHierarchyDelete>

`<cfa_metadataHierarchyDelete>` deletes a meta data hierarchy, including all categories under the hierarchy.

Syntax:

```
<cfa_metadataHierarchyDelete dataSource=""
                             hierarchyID=""
>
```

Attributes:

Attribute	Description
dataSource	Required datasource of ContentObject Database
hierarchyID	Required hierarchy ID to be deleted

<cfa_metadataHierarchyEditor>

`<cfa_metadataHierarchyEditor>` creates a tree control that can be used to add or remove hierarchy categories.

Syntax:

```
<cfa_metadataHierarchyEditor bNewWindow=""
                             dataSource=""
                             hierarchyID=""
>
```

Attributes:

Attribute	Description
bNewWindow	Optional flag specifying whether the tree control should be displayed in a new window or the existing window. The default is `NO`.
dataSource	Required datasource of ContentObject Database.
hierarchyID	Optional hierarchy ID.

<cfa_metadataHierarchyGet>

`<cfa_metadataHierarchyGet>` creates a meta data category.

Syntax:

```
<cfa_metadataHierarchyGet dataSource=""
                          hierarchyID=""
                          r_stHierarchy=""
>
```

Attributes:

Attribute	Description
dataSource	Required datasource of ContentObject Database
hierarchyID	Required hierarchy ID
r_stHierarchy	Optional variable to contain hierarchy structure

<cfa_metadataHierarchyUnAssignRelatedType>

<cfa_metadataHierarchyUnAssignRelatedType> removes a list of object types from a meta data hierarchy.

Syntax:

```
<cfa_metadataHierarchyUnAssignRelatedType dataSource=""
                                          hierarchyID=""
                                          lRelatedTypes=""
>
```

Attributes:

Attribute	Description
dataSource	Required datasource of ContentObject Database
hierarchyID	Required hierarchy ID
lRelatedTypes	Required list of object IDs to be removed from specified hierarchy

<cfa_metadataHierarchyUpdate>

<cfa_metadataHierarchyUpdate> updates a meta data category.

Syntax:

```
<cfa_metadataHierarchyUpdate dataSource=""
                             hierarchyID=""
                             stHierarchy=""
>
```

Attributes:

Attribute	Description
dataSource	Required datasource of ContentObject Database
hierarchyID	Required hierarchy ID
stHierarchy	Required updated hierarchy structure

<cfa_metadataIndexAll>

`<cfa_metadataIndexAll>` reindexes all meta data.

Syntax:

```
<cfa_metadataIndexAll dataSource="">
```

Attribute:

Attribute	Description
dataSource	Required datasource of ContentObject Database

<cfa_metadataIndexDelete>

`<cfa_metadataIndexDelete>` removes meta data from an index for specified objects.

Syntax:

```
<cfa_metadataIndexDelete dataSource=""
                         lObectIDs=""
>
```

Attributes:

Attribute	Description
dataSource	Required datasource of ContentObject Database
lObjectIDs	Required list of objects to remove

<cfa_metadataIndexUpdate>

`<cfa_metadataIndexUpdate>` indexes meta data for specified objects.

Syntax:

```
<cfa_metadataIndexUpdate dataSource=""
                         lObectIDs=""
>
```

Attributes:

Attribute	Description
dataSource	Required datasource of ContentObject Database
lObjectIDs	Required list of objects to update

<cfa_metadataKeywordObjectFind>

`<cfa_metadataKeywordObjectFind>` retrieves content items associated with specific keywords.

Syntax:

```
<cfa_metadataKeywordObjectFind dataSource=""
                               keywords=""
                               lCategoryIDs=""
                               lTypeIDs=""
                               r_qObjects=""
                               r_stObjects=""
                               resultSet=""
>
```

Attributes:

Attribute	Description
`dataSource`	Required datasource of ContentObject Database.
`keywords`	Required list of keywords for which to search.
`lCategoryIDs`	Required comma-delimited list of category IDs.
`lTypeIDs`	Optional list of type IDs for which to search.
`r_qObjects`	Optional name of query to store retrieved items.
`r_stObjects`	Optional name of the structure to store retrieved items.
`resultSet`	Optional result desired specifier, either `FULL` (for all data) or `KEY` (for object IDs). The default is `KEY`.

<cfa_metadataObjectKeywordAssign>

`<cfa_metadataObjectKeywordAssign>` assigns keywords to an existing content item.

Syntax:

```
<cfa_metadataObjectKeywordAssign dataSource=""
                                 objectID=""
                                 stKeywords=""
>
```

Attributes:

Attribute	Description
`dataSource`	Required datasource of ContentObject Database
`objectID`	Required object ID
`stKeywords`	Required structure containing meta data in key value pairs

<cfa_metadataObjectKeywordRemove>

`<cfa_metadataObjectKeywordRemove>` removes keywords from a content item.

Syntax:

```
<cfa_metadataObjectKeywordRemove dataSource=""
                                 objectID=""
                                 stKeywords=""
>
```

Attributes:

Attribute	Description
dataSource	Required datasource of ContentObject Database
objectID	Required object ID
stKeywords	Required structure containing meta data in key value pairs

<cfa_metadataPicker>

`<cfa_metadataPicker>` creates a tree control that can be used to assign or remove object keywords.

Syntax:

```
<cfa_metadataPicker bNewWindow=""
                    dataSource=""
                    objectID=""
>
```

Attributes:

Attribute	Description
bNewWindow	Optional flag specifying whether the tree control should be displayed in a new window or the existing window. The default is NO.
dataSource	Required datasource of ContentObject Database.
objectID	Required object ID.

Object Packager Tags

These tags are used to install objects and to package (prepare) objects for moving or copying between installations.

<cfa_objectInstallCOAPI>

`<cfa_objectInstallCOAPI>` is used to install objects and handlers.

Syntax:

```
<cfa_objectInstallCOAPI bOverwriteFiles=""
                        dataSource=""
                        installationPath=""
                        r_bSuccessful=""
                        stObject=""
>
```

Attributes:

Attribute	Description
bOverwriteFiles	Optional flag specifying whether to overwrite existing files. The default is YES.
dataSource	Required datasource of ContentObject Database.
installationPath	Required absolute installation path.
r_bSuccessful	Required name of variable to contain operation success flag.
stObject	Required object to install.

<cfa_objectInstaller>

`<cfa_objectInstaller>` is used to install an object package previously prepared with `<cfa_objectPackager>`.

Syntax:

```
<cfa_objectInstaller dataSource=""
                     installationPath=""
                     label=""
                     r_bSuccessful=""
                     wstObject=""
>
```

Attributes:

Attribute	Description
dataSource	Required datasource of ContentObject Database.
installationPath	Optional absolute installation path. The default is the cfa root.
label	Optional object name (overrides the name in the package).
r_bSuccessful	Optional name of variable to contain operation success flag.
wstObject	Required object to install (in WDDX format).

<cfa_objectInstallPLP>

`<cfa_objectInstallPLP>` is used to install a PLP object and its handlers.

Syntax:

```
<cfa_objectInstallPLP bOverwriteFiles=""
                      dataSource=""
                      installationPath=""
                      r_bSuccessful=""
                      stObject=""
>
```

Attributes:

Attribute	Description
`bOverwriteFiles`	Optional flag specifying whether to overwrite existing files. The default is `YES`.
`dataSource`	Required datasource of ContentObject Database.
`installationPath`	Required absolute installation path.
`r_bSuccessful`	Required name of variable to contain operation success flag.
`stObject`	Required object to install.

<cfa_objectPackager>

`<cfa_objectPackager>` is used to package up an object or PLP for distribution or migration. The packaged object is in WDDX format. This tag calls either `<cfa_objectPackCOAPI>` or `<cfa_objectPackPLP>` (which may be called directly too).

Syntax:

```
<cfa_objectPackager dataSource=""
                    dataType=""
                    ID=""
                    r_wstObject=""
>
```

Attributes:

Attribute	Description
`dataSource`	Required datasource of ContentObject Database.
`dataType`	Required type. Valid values are `COAPI` or `PLP`.
`ID`	Required ID of object or PLP (based on `dataType`).
`r_wstObject`	Required variable to store generated WDDX package.

<cfa_objectPackCOAPI>

`<cfa_objectPackCOAPI>` is used to package up an object for distribution or migration. The packaged object is in WDDX format.

Syntax:

```
<cfa_objectPackCOAPI dataSource=""
                     typeID=""
                     r_wstObject=""
>
```

Attributes:

Attribute	Description
dataSource	Required datasource of ContentObject Database
typeID	Required ID of object
r_wstObject	Required variable to store generated WDDX package

<cfa_objectPackPLP>

`<cfa_objectPackPLP>` is used to package up a PLP for distribution or migration. The packaged object is in WDDX format.

Syntax:

```
<cfa_objectPackPLP dataSource=""
                   objectID=""
                   r_wstObject=""
>
```

Attributes:

Attribute	Description
dataSource	Required datasource of ContentObject Database
objectID	Required ID of PLP object
r_wstObject	Required variable to store generated WDDX package

Object Store Tags

These tags are used to provide basic object store interaction.

<cfa_getNewObjectStruct>

`<cfa_getNewObjectStruct>` is used to get a new object structure without writing it to the object database.

Syntax:

```
<cfa_getNewObjectStruct dataSource=""
                        objectID=""
                        r_stObject=""
                        typeID=""
>
```

Attributes:

Attribute	Description
dataSource	Required datasource of ContentObject Database
objectID	Required object ID
r_stObject	Optional name of the structure to store result data
typeID	Required type ID

<cfa_objectEditFormFields>

<cfa_objectEditFormFields> is used to edit and update default object handlers. One of either objectID or typeID is required.

Syntax:

```
<cfa_objectEditFormFields dataSource=""
                          objectID=""
                          tyepID=""
>
```

Attributes:

Attribute	Description
dataSource	Required datasource of ContentObject Database
objectID	Object ID, required if typeID isn't provided
typeID	Type ID, required if objectID isn't provided

<cfa_objectType>

<cfa_objectType> is used to manage the basic description of an object type.

Syntax:

```
<cfa_objectType action=""
                bSystemEnabled=""
                dataSource=""
                description=""
                handlerRoot=""
                label=""
                r_typeID=""
                typeID=""
>
```

Attributes:

Attribute	Description
action	Required action. Valid values are CREATE, DELETE, or UPDATE.
bSystemEnabled	Optional flag protecting the system from definitions being updated or deleted. If this value is NO, an error will be thrown if an UPDATE or DELETE action is attempted on a system type. The default is NO.
dataSource	Required datasource of ContentObject Database.
description	Optional object description.
handlerRoot	Optional relative handler root.
label	Optional object name.
r_typeID	Optional variable to contain ID of new type.
typeID	Required type ID for DELETE or UPDATE actions.

<cfa_objectTypeGet>

<cfa_objectTypeGet> retrieves information about a specified object.

Syntax:

```
<cfa_objectTypeGet bUseCache=""
                   dataSource=""
                   r_stType=""
                   r_stAllMethodDefinitions=""
                   typeID=""
>
```

Attributes:

Attribute	Description
bUseCache	Optional flag specifying whether to cache the requested data. The default is YES.
dataSource	Required datasource of ContentObject Database.
r_stType	Optional string containing the name of the structure to store result data.
r_stAllMethodDefinitions	Optional string containing the name of the structure to store method definition structures.
typeID	Required type ID.

<cfa_objectTypeGetMultiple>

<cfa_objectTypeGetMultiple> retrieves information about one or more objects.

Syntax:

```
<cfa_objectTypeGetMultiple bUseCache=""
                           dataSource=""
                           r_stTypes=""
                           lTypeIDs=""
>
```

Attributes:

Attribute	Description
bUseCache	Optional flag specifying whether to cache the requested data. The default is YES.
dataSource	Required datasource of ContentObject Database.
r_stTypes	Optional string containing the name of the structure to store result data.
lTypeIDs	Optional comma-delimited list of type IDs.

<cfa_objectTypeMethod>

<cfa_objectTypeMethod> is used to manage object type methods.

Syntax:

```
<cfa_objectTypeMethod action=""
                      alias=""
                      bSystemEnabled=""
                      dataSource=""
                      description=""
                      handlerURL=""
                      typeID=""
                      method=""
>
```

Attributes:

Attribute	Description
action	Required action. Valid values are CREATE, DELETE, or UPDATE.
alias	Optional descriptive name for method.
bSystemEnabled	Optional flag protecting the system from definitions being updated or deleted. If this value is NO, an error will be thrown if an UPDATE or DELETE action is attempted on a system type. The default is NO.
dataSource	Required datasource of ContentObject Database.
description	Optional object description.
handlerURL	Required URL of the directory containing the handler for this method.

Attribute	Description
typeID	Required type ID for DELETE or UPDATE actions.
method	Required name of the method to be created, updated, or deleted.

<cfa_objectTypeProperty>

<cfa_objectTypeProperty> is used to manage object type properties.

Syntax:

```
<cfa_objectTypeProperty action=""
                         bArray=""
                         bIndexed=""
                         bRequired=""
                         bSearachable=""
                         dataSource=""
                         defaultValue=""
                         lCollections=""
                         propertyDefintionID=""
                         propertyName=""
                         typeID=""
                         bSystemEnabled=""
>
```

Attributes:

Attribute	Description
action	Required action. Valid values are CREATE or DELETE.
bArray	Optional flag specifying whether property is an array. The default is NO.
bIndexed	Optional flag specifying whether property is to be indexed for full text searching. The default is NO.
bRequired	Optional flag specifying whether property is required. The default is NO.
bSearchable	Optional flag specifying whether property is searchable. The default is NO.
bSystemEnabled	Optional. Protects the system type property definitions from being updated or deleted. If the value is NO, an error is thrown when the tag is used with a system type. The default is NO.
dataSource	Required datasource of ContentObject Database.
defaultValue	Optional default value.

continues

continued

Attribute	Description
lCollections	Optional list of collections in which the property is indexed (if bIndexed is YES).
propertyDefintionID	Property ID required if ACTION is CREATE.
propertyname	Required property name.
typeID	Required type ID.

<cfa_propertyDefinition>

<cfa_objectTypeDefinition> is used to manage object type property definitions.

Syntax:

```
<cfa_objectTypeDefinition action=""
                          bIndexed=""
                          bRequired=""
                          bSearachable=""
                          dataSource=""
                          dataType=""
                          defaultValue=""
                          description=""
                          inputType=""
                          label=""
                          lCollections=""
                          propertyDefintionID=""
                          r_ID=""
                          wstInputOptions=""
                          wstValidate=""
                          bSystemEnabled=""
>
```

Attributes:

Attribute	Description
action	Required action. Valid values are CREATE, DELETE, or UPDATE.
bIndexed	Optional flag specifying whether property is to be indexed every time it's updated. The default is NO.
bRequired	Optional flag specifying whether property is required for objects that use it. The default is NO.
bSearchable	Optional flag specifying whether property is stored in the properties table for improved searching. The default is NO.

Attribute	Description
`bSystemEnabled=""`	Optional. Protects the system property definitions from being updated or deleted. If the value is `NO`, an error is thrown when the tag is used with a system property definition and the action is either `UPDATE` or `DELETE`. The default is `NO`.
`dataSource`	Required datasource of ContentObject Database.
`dataType`	Required id `ACTION` is `CREATE` (ignored for other actions). Valid values are `Char`, `DateTime`, `Integer`, `Longchar`, or `Numeric`.
`defaultValue`	Required default value.
`description`	Optional property description.
`inputType`	Optional input type. Valid values are `Checkbox`, `MultiSelect`, `Radio`, `Select`, `Text`, `TextArea`, or `WDDX`. No default.
`label`	Required definition name.
`lCollections`	List of collections in which the property is indexed, required if `bIndexed` is `YES`.
`propertyDefintionID`	Property ID required if `ACTION` is `DELETE` or `UPDATE`.
`r_ID`	Optional name of variable to contain the property definition ID.
`wstInputOptions`	Optional WDDX packet containing options for `MultiSelect`, `Radio`, and `Select` input types.
`wstValidate`	Optional WDDX packet containing validation rules.

<cfa_propertyDefinitionGetMultiple>

`<cfa_propertyDefinitionGetMultiple>` retrieves information for one or more property definitions.

Syntax:

```
<cfa_propertyDefinitionGetMultiple dataSource=""
                                   lPropertyDefintionIDs=""
                                   r_stDefinitions=""
>
```

Attributes:

Attribute	Description
`dataSource`	Required datasource of ContentObject Database.
`lPropertyDefinitionIDs`	Optional list of property definitions to retrieve. The default is all properties.
`r_stDefinitions`	Required name of the structure to contain retrieved definitions.

<cfa_propertyIndexKeyDelete>

`<cfa_propertyIndexKeyDelete>` deletes a property from indexes.

Syntax:

```
<cfa_propertyIndexKeyDelete dataSource=""
                            property=""
                            qPropertyData=""
>
```

Attributes:

Attribute	Description
dataSource	Required datasource of ContentObject Database
property	Required name of property to delete
qPropertyData	Required query containing property to be deleted

<cfa_propertyIndexKeyUpdate>

`<cfa_propertyIndexKeyUpdate>` indexes property values associated with a property definition.

Syntax:

```
<cfa_propertyIndexKeyUpdate dataSource=""
                            property=""
                            qPropertyData=""
>
```

Attributes:

Attribute	Description
dataSource	Required datasource of ContentObject Database
property	Required name of property to delete
qPropertyData	Required query containing property data to be indexed

PLP (Process Logic Path) Tags

These tags are used to create, manage, and execute PLP processes.

<cfa_PLP>

`<cfa_PLP>` executes a defined PLP.

Syntax:

```
<cfa_PLP bDebug=""
         bForceNewInstance=""
         dataSource=""
         instanceHandle=""
         iTimeout=""
         name=""
         PLPID=""
         queryString=""
         r_instanceHandle=""
         r_bPLPIsComplete=""
         r_stOutput=""
         stExtendedInfo=""
         stInput=""
         userName=""
>
```

Attributes:

Attribute	Description
`bDebug`	Optional flag specifying whether to display debug information. The default is `NO`.
`bForceNewInstance`	Optional flag specifying whether to create a new instance for the PLP. The default is `NO`.
`dataSource`	Required datasource of ContentObject Database.
`instanceHandle`	Reserved.
`iTimeout`	Optional timeout interval in minutes. This overrides the value specified at PLP creation time.
`name`	Name of the PLP to be executed. Required only if `PLPID` isn't specified.
`PLPID`	ID of the PLP to be executed. Required only if `name` isn't specified. (Using `PLPID` rather than `name` is recommended for performance reasons).
`queryString`	Optional query string in the format of `name=value` separated by ampersands (the `&` character).
`r_instanceHandle`	Reserved.
`r_bPLPIsComplete`	Optional name of variable to contain a flag indicating whether the PLP has completed.
`r_stOutput`	Optional name of the structure into which the complete DDO is to be placed. The default is `output`.
`stExtendedInfo`	Optional structure containing the data to be added to the DDO for this instance.
`stInput`	Optional structure containing the comma-delimited DDO to be passed to the PLP.
`userName`	Optional name of the owner of this instance. The default is `system`.

<cfa_PLPCreate>

<cfa_PLPCreate> is used to create a new PLP definition.

Syntax:

```
<cfa_PLPCreate bCreateStructure=""
               dataSource=""
               handlerRelativePath=""
               iTimeout=""
               name=""
               PLPID=""
               r_bStructureWasCreated=""
               r_objectID=""
               r_stOutput=""
               stDDO=""
>
```

Attributes:

Attribute	Description
bCreateStructure	Optional flag specifying whether to create a directory for the PLP. The default is NO.
dataSource	Required datasource of ContentObject Database.
handlerRelativePath	Optional path to handlers.
iTimeout	Optional timeout interval in minutes. This The default is 15.
name	Required PLP name.
PLPID	Optional PLP ID.
r_bStructureWasCreated	Optional variable to contain a flag indicating whether a new directory structure was created.
r_objectID	Optional name of variable to contain the new object ID.
r_stOutput	Optional name of the structure into which the new transaction data object is to be placed. The default is output.
stDDO	Optional name of the structure to contain the new defined data object.

<cfa_PLPDelete>

<cfa_PLPDelete> is used to delete existing PLP definitions.

Syntax:

```
<cfa_PLPDelete dataSource=""
               name=""
               PLPID=""
>
```

Attributes:

Attribute	Description
dataSource	Required datasource of ContentObject Database
name	PLP name, required if PLPID not specified
PLPID	PLP ID, required if name not specified

<cfa_PLPGet>

<cfa_PLPGet> is used to retrieve a PLP definition.

Syntax:

```
<cfa_PLPGet bCleanInstances=""
            dataSource=""
            iTimeout=""
            PLPID=""
            PLPName=""
            r_objectID=""
            r_stInstances=""
            r_stOutput=""
            stDDO=""
>
```

Attributes:

Attribute	Description
bCleanInstances	Optional flag specifying whether to destroy all PLP instances. The default is NO.
dataSource	Required datasource of ContentObject Database.
iTimeout	Optional timeout interval in minutes. This The default is the value specified when the PLP was created.
PLPID	PLP ID, required if PLPName not specified.
PLPName	PLP name, required if PLPID not specified.
r_objectID	Optional name of variable to contain the PLP object ID.
r_stOutput	Optional name of the structure to store the transaction data object (TDO).
stDDO	Optional name of the structure to contain the defined data object (DDO).

<cfa_PLPHandler>

<cfa_PLPHandler> is used to define a PLP handler and encloses the handler code.

Syntax:

```
<cfa_PLPHandler>
        ...handler_code...
</cfa_PLPHandler>
```

<cfa_PLPHandler> takes no attributes.

<cfa_PLPShow>

<cfa_PLPShow> is used to generate a view of a PLP.

Syntax:

```
<cfa_PLPShow dataSource=""
             PLPID=""
             r_generatedHTML=""
>
```

Attributes:

Attribute	Description
dataSource	Required datasource of ContentObject Database
PLPID	Required PLP ID
r_generatedHTML	Optional variable to contain generated HTML

<cfa_PLPStepCreate>

<cfa_PLPStepCreate> creates a PLP step.

Syntax:

```
<cfa_PLPStepCreate bCreateFile=""
                   condition=""
                   dataSource=""
                   else=""
                   handler=""
                   input=""
                   logic=""
                   nextStep=""
                   nOrder=""
                   onError=""
                   output=""
                   PLPID=""
                   PLPName=""
                   r_bFileWasCreated=""
                   r_bStepWasCreated=""
                   stepName=""
>
```

Attributes:

Attribute	Description
bCreateFile	Optional flag specifying whether this step creates a default template. The default is NO.
condition	Optional condition that must be TRUE to allow proceeding to the next step.
dataSource	Required datasource of ContentObject Database.
else	PLP step to execute if condition is FALSE and logic is either Iterate or IterateConditional.
handler	Required handler filename (no path).
input	Optional input scope.
logic	Required execution option. Must be one of Run, Conditional, Iterate, ConditionalIterate.
nextStep	Optional next step to execute when step has been completed.
nOrder	Optional execution order.
onError	Optional PLP step to execute if an error occurs.
output	Optional output scope.
PLPID	ID of the PLP into which step is being defined. Required only if name isn't specified. (Using PLPID rather than PLPname is recommended for performance reasons.)
PLPname	Name of the PLP into which step is being defined. Required only if PLPID isn't specified.
r_bFileWasCreated	Optional variable to contain a flag indicating whether file creation was successful.
r_bStepWasCreated	Optional variable to contain a flag indicating whether step creation was successful.
stepName	Required step name.

<cfa_PLPStepDelete>

<cfa_PLPStepDelete> deletes a PLP step.

Syntax:

```
<cfa_PLPStepDelete bDeleteFile=""
                   dataSource=""
                   PLPName=""
                   r_bFileWasDeleted=""
                   stepName=""
>
```

Attributes:

Attribute	Description
`bDeleteFile`	Optional flag specifying whether to delete the template for this step. The default is `NO`.
`dataSource`	Required datasource of ContentObject Database.
`PLPname`	Required PLP name.
`r_bFileWasDeleted`	Optional variable to contain a flag indicating whether file deletion was successful.
`stepName`	Required step name.

<cfa_PLPStepUpdate>

`<cfa_PLPStepUpdate>` updates a PLP step.

Syntax:

```
<cfa_PLPStepUpdate condition=""
                   dataSource=""
                   else=""
                   handler=""
                   input=""
                   logic=""
                   nextStep=""
                   nOrder=""
                   onError=""
                   output=""
                   PLPID=""
                   PLPName=""
                   r_bStepWasUpdated=""
                   stepName=""
>
```

Attributes:

Attribute	Description
`condition`	Optional condition that must be `TRUE` to allow proceeding to the next step.
`dataSource`	Required datasource of ContentObject Database.
`else`	PLP step to execute if `condition` is `FALSE` and `logic` is either `Iterate` or `IterateConditional`.
`handler`	Optional new handler filename (no path).
`input`	Optional input scope.
`logic`	Required new execution option. Must be one of `Run`, `Conditional`, `Iterate`, `ConditionalIterate`.

Attribute	Description
nextStep	Optional next step to execute when step has been completed.
nOrder	Optional execution order.
onError	Optional PLP step to execute if an error occurs.
output	Optional output scope.
PLPID	ID of the PLP into which step is being defined. Required only if name isn't specified. (Using PLPID rather than PLPname is recommended for performance reasons).
PLPname	Name of the PLP into which step is being defined. Required only if PLPID isn't specified.
r_bStepWasUpdated	Optional variable to contain a flag indicating whether step update was successful.
stepName	Required step name.

<cfa_PLPUpdate>

<cfa_PLPUpdate> is used to update a PLP definition.

Syntax:

```
<cfa_PLPUpdate bCreateStructure=""
               dataSource=""
               handlerRelativePath=""
               handlerRoot=""
               iTimeout=""
               PLPID=""
               PLPName=""
               r_bStructureWasCreated=""
               r_stOutput=""
               stDDO=""
>
```

Attributes:

Attribute	Description
bCreateStructure	Optional flag specifying whether to create a directory for the PLP. The default is NO.
dataSource	Required datasource of ContentObject Database.
handlerRelativePath	Optional path to handlers.
handlerRoot	Required handler root.
iTimeout	Optional timeout interval in minutes.

continues

continued

Attribute	Description
PLPID	PLP ID, required if PLPName not specified.
PLPName	PLP name, required if PLPID not specified.
r_bStructureWasCreated	Optional variable to contain a flag indicating whether a new directory structure was created.
r_stOutput	Optional name of the structure into which the new transaction data object is to be placed. The default is output.
stDDO	Optional name of the structure to contain the new defined data object.

Schedule Tags

These tags are used in event scheduling and management.

<cfa_scheduleCreate>

<cfa_scheduleCreate> is used to define and create scheduled events. This tag is essentially a Spectra wrapper around the ColdFusion <CFSCHEDULE> tag.

Syntax:

```
<cfa_scheduleCreate bResolveURL=""
                    bPublish=""
                    endDate=""
                    endTime=""
                    file=""
                    interval=""
                    method=""
                    objectID=""
                    password=""
                    path=""
                    proxyServer=""
                    r_bSuccess=""
                    requestTimeout=""
                    startDate=""
                    startTime=""
                    userName=""
>
```

Attributes:

Attribute	Description
bResolveURL	Optional flag specifying whether to resolve URLs within retrieved pages. The default is NO.
bPublish	Optional flag specifying whether to save results to a file. The default is NO.
endDate	Optional end date.
endTime	Optional end time.
file	Output file. Required if bPublish is YES.
interval	Required execution interval. Value must be one of Once, Daily, Weekly, Monthly, Execute, or a number (in seconds). The default is 3600 (1 hour).
method	Required name of associated method.
objectID	Required ID of object to be associated with scheduled task.
password	Optional password for secure URLs.
path	Optional output file path.
proxyServer	Optional proxy server host name or IP address.
r_bSuccess	Required variable to contain success flag.
requestTimeout	Optional request timeout (in seconds). The default is 60.
startDate	Required start date.
startTime	Required start time (in seconds).
userName	Optional username for secure URLs.

<cfa_scheduleDelete>

<cfa_scheduleDelete> is used to delete a scheduled event.

Syntax:

```
<cfa_scheduleDelete method=""
                    objectID=""
                    r_bSuccess=""
>
```

Attributes:

Attribute	Description
method	Required name of associated method
objectID	Required ID of object to be associated with scheduled task
r_bSuccess	Required variable to contain success flag

<cfa_scheduleGet>

<cfa_scheduleGet> is used to retrieve the details pertaining to a scheduled event.

Syntax:

```
<cfa_scheduleGet method=""
                 objectID=""
                 r_stSchedule=""
>
```

Attributes:

Attribute	Description
method	Required name of associated method
objectID	Required ID of object to be associated with scheduled task
r_stSchedule	Required variable to contain structure of event details

<cfa_scheduleRun>

<cfa_scheduleRun> is used to immediately execute a scheduled event.

Syntax:

```
<cfa_scheduleRun method=""
                 objectID=""
                 r_stSuccess=""
>
```

Attributes:

Attribute	Description
method	Required name of associated method
objectID	Required ID of object to be associated with scheduled task
r_bSuccess	Required variable to contain success flag

<cfa_scheduleUpdate>

`<cfa_scheduleUpdate>` is used to update the properties of a scheduled event.

Syntax:

```
<cfa_scheduleUpdate bResolveURL=""
                    bPublish=""
                    endDate=""
                    endTime=""
                    file=""
                    interval=""
                    method=""
                    objectID=""
                    password=""
                    path=""
                    proxyServer=""
                    r_bSuccess=""
                    requestTimeout=""
                    startDate=""
                    startTime=""
                    userName=""
>
```

Attributes:

Attribute	Description
`bResolveURL`	Optional flag specifying whether to resolve URLs within retrieved pages. The default is `NO`.
`bPublish`	Optional flag specifying whether to save results to a file. The default is `NO`.
`endDate`	Optional end date.
`endTime`	Optional end time.
`file`	Output file. Required if `bPublish` is `YES`.
`interval`	Required execution interval. The value must be one of `Once`, `Daily`, `Weekly`, `Monthly`, `Execute`, or a number (in seconds). The default is `3600` (1 hour).
`method`	Required name of associated method.
`objectID`	Required ID of object to be pdated.
`password`	Optional password for secure URLs.
`path`	Optional output file path.
`proxyServer`	Optional proxy server host name or IP address.
`r_bSuccess`	Required variable to contain success flag.
`requestTimeout`	Optional request timeout (in seconds). The default is `60`.
`startDate`	Required start date.
`startTime`	Required start time (in seconds).
`userName`	Optional username for secure URLs.

Search and Index Tags

These tags are used to index and search data using the Verity search engine.

<cfa_allTypeSearch>

`<cfa_allTypeSearch>` is used to search the ContentObject Database for all objects of all types.

Syntax:

```
<cfa_allTypeSearch bDistinctObject=""
                   dataSource=""
                   lProperties=""
                   lTypes=""
                   r_qResults=""
                   r_stResults=""
                   resultSet=""
                   searchTerms=""
>
```

Attributes:

Attribute	Description
bDistinctObject	Optional flag specifying whether to remove duplicates from search results. The default is NO.
dataSource	Required datasource of ContentObject Database.
lProperties	Optional list of properties for which to search. The default is all properties.
lTypes	Optional list of types for which to search. The default is all types.
r_qResults	Optional name of query to store retrieved items.
r_stResults	Optional name of the structure to store retrieved items.
resultSet	Optional result desired specifier, either FULL (for all data) or KEY (for object IDs). The default is KEY.
searchTerms	Required search terms.

<cfa_propertySearch>

`<cfa_propertySearch>` is used to search property indexes.

Syntax:

```
<cfa_propertySearch bDistinctObject=""
                    dataSource=""
                    lProperties=""
                    property=""
```

```
                  r_qResults=""
                  r_stResults=""
                  resultSet=""
                  searchTerms=""
>
```

Attributes:

Attribute	Description
bDistinctObject	Optional flag specifying whether to remove duplicates from search results. The default is NO.
dataSource	Required datasource of ContentObject Database.
lProperties	List of properties for which to search. Required if property not specified.
property	ID of property to retrieve. Required if lProperties not specified.
r_qResults	Optional name of query to store retrieved items.
r_stResults	Optional name of the structure to store retrieved items.
resultSet	Optional result desired specifier, either FULL (for all data) or KEY (for object IDs). The default is KEY.
searchTerms	Required search terms.

<cfa_typeIndex>

<cfa_typeIndex> indexes all properties for a specified object type.

Syntax:

```
<cfa_typeIndex dataSource=""
               typeID=""
>
```

Attributes:

Attribute	Description
dataSource	Required datasource of ContentObject Database
typeID	Required type ID

<cfa_typeIndexAll>

<cfa_typeIndexAll> indexes all properties for all objects.

Syntax:

```
<cfa_typeIndexAll dataSource="">
```

Attribute:

Attribute	Description
dataSource	Required datasource of ContentObject Database

<cfa_typeIndexCreate>

<cfa_typeIndexCreate> creates a Verity collection and indexes the properties for all objects of a specific type.

Syntax:

```
<cfa_typeIndexCreate collectionPath=""
                     dataSource=""
                     r_lCollectionCreated=""
                     typeID=""
>
```

Attributes:

Attribute	Description
collectionPath	Optional path for new Verity collection. The default is the system collections path.
dataSource	Required datasource of ContentObject Database.
r_lCollectionsCreated	List of variables to store the names of the created collections.
typeID	Required type ID.

<cfa_typeIndexDelete>

<cfa_typeIndexDelete> deletes the collections associated with a specified object type.

Syntax:

```
<cfa_typeIndexDelete dataSource=""
                     typeID=""
>
```

Attributes:

Attribute	Description
dataSource	Required datasource of ContentObject Database
typeID	Required type ID

<cfa_typeIndexKeyDelete>

`<cfa_typeIndexKeyDelete>` deletes specified content from all property indexes.

Syntax:

```
<cfa_typeIndexKeyDelete dataSource=""
                        lObjectIDs=""
                        typeID=""
>
```

Attributes:

Attribute	Description
dataSource	Required datasource of ContentObject Database
lObjectIDs	Required list of object IDs to delete
typeID	Required type ID

<cfa_typeIndexKeyUpdate>

`<cfa_typeIndexKeyUpdate>` indexes the properties for the specified content.

Syntax:

```
<cfa_typeIndexKeyUpdate dataSource=""
                        lObjectIDs=""
                        typeID=""
>
```

Attributes:

Attribute	Description
dataSource	Required datasource of ContentObject Database
lObjectIDs	Required list of object IDs to be updated
typeID	Required type ID

<cfa_typeSearch>

`<cfa_typeSearch>` is used to search the ContentObject Database for all objects of specified types.

Syntax:

```
<cfa_allTypeSearch bDistinctObject=""
                   dataSource=""
                   lProperties=""
                   lTypes=""
                   r_qResults=""
                   r_stResults=""
                   resultSet=""
                   searchTerms=""
                   typeID=""
>
```

Attributes:

Attribute	Description
bDistinctObject	Optional flag specifying whether to remove duplicates from search results. The default is NO.
dataSource	Required datasource of ContentObject Database.
lProperties	Optional list of properties for which to search. The default is all properties.
lTypes	List of types for which to search. The default is all types. Required if typeID isn't specified.
r_qResults	Required name of query to store retrieved items.
r_stResults	Optional name of the structure to store retrieved items.
resultSet	Optional result desired specifier, either FULL (for all data) or KEY (for object IDs). The default is KEY.
searchTerms	Required search terms.
typeID	List of types for which to search. The default is all types. Required if lTypes isn't specified.

Security Tags

These tags are used to manage and maintain users and user groups as well as policies, authentication, and other security related features.

<cfa_authenticate>

<cfa_authenticate> is used to authenticate users using provided usernames and passwords. This tag is essentially a wrapper around the ColdFusion <CFAUTHENTICATE> tag.

Syntax:

```
<cfa_authenticate bSetCookie=""
                  bThrowOnFailure=""
                  password=""
                  r_bResult=""
                  securityContext=""
                  userName=""
>
```

Attributes:

Attribute	Description
bSetCookie	Optional flag specifying whether to set cookie containing the username and password. The default is YES.
bThrowOnFailure	Optional flag specifying whether to throw an error upon unsuccessful authentication. The default is YES.

Attribute	Description
password	Required user password.
r_bResult	Required name of variable to contain authentication status.
securityContext	Required security context name.
userName	Required username.

<cfa_group>

<cfa_group> is used to create and manage user groups.

Syntax:

```
<cfa_group action=""
           description=""
           groupName=""
           userDirectory=""
>
```

Attributes:

Attribute	Description
action	Required action. The value can be Create, Delete, or Update.
description	Optional group description.
groupName	Required unique group name.
userDirectory	Required user directory name.

<cfa_groupCreate>

<cfa_groupCreate> is used to create user groups.

Syntax:

```
<cfa_groupCreate description=""
                 groupName=""
                 userDirectory=""
>
```

Attributes:

Attribute	Description
description	Required group description
groupName	Required unique group name
userDirectory	Required user directory name

<cfa_groupDelete>

<cfa_groupDelete> is used to delete user groups.

Syntax:

```
<cfa_groupDelete groupName=""
                 userDirectory=""
>
```

Attributes:

Attribute	Description
groupName	Required group name
userDirectory	Required user directory name

<cfa_groupGet>

<cfa_groupGet> is used to retrieve group information.

Syntax:

```
<cfa_groupGet groupName=""
              r_lUsernames=""
              r_stGroup=""
              r_stUsers=""
              userDirectory=""
>
```

Attributes:

Attribute	Description
groupName	Required group name
r_lUserNames	Optional variable into which to store the retrieved groups users
r_stGroup	Required structure to store group information
r_stUsers	Optional structure to store group users
userDirectory	Required user directory name

<cfa_groupGetMultiple>

<cfa_groupGetMultiple> is used to retrieve for all groups.

Syntax:

```
<cfa_groupGetMultiple r_stGroups=""
                      userDirectory=""
                      userName=""
>
```

Attributes:

Attribute	Description
r_stGroups	Required structure to store group information
userDirectory	Required user directory name
userName	Optional username to restrict search to groups of which the user is a member

<cfa_groupUpdate>

<cfa_groupUpdate> is used to update user groups.

Syntax:

```
<cfa_groupUpdate description=""
                 groupName=""
                 userDirectory=""
>
```

Attributes:

Attribute	Description
description	Required group description
groupName	Required group name
userDirectory	Required user directory name

<cfa_LDAPUserParse>

<cfa_LDAPUserParse> is used to separate users in an LDAP list by semi-colons (making parsing and manipulation easier).

Syntax:

```
<cfa_LDAPUserParse lUsers=""
                   r_lUsers=""
>
```

Attributes:

Attribute	Description
lUsers	Required LDAP list
r_lUsers	Required variable to store converted list

<cfa_policy>

<cfa_policy> is used to create and update policies, adding or removing users.

Syntax:

```
<cfa_policy action=""
            lAddUsers=""
            lRemoveUsers=""
            policyName=""
            resource=""
            resourceMethod=""
            securityContext=""
            userDirectory=""
>
```

Attributes:

Attribute	Description
action	Required action. Valid values are ADDUSERS, CREATE, DELETE, REMOVEUSERS, or UPDATE
lAddUsers	Optional comma-delimited list of users to add to policy
lRemoveUsers	Optional comma-delimited list of users to remove from policy
policyName	Required policy name for all actions other than CREATE
resource	Required resource ID for CREATE action
resourceMethod	Optional resource method, only used if ACTION is CRE-ATE
securityContext	Required security context
userDirectory	Required user directory

<cfa_policyCreate>

<cfa_policyCreate> is used to create a security policy and optionally add users to it.

Syntax:

```
<cfa_policyCreate lUsers=""
                  resource=""
                  resourceMethod=""
                  securityContext=""
                  userDirectory=""
>
```

Attributes:

Attribute	Description
lUsers	Optional comma-delimited list of users to add to policy
resource	Required resource ID
resourceMethod	Required resource method
securityContext	Required security context
userDirectory	Required user directory

<cfa_policyDelete>

<cfa_policyDelete> is used to delete a security policy.

Syntax:

```
<cfa_policyDelete policyName=""
                  securityContext=""
>
```

Attributes:

Attribute	Description
policyName	Required policy name
securityContext	Required security context

<cfa_policyGet>

<cfa_policyGet> is used to retrieve policy information.

Syntax:

```
<cfa_policyGet policyName=""
               r_bPolicyExists=""
               r_lUsers=""
               securityContext=""
               userDirectory=""
>
```

Attributes:

Attribute	Description
policyName	Required policy name
r_bPolicyExists	Optional name of variable to contain a flag indicating whether policy exists
r_lUsers	Optional name of variable to contain policy user list
securityContext	Required security context
userDirectory	Required user directory

<cfa_policyGetMultiple>

`<cfa_policyGetMultiple>` is used to retrieve policy information for multiple policies.

Syntax:

```
<cfa_policyGetMultiple r_lPolicies=""
                       securityContext=""
                       userDirectory=""
>
```

Attributes:

Attribute	Description
r_lPolicies	Optional name of variable to contain list of policies
securityContext	Required security context
userDirectory	Required user directory

<cfa_policyUser>

`<cfa_policyUser>` is used to associate or disassociate a user with a policy.

Syntax:

```
<cfa_policyUser action=""
                policyName=""
                securityContext=""
                userDirectory=""
                userName=""
>
```

Attributes:

Attribute	Description
action	Required action. The values can be CREATE or DELETE.
policyName	Required name of policy.
securityContext	Required security context.
userDirectory	Required user directory.
userName	Required name of user to be associated or disassociated.

<cfa_profile>

`<cfa_profile>` is used to track and manage user profile information, including managing related cookie.

Syntax:

```
<cfa_profile expires=""
             dataSource=""
             r_stUserProfile=""
             sessionExpires=""
             storageType=""
userName=""
>
```

Attributes:

Attribute	Description
expires	Optional number of days for cookie to persist. The default is 30.
dataSource	Datasource of ContentObject Database. Required is r_stUserProfile is specified.
r_stUserProfile	Optional variable to store user profile structure.
sessionExpires	Optional session expiration time in minutes, The default is 30 minutes.
storageType	Optional storage type, valid values are COOKIE or SESSION. The default is COOKIE.
userName	Optional username, The default is anonymous.

<cfa_secure>

<cfa_secure> provides integrated access to application security authentication and access control. Internally, this tag calls <cfa_authenticate>, <cfa_session>, and <cfa_userProfileGet>.

Syntax:

```
<cfa_secure authenticationURL=""
            dataSource=""
            password=""
            r_bResult=""
            r_stUserProfile=""
            securityContext=""
            sessionExpires=""
            storageType=""
            userName=""
>
```

Attributes:

Attribute	Description
authenticationURL	Optional URL form to be used for login and password prompt.
dataSource	Datasource of ContentObject Database. Required if r_stUserProfile is specified.
password	Required password of user to be authenticated.
r_bResult	Optional variable to store operation success flag.
r_stUserProfile	Optional variable to store user profile structure.
securityContext	Required security context.
sessionExpires	Optional session expiration time in minutes, The default is 30 minutes.
storageType	Optional storage type, valid values are COOKIE or SESSION. The default is COOKIE.
userName	Optional username. The default is anonymous.

<cfa_user>

<cfa_user> is used to add, update, or remove a user from a user database. Individual actions can also be performed using the <cfa_userCreate>, <cfa_userDelete> and <cfa_userUpdate> tags.

Syntax:

```
<cfa_user action=""
          description=""
          password=""
          userDirectory=""
          userName=""
>
```

Attributes:

Attribute	Description
action	Required action. The valid values are CREATE, DELETE, or UPDATE.
description	Optional user description.
password	Optional user password, required if ACTION is DELETE.
userDirectory	Required user directory.
userName	Required username.

<cfa_userAddGroups>

`<cfa_userAddGroups>` is used to add a user to one or more groups.

Syntax:

```
<cfa_userAddGroups lGroupNames=""
                   userDirectory=""
                   userName=""
>
```

Attributes:

Attribute	Description
lGroupNames	Required list of groups
userDirectory	Required user directory
userName	Required username

<cfa_userCreate>

`<cfa_userCreate>` is used to add a new user to the user database.

Syntax:

```
<cfa_userCreate description=""
                password=""
                userDirectory=""
                userName=""
>
```

Attributes:

Attribute	Description
description	Required user description
password	Required user password
userDirectory	Required user directory
userName	Required username

<cfa_userDelete>

`<cfa_userDelete>` is used to delete a user from the user database.

Syntax:

```
<cfa_userDelete password=""
                userDirectory=""
                userName=""
>
```

Attributes:

Attribute	Description
password	Required user password
userDirectory	Required user directory
userName	Required username

<cfa_userDirectoryGet>

<cfa_userDirectoryGet> is used to retrieve information about a user directory.

Syntax:

```
<cfa_userDirectoryGet r_stUserDirectory=""
                      userDirectory=""
>
```

Attributes:

Attribute	Description
r_stUserDirectory	Required variable to contain user directory structure
userDirectory	Required user directory

<cfa_userDirectoryGetMultiple>

<cfa_userDirectoryGetMultiple> is used to retrieve information about all user directories in a specified security context.

Syntax:

```
<cfa_userDirectoryGet r_stUserDirectories=""
                      securityContext=""
>
```

Attributes:

Attribute	Description
r_stUserDirectory	Required variable to contain user directory structure
securityContext	Required security context

<cfa_userGet>

<cfa_userGet> is used to retrieve information about a user.

Syntax:

```
<cfa_userGet r_stGroups=""
             r_stUser=""
             userDirectory=""
             userName=""
>
```

Attributes:

Attribute	Description
r_stGroups	Optional variable to contain associated group information
r_stUser	Required variable to contain user structure
userDirectory	Required user directory
userName	Required username

<cfa_userGetMultiple>

<cfa_userGetMultiple> is used to retrieve information about all user or users in a specific group.

Syntax:

```
<cfa_userGetMultiple groupName=""
                     r_stUsers=""
                     userDirectory=""
>
```

Attributes:

Attribute	Description
groupName	Optional name of group whose members are to be returned
r_stUsers	Required variable to contain user structure
userDirectory	Required user directory

<cfa_userIsAuthorized>

<cfa_userIsAuthorized> is used to determine if a user has the rights to invoke specific methods for specific objects.

Syntax:

```
<cfa_userIsAuthorized bSecure=""
                      bTypePriority=""
                      dataSource=""
```

```
                         method=""
                         objectID=""
                         r_bResult=""
                         typeID=""
>
```

Attributes:

Attribute	Description
`bSecure`	Optional flag specifying whether to check user permission before proceeding. The default is `NO`.
`bTypePriority`	Optional flag specifying whether type has priority over object. The default is `YES` (type has priority).
`dataSource`	Datasource, required if `objectID` is specified.
`method`	Required method to be checked.
`objectID`	Object ID, required if `typeID` isn't specified.
`r_bResult`	Required variable to contain authorization flag.
`typeID`	Type ID, required if `objectID` isn't specified.

<cfa_userRemoveGroups>

`<cfa_userRemoveGroups>` is used to remove a user from one or more groups.

Syntax:

```
<cfa_userRemoveGroups lGroupNames=""
                      userDirectory=""
                      userName=""
>
```

Attributes:

Attribute	Description
`lGroupNames`	Required list of groups
`userDirectory`	Required user directory
`userName`	Required username

<cfa_userUpdate>

`<cfa_userUpdate>` is used to update a user in the user database.

Syntax:

```
<cfa_userUpdate description=""
                password=""
                userDirectory=""
                userName=""
>
```

Attributes:

Attribute	Description
`description`	Optional new user description
`password`	Optional new user password
`userDirectory`	Required user directory
`userName`	Required username

Session Management Tags

These tags are used in application and session management.

<cfa_applicationInitialize>

`<cfa_applicationInitialize>` is used to initialize an application. This process defines scopes used by the application and also establishes settings for session state management.

Syntax:

```
<cfa_applicationInitialize applicationID=""
                           applicationTimeout=""
                           bActiveApp=""
                           bActiveLog=""
                           clientManagement=""
                           clientStorage=""
                           mode=""
                           name=""
                           sessionManagement=""
                           sessionTimeout=""
                           setClientCookies=""
>
```

Attributes:

Attribute	Description
`applicationID`	Application ID, required if `name` isn't specified.
`applicationTimeout`	Optional application variable timeout (as a `CreateTimeSpan()`). The default is the ColdFusion administrator setting.
`bActiveApp`	Optional flag specifying whether this is the active application. The default is `YES`.
`bActiveLog`	Optional flag specifying whether to write to the active log as needed. The default is `YES`.

continues

continued

Attribute	Description
clientManagement	Optional flag specifying whether to use client state management. The default is NO.
clientStorage	Optional location for client variable storage. Valid values are COOKIE, REGISTRY, or the name of a datasource.
mode	Optional application mode. Valid values are BROWSE, DESIGN, or SUBSCRIBE.
name	Application name, required if applicationID isn't specified.
sessionManagement	Optional flag specifying whether to use session state management. The default is NO.
sessionTimeout	Optional session variable timeout (as a CreateTimeSpan()). The default is the ColdFusion administrator setting.
setClientCookies	Optional flag specifying whether client identification cookies are set automatically. The default is YES.

<cfa_session>

<cfa_session> is used to control session management.

Syntax:

```
<cfa_session customHandlerURL=""
             lengthUnit=""
             storageType=""
             timeOut=""
             timeOutLength=""
>
```

Attributes:

Attribute	Description
customHandlerURL	Required if storageType is CUSTOM.
lengthUnit	Date specifier string, required if timeout not specified.
storageType	Optional storage type. Valid values are CLIENTVAR, COOKIEPERM, COOKIETEMP, CUSTOM, or SESSIONVAR. The default is COOKIEPERM.
timeOut	Timeout interval, required if lengthUnit not specified.
timeOutLength	Timeout units, required if lengthUnit is specified.

<cfa_sessionCreate>

`<cfa_sessionCreate>` creates a new session.

Syntax:

```
<cfa_sessionCreate customHandlerURL=""
                   dtTimeOutDateTime=""
                   nTimeOutInterval=""
                   r_nSessionID=""
                   sIntervalDateTimeUnit=""
                   storageType=""
>
```

Attributes:

Attribute	Description
customHandlerURL	Required if storageType is CUSTOM.
dtTimeOutDateTime	Session expiration date and time, required if nTimeOutInterval and sIntervalDateTimeUnit aren't specified.
nTimeOutInterval	Number of intervals until timeout, required if dtTimeOutDateTime not specified.
r_nSessionID	Optional variable to store session ID.
sIntervalDateTimeUnit	Timeout units, required if dtTimeOutDateTime not specified.
storageType	Optional storage type. Valid values are CLIENTVAR, COOKIEPERM, COOKIETEMP, CUSTOM, or SESSIONVAR. The default is COOKIEPERM.

<cfa_sessionExpire>

`<cfa_sessionExpire>` is used to force the expiration of a session.

Syntax:

```
<cfa_sessionExpire customHandlerURL=""
                   nSessionID=""
                   storageType=""
>
```

Attributes:

Attribute	Description
customHandlerURL	Required if storageType is CUSTOM.
nSessionID	Required session ID.
storageType	Optional storage type. Valid values are CLIENTVAR, COOKIEPERM, COOKIETEMP, CUSTOM, or SESSIONVAR. The default is COOKIEPERM.

<cfa_sessionGetAll>

`<cfa_sessionGetAll>` retrieves all session data for the current user.

Syntax:

```
<cfa_sessionGetAll r_stAllSessions="">
```

Attribute:

Attribute	Description
r_stAllSessions	Required name of the structure to store session information

<cfa_sessionIsDefined>

`<cfa_sessionIsDefined>` is used to determine if a client session exists.

Syntax:

```
<cfa_sessionIsDefined customHandlerURL=""
                      r_bSessionIsDefined=""
                      r_nSessionID=""
                      r_storageType=""
                      storageType=""
>
```

Attributes:

Attribute	Description
customHandlerURL	Required if storageType is CUSTOM.
r_bSessionIsDefined	Required variable to store session defined flag.
r_nSessionID	Optional variable to store the session ID.
r_storageType	Optional variable to store type of storage used.
storageType	Optional storage type. Valid values are CLIENTVAR, COOKIEPERM, COOKIETEMP, CUSTOM, or SESSIONVAR. The default is COOKIEPERM.

<cfa_sessionManage>

`<cfa_sessionManage>` changes a session's timeout and expiration settings.

Syntax:

```
<cfa_sessionManage customHandlerURL=""
                   dtTimeOutDateTime=""
                   nSessionID=""
```

```
                        nTimeOutInterval=""
                        nTimeOutIntervalFromNow="
                        sIntervalDateTimeUnit=""
                        storageType=""
>
```

Attributes:

Attribute	Description
customHandlerURL	Required if storageType is CUSTOM.
dtTimeOutDateTime	Session expiration date and time, required if nTimeOutInterval, sIntervalDateTimeUnit and nTimeOutIntervalFromNow aren't specified.
nSessionID	Required session ID.
nTimeOutInterval	Number of intervals until timeout, required if dtTimeOutDateTime and nTimeOutIntervalFromNow aren't specified.
nTimeOutIntervalFromNow	Number of interval units timeout from now, required if dtTimeOutDateTime and nTimeOutInterval aren't specified.
sIntervalDateTimeUnit	Timeout units, required if dtTimeOutDateTime not specified.
storageType	Optional storage type. Valid values are CLIENTVAR, COOKIEPERM, COOKIETEMP, CUSTOM, or SESSIONVAR. The default is COOKIEPERM.

<cfa_sessionStatusGet>

<cfa_sessionStatusGet> is used to retrieve session status information.

Syntax:

```
<cfa_sessionStatusGet customHandlerURL=""
                      nSessionID=""
                      r_bSessionStatus=""
                      r_dtSessionExpires=""
                      r_dtSessionStart=""
                      r nTimeOutInterval=""
                      r_sIntervalDateTimeUnit=""
                      r_storageType=""
                      storageType=""
>
```

Attributes:

Attribute	Description
customHandlerURL	Required if storageType is CUSTOM.
nSessionID	Required session ID.
r_bSessionStatus	Optional variable to store a flag indicating whether the session is active.
r_dtSessionExpires	Optional variable to store session expiration date and time.
r_dtSessionStart	Optional variable to store session start date and time.
r_nTimeoutInterval	Optional variable to store session timeout interval.
r_sIntervalDateTimeUnit	Optional variable to store session interval units.
r_storageType	Optional variable to store session storage type.
storageType	Optional storage type. Valid values are CLIENTVAR, COOKIEPERM, COOKIETEMP, CUSTOM, or SESSIONVAR. The default is COOKIEPERM.

Site Modeling Tags

These tags are used in site layout and design.

<cfa_container>

<cfa_container> is used to define a region on a page containing data or other content.

Syntax:

```
<cfa_container bUseCache=""
               cacheDir=""
               cacheType=""
               dataSource=""
               dtCacheTimeout=""
               name=""
>
```

Attributes:

Attribute	Description
bUseCache	Optional flag to specify whether to use cached copy of object if it exists (or create one). The default is NO.
cacheDir	Required only if cacheType is FILE. Path for cache files.
cacheType	Optional cache type (only used if bUseCache is YES). Options are SESSION, REQUEST, SERVER, and FILE. The default is SESSION.

Attribute	Description
dataSource	Optional datasource of ContentObject Database. The default is the contents of request.cfacontentObject.dsn.
dtCacheTimeout	Optional cache reset time used if cacheType is SESSION. The default is 0.
name	Required container name. Must be unique on its page.

<cfa_containerGetId>

<cfa_containerGetId> is used to register and determine the ID of containers.

Syntax:

```
<cfa_containerGetId containerName=""
                    dataSource=""
                    pageID=""
                    r_containerID=""
                    r_bIsNewContainer=""
>
```

Attributes:

Attribute	Description
containerName	Required container name.
dataSource	Optional datasource of ContentObject Database. The default is the contents of request.cfacontentObject.dsn.
pageID	Required page ID.
r_containerID	Optional variable to store container ID.
r_bIsNewContainer	Optional flag indicating whether this is a new container that was just registered.

<cfa_page>

<cfa_page> is used to define and use pages.

Syntax:

```
<cfa_page bPreLoadPageObjects=""
          bSecure=""
          dataSource=""
          pageName=""
          r_PageID=""
          sectionName=""
          siteName=""
>
...
</cfa_page>
```

Attributes:

Attribute	Description
bPreLoadPageObjects	Optional flag to specify whether objects should be preloaded for use by page containers. The default is NO.
bSecure	Optional flag to specify whether to check user permission before proceeding. The default is NO.
dataSource	Optional datasource of ContentObject Database. The default is the contents of request.cfacontentObject.dsn.
pageName	Required page name.
r_PageID	Optional variable to contain the assigned page ID.
sectionName	Optional section name. The default is the section specified in the site model.
siteName	Optional site name. The default is the section specified in the site model.

<cfa_pageCacheFlush>

<cfa_pageCacheFlush> is used to flush the cache for a specific page.

Syntax:

```
<cfa_pageCacheFlush dataSource=""
                    pageName=""
>
```

Attributes:

Attribute	Description
dataSource	Optional datasource of ContentObject Database. The default is the contents of request.cfacontentObject.dsn.
pageName	Required page name.

<cfa_refreshPageModel>

<cfa_refreshPageModel> is used to force a page model refresh.

Syntax:

```
<cfa_refreshPageModel dataSource="">
```

Attribute:

Attribute	Description
dataSource	Optional datasource of ContentObject Database. The default is the contents of `request.cfacontentObject.dsn`.

<cfa_refreshSectionModel>

`<cfa_refreshSectionModel>` is used to force a section model refresh.

Syntax:

```
<cfa_refreshSectionModel dataSource="">
```

Attribute:

Attribute	Description
dataSource	Optional datasource of ContentObject Database. The default is the contents of `request.cfacontentObject.dsn`.

<cfa_refreshSiteModel>

`<cfa_refreshSiteModel>` is used to force a site model refresh.

Syntax:

```
<cfa_refreshSiteModel dataSource="">
```

Attribute:

Attribute	Description
dataSource	Optional datasource of ContentObject Database. The default is the contents of `request.cfacontentObject.dsn`.

<cfa_siteElementGetChildren>

`<cfa_siteElementGetChildren>` is used to retrieve the children of site elements.

Syntax:

```
<cfa_siteElementGetChildren bIncludeContainers=""
                            bIncludePages=""
                            bIncludeSections=""
                            dataSource=""
                            elementName=""
                            elementType=""
                            r_qChildren=""
                            r_stChildren=""
>
```

Attributes:

Attribute	Description
bIncludeContainers	Optional flag specifying whether to include containers in the search. The default is YES.
bIncludePages	Optional flag specifying whether to include pages in the search. The default is YES.
bIncludeSections	Optional flag specifying whether to include sections in the search. The default is YES.
dataSource	Optional datasource of ContentObject Database. The default is the contents of request.cfacontentObject.dsn.
elementName	Required name of element to retrieve.
elementType	Optional element type. Default precedence is SECTION followed by PAGE.
r_qChildren	Optional query to contain retrieved children.
r_stChildren	Optional variable to contain retrieved children.

User Interface Tags

These user interface tags aren't actually tied to a particular service but are wrappers around UI elements that can be used within Spectra applications.

<cfa_button>

<cfa_button> creates a text or image button.

Syntax:

```
<cfa_button action=""
            actionData=""
            controlHandlerEventData=""
            description=""
            id=""
            label=""
            state=""
            stDownImage=""
            stDownStyle=""
            stNormalImage=""
            stNormalStyle=""
            stOverImage=""
            stOverStyle=""
            stPressedImage=""
            stPressedStyle=""
            stUnAvailableImage=""
```

```
            stUnAvailablePressedImage=""
            stUnAvailablePressedStyle=""
            stUnAvailableStyle=""
            target=""
>
```


Attributes:

Attribute	Description
action	Required action. Valid values are controlHandlerEvent, javascript, or url.
actionData	Required structure defining action.
controlHandlerEventData	Optional data to be sent to control handler if ACTION is controlHandlerEvent.
description	Optional tooltip description.
id	Required UUID (created with CreateUUID() function).
label	Optional button text.
state	Optional button state. Valid values are NORMAL, UNAVAILABLE, PRESSED, and UNAVAILABLEPRESSED.
stDownImage	Optional image structure for when mouse is clicked.
stDownStyle	Optional style sheet structure for when mouse is clicked.
stNormalImage	Optional normal image structure.
stNormalStyle	Optional normal style sheet structure.
stOverImage	Optional image structure for mouse-over.
stOverStyle	Optional style sheet structure for mouse-over.
stPressedImage	Optional image structure for mouse button pressed.
stPressedStyle	Optional style sheet structure for mouse button pressed.
stUnAvailableImage	Optional image structure for when button is unavailable.
stUnAvailablePressedImage	Optional image structure for when unavailable button is locked in pressed state.
stUnAvailablePressedStyle	Optional style sheet structure for when unavailable button is locked in pressed state.
stUnAvailableStyle	Optional style sheet structure for when button is unavailable.
target	Optional TARGET attribute if ACTION is url.

<cfa_colorSelector>

`<cfa_colorSelector>` is used to display a color selector interface that can be used for the selection of safe and named Web colors.

Syntax:

```
<cfa_colorSelector closeConfirm=""
                   color=""
                   fieldLabel=""
                   fieldMaxLength=""
                   fieldName=""
                   fieldSize=""
                   formAction=""
                   formName=""
                   headerText=""
                   height=""
                   includeCloseButton=""
                   includeFormTags=""
                   includeHeader=""
                   includeTableTags=""
                   includeTDTags=""
                   includeTRTags=""
                   width=""
                   xPosition=""
                   yPosition=""
>
```

Attributes:

Attribute	Description
`closeConfirm`	Optional flag specifying whether to confirm closing of control window if `includeCloseButton` is `NO`. The default is `YES`.
`color`	Optional initial color.
`fieldLabel`	Required field label.
`fieldMaxLength`	Optional maximum field length. The default is `50`.
`fieldName`	Required field name.
`fieldSize`	Optional field size. The default is `25`.
`formAction`	Optional form action page.
`formName`	Optional form name in which to include selector control.
`headerText`	Optional header text. Default text is `Select any color below to change the value in the form. These colors are safe across browsers and platforms.`
`height`	Optional control height in pixels. The default is `250`.

Attribute	Description
includeCloseButton	Optional flag specifying whether to include a close button. The default is YES.
includeFormTags	Optional flag specifying whether to include <FORM> tags. The default is YES.
includeHeader	Optional flag specifying whether to include <TH> tags. The default is YES.
includeTableTags	Optional flag specifying whether to include table tags. The default is YES.
includeTDTags	Optional flag specifying whether to include <TD> tags. The default is YES.
includeTRTags	Optional flag specifying whether to include <TR> tags. The default is YES.
width	Optional control width in pixels. The default is 530.
xPosition	Optional distance from left edge of screen in pixels. The default is 10.
yPosition	Optional distance from top edge of screen in pixels. The default is 10.

<cfa_controlHandler>

<cfa_controlHandler> is used to bind the controls within a handler block to unique client events. This tag is used with one or more <cfa_controlHandlerEvent> tags.

Syntax:

```
<cfa_controlHandler bSuppressForm=""
name=""
                    r_contextName=""
                    r_stContextData=""
>
...
</cfa_controlHandler>
```

Attributes:

Attribute	Description
bSuppressForm	Optional flag specifying whether to suppress display of form. The default is NO.
name	Required unique control name.
r_contextName	Optional name of variable to return context.
r_stContextData	Optional name of the structure in which context data is returned.

<cfa_controlHandlerEvent>

<cfa_controlHandlerEvent> is used associate code with specific controls allowing that code to be executed upon the occurrence of specific events. This tag must be used within <cfa_controlHandler> and </cfa_controlHandler> tags.

Syntax:

```
<cfa_controlHandlerEvent name="">
...
</cfa_controlHandlerEvent>
```

Attribute:

Attribute	Description
name	Required event name

<cfa_dataSheet>

<cfa_dataSheet> is used to create a grid style data sheet.

Syntax:

```
<cfa_dataSheet aDataRows=""
               dataSource=""
               id=""
               navigationControlRegion=""
               stView=""
>
```

Attributes:

Attribute	Description
aDataRows	Optional array of structures containing data to be displayed.
dataSource	Required datasource of ContentObject Database.
id	Required page UUID.
navigationControlRegion	Optional location of navigation controls, valid values are BOTTOM or TOP. The default is BOTTOM.
stView	Required structure containing viewing information.

<cfa_dataSheetArrayGet>

<cfa_dataSheetArrayGet> is used to transform data into a format to be used with <cfa_datasheet>.

Syntax:

```
<cfa_dataSheetArrayGet dataSource=""
                       r_aRows=""
                       stFilter=""
                       stObjects=""
>
```

Attributes:

Attribute	Description
dataSource	Required datasource of ContentObject Database
r_aRows	Required name of variable to contain transformed data
stFilter	Required structure containing data filter information
stObjects	Required structure containing the record sets to be transformed

<cfa_datePicker>

<cfa_datePicker> is used to display an HTML- and JavaScript-based date selection control.

Syntax:

```
<cfa_datePicker bDisplayMonthNames=""
                bShowLabels=""
                bSubmitMonthNames=""
                bUseEuroDates=""
                bUseTextBox=""
                defaultDate=""
                endYear=""
                formName=""
                name=""
                startYear=""
>
```

Attributes:

Attribute	Description
bDisplayMonthNames	Optional flag specifying whether to display month names instead of numbers. The default is NO.
bShowLabels	Optional flag specifying whether to display month, day, and year labels at the start of the list. The default is NO.
bSubmitMonthNames	Optional flag specifying whether to submit month names instead of numbers. The default is NO.
bUseEuroDates	Optional flag specifying whether to use European format dates (day, month, year). The default is NO.

continues

continued

Attribute	Description
defaultDate	Optional date string specifying default value of date picker. The default is 1/31/2000.
bUseTextBox	Optional flag specifying whether to display a single text box for date entry. The default is NO.
endYear	Optional last allowed year. The default is 2100.
formName	Optional form name.
name	Required field name.
startYear	Optional first allowed year. The default is 1900.

<cfa_dropDownMenu>

<cfa_dropDownMenu> is used to render a drop-down menu.

Syntax:

```
<cfa_dropDownMenu dataSource=""
                  id=""
                  label=""
                  stLabelNormalStyle=""
                  stLabelOverStyle=""
                  stMenuStyle=""
>
```

Attributes:

Attribute	Description
dataSource	Required datasource of ContentObject Database
id	Required UUID
label	Required menu label
stLabelNormalStyle	Optional style sheet structure for label properties
stLabelOverStyle	Optional style sheet structure for mouse-over label properties
stMenuStyle	Optional style sheet structure for menu style

<cfa_font>

<cfa_font> is used to create a font style.

Syntax:

```
<cfa_font id=""
          stStyle=""
>
```

Attributes:

Attribute	Description
id	Required ID for style object
stStyle	Required style sheet structure for font style

<cfa_HTMLEditor>

<cfa_HTMLEditor> is used to create an HTML editor screen. The exact editor feature set will vary, based on detected browser capabilities.

Syntax:

```
<cfa_HTMLEditor form=""
                height=""
                name=""
                stFormatting=""
                value=""
                width=""
>
```

Attributes:

Attribute	Description
form	Optional name of form to contain control. The default is first form in page.
height	Required editor height in pixels.
name	Required field name.
stFormatting	Optional formatting information structure.
value	Optional initial value.
width	Required editor width in pixels.

<cfa_HTMLHead>

<cfa_HTMLHead> is used to write a block of text into a page's HTML header section. This tag is essentially a wrapper around the ColdFusion <CFHTMLHEAD> tag.

Syntax:

```
<cfa_HTMLHead>
...
</cfa_HTMLHead>
```

<cfa_HTMLHead> takes no attributes.

<cfa_menuItem>

<cfa_menuItem> is used to populate lists that use menu item tags.

Syntax:

```
<cfa_menuItem controlHandlerEventName=""
              description=""
              javascript=""
              label=""
              selected=""
              stNormalStyle=""
              stOverStyle=""
              target=""
              url=""
>
```

Attributes:

Attribute	Description
controlHandlerEventName	Optional associated server event.
description	Optional tooltip text.
javascript	Optional JavaScript code to be executed upon item activation.
label	Required menu item label.
selected	Optional flag specifying whether this item is currently selected. The default is NO.
stNormalStyle	Optional style sheet structure for item properties.
stOverStyle	Optional style sheet structure for mouse-over item properties.
target	Optional URL target.
url	Optional URL to relocate to upon selection.

<cfa_span>

<cfa_span> is used to wrap a block of text with <SPAN> tags, optionally associating the block with a specified style.

Syntax:

```
<cfa_span dataSource=""
          stStyle=""
>
...
</cfa_span>
```

Attributes:

Attribute	Description
dataSource	Required datasource of ContentObject Database
stStyle	Required style sheet structure

<cfa_tabArea>

`<cfa_tabArea>` is used to create a tabbed dialog style interface. This tag must include one or more tabs created using `<cfa_tabPage>`.

Syntax:

```
<cfa_tabArea height=""
             layout=""
             minimumTabWidth=""
             mode=""
             stNormalStyle=""
             stSelectedStyle=""
             tabHeight=""
             tabType=""
             tabWidth=""
             width=""
>
...
</cfa_tabArea>
```

Attributes:

Attribute	Description
height	Optional minimum box height in pixels.
layout	Optional layout type specifying position of tabs, valid values are BOTTOM, LEFT, RIGHT, or TOP. The default is TOP.
minimumTabWidth	Optional minimum tab width in pixels.
mode	Optional execution mode, valid values are DEFAULT (which will attempt to use client side capabilities if supported by the browser) or SERVERSIDE.
stNormalStyle	Optional style sheet structure for item properties.
stOverStyle	Optional style sheet structure for mouse-over item properties.
tabHeight	Optional minimum height in pixels.
tabType	Optional tab type, valid values are BUTTON, BUTTONLINK, HTMLBUTTON, LINK. The default is LINK.
tabWidth	Optional minimum tab width in pixels.
width	Optional minimum box width in pixels.

<cfa_tabPage>

<cfa_tabPage> is used to define pages within a tabbed dialog. This tag must be used in between <cfa_tabArea> and </cfa_tabArea> tags.

Syntax:

```
<cfa_tabPage name=""
             selected=""
             stButton=""
>
...
</cfa_tabPage>
```

Attributes:

Attribute	Description
name	Required page name.
selected	Optional flag specifying whether this page is selected. The default is NO.
stButton	Button style sheet structure, required if <cfa_tabArea> tabType attribute is BUTTON.

<cfa_tree>

<cfa_tree> is used to display a tree control (similar to the control created by the ColdFusion <CFTREE> tag). This tag can be used with one or more child tags to further control and define tree contents and appearance.

Syntax:

```
<cfa_tree aItems=""
          bReset=""
          bShowItemIcon=""
          clientSideItemLimit=""
          itemCount=""
          mode=""
          name=""
          onSelect=""
          skin=""
          stHighlightStyle=""
          stLinkStyle=""
          stNormalStyle=""
          treeImagesDir=""
          width=""
>
...
</cfa_tree>
```

or

```
<cfa_tree aItems=""
          bReset=""
          bShowItemIcon=""
          clientSideItemLimit=""
          itemCount=""
          mode=""
          name=""
          onSelect=""
          skin=""
          stHighlightStyle=""
          stLinkStyle=""
          stNormalStyle=""
          treeImagesDir=""
          width=""
>
```

Attributes:

Attribute	Description
aItems	Array of tree items, required if <cfa_treeItems> not used.
bReset	Optional flag specifying whether to refresh the tree control which is usually stored in session variables. The default is NO.
bShowItemIcon	Optional flag specifying whether to display icons along-side items. The default is YES.
clientSideItemLimit	Optional maximum number of items to send to client. The default is 750.
itemCount	Optional number of items in aItems.
mode	Optional mode, valid values are MULTISELECT, NAV, or SELECT. The default is MULTISELECT.
name	Required form element name.
skin	Optional set of images to use for icons.
stHighlightStyle	Optional style sheet structure for highlighted item properties.
stLinkStyle	Optional style sheet structure for link item properties.
stNormalStyle	Optional style sheet structure for item properties.
treeImagesDir	Optional directory containing tree icon images.
width	Optional width in pixels or percentage of screen width.

<cfa_treeColumn>

<cfa_treeColumn> is used to populate columns within a tree control created with <cfa_tree>. Column headers are defined with <cfa_treeColumnHeader>.

Syntax:

```
<cfa_treeColumn icon=""
                label=""
                name=""
>
```

Attributes:

Attribute	Description
icon	Optional icon to display. Cannot be used if LABEL is specified.
label	Optional text to display. Cannot be used if ICON is specified.
name	Required column name as defined by <cfa_treeColumnHeader>.

<cfa_treeColumnHeader>

<cfa_treeColumnHeader> is used to define columns within a tree control created with <cfa_tree>. Columns are populated with <cfa_treeColumn>.

Syntax:

```
<cfa_treeColumnHeader label=""
                      name=""
                      width=""
>
```

Attributes:

Attribute	Description
label	Optional text to display in the column header
name	Required unique column name
width	Optional width in pixels or percentage of tree width

<cfa_treeItem>

<cfa_treeItem> is used to populate a tree control created with <cfa_tree>. Tree items can be nested, and so both forms of syntax are supported.

Syntax:

```
<cfa_treeItem expand=""
              icon=""
              label=""
              target=""
              value=""
>
...
</cfa_treeItem>
```

or

```
<cfa_treeItem expand=""
              icon=""
              label=""
              target=""
              value=""
/>
```

Attributes:

Attribute	Description
expand	Optional flag specifying whether to initially display the tree item expanded. The default is NO.
icon	Optional icon to display. The default is FOLDER.
label	Required item text.
target	Optional HREF target.
value	Optional item value.

User Profile and Preference Tags

These tags are used to manage user profiles and preferences.

<cfa_getCurrentUserProfile>

<cfa_getCurrentUserProfile> checks whether a user profile has been loaded, and if not, it's retrieved into the request scope.

Syntax:

```
<cfa_getCurrentUserProfile dataSource=""
                           r_stUserProfile=""
>
```

Attributes:

Attribute	Description
dataSource	Required datasource of ContentObject Database
r_stUserProfile	Required name of the structure to contain retrieved profile

<cfa_userProfileCreate>

<cfa_userProfileCreate> is used to create a new user profile.

Syntax:

```
<cfa_userProfileCreate bActivate=""
                       dataSource=""
                       r_stUserProfile=""
                       userName=""
>
```

Attributes:

Attribute	Description
bActivate	Optional flag specifying whether to activate this user profile. The default is YES.
dataSource	Required datasource of ContentObject Database.
r_stUserProfile	Optional variable to contain user profile structure.
userName	Required username.

<cfa_userProfileFind>

<cfa_userProfileFind> is used to retrieve a user profile by its properties.

Syntax:

```
<cfa_userProfileFind dataSource=""
                     r_stUserProfiles=""
                     stProperties=""
>
```

Attributes:

Attribute	Description
dataSource	Required datasource of ContentObject Database
r_stUserProfiles	Required variable to contain user profile structure
stProperties	Required properties

<cfa_userProfileGet>

`<cfa_userProfileGet>` is used to retrieve a user profile.

Syntax:

```
<cfa_userProfileGet dataSource=""
                    r_stUserProfile=""
                    userName=""
>
```

Attributes:

Attribute	Description
dataSource	Required datasource of ContentObject Database
r_stUserProfile	Required variable to contain user profile structure
userName	Required username

<cfa_userProfileGetMultiple>

`<cfa_userProfileGetMultiple>` is used to retrieve user profiles for a specified list of users.

Syntax:

```
<cfa_userProfileGetMultiple dataSource=""
                            nMaxCount=""
                            r_stUserProfiles=""
                            userNames=""
>
```

Attributes:

Attribute	Description
dataSource	Required datasource of ContentObject Database.
nMaxCount	Optional maximum number of profiles to retrieve. The default is all profiles.
r_stUserProfiles	Required variable to contain user profile structures.
userNames	Optional comma-delimited list of usernames.

<cfa_userProfileSet>

`<cfa_userProfileSet>` is used to update a user profile.

Syntax:

```
<cfa_userProfileSet dataSource=""
                    stUserProfile=""
                    userName=""
>
```

Attributes:

Attribute	Description
dataSource	Required datasource of ContentObject Database
stUserProfile	Required user profile structure
userName	Required username

Utility Tags

The utility tags are a collection of miscellaneous tags that can be used anywhere within a Spectra application.

<cfa_assocAttribs>

`<cfa_assocAttribs>` is used to associate a base tag with a child tag.

Syntax:

```
<cfa_assocAttribs callerTag="">
```

Attribute:

Attribute	Description
callerTag	Required name of caller tag

<cfa_associate>

`<cfa_associate>` is used to associate a child tag with a base tag.

Syntax:

```
<cfa_associate baseTag=""
               callerTag=""
               dataCollection=""
>
```

Attributes:

Attribute	Description
baseTag	Required name of base tag.
callerTag	Required name of caller tag.
dataCollection	Optional data collection name. The default is AssocAttribs.

<cfa_cfformIsUniqueItem>

`<cfa_cfformIsUniqueItem>` is used to generate JavaScript code to check that a list of items in a form is unique.

Syntax:

```
<cfa_cfformIsUniqueItem functionName=""
                        lItems=""
>
```

Attributes:

Attribute	Description
functionName	Required name of JavaScript function to generate
lItems	Required list of items to check

<cfa_datasourceGetList>

`<cfa_datasourceGetList>` is used to retrieve a list of available data sources.

Syntax:

```
<cfa_dataSourceGetList r_qDatasource="">
```

Attribute:

Attribute	Description
r_qDatasource	Required name of query to contain retrieved data source list

<cfa_deepCopy>

`<cfa_deepCopy>` is used to copy a complete set of structures, arrays, or other data types. This is also referred to as a *copy by value.*

Syntax:

```
<cfa_deepCopy input=""
              output-""
>
```

Attributes:

Attribute	Description
input	Required source
output	Required destination

<cfa_dump>

`<cfa_dump>` is used to display a specified variable. Data can be a simple variable, a query, a structure, an array, or a WDDX packet. This tag is primarily used in debugging.

Syntax:

```
<cfa_dump var="">
```

Attribute:

Attribute	Description
var	Required variable's data to dump

<cfa_dumpObject>

`<cfa_dumpObject>` is used to display the contents of an object. This tag is primarily used in debugging.

Syntax:

```
<cfa_dumpObject dataSource=""
                objectID=""
>
```

Attributes:

Attribute	Description
dataSource	Required datasource of ContentObject Database
objectID	Required object ID

<cfa_executionTime>

`<cfa_executionTime>` is used to display the time taken to execute a block of code. This tag is primarily used in debugging.

Syntax:

```
<cfa_executionTime label="">
```

Attribute:

Attribute	Description
label	Optional label to display next to execution time

<cfa_fetchGeneratedContent>

`<cfa_fetchGeneratedContent>` is used to retrieve generated content returning it in a variable.

Syntax:

```
<cfa_fetchGeneratedContent bReset=""
                           r_generatedContent=""
>
```

Attributes:

Attribute	Description
bReset	Optional flag specifying whether to clear the content once it has been fetched. The default is YES.
r_generatedContent	Required variable to contain fetched content.

<cfa_formDetect>

`<cfa_formDetect>` is used to detect if a form exists within a block of code, in which case, its contents are suppressed.

Syntax:

```
<cfa_formDetect r_bContainsForm=""
                r_generatedContent=""
>
```

Attributes:

Attribute	Description
r_bContainsForm	Required variable to contain form exists flag
r_generatedContent	Required variable to contain suppressed contentis used to detect if a form exists

<cfa_formfields2Struct>

`<cfa_formfields2Struct>` is used to detect if a form existsis used to create a structure containing form fields and values.

Syntax:

```
<cfa_formfields2Struct lExclude=""
                       lformFields=""
                       r_struct=""
>
```

Attributes:

Attribute	Description
lExclude	Optional list of fields to ignore.
lformFields	Optional list of fields to include. The default is all form fields.
r_struct	Required variable to contain generated structure.

<cfa_generatedContentCache>

`<cfa_generatedContentCache>` is used to cache generated content.

Syntax:

```
<cfa_generatedContentCache bUseCache=""
                           cacheDir=""
                           cacheName=""
                           cacheType=""
                           dtCacheTimeout=""
                           nLockTimeout=""
                           r_stParams=""
>
```

Attributes:

Attribute	Description
bUseCache	Optional flag to specify whether to use cached copy of object if it exists (or create one). The default is NO.
cacheDir	Required only if cacheType is FILE. Path for cache files.
cacheName	Required unique cache name.
cacheType	Optional cache type (only used if bUseCache is YES). Options are SESSION, REQUEST, SERVER, and FILE. The default is SESSION.
dtCacheTimeout	Optional cache reset time used if cacheType is SESSION. The default is 0.
nLockTimeout	Optional lock timeout in milliseconds. The default is 20.
r_stParams	Optional name of variable into which content item parameters are stored.

<cfa_generatedContentCacheFlush>

<cfa_generatedContentCacheFlush> is used to flush a specific cache.

Syntax:

```
<cfa_generatedContentCacheFlush cacheDir=""
                                cacheName=""
                                cacheType=""
>
```

Attributes:

Attribute	Description
cacheDir	Required only if cacheType is FILE. Path for cache files.
cacheName	Required unique cache name.
cacheType	Optional cache. Options are SESSION, REQUEST, SERVER, and FILE. The default is SESSION.

<cfa_getCurrentUsername>

<cfa_getCurrentUsername>is used to obtain the current logged in user.

Syntax:

```
<cfa_getCurrentUsername r_userName="">
```

Attribute:

Attribute	Description
r_userName	Required name of variable to contain retrieved username

<cfa_getFileExtension>

<cfa_getFileExtension> is used to retrieve the extension of a specified filename.

Syntax:

```
<cfa_getFileExtension file=""
                      r_extension=""
>
```

Attributes:

Attribute	Description
file	Required filename
r_extension	Required variable to contain file extension

<cfa_getStringInfo>

`<cfa_getStringInfo>` is used to check string properties.

Syntax:

```
<cfa_getStringInfo r_bIsAllowedVarName=""
                   r_bIsUUID=""
                   string=""
>
```

Attributes:

Attribute	Description
`r_bIsAllowedVarName`	Optional variable to store flag indicating if the string is a valid variable name
`r_bIsUUID`	Optional variable to store flag indicating if the string is a valid UUID
`string`	Required string

<cfa_globalSettings>

`<cfa_globalSettings>` is used establish global settings using the request scope.

Syntax:

```
<cfa_globalSettings>
```

`<cfa_globalSettings>` takes no attributes.

<cfa_handler>

`<cfa_handler>` creates a scope for the handled object. Loops automatically if multiple content items are being handled.

Syntax:

```
<cfa_handler ISOLanguage=""
             object=""
             result=""
             separator=""
>
...
</cfa_handler>
```

Attributes:

Attribute	Description
`ISOLanguage`	Optional two character ISO language code. The default is `en` (English).
`object`	Optional object name.
`result`	Optional variable to store result exposed by handler.
`separator`	Optional text delimiter.

<cfa_isCollection>

`<cfa_isCollection>` is used to check whether a specified collection exists.

Syntax:

```
<cfa_isCollection collection=""
                  r_bIsCollection=""
>
```

Attributes:

Attribute	Description
`collection`	Required collection name
`r_bIsCollection`	Required variable to store flag indicating if collection exists

<cfa_isDataSource>

`<cfa_isDataSource>` is used to check whether a specified data source exists.

Syntax:

```
<cfa_isDataSource dataSource=""
                  r_bIsDataSource=""
>
```

Attributes:

Attribute	Description
`dataSource`	Required data source name
`r_bIsDataSource`	Required variable to store flag indicating if data source exists

<cfa_isEmbeddedObject>

<cfa_isEmbeddedObject> is used to check if an object ID belongs to an embedded object.

Syntax:

```
<cfa_isEmbeddedObject objectID=""
                      r_bIsEmbeddedObject=""
                      r_ownerObjectID=""
                      r_scope="
>
```

Attributes:

Attribute	Description
objectID	Required object ID
r_bIsEmbeddedObject	Required variable to store flag indicating if object is an embedded object
r_ownerObjectID	Optional variable in which to store the owner object ID
r_scope	Optional variable in which to store the object scope.

<cfa_isWDDX>

<cfa_isWDDX> is used to check whether a string is a valid WDDX packet. If the string is a WDDX packet, it's decoded.

Syntax:

```
<cfa_isWDDX input=""
            r_bIsWDDX=""
            r_output="
>
```

Attributes:

Attribute	Description
input	Required string to check
r_output	Required variable to store decoded WDDX
r_bIsWDDX	Required variable to store flag indicating whether the string is valid WDDX

<cfa_listMakeDistinct>

<cfa_listMakeDistinct> is used to remove all duplicate items from a list.

Syntax:

```
<cfa_listMakeDistinct bCaseSensitive=""
                      delimiters=""
                      lInput=""
                      r_lOutput="
>
```

Attributes:

Attribute	Description
bCaseSensitive	Optional flag specifying whether to treat the list as case sensitive. The default is YES.
delimiters	Optional list delimiters.
lInput	Required list to process.
r_lOutput	Required variable to store output.

<cfa_newWindow>

<cfa_newWindow> is used to create a link which, when clicked, opens a new window.

Syntax:

```
<cfa_newWindow height=""
               imageAlt=""
               imageSource=""
               left=""
               method=""
               newWindowName=""
               source=""
               top=""
               width=""
>
```

Attributes:

Attribute	Description
height	Required window height in pixels.
imageAlt	Optional alternate image text.
imageSource	Image source, required if METHOD is IMAGE.
left	Required window offset from left in pixels.
method	Optional method, valid values are BUTTON, IMAGE, or LINK. The default is LINK.
newWindowName	Required JavaScript window object name.
source	Required HTTP source for new window.
top	Required window offset from top in pixels.
width	Required window width in pixels.

<cfa_resolveCFMapping>

<cfa_resolveCFMapping> is used to convert a ColdFusion mapping to an absolute path.

Syntax:

```
<cfa_resolveCFMapping b_returnUNIXCompatible=""
                      mapping=""
```

```
                     r_bMappingExists=""
                     r_resolvedMapping="
>
```

Attributes:

Attribute	Description
b_returnUNIXCompatible	Optional flag specifying whether to return a UNIX-compatible path. The default is YES.
mapping	Required mapping to convert.
r_bMappingExists	Optional variable to store mapping exists flag.
r_resolvedMapping	Optional variable to store resolved mapping.

<cfa_sort2dArray>

<cfa_sort2dArray> is used to sort a two-dimensional array by one or more specified fields.

Syntax:

```
<cfa_sort2dArray array=""
                 liIndex=""
                 r_array=""
                 type="
>
```

Attributes:

Attribute	Description
array	Required array to sort.
liIndex	Required comma-delimited list of fields to sort by.
r_array	Optional variable to store sorted array.
type	Optional sort order. Valid values are ASC or DESC. The default is ASC.

<cfa_stripDebug>

<cfa_stripDebug> is used to strip debug output from the bottom of a ColdFusion generated page.

Syntax:

```
<cfa_stripDebug input=""
                r_output=""
>
```

Attributes:

Attribute	Description
`input`	Required input page
`r_output`	Required variable to contain stripped output

<cfa_structGet>

`<cfa_structGet>` is used to check for the existence of a structure or structure key, creating it if it doesn't exist.

Syntax:

```
<cfa_structGet r_struct=""
               structName=""
>
```

Attributes:

Attribute	Description
`r_struct`	Required variable to contain newly created structure
`structName`	Required structure or structure key name

<cfa_structSortCommonSubkeys>

`<cfa_structSortCommonSubkeys>` is used to return an array of key names from an associative array.

Syntax:

```
<cfa_structSortCommonSubkeys commonSubKey=""
                             r_aSortedKeys=""
                             sortOrder=""
                             sortType=""
                             struct=""
>
```

Attributes:

Attribute	Description
`commonSubKey`	Required sub key by which to sort.
`r_aSortedKeys`	Required variable to contain sorted array.
`sortOrder`	Optional sort order. Valid values are `ASC` or `DESC`. The default is `ASC`.
`sortType`	Optional sort order, valid values are `NUMERIC`, `TEXT`, or `TEXTNOCASE`. The default is `TEXTNOCASE`.
`struct`	Required array or associative array of structures.

<cfa_URL2Struct>

`<cfa_URL2Struct>` is used to convert a URL into a structure of name value pairs.

Syntax:

```
<cfa_URL2Struct lExclude=""
                queryString=""
                r_struct=""
>
```

Attributes:

Attribute	Description
lExclude	Optional list of parameters to exclude
queryString	Optional query string, defaults to complete current query string
r_struct	Required variable to store new structure

<cfa_URLAppendTrailingSlash>

`<cfa_URLAppendTrailingSlash>` is used to append a slash at the end of a URL if needed.

Syntax:

```
<cfa_URLAppendTrailingSlash input=""
                            output=""
>
```

Attributes:

Attribute	Description
input	Required URL to be tested
output	Required name of variable to store converted URL

<cfa_URLRemoveTrailingSlash>

`<cfa_URLRemoveTrailingSlash>` is used to remove a slash from the end of a URL if it exists.

Syntax:

```
<cfa_URLRemoveTrailingSlash input=""
                            r_output=""
>
```

Attributes:

Attribute	Description
input	Required URL to be tested
r_output	Required name of variable to store converted URL

<cfa_URLSet>

<cfa_URLSet> is used to create a well-formed URL.

Syntax:

```
<cfa_URLSet protocol=""
            r_URL=""
            server=""
            URL=""
>
```

Attributes:

Attribute	Description
protocol	Optional protocol
r_URL	Required variable to store created URL
server	Optional server name or IP address
URL	Required absolute or relative URL

Workflow Tags

These tags are used to create and manage tasks and workflow.

<cfa_taskBegin>

<cfa_taskBegin> is used to mark a task as having begun.

Syntax:

```
<cfa_taskBegin dataSource=""
               taskID=""
>
```

Attributes:

Attribute	Description
dataSource	Required datasource of ContentObject Database
taskID	Required task ID

<cfa_taskDependency>

`<cfa_taskDependency>` is used to establish dependencies among tasks in a workflow.

Syntax:

```
<cfa_taskDependency action=""
                    dataSource=""
                    lPredecessorTaskIDs=""
                    taskID=""
                    workflowID=""
>
```

Attributes:

Attribute	Description
action	Required action. Valid values are CREATE or DELETE.
dataSource	Required datasource of ContentObject Database.
lPredecessorTaskIDs	Required list of tasks that must be completed before this task can begin.
taskID	Required task ID.
workflowID	Required workflow ID.

<cfa_taskEnd>

`<cfa_taskEnd>` is used to mark a task as having been completed.

Syntax:

```
<cfa_taskEnd dataSource=""
             taskID=""
             workflowID=""
>
```

Attributes:

Attribute	Description
dataSource	Required datasource of ContentObject Database
taskID	Required task ID
workflowID	Required related workflow ID

<cfa_taskExecute>

`<cfa_taskExecute>` is used to execute a specified task.

Syntax:

```
<cfa_taskExecute dataSource=""
                 taskID=""
>
```

Attributes:

Attribute	Description
dataSource	Required datasource of ContentObject Database
taskID	Required task ID

<cfa_taskInstanceCreate>

<cfa_taskInstanceCreate> is used to create an instance of a specific task type.

Syntax:

```
<cfa_taskInstanceCreate autoExecute=""
                        dataSource=""
                        description=""
                        dtTaskDue=""
                        method=""
                        name=""
                        notificationMethod=""
                        notificationType=""
                        owner=""
                        PLPID=""
                        r_taskID=""
                        taskTypeID=""
>
```

Attributes:

Attribute	Description
autoExecute	Optional flag specifying whether to initially flag this task as begun. The default is NO.
dataSource	Required datasource of ContentObject Database.
description	Optional instance description.
dtTaskDue	Optional due date.
method	Optional method for this task. Cannot be used if PLPID is specified.
name	Optional instance name.
notificationMethod	Notification method, required if notificationType is CUSTOM.
notificationType	Optional notification type. Valid values are CUSTOM, EMAIL, NONE, or PAGER. The default is EMAIL.
owner	Required instance owner.
PLPID	Optional ID of PLP for this task. Cannot be used if METHOD is specified.
r_taskID	Required variable to store ID of task instance.
taskTypeID	Required task type ID.

<cfa_taskRedo>

`<cfa_taskRedo>` is used to restart a specific task.

Syntax:

```
<cfa_taskRedo dataSource=""
              taskID=""
              workflowID=""
>
```

Attributes:

Attribute	Description
dataSource	Required datasource of ContentObject Database
taskID	Required task ID
workflowID	Required workflow ID

<cfa_taskType>

`<cfa_taskType>` is used to create, update, and delete task types.

Syntax:

```
<cfa_taskType action=""
              dataSource=""
              description=""
              method=""
              name=""
              owner=""
              r_taskTypeID=""
              taskTypeID=""
>
```

Attributes:

Attribute	Description
action	Required action. Valid values are CREATE, DELETE, or UPDATE.
dataSource	Required datasource of ContentObject Database.
description	Optional task type description.
method	Optional method to invoke.
name	Optional task type name.
owner	Optional default owner.
r_taskTypeID	Variable for task type ID, required if ACTION is CREATE.
taskTypeID	Task type ID, required if ACTION is DELETE or UPDATE.

<cfa_taskTypeDependency>

`<cfa_taskTypeDependency>` is used to establish dependencies between tasks types.

Syntax:

```
<cfa_taskTypeDependency action=""
                        dataSource=""
                        lPredecessorTaskTypeIDs=""
                        taskTypeID=""
                        workflowTypeID=""
>
```

Attributes:

Attribute	Description
action	Required action. Valid values are CREATE or DELETE.
dataSource	Required datasource of ContentObject Database.
lPredecessorTaskTypeIDs	Required list of tasks types that must be completed before this task type can begin.
taskTypeID	Required task ID.
workflowTypeID	Required workflow ID.

<cfa_taskUpdate>

`<cfa_taskUpdate>` is used to update specific tasks.

Syntax:

```
<cfa_taskUpdate autoExecute=""
                dataSource=""
                description=""
                dtTaskDue=""
                method=""
                name=""
                notificationMethod=""
                notificationType=""
                owner=""
                PLPID=""
                taskID=""
>
```

Attributes:

Attribute	Description
autoExecute	Optional flag specifiying whether to initially flag this task as begun. The default is NO.
dataSource	Required datasource of ContentObject Database.

continues

continued

Attribute	Description
description	Optional new task description.
dtTaskDue	Optional new due date.
method	Optional new method for this task. Cannot be used if PLPID is specified.
name	Optional new task name.
notificationMethod	Notification method, required if notificationType is CUSTOM.
notificationType	Optional new notification type. Valid values are CUSTOM, EMAIL, NONE, or PAGER. The default is EMAIL.
owner	Optional new task owner.
PLPID	Optional ID of new PLP for this task. Cannot be used if METHOD is specified.
taskID	Required task ID.

<cfa_workflowDelete>

<cfa_workflowDelete> is used to delete a workflow instance and any related tasks.

Syntax:

```
<cfa_workflowDelete dataSource=""
                    workflowID=""
>
```

Attributes:

Attribute	Description
dataSource	Required datasource of ContentObject Database
workflowID	Required workflow ID

<cfa_workflowExecute>

<cfa_workflowExecute> is used to begin (or refresh) a workflow instance.

Syntax:

```
<cfa_workflowExecute dataSource=""
                     r_bTargetTaskEnd=""
                     workflowID=""
>
```

Attributes:

Attribute	Description
`dataSource`	Required datasource of ContentObject Database
`r_bTargetTaskEnd`	Optional variable to contain target end flag
`workflowID`	Required workflow ID

<cfa_workflowGetList>

`<cfa_workflowGetList>` is used to retrieve information about a workflow instance.

Syntax:

```
<cfa_workflowGetList dataSource=""
                     r_stWorkflowAgenda=""
                     workflowID=""
>
```

Attributes:

Attribute	Description
`dataSource`	Required datasource of ContentObject Database
`r_stWorkflowAgenda`	Required structure to store retrieved workflow details
`workflowID`	Required workflow ID

<cfa_workflowGetUserWorkList>

`<cfa_workflowGetUserWorkList>` is used to retrieve information about active workflow tasks for a specific user.

Syntax:

```
<cfa_workflowGetUserWorkList dataSource=""
                             r_stWorkflowUserWorkList=""
                             userName=""
                             workflowID=""
>
```

Attributes:

Attribute	Description
`dataSource`	Required datasource of ContentObject Database
`r_stWorkflowUserWorkList`	Required structure to store retrieved workflow details
`userName`	Required username
`workflowID`	Required workflow ID

<cfa_workflowInstanceCreate>

<cfa_workflowInstanceCreate> is used to create an instance of a workflow.

Syntax:

```
<cfa_workflowInstanceCreate dataSource=""
                            description=""
                            name=""
                            r_workflowID=""
                            workflowDirector=""
                            workflowTypeID=""
>
```

Attributes:

Attribute	Description
dataSource	Required datasource of ContentObject Database.
description	Optional description.
name	Optional name.
r_workflowID	Required variable to store new workflow ID.
workflowDirector	Optional workflow director. The default is the director specified in the workflow specification.
workflowTypeID	Required workflow type ID.

<cfa_workflowReset>

<cfa_workflowReset> is used to reset a workflow instance back to its original state.

Syntax:

```
<cfa_workflowReset dataSource=""
                   workflowID=""
>
```

Attributes:

Attribute	Description
dataSource	Required datasource of ContentObject Database
workflowID	Required workflow ID

<cfa_workflowShow>

<cfa_workflowShow> is used to generate HTML code providing a workflow visualization.

Syntax:

```
<cfa_workflowShow dataSource=""
                  workflowID=""
>
```

Attributes:

Attribute	Description
dataSource	Required datasource of ContentObject Database
workflowID	Required workflow ID

<cfa_workflowTarget>

<cfa_workflowTarget> is used to mark or unmark tasks as workflow targets.

Syntax:

```
<cfa_workflowTarget action=""
                    dataSource=""
                    taskID=""
                    workflowID=""
>
```

Attributes:

Attribute	Description
action	Required action. Valid values are CREATE or DELETE.
dataSource	Required datasource of ContentObject Database.
taskID	Required task ID.
workflowID	Required workflow ID.

<cfa_workflowTaskBind>

<cfa_workflowTaskBind> is used to associate or disassociate task instances with workflow instances.

Syntax:

```
<cfa_workflowTaskBind action=""
                      dataSource=""
                      ltaskIDs=""
                      workflowID=""
>
```

Attributes:

Attribute	Description
action	Required action. Valid values are CREATE or DELETE.
dataSource	Required datasource of ContentObject Database.
ltaskIDs	Required list of task IDs.
workflowID	Required workflow ID.

<cfa_workflowTaskTypeBind>

`<cfa_workflowTaskTypeBind>` is used to associate or disassociate task types with workflow specifications.

Syntax:

```
<cfa_workflowTaskTypeBind action=""
                          dataSource=""
                          ltaskTypeIDs=""
                          workflowTypeID=""
>
```

Attributes:

Attribute	Description
`action`	Required action. Valid values are `CREATE` or `DELETE`.
`dataSource`	Required datasource of ContentObject Database.
`ltaskTypeIDs`	Required list of task type IDs.
`workflowTypeID`	Required workflow type ID.

<cfa_workflowType>

`<cfa_workflowType>` is used to create, update, and delete workflow types.

Syntax:

```
<cfa_workflowType action=""
                  artifactTypeID=""
                  dataSource=""
                  description=""
                  name=""
                  r_workflowTypeID=""
                  workflowDirector=""
                  workflowTypeID=""
>
```

Attributes:

Attribute	Description
`action`	Required action. Valid values are `CREATE`, `DELETE`, or `UPDATE`.
`artifiactTypeID`	Optional type ID of the content type to be built by the workflow.
`dataSource`	Required datasource of ContentObject Database.
`description`	Optional task type description.

Attribute	Description
name	Optional task type name.
r_workflowTypeID	Variable for workflow type ID.
workflowDirector	Optional user who will act as workflow director for all instances of this workflow type.
workflowTypeID	Workflow type ID, required if ACTION is DELETE or UPDATE.

APPENDIX B

Spectra Structures

In this appendix

Spectra makes extensive use of ColdFusion structures for data storage and manipulation. An integral part of writing Spectra code requires an understanding of these structures. This appendix lists the structures and their members, with a brief explanation of each.

NOTE *Structures* are a hierarchical ColdFusion data type used to store related information under a single variable. For more information on basic structure usage and the ColdFusion structure manipulation functions, refer to your ColdFusion documentation.

Category

Description: Stores metadata category information.

Referred to as: `r_stCategory`

Category Structure Keys

Key	Description
`Hierarchy`	Hierarchy ID; 0 is the root
`Label`	Category label (name)
`stChildren`	Structure containing IDs of child categories
`stKeywords`	Structure containing related keywords
`stParents`	Structure containing IDs of parent categories

See also: Child Element, Hierarchy

Child Element

Description: Stores child element information; used by site modeling.

Referred to as: `r_stChildren`

Child Element Structure Keys

Key	Description
`AbsolutePath`	Child element absolute path
`AbsoluteURL`	Child element full URL
`ID`	Child element unique ID (as UUID)
`Label`	Child element label (name)
`RelativePath`	Child element relative path

Key	Description
RelativeURL	Child element relative URL
Type	Child element type

See also: Category

ContentObject Type

Description: Core object type used for content storage.

Referred to as: st_Type, r_stType

ContentObject Type Structure Keys

Key	Description
Description	Brief object description
HandlerRoot	URL for directory containing object handlers for the ContentObject Type
Label	Object label (name)
nSysAttributes	Reserved
stTypePropertyDefinitions	Array of Type Property Definition structures (of type Group)
stTypeMethodDefinitions	Array of type method definitions (of type Method Definition)
TypeID	Object type ID

See also: Group, Object, Type Method Definition

Error Data

Description: Error information based on the tag being used. The contents of this structure vary, based on the tags being used.

Group

Description: Group definition information.

Referred to as: st_Groups, r_stGroups

Group Structure Keys	
Key	**Description**
`Description`	Brief group description
`GroupName`	Group name

Hierarchy

Description: Meta data hierarchy.

Referred to as: `r_stHierarchy`

Hierarchy Structure Keys	
Key	**Description**
`0`	Structure containing labels and IDs of child categories in the structure. Each level contains a label and 0 or more category IDs. The presence of a category ID indicates the existence of a lower level.
`Label`	Hierarchy label (name)
`stCategories`	Structure containing the IDs of categories defined in the hierarchy

Log File

Description: Log file entry format.

Log File Structure Keys	
Key	**Description**
`dtTimeStamp`	Date and time error occurred
`Label`	Object label (name)
`Method`	The method being executed when the error occurred
`ObjectID`	ID of the object being used when the error occurred
`PageID`	ID of the page being processed when the error occurred
`RemoteAddr`	IP address of the requesting client
`SectionID`	ID of the section being processed when the error occurred
`SessionID`	ID of the user session in which the error occurred

Key	Description
SiteID	ID of the site in which the error occurred
TypeID	ID of the ContentObject Type being processed when the error occurred
UserAgent	Description of the user agent
UserID	ID of the user running the session in which the error occurred

See also: ContentObject Type

Message Data

Description: Message data.

Referred to as: `stMessageData`

Message Data Structure Keys

Key	Description
Body	Message body structure
Header	Message header structure

See also: Message Queue

Message Queue

Description: Message queue.

Referred to as: `stMessageQueue`

Message Queue Structure Keys

Key	Description
HandlerRoot	Directory containing message queue handlers (uses ColdFusion mapping)
Label	Message queue label (name)
Messages	Array of messages in message queue
Methods	Array of methods defined for message queue
ObjectID	Message queue unique ID

See also: Message Data

Object

Description: Structure for objects or content items.

Referred to as: `stObject`, `r_stObject`, `stObjects`, `r_stObjects`

Object Structure Keys

Key	Description
`Attr_Active`	Object is active flag
`Attr_Archived`	Object is archived flag
`Attr_CreatedBy`	Name of user who created the object
`Attr_DateTimeCreated`	Date and time of object creation
`Attr_DateTimeLastUpdate`	Date and time object was last updated
`Attr_LastUpdatedBy`	Name of user who last updated the object
`Attr_Locked`	Object is locked flag
`Attr_LockedBy`	Name of user who has locked the object (if `Attr_Locked` is true)
`Attr_System`	Object has system flag
`Attr_Published`	Reserved
`Attr_Secure`	Reserved
`Attr_Public`	Reserved
`Label`	Object label (name)
`nSysAttributes`	Reserved
`ObjectID`	Object unique ID
`PropertyName`	Property definition structure
`stKeywords`	Meta data keywords associated with this object
`TypeID`	ID of the associated ContentObject Type

See also: ContentObject Type, Property Definition

PLP

Description: Process logic path (PLP) definition.

PLP Structure Keys

Key	Description
`Completed`	PLP finished flag.
`CurrentStep`	Current step is active flag.

Key	Description
`HandlerRelativePath`	Relative path to directory containing PLP handlers.
`HandlerRoot`	Full path to directory containing PLP handlers.
`Input`	Data received during current step.
`IsActive`	PLP is active flag. Set to `YES` when PLP is active.
`LastModified`	Data and time of last modification to PLP.
`LastStep`	Last step is active flag.
`Name`	Name of the PLP.
`NextStep`	Name of the next step.
`Result`	PLP result.
`Started`	Date and time PLP was started.
`Steps`	Array containing PLP steps.
`TimeOut`	PLP step timeout interval, in minutes. Default value is `15`.

See also: PLP `ThisStep`

PLP *ThisStep*

Description: Process logic path (PLP) step definition.

PLP *ThisStep* Structure Keys

Key	Description
`Advance`	PLP step is complete and ready to advance to next step flag.
`CurrentRow`	Current iteration.
`DataSource`	Datasource passed to PLP processing tags.
`IsComplete`	PLP step is complete flag.
`IterateKey`	Current iteration value.
`IterateList`	List of keys iterated over.
`NextStep`	Override next step name.
`QueryString`	Variable to be appended to URL when advancing.
`URL`	URL of current template.

See also: PLP

Property Definition

Description: Property definition.

Referred to as: `stPropertyDefinitions`, `r_stPropertyDefinitions`, `stDefinitions`, `r_stDefinitions`

Property Definitions Structure Keys

Key	Description
`aInputOptions`	Array of option structures
`ClientValidationExpression`	JavaScript client-side validation rule
`DataType`	Property definition data type (Integer, Numeric, Char, LongChar, DateTime)
`Description`	Brief description
`InputType`	Form input type (Text, TextArea, Select, MultiSelect, Checkbox, Radio, WDDX)
`Label`	Property label (name)
`nSysAttributes`	Reserved
`PropertyDefinitionID`	Property definition unique ID
`ServerValidationExpression`	CFML server-side validation rule
`ValidationErrorMessage`	Message to be displayed on validation failure

Property Search

Description: Property search results.

Referred to as: `r_qResults`, `r_stResults`

Property Search Structure Keys

Key	Description
`Label`	Current item label (name)
`ObjectID`	Object unique ID
`Property`	Property name
`Score`	Search results relevancy score
`stProperties`	Complete object structure
`Type`	Associated ContentObject Type ID

See also: ContentObject Type

Schedule

Description: Scheduled task structure.

Referred to as: `r_stSchedule`

Schedule Structure Keys

Key	Description
EndDate	Schedule end date
EndTime	Schedule end time
File	Filename if publishing
Interval	Execution interval
Operation	Operation type
Password	Password to be used for secure URLs
Path	Full path of directory if publishing
ProxyServer	Name or IP address of proxy server if needed
Publish	Publish (save) results flag
RequestTimeOut	Request time out value
ResolveURL	Resolve URL in results flag
StartDate	Schedule start date
StartTime	Schedule start time
TaskName	Method to be executed
UserName	Username to be used for secure URLs

Style Object

Description: Style encapsulation object.

Style Object Structure Keys

Key	Description
Background_Color	Background color or RGB value
Border_Color	Border color or RGB value
Border_Style	CSS border style specifier
Border_Width	Width of border in pixels
Color	Color name or RGB value
Font_Family	Font family designator

continues

continued

Style Object Structure Keys	
Key	**Description**
`Font_Size`	CSS font size specifier
`Font_Weight`	Font weight value
`Padding_Left`	Number of pixels to pad left side of cells
`Padding_Right`	Number of pixels to pad right side of cells

Type Method Definition

Description: Type method definition.

Referred to as: `stMethodDefinitions`, `r_stMethodDefinitions`

Type Method Definition Structure Keys	
Key	**Description**
`Alias`	Alias (alternate name) for method
`Description`	Brief method description
`HandlerURL`	URL of the method handler
`Method`	Method name

User

Description: User definition.

Referred to as: `stUsers`, `r_stUsers`

User Structure Keys	
Key	**Description**
`Description`	User description
`Password`	Password
`UserName`	Username

See also: User Directory, User Worklist

User Directory

Description: User directory definition.

Referred to as: `stUserDirectory`, `r_stUserDirectory`

User Directory Structure Keys

Key	Description
`Description`	Directory description
`Lookup_Start`	Lookup prefix
`NameSpace`	Type of directory (LDAP or NT)
`Password`	Login password
`Search_Scope`	Depth of search to be performed
`Search_Root`	LDAP search root
`SecureConnect`	Secure connection required flag (uses SSL)
`Server`	Domain server name if `NameSpace` is Windows NT; LDAP server if `NameSpace` is LDAP
`UserName`	Login username

See also: User

User Worklist

Description: User workflow list definition.

Referred to as: `stWorkflowUserWorkList`, `r_WorkflowUserWorkList`

User Worklist Structure Keys

Key	Description
`Tasks`	Structure of tasks for specified user
`Workflow`	Workflow ID

See also: User, Workflow Agenda

Workflow Agenda

Description: Workflow Agenda definition.

Referred to as: `stWorkflowAgenda`, `r_WorkflowAgenda`

Workflow Agenda Structure Keys

Key	Description
`Tasks`	Structure of all workflow tasks
`Workflow`	Workflow ID

See also: User, User Worklist

APPENDIX C

COAPI Data Types

In this appendix

Spectra provides support for commonly used data types in the form of Core Object Types (known as Media Assets in the Webtop). These are traditional style objects with both properties (attributes) and methods (functions).

This appendix lists the four Core Object Types provided, with the properties and methods for each (including parameters where appropriate).

NOTE It's highly likely that future versions of Spectra will include additional or enhanced Core Object Types. To prevent possible naming conflicts in the future, name any custom types (types you yourself create) with a naming convention that does not use generic names (like File and Image).

File

The File object type is used for all file access and manipulation and can be used with files of any MIME type.

Properties

The File object type contains the following properties:

Property	Description
`FileName`	Filename (no path)
`FilePath`	Complete path (including filename)
`FileURL`	Complete URL (including filename)

Methods

The File object type supports the following six methods:

- The `Create` method is used to create new file objects. `Create` takes the following parameters:

Parameter	Description
`stParams.FilePath`	Full path for new file
`stParams.FileName`	New filename
`stParams.FileURL`	URL to new file

- The `Delete` method is used to delete file objects. `Delete` takes no parameters.
- The `Display` method is used to create and display links to files. `Display` takes no parameters.
- The `Edit` method is used to edit files. `Edit` takes no parameters.

- The `Picker` method is used to display a file selection interface. Once a file has been selected, the object is updated with the selection information. `Picker` takes the following parameters:

Parameter	Description
`stParams.DirectoryPath`	Required full path of directory to be displayed
`stParams.DirectoryURL`	Required URL for directory to be displayed
`stParams.lExtensionFilter`	Optional list of extensions to use for file filtering
`stParams.DefaultFile`	Optional default file selection

- The `Upload` method is used to display a file upload window and then process a file uploaded via HTTP file upload. `Upload` takes the following parameters:

Parameter	Description
`stParams.DirectoryPath`	Required full path to save the file to
`stParams.DirectoryURL`	Optional URL specifying the file path

Flash

The Flash object type is used to interact with Macromedia Flash files, including audio, graphics, and MP3 files.

Properties

The Flash object type contains the following properties:

Property	Description
`BGColor`	Background color in RGB form.
`Height`	Movie window height.
`Loop`	Repeat movie until user intervention flag. Default is `No`.
`Menu`	Display user menu flag. Default is `No`.
`Play`	Play immediately on download flag. Default is `Yes`.
`PlugInsPage`	Optional link to plug-ins.
`Quality`	Image playback quality (`Low`, `High`, `Autolow`, `Autohigh`, `Best`). Default is `High`.
`SAlign`	Position for scaled movie (within specified `Height` and `Width`).
`Scale`	Scale to window flag. Default is `Yes`.
`SourceFile`	Optional file source.
`Width`	Movie window width.

Methods

The Flash object type supports the following two methods:

- The `Display` method is used to display an embedded Flash player (and possibly initiate the play sequence). `Display` takes the following parameter:

`stParams.bAutoStart`	Start playing automatically flag. Default is Yes.

- The `Edit` method is used to edit Flash object properties. `Edit` takes the following parameters:

Parameter	Description
`stParams.FileDirectoryPath`	Full file path
`stParams.FileDirectoryURL`	Full file URL

Image

The Image object type is used for working with standard browser graphic files (usually GIF and JPEG images).

Properties

The Image object type contains the following properties:

Property	Description
`Align`	Image alignment (values are those supported by the `<IMG> ALIGN` attribute).
`Alt`	Alternate display text.
`Border`	Border flag and size (values are those supported by `<IMG> BORDER` attribute).
`File`	Filename.
`Height`	Height (in pixels).
`HSpace`	Horizontal spacing (in pixels).
`Title`	Image title.
`VSpace`	Vertical spacing (in pixels).
`Width`	Width (in pixels).

Methods

The Image object type supports the following four methods:

- The `Create` method is used to create a new image object. `Create` takes the following parameter:

`stParams.File`	Image file information.

- The `Delete` method deletes an image object. `Delete` takes no parameters.
- The `Display` method creates an `<IMG>` tag with which to display an image. `Display` takes no parameters.
- The `Edit` method is used to edit Image object properties. `Edit` takes the following parameters:

Parameter	**Description**
`stParams.FileDirectoryPath`	Full file path
`stParams.FileDirectoryURL`	Full file URL

RealMedia

The RealMedia object type is used for interaction with RealMedia audio and video files.

Properties

The RealMedia object type contains the following properties:

Property	**Description**
`Height`	RealPlayer window height (in pixels)
`Width`	RealPlayer window width (in pixels)
`SourceFile`	A file object (see File type) containing the RealMedia file

Methods

The RealMedia object type supports the following five methods:

- The `Create` method initializes object properties. `Create` takes no parameters.
- The `Display` method is used to display an embedded RealMedia player using the `Height` and `Width` properties (and possibly initiate the play sequence). `Display` takes the following parameter:

`stParams.bAutoStart`	Start playing automatically flag. Default is Yes.

- The `Edit` method displays the form used to edit RealMedia object properties. `Edit` takes no parameters.
- The `Play` method generates data to be sent to a RealPlayer, including any needed info files or MIME types. `Play` takes the following attributes:

Parameter	Description
`stParams.bEmbedded`	Use embedded player flag. Default is `No`.
`stParams.bRealServer`	Use Real's streaming protocol instead of HTTP. Default is `No`.
`stParams.realServerVersion`	Server version compatibility options (`G2`, `3`, `4`, `5`). Default is `G2`.

- The `PlayBackground` method plays a RealAudio file in the background. `PlayBackground` takes no parameters.

Index

SYMBOLS

A

B

C

D

E

F

G-H

I

L

N

O

Q

R

S

T

V

W-Z

Other Related Titles

From Que Publishing:

Special Edition Using Microsoft Access 2000
Roger Jennings
ISBN: 0-7897-1606-2
$39.99 U.S./$59.95 CAN

JavaScript Goodies
Joe Burns
ISBN: 0-7897-2024-8
$19.99 U.S./$29.95 CAN

Java 2 from Scratch
Steven Haines
ISBN: 0-7897-2173-2
$29.99 U.S./$44.95 CAN

Special Edition Using Microsoft SQL Server 7.0
Stephen Wynkoop
ISBN: 0-7897-1523-6
$39.99 U.S./$59.95 CAN

Using Microsoft Access 2000
Susan Sales Harkins, Ken Hansen, Tom Gerhart
ISBN: 0-7897-1604-6
$29.99 U.S./$44.95 CAN

From Sams Publishing:

Sams Teach Yourself Microsoft SQL Server 7.0 in 21 Days
Richard Waymire, Rick Sawtell
ISBN: 0-672-31290-5
$39.99 U.S./$59.95 CAN

Pure JavaScript
R. Allen Wyke, Charlton Ting, Jason Gilliam
ISBN: 0-672-31547-5
$34.99 U.S./$52.95 CAN

Developing Java Servlets
James Goodwill
ISBN: 0-672-31600-5
$29.99 U.S./$44.95 CAN

Building Java Enterprise Systems with J2EE
Paul Perrone
ISBN: 0-672-31795-8
$59.99 U.S./$89.95 CAN

Developing Java Server Pages
Ben Forta, Scott Stirling, Andre Lei
ISBN: 0-672-31939-X
$39.99 U.S./$59.95 CAN

www.quecorp.com

Sams Teach Yourself SQL in 10 Minutes
Ben Forta
ISBN: 0-672-31664-1
$12.99 U.S./
$19.95 CAN

Special Edition Using HTML 4, Sixth Edition
Molly E. Holzschlag
ISBN: 0-7897-2267-4
$39.99 U.S./
$59.95 CAN

Special Edition Using XML
Lee Anne Phillips
ISBN: 0-7897-1996-7
$39.99 U.S./
$59.95 CAN

All prices are subject to change.

CD Installation Instructions

Windows 9x, Windows NT 4, and Windows 2000

If Windows 9x, Windows NT 4, or Windows 2000 is installed on your computer and you have the AutoPlay feature enabled, the `start.exe` program starts automatically whenever you insert the disc into your CD-ROM drive. If the file doesn't start up automatically, follow these steps:

1. From the Windows desktop, double-click the My Computer icon.
2. Double-click the icon representing your CD-ROM drive.
3. Double-click the icon titled `START.EXE` to run the program.

Solaris

Look in the individual directories for software. Untar the software package. Follow the instructions in Chapter 4, "Installing and Configuring Spectra," to install the Spectra application.

Using the Code Included on the CD

This CD includes a full version of the a2zBooks application developed in this book.

- The `readme.txt` file explains how to install the application. As you progress through the chapters, you will develop the same application.
- A folder named `Book Examples` contains the code for each chapter, so you don't have to type it in if you choose to develop the application incrementally.